REGIONALISM IN INTERNATIONAL INVESTMENT LAW

Regionalism in International Investment Law

Edited by
Leon E. Trakman
and
Nicola W. Ranieri

OXFORD
UNIVERSITY PRESS

OXFORD
UNIVERSITY PRESS

Oxford University Press is a department of the University of Oxford. It furthers the University's objective of excellence in research, scholarship, and education by publishing worldwide.

Oxford New York
Auckland Cape Town Dar es Salaam Hong Kong Karachi Kuala Lumpur Madrid
Melbourne Mexico City Nairobi New Delhi Shanghai Taipei Toronto

With offices in
Argentina Austria Brazil Chile Czech Republic France Greece Guatemala Hungary
Italy Japan Poland Portugal Singapore South Korea Switzerland Thailand
Turkey Ukraine Vietnam

Published in the United States of America by
Oxford University Press
198 Madison Avenue, New York, NY 10016

Library of Congress Cataloging-in-Publication Data
Regionalism in international investment law / edited by Leon E. Trakman and Nicola W. Ranieri
p. cm.
Includes bibliographical references and index.
ISBN 978-0-19-538900-5 ((hardback) : alk. paper)
1. Investments, Foreign (International law) 2. Investments, Foreign—Law and legislation.
3. Canada. Treaties, etc. 1992 Oct. 7. I. Trakman, Leon E. II. Ranieri, Nicola (Nicola William)
K3830.R435 2013
346'.092—dc23
2012033074

Note to Readers
This publication is designed to provide accurate and authoritative information in regard to the subject matter covered. It is based upon sources believed to be accurate and reliable and is intended to be current as of the time it was written. It is sold with the understanding that the publisher is not engaged in rendering legal, accounting, or other professional services. If legal advice or other expert assistance is required, the services of a competent professional person should be sought. Also, to confirm that the information has not been affected or changed by recent developments, traditional legal research techniques should be used, including checking primary sources where appropriate.

(Based on the Declaration of Principles jointly adopted by a Committee of the American Bar Association and a Committee of Publishers and Associations.)

Table of Contents

Acknowledgments

THIS BOOK IS the product of many fruitful conversations with scholars across the globe. The different chapters have been written by authors with different backgrounds and perspectives, working in disparate settings. Their inspirations have come from their participation in the academic life of the universities they serve, their experiences advising states and investors, and their different roles in investment disputes and their settlement. Their experiences include participating in international investment conferences, workshops, and symposia from Lima, Peru to Xi'an, China, and across Europe and North America and Australia. Each contributing author has added exciting new perspectives to the unfolding history of international investment law. Each has provided inspirations and insights to his or her fellow authors.

The editing authors are indebted to their academic mentors. Leon E. Trakman dedicates his contributions to this book to the memory of Harold Berman, David Cavers, and Arthur von Mehren, for their inspiration as his doctorate supervisors at the Harvard Law School. In many respects, they foreshadowed the liberalization of trade and investment law through their remarkable understanding of global legal systems, comparative law, and the conflicts of law.

Leon Trakman also thanks Kunal Sharma for his research assistance and Anita Wise for proof-reading parts of this book.

Nicola W. Ranieri dedicates his contributions to this book to Edward Sherman for his inspiration as his doctorate supervisor at the Tulane Law School. His dedication to task, vision, and ability for building consensus among diverse interests facilitated a multitude of projects that were instrumental to forming a deeper understanding of alternative dispute resolution.

The authors also owe a debt of gratitude to their families who put up with many hours of late work and endless teleconferencing across multiple time zones.

Notes on Editors and Contributors

Leon E. Trakman is Professor of Law and Immediate Past Dean, Faculty of Law, University of New South Wales. He has been appointed distinguished or visiting professor at, inter alia, the University of California, Davis; Wisconsin; McGill; Tulane; and Cape Town. He has been awarded a Bora Laskin National Fellowship and a Killam Senior Fellowship, both in Canada. Author and editor of eight books, he has written over one hundred articles on, inter alia, international commercial arbitration and international trade and investment law. An international commercial arbitrator and mediator, he chairs or serves on arbitration and mediation panels, boards, and associations on four continents. He has served extensively as an intergovernmental trade adjudicator, appointed by U.S., Canadian, and Mexican governments under the North American Free Trade Agreement (NAFTA) and before then, under the U.S.–Canada Free Trade Agreement.

Professor Trakman is a barrister in New South Wales, Australia, a barrister and solicitor in Nova Scotia, Canada, and an advocate in South Africa. He holds masters and doctorate degrees in Law, both earned at the Harvard Law School.

Nicola W. Ranieri obtained his doctorate from the Tulane School of Law. He is admitted to the Bars of Ontario and New York, as well as other bars in the United States. He was the Director of the Centro Juridico Para el Comercio Inter-Americana in Monterrey, Mexico, and has served as a Panelist under the NAFTA Chapter 19 panel process dealing with antidumping and subsidies matters. His professional experience has included counseling state entities on the creation of free trade zones, as well as counseling private entities on issues dealing with foreign investment and expropriation. He has written on subjects relating to international trade and investment, and has lectured at the ITESM School of Law. He was a founding member of the NAFTA Consortium on Legal Education and served on various alternative dispute resolution bodies throughout North America. He is presently in private practice counseling clients on NAFTA-related issues.

Professor Muthucumaraswamy Sornarajah LL B (Ceylon), LLM (Yale), LLM, PhD, and LLD (London) is C.J. Koh Professor of Law at the National University of Singapore. He was previously the Tunku Abdul Rahman Professor of Public International Law at the University of Malaya, Kuala Lumpur, and Head of the Law School of the University of Tasmania, Australia. He is the author of the *International Law on Foreign Investment* (3d ed. 2010) and several other books. He has been counsel or arbitrator in several investment arbitrations.

Anna De Luca is a Research Fellow in International Law at Bocconi University in Milan. She holds a PhD in International Law from the University of Milan and specializes in international investment law and arbitration, and EU law. She has authored many articles in the field and two treatises on investment treaty-based arbitration and EU investment policy under the Lisbon Treaty ("L'arbitrato internazionale treaty-based sugliinvestimentiesteri", Comunicazioni e studi, vol. XXIII, 2007, at 977–1086 and "New Developments on the Scope of the EU Common Commercial Policy under the Lisbon Treaty, Investment Liberalization versus Investment Protection?," in *Yearbook on International Investment Law & Policy 2010/2011*, ch. 5 (2012) edited by K.P. Sauvant) respectively. She is a member of the editorial committee of the *Rivista dell'arbitrato*, the leading Italian review on arbitration law. She has been an Adjunct Professor of International Health Law at the University of Milan and regularly lectures on international investment law and arbitration at Bocconi University.

She has acted as assistant to the President of the ICSID Tribunal (Prof. Giorgio Sacerdoti) in *Continental Casualty Company v. Argentine Republic* (closed) and *Total S.A. v. Argentine Republic* (pending). She is a member of the Milan Bar and is currently acting as counsel for the Claimants in *Marco Gavazzi and Stefano Gavazzi v. Romania;* ICSID Case No. ARB/12/25 (pending).

Vivienne Bath is Professor of Chinese and International Business Law at Sydney Law School, University of Sydney, Director of the Centre for Asian and Pacific Law, and Chair of the China Studies Centre Research Committee at the University of Sydney. Her teaching and research interests are in international business law and Chinese law (particularly Chinese investment and commercial law). She has first class honors in Chinese and in Law from the Australian National University, and a Master of Laws from Harvard University. She is admitted to practice in Australia, New York, England and Wales, and Hong Kong and prior to joining Sydney Law School was a partner in the international law firm, Coudert Brothers. She has extensive professional experience in Sydney, New York, and Hong Kong, specializing in commercial law, with a focus on foreign investment and commercial transactions in the People's Republic of China and the Asian region. Representative publications include: "Foreign Investment, the National Interest and National Security—Foreign Direct Investment in Australia and China," 34 *Sydney Law Review* 5–34 (2012); Vivienne Bath and Luke Nottage (editors), *Foreign Investment and Dispute Resolution Law and Practice in Asia* (2011); Robin Burnett and Vivienne Bath, *Law of International Business in Australasia* (2009). Professor Bath speaks Chinese (Mandarin) and German.

Gisela Bolívar is an International Trade Consultant. She has acted as a panelist for the World Trade Organization ("DSB") and in NAFTA dispute settlements. She has served as trade partner, of counsel, and senior advisor to top law firms in Mexico, the United States, and Europe. She is professor in the LLM and JD programs of Law and Business schools at the Universidad Iberoamericana in Mexico City and has lectured at other leading Mexican universities. She worked for the Mexican government during the opening up of trade negotiations, and was in charge of the bilateral dispute settlement directorate. She holds a JD degree in Law, an LLM in European Union Law, and several diplomas on lobbying, antitrust, arbitration, and trade matters. She specializes in international law, international trade law, trade litigation, customs law, antidumping and countervailing investigations, dispute settlement mechanisms, arbitration, and European Union law. She has been appointed by the Mexican government as a member on the list of trade experts to act as a panelist on dispute settlement mechanisms, before international organizations.

Luke Nottage (BCA, LLB, PhD VUW, LLM Kyoto) specializes in contract law, consumer product safety law, and arbitration, with a particular interest in Japan and the Asia–Pacific. He is Professor of Comparative and Transnational Business Law at Sydney Law School, founding Co-Director of the Australian Network for Japanese Law, Associate Director of the Centre for Asian and Pacific Law at the University of Sydney, and Comparative and Global Law Program coordinator for the Sydney Centre for International Law. His publications include *Product Safety and Liability Law in Japan* (2004), *Corporate Governance in the 21st Century: Japan's Gradual Transformation* (2008), *International Arbitration in Australia* (2010), *Foreign Investment and Dispute Resolution in Asia* (2011), and four other books. He has executive roles in the Law Council of Australia's International Section, the Australian Centre for International Commercial Arbitration, and the Australasian Forum for International Arbitration. He has also consulted for law firms world-wide, the EC, the OECD, the UNDP, and the Japanese government.

Colin Picker is an associate professor on the University of New South Wales Law Faculty. He specializes in Transnational Litigation and Arbitration, International Law, International Trade, Comparative Law, Conflicts of Laws, and the U.S. Legal System. Prior to joining UNSW in 2010, he was the Daniel L. Brenner/UMKC Scholar & Professor of Law at the University of Missouri–Kansas City School of Law. He is the author of one of the primary comparative law textbooks in the United States. Picker was also a founder of the Society of International Economic Law (SIEL), and has served as SIEL Executive Vice President since its formation. He has also been active in the American Society of Comparative Law, the Law & Development Institute, and the American Society of Comparative Law's IEL Group. He entered academia in 2000, after practicing in the International Group of the Washington, D.C. law firm of Wilmer, Cutler & Pickering and after clerking for the Honorable Jose Cabranes of the U.S. Second Circuit

Court of Appeals. Among other qualifications, he holds a JD from Yale Law School and is a member of the Maryland Bar.

Wenhua Shan PhD (Cantab), is the Dean and Ministry of Education Changjiang Chair Professor of International Economic Law of Xi'an Jiaotong University School of Law, and Professor of International Law at Oxford Brookes University, UK. He is a National Special Advisor appointed by the Chinese Central Government under the national "1000Plan", Titular Member of the International Academy of Comparative Law, Editor-in-Chief of the *Chinese Journal of Comparative Law*, and Editor-in-General of the China and International Economic Law Series (Hart Publishing) and the Overseas Chinese Law Scholars Series (Peking University Press). His eight books have been published by several publishers (Oxford University Press, Hart, People's Press, and the Peking University Press), and he has numerous articles in journals such as the *European Journal of International Law*, *American Journal of Comparative Law*, and *ICSID Review*. He has practiced international and Chinese law since 1992 as Arbitrator of the China International Economic and Trade Arbitration Commission (CIETAC), among other arbitration institutions, and Senior Consultant of HaiLiWen PRC Attorneys, Shanghai.

Stephan Schill is a Senior Research Fellow at the Max Planck Institute for Comparative Public Law and International Law in Heidelberg. Prior to that, he clerked for the Honorable Charles N. Brower, 20 Essex Street, London, and for Judge Abdul G. Koroma at the International Court of Justice. He holds a degree of Dr. iur. from Johann Wolfgang Goethe-Universität, Frankfurt/Main, and an LL.M. from New York University. His expertise covers general international law and international dispute settlement, international investment law and arbitration, EU law, the European Convention on Human Rights, and comparative public law. He is admitted to the bar in Germany and New York and has acted as counsel before the European Court of Human Rights. He has published numerous articles and two books on international investment law: *The Multilateralization of International Investment Law* (2009); and, as editor, *International Investment Law and Comparative Public Law* (2010).

Romesh Weeramantry was an Associate Professor of at the City University of Hong Kong until September 2012. In September 2012, he joined the Hong Kong Office of King & Wood Mallesons where he works with Neil Kaplan QC. Romesh Weeramantry has worked in the field of international arbitration and dispute settlement at the Iran–United States Claims Tribunal (The Hague), the United Nations Compensation Commission (Geneva), and at a leading Swiss law firm. He has also advised a number of international organizations and trained government officials on dispute settlement and international investment law issues. His publications include *Treaty Interpretation in Investment Arbitration* (2012), *International Commercial Arbitration: An Asia–Pacific Perspective* (2011) (coauthored with Simon Greenberg and Chris Kee), and *The Hong Kong Arbitration Ordinance: Commentary and Annotations* (2011) (coedited with John Choong). He was a founding Co-Chair of the Australasian Forum for International Arbitration (AFIA).

Preface

Investment treaties are complex international economic agreements. They are crafted to provide predictability, and security to foreign investors, while protecting the national interests of host countries and remaining legitimate in the eyes of civil society. These competing objectives are variously expressed through principles developed in international customary law, as well as in a plethora of free trade and bilateral investment treaties. These customary and treaty laws prescribe, not always consistently, who is an investor, what is an investment, and what is an expropriation. They highlight sometimes disparate standards of treatment that states are required to accord to foreign investors, such as national treatment, the minimum standards of justice, and fair and equitable treatment. They also provide for the protection of the national interests of different states, such as essential national security, public health, and protection of the environment. They, more recently, echo the sentiments of civil society by providing, or referencing, transparency and public input. In the event of a conflict, these treaties rely primarily on investor–state arbitration to resolve claims brought by foreign investors against host states, but again with variable results.

The problem for international investment law is that there are a myriad of different bilateral investment treaties that diverge in how they provide for and regulate international investment. Further atrophying potential homogeneity in the application of investment regulations is the reliance that international investment law places on property. Property is conceived of differently between one jurisdiction and the next as notions of culture, tradition, heritage, and even language have continually impacted on the evolution of this basic concept. As a result, the study of international investment law is unavoidably complex.

In contest, too, are the potentially competing interests of different stakeholders. The interests of investors, states, and civil society, often mutually compatible at the outset, sometimes diverge over time, place, and space. The interests of investors and states are seldom aligned. Moreover, the public and private interests they represent are often multifaceted and at times incongruous. Simply ponder the ostensibly incongruous objectives of states in attracting foreign capital into the domestic economy and protecting their investors abroad, while simultaneously wanting to control the impact of foreign capital on local domestic interests. The countervailing interests of states in attracting foreign investment, through clear and transparent rules, while also preserving their discretion to circumvent those rules in the national interest, can lead states into espousing what might appear to be a schizophrenic policy. On the one hand, policy is often geared to ensuring that domestic investors are treated fairly abroad and preventing the flight of foreign investor capital from the domestic economy based on fears of arbitrary laws and discrimination. On the other hand, policies simultaneously attempt to imbue states with the discretion necessary to regulate foreign investment for the national good.

Some contributors to the book will argue that one way forward is through the internationalization of foreign investment law. However, any such realization must begin with the recognition that foreign investment law has developed significantly at a regional level. Recognition of regional differences will assist multistate and state regulators to arrive at both principled and practical ways by which to level the playing field within the international community of states. This will necessitate refining the rules that circumscribe foreign investment regulations to ensure that they are transparent in nature, to hold states accountable for their actions toward foreign investors, and to take account of socioeconomic and political differences among both states and investors. A tension here is for investment regulators to devise a predictable framework for international investment that seeks uniformity in the treatment of foreign investors, while also endorsing differences in the interests and propensities of states that are often manifest regionally.

This book will examine the history and development of foreign direct investment in international investment law. In so doing, it will evaluate the protection accorded to foreign investors in particular regions, such as the European Union, under the North American Free Trade Agreement, among ASEAN countries, and in China, Latin America, and Australia. Given the vast number of multilateral and regional instruments regulating foreign investment, with thousands of bilateral investment agreements in play, the analysis will necessarily be selective. Emphasis will be given to those investment laws that have the greatest significance economically, politically, and socially in the global community and in the regions selected for specific study.

The focus will be on developments in international investment laws arising regionally and bilaterally. Particular attention will be given to salient differences among investment treaty protocols, the distinctive manner in which investment arbitrators have construed them in discrete contexts, and how those constructions have influenced both investor and state practice. Importance will also be placed on competing regional and bilateral policies and principles governing the protection of foreign direct investors against expropriation, the standards that bind states in resorting to such expropriation, and the manner in which foreign investors can arrive at reasonably informed investment decisions in light of those policies, principles, and standards.

The book will strive to imbue the reader with the essential tools to better understand evolving trends in treaty practice. Analysis will move from the history and practice of international law governing foreign direct investment (such as under the World Trade Organization) to its regional application (such as under the law of the European Union) to its development through a series of bilateral investment treaties. Particular importance will be placed on "first-generation" investment treaties such as Chapter 11 of the North American Free Trade Agreement (NAFTA), as well as on more recent bilateral treaties among developed and developing states alike. The book will stress the growing importance of China for both inbound and outbound investments and its significant impact on regional and international investment law and practice. Emphasis will also be given to the significance of ASEAN countries, Latin America, and Australia in the evolution of customary and treaty law governing international investment.

The book will highlight topical dispute-resolution trends in investment law. It will utilize illustrations of institutions created to resolve particular kinds of investor–state disputes, such as the U.S.–Iran expropriation claims process. Attention will also be given to the evolving body of investor–state arbitration resulting from leading international investment regimes, notably the International Centre for Settlement of Investment Disputes (ICSID) and the United Nations Commission on International Trade Law (UNCITRAL).

The book has practical aspirations. Key among these is to provide a sound understanding of the issues faced by foreign investors who engage in direct trans-border investment. This understanding will be directed at identifying differences in substantive laws and procedures governing direct foreign investment and assisting investors to plan their investments in light of these laws and procedures.

The book avoids the one-size-fits-all solution to direct foreign investment decision making. It stresses the variable character of foreign direct investment law identified with multilateral, regional, and bilateral treaties. It addresses the sometimes inconsistent traditional principles of customary and treaty laws that are differently modernized to meet the needs of today's and tomorrow's investors across different regions of the globe.

In conducting this analysis, attempts will be made to identify competing forces that influence the liberalization of modern international investment law, as well as their incongruous application in different treaty and investor–state contexts.

Given the constantly changing character of international investment law, the intention is not to provide predictable legal responses to the full spectrum of global or regional investment practices. What is sought instead is an understanding of the key issues arising in planning foreign direct investment in principle as in practice. The book emphasizes variations in international investment laws and how investors can take advantage of those laws in exercising investment choices. It stresses the virtue of investors understanding how to avoid investor–state disputes. Failing that, it highlights fundamental issues arising in resolving those disputes. Ultimately, the book covers the issues that tend to recur most frequently in investment practice: the disparate nature of investment laws, the lack of transparency in their application, and the way to address those disparities in a functional and equitable manner.

Introduction

INVESTMENT TREATIES ARE significantly concerned with balancing the sometimes competing interests of foreign investors and host countries. On the one hand, they strive to provide legitimacy, predictability, and security to foreign investors. On the other hand, they also purport to protect the interests of host countries. At the crux of this delicate balancing act is the interest of foreign investors in avoiding arbitrary action by nation states and being unfairly treated. These goals are expressed through sometimes divergent policies and principles governing foreign investment, variable standards upon which they are based, and a plethora of rules through which they are applied. In contest is the public interest of host states in protecting their domestic interests from the influx of foreign investment and the concern of foreign investors not to be arbitrarily shackled by intrusive domestic requirements. Also in contest is the tension between the interest of states in attracting foreign investment and the perception that states obfuscate the property of foreign investors through practices that are neither clearly nor transparently applied. In issue, too, is the dislocation of international investment markets arising from the flight of investment capital in response to laws that investors perceive to be arbitrary. Finally and significantly, international investment law is increasingly regionalized. International principles of investment law are tailored to regional interests, notably through regional free trade and investment regions, and also bilateral investment agreements.

This book will explore these issues. It will debate principled and practical ways in which to level the playing field among states and foreign investors. It will evaluate often contentious international principles that govern foreign investment. It will explore investment practices that purport to regulate foreign investment transparently, while trying to ensure that states are accountable for their actions toward foreign investors. In issue will be the tension between the need for an international investment framework in which foreign investors are treated fairly while acknowledging that states sometimes conceive of fairness quite differently from one another, including in response to regional factors. Given the vast number of multilateral and regional instruments regulating foreign investment, with over 3,000 bilateral investment agreements in force by the end of 2012, the contributing authors will necessarily be selective in addressing these issues. They will stress key developments in international and regional investment law including their often-changing impact upon foreign direct investment. Leon Trakman and Nick Ranieri will examine the nature of an investment in Chapter 1 and the history of international investment law in Chapter 2. In Chapter 3, Colin Picker will evaluate the intersection of comparative and international trade and investment law in relation to institutions such as the World Trade Organization. Leon Trakman will highlight the development and significance of regional and bilateral investment agreements in Chapter 4. In Chapter 5, Nick Ranieri will provide an overview of the North American Free Trade Agreement (NAFTA) as a template for regional trade and investment agreements. In Chapter 6, Anna de Luca will explore the legal framework for foreign investments in the European Union. Gisela Bolivar will examine in Chapter 7 the protection of investments in Latin America through survival and withdrawal clauses in investment treaties. In Chapter 8, Vivienne Bath will address the liberalization of investment among the ASEAN nations. Wenhau Shan will demonstrate in Chapter 9 how international investment law has developed in China. In Chapter 10, Leon Trakman will evaluate the role of the International Centre for the Settlement of Investment Disputes (ICSID). Romesh Weeramantry will discuss in Chapter 11 the history, development, and significance of the Iran–U.S. case law on expropriation. In Chapter 12, Leon Trakman will evaluate the significance of Australia's rejection of investor–state arbitration. Stephan Schill will study in Chapter 13 the complex relationship between the European Union and its member states in investor–state arbitration. In Chapter 14, Nick Ranieri will scrutinize the delicate balance between investors' rights and the public interest under Chapter 11 of the NATFA that regulates investment. Luke Nottage will explore in Chapter 15 the unfolding dispute between Philip Morris and Australia over Australia's consumer product safety legislation. In Chapter 16, Muthucumaraswamy Sornarajah will conclude the book by challenging the foundations of international investment law. In the Appendix, Leon Trakman and Muthucumaraswamy Sornarajah will debate the case for and against the liberalization of international investment law.

These chapters together will highlight salient differences among investment treaty treaties, the distinctive manner in which investment treaties and laws are applied in discrete national regional and international contexts, and how their application has influenced investor and state practice. They will focus on competing policies that govern the expropriation of foreign direct investors. They will analyze the significance of standards of treatment accorded to foreign investors, such as the national standard by which countries are expected to accord comparable standards to foreign investors as to their own nationals. Finally, they will suggest ways in which states can apply investment standards to foreign investors and ways in which investors can respond, including in different national, regional, and international contexts.

The analyses will move from the history and practice of international law governing foreign direct investment, such as under the World Trade Organization, to its regional application, such as under the NAFTA and the EU, to its development through a series of bilateral investment treaties. Particular importance will be placed on "first generation" investment treaties, such as Chapter 11 of the North American Free Trade Agreement (NAFTA) as well as upon more recent bilateral treaties among developed and developing states alike. The book will consider how investor–state disputes are resolved through arbitration, varying from investor–state arbitration before the ICSID to binding third-party arbitration on claims by nationals of Iran and the United States. It will also consider alternatives to investor–state arbitration, varying from conciliation proceedings to reliance on domestic courts to resolve investor–state disputes.

The contributing editors and authors have practical and theoretical aspirations. Key among these is to provide a sound understanding of the issues faced by foreign investors that engage in direct transborder investment. These issues are analyzed in the context of the differences in the substantive laws and procedures governing foreign investment, in planning direct foreign investments in light of those laws and procedures, in making investment decisions as a result of such planning, and in deriving legal consequences from the exercise of those choices.

The book in general will avoid a one-size-fits-all solution to direct foreign investment decision making. It will propose that the development of international investment law is best understood in light of the competing cultural influences and legal traditions that have influenced it. It will stress how these competing influences affect multilateral, regional, and bilateral treaties.

Given the constantly changing and sometimes disputed character of international investment principles and laws, the book will concentrate on developing a better understanding of some of the key issues faced by countries and investors alike in investment planning, the underlying complexities in such planning, and the capacity to arrive at functional outcomes in light of this. It will explore the disparate impact of domestic and international laws on the needs of today's and tomorrow's investors, together with the interests of host and home states. It will consider strategies to avoid investment disputes, and failing that, to resolve them, without purporting to provide perfectly predictable outcomes to the full spectrum of potential investor–state disputes.

A final purpose of the book is to recognize that international investment law is not an entirely value-neutral means of resolving investor–state disputes. It consists of a disputable body of institutions and laws whose operations are subject to challenge and whose application does not ensure unified, harmonious, or fair results in every case.

1

FOREIGN DIRECT INVESTMENT: AN OVERVIEW

Leon E. Trakman and Nicola W. Ranieri

Introduction

This first chapter commences with an analysis of the nature of foreign direct investment, including its meaning and perceived significance to foreign direct investors and host states. It analyzes key ways of regulating foreign direct investment both historically and today. It highlights the principles, standards, and rules governing direct foreign investment that have evolved in modern times. Finally, it underscores direct foreign investment's most salient impact upon conventional international investment law and practice.

The remainder of the chapter identifies the basic elements of foreign direct investment and provides the context within which they are best understood. We discuss the basic components of foreign direct investment in order to facilitate the foundation for further analysis.

I. Defining Foreign Direct Investment

Foreign direct investment (FDI) is a significant part of international business and of the global economy. Companies that engage in FDI can expand to new marketplaces; shift their production facilities across national boundaries; and secure more advanced technologies, products, skills, and modes of financing. Foreign companies can provide host countries and their domestic economies with the infusion of capital, updated technologies, improved and more efficient production processes, organizational capacities, management skills, market networks, improved job prospects and employment skills, access to more competitive products, and prospects of economic development generally.[1]

A World Trade Organization (WTO) report on trade and investment provides the following definition of FDI:

> Foreign direct investment (FDI) occurs when an investor based in one country (the home country) acquires an asset in another country (the host country) with the intent to manage that asset. The management dimension is what distinguishes FDI from portfolio investment in foreign stocks, bonds and other financial instruments. In most instances, both the investor and the asset it manages abroad are business firms. In such cases, the investor is typically referred to as the "parent firm" and the asset as the "affiliate" or "subsidiary".
>
> There are three main categories of FDI:
>
> 1. Equity capital is the value of the multinational corporation's (MNC) investment in shares of an enterprise in a foreign country. An equity capital stake of 10 per cent or more of the ordinary shares or voting power in an incorporated enterprise, or its equivalent in an unincorporated enterprise, is normally considered as a threshold for the control of assets. This category includes both mergers and acquisitions and Greenfield investments (the creation of new facilities). Mergers and acquisitions are an important source of FDI for developed countries, although the relative importance varies considerably.
> 2. Reinvested earnings are the MNC's share of affiliate earnings not distributed as dividends or remitted to the MNC. Such retained profits by affiliates are assumed to be reinvested in the affiliate. This can represent up to 60 per cent of outward FDI in countries such as the USA and the UK.
> 3. Other capital refers to short- or long-term borrowing and lending of funds between the MNC and the affiliate.[2]

FDI can therefore assume various forms. For example, it may involve a company from one country making a physical investment or taking a management interest in an industry in another country. Typically, a purchase by a company located in one country of a factory, machinery, or equipment in a neighboring country would constitute FDI. Similarly, building a plant or factory where none previously existed in that neighboring country would also constitute FDI.

In contrast, acquiring stock or shares as part of a portfolio investment in another country would ordinarily not be considered as FDI, unless some element of management

---

1 *See* http://www.going-global.com/articles/understanding_foreign_direct_investment.htm.

2 WTO, "Trade and Foreign Direct Investment", Oct. 9, 1996, *available at* www.wto.org/english/news_e/pres96_e/pr057_e.htm.

control is attached to the purchase. Precisely how much control would give rise to FDI is primarily a question of fact, one answered by demonstrating that the investment establishes sufficient de facto control to be considered a "direct" as distinct from an "indirect" investment. The factual test would ordinarily be both quantitative and qualitative. De facto control would usually involve owning 50 percent or more of the stock in a foreign company. However, a significantly lesser investment might qualify as a "direct" investment. The qualitative nature of "control" may be equally variable, depending on the nature and extent of that control, such as it being through voting rights, a voice on the board of directors, or some other means of "control."

FDI can also be determined by its "direction" or by its "target." In classifying it by direction, "inward FDI" occurs when foreign capital is invested in local resources. "Outward" FDI—sometimes referred to as "direct investment abroad"—arises when local capital is invested in foreign resources. In classifying FDI by "target," the target may be expressed through a so-called "Greenfield investment," or through a merger or acquisition. FDI that takes place through new facilities, or the expansion of existing facilities, is referred to as a "Greenfield investment," which is sometimes described as "insourcing."

Greenfield investments often are controversial. Host nations often favor them in particular on grounds that they are capital investments that may directly create new jobs, conceivably at higher rates than is generated by local firms. Greenfield investments may also increase production capacity, such as through the transfer of technology and know-how, through investments in research and development, and through increased linkages to the global market.

However, Greenfield investments may lead to a reduction in market share for competing domestic firms that may be less efficient or cannot produce to the same standards as can the Greenfield investment. Greenfield investments may also be attacked for channeling profits away from the domestic economy to the home economy of the MNC, or to a third country in which that MNC or other entity has economic interests.[3]

Notwithstanding the growth of Greenfield investments, the main category of FDI is through mergers and acquisitions. Such mergers and acquisitions occur through the transfer of existing assets from local firms to foreign firms. For example, a cross-border merger may occur when the assets and operations of firms from different countries are combined in order to establish a new legal entity. A cross-border acquisition may arise when the control of assets and operations is transferred from a local to a foreign company, including when the local company becomes an affiliate of that foreign company.[4]

[3] On Greenfield Investments, *see* http://www.investopedia.com/terms/g/greenfield.asp.

[4] Horst Raff, Michael Ryan & Frank Stähler, *The Choice of Market Entry Mode: Greenfield Investment, M&A and Joint Venture*, 18 INT'L. L. REV. ECON. & FIN. 3–9 (2009); Holger Gorg, *Analysing Foreign Market Entry—The Choice between Greenfield Investment and Acquisitions*, 27 J. ECON. STUD. 165 (2000).

A growing feature of modern FDI is the development of joint ventures across national boundaries. FDI joint ventures arise when parties based in different home states engage in joint enterprises in one or the other home states and/or in third jurisdictions. Such joint ventures often are employed to capitalize investments; to secure know-how, such as specialized skills in conducting that joint venture; and to gain access to foreign markets.

Joint ventures may include a combination of investment options discussed above, as when they engage Greenfield investments, mergers, and acquisitions. Joint ventures are also important to developing countries whose governments are keen to avoid majority foreign ownership or material control of domestic companies. Joint ventures provide useful vehicles by which those governments can engage the partnership of a foreign company without relinquishing control to it.[5]

II. What Is the Value of FDI?

Debate over the value of FDI in general and in its different manifestations is understandably intense. Much depends on the position adopted by the proponent and the economic, political, and social interests involved. Strong supporters of FDI in general argue that it usually provides economic benefits to both host and home countries and to individuals and companies engaged in FDI, as well as socially through spill-off benefits such as higher standards of living, a wider choice of goods and services, more and better paying jobs, etc. The central argument is that FDI creates "more," and that "more" is better than "less."[6]

A countervailing argument is that FDI privileges the already privileged. Given that MNCs traditionally dominated FDI and that MNCs are identified with developed states and their economic interests, critics of FDI contend that these interests benefit at the expense of developing countries, fledging industries in such countries, and their local interests. Critics argue, too, that even the benefits of FDI to developing countries, such as through specialized products and services, are undermined by the fact that products and services produced domestically may be destined for foreign markets. FDI may also lead to the increased employment of foreign workers who are brought in from developed countries to develop FDI markets at the expense of domestic workers.[7]

A mixed concern is that FDI may benefit select sectors of the domestic economy at the expense of others. FDI may satisfy discrete domestic markets for goods and services while undermining other sectors of the domestic economy that cannot compete

---

5 Useful Web sites include: www.unctad.org; www.oecd.org; www.columbia.edu/cu/libraries/indiv/business/guides/fordinv.html; www.doc.gov; www.ita.gov; and www.worldbank.org; www.opic.gov.

6 *See generally* Danachi Tan, *Foreign Market Entry Strategies and Post-Entry Growth: Acquisitions vs. Greenfield Investments*, J. INT'L. BUS. STUD. 1046 (2009).

7 *See generally* H. DUNNING, GLOBAL CAPITALISM AT BAY? (2001).

effectively with the FDI. These concerns are endemic to both developed and developing countries.[8]

An attempt to present a balanced view of the virtues and pitfalls associated with FDI is expressed by Jeffrey P. Graham and R. Barry Spaulding in "Understanding Foreign Direct Investment" (2004):

> Proponents of foreign investment point out that the exchange of investment flows benefits both the home country (the country from which the investment originates) and the host country (the destination of the investment). Opponents of FDI note that multinational conglomerates are able to wield great power over smaller and weaker economies and can drive out much local competition. The truth lies somewhere in the middle.
>
> For small and medium sized companies, FDI represents an opportunity to become more actively involved in international business activities. In the past 15 years, the classic definition of FDI . . . has changed considerably. This notion of a change in the classic definition, however, must be kept in the proper context. Very clearly, over 2/3 of direct foreign investment is still made in the form of fixtures, machinery, equipment and buildings. Moreover, larger multinational corporations and conglomerates still make the overwhelming percentage of FDI. But, with the advent of the Internet, the increasing role of technology, loosening of direct investment restrictions in many markets and decreasing communication costs means that newer, non-traditional forms of investment will play an important role in the future. Many governments, especially in industrialized and developed nations, pay very close attention to foreign direct investment because the investment flows into and out of their economies can and does have a significant impact. In the United States, the Bureau of Economic Analysis, a section of the US Department of Commerce, is responsible for collecting economic data about the economy, including information about foreign direct investment flows. Monitoring this data is very helpful in trying to determine the impact of such investments on the overall economy, but is especially helpful in evaluating industry segments. State and local governments watch closely because they want to track their foreign investment attraction programs for successful outcomes.[9]

---

8 *See, e.g.*, FOREIGN OWNERSHIP AND THE CONSEQUENCES OF DIRECT FOREIGN INVESTMENT IN THE UNITED STATES (Douglas Woodward & Douglas Nygh eds., 1998).

9 *Available at* http://www.going-global.com/articles/understanding_foreign_direct_investment.htm.

III. What Is the Future of FDI?

A. FDI IN NEW TECHNOLOGIES

A growing trend in FDI is in a shift from traditional models associated with investments in goods and services toward investments in "new" goods and services that do not involve extensive outlays on plant and facilities, but rely instead on the development and transfer of high-tech information and know-how. These developments are accentuated by the growth of the World Wide Web and the use of the Internet. They are also evident in different kinds of foreign investors than traditional MNCs, such as "start-up" companies that make limited financial outlays and function in a virtual world without physical facilities and labor support beyond a few individuals, a computer, and limited office space. In place of complex manufacturing facilities, stores and warehousing and stockpiling of goods are new forms of FDI devoted to developing and protecting intellectual property rights, such as through patents and copyright. Under development may be a software program or process that is pioneered in a single office, or even in someone's home.

These new manifestations of FDI are important both quantitatively and qualitatively. Although it is difficult to assess the percentage of FDI that is identified with such new technologies, it is apparent that they are growing in both number and variety. It is also apparent that successful start-ups can evolve into massive businesses, as is evident by once-upon-a-time start-up companies such as eBay.

At the same time, these new developments may sometimes operate below the radar of regulators of FDI (i.e., not per se illegally), as such activities are often associated with a subsector industry that is neither resource intensive nor often profitable in fact. Most start-ups do not progress to profitability, and cross-border venture capital is often prefaced on the expectation that twenty or more FDI investments may fail for every one that succeeds. However, with limited capital outlay associated with start-up investments, the benefit of an occasional success may well be worth the risk associated with those that fail.

A further feature of these new FDI developments is that they often function under the rubric of more traditional trans-border FDI. One-time start-ups (the likes of Microsoft) invest billions in developing and protecting their software and licenses in that software including through FDI. They also engage in technology start-ups, or more often technology "buy ups," as when they purchase the technology of start-up innovators that they either absorb into their own software, or sublimate the technology to avoid software competition with their own developments.

B. FDI IN THE DEVELOPING WORLD

A further development in FDI is the realization that new technologies are not limited to the developed countries that resource and export FDI. In some respects, new technologies can evolve anywhere at anytime. Just as the Republic of Ireland and Israel became second "Silicone" havens to California in decades past by attracting FDI investment and expertise, developing countries that are receptive to new technologies can do the same. Such is already clearly the case in developing countries such as India.[10] Coupled with this is the realization that developing countries, not least of all China, are not only well resourced in attracting FDI, but in recent years have engaged increasingly in both in- and outbound-FDI at levels not foreseen historically.[11]

C. ILLUSTRATIONS OF FDI AT WORK

Here are a few illustrations of categories of high technology in which FDI takes place, identified by Jeffrey P. Graham and R. Barry Spaulding in *Understanding Foreign Direct Investment* (2004):[12]

- **Licensing and technology transfer.** Licensing and technology transfer have been essential in promoting collaboration between the academic and business communities. Ever since legal hurdles were removed that allowed universities to hold title to research and development done in their labs, licensing agreements have helped turned [*sic*] raw technology into finished products that are viable in competitive marketplaces. With some help from a variety of government agencies in the form of grants for R&D as well as other financial assistance for such things as incubator programs, once timid college researchers are now stepping out and becoming cutting edge entrepreneurs. These strategic alliances have had a serious impact in several high tech industries, including but not limited to: medical and agricultural biotechnology, computer software engineering, telecommunications, advanced materials processing, ceramics, thin materials processing, photonics, digital multimedia production and publishing, optics and imaging and robotics and automation. Industry clusters are now growing up around the university labs where their derivative technologies were first discovered and nurtured. Licensing agreements allow companies to take full advantage of new and exciting technologies, while limiting their overall risk to royalty payments until a particular technology is fully developed and thus ready to put new products into the manufacturing pipeline.
- **Reciprocal distribution agreements**. Actually, this type of strategic alliance is more trade-based, but in a very real sense it does in fact represent a type of direct investment. Basically, two companies, usually within the same or affiliated

[10] *See, e.g.*, DIZAN SHIRA & ASSOCIATES, DOING BUSINESS IN INDIA, chs 1–3 (2012).

[11] On China's spectacular emergence in inbound and outbound investment, *see* ELIYATHAMBY A. SELVANATHAN, SAROJA SELVANATHAN & SUMEI TANG, CHINA'S ECONOMIC MIRACLE: DOES FDI MATTER? (2012); CHUNLAI CHEN, FOREIGN DIRECT INVESTMENT IN CHINA: LOCAL DETERMINANTS, INVESTOR DIFFERENCES AND ECONOMIC IMPACTS (2012); NICK J. FREEMAN AND FRANK L. BARTELS, THE FUTURE OF FOREIGN INVESTMENT IN SOUTHEAST ASIA (2012).

[12] *See* http://www.going-global.com/articles/understanding_foreign_direct_investment.htm.

industries, agree to act as a national distributor for each other's products. The classical example is to be found in the furniture industry. A US based manufacturer of tables signs a reciprocal distribution agreement with a Spanish-based manufacturer of chairs. Both companies gain direct access to the other's distribution network without having to pay distributor support payments and other related expenses found within the distribution channel and neither company can hurt the other's market for its products. Without such an agreement in place, the Spanish manufacturer might very well have to invest in a national sales office to coordinate its distributor network, manage warehousing, inventory and shipping as well as to handle administrative tasks such as accounting, public relations and advertising.

- **Joint venture and other hybrid strategic alliances**. The more traditional joint venture is bilateral, that is it involves two parties who are within the same industry who are partnering for some strategic advantage. Typical reasons might include a need for access to proprietary technology that might tip the competitive edge in another competitor's favor, desire to gain access to intellectual capital in the form of ultra-expensive human resources, access to heretofore closed channels of distribution in key regions of the world. One very good reason why many joint ventures only involve two parties is the difficulty in integrating different corporate cultures. With two domestic companies from the same country, it would still be very difficult. However, with two companies from different cultures, it is almost impossible at times. This is probably why pure joint ventures have a fairly high failure rate only five years after inception. Joint ventures involving three or more parties are usually called syndicates and are most often formed for specific projects such as large construction or public works projects that might involve a wide variety of expertise and resources for successful completion. In some cases, syndicates are actually easier to manage because the project itself sets certain limits on each party and close cooperation is not always a prerequisite for ultimate success of the endeavor.
- **Portfolio investment.** Recall our definition of foreign direct investment as it pertains to controlling interest. For most of the latter part of the 20th century when FDI became an issue, a company's portfolio investments were not considered a direct investment if the amount of stock and/or capital was not enough to garner a significant voting interest amongst shareholders or owners However, two or three companies with "soft" investments in another company could find some mutual interests and use their shareholder power effectively for management control. This is another form of strategic alliance, sometimes called "shadow alliances." So, while most company portfolio investments do not strictly qualify as a direct foreign investment, there are instances within a certain context that they are in fact a real direct investment.[13]

[13] *Id.*

D. LOOKING AHEAD

The precise future of FDI in new technologies, as well as shifts from developed to emerging and developing countries, remains somewhat uncertain. Developments in FDI seldom occur overnight. Competition is often fierce, and investment products and services in the marketplace are often in constant flux. As an illustration, the value of FDI in new technologies is often uncertain for a significant part of their incubation periods, and profitability is often a distant aspiration that may pleasantly surprise proponents just as it may disappoint them.

What is apparent is that, despite the collapse of many so called "dot.com" FDI initiatives at the turn of this century, the "dot.com" bubble has not fully burst. If anything, it has grown in value and momentum, and by all accounts will continue to do so. Considering that online shopping was a novel technology just a decade ago, and software technology that supported it was in its infancy, one can anticipate that FDIs in online consumer and producer industries will reinvent themselves repeatedly as they become the dominant means of engaging in both international trade and investment.

IV. How Significant Is FDI to Internationalization?

FDI has important strategic economic, social, and political significance beyond its immediate investment prospects. In particular, it may enable foreign investors to limit direct and indirect trade barriers on FDI, to build joint ventures with partners in host countries, to shift from domestic export sales to sales both in and out of those host countries, to increase total production capacity, etc. It may also function to avoid pressure from home states to confine production and services to domestic consumption.

The result is that foreign investors, not limited to MNCs, can build global markets through strategic investments in selected host states. In some measure, this enables foreign investors to cater to foreign markets in accordance with their respective financial, production, and related capacities, rather than force them to operate at a global level with multiple international points of entry into and out of international investment markets. These developments favoring small and middle-sized foreign investors do not offset the capacity of MNCs to compete both globally and through specific host states.

Rather, they enable foreign investors who historically lacked capacity to enter international markets incrementally, and to build strategic relationships with host governments without having to overextend their foreign commitments. They are assisted in doing so in some measure by the greater ease involved in communication across national boundaries, most recently with the advent of the Internet, along with e-mail and podcasting, and other new developments in technology. An attendant result is the capacity of small and middle-sized foreign investors to run foreign operations with limited capital outlays, limited operational costs, and limited costs of travel to and in host countries. These advantages are most evident in high-technology industries, such as software development and e-production and e-commerce generally. These new technologies also provide greater access, not only to foreign investors and host country partners, but also to markets and customers.

A related benefit, not to be underestimated, is the capacity to conduct sophisticated analysis of market conditions and improve market access from a distance. While cultural barriers to international investment ought not to be underestimated, the Internet has contributed both its own cultural dynamics, as well as technological means of overcoming traditional cultural barriers, such as are associated with national legal systems and the distinctiveness of domestic markets. Access to host country legal systems, statutes and their interpretation, and to customs and usages among trades and industries in foreign markets is increasingly possible, including through the Internet. In fact, it is often a key to the success of FDI ventures. Not to be underestimated, too, is the extent to which foreign investors can identify, record and respond to domestic, foreign and international competition by these and related means.

The result is that foreign investors are generally better able to assess their own capabilities in relation to intrusive—subtle or otherwise—government regulation and market forces in host countries. Adept foreign investors also have far more sophisticated means of utilizing their capabilities in addressing these political, economic, and social forces than was available to them historically.

None of these results are assured in particular cases. Typically, readily available information on the Internet about foreign laws, regulations, and competition may be overly voluminous, unreliable, outdated, and subject to manipulation. However, foreign investors also have access to a variety of quantitative and qualitative means of assessing such information, not least of all by hiring local law firms and by employing local marketing firms and personnel to lobby governments and to both gauge and counter competitors in host countries.[14]

V. How Should Governments Regulate FDI?

Just as foreign investors face a variety of competitive forces in deciding when, how, and to what extent to invest abroad, host countries need to develop policies, principles, standards, and rules of application by which to regulate FDI. Like foreign investors who face the risk of economic exclusion or sublimation at the hands of both market forces and government regulations in host countries, host countries face the risk of having their domestic needs marginalized as a result of FDI. In the same way as foreign investors can gain access to less expensive capital, labor, production, transportation, and regulatory costs, not least of all taxation, host governments need to ensure that

[14] On the issue of whether FDI promotes developments, *see* Does Foreign Direct Investment Promote Development? (Theodore H. Moran, Edward M. Graham & Magnus Blomström eds., 2005).

these benefits do not erode local interests. At issue for foreign investors and host governments are a series of political, economic, and social risks that FDI may facilitate rather than redress.

Among these risks is an assortment of the following:

- Corruption;
- Policy instability or uncertainty;
- Crime, theft, kidnapping, or social disorder;
- Presence of organized crime or localized mafia;
- Reintroduction of inflation;
- Problems securing financing;
- Exchange rate difficulties;
- Anticompetitive practices;
- Infrastructure deficiencies;
- Unclear systems of taxation and unclear tax regulations;
- Unreliable judiciary and differences in the legal system; and
- Property seizures, such as confiscation, expropriation, and nationalization.

For the host nation, positive impacts of foreign investment include:

- Increased domestic capital formation;
- Innovation and advanced technology transfer;
- Management skill transfer;
- Increased marketing networks;
- Targeted regional and sector development;
- Fostering of internal competition and entrepreneurship;
- Favorable effect on balance of payments;
- Increased domestic employment; and
- Increased economic development.

Potential negative impacts of foreign investment may include, among others:

- Industrial sector dominance in the domestic market;
- Technological dependence on foreign technology sources;
- Disturbance of domestic economic plans in favor of FDI-directed projects;
- Cultural change created by the infusion of foreign culture and foreign business practices;
- Corruption of local officials by unethical foreign investors; and
- Potential interference in domestic economic and political decision making in the host country by the home government of the multinational corporation.

These risks are unlikely to deter FDI, especially when the benefits of FDI are seen to outweigh the costs. However, what ought not to be trumpeted is the view that FDI is a panacea for foreign investors and host countries. Developing reliable, profitable, and socially responsive FDI bridges across national boundaries usually requires inspiration, innovation, and ultimately, hard work. Some of the greatest challenges to FDI may arise in times of recession.[15] But negative economic and political conditions sometimes are themselves the source of inspiration in overcoming barriers to foreign investment and taking FDI to greater heights than in eras past.[16]

VI. The Future of FDI

Risks to the geometric development of FDI notwithstanding, the extent and reach of FDI has grown dramatically in recent decades. Most notable was its growth between 1985 and 1995 during which the total FDI globally increased from US$60 billion to US$315 billion. Notable, too, is the estimate that in 2007 the total flow of FDI had reached an estimated US$1.5 trillion.[17] That growth continues notwithstanding the 2008 recession. Important, too, is the across-the-board growth of FDI, with FDI flows increasing from 2006 levels among developed countries, developing countries, and countries in transition alike; and with countries such as China, India, and Brazil leading the outbound growth of FDI globally.[18]

Also significant is the observation that the sales of foreign affiliates of MNCs now exceed the value of world trade in goods and services. In particular, intra-firm trade among MNCs accounts for approximately one-third of world trade; MNC exports to nonaffiliates account for another one-third of world trade, while the remaining one-third accounts for trade among national (non-MNC) firms.[19] These high levels of FDI and intra-firm trade would not have been possible without the reduction of tariffs and other barriers to FDI that are wrought by a combination of formidable forces: the General Agreement on Trade and Tariffs (GATT) and the World Trade Organization (WTO); advances in communication, information systems, and shipping technologies;

---

[15] *See, e.g.*, discussion on the growth of transatlantic investment as a response to the global recession; *see also, e.g.*, http://www.europesworld.org/NewEnglish/Home/Article/tabid/191/ArticleType/ArticleView/ArticleID/21380/Default.aspx; World Bank Group, World Investment and Political Risk (2010), *available at* http://books.google.com.au/books?id=pZ-WHvkSd_AC&printsec=frontcover&dq=foreign+direct+investment+2010&source=bl&ots=-wMOQoPBYL&sig=ebITIs8B1Epfm1PfLuaVOVShxfU&hl=en#.

[16] *See generally,* Peterson Institute, Does Foreign Direct Investment Promote Development? New Methods, Outcomes and Policy Approaches (2005); Theodore H. Moran, Beyond Sweatshops: Foreign Direct Investment and Globalization in Developing Nations (2002).

[17] *See* Press Release, United Nations Conference on Trade and Development (UNCTAD), Foreign Direct Investment Reached New Record in 2007 (Jan. 8, 2008), *available at* www.unctad.org/Templates/webflyer.asp?docid=9439&intItemID=1528&lang=1.

[18] On these emerging markets, see Siegfried Hotter, International Joint Ventures in Brazil's Markets (2012); China and the Multinationals: International Business and the Entry of China into the Global Economy (Robert Pearce ed., 2012). *See also supra* notes 10–11.

[19] *See* WTO, "Trade and Foreign Direct Investment," Oct. 9, 1996, *available at* www.wto.org/english/news_e/pres96_e/pr057_e.htm.

and the willingness of host countries to permit foreign investment, albeit so as to further their own domestic development.

It is too early to predict the extent of the impact of the financial and credit crisis that began in late 2007 that worsened in 2008 and began to abate in 2009, only to be heightened in 2011 with the economic crises in Europe. The most likely scenario is that these developments will impact on the total volume of FDI, as companies struggle worldwide to deal with declining demand and experience difficulties in raising capital and securing credit, and as companies across the globe again may issue profit warnings that reverberate across national boundaries. Preliminary data affirm these concerns with an estimated reduction in total FDI of more than 20 percent in 2008 and with the United States and European countries being viewed as particularly vulnerable to these economic forces.[20] Uncertainty remains over the recovery predicted for the global community into the future and its impact on FDI,[21] and over the impact of politics on foreign investments.[22]

What can be fairly stated is that the development of FDI, like any other global economic phenomenon, cannot be expected to rise each year, despite China's meteoric growth as an outbound and now, inbound FDI destination. Nor can the development of FDI be immune to global and domestic political forces that inevitably impact on it. What is reasonably likely is that FDI will not only recover its monumental foothold in the development of commerce globally, but also provide leadership in economic, political, and social reform in the future.[23]

---

[20] Reduction in Europe includes the UK being down 51 percent, Germany down 49 percent, and Italy down 94 percent. FDI in Singapore dropped 57 percent, while in the United States it dropped only 6 percent. Russia (18 percent), China (11 percent), and Brazil (21 percent) all gained. *See* Press Release, UNCTAD, Global Foreign Direct Investment Now in Decline—and Estimated to Have Fallen during 2008, (Jan. 19, 2009), *available at* www.unctad.org/Templates/webflyer.asp?docid=10930&intItemID=1528&lang=1. *See also* THE FUTURE OF FOREIGN DIRECT INVESTMENT AND THE MULTINATIONAL ENTERPRISE (RESEARCH IN GLOBAL STRATEGIC MANAGEMENT) (Ravi Ramamurti & Niron Hashai eds., 2012)

[21] *Id. See generally* ANGELOS DIMOPOULOS, EU FOREIGN INVESTMENT LAW (2012).

[22] *See* NATHAN M. JENSEN ET AL., POLITICS AND FOREIGN DIRECT INVESTMENT (2012).

[23] *See e.g. UPDATE 2-Brazil Raises 2012 FDI Forecast Despite Global Slowdown: Economic Recovery Attracting Foreign Investment*, Sept. 25, 2012, *available at* http://in.reuters.com/article/2012/09/25/brazil-economy-currentaccount-idINL1E8KP4XO20120925.

2

FOREIGN DIRECT INVESTMENT: A HISTORICAL PERSPECTIVE

Leon E. Trakman and Nicola W. Ranieri

THE EVOLUTION OF FDI protocols has attracted much attention. This scrutiny has led many critics to call for reform amid allegations that the protections are being manipulated to raise corporate agendas over societal well-being. Underlying these concerns is the belief that the development of FDI protections has been unexpectedly hijacked by special interests and set on an unforeseen and irreversible path.[1]

However, on closer analysis, the notion that the trends underlying modern FDI protocols have undergone radical rethinking is subject to challenge. Rather, these trends reflect an evolutionary progression of thinking on the subject. They are steeped in established international law obligations and evolving treaty commitments. Although the speed with which these changes have taken place is often the result of political exigencies, the trends nonetheless reflect a predictable progression of thinking on the evolution and value of FDI.

Some FDI progress has been made multilaterally, but more often, regionally and bilaterally. Investor protection is now commonly addressed in comprehensive regional and bilateral trade agreements, or in stand-alone Bilateral Investment Treaties (BITs). Regardless of the type of agreement that embodies them, investment provisions are

[1] For concern about the influence of special interests on WTO and other global trade and investment institutions, notably in relation to human rights, *see, e.g.*, BERNARD M. HOEKMAN & MICHEL M. KOSTECKI., THE POLITICAL ECONOMY OF THE WORLD TRADING SYSTEM: THE WTO AND BEYOND (3rd Ed, 2009); LORI WALLACH & MICHELLE SFORZA, THE WTO: FIVE YEARS OF REASONS TO RESIST CORPORATE GLOBALIZATION (2000). *See generally*, GIORGIO BARBA NAVARETTI & ANTHONY J. VENABLES, MULTINATIONAL FIRMS IN THE WORLD ECONOMY (2004). Caroline Dommen, *Raising Human Rights Concerns in the World Trade Organization—Actors, Processes and Possible Strategies*, 24 HUMAN RIGHTS Q. 1 (2002). *See also* KENT ALBERT JONES, WHO'S AFRAID OF THE WTO? (2003); BENJAMIN HEIM SHEPARD & RONALD HAYDUK, FROM ACT UP TO THE WTO: URBAN PROTEST AND COMMUNITY BUILDING IN THE ERA OF GLOBALIZATION (2002); Robin Broad, GLOBAL BACKLASH: CITIZEN INITIATIVES FOR A JUST WORLD ECONOMY (2002).

generally aimed at facilitating the flow of investments between countries and creating standard investor protection protocols. In essence, they seek to imbue certainty and predictability in the FDI decision-making process and limit political interference, albeit selectively.

Historical events are also instrumental in gleaning a true understanding of modern FDI protocols. These events shape the global investment environment, which continues to spawn novel refinements in FDI protocols. Modern FDI protections have also been shaped by a history that is attributable, inter alia, to neocolonial imperialism, ideological tension between capital-importing and exporting-countries, the growth of civil society activism, and developments in international economic law. The modern history of FDI protocols is usefully analyzed in four distinct phases, which include regulation in historical societies, the period of regulation prior to the end of World War II, the period subsequent to that war, and the present global era.[2]

The regulation of foreign investment can be traced back over many centuries. The early trading nations, such as the Phoenicians, maintained a constant vigilance over investments in their territories. Versions of what we now know as eminent domain can be found in ancient Rome. The Roman Empire confiscated property from non-Romans in the course of conquest and eventually developed the practice using private Roman property in the furtherance of public projects.

These practices that developed in the Roman Empire were adopted by the Civil Codes in the ensuing centuries, and the common law adopted similar practices from civil law. In the early eighteenth century, the British Parliament developed the practice of paying compensation when appropriating land for public purposes. Shortly after the American Revolution, the United States and Britain signed the Jay Treaty, which, among other things, stipulated the protection of their investor nationals from the host government.[3]

Over time, the political sensitivities of taking property from private citizens, in furtherance of public works, were exacerbated in those cases in which the property belonged to foreigners. Ad hoc tribunals became a useful tool to diffuse sensitive political claims over the expropriation of private property. The once inalienable sovereign right of states to expropriate property was gradually but unevenly tempered. Host governments sometimes bowed in response to political pressure, in times of military or civil instability, to limit their powers to act in the "public interest." Foreigners who

---

[2] *See* Kenneth Vandevelde, *A Brief History of International Investment Agreements*, 12 U.C. Davis J. Int'l L. & Pol'y 157 (2005) (reviewing the history of BITs from the perspective of three eras: colonial era, post-colonial era, and global era.) *See also* O. Thomas Johnson, Jr. & Jonathan Gimblett, From Gunboats to Bits: The Evolution of Modern International Investment Law, *in* Yearbook on International Investment Law & Policy 2010–2011 (Karl P. Sauvant ed., 2012).

[3] Treaty of Amity, Commerce and Navigation, between His Britannic Majesty and the United States of America, Ratified June 24, 1795 [the Jay Treaty].

were subject to expropriation, in turn, came to expect access to nondomestic tribunals to resolve expropriation issues.[4]

The history of relations between the United States and Mexico is replete with examples of resolution of disputes through arbitration. Arbitration has been successfully used to diffuse armed conflict and settle boundary disputes, as well as to indemnify private investors. Notably, the Mexico–U.S. Claims Tribunal was an arbitral mechanism employed by Mexico and the United States in 1868 to resolve politically sensitive expropriations claims.[5] The Tribunal resolved thousands of claims and, in so doing, was instrumental in fostering sovereign respect for an extrajudicial process for lodging investment claims.[6]

The Allied–German Tribunal, established after the conclusion of World War I, provided another opportunity to advance thinking on extrajudicial claims against a host state. It was set up to arbitrate the claims of individuals against the German state for losses incurred during that war. The Tribunal created a novel model for the resolution of disputes between the state and individuals, which would eventually come to serve as a useful model for subsequent arbitral bodies.

Prior to the end of World War II, global economic relations were fostered by establishment of commercial trade ties. However, in this environment, many states were distinctly protectionist in regulating foreign investment. As a result, investment protections for foreign investors were invariably relegated to a subsidiary concern. Friendship, Commerce and Navigation Treaties (FCNTs) became the primary instrument by which global economic relations were regulated in the late eighteenth century. Their prominence endured to the end of World War II. FCNTs focused on enhancing trade relations between nations, but also contained subsidiary provisions protecting property. As these treaties did not provide enforcement mechanisms, vulnerable investors seeking protection were forced to rely on their government's assistance. Such assistance was usually channeled through the diplomatic espousal of an investor's claim, or at the behest of coercive military forces.[7]

The post–World War II era ushered in a new reality in global economic relations. Geopolitical developments became the driving force behind FDI protection protocols between the end of World War II and the collapse of the Soviet Union. The end of that war ushered in a new era of neoliberal global economic relations as the Allied victors sought to establish a global framework to ensure economic prosperity as they envisaged it. The Bretton-Woods System was intended to liberalize global trade and guard against the protectionist sentiment that many believed had precipitated that war.[8]

---

4 *See generally*, JOHN HOWARD JACKSON, SOVEREIGNTY, THE WTO AND CHANGING FUNDAMENTALS OF INTERNATIONAL LAW (2006).

5 Convention between the United States of America and the Republic of Mexico for the Adjustment of Claims, July 4, 1868, US–MEX, art. 11, 115 Stat. 679.

6 A.H. FELLER, THE MEXICAN CLAIMS COMMISSIONS (1935).

7 Vandevelde, *supra* note 2, at 157–61.

8 *See, e.g.*, MARTIN WOLF, WHY GLOBALIZATION WORKS (2004); Jagdish Bhagwati & Arvind Panagariya, *The Theory of Preferential Trade Agreements: Historical Evolution and Current Trends*, 86(2) AM. ECON.

This system envisioned global trade and investment rules, along with supranational institutions to oversee the regulation of trade and investment. The General Agreement on Trade and Tariffs (GATT) was established in 1947, but the Havana Charter, which was to establish an investment regime, and the institutional makeup for the GATT, did not materialize. Over time, the GATT became the principal multilateral engine for trade liberalization, while investment issues were dealt with separately outside the multilateral arena. As trade liberalization flourished, multilateral agreements displaced the importance of bilateral treaties.[9]

However, this neoliberal philosophy did not develop in isolation. It was soon challenged by the rising socialist tide, which swept in as a result of the process of decolonization. This process both highlighted the great disparity between the developed and developing worlds and brought into focus the competing ideologies over investment policy. The effect of this debate manifested itself in a questioning of the fundamental underpinnings of neoliberal global economic relations.

The decolonization, which occurred after World War II, greatly influenced the FDI debate. Many newly independent but underdeveloped nations came together to decry FDI as a modern form of neocolonialism. These countries, fiercely protective of their newfound sovereignty, looked suspiciously at any attempt by foreigners from developed states to control their means of production and to influence domestic affairs. Under the banner of ending the cycle of exploitation, these developing countries engaged in a course of import substitution, which was less than hospitable to FDI.[10]

Similarly, the socialist block also became a driving force in the FDI debate. As the Soviet Union emerged into a superpower after World War II, socialist states openly rejected free market principles in favor of state regulation. This philosophy decried foreign investment as an oppressive capitalist tool and led to extensive expropriations of private investments.[11]

REV. 82 (1996); A.O. Krueger, *Are Preferential Trading Arrangements Liberalizing or Protectionist?* 13(4) J. ECON. PERSPECTIVE 105 (1999); Raymond Riezman, *Can Bilateral Trade Agreements Help to Induce Free Trade?*, 32 CAN. J. ECON.751 (1999); Kyle Bagwell & Robert W. Staiger, *Will Preferential Agreements Undermine the Multilateral Trading System?* 108 THE ECON. J. 1162 (1998); Philip I. Levy, *A Political-Economic Analysis of Free Trade Agreements*, 87 AM. ECON. REV. 506 (1997).

[9] *See, e.g.*, YONG-SHIK LEE, RECLAIMING DEVELOPMENT IN THE WORLD TRADING SYSTEM (2006); ANDREW G. BROWN, RELUCTANT PARTNERS: A HISTORY OF MULTILATERAL TRADE COOPERATION, 1850–2000 (2003); BERNARD HOEKMAN & MICHEL KOSTECKI, THE POLITICAL ECONOMY OF THE WORLD TRADING SYSTEM, FROM GATT TO WTO (2001); JAGDISH NATWARLAL BHAGWATI, IN DEFENSE OF GLOBALIZATION (2004); John H. Jackson, THE JURISPRUDENCE OF GATT AND THE WTO: INSIGHTS ON TREATY LAW AND ECONOMIC RELATIONS (2000).

[10] For example, in the case of Mexico, it was not until 1993 that Mexico's highly restrictive approach to foreign investment was replaced with a new investment law that was seen as being more favorable to foreign investment in Mexico and as promoting international trade. *See generally*, JORGE A. VARGAS, MEXICAN LAW: A TREATISE FOR LEGAL PRACTITIONERS AND INTERNATIONAL INVESTORS, Vol. 1, at 105–39 (1998).

[11] Vandevelde, *supra* note 2, at n.52.

In response, the United States embarked upon a new series of FCNTs, which sought to prioritize FDI protections.[12] These FCNTs granted foreign investors both national treatment and most-favored-nation status. These protections were also, for the first time, extended to corporations and included dispute resolution clauses.

These dispute resolution clauses obliged host governments to consent to the jurisdiction of the International Court of Justice. Host governments could no longer use their consent to sublimate the jurisdiction of an international tribunal. However, investors still had to exhaust local remedies and were usually put to the task of persuading their home state governments to espouse investor claims with host states. Although this new generation of FCNTs created many innovations, its utility faded because, in essence, FCNTs were still seen as being primarily trade-based, and trade was increasingly being dealt with through the GATT.[13]

The developing countries and the socialist block eventually combined resources to form a formidable presence on the global stage. By the mid 1970s, this group, holding a numerical majority in the United Nation's General Assembly, vigorously fought for the recognition of their right to expropriate foreign investments without paying compensation at fair market value. In 1974, the General Assembly of the United Nations adopted the Declaration of the New International Economic Order, which recognized state sovereignty over natural resources and other economic activities. The declaration further recognized the right of states to nationalize domestic industries and declined to articulate any specific obligation to pay compensation for such nationalization.[14]

The General Assembly eventually also adopted the Charter of Economic Rights and Duties of States. That UN Charter banned the use of military force, in all circumstances, except in self-defense. The Charter also recognized the right of states to expropriate, and opted for the requirement that compensation "should," rather than "must" be paid.[15] This obligation on states was further diluted by the adoption of a national, rather than an international law standard that was applied to questions of compensation. Given that many national laws did not provide for any, much less adequate, compensation, the significance of this distinction should not be overstated.[16] Also problematic was the fact that customary international law continued to offer investors only very limited protection, and was routinely proven to be inadequate, in the context of growing nationalizations and expropriations.

---

[12] *See id.*, at 161–62. *See also* Calvin Hamilton & Paula L. Rochwerger, *Trade and Investment: Foreign Direct Investment through Bilateral and Multilateral Treaties*, 18 N.Y. INTL L. REV. 1 (2005).

[13] *See* Vandevelde, *supra* note 2.

[14] *See* Vandevelde, *supra* note 2, at 167–68.

[15] United Nations General Assembly, Charter of Economic Rights and Duties of States, G.A. Res. 3281 (XXIX), U.N. GAOR, 29th Sess., 2315th Plen. Mtg., U.N. Doc. A/RES/3281 (XXIX) (Dec. 12, 1974), *reprinted* in 14 I.L.M. 251 (1975).

[16] *See* Vandevelde, *supra* note 2, at 168. *See also* Charles N. Brower & John Tepe, Jr., *The Charter of Economic Rights and Duties of States: A Reflection or a Rejection of International Law?*, 9 INT'L L. 295 (1975) and Burns Weston, *The Charter of Economic Rights and Duties of States and the Deprivation of Foreign-Owned Wealth*, 75 AM. J. INT'L L. 437 (1981).

Treaties became the only viable tool to protect against uncompensated, or under-compensated, takings. As such, developed states increasingly adopted BITs as a means of protecting foreign investors who lacked protection both under multilateral treaties and customary international law.[17] The first BIT was concluded between West Germany and Pakistan in 1959. Following further BIT development, Western European countries increasingly pioneered the use of modern BITs throughout the 1960s. The 1970s saw most of the developed Western world follow suit.[18] The United States inaugurated its BIT program in 1997, and quickly concluded its first BIT in 1998.[19] The American BIT Program supported several key economic policy objectives ranging from the protection of investment interests overseas to the promotion of market-oriented policies and exports.[20]

The BITs programs were straightforward. A basic aim of BITs was to protect investments abroad where investors' rights were not already protected through existing agreements. These BITs encouraged the adoption of market-oriented domestic policies that treated private investment in a transparent and nondiscriminatory fashion. BITs were also used to support the development of international law standards that were consistent with these objectives.[21] "Core" BIT principles included:

- the treatment for the life of the investments to be the better of most-favored nation or national treatment;
- disciplines on expropriation and the payment of prompt compensation;
- funds transferability into and out of the host country at market exchange rates;
- limits on performance requirements;
- the right of the investor to submit investment disputes to international arbitration, without need to resort to domestic courts;
- the right of the investor to hire the management personnel of their choice, regardless of nationality.[22]

---

[17] *See* Carlos Garcia, *All The Dirty Little Secrets: Investment Treaties, Latin America and the Necessary Evil of Investor—State Arbitration*, 16 FLA. J. INT'L L. 301 (discussing the debate over whether investment treaties establish good policies that encourage FDI in the developing world, or whether they amount to economic imperialism that binds the developing world).

[18] Notably, the United Kingdom, Japan, Australia. *See* Vandevelde, *supra* note 2, at 169–70. *See also* Tarcisio Gazzini, *Bilateral Investment Treaties*, *in* INTERNATIONAL INVESTMENT LAW: THE SOURCES OF RIGHTS AND OBLIGATIONS (Tarcisio Gazzini & Eric De Brabandere eds., 2012).

[19] Vandevelde, *supra* note 2 (discussing various American BITs and the problems associated with interpretation). *See also* ANGELOS DIMOPOULOS, EU FOREIGN INVESTMENT LAW (2011).

[20] US Bilateral Investment Treaties, Policy Issues, U.S. Department of State, *available at* http://www.ustr.gov/node/4375/206/0. *See also* JEFFREY J. SCOTT, FREE TRADE AGREEMENTS. US STRATEGIES AND PRIORITIES (2004).

[21] SCOTT, *supra* note 20. *See also* ALEXANDRA DIEHL, THE CORE STANDARD OF INTERNATIONAL INVESTMENT PROTECTION (2012).

[22] *Id.*

Modern BITs were uniform among nations as they were modeled on provisions found in the modern American FCNTs. Specifically, they guaranteed foreign investors, inter alia, both national and most-favored-nation treatment.[23] Notably, they dealt exclusively with the protection of investments, opting not to get bogged down on non-investment issues. Trade issues were left in the exclusive domain of the GATT.[24]

At this juncture, FDI was in the process of depoliticization. It was moving from a policy toward a rule-based regimen. In providing foreign investors with legal remedies, FDI protections were less dependent on diplomacy. Furthermore, modern BITs opted largely for international investment arbitration, as distinct from reliance on the domestic courts of member states. The result was that it was no longer required that foreign investors exhaust local remedies in the host country; instead, such investors could proceed directly to international investment arbitration. Although BITs largely preserved the dispute resolution process between the state and the investor, they broke new ground by subjecting investment disputes to especially constituted ad hoc international arbitral tribunals rather than the International Court of Justice. The establishment of the International Centre for the Settlement of Investment Disputes (ICSID) in 1965 further expanded the potential scope of arbitrability to include disputes over the interpretation of the ICSID Convention.[25]

BITs that were concluded between developed and developing nations included provisions that dealt with ideological concerns. Developing countries signed BITs largely in order to attract FDI. Developed countries signed BITs primarily to protect their nationals investing abroad. These BITs were, for the most part, boilerplate. They contained expansive investor protections, but they were, essentially, presented to developing countries as take-it-or-leave-it propositions for signature, without negotiation. Although these agreements theoretically contained reciprocal obligations, the reality was that capital-exporting countries were often advantaged in responding to the claims of nationals from capital-importing countries on account of the capital-exporting countries having already liberalized their investment regimes to deal with investors from developed countries. Developing countries that lacked such a liberalized investment infrastructure sometimes were disadvantaged in having to devise regimes to accommodate foreign investors from developed countries who were often accustomed to significant liberalization in dealing with developed states.[26]

---

23 Vandevelde, *supra* note 2, at 170.

24 *See further* Bryan Mercurio & Simon Lester, Bilateral and Regional Trade Agreements: Analysis and Commentary (2007); Lorand Bartels & Federico Ortino, Regional Trade Agreements and the WTO Legal System (2006).

25 Convention on the Settlement of Investment Disputes between States and Nationals of Other States, Mar. 18, 1965, 17 U.S.T. 1270, T.I.A.S. No. 6090. Documents pertaining to the ICSID and its Rules are available at http://www.worldbank.org/icsid.

26 *See, e.g.*, T.N. Srinivasan, Developing Countries and the Multilateral Trading System after Doha (2002). *See further* Bernard Hoekman & Will Martin, Developing Countries and the WTO: A Pro-Active Agenda (2005); Merlinda D. Ingco & John D. Nash, Agriculture and the WTO: Creating a Trading System for Development (2004); Commonwealth Secretariat,

The ensuing tension over the wording of treaties also delayed the progression of BITs. The United States sought to establish FDI protections through customary international law. The U.S. strategy was to create a sufficiently large network of BITs that would reflect norms of customary international law, especially prompt, adequate, and effective compensation for expropriations. In keeping with this objective, the United States would not sign a treaty in the absence of such wording. Not surprisingly, developing countries, in response, were often hesitant to conclude such agreements. They were reluctant to be drawn into treaties employing such compromising wording that might not only be used against them under a particular agreement, but would also further entrench the U.S. view of customary international law.[27]

While progress on bilateral investment treaties stalled, political exigency, once again, created the opportunity to advance FDI protocols. The Iran–U.S. Tribunal was established as a measure to diffuse the crisis between the United States and Iran resulting from the detention of U.S. nationals at the U.S. embassy in Tehran in November 1979 and the subsequent seizure of Iranian assets by the United States. The Tribunal was the mechanism used to bring about binding third-party arbitration of claims between nationals of either country against the host governments. This Tribunal effectively usurped judicial authority from the domestic courts in the United States and Iran. The Tribunal, in accordance with the UNCITRAL Rules, yielded substantial decisions that further legitimized the use of arbitral mechanisms and also synthesized the international jurisprudence on takings.

The global era continues to evolve in a dynamic context. The conclusion of the Uruguay Round created the World Trade Organization (WTO) to oversee international trade, under the auspices of the GATT.[28] The WTO was also endowed with jurisdiction over investment-related issues, most notably under the auspices of the General Agreement on Trade-Related Services (GATS).[29] As services are often provided by establishing a presence in a foreign market, the GATS obligation to liberalize trade in services in many ways is an obligation to liberalize and protect foreign investment.

Other multilateral and plurilateral agreements further expanded the WTO's jurisdiction over investment and restricted the authority of governments over foreign investments. These agreements included the Agreement on Trade Related Investment Measures (TRIMS)[30] which, inter alia, prohibits inflicting certain trade-distorting performance requirements on foreign investments. The Agreement on Trade-Related Intellectual Property Rights (TRIPS),[31] obligating countries to protect intellectual

---

Developing Countries and the WTO: A Compelling Case for Full Participation in the New Round (2002).

[27] By 1969 only seventy-five BITs were negotiated. By the 1970s, BITs were being negotiated at the rate of nine per year, and the rate doubled during the 1980s. *See*, Vandevelde, *supra* note 2, at 172.

[28] World Trade Organization (WTO) documentation is available at the WTO Website, http://www.wto.org. *See also* Peter Gallagher, The First Ten Years of the WTO: 1995–2005 (2005).

[29] GATS documentation is available at the WTO Website, http://www.wto.org.

[30] TRIMS documentation is available at the WTO Website, http://www.wto.org.

[31] TRIPS documentation is available at the WTO Website, http://www.wto.org.

property rights, represents a further restriction on the capacity of governments to regulate FDI.

The international investment regime has also witnessed a pronounced intermingling between trade and investment, coupled with a corresponding explosion in the number of investment protocols. There are anticipated to be over 3,000 negotiated BITs by the end of 2012, as well as a growing number of FTAs with investment provisions.[32] International trade and investment are now increasingly carried out between different subsidiaries of the same multinational entities. As such, trade and investment are more integrated, encompassing various emerging elements of international commerce: exports, imports used in exports, use of foreign affiliates for sale, globalized production and distribution, and FDI.

The economic integration brought about by the expansion of multilateral agreements has also encouraged the negotiation of regional FTAs. These agreements, which are increasingly negotiated between developed and developing countries, also include investment provisions.[33] This phenomenon is attributable to at least three developments. First, the traditional distinction between capital-importing and capital-exporting countries had receded. The reasons underlying this change were both political and practical. Second, as a matter of practice, a number of countries that were previously viewed as developing, such as China, had advanced to the point where they had grown sufficiently to be viewed as capital exporters of their newfound wealth. Many countries that were traditionally viewed as capital exporters, including the United States, had gradually become dependent on importing capital, which increasingly came from developing countries. Third, as a political and economic reality, new trade and investment agreements were being forged between countries in distinct regions of the world. This further intensified regional preferential economic agreements, including the political–economic alliances that ensued.[34]

The global era also bore witness to a further phenomenon: the race among states to attract FDI. The collapse of the Soviet Union gave rise to the prominence of market-oriented developing countries that relied on FDI. The ideological divisions, which separated the developing world from the capital-exporting developed world, also succumbed to a new pragmatic and seemingly cooperative relationship. Developing countries came to rely on FDI as a means to develop, whereas developed countries saw FDI as another lucrative export. In addition, socialist countries such as China increasingly engaged in a bifurcated economic policy. They continued to preserve socialist restrictions on domestic commerce, albeit with less rigor than in decades past. At the same time, they embraced market-based principles in their international

---

32 *See Research Note: Recent Developments in International Investment Agreements,* United Nations Conference on Trade and Development (Aug. 30, 2005) (UNCTAD), http://www.unctad.org. *See also* http://www.cfr.org/publication/10890/.

33 By 2005, 39% of all preferential trade agreements containing investment provisions were concluded between countries with dissimilar levels of development. *See* Vandevelde, *supra* note 2, at 182.

34 By 2005, 44% of all preferential trade arrangements were concluded between countries in different regions. *See id.* at 182.

trade and investment relations. This includes both selective access provided to foreign investors to domestic Chinese markets and support for Chinese investors abroad.[35]

The fermenting global dependence on FDI and the economic wealth it generated further spawned a movement to democratize global institutions. This was, in part, a response to the perception that international economic institutions had ignored the role otherwise played by individuals and non-state actors in global governance.[36] The result was a hurried attempt to make up for lost time as civil society responded to modern challenges by demanding a more vocal participation in global governance.

Overall, despite the efforts to democratize global institutions, the results have been somewhat disappointing. On the one side, active segments of civil society continue to decry the illegitimacy of global institutions, arguing that the corrective measures that have been undertaken do not go far enough. On the other side, many countries have begun questioning the legitimacy of global institutions that embrace such fundamental change without the consensus of their constituent members. Those following the cultures and legal traditions of many non-Western countries may not adequately value and, in fact, sometimes may resent the participation of private investors in what they deem to be exclusively a sovereign function.[37]

The perceived deficiencies of liberalized global institutions are further fermented in current recessionary times. Trade and investment isolation may now be a by-product of new fears in regard to the intrusion of foreign competition into domestic markets. These concerns are expressed both through restrictions placed by governments on international investments in domestic economies and by negative reactions towards FDI within civil society. These include, among others, lobbying by labor groups against competition that undermines local employment and agitation by environmental groups against the ecological impact of FDI. Domestic alarm about the perceived lack of safety of foreign-made goods and services are also a prospective reason for growing protectionism in both trade and investment. Coupled with this is the desire of governments to secure both greater advantage and greater protection from investment treaties than in decades past.

---

[35] *See, e.g.*, GUIGUO WANG, CHINESE PERSPECTIVES ON INTERNATIONAL INVESTMENT LAW (2013); Vivienne Bath, *Foreign Investment, The National Interest and National Security—Foreign Direct Investment in Australia and China*, 34 SYDNEY L. REV. 5 (2012); GERALD CHAN, CHINA'S COMPLIANCE IN GLOBAL AFFAIRS: TRADE, ARMS CONTROL, ENVIRONMENTAL PROTECTION, HUMAN RIGHTS (2006); YONG DENG & FEI-LING, CHINA RISING: POWER AND MOTIVATION IN CHINESE FOREIGN POLICY (2005).

[36] *See* ANDREAS KULICK, GLOBAL PUBLIC INTEREST IN INTERNATIONAL INVESTMENT LAW (2012); David Schneiderman, *Investing in Democracy? Political Process and International Investment Law*, 60 U. TORONTO L.J. 909 (2012); DANIEL VERDIER, DEMOCRACY AND INTERNATIONAL TRADE: BRITAIN, FRANCE, AND THE UNITED STATES, 1860–1990 (1995). *See also* Noemi Gal-Or, *Private Party Access: A Comparison of NAFTA and the EU Disciplines*, 21 B.C. INTL & COMP. L. REV. 1 (1988).

[37] *See, e.g.*, PHILIP DAVID MCMICHAEL, DEVELOPMENT AND SOCIAL CHANGE: A GLOBAL PERSPECTIVE (3rd ed., 2004); ROURDES BENERIA & SAVITRI BISNATH, GLOBAL TENSIONS: CHALLENGES AND OPPORTUNITIES IN THE WORLD ECONOMY (2003).

These perceived deficiencies in the growth of a receptive global environment for international investment are offset by significant structural changes in the international regime that continue to support FDI, including in bad economic times. Individuals continue to enjoy the right to bring direct claims for the infringement of their investment rights—especially as they relate to property ownership—before international investment tribunals. International law has evolved after World War II in ways in which the traditional approach that limited access to international legal remedies to state actors has been significantly replaced by recognition that individuals should enjoy a role in the development of FDI. Particularly important in this process was the growth of the international human rights movement. The once-clear demarcation between human rights and other rights has been obfuscated in some measure.[38]

Today, the issue is less whether, and more how, civil society will participate in global governance.[39] In this context, the right of citizens to bring actions and secure standing (*locus standi*) to assert public interest claims has become increasingly significant. The right of private parties to assert their rights and interests is relevant in three related, but different contexts. First, the right of private parties to assert these interests is understood in the context of state-to-state adjudication. Second, it is important in the context of disputes between private parties and states. Third, the right of private parties to assert claims against states is often meaningful only when those parties are resourced companies and individuals with the ability to sustain a costly and often protracted claims process.

The global FDI era has also led to a collision course between an emboldened civil society and an insatiable global demand for FDI. Proponents of global investment envisioned the need for a multilateral investment agreement to provide predictable and transparent investment rules in a world in which competition for FDI is growing. In contrast, energized civil society groups have actively sought to restrain the development of a multilateral investment regime that they considered corporate-driven, repugnant to the notions of governmental sovereignty and socially regressive. This battle came to a head in 1998 when public pressure effectively derailed negotiations on the Multilateral Agreement on Investment (MAI). That failure to reach consensus on the MAI at the Organization for Economic Development and Cooperation (OECD) is often cited as the end to multilateral progress on FDI protocols.[40]

---

38 *See* Diane Alferez Desierto, *Calibrating Human Rights and Investment in Economic Emergencies: Prospects of Treaty and Valuation Defenses*, MANCHESTER J. INT'L ECON. L, 280 (2012), *available at* http://ssrn.com/abstract=2062367.

39 *See* THE FUTURE OF THE WTO: ADDRESSING INSTITUTIONAL CHALLENGES IN THE NEW MILLENNIUM 41, Report by the Consultative Board to the Director—General Supachai Panitchpakdi (2004). *See also* Alan O. Sykes, *Public Versus Private Enforcement of International Economic Law: Standing and Remedy*, 34 J. LEGAL STUD. 631 (2005) (arguing that private enforcement of governmental commitments is more efficient in the context of international investment agreements than in international trade agreements).

40 Negotiations on the Multilateral Agreement on Investment (MAI), under the auspices of the Organization for Economic Cooperation and Development, failed in 1998, in large part due to effective public criticism. For an overview of the MAI and its implications to sovereignty and the federal–state

Having failed to arrive at a multilateral investment accord before the OECD, the only other multilateral forum available for FDI was the WTO. However, the WTO, as it presently stands, addresses FDI only indirectly. The Doha Round has provided faint hope for progress on a more holistic basis.[41] The lack of an overarching FDI multilateral instrument also renders the emerging FDI regime into a patchwork quilt of disparate obligations. In effect, the global FDI regime consists of obligations expressed through an ever-expanding network of international instruments. These include regional FTAs and BITs, specialized multilateral treaties (such as TRIMs), services agreements, the OECD's code of Capital Movements, and Europe's Energy Charter, as well as soft-law instruments, such as the World Bank's FDI Guidelines.[42]

In the absence of multilateral progress, the NAFTA offered a way forward. Its investment protection provisions were initially looked upon as a model, or prototype, for evolving investment protocols.[43] As many trade agreements negotiated after NAFTA tracked its investment provisions, there was an expectation that NAFTA Chapter 11 would provide the framework for investment in future FTAs, especially the anticipated FTAA.[44] However, more recent agreements appear to be trying to cut back on many of the investor safeguards contained in the NAFTA, and new BITs and FTAs have chosen an alternative pathway to the NAFTA, which is increasingly regarded as a past-order treaty.[45]

In the dearth of a multilateral structure, the history of NAFTA Chapter 11 has nevertheless played a pivotal role in shaping the evolving FDI regime, particularly in regard to FDI decisions. In many respects, Chapter 11 has become the theater for cutting-edge

balance of powers, *see* Robert Stumberg, *Sovereignty by Subtraction: The Multilateral Agreement on Investment*, 31 CORNELL INT'L L.J. 491 (1998). *See generally* MAI Negotiating Text (Apr. 24, 1998), http://www.oecd.org/daf/cmis/mai/maitext.pdf and Katie Tieleman, *The Failure of the Multilateral Agreement on Investment and the Absence of a Global Public Policy Network* (2000), http://www.gppi.net.

41 Doha Ministerial declaration, Fourth Ministerial Conference in Doha, Qatar, ¶¶ 20–22 (Nov. 2001), http://www.wto.org.

42 *See, e.g.*, Jose Alvarez, *The Emerging Foreign Direct Investment Regime*, 99 AM. SOC'Y INT'L L. PROC. 94. *See also* UNCTAD, *supra* note 32. On these different investment regimes, *see generally* RUDOLF DOLZER & CHRISTOPH SCHREUER, PRINCIPLES OF INTERNATIONAL INVESTMENT LAW (2nd ed. 2012); INTERNATIONAL INVESTMENT LAW, *supra* note 18.

43 *See generally* Jacqueline Granados, *Investor Protection and Foreign Investment under NAFTA Chapter 11: Prospects for the Western Hemisphere under Chapter 17 of the FTAA*, 13 CARDOZO J. INT'L & COMP. L. 189 (2005).

44 The FTAA contemplates a hemispheric wide trade agreement among thirty-four countries in the Americas. The draft FTAA text may be consulted at http: //www.ftaa.alca.org.

45 Earlier agreements that appeared to track the NAFTA include: The Canada-Chile FTA, concluded Dec. 5, 1996, *reprinted* in 36 I.L.M. 1067, 1114 (1997) and the Mexico–Northern triangle FTA. *See*, Guillermo Pereira, *Mexico–Northern Triangle Free Trade Agreement*, 7 L. & BUS. REV. AM. 383 (2001). However, more recent agreements based on the 2002 Trade Promotions Act, such as the CAFTA and the U.S.–Chile FTA, appear to cut back on some of the NAFTA safeguards. *See* David Gantz, *The Evolution of FTA Investment Provisions: From NAFTA to the United States–Chile Free Trade Agreement*, 19 AM. U. INT'L L. REV. 679.

twenty-first–century issues, which has shaped international law and adjudication.[46] It has become the focal point for debate over the liberalization of trade and investment, in general and, more specifically, the evolution of FDI protection protocols. It also has become both the lightning rod for antiglobalization critics as well as the beacon of light for internationalists.

[46] *See* Ari Afilalo, *Meaning, Ambiguity and Legitimacy: Judicial (Re-) Construction of NAFTA Chapter 11*, 25 NW. J. INT'L L. & BUS. 279 (2005). *See also* Patricia Isela Hansen, *Dispute Settlement in NAFTA and Beyond*, 40 TEX. INT'L L.J. 417 (arguing that the NAFTA experience may prove helpful in building models for dispute settlement in other agreements, especially in the areas of private rights of action, transparency, and public participation).

3

INTERNATIONAL INVESTMENT LAW: SOME LEGAL CULTURAL INSIGHTS

*Colin B. Picker**

I. Introduction

A legal cultural analysis can be a very useful device when considering legal systems and traditions. Previous such analyses by the author have provided interesting insights into the legal culture of international fields and organizations.[1] Each of those examinations presented new challenges for the methodology as well as new opportunities for the methodology to be tested and expanded. This chapter will apply that methodological approach to international investment law. In the process of that examination, this chapter will confront fresh obstacles and issues and consequently will further develop

* Associate Professor, University of New South Wales, Sydney, Australia. A.B. (Bowdoin College), J.D. (Yale Law School). The research here is part of a larger study by the author on legal culture and international economic law that will be part of the author's PhD dissertation.

1 *See, e.g.*, Colin B. Picker, *An Introduction to Comparative Analyses of International Organizations*, *in* COMPARATIVE LAW AND INTERNATIONAL ORGANIZATIONS: COOPERATION, COMPETITION AND CONNECTIONS (Lukas Heckendorn & Colin Picker eds., forthcoming 2012–13) [hereinafter Picker, *IOs*]; Colin B. Picker, *WTO Governance: A Legal Cultural Critique*, *in* GOVERNANCE IN CONTEMPORARY JAPAN (Kenji Hirashima ed., 2011) [hereinafter Picker, *Governance*]; Colin B. Picker, *A Framework for Comparative Analyses of International Law and Its Institutions: Using the Example of the World Trade Organization*, *in* COMPARATIVE LAW AND HYBRID LEGAL SYSTEMS (Eleanor Cashin Ritaine, Seán Patrick Donlan & Martin Sychold eds., 2010) [hereinafter Picker, *WTO*]; Colin B. Picker, *China, Global Governance & Legal Culture: The Example of China & the WTO* (J. Nakagawa ed., 2011) [hereinafter Picker, *China*); Colin B. Picker, *International Trade & Development Law: A Legal Cultural Critique*, 4(2) L. & DEVEL. REV. 4 (2011) [hereinafter Picker, *Development*"); Colin B. Picker, *Comparative Law Methodology & American Legal Culture: Obstacles and Opportunities*, 16 ROGER WILLIAMS UNIV. L. REV.86–99 (2011).

the methodology. It should not be surprising that international investment law presents its own challenges and requires its own individual approach, for it is a dynamic and expansive field in its own right. Nonetheless, as will be shown below, the methodology once again proves its worth by providing insights for those involved in international investment law—from scholars to practitioners to arbitrators and regulators. Any insights that can help develop our understanding of the field should be welcomed, for international investment law, despite the many controversies surrounding it, is a field that has tremendous ability to enhance the lives of people around the world by providing employment, infrastructure, and better living conditions, and generally contributing to the improvement of people's lives.[2]

Typically legal discussions of investment focus on the technical substantive landscape—from the restrictions and incentives that may be present at the start of an investment transaction to the resolution of disputes when investments go awry. Yet, there is also a human angle that is relevant to any examination of the legal aspects of investments. The legal analysis of that human angle is represented by the legal culture of the participants. Those legal cultures will be reflected in the law-related behaviors of: the individual investors, the investments recipients, the lawyers for both parties, the different governments' regulators and institutions, and the international civil servants and international institutions relevant to the investments. Additionally, the role of legal culture will be relevant at all stages of an investment from initiation of the investment to the operation of the investment, and to any investment disputes and their resolutions. Furthermore, those legal cultures will themselves impact the interpretation, application, and development of international investment law and will as a whole contribute to the creation of a legal culture for international investment law itself. Any insights ensuing from analyses of those legal cultural issues should prove beneficial to all the participants in international investments.

The most straightforward consideration of legal culture and international investment law would be simply to describe some common legal cultural characteristics for each aspect of international investment law. Those characteristics might include such features as the fact that Scandinavian investment contract negotiations may result in shorter or "less formal" agreements than is typically the case in the United States or Britain,[3] or that "saving face" is critical during investment negotiations in China.[4] These and the many other valuable discussions of specific legal cultural characteristics relevant to international investment law may be described as a "how-to" or guidebook legal cultural method. As the many citations in this chapter attest, there is no shortage

---

[2] *See, e.g.*, Efi Chalamash, *The Future of Bilateral Investment Treaties: A De Facto Multilateral Agreement?* 34 Brook. J. Int'l L. 303, 308 (2009) ("...during the 1990s [] when foreign investment became a central aspect of the global economy and effectively the principal engine of sustainable growth and development.").

[3] Sanna Suvanto, *Negotiating International Business Transactions—A Scandanavian Approach*, http://www.dundee.ac.uk/cepmlp/car/html/car7_article19.pdf (last visited Apr. 16, 2011) at 5.

[4] George O. White III, *Navigating the Cultural Malaise: Foreign Direct Investment Dispute Resolution in the People's Republic of China*, 5 Transactions: Tenn. J. Bus. L. 55, 58 (2003).

of international investment law publications that have taken that approach. This chapter's legal cultural analysis of international investment law, however, will not take that approach. Indeed, such an approach is clearly not possible within one chapter. After all, each region, state, and municipality will have its own discrete legal cultural issues that must be identified and understood for each interaction of every part of international investment law. Similarly, each of the many international institutions and organizations involved with the field will have its own legal cultures that will also vary with their interaction with international investment law.

Rather, and despite the value of such "guidebooks," this chapter will consider deeper conceptual and systemic legal cultural issues that should be considered when working within the field—either as a scholar or as a practitioner "on-the-ground." Of course, the broader issues that will be discussed will be illustrated with specific legal cultural characteristic examples that may be associated with that aspect of international investment law under examination. But, at its heart, this chapter is concerned with presenting the broader more systemic legal cultural issues facing the field of international investment law. This chapter will consider international investment law as a whole, and will leave the detailed legal cultural analysis of the many specific issues within domestic international investment regulation for other and later examinations.[5]

Nor will this chapter suggest which legal cultural characteristics may be better or worse for international investment law. Such a normative approach is rife with difficulties and entirely too contentious for a work that merely seeks to provide insights to what is presently going on within the international investment law field. Accordingly, this chapter will not enter the debate of which legal culture, systems, or traditions are more suited to an international investment climate or for specific aspects of international investment law.[6] That being said, it is likely that some of the insights provided in this chapter may be invoked in those debates. To the extent this chapter enters the fray at all it will merely be to suggest legal cultural characteristics within the field that may exist or be emerging and which may be relevant to those discussions about the direction of development of international investment law.

In order to provide the necessary background and context, this chapter will first explain the methodology and then discuss the unique obstacles international economic law presents for an application of the methodology. The chapter will then examine the field, with those difficulties in mind, and will identify systemic or macro-legal cultural

---

[5] Many such works already exist. *See, e.g.*, Talal A. Al-Emadi & Maryam A. Al-Asmakh, *Cultural Differences and Their Impact: Some Brief Comments*, 5 CHINESE J. INT'L L. 807, 807 n.1 (2005) (providing a detailed list of many such "how-to" works for negotiations and culture); Leon E. Trackman, *"Legal Traditions" and International Commercial Arbitration*, 17 AM. REV. INT'L ARB.1 (2006) (discussing legal traditions and cultures in the context of the main international fora for international investment dispute resolution); Don Peters, *Can We Talk? Overcoming Barriers to Mediating Private Transborder Commercial Disputes in the Americas*, 41 VAND. J. TRANSNAT'L L. 1251 (2008); and so on.

[6] *See, e.g.*, Claire Moore Dickerson, *Harmonizing Business Laws in Africa: OHADA Calls the Tune*, 44 COLUM. J. TRANSNAT'L L. 17, 29–37 (2005) (discussing the many claims that the French and civil law systems are less conducive to economic development).

consideration of the legal cultural issues present in international arbitrations.[10] As an example within the arbitration context, which also highlights the difference between legal culture and tradition, the following observation is best described as an observation of legal culture:

> [A] common law attorney representing a party in drafting an arbitration agreement would likely prefer substantial pre-hearing discovery, where each side provides considerable amounts of documents and depositions of key players are taken. On the other hand, a civil law attorney would likely prefer, or at least be more comfortable with, minimal or no discovery, such as a procedure disallowing depositions and permitting only a limited exchange of documents.[11]

Although the author attributes the difference to legal tradition,[12] in fact the legal traditions do not have a monolithic view on pretrial discovery. Each of the traditions include legal systems that approach pretrial discovery differently. For example, within the common law legal tradition, the English and the Americans take very different approaches to pretrial discovery—the Americans tending to favor expansive discovery, while the English oppose such "fishing expeditions."[13] Nor will it be the legal system's rules that determine lawyer's views on evidence production, for arbitration is neutral on the issue, leaving the decision to the parties. Rather, it will be the legal culture of the attorneys that is at issue in determining their views about extensive evidence production.

The above example also points to the fact that a great deal of legal culture is closely connected to the major legal traditions of the world—even as those systems are in the process of some level of convergence.[14] Thus, as a system becomes more common law, we might expect to see more of a pragmatic and ad hoc approach to the law.[15] Similarly, as a system becomes more civilian, we may expect to see more passive attorneys in

---

10 *See generally* Valentina Vadi, *Critical Comparisons: The Role of Comparative Law in Investment Treaty Arbitration*, 39 DENV. J. INT'L L. & POL'Y 67 (2010); White, *supra* note 4.

11 David J. McLean, *Toward a New International Dispute Resolution Paradigm: Assessing the Congruent Evolution of Globalization and International Arbitration*, 30 U. PA. J. INT'L L. 1087, 1094 (2009). As the author notes, there has been a compromise between the two with a middle ground–style of evidence production now in standard use. *Id.*

12 *Id.*

13 *See* Steven Loble, *Jurisdiction and Evidence—An English Perspective*, 4 ILSA J. INT'L & COMP. L. 489, 503–04 (1998); *see also* Elizabeth G. Thornburg, *Just Say "No Fishing": The Lure of Metaphor*, 40 U. MICH. J.L. REFORM 1 (2006).

14 *See* Mary Ann Glendon, Paolo G. Carozza & Colin B. Picker, COMPARATIVE LEGAL TRADITIONS: TEXTS, MATERIALS AND CASES ON WESTERN LAW 799 (3rd ed. 2007). *But see* Vivian Grosswald Curran, *Romantic Common Law, Enlightened Civil Law: Legal Uniformity and the Homogenization of the European Union*, 7 COLUM. J. EUR. L. 63, 71–72 (2001) (noting the enduring fundamental differences between the common and civil law systems).

15 J. Bédard, *Transsystemic Teaching of Law at McGill: "Radical Changes, Old and New Hats,"* 27 QUEEN'S L.J. 237, 288 (2001).

dispute settlement contexts, such as in court or arbitration hearings.[16] Of course, legal culture is derived from more than the larger legal traditions, for as the example above shows, the specific legal cultural attitude toward discovery is independent of the legal traditions. Nonetheless, noting a tendency toward a legal tradition's approach within a legal system will necessarily and strongly suggest the existence or emergence of associated legal cultural characteristics typically associated with that tradition.

The analysis of the example above, concerning discovery or pretrial evidence production, highlights the employment of a micro- or specific legal cultural analysis—the sort that typically finds itself in those valuable "how to" or "guidebook" considerations of the legal culture of international investment law. Another example of such a specific legal cultural analysis may help to show the detailed level that can be considered. For example, the late and distinguished Thomas Wälde noted that at the contract formation stage of an investment:

> [T]here is a cultural element involved; common law practitioners have always preferred to regulate in utmost detail, depth, and scope the salient behavior of, preferably, the other party to an agreement, either because of the absence of relatively specific, comprehensive, and credible law, because of a tradition of narrow and literal interpretation, or simply for reasons of habit and precedent. Conversely, in societies such as Asia, where law is not such an important regulator of commercial relationships and the contract is rather a statement of good will and the start-up of a relationship . . .[17]

Identification of specific legal cultural characteristics is especially useful for those fields where culture has been ignored or simply not considered. This was the case with earlier legal cultural analysis for such fields as international trade law and its governing institution, the World Trade Organization.[18] But, identification of specific or micro-legal cultural issues is insufficient on its own, for it is those legal cultural issues that span the field, at the macro, systemic, or holistic level, that drive the development of a field in particular and identifiable directions. Indeed, that form of macro-legal cultural analysis has also been undertaken and has successfully provided insights into the development of examined fields.[19] Of course, sometimes it can be difficult to separate the micro- and macro-legal cultural analyses because the identification of the specific legal cultural issues at the specific or micro-level will clearly suggest larger trends and issues within the field. Similarly, the identification of the macro- or systemic legal cultural issues may have implications at the micro- or specific level, and may itself rely on data generated by micro-legal analyses. As discussed further below, the analysis here

---

16 Picker, *WTO*, *supra* note 1, at 129.

17 Thomas W. Wälde & George Ndi, *Stabilizing International Investment Commitments: International Law versus Contract Interpretation*, 31 TEX. INT'L L.J. 215, 220–21 (1996).

18 *See* Picker, *WTO*, *supra* note 1.

19 *See* Picker, *Governance*, *supra* note 1.

will focus more on the macro- or systemic legal cultural issues present within international investment law.

Regardless of whether the legal cultural issue would be considered to be specific or general, international investment law is a field particularly suited to a legal cultural analysis at both specific and systemic levels. The human element, and hence the legal cultural element, is present to such a significant level in international investments that it impacts the detailed and the overarching regulation of international investments. That human involvement is present as a result of the very many human interactions necessary to make such a difficult business opportunity work. Foreign investments, as is the case with all human activities that take place far from home, necessarily require trust and good communications to make them work. As a result, understanding the different cultures, including the legal cultures involved, will be critical to an investment's success.

The human element is also there because foreign investments may stir passions within the host state, as they concern issues of sovereignty, foreign culture, competition, national security, economic policies, the environment, local community, and so on. Indeed, it has been said that "[f]ew areas of international law excite as much controversy as the law relating to foreign investment."[20] The controversy is said to be a result of the competition between different political and economic ideologies and between groups at different levels of development and power.[21] But, whether at the treaty formation, the investment agreement, or the dispute resolution stage, the conflict may also be a result of differences in legal cultures that have resulted in miscommunication and misunderstanding. Such missteps could be ameliorated by consideration of legal cultural issues at the different stages of the investment relationship. Of course, it may be that the difference in legal culture may itself lead to a conflict, but knowing that possibility in advance might save a great deal of trouble, and perhaps permit proactive attempts to get around the legal cultural obstacles and conflicts.

This chapter is not intended to suggest that considerations of legal culture alone are sufficient when trying to identify the disconnects between the very many participants in an international investment. There are, of course, often true substantive law, political, sociological, sociopolitical,[22] historical,[23] anthropological, and economic issues that need to be understood and taken into account. Furthermore, each of those approaches and concerns, along with legal cultural approaches and concerns, are related to and overlap with each other. In an ideal world, each would need to be mastered for the investment to be successful, however one measures such success. But, an understanding of the legal cultural issues in international investment law could go a long way to

---

20 M. Sornarajah, The International Law on Foreign Investment 1 (2nd ed. 2004).

21 *Id.*

22 Kate Miles, *International Investment Law: Origins, Imperialism and Conceptualizing the Environment*, 21 Colo. J. Int'l Envtl. L. & Pol'y 1, 1 (2010).

23 *Id.* at 1.

reducing typically difficult transactions and relationships by providing helpful insights that may lead to improvements in the field's development and operation.

III. Obstacles to a Legal Cultural Analysis of International Investment Law

International law comprises many fields, including the subject of the present legal cultural analysis. But, some fields more than others are more amenable to that analysis. The difference may relate to the fact that some fields include parent institutions and broad-based treaties that help to center the field for the analysis.[24] Some fields even include a long history of customary international law from which long-term legal cultural insights can be gleamed.[25] Indeed, at a basic level, some of those fields are easier to define than others. Those fields of international law that are controversial or relatively new tend to be less well defined—in substance and scope. Those diffuse fields may not have broad-based treaties or global institutions, and in some cases may have little hard international law, but will instead include mostly "soft law."[26] Nonetheless, those fields will also have a legal culture associated with them, for they will still involve humans interacting and responding to legal issues in conscious and subconscious ways.

Yet, despite being a subject peculiarly amenable to a legal cultural analysis, and despite the fact that it, perhaps more than other international economic law fields, has been the subject of specific legal cultural examinations (those "how to" or "guidebook" works), it is a field that presents numerous obstacles to a systemic legal cultural analysis. As an initial matter, notwithstanding the fact that international investment law has existed for hundreds if not thousands, of years[27], it is without a global institution, includes many issues that are controversial, and is responding in novel ways to many new issues that have arisen in the post–World War II period as the impacts of globalization have become ever more ubiquitous. International investment law can thus be said in many ways to be new, controversial, and without a parent.

Being new and without an overarching treaty or institution, it may even be unclear what is meant by "international investment law." Clearly, it is a field that is difficult to define, as opposed to such fields as international trade law with its WTO.[28]

---

[24] *E.g.*, international trade law with its World Trade Organization, or international criminal law with the International Criminal Court.

[25] The Law of the Sea has a long history that includes significant customary international law, much of which has now been reduced to treaty form. *See, e.g.*, Marko Pavliha & Norman A. Martinez Gutierrez, *Marine Scientific Research and the 1982 United Nations Convention on the Law of The Sea*, 16 OCEAN & COASTAL L.J. 115, 131 (2010).

[26] *See generally* Gregroy C. Shaffer & Mark Pollack, *Hard vs. Soft Law: Alternatives, Complements, and Antagonists in International Governance*, 94 MINN. L. REV. 706 (2010).

[27] Rafael Leal-Arcas, *The Multilateralization of International Investment Law*, 35 N.C. J. INT'L L. & COM. REG. 33, 36 (2009).

[28] With significant global membership, the WTO regulates almost all of the world's trade, with even the many regional and other trade agreements, as a de jure matter, subservient to the WTO.

Nonetheless, we can at least broadly describe the contours of international investment law. It includes:

> a patchwork of [BITs], regional provisions... and multilateral instruments (signed in the framework of the WTO, OECD, World Bank, or the [UNCTAD]). One should add to this list the unilateral liberalization measures taken by both developed and developing countries during the 1980s and 1990s... [and] the coexistence of voluntary, non-binding and binding rules that impose on the State an obligation and the responsibility to implement.[29]

As this "definition" shows,[30] even calling this collection of regulations a field is a challenge—for it is diffuse, fragmented, and uncoordinated. It has even been claimed that it is in "disarray."[31] Indeed, an estimate of the field suggested that there are "2,700 BITs, 200 regional cooperation arrangements, and 500 multilateral conventions governing cross border investment flows."[32] All this makes comparative legal cultural analysis difficult, though not impossible.[33]

But, even as the field is incredibly diffuse and fragmented, so too it is highly focused. Investments are by their nature the product of detailed contracts and agreements, and as such they will be governed by highly specific and often individual and bespoke legal regimes. For example, the primary modern investment regulatory regime is the Bilateral Investment Treaties, the "BITS." Those treaties, although often appearing to come from a "cookie cutter" due to their frequent use of common provisions in so many of the different BITs,[34] are in fact designed to deal just with the specific investment relations between two states, and to be implemented between just those two states. Even more specifically, many times there will be investment agreements created ad hoc, involving the host state, the investor, the investor's home state, and perhaps an international institution or two, such as a regional development bank. A field made up of such particular and often highly detailed regimes may prove especially difficult for a systemic analysis of a field such as is attempted in this chapter.

As noted above, the field is also in many ways new, and dynamic—both of which are a problem for a legal cultural analysis. Since the first modern international agreement concerning investment in 1907, the Drago-Porter Convention[35], the field has come

---

[29] Leal-Arcas, *supra* note 27, at 51–52 (2009).

[30] *See id.* at 38–41 (providing some definitions of foreign direct investors and examples of the types of different investments).

[31] Carlos G. Garcia, *All the Other Dirty Little Secrets: Investment Treaties, Latin America, and the Necessary Evil of Investor–State Arbitration*, 16 FLA. J. INT'L L. 301, 347 (2004).

[32] *See* Leal-Arcas, *supra* note 27, at 124.

[33] *See generally* Picker, *Development*, *supra* note 1 (providing a legal cultural analysis of the diffuse field of international development law).

[34] Americo Beviglia Zampetti & Pierre Sauvé, *International Investment*, in RESEARCH HANDBOOK IN INTERNATIONAL ECONOMIC LAW 215 (Andrew T. Guzman & Alan O. Sykes eds., 2007).

[35] See Hague Convention II on the Limitations of the Employment of the Use of Force for the Recovery of Contract Debts, signed on Oct. 18, 1907, 36 Stat. 2241; Treaty Series 537.

a long way. However, it is for the most part relatively new. Although international investment law was discussed in the Havana Charter negotiations,[36] it was not until the 1960s, under the auspices of the OECD[37] and then through the UN in the 1970s that we began to see the beginning of what is today an incredibly broad field. The impressive and massive expansion of the BITs started in the 1980s and does not appear to be abating.[38] The field's dynamism is apparent in the fact that in those last fifty years the field has undergone some substantial transformations—both qualitatively and quantitatively. Those developments span the thousands of BITs to the substantively binding and enforceable investor–state arbitrations, with their deep and sophisticated *jurisprudence constante*.[39] This relatively young and correspondingly immature field is therefore harder to consider from a legal cultural perspective than is the case with a more mature field.

Even as the field's relative youth presents difficulties for a legal cultural analysis, surprisingly, so too does its sophistication. Unlike some fields that are now well regulated, such as those of trade in services and international intellectual property,[40] investment law is already relatively complex. In contrast, the international fields regulating trade in services and intellectual property were essentially created anew—"from scratch." Those other fields were more easily brought into the international legal order, as they had no confusing and contradictory history to confuse the development of a cohesive legal culture. Yet, at the same time, international investment law is relatively undeveloped in comparison to those fields that had a long history of international regulation and institutions, such as trade in goods. International investment consequently faces the difficult situation of being both too developed and insufficiently developed.

Finally, another obstacle to a legal cultural analysis is that much international investment law is found within domestic legal systems, and hence varies tremendously across the globe. That diverse local investment law will itself be solidly anchored in the domestic legal culture and hence does not easily contribute to a systemic legal cultural examination of the field as a whole. Nonetheless, this issue too, like the other obstacles, can be overcome with sufficient imagination and flexibility. Of course, there is a risk that the conclusions will be too general, insufficiently "scientific," and somewhat conclusory. That concern, however, is one that will typically arise in all comparative analyses that go beyond micro examinations, and sometimes even in those ones. Generalizations and approximations are simply the cost of doing macro examinations. So long as they are noted and always kept in mind, they should not serve as obstacles

36 *See* Leal-Arcas, *supra* note 27, at 55.

37 *Id.* at 57–58.

38 *Id.* at 59 (noting 1986 is considered to be the start of the expansion).

39 *See* Andrew Newcombe & Lluis Paradell, LAW & PRACTICE OF INVESTMENT TREATIES: STANDARDS OF TREATMENT 47–49 (2009); *see also generally* Andrea K. Bjorklund, *Investment Treaty Arbitral Decisions as Jurisprudence Constante*, *in* INTERNATIONAL ECONOMIC LAW: THE STATE AND FUTURE OF THE DISCIPLINE 265 (Colin B. Picker, Isabella D. Bunn & Douglas W. Arner eds., 2008).

40 *See* Leal-Arcas, *supra* note 27, at 125.

to the underlying goal—the identification of insights and issues for the legal system under what is, in any event, a holistic examination.[41]

If the field is to move forward it must find some coherence across the new and the old, and it must address the incredible fragmentation of the field, described above. Understanding the legal cultural issues within and facing the field is one critical piece in the eventual puzzle.

IV. The Legal Cultural Analysis

Despite the obstacles noted above, there are some common legal cultural characteristics and questions that are amenable to consideration and examination and that play a large role in shaping and influencing major parts of the field. These few issues should be sufficient to show the utility of examining international investment law under a legal cultural analysis. Of course, considerably more issues would need to be considered in order to obtain a complete understanding of the role of legal culture for the whole field.

A. THE LEGAL CULTURAL IMPACT OF PUBLIC INTERNATIONAL LAW

The legal culture of international law has been explored before, and some general legal cultural insights have been generated from those examinations.[42] If international investment law can be legitimately placed within international law, then it can be expected that the legal culture of international law will be present to some degree in international investment law. The question is then raised as to whether international investment law is truly a field within public international law. To the extent that it is regulated by public international law devices, such as treaties and customary international law, then it is clearly within the scope of public international law. BITs, which are the primary form of international investment law, are treaties and have the full force provided by international treaty law and are therefore clearly a part of international law.[43] In addition, the provisions found within the typical BIT are themselves often part of the substance of international law, with other parts serving as a model for the development of new international law.[44] For example, BITs typically provide that:

> The contracting state parties agree to grant foreign investors the following: 1) admission into the host country; 2) *national treatment* vis-a-vis their own investors; 3) *most-favored nation* treatment vis-a-vis investors of other nations

---

[41] *See* Picker, *IOs*, *supra* note 1, at 12.

[42] *See, e.g.*, Colin B. Picker, *International Law's Mixed Heritage: A Common/Civil Law Jurisdiction*, 41 VANDERBILT J. TRANS. L. 1093, 1094 (2008) [hereinafter Picker, *International*].

[43] *See generally* José E. Alvarez, *A BIT on Custom*, 42 N.Y.U. J. INT'L L. & POL. 17 (2009).

[44] *See generally* Andreas F. Lowenfeld, *Investment Agreements and International Law*, 42 COLUM. J. TRANSNAT'L L. 123 (2003).

not party to the treaty; 4) "fair and equitable treatment" under *international law*; 5) "full protection and security" under *international law*; and 6) compensation in the event of an *expropriation*.[45]

Expropriation compensation,[46] national treatment, and most-favored-nation provisions are also parts of international law.[47] It is safe to say that international investment law is thoroughly immersed in international law and particularly includes substantial "hard" international law—law with real application and enforcement. Indeed, one scholar noted that "even if there is no complete uniformity yet, there is enough convergence to be able to speak of international investment law as an existing international law discipline made up of uniform investment law principles."[48]

Although BITS and international investment law institutions such as the ICSID are quite clearly a part of international law, international investment law also includes within it law that would seem to have a less immediate connection to public international law, such as that part of international investment law that would be found within domestic regulations or within private international law. But, if the underlying investment transactions and the resultant legal issues that follow from it are the sort of legal issues with which international law would normally be involved, then we can assume that they will also be influenced by international law and its legal culture, although not to quite the same degree as those parts of international investment law that are more clearly part of public international law. For those situations where a state is a party and nationals of another state are the other party, then we would expect international law to be relevant. Although purely private international investments would appear not to have an international law nexus, they are nonetheless transnational, and hence borders are crossed and the means of international commerce are utilized. The presence of international law exists in the interstices of those transactions. International law is further relevant to these transactions when problems start to appear between the foreign parties. At that time, the foreign investor may seek assistance from its own state, and international law is relevant as the extraterritorial actions of a state are regulated by international law, in one form or another.[49] If eventually there is litigation, through domestic courts, arbitration, or otherwise, there may be issues involving enforcement of foreign judgments, service of process, foreign evidence gathering, and so on—all regulated by international law. So, even the domestic and private components of international investment law appear to have a serious relationship with public international law and hence to its associated legal culture.

The concordance between international investment law and international law suggests that international investment law will be impacted to some degree by the

45 Garcia, *supra* note 31, at 311–12 (citations omitted, emphasis added).

46 *See, e.g.*, Zampetti & Sauvé, *supra* note 34, at 225.

47 *See generally* Newcombe & Paradell, *supra* note 39, at 147, 193, and 321.

48 Leal-Arcas, *supra* note 27, at 67.

49 *See* Miles, *supra* note 22, at 15; Newcombe & Paradell, *supra* note 39, at 5–7.

overarching legal culture of international law. Although the legal culture of international law is difficult to identify, previous considerations of the issue have managed to discern its general contours and to identify some legal cultural themes that pervade it as a whole.[50] Without going into too much detail, the legal culture of international law is predominantly Western.[51] Furthermore, international law:

> comprises some unique legal cultural elements, after all, the subjects of international law are sovereign states, but that it also draws heavily from both the civil law and common law traditions—but in a specific style and composition . . . they resemble the classical mixed jurisdiction systems of the world (such as Quebec, Scotland, etc).[52]

To the extent international investment law reflects international law's legal culture, then one would expect international investment law's legal culture to reflect strong civil and common law legal cultures, but with each present to a greater or lesser degree in the different parts of the law. For example, with respect to procedure and dispute settlement, the mixed jurisdictions[53] and international law tend to be more common law–like, while the private law, to the extent one can analogize to it within public international law, will tend to be more civilian.[54] A detailed consideration of international investment law under the rubric developed to consider international law as a mixed jurisdiction would be detailed work that would likely provide some interesting and useful insights. Such an examination is not, however, provided here for it tends to quickly become very specific and detailed, and the goal in this chapter is to consider international investment law from a systemic legal cultural perspective. But, the more relevant of those commonalities and insights will be considered in greater detail below.

---

50 *See generally,* Colin B. Picker, *International Law's Mixed Heritage: A Common/Civil Law Jurisdiction*, 41 VANDERBILT J. TRANS. L. 1093 (2008) [hereinafter Picker, *International*); Colin B. Picker, *Beyond the Usual Suspects: Application of the Mixed Jurisdiction Jurisprudence to International Law and Beyond*, 3 J. COMP. L. 160 (2008); Colin B. Picker, *Beyond the Usual Suspects: Applications of the Mixed Jurisdiction Methodology to Public International and International Economic Law*, *in* MIXED LEGAL SYSTEMS AT NEW FRONTIERS (Esin Örücü ed., 2010).

51 *See* Picker, *International, supra* note 50, at 1095–1100.

52 Picker, *Development, supra* note 1, at 50, citing Picker, *International, supra* note 50, at 1102.

53 The mixed jurisdictions "were first defined more than one hundred years ago as 'legal systems in which the Romano–Germanic tradition has become suffused to some degree by Anglo–American law.' The origin of mixed jurisdictions typically lies in the many transfers of colonial power, usually from French or Dutch to British control and from Spanish to American control." Picker, *International, supra* note 50, at 1102 (quoting and citing William Tetley, *Mixed Jurisdictions: Common Law v. Civil Law (Codified and Uncodified)*, 60 LA. L. REV. 677, 679 (2000) (quoting Maurice Tancelin, *Introduction* to F.P. Walton, THE SCOPE AND INTERPRETATION OF THE CIVIL CODE 1 (Butterworths 1980) (1907)); *see also* Kenneth G. C. Reid, *The Idea of Mixed Legal Systems*, 78 TUL. L. REV. 5, 7 (2003).

54 *See* Vernon Valentine Palmer, *Introduction to the Mixed Jurisdictions*, *in* MIXED JURISDICTIONS WORLDWIDE: THE THIRD LEGAL FAMILY 3, 4–5, 63 (Vernon Valentine Palmer ed., 2001); Picker, *International, supra* note 50, at 1117, 1127; Stephen Goldstein, *The Odd Couple: Common Law Procedure and Civilian Substantive Law*, 78 TUL. L. REV. 291, 292 (2003).

Of course, there is an open question as to whether it is the connection to international law that would result in similar legal cultural issues being present within international investment law or whether international investment law would of its own accord have independently developed similar legal cultural characteristics. Although an interesting question, and with some limited relevance, regardless of the causality it is through comparison with and reflection on international law's legal cultural characteristics that it is possible to explore whether similar characteristics exist within international investment law. Indeed, frequently a legal cultural characteristic will exist, but until it is explicitly noted, it will often go unnoticed. For example, the fact that common law procedure and dispute settlement styles exist within both the legal culture of international investment law, as discussed below, and within international law could mean that those two similar characteristics were arrived at independently, or that international law led the way for international investment law to follow. Yet, without the issue having being considered as part of international law or within the mixed jurisdictions, it likely would not have been explored in the same way in the international investment context—which is the more critical issue.

Although not considered in depth here, a few examples will show the value of considering a shared international law and international investment law legal culture. The Western legal cultural tradition of international law suggests that international investment law would also be largely Western. Although being "Western" implies the presence of many different legal cultural characteristics, one in particular is troubling for international law, and perhaps then equally troubling for international investment law—the requirement that Western legal systems embrace "legal pluralism, accepting the existence of competing legal systems and jurisdictions."[55] Specifically, and despite international law being solidly within the Western legal tradition, it has problems reflecting the legal pluralism considered to be one of the defining characteristics of the Western legal system.[56] Of course, within it, international law welcomes many different sources of international law and accepts different regimes covering different fields. The pluralism issue, however, arises because international law believes itself, almost by definition, to be hierarchically superior to all other laws and legal systems.[57] To the extent there is a conflict, international law will find its own laws to be supreme, and the question as to the existence of a conflict will be determined under international law. Although such a position is necessary for the existence of international law, it

[55] Picker, *International*, *supra* note 50, at 1082 (citing Harold J. Berman, LAW AND REVOLUTION: THE FORMATION OF THE WESTERN LEGAL TRADITION 10 (1983).

[56] *See* Berman, *supra* note 55, at 7–10; *see also* Glendon, *supra* note 14, at 46.

[57] Nor is this issue saved by the fact that international law is mainly a positivist system. The very strong positivism present within international law is itself a form of legal pluralism, for the respect given to each state by only holding the state to that international law to which it has consented suggests a respect for the individual states' legal systems regardless of what sort of legal system the state employs. But, international law is not entirely positivist, for there also exists peremptory norms, *jus cogens*. *See*, *e.g.*, Alfred von Verdross, *Forbidden Treaties in International Law*, 31 AM. J. INT'L L. 571 (1937). The existence of *jus cogens*, and the fact that it is up to international law to determine its existence, undermines the ultimate respect international law might have for domestic legal systems.

creates a legal cultural sheen to international law that will tend to denigrate legal systems alien to international law. Although this may not be a problem for Western legal systems, it may undermine international law's acceptance of the legitimacy of non-Western legal systems. The consequence for international investment law, which often regulates investments in non-Western legal systems, is particularly troubling, for it may then take on that legal chauvinism within its legal culture despite the very real need to take into account the different legal systems in which it operates. This problem is reinforced, as discussed later in this chapter, as a result of the power asymmetries that are pervasive throughout the field.

In sum, international investment law's connection to international law will likely serve as a major factor in the development of the legal culture of international investment law. At a minimum, consideration of the congruence will permit examination of some specific legal cultural trends and factors that will influence the practice and development of international investment law.

B. THE ROLE OF LANGUAGE

The role of languages is increasingly understood to be a critical and determinative factor in the development of a legal culture.[58] This is especially true for relatively undeveloped legal cultures, the sort one tends to find among the many new fields and institutions of international law, such as international investment law.

The role of language as a determinative factor in the development of a legal culture has been best explored in the context of those legal systems that serve as comparative law laboratories—the mixed jurisdictions.[59] The impact in those systems is more easily observed due to the very constant and easily visible clash between the legal cultures within those mixed systems. For example, where the civil law language was healthy, as in Quebec, the civil law has remained strong. Where the civil law language was weak, as in Louisiana and will be in South Africa now that Afrikaans is but one of many official languages, the civil law will wither and the common law legal culture will slowly dominate and replace the civil law legal culture.[60] Yet, the same pressures are present, albeit less visibly, in all other systems including those within the international legal order.[61]

With respect to international investment law, language is visible as an issue in international investment law in numerous ways, from the negotiations of the contract to any resultant disputes. As such, it has the ability to influence the legal cultural character of the field as a whole, and of the specific transactions at issue. To the extent one language becomes dominant in the negotiations, contract, treaty, or dispute reso-

58 *See* Glendon, *supra* note 14, at 972–82.

59 Celia Wasserstein Fassberg, *Language and Style in a Mixed System*, 78 TUL. L. REV. 151 (2003); Max Loubser, *Linguistic Factors into the Mix: The South African Experience of Language and the Law*, 78 TUL. L. REV. 105, 144–47 (2003).

60 Loubser, *supra* note 59, at 121.

61 Picker, *International*, *supra* note 50, at 1123–24.

lutions, then the legal systems associated with that specific language will inexorably exert their legal cultural influence. Of course, and without question, the language at issue in influencing the legal culture of international investment law is English.[62] Indeed, all aspects of the world of international investment law are finding English to be increasingly the dominant language.

> Where only one or even neither of disputing parties, for example, has English as their native tongue, the parties will nevertheless default to English (and arbitrators who speak or at least understand English) as the most practical language in which to conduct proceedings.[63] This predilection spreads even to the interpretation of the language of the BITs themselves as in some instances of treaties between Latin American and non-English speaking countries, English is added as a third official text and deemed to prevail in the event of a difference in interpretation between the versions of the languages of the contracting parties.[64]

The role of language, and in particular the English language, was discussed by the author in a recent work concerning legal cultures and international organizations, but is equally applicable in the present context of international investment law:

> Language and legal tradition are closely tied together, with, for example, English associated with the common law and French, German, Spanish and Italian tied to the civil law tradition.[65] Furthermore, Chinese and Arabic are also typically associated with non-common law legal systems—be they civilian, socialist, or Islamic legal systems. After all, any major western language employed other than English will tend to end up reflecting more civilian, or rather, less Anglo-American and hence common law legal culture within the institution.[66] Whereas the use of English will tend to strengthen the emergence and perhaps dominance of a common law legal culture.[67] Of course, the ever increasing role of English, as the common second language of the world, suggests a continuing and potentially expanding influence of common law legal cultural characteristics.[68]

---

62 McLean, *supra* note 11, at 1095; Lawrence M. Friedman, *Erewhon: The Coming Global Legal Order*, 37 STAN. J. INT'L L. 347, 355 (2001). One scholar–practitioner noted that "you take account of the peculiarities of national law, but the agreements look the same and they will almost always be in the English language [while even] in France where it's technically illegal, ... [people will] pay their €300 fine for having their agreement in English." Flood, *supra* note 74, at 64. (internal quotation marks omited). *See also* Suvanto, *supra* note 3, at 5–7 (noting an increasing use of use of English within Scandinavian companies and in inter-Scandinavian deals).

63 Driven in not insignificant respect by the fact that few native English speakers will have non-English language fluency. *See* Clark, *supra* note 83, at 1076–77.

64 Garcia, *supra* note 31, at 362 (footnote added).

65 *See* Picker, *International*, *supra* note 50, at 1124.

66 *Id.* at 1123–25; *see also* Loubser, *supra* note 59, at 144–47.

67 Loubser, *supra* note 59, at 107–08; *see also* Esin Örücü, *The Judge and Jurist in Scotland: On the Verge of a Second Renaissance*, 78 TUL. L. REV 89, 102 (2003).

68 Picker, *IOs*, *supra* note 1, at 17–18.

In some cases even domestic statutes are written in English so as to properly capture an intended common law approach—for the purpose of facilitating investment.[69]

Of course, the move toward the English language will not necessarily lead to employment of a common law legal culture.[70] As an initial matter, there may be a counterweight as more civil law scholars and practitioners write in English and introduce non–common law ideas into English language sources. But, language can be very closely tied to culture, including legal culture, and the strict meanings of words can curtail the use of foreign concepts in another language. Another potential counter to the common law invasion through English is some investment-related efforts that have not followed the common law or relied upon the use of English. For example, the Organization for Harmonization in Africa of Business Laws (OHADA) have implemented a French civil law approach to its shared pro-investment legal regime, with French remaining the primary language. It should be noted, however, that even this endeavor has made overtures toward non-French legal devices and toward the common law and Anglo-phone neighbors of the members of the OHADA.[71]

For international investment law, the dominance of English should be viewed as a warning and sign that the common law and its associated legal cultural characteristics may be entering the field in greater force and vigor than otherwise expected. Furthermore, given the foreseeable continued dominance of English, this process shows no signs of abating. The legal culture of the field may therefore continue to feel a pressure to develop along common law lines, with its associated legal culture.

C. PARTICIPANT-DRIVEN LEGAL CULTURE IN INTERNATIONAL INVESTMENT

One of the main areas of consideration in a legal cultural analysis will be the participants and actors within the legal system under analysis. Those participants include lawyers, individuals, and corporations with a legal relationship to the issue;[72] judges; jurors; legislators; regulators; civil servants; international officials; NGO and MNC officers and directors; and even the general public. Any humans actively involved in

---

[69] *E.g.* Dubai's International Financial Centre. *See* Damien P. Horigan, *The New Adventures of the Common Law*, 1(5) PACE INT'L L. REV. ONLINE COMPANION 1, 10, 22 (2009).

[70] Laura J. Macgregor, *The Effect of Unexpected Circumstances on Contracts in Scots and Louisiana Law*, *in* MIXED JURISDICTIONS COMPARED: PRIVATE LAW IN LOUISIANA AND SCOTLAND 272, 279 (Vernon Palmer & Elspeth Reid eds., 2009) (using the mixed jurisdictions as the laboratory, and pointing out that language will not always be the determinative factor, noting that despite employment of different language, Scottish and French contract law can be remarkably similar, and also that the lack of French in Louisiana did not stop the civilian notion of "cause from thriving in Louisiana").

[71] Dickerson, *supra* note 6, at 21 (2005). The OHADA is the Traité Relatif à l'Harmonisation en Afrique du Droit des Affaires (the Organization for Harmonization in Africa of Business Laws), which includes Benin, Burkina Faso, Central African Republic, Chad, Cameroon, Comores, Congo, Côte d'Ivoire, Equatorial Guinea, Gabon, Mali, Niger, Senegal, and Togo as well as Guinea and Guinea-Bissau. *Id.* at n.2.

[72] In a legal cultural setting individuals are very relevant—but only to the extent they have a direct connection with the law through their roles as voters, clients, litigants, victims (broadly construed), witnesses, and so on.

the legal system can have a role in the creation and development of the legal culture, just as they will also reflect the legal culture in their conscious and subconscious interactions with the legal system. In this section just a few of the more central participants will be considered, chosen for their legal cultural influence across the international investment field as a whole, as opposed to their legal cultural impact at a more specific level within an investment. As an initial matter, lawyers, law schools, and artificial persons will be considered. Specifically, this means consideration of the dominant Anglo-American law firms and legal education of non–common law lawyers in Anglo-American law schools; finally, there will be a brief consideration of the role of multinational corporations (MNCs).

The large Anglo-American law firms are perhaps one of the most influential groups of participants within international economic law in general.[73] Their significant place in the international investment law can be attributed to a number of causes including historic, economic, and regulatory factors, and even as a result of some legal cultural factors. Historically, the fact that America first developed the large law firms is important to their later joint dominance.[74] Additionally, the dominance of the Anglo-American firms is also a result of the fact that there are really only two jurisdiction of great importance to finance—London and New York, with the result that their law firms will have the edge over the law firms of other jurisdictions, especially over those from very different legal traditions and cultures.[75] In addition, the comparatively deregulated legal market in England and America has allowed their law firms to expand to positions that then enabled them to dominate the field.[76] In contrast, in much of the rest of the developed world, law firms are heavily regulated, with some jurisdictions even prohibiting partnerships.[77] The view of "free competition" is different in different countries, with the United States on one extreme, going even so far as to free its lawyers to advertise and set their own fees and style of compensation in comparison to such jurisdictions as Italy where fees are fixed and there is much less competition.[78] One consequence of the regulations is that for many countries solo practice or small firms is the norm.[79] In addition, those jurisdictions' smaller markets then further hinder the development of very large firms that could compete with the Anglo-American ones. Sometimes the legal culture in those jurisdictions itself inhibits their law firms' growth. For example, in some legal cultures lawyers are primarily hired remedially, not proactively, as businesses have the attitude that they can get along just fine without

[73] *See* Junji Nakagawa, *A Comment on Professor Colin Picker's Paper on "WTO Governance: A Legal Cultural Critique," in* GOVERNANCE IN CONTEMPORARY JAPAN (Kenji Hirashima ed., 2011); *see also* Picker, *WTO*, *supra* note 1, at 130.

[74] John Flood, *Lawyers as Sanctifiers: The Role of Elite Law Firms in International Business Transactions*, 14 IND. J. GLOBAL LEGAL STUD. 35, 42 (2007).

[75] *Id.* at 48–49.

[76] McLean, *supra* note 11, at 1095.

[77] Stefano Agostino, *Advertising and Solicitation: A Comparative Analysis of Why Italian and American Lawyers Approach Their Profession Differently*, 10 TEMP. INT'L & COMP. L.J. 329, 335 (1996).

[78] *Id.* at 354.

[79] *Id.* at 335. For example, in Italy a forty-lawyer law firm would be considered huge. *Id.*

legal assistance, leading to significantly lower demand for lawyers and making larger firms less feasible.[80]

Reflecting these and other factors, a recent survey of the top hundred law firms of the world identified only two that were not from a common law country, and only seven that were not from the United States or Britain.[81] This dominance by Anglo-American law firms has and will continue to have a long-term impact on the development of the legal culture of international investment law. Indeed, it has been argued that at this point "globalization cannot succeed without the large law firm."[82] Certainly, the large law firms are having a very large impact on the legal culture of international investment law.

> The term imperialism, implied to the spread of United States law and United States lawyering abroad, may be a shade too strong. In part, what we have is a matter of taste, like the spread of Coca-Cola. It is perhaps also sheer convenience and the fact that Americans were in the field... fairly early, and because their style of lawyering suits the needs of the international order.[83]

However, this same author quickly notes that his comments are not just confined to the role of U.S. law firms, but to law firms from throughout the common law world.[84] It also casts a common law sheen or gloss, and associated legal culture, over the field that in turn makes it even more difficult for non–common law lawyers to enter the field.[85]

This legal cultural impact is in all areas of international investment law. For example, the Anglo-American law firms and their legal cultures are having an impact in negotiations and in the resultant legal instruments. For example, Scandinavian contracts have been influenced by American lawyers in a very physical manner—their contracts are getting longer.[86] Another area where there has been a legal cultural impact from the Anglo-American law firms is in the issue of mediation versus litigation for international investment dispute resolution. There is reportedly a bias within the American law firms away from mediation and toward litigation. As a matter of legal culture, this will likely contribute to a more litigious, combative, and adversarial approach to dispute resolution in the field than would otherwise have been the case.[87] However, it should be noted that it is not just the law firms, but their clients as well (though

---

80 *Id.* at 353.

81 *See* http://www.thelawyer.com/global100/2006/index.html (last visited Apr. 23, 2010) (of the seven, one is French, one Dutch, one Canadian, and four Australian; those seven are all listed in the seventy-five to one hundred tranche).

82 Flood, *supra* note 74, at 41.

83 Garcia, *supra* note 31, at 362.

84 *Id.*

85 *Id.* at 362.

86 *See* Suvanto, *supra* note 3, at 5–7.

87 *See* Don Peters, *Can We Talk? Overcoming Barriers to Mediating Private Transborder Commercial Disputes in the Americas*, 41 VAND. J. TRANSNAT'L L. 1251, 1276–77 (2008) ("The professional culture of U.S. lawyers

perhaps more accurately, the in-house counsel) at those businesses that are pushing for U.S. or Anglo-American styles in those international arbitrations.[88]

The large Anglo-American law firms are clearly having and going to continue to have an influence on the development of the legal culture of the field. But, those law firms are international and employ many non–common law attorneys, and so one might have expected them to counterbalance the impact of the common law attorneys in those firms. But, those large firms will have an internal culture, reflecting their common law parentage that will acculturate non–common law lawyers into the Anglo-American way of doing things. Consequently, even the large number of non–common law lawyers within the large Anglo-American law firms will likely cast a common law sheen over the field.

The common law acculturation of the non–common law lawyers in the big firms will have started even before the non–common law lawyers were hired as a significant number of them will already have studied at law schools in the common law world. But, it is not just the Anglo-American law firms that place a premium on such training. Lawyers, scholars, government, and international organization officials throughout the non–common law world increasingly seek and feel they require such an experience.[89] Indeed, the increasing number of legal practitioners, officials, and scholars from non-Anglo-American backgrounds who have spent time in Anglo-American legal education establishments cannot be ignored—both for what they become and what they bring back with them to their home legal systems.[90]

> Young lawyers from jurisdictions outside the Anglo-American nexus now find it essential to obtain an LL.M. degree at a major U.S. or U.K. law school, otherwise they will not be conversant with global legal techniques.[91]

Perhaps of greatest and ever increasing impact is that there will be some common law acculturation even for those who did not receive such education in the common law world. This issue, and some potential responses to it, were previously considered in the context of the legal culture of international organizations, though it is directly on point with respect to the legal culture of international investment law.

> [E]ven when law students do not attend common law system law schools, it will often be the case that their lecturers and advisors studied or have spent

---

also erects barriers to recommending and using mediation to resolve trans-border disputes . . . ," with the article then describing the reasons for this phenomenon).

[88] McLean, *supra* note 11, at 1094–95. The in-house counsel are themselves likely to have had their training in those large law firms.

[89] David S. Clark, *American Law Schools in the Age of Globalization: A Comparative Perspective*, 61 RUTGERS L. REV. 1037, 1061 (2009). *See generally* Carole Silver, *Internationalizing U.S. Legal Education: A Report on the Education of Transnational Lawyers*, 14 CARDOZO J. INT'L & COMP. L. 143 (2006); Picker, *WTO*, *supra* note 1, at 133.

[90] McLean, *supra* note 11, at 1095.

[91] Flood, *supra* note 74, at 54.

> considerable time at universities in common law countries.[92] But, education institutions outside the common law world have now entered into competition with the common law universities for the valuable foreign student market—even going so far as to teach in English.[93] . . . [But], it is debatable just how much those civil law institutions can influence the common law scholars, practitioners, officials and students that attend those organizations. It is likely that there will not be the same large influence, due as much to the issue of language as anything else . . . Consequently the common law countries' education institutions' current domination may not be so easily displaced.[94]

Anglo-American legal education's impact is thus far-reaching, though not unprecedented—the role of late–Middle Ages' Northern Italian legal education was even more significant in spreading the *ius commune* and the Corpus Juris Civilis to almost all of Europe;[95] however, this time the spread of Anglo-American legal culture is global.

Another global character in international law in general is the major presence and employment of artificial persons. This is especially the case in international economic law, and in international investment law in particular. The question is then raised as to whether those artificial persons, typically multinational corporations and almost always set up as limited liability entities, impact the legal culture of international investment law. It has been suggested that their presence provides a sense of immunity and lack of connection between the people who actually make the decisions and any consequences for those decisions.

> It would seem that the use of international comity, forum non conveniens, and the doctrine of separate corporate legal personality to preclude foreign investor liability for environmental damage in host states also replicates this pattern. Rogge describes the character of the current legal framework as constituting the "best of both worlds" for multinational corporations—they are permitted to operate in other states and to profit from politically oppressive regimes or environmentally lax regulation, but are shielded from liability for damage resulting from those activities. The same system that enables foreign investors to engage in transnational operations withholds protection from those they damage.[96]

Even as corporations benefit from limited liability on a personal level, the wider investment regime also permits them to benefit from investments without having to concern

92 Many will also submit articles to the numerous and less-demanding student-run law reviews in the United States, and thus will, to some extent, be forced to adopt to American legal culture in order to have their scholarship accepted.

93 *See* Clark, *supra* note 83, at 1075.

94 *See* Picker, IOs, *supra* note 1, at 17.

95 *See* Glendon, *supra* note 14 at 56–57; *see also* Clark, *supra* note 89, at 1075 n.165 (noting the dominance of German legal education as recently as the nineteenth century).

96 Miles, *supra* note 22, at 34 *et seq.* (citations ommited).

themselves with many of the so-called noneconomic externalities of their investments: "The law of capital-exporting states enables their multinational corporations to pursue economic activities globally, but disengages when called upon to protect the local communities and environments within which those companies operate."[97] Indeed, their immunity may, as a de facto matter, be even greater due to the fact that their multinational character may also be a way to escape the effective jurisdiction and control by any one government—either official control or moral control. Furthermore, to the extent they may fall within the control of a state, they may always resort to lobbying to have the regulations or laws changed.[98]

The role and protections offered to those MNCs will likely have an impact on the legal culture of the field. One should expect a larger focus on legal and technical compliance as opposed to compliance with larger social justice obligations as MNCs operate behind their limited liability and other shields. The legal culture may also tend to be more myopic, viewing externalities and other issues as outside the scope of the field. Like the issues raised in the discussion of asymmetries within the field, one consequence of those types of MNC behaviors, and of a corresponding legal culture for the field, is that the MNCs may end up being considered less legitimate, along with the field itself.[99] Few of these legal cultural attributes would be considered positive by most observers. This is so even though there are good reasons to permit the use of limited liability: not all the negative consequences of investment can be solved by corporations, and MNCs have shareholders monitoring the corporate profitability and share price.

The consideration of the legal cultural impact of the actors, the participants, within the field is helpful in providing insights into the development and operation of the field. Clearly, consideration of all the other participants would be useful for the field, though in a short chapter such as this one, that is not possible.

D. THE DIVERSITY OF THE FIELD

International investment law is a very diverse field—at the substantive and participant levels. Those diversities will clearly have an impact on the legal culture of the field.

1. Ideological Diversity

One of the more important diversities within the field relates to how the field is viewed, with a strong division between a positive view and a negative view of international investment law. Of course, there will be very few opinions about the field that are

---

97 *Id.* at 37.

98 *See* Sornoraja, *supra* note 20, at 2, 183.

99 Another impact of the large role of MNCs in the field is the consequent separation of the human actors from the legal entities involved, a result of the demise of the "company man." This in turn may also lead to a "short termism" within the legal culture, as corporate officers understand their likely short tenure. That short termism fits well with and mutually enforces the other MNC legal cultural issues discussed above.

wholly positive or wholly negative. As a sophisticated body of law, reflecting many different demands and needs, it is simply not possible that the field could serve all goals and all constituencies equally well or equally badly. Nonetheless, there are deep divisions within the field, and it is the existence of those deep divisions and their impact on the legal culture of the field that is considered.

Some fields are more controversial than others, though all fields will include within them some parts that are hotly disputed. The deep seabed provisions of the Law of the Sea are an excellent example of a highly contentious area within a generally uncontroversial field.[100] International investment, however, is one of the more controversial fields within international law. The failure of the Multilateral Agreement on Investment (MAI)[101] was perhaps the most visible expression of such intense feelings about international investment law.[102] The divisive disagreements within and about international investment law span the entire field, including, among other issues, its BITs, investment provisions in RTAs, international institutions, and impact on the target economies.[103] The rancor is not just confined to investments in specific levels of economic development, for the controversy can be found to concern investments in both the developing and in the developed world. For example, the regional investment law in North America, pursuant to NAFTA's Chapter 11 investor protection provisions, has also had a tumultuous time since its inception in 1994.[104]

Part of the divisiveness is a legacy of the colonial and imperial expansionism of the West.[105] Part of the divisiveness is also due to there being little agreement in the field about the macroeconomics and "what constitutes investment stability."[106] The divisiveness is further accentuated when investments become pawns in the relations between states. For example, during times of crisis when foreign nationals' investments are expropriated, sometimes just property of nationals of specific states are targeted, or where the foreign state imposes investment restrictions as a foreign policy tool.[107]

The divisiveness is made worse by the fact that many other issues get pulled into the international investment law debate—issues that are of close personal concern

---

100 John Charles Kunich, *Losing Nemo: The Mass Extinction Now Threatening the World's Ocean Hotspots*, 30 COLUM. J. ENVTL. L. 1, 44 (2005).

101 *See* Leal Arcas, *supra* note 27, at 67–68 ("the MAI sought to set strict global rules limiting governments' rights and abilities to regulate currency speculation and set public interest policies regarding investment in land, factories, service sectors and stocks [and...] would have expanded worldwide key NAFTA investment provisions, including... the right to establish an investment in another country, the ability for corporations to sue governments for cash damages over any regulatory action affecting profits, and an expansive definition of investment...").

102 *See* Leal-Arcas, *supra* note 27, at 67–70, 110 (discussing the MAI and its failure, and showing the long-lasting impact of the failure for the field).

103 *See generally*, Peter Muchlinski, *Policy Issues*, *in* the OXFORD HANDBOOK OF INTERNATIONAL INVESTMENT 3 *et seq.* (Peter Muchlinski, Federico Ortino & Christoph Shreuer eds., 2008).

104 *See generally* Catherine M. Amirfar & Elyse M. Dreyer, *Thirteen Years of NAFTA's Chapter 11: The Criticisms, the United States's Responses, and Lessons Learned*, 20 N.Y. INT'L L. REV. 39 (2007).

105 *See generally* Miles, *supra* note, 22.

106 Leal-Arcas, *supra* note 27, at 125.

107 Garcia, *supra* note 31, at 316–17.

to states. These sensitive subjects include matters of governance, corruption, discrimination, labor and human rights, environmental protections, high-profile investor misconduct, and so on. All of those issues are controversial, from the content of their principles to their application. Yet, investments touch on all them and very often require that a position be taken on them by the foreign investor and the host state—even if that position is to ignore the issue. For example, when investing in a new power plant, the environmental issues must be resolved. When investing in a country known for corruption, the foreign investor must navigate those demands—one way or another. When investing in a manufacturing or service industry in a country not known for implementation of health and safety laws, the investor must decide how to cope with those issues. Furthermore, the foreign investor's own state, through its ability to regulate its own nationals in their extraterritorial behavior, will also be deemed to be taking a position on all these issues.[108] Similarly, the international institutions involved, from those insuring or directly funding the investment to those responsible for the regulation of the substantive law, must also be deemed to have taken a side on the issue. Silence or a lack of decisions on the issue is itself a position in the debate. In some ways, international investments are one of the primary flash points of the many contentious issues arising from globalization. These controversies are further inflamed by the general failure of investor arbitration to take into account these many issues.[109] Being largely driven by investors, with no room for third parties (such as NGOs) representing these other views, it is no wonder that the law, itself driven mostly by disputes, will then fail to adequately deal with these issues. This will in turn further stir up the debate and potentially undermine the legitimacy of the law itself.

The consequences as a legal cultural matter for the field are a constant defensive posture, and an inability for the field to mature. The development of fundamental principles and long-term strategy are stymied by a need to constantly defend the basics as well as to handle issues outside the usual competences of investment experts. Furthermore, there is no normative consensus, leaving the discipline resting on few common principles, in a time when international law, and the law in general, has taken on a greater acceptance of the important role of context and an understanding that commonly accepted principles are necessary to secure legitimacy in a world with incredible diversity. Although individual transactions may be free of the different perspectives, due to the unsettled and divided nature of the field, the long-term viability of the transaction and investment may itself be unsettled. Also, no international organization can be created, nor can there be better harmonization with the other fields and international organizations within the international legal order so long as the field is itself divided.

---

108 A good example is the recent developments of anticorruption rules for overseas business activities in most developed countries, initially via the OECD's Anti-Bribery Convention. Organization for Economic Cooperation and Development(OECD), Convention on Combating Bribery of Foreign Public Officials in International Business Transactions, Nov. 21, 1997 available at http:// www.oecd.org/dataoecd/4/18/38028044.pdf (last visited Oct., 2012).

109 Miles, *supra* note 22, at 19.

In a field that is so fragmented and unable to mature, one can expect the legal culture to be replete with the legal cultural equivalent of an identity crisis, a lack of legitimacy, and insecurity, anger, and confusion. These legal cultural "characteristics" will be reflected in the role played by national politicians and international organization leaders in the development of the field as those "leaders" will likely be reluctant to assert leadership and provide direction. A "hunker down" or bunker approach may be evident. One may expect a lack of transparency, for transparency will just expose activities to censure. In such an atmosphere the field will be hard-pressed to secure rational development.

2. Power Diversity

Another aspect of the diversity of the field is the significant difference in economic and other power measurements between the many different participants in the field. Although international investments are very often between similarly developed economies, there are also many investments from more-developed states into less-developed states. Historically, although the early international investment law was created as a result of investment between largely equal states, in the modern period it has been developed largely in the context of investments from more powerful into weaker states, often reflecting post-colonial relationships and dependencies.[110] Indeed, the main international investment law development in the modern period has been the tremendous growth of the BITs that are typically avenues for investment from the developed to the less-developed world. It has been noted that outside the NAFTA Chapter 11 context, "BITs amongst developed countries inter se are virtually unheard of."[111] After all, the great gains from investment are often from investments in untapped or emerging economies.[112] The ubiquity of these asymmetric investments suggests many legal cultural issues for the field.

One aspect of these asymmetric investments is that they and their associated BITs are very often offered from the more- powerful to less-powerful parties on a "take-it-or-leave-it" basis.[113] As a legal cultural matter, such asymmetries are chauvinist and contrary to the legal pluralism culture that should be a part of the Western legal tradition. As noted above when discussing the legal culture of international law, this "anti-pluralism" or "legal cultural myopia" may have an enduring and pernicious impact in the very substantive concerns of the field. That history and continuing legacy of power

110 *Id.* at 3–4.

111 Garcia, *supra* note 31, at 315; Leal-Arcas, *supra* note 27, at 60 (noting that BITS are between developed and developing countries); *but see* Newcombe & Paradell, *supra* note 39, at 43 (noting some exceptions to the usual asymmetry between the parties, even as noting those asymmetries were the usual case).

112 *See* Garcia, *supra* note 31, at 320.

113 *Id.* at 316 (quoting Jose Alvarez discussing his experience as a U.S. BIT negotiator, who noted among other things that "the United States call[ed] the shots and the BIT partner [was like a] supplicant").

asymmetry has been credited by some scholars with creating some specific legal cultural characteristics:

> [An] inherent investor bias of international investment law in the twentieth and twenty-first centuries [which finds] a modern manifestation in its excessive focus on the rights of the investor, its obsessive promotion of foreign investment to the exclusion of the interests of the host state and of other stakeholders, the manner in which it is used by foreign investors and their states to secure commercial interests, and the investor–state arbitral system of dispute resolution.[114]

In addition to representing specific substantive issues, these qualities are also manifestations of the legal culture within the field. Indeed, these are as much legal culture as might be an anti-defendant bias among middle-class jurors in a domestic legal system. These are attitudes with legal significance that drive the substantive body of the law as well as other aspects of the development of the field. These legal cultural conditions are likely present throughout the legal culture of international investment law at this stage. This may be the rare case of legal cultural attributes that are applicable across the whole field. The acceptance of this situation has not gone unchallenged,[115] but has rather contributed to the divisiveness within the field, helping to generate those legal cultural characteristics that are related to such divisiveness.

Another legal cultural consequence of the asymmetric condition of the field is that the historic European conception of international law and of those parts of the law relevant to investment have apparently triumphed over non-Western approaches.[116] This has important legal cultural consequences when so much of the investments are into non-Western states. The legal cultural imperialism is not diminished by the fact that most states, even in the non-Western world, have an overlay, often superficial, of a Western legal system—be it civil or common law in origin, itself often a colonial legacy.[117] The legal cultural issues that arise from this situation have been previously discussed in the other recent legal cultural analyses, for it is a common situation among the many parts of international law.[118] In those earlier examinations, many points of legal cultural conflict between the local and Western international field were noted, such as: the very large informal legal systems operating in many non-Western states,[119] the tenuous hold of positivism in many non-Western systems,[120] and the transparency

---

114 Miles, *supra* note 22, at 11.

115 *See, e.g.*, Zampetti & Sauvé, *supra* note 34.

116 Miles, *supra* note 22, at 4.

117 *Id.*

118 *See generally* Picker, *IOs*, *supra* note 1, at 14; Picker, *Development*, *supra* note 1, at 65–68.

119 *See, e.g.*, PITMAN B. POTTER, THE CHINESE LEGAL SYSTEM: GLOBALIZATION AND LOCAL LEGAL CULTURE 12–13 (2001).

120 *See, e.g.*, Daniel Etounga-Manguelle, *Does Africa Need a Cultural Adjustment Program?*, *in* CULTURE MATTERS: HOW VALUES SHAPE HUMAN PROGRESS 67 (Lawrence E. Harrison & Samuel P. Huntington eds., 2000).

difficulties in indigenous oral legal traditions.[121] Clearly there is a need for non-Western legal cultural issues to be taken into account at the specific legal cultural analysis level. But, at the systemic level, the failure of the field to adequately take into account those issues is further evidence of the Western legal cultural character of the field—a character that is likely to raise legitimacy concerns given the very large non-Western legal culture present throughout the world.

Another legal cultural issue related to the power asymmetries within the field is the issue of legal cultural transplantation that may be taking place through the conduit of international investment law. For example, it has been claimed that through its BITs the United States has been exporting aspects of its legal system, and associated legal culture, around the world.[122] Given the United States is one of the few common law systems in the world, it is quite likely that it is exporting a common law legal culture to non–common law systems. Although it may be said that the EU and other economic powers are also exporting their own legal cultures, they and most investment target states will more likely share the same legal tradition and hence many of the same legal cultural characteristics. Of course, there may be instances where there are investment relations between an economically powerful civil law country and a developing country from the common law world, in which case there may be a corresponding spread of civilian notions into those common law countries. But, that potential transplantation is likely to have been offset by the powerful economic relations those common law systems would have with the United States or the UK or the other common law economic powers (Australia and Canada to name just two). This is especially likely as those common law developing countries would probably have been former colonies or have been in other similar relationships for the common law to have been originally transplanted into their system.[123] Furthermore, with the general trend of international investment and commercial law toward a more common law feel, it is likely that the trend would also counter the influence of the civil law system on the developing common law system. Indeed, if the mixed jurisdictions are predictive, the almost invariable trend of legal cultural drift is from civil to common law, and almost never in the opposite direction.[124]

3. International–Domestic Diversity

Another source of diversity is that international investment law, like most international law fields, takes place on two planes—both international and domestic. One might then expect that the legal culture of the field will reflect these two planes. Indeed, the legal culture present in an international investment law context will in broad terms reflect the legal culture of the domestic legal systems involved, typically

---

121 *See* H. PATRICK GLENN, LEGAL TRADITIONS OF THE WORLD 64 (4th ed. 2010).

122 *See, e.g.*, Eric Gillman, *Legal Transplants in Trade and Investment Agreements: Understanding the Exportation of U.S. Law to Latin America*, 41 GEO. J. INT'L L. 263, 265 (2009).

123 *See* Glendon, *supra* note 14, at 320–24 (discussing the common law's "distribution" methods).

124 Glendon, *supra* note 14, at 968. But note Israel as an exception in its early years when the influx of civil law–trained lawyers after World War II shifted the system toward the civil law. Palmer, *supra* note 54, at 6.

civilian or common law systems. But, the field would also reflect the legal culture of international law and any relevant international institutions.[125]

This diversity or duality will impact the legal culture of international investment law in a number of ways. For example, the domestic legal culture may prove more powerful than the international legal culture, for despite the existence of an international legal culture, that legal culture will simply be less entrenched and robust than a domestic legal culture. As such the domestic legal culture may inhibit the role of the legal culture of international law on the legal culture of international investment law. This may be more of an issue for international investment law perhaps than many other international law fields for it is one of the fields of international law that has exceptionally close connection to states' domestic laws. Once again, this is an issue that will empower those states and the attorneys who are frequent participants in international investments, for their legal cultures will be more strongly reflected in international transactions. Most likely, those states will disproportionately tend to be the United States and Britain, due to the dominance of their law firms as well as the fact that London and New York are the financial capitals of the world.

* * *

In conclusion, a field's broad diversity does not mean a legal cultural analysis is inapplicable. Although the existence of strong diversity within a legal field may provide obstacles for a legal cultural analysis, the above discussion shows that the nature or character of the diversity may itself contribute to the legal culture of the field, and its analysis may then lead to broadly applicable insights for the whole field.

E. THE DISPUTE-CENTERED DEVELOPMENT OF THE FIELD

Investment disputes are a major focus of those studying and working in international investment law. The resolutions of those disputes with their published decisions are significant sources of international investment law. The fact that the field is being developed by disputes is a significant factor in the ongoing development and maturation of the legal culture of international investment law.

Although it is true that a major part of the law in any field and system involves resolution of disputes, it is not the case that all systems, or even a majority, are significantly developed as a result of dispute resolutions. Dispute-driven law formation, although it exists in all systems either as a de jure or de facto matter, is a primary

---

[125] At the formation stage of the investment, those institutions might include (among others) one of the regional development banks, or if at the dispute stage, the arbitration facilities of the International Chamber of Commerce in Paris. Legal cultural analyses of these institutions would be helpful, but at the moment the author is not aware of any such works. However, a recent symposium of the Swiss Institute of Comparative Law invited representatives of many international institutions to discuss the role of legal traditions and cultures within their institutions. For a volume including some of those reports, see COMPARATIVE LAW & INTERNATIONAL ORGANIZATIONS: COOPERATION, COMPETITION AND CONNECTIONS (Lukas Heckendorn & Colin Picker eds., 2011).

feature of the common law or Anglo-American legal systems[126]—with its associated common law legal cultural characteristics. Civil law or the "continental" legal systems have elements of dispute-driven law creation, but are, as a conceptual matter if not as a practical one, developed through scholarship and legislation.[127] In contrast, in the common law world, and to a significant extent in the international investment law world, the law is developed as a result of judicial opinions and the employment of precedent. Even when it is not the judiciary that is the driving force of the law but rather the regulators and legislators, in the common law world such legislation and regulation is often today created in response to disputes, and is very quickly subject to judicial interpretation that is then the main source of the law.

Dispute-centered law creation in the common law world is a reflection of the common law's pragmatism, in contrast to the civil law's traditional proactive approach of creating law from principles, in advance of disputes.[128] The legal culture associated with dispute settlement–driven systems is accordingly more pragmatic and less focused on principles. It also supports a larger role for judges and arbitrators, and a correspondingly smaller role for academics and legislators. However, those academics that are important in the development of international investment law may themselves contribute to the common-law gloss by their focus on disputes and the law created from those disputes. Even when some of those scholars argue that there is no precedent in international investment law, eventually they will have to admit that there is "de facto" precedent.[129] This is not to suggest that scholars and legislators are irrelevant. It may be the case that scholars in particular, more so than the legislators, play an ongoing and important role in the development of this diffuse body of law. Indeed, they are likely more relevant than is typically the case in the Anglo-American legal culture.[130] That may be a reflection of the fact that international investment law, like international law in general, is a mixed system, with some civilian characteristics still strongly present, even as the common law looms at the gate, voracious to devour everything. "Legislators" too, domestic or international (in the sense of state officials or diplomats negotiating treaties) are a part of the international investment order. The many efforts to create investment law proactively, either in the context of the BITs or other multilateral disputes, are proof of their existence. But, the resultant "legislation," in the form of BITS and other treaties and agreements, are too often written in vague

---

[126] *See, e.g.*, Peter L. Strauss, *The Common Law and Statutes*, 70 U. COLO. L. REV. 225, 240 (1999).

[127] *See, e.g.*, Wayne R. Barnes, *Contemplating a Civil Law Paradigm for a Future International Commercial Code*, 65 LA. L. REV. 677, 731 (2005). Legislation can be broadly defined here to include codes, regulations, executive legislation, treaties, and so on.

[128] Picker, *WTO*, *supra* note 1, at 121–22..

[129] Christoph Shreuer & Matthew Weiniger, *A Doctrine of Precedent*, in OXFORD HANDBOOK OF INTERNATIONAL INVESTMENT 1197 (Peter Muchlinski, Federico Ortino & Christph Shreuer eds., 2008).

[130] Glendon, *supra* note 14, at 179.

generalities, allowing the jurisprudence to both inform the meaning and to develop the future path of the BIT or other treaty.[131]

The fact that international investment law is being developed increasingly by dispute resolutions suggest a greater role for the common law than might otherwise have been the case. The consequences for the legal culture of the field, at the macro- and micro-levels could be significant, as common law methods and approaches are increasingly employed, slowly shaping the legal culture, which then feeds back into the selection of common law devices to match that legal culture. Given how few legal systems in the world are in fact common law,[132] this suggests an advantage to those that hail from common law jurisdictions, or for those able to assimilate common law legal cultural characteristics into their own legal systems.

V. Conclusion

The mechanics and specifics of international investments have been subject to numerous valuable legal cultural analyses. Many papers have been written on the legal cultural issues that arise in investment arbitration and investment negotiation, and in the operations of investments in different legal systems. But, the field has not really been subject to a legal cultural examination at the system level. Although difficult and rife with obstacles, doing so can be a rewarding experience.

As this short attempt shows, despite necessary generalizations and simplifications, some critical legal cultural issues have been identified. Those issues include consideration of some of the legal cultural factors that may be driving the development of the field to some specific legal cultural characteristics that may be applicable across the field, with wide-ranging implications for its operation and growth. Those factors extend from the use of English to the limited liability of the MNCs involved in international investment. The legal cultural characteristics that may span the field range from such different attributes as a defensiveness associated with the divisiveness of the

[131] Olivia Chung, *The Lopsided International Investment Law Regime and Its Effect on the Future of Investor–State Arbitration*, 47 VA. J. INT'L L. 953, 959 (2007).

[132] *See* Barnes, *supra* note 127, at 684 (showing that fifty-one nations utilize common law systems, whereas 115 nations have civil law systems). Civil law systems include most of Europe, save Ireland and England, and also include Russia, China, Mexico, South and Central America, and significant parts of Africa. In contrast, the common law systems include the United States, Anglo-Canada, England, Ireland, Australia, some African countries, most of south Asia (although family law tends to be based on religious law), and a few other countries around the world. *See id.* at 685.

> Common law (exclusive of any civil law), whether in "pure" or "mixed" form, is utilized by some fifty-one nations, or 26.7% of all nations of the world. These nations account for 34.81% of the world's population.... Civil law (exclusive of any common law), whether in "pure" or "mixed" form, is utilized by some 115 nations, or 60.21% of all nations of the world. These nations account for 59.01% of the world's population.
>
> *Id.*

field to a common law pragmatism created by the significant role of dispute resolution on the development of the field.

Finally, if there is ever to be an international agreement on investment, and perhaps even a global institution, it would be helpful to understand the field from all perspectives. Legal culture is one of the perspectives that should be understood for it too often operates at a subconscious level, but has the ability to affect all aspects of the operation of the field. Furthermore, because the field, including any overarching treaty or institution, must interact with other fields and systems, each with its own legal cultures, it would be very helpful to know if there are likely to be any legal cultural disconnects in those interactions. Certainly, these and other legal cultural issues must be taken into account, for failure to do so could undermine the success of any future multilateral agreement or institution for the field.

4

BILATERAL TRADE AND INVESTMENT AGREEMENTS*

*Leon E. Trakman***

THIS CHAPTER EXPLORES the rationale behind the development of bilateral trade and investment agreements as measures of state action. In examining the arguments in support of such bilateral agreements, it scrutinizes the virtues and deficiencies associated with each. It concludes by considering whether bilateralism contributes to the development of principles and standards governing multilateral trade and investment.

The proliferation of bilateral trade and investment agreements has helped to fill lacunae in a multilateral trade process that is impeded by the impasse of negotiations in the World Trade Organization (WTO).[1] At the same time, the development of bilateral agreements arguably has discouraged some states from engaging in multilateral negotiations.[2] The result is a new genre of trade and investment relations in which

---

* An earlier version of this chapter titled *The Proliferation of Free Trade: Bane or Beauty*? was published in the *Journal of World Trade* in 2008. A particular thanks is extended to that journal and to Kluwer International, its publisher, for the kind permission to republish it as this modified chapter.

** UNSW Professor of Law and Immediate Past Dean, Faculty of Law, University of New South Wales. The author's earned degrees are B.Com, LLB (Cape Town), and LLM, SJD (Harvard). He is a certified mediator and arbitrator on four continents, specializing in trade and investment law. This chapter is dedicated to the memory of the author's supervisors at Harvard Law School, Professors Harold Berman, Arthur von Mehren, and David Cavers for their insights on this and related topics. Further thanks are owed to the Social Sciences and Humanities Research Council of Canada for funding the original project upon which this chapter is based, and to the University of New South Wales for a decanal grant to write it.

[1] On the changing character of the WTO, *see* Julia Ya Qin, *The Challenge of Interpreting "WTO-Plus" Provisions*, 44 J. WORLD TRADE 127 (2010); PETER GALLAGHER, THE FIRST TEN YEARS OF THE WTO: 1995–2005 (2005); PETER VAN DEN BOSSCHE, THE LAW AND POLICY OF THE WORLD TRADE ORGANIZATION: TEXT, CASES AND MATERIALS (2005). On the history of global trade negotiations, *see, e.g.*, THOMAS R. HOWELL, ALAN WILLIAM WOLFF, BRENT L. BARTLETT & R. MICHAEL GADBAW, CONFLICT AMONG NATIONS: TRADE POLICIES IN THE 1990S (1993); FATOUMATA JAWARA & AILEEN KWA, BEHIND THE SCENES AT THE WTO—THE REAL WORLD OF INTERNATIONAL TRADE NEGOTIATION (2003).

[2] For convenience, bilateral investment agreements are referred to as BITs, and free trade agreements are referred to as FTAs. On the relationship between BITs and FTAs, *see, e.g.*, TRADE AND INVESTMENT

bilateral and regional mechanisms are increasingly adopted in substitution for multilateral trade and investment processes, including in dispute resolution.[3] Although bilateral agreements diverge significantly in their form and substance, including in relation to trade as distinct from investment, they have an important, albeit controversial, impact upon multilateral commerce. One view is that bilateralism reflects a shift back toward a consensual relationship between sovereign states from a multilateral process based on a *ius cogens* that transcends state power. The contrary view is that such bilateralism advances the multilateral process, binding states to peremptory norms such as in their dealings with foreign traders and investors.

This chapter examines different arguments for asserting that bilateral trade and investment agreements have advanced multilateral commercial relations. It poses a variety of questions. To what extent is the development of bilateral agreements founded on sound trade and investment principles?[4] Have bilateral agreements added value to or detracted from the perceived demands of multilateral trade and investment? Are states subject to suitable guidelines grounded in a multilateral *ius cogens* in negotiating and concluding such bilateral agreements? To what extent are they required to redress the practices of recalcitrant states based on universal legal norms, or by such practical measures as trade and investment boycotts and other sanctions for violating international trade law or for treating direct foreign investors unfairly?[5]

RULE-MAKING: ROLE OF REGIONAL AND BILATERAL AGREEMENTS (S. Woolcock ed., 2006). On the proliferation of FTAs, *see* http://www.cfr.org/publication/10890/. On the history of BITs, see K.J. Vandevelde, *A Brief History of International Investment Agreements*, 12 U.C. DAVIS J. INT'L L. & POL'Y 157 (2005). *See generally* RUDOLF DOLZER & CHRISTOPH SCHREUER, PRINCIPLES OF INTERNATIONAL INVESTMENT LAW (2nd ed. 2012); ANDREAS KULICK, GLOBAL PUBLIC INTEREST IN INTERNATIONAL INVESTMENT LAW (2012).

[3] On dispute resolution under the WTO, *see* YANG GUOHUA, BRYAN MERCURIO & LI YONGJIE, WTO DISPUTE SETTLEMENT UNDERSTANDING: A DETAILED INTERPRETATION (2005); Colin B. Picker, *Regional Trade Agreements V. The WTO: A Proposal for Reform of Article XXIV to Counter This Institutional Threat*, 26 U. PA. J. INTL ECON. L. 267 (2005); PETROS C. MAVROIDIS & N. DAVID PALMETER, DISPUTE SETTLEMENT IN THE WORLD TRADE ORGANIZATION: PRACTICE AND PROCEDURE (2004); ERNST-ULRICH PETERSMANN, THE GATT/WTO DISPUTE SETTLEMENT SYSTEM: INTERNATIONAL LAW, INTERNATIONAL ORGANIZATIONS AND DISPUTE SETTLEMENT (1997). On regional trade agreements, *see, e.g.*, JAMES H. MATHIS, REGIONAL TRADE AGREEMENTS IN THE GATT/WTO: ARTICLE XXIV AND THE INTERNATIONAL TRADE REQUIREMENT (2002).

[4] For illustrations of structural changes wrought by bilateral trade agreements upon multilateral trade, particularly in regard to trade liberalization and protectionism, *see* Scott L. Baier & Jeffrey H. Bergstrand, *The Growth of World Trade: Tariffs, Transport Costs and Income Similarity*, 53 J. INT'L ECON. 27 (2001); Anne O. Krueger, *Are Preferential Trading Arrangements Trade-Liberalizing or Protectionist?* 13(4) J. ECON. PERSPECTIVES 105 (1999); Paul Krugman, *The Move towards Free Trade Zones, available at* http://www.kansascityfEd.org/publicat/Sympos/1991/S91krugm.pdf. *See generally* SURYA P. SUBEDI, INTERNATIONAL INVESTMENT LAW: RECONCILING POLICY AND PRINCIPLE (2nd ed. 2012); Jan Wouters, Sanderijn Duquet & Nicolas Hachez, *International Investment Law: The Perpetual Search for Consensus, available at* http://papers.ssrn.com/sol3/papers.cfm?abstract_id=2031552.

[5] *See generally* Robert McMahon, *The Rise in Bilateral Free Trade Agreements*, Council on Foreign Relations, June 13, 2006, *available at* http://www.cfr.org/publication/10890/. *But see* http://www.bilaterals.org/article.php3?id_article=1227 (a Web site devoted to the downfall of bilateral free trade agreements). On the development of bilateral investment treaties, *see, e,g.*, KENNETH J. VANDEVELDE, BILATERAL

Related to these questions are tensions between policies over the nature of trade and investment liberalization. One nineteenth-century policy is grounded in principles of state autonomy: that states should be comparatively unchecked in concluding bilateral trade and investment agreements, in the interests of both promoting the free exchange of goods and services and international investment. This policy is grounded in the sovereignty of states and the assertion that international trade and investment law is no greater than the sum of agreements to which states are parties, with a limited override of customary international law.

Another policy holds that states are bound to respect their bilateral agreements and that violating them ought to lead to the censuring of offending states according to peremptory principles of law. In support of reconciling these two policies is the claim that states that consent to bilateral agreements both surrender their sovereignty and territoriality bilaterally and subject themselves to international standards of compliance not limited to those embodied in the General Agreement on Tariffs and Trade (GATT) and its WTO successor, including in their treatment of investors from partner states.[6]

The first two sections of this chapter evaluate the reasoning behind the liberalization of trade and investment and the assumptions in favor of free trade agreements (FTAs) and bilateral investment treaties (BITs). The third section critiques different arguments in favor of negotiating and concluding BITs and FTAs. The fourth section proposes legal principles and standards to guide the application of bilateral trade and investment agreements in the future.

The purpose is to contrast the divergence among FTAs and BITs, with the convergence of a multilateral system of trade and investment law, and to determine whether the two are reconcilable, ideologically, conceptually, and functionally.[7] Another purpose, developed in Section III, is to present the chapter through the eyes of developing states, in particular the extent to which FTAs and BITs promote their individual and collective interests.

INVESTMENT TREATIES: HISTORY, POLICY, AND INTERPRETATION (2010); Leon E. Trakman, *Foreign Direct Investment: Hazard or Opportunity?*, 41(1) GEO. WASH. INT'L. L. REV. 1–65 (2010).

[6] *See, e.g.*, Chad P. Bown, *Participation in WTO Dispute Settlement: Complainants, Interested Parties, and Free Riders*, 19(2) WORLD BANK ECON. REV. 287 (2005); Chad P. Bown, *On the Economic Success of GATT/WTO Dispute Settlement*, 86(3) REV. ECON. & STAT. 811 (2004); James McCall Smith, *The Politics of Dispute Settlement Design: Explaining Legalism in Regional Trade Pacts*, 54 INT'L. ORG. 137 (2003); MICHAEL J. TREBILCOCK & ROBERT HOWSE, THE REGULATION OF INTERNATIONAL TRADE (1995). Marc L. Busch & Eric Reinhardt, *Testing International Trade Law: Empirical Studies of GATT/WTO Dispute Settlement*, *available at* http://www.carleton.ca/ctpl/pdf/conferences/REINHARDT-BUSCH!95.pdf. For a comprehensive list of publications on global commerce and the WTO, see http://henningcenter.berkeley.edu/gateway/wto.html.

[7] On this divergence leading to convergence, *see, e.g.*, STEPHAN W. SCHILL, THE MULTILATERALIZATION OF INTERNATIONAL INVESTMENT LAW (2009); Jeffery P. Commission, *Precedent in Investment Treaty Arbitration—A Citation Analysis of a Developing Jurisprudence*, 24 J. INT'L ARB. 129, 148 (2007); ANDREAS F. LOWENFELD, INTERNATIONAL ECONOMIC LAW 467–591 (2008); RUDOLF DOLZER & CHRISTOPH SCHREUER, PRINCIPLES OF INTERNATIONAL INVESTMENT LAW (2008).

I. The Liberalization of Trade and Investment

The post–World War II era has heralded two not always harmonious developments: a commitment by nation states to reduce barriers to trade and investment, and an effort to establish principles and guidelines for the free flow of goods, services, and investments across national boundaries.[8] In particular, the General Agreement on Tariffs and Trade (GATT) sought to unify multilateral trade practice through a pervasive, transparent, and commonly understood set of principles directed at harmonizing trade and investment practice and maximizing cooperation in the global interest. The underlying rationale was that these principles were the product of the multilateral consent of states, and reflected unifying norms of conduct that bound them in the conduct of trade including their treatment of foreign traders and investors.[9]

Despite these developments, global liberalization of trade and investment has fallen short of a resounding success. The trade protectionism and investment selectivity that marked the era prior to World War II has remained a serious impediment to liberalized trade and investment, along with disparities in the power of trading states and the more recent fragmentation of trade and investment agreements along bilateral lines.[10] Although the GATT purported to incorporate both bilateral and regional trade and investment practices on the grounds that they furthered multilateralism, such bilateralism arguably has chipped away at the development of global principles of trade

---

[8] *See infra* Section II(i). On challenges to the WTO, *see, e.g.*, KENT ALBERT JONES, WHO'S AFRAID OF THE WTO? (2003); BENJAMIN HEIM SHEPARD & RONALD HAYDUK, FROM ACT UP TO THE WTO: URBAN PROTEST AND COMMUNITY BUILDING IN THE ERA OF GLOBALIZATION (2002); ROBIN BROAD, GLOBAL BACKLASH: CITIZEN INITIATIVES FOR A JUST WORLD ECONOMY (2002).

[9] This conception of cooperation is exemplified by the requirements under the WTO, as distinct from the GATT, that China satisfy three levels of commitment in order to be admitted as a member of the WTO. First, China was obliged to commit itself to the objectives of the WTO, such as to the most-favored-nation's clause, national treatment, and transparency requirements, as exemplified in the GATT and developed in the ensuing WTO agreements. Second, China had to demonstrate in its accession protocol its commitment to establishing and complying with a series of WTO trade rules applicable in specific sectors, such as in relation to agriculture and textiles, information technology, and telecommunications. Third, China had to establish its commitment to its bilateral agreements with its major trading partners, and that it had their support in negotiating its entry into the WTO. *See further infra* notes 41, 42, and 62. On transparency requirements in investment law, *see* Julie A. Maupin, *Transparency in International Investment Law: The Good, the Bad, and the Murky*, *in* TRANSPARENCY IN INTERNATIONAL LAW (Andrea Bianchi & Anne Peters eds., 2013).

[10] For the argument that the liberalization of trade through free trade agreements generally benefits multilateral trade, *see* Emanuel Ornelas, *Endogenous Free Trade Agreements and the Multilateral Trading System*, 67(2) J. INT'L. ECON. 471 (2005). On the tension between trade liberalization and protectionism, *see* Gea M. Lee, *Trade Agreements with Domestic Policies as Disguised Protection*, 71(1) J. INT'L ECON. 241–59 (2007). *See generally* JOHN HOWARD JACKSON, SOVEREIGNTY, THE WTO AND CHANGING FUNDAMENTALS OF INTERNATIONAL LAW (2006). *But see* Judith L. Goldstein & Lisa Martin, *Legalization, Trade Liberalization, and Domestic Politics: A Cautionary Note*, 54 INT'L ORG. 63 (2003).

and investment in particular that some viewed as unduly protective of the national interests of developed states and their investors.[11]

Against this background, the tension between bilateralism and multilateralism has re-arisen with a vengeance as states have repeatedly failed to reach multilateral accord on account of their conflicting domestic interests.[12] A by-product of this tension has been the growth of bilateral agreements between selected trade and investment partners on supposedly mutually satisfying terms. The result of this by-product has been applauded as evidence of trade and investment development by those who favor bilateralism as a legitimate and efficacious development,[13] but a source of concern for those who worry about lost opportunities for the multilateral trade and investment processes. At issue, too, are systemic differences over the extent to which bilateralism undermines the multilateral process by marginalizing common principles that underlie it and imposing discriminatory standards of treatment upon foreign traders and investors.[14]

II. Reconciling Multilateralism and Bilateralism

Despite inevitable tensions between bilateral and multilateral trade and investment processes, international instruments historically have tried to reconcile them. In particular, the GATT sought to do so as a matter of policy, principle, and practice.[15] Article

---

[11] It is arguable that BITs should be primarily regulated by the General Agreement on Trade and Services (GATS) not by the WTO. *See* Art. 2(2), Annex., General Agreement on Trade in Services, Apr. 15, 1994, Marrakesh Agreement Establishing the World Trade Organization, annex 1B, 1869 U.N.T.S. 183. *See generally* Eyal Benvenisti & George W. Downs, *The Empire's New Clothes: Political Economy and the Fragmentation of International Law*, 60 STAN. L. REV. 595 (2007). *See infra* Section II(vi).

[12] Despite the image of a liberalizing trade and investment culture shifting from multilateralism to bilateralism, multilateralism is sometimes quietly resurrected through diplomacy. On the "quiet" resurrection of the Doha Talks through to Hong Kong, see for example comments of the U.S. Trade Representative, Susan Schwab, *available at* http://www.iht.com/articles/ap/2007/02/23/business/NA-FIN-US-Doha-Talks.php. On different WTO negotiation strategies since Doha, *see* http://www.twnside.org.sg/trade_1.htm. *See also* Robert M. Stern, *Perspectives on the WTO Doha Development*, 5(4) GLOBAL ECON. J. (2005).

[13] On the contribution of BITs to the unification of a multilateral law governing investment, *see, e.g.*, T. Rixen & I. Rohlfing, *The Institutional Choice of Bilateralism and Multilateralism in International Trade and Taxation*, 12 INT'L NEGOT. 389 (2007); CAMPBELL MCLACHLAN, LAURENCE SHORE & MATTHEW WEINIGER, INTERNATIONAL INVESTMENT ARBITRATION—SUBSTANTIVE PRINCIPLES (2007); Stephan Schill, *International Investment Law and the Host State's Power to Handle Economic Crises*, 24 J. INT'L ARB. 265 (2007). In defense of bilateral free trade agreements, *see, e.g.*, Daniel Griswald, *Bilateral Deals Are No Threat to Global Trade*, FIN. TIMES (July 27, 2003); CBO, *The Pros and Cons of Pursuing Free Trade Deals*, Congressional Economic and Budget Issue Brief (Congressional Budget Office, July 31, 2003).

[14] *See, e.g.*, BRYAN MERCURIO & SIMON LESTER, BILATERAL AND REGIONAL TRADE AGREEMENTS: ANALYSIS AND COMMENTARY (2007); LORAND BARTELS & FEDERICO ORTINO, REGIONAL TRADE AGREEMENTS AND THE WTO LEGAL SYSTEM (2006).

[15] On the history of Article XXIV of the GATT and divisions among developing states over its virtues, *see* MATHIS, *supra* note 3; J. Goto & K. Hamada, *Regional Economic Integration and Article XXIV of the GATT*, 7(4) REV. INT'L. ECON. 555 (1999).

XXIV of the GATT specifically endorsed customs unions and free trade agreements between members, noting that

> The contracting parties recognize the desirability of increasing freedom of trade by the development, through voluntary agreements, of closer integration between the economies of [those] countries.[16]

The rationale behind the GATT's endorsement of regional and bilateral trade and arguably also investment agreements was that by reducing barriers to entry between two or more members, the presupposed net result was the enhancement of global trade and investment.[17] The inferred result was an overall increase in total global trade and investment arising from the accretion of a series of profitable regional and bilateral agreements that exceeded their net cost.[18]

Whether these assumptions in Article XXIV have been satisfied depends on careful scrutiny of the arguments favoring regional and bilateral trade and investment, and an assessment of their impact on trade and investment practice. What follows are reflections on different rationales favoring bilateral trade and investment agreements, followed in each case by arguments challenging them. The intention is neither to echo nor gainsay the principles or the arguments that gave rise to Article XXIV of the GATT, but to consider how they applied to conventional trade and investment practice.[19]

I. THE RATIONALE FAVORING LIBERALIZED TRADE AND INVESTMENT

The liberalization of trade and investment along bilateral lines is grounded in a set of interrelated political, economic, and social assumptions. The first is that the liberalization of trade law in general is most effective when states reduce barriers to trade and investment, including through bilateral agreements; when buyers, sellers, and investors have greater freedom to transact within regional and bilateral free trade zones; when avenues to foreign investment are opened; and when

---

[16] The text of Article XXIV, clause 4, continues that the contracting parties "recognize that the purpose of a customs union or of a free-trade area should be to facilitate trade between the constituent territories and not to raise barriers to the trade of other contracting parties with such territories." *See further* http://www.wto.org/english/tratop_e/region_e/regatt_e.htm#gatt.

[17] The rules of the GATT and WTO provide that, except in relation to free trade areas (which would include bilateral trade agreements), a state may not impose a higher tariff against one member state than another, so that any diminution in a state's barriers to trade must apply equally to imports from all other member countries. As a result, reducing a state's barriers to trade supposedly promotes the competitiveness of all imports equally, so that the growth in imports from one state will displace domestic production and not imports from other states.

[18] *See* Fred C. Bergsten, *Competitive Liberalization and Global Free Trade: A Vision for the Early 21st Century*, APEC Working Paper No. 96-15 (1996). It is through this "competitive liberalism" that GDP is expected to grow.

[19] *See generally* ELHANAN HELPMAN, THE MYSTERY OF ECONOMIC GROWTH (2004); J.R. MACARTHUR, THE SELLING OF FREE TRADE (2000).

the cost and prices of goods and services are reduced as a result of lower economies of scale in the production, distribution, and sale of such goods and services within such regional or bilateral markets.[20] A second and related assumption is that trade and investment is more effectively liberalized when barriers to the supply of goods and services between particular states and their investors are reduced selectively, including when bilateral agreements are devised to have that effect.[21] A third assumption is that bilateral trade and investment agreements that reduce barriers to trade and investment between specific parties and their respective investors ordinarily liberalize trade and investment multilaterally as well.[22] A fourth qualifying assumption is that bilateral agreements benefit global trade and investment when the benefit of expanded trade and investment between bilateral parties more than offsets the loss of trade and investment to states and their investors who are not parties to those agreements.[23] A fifth assumption is that liberalized trade and investment can and should have a positive distributive effect, namely, when the accretion in wealth derived from expanded trade and investment is distributed by partner states to bilateral trade and investment agreements to those subjects who have the greatest need.[24]

These assumptions are best examined in light of the principles underlying global trade and investment and in applying those principles to relationships among states engaged in bilateral, regional, and multilateral trade and investment in particular.

---

20 For a historical debate over the extent to which global competition promotes trade liberalization, *see, e.g.*, EDWARD MONTGOMERY GRAHAM & J. DAVID RICHARDSON, GLOBAL COMPETITION POLICY (1997); MICHAEL STORPER, THE REGIONAL WORLD: TERRITORIAL DEVELOPMENT IN A GLOBAL ECONOMY (1997); ELHANAN HELPMAN & PAUL ROBIN KRUGMAN, MARKET STRUCTURE AND FOREIGN TRADE PRESENTS A COHERENT THEORY OF TRADE IN THE PRESENCE OF MARKET STRUCTURES OTHER THAN PERFECT COMPETITION (1985).

21 For a debate over the extent to which bilateral trade and investment is selective and exclusionary, *see, e.g.*, MARTIN WOLF, WHY GLOBALIZATION WORKS (2004); Jagdish Bhagwati & Arvind Panagariya, *The Theory of Preferential Trade Agreements: Historical Evolution and Current Trends*, 86(2) AM. ECON. REV. 82 (1996); A.O. Krueger, *Are Preferential Trading Arrangements Liberalizing or Protectionist?* 13(4) J. ECON. PERSPECTIVE 105 (1999); Raymond Riezman, *Can Bilateral Trade Agreements Help to Induce Free Trade*, 32 CAN. J. ECON. 751 (1999); Kyle Bagwell & Robert W. Staiger, *Will Preferential Agreements Undermine the Multilateral Trading System?* 108 ECON. J. 1162 (1998); Philip I. Levy, *A Political-Economic Analysis of Free Trade Agreements*, 87 AM. ECON. REV. 506 (1997).

22 On the impact of bilateral trade agreements upon nonparties, *see* Kyle Bagwell & Robert W. Staiger, *Erratum to Multilateral Trade Negotiations, Bilateral Opportunism and the Rules of GATT/WTO*, 67(2) J. INT'L ECON. 268 (2004). *See also* Ornelas, *supra* note 10.

23 This relative decrease in barriers to trade occurs when the parties to bilateral or regional trade agreements erect barriers to trade as to nonparties that do not exceed the reduced trade barriers between the parties to those agreements. *See, e.g.*, HELPMAN & KRUGMAN, *supra* note 20. For criticisms that the economic benefits of BITs outweigh their costs, *see* J.W. Salacuse, *The Treatification of International Investment Law*, 8 STUD. INT'L FIN. ECON. & TECH. L. 241, 245 (2007).

24 For an analysis of the distribution effect of trade policy, *see* Guido G. Porto, *Using Survey Data to Assess the Distributional Effects of Trade Policy*, 70(1) J. INT'L ECON. 140 (2006).

II. PRINCIPLED REASONS FOR LIBERALIZING TRADE AND INVESTMENT

The philosophical basis for enhanced freedom to trade and invest is grounded in the interrelated principles of democratic liberalism affirmed in the nineteenth century[25] coupled with economic rationality that evolved primarily in the twentieth century.[26] Democratic liberalism implies that states ought to empower their subjects to engage in the free flow of goods and services across national boundaries as a democratic entitlement. Freedom within a liberal democracy includes not only the personal liberty of individuals, but also their rights to profit from state-sponsored trade and investment, including from bilateral trade and investment. Coupled to this notion is the view that states that liberalize trade and investment bilaterally act in an economically rational manner in reducing barriers to the free flow of goods and services between bilateral parties and their investors. The result of the coalescence of democratic liberalism and economic rationalism is that trade and investment becomes more profitable for the benefit of the state parties as well as their traders and investors.[27]

To these principles is added a controversial third principle of equitable treatment, namely that a by-product of the liberalization of trade and investment between states is the promotion of "fairer trade and investment, an outgrowth of the early 20th century welfare state."[28] Fairer trade and investment is achieved on a level playing field of equal opportunity when state parties to bilateral trade and investment agreements seek to benefit the subjects of treaty partners through "most favored nation" treatment, or "national" treatment. Fairer trade and investment is presumably economically rational as well in helping to sustain trade and investment between parties who are more equal in status and capacity.[29]

---

25 In rooting multilateral trade, including bilateral trade agreements, in the traditions of a liberal democracy, *see, e.g.*, DANIEL VERDIER, DEMOCRACY AND INTERNATIONAL TRADE: BRITAIN, FRANCE, AND THE UNITED STATES, 1860–1990 (1995).

26 *See generally* D. SCHNEIDERMAN, CONSTITUTIONALIZING ECONOMIC GLOBALIZATION 71–108 (2008); D. HARVEY, A BRIEF HISTORY OF NEOLIBERALISM 15–19 (2005); RAZEEN SALLY, CLASSICAL LIBERALISM AND INTERNATIONAL ECONOMIC ORDER: STUDIES IN THEORY AND INTELLECTUAL HISTORY (1998). For a criticism of "economic rationality" attributed primarily to the United States, *see, e.g.*, Peter Karl Kresl, *The United States, Canada, and the Market Mentality*, 14 (1) J. INTERAMERICAN STUD. & WORLD AFFAIRS 3 (1972).

27 *See* ROGER B. PORTER, EFFICIENCY, EQUITY, AND LEGITIMACY: THE MULTILATERAL TRADING SYSTEM AT THE MILLENNIUM (2001).

28 *See, e.g.*, Benedict Kingsbury & Stephan Schill, *Investor-State Arbitration as Governance: Fair and Equitable Treatment, Proportionality, and the Emerging Global Administrative Law*, IILJ Working Paper 2009/6 (Global Administrative Law Series), pp. 1–2, *available at* http://www.iilj.org/publications/2009-6Kingsbury-Schill.asp (last visited Mar. 31, 2010): JAN PAULSSON, DENIAL OF JUSTICE IN INTERNATIONAL LAW CH. 9 (2005), ch.9; PORTER, *supra* note 27. *But see* Jagdish Bhagwati, *After Seattle: Free Trade and the WTO*, 77(1) INT'L AFFAIRS 15–30 (2001).

29 On the "most favored nation" treatment in international trade, *see, e.g.*, Faya Rodriguez, *The Most-Favored-Nation Clause in International Investment Agreements*, 25 J. INT'L ARB. 89 (2008); Endre Ustor, *Most-Favoured-Nation Clause*, *in* ENCYCLOPEDIA OF PUBLIC INTERNATIONAL LAW 468 (Vol. III) (Rudolf Bernhardt & Peter Macalister-Smith eds., 1997); Kamal Saggi, *Tariffs and the Most Favored Nation*

These philosophical assumptions behind bilateralism are at best generalizations. However much bilateralism may expand trade and investment between partner states and their subjects, the process of bilateral agreement is both selective and exclusionary in inception, application, and operation. In particular, it leads to the privileging of some states and their subjects over other states and their subjects. However rational states may appear to be and however much they may propose to liberalize trade and investment practices bilaterally, acting in their rational self-interest does not ensure that the results are fair. Self-interest sometimes supports decisions to act inequitably, including by granting trade and investment benefits differentially on political grounds. It also accounts in part for the observation that many BITs are viewed as overly favoring a dominant party at the expense of a subservient one. The perceived inequities that are associated with BITs partially explain why up to one-third of BITs are not ratified.[30]

Nevertheless, bilateralism does have wide appeal. The rhetoric is that, in the absence of viable alternatives, bilateralism renders trade and investment across national boundaries more cost effective and ultimately more profitable. Insofar as bilateral trade and investment furthers these objectives, however questionable it may be in particular cases, one would expect states to support FTAs and BITs.[31] One would also expect states to act "rationally" in seeking the economic good of other states so long as doing so is consistent with furthering their own good.[32] One would presuppose, too, that most states would support the "invisible hand" of a free market of rational states, traders, and investors in which bilateral agreements reduce barriers to trade

---

Clause, 63 J. INT'L ECON. 341 (2005); Andrew F. Daughety & Jennifer F. Reinganum, *Exploiting Future: Settlements: A Signaling Model of Most-Favored National Clauses in Settlement Bargaining*, 35(3) RAND J. ECON. 467 (2004); Andrew A. Faye, *APEC and the New Regionalism: GATT Compliance and Prescriptions for the WTO*, 28 LAW & POLICY INT'L. BUS. 175 (1996).

[30] There is evidence that BITs have played only a "minor and secondary role in influencing FDI Flows. . . ." *See* UNCTAD, *Bilateral Investment Treaties in the Mid-1990s*, UN DOC. UNCTAD/ITE/IIT/7 (1998), at 141–42. For the observation that only 800 out of 2,500 BITs were ratified, *see* M. Sornarajah, *The Fair and Equitable Standard of Treatment: Whose Fairness? Whose Equity? in* INVESTMENT TREATY LAW (Federico Ortino et al. eds., 2007); E. Neumayer & L. Spess, *Do Bilateral Investment Treaties Increase Foreign Direct Investment to Developing Countries?*, at 5, LSE Research Online, *available at* http://eprints.lse.ac.uk/archive/00000627; L.S. Poulsen, *The Importance of BITs for Foreign Direct Investment and Political Risk Insurance: Revisiting the Evidence, in* YEARBOOK ON INTERNATIONAL INVESTMENT LAW AND POLICY 2009/2010 (K. Sauvant ed., 2010); GUS VAN HARTEN, INVESTMENT TREATY ARBITRATION AND PUBLIC LAW 30–31 (2007).

[31] *See generally* ADAM SZIRMAI, THE DYNAMICS OF SOCIO-ECONOMIC DEVELOPMENT: AN INTRODUCTION (2005); PHILIP DAVID MCMICHAEL, DEVELOPMENT AND SOCIAL CHANGE: A GLOBAL PERSPECTIVE (3rd ed. 2004); ROURDES BENERIA & SAVITRI BISNATH, GLOBAL TENSIONS: CHALLENGES AND OPPORTUNITIES IN THE WORLD ECONOMY (2003).

[32] For example, it is presumably rational for states to use bilateral free trade agreements as ways of "encouraging" states to engage in social reform in the interests of more stable, and mutually profitable, trade over the longer term. *See further infra* Section II(iv).

and investment, lower the costs of goods and services, and help to promote higher standards of living in partner states.[33]

III. BENEFITS ASCRIBED TO BILATERALISM

Bilateral trade and investment agreements, formally at least, are reciprocal, consensual, and inclusive of the state parties while being exclusionary of other states.

As a matter of practice, however, FTAs and BITs are internally different from one another. Some are seemingly all-encompassing in liberalizing trade and investment and in seeking to provide unrestricted access to local markets.[34] Others are distinctly protectionist.[35] Some set clear shields around sensitive industries such as education, the media, and healthcare.[36] Others do so generically through open-ended protection of "the national interest."[37] Some bilateral trade and investment agreements resemble treaties of friendship more than instruments of trade and investment liberalization. Some states, such as Ecuador, withdraw from BITs on the economic grounds that they fail adequately to benefit the domestic economy.[38]

---

33 The conception of the "invisible hand" in the free market is attributed to Adam Smith and his "wealth of nations," although in the two passages in which he refers to the invisible hand, it is of the individual, not the state. *See* ADAM SMITH, AN INQUIRY INTO THE NATURE AND CAUSES OF THE WEALTH OF NATIONS, ¶¶ IV.2.9 & IV.I.10 (1776).

34 *See* LEON TRAKMAN, DISPUTE SETTLEMENT UNDER THE NAFTA: MANUAL AND SOURCEBOOK (1997); ROBERT E. LITAN & PETER HAKIM, THE FUTURE OF NORTH AMERICAN INTEGRATION: BEYOND NAFTA (2002).

35 Protectionism is often based on the "infant industry" syndrome, namely, that a state needs to protect an industry that is as yet underdeveloped and would be undermined by foreign competition in the absence of such protection. Equally often, such protection is girded by the interest of a government in preserving relationships with particular industries, as when a government supports farmers who represent significant voting strength in rural constituencies. On infant industries, *see, e.g., Symposium on Infant Industries: A Comment*, 31(1) OXFORD DEVELOP. STUD 33 (2003); Steven M. Suranovic, *International Trade Theory and Policy, available at* http://internationalecon.com/Trade/Tch100/T100-4.php. *See generally* Olivier De Schutter & Peter Rosenblum, *Large-Scale Investments in Farmland: The Regulatory Challenge, in* YEARBOOK ON INTERNATIONAL INVESTMENT LAW & POLICY 2010–2011 (Karl P. Sauvant ed., 2012).

36 For instance, the U.S.–Australia Free Trade Agreement. *See, e.g.*, JEFFREY J. SCOTT, FREE TRADE AGREEMENTS: U.S. STRATEGIES AND PRIORITIES (2004); Peter Drahos & David Henry, *The Free Trade Agreement between Australia and the United States*, BMJ. COM. 27 (Feb. 2007); P.I. Levy, *A Political-Economic Analysis of Free-Trade Agreements*, 87(4) AM. ECON. REV. (2003).

37 Such protectionism is apparent when smaller states wish to protect their "cultural heritage" in negotiating FTAs and BITs with more powerful trade partners. Both Canada and Mexico under the NAFTA, and Australia under the U.S.–Australia Free Trade Agreements, were so preoccupied. *See, e.g.*, John A. Ragosta, *The Cultural Industries Exemption from NAFTA—Its Parameters*, 3 CANADA-U.S. L.J. (1997); Report, DEPARTMENT OF FOREIGN AFFAIRS AND TRADE, AN AUSTRALIA–UNITED STATES FREE TRADE AGREEMENT (Australian Government, DFAT, 2001, *available at* http://www.dfat.gov.au/publications/aus_us_fta_mon/.

38 *See* L.E. Peterson, *Ecuadorian President Reportedly Asks Congress to Terminate 13 BITS; Move Comes on Heels of Earlier Termination of Multiple BITS*, 2(17) INV. ARB. REP. (Oct. 30, 2009).

Against such a background of difference,[39] one ought not to expect bilateral agreements to represent comparable patterns of reciprocity, inclusiveness for the parties to such agreements and their investors, or the exclusion of nonparties and their investors. Nor should one expect such differences to derive solely from the changing normative attitudes of states toward democratic liberalism or their disparate support for economic rationality. Different values ascribed to bilateral agreements also derive functionally from a quantitative assessment of economic data such as the impact of foreign direct investment upon the balance of trade and investment upon gross domestic production.[40]

Nor should one expect bilateral trade and investment practice to follow a consistent pathway. States conclude FTAs and BITs for a multiplicity of reasons that also change over time, place, and space. For example, China's interest in bilateral trade and investment has changed with its accession to global markets for exports and investment,[41] yet it has continued to restrict trade and foreign investment that otherwise would threaten its vulnerable rural economy.[42]

Similarly, bilateral trade and investment practices vary according to a shifting balance of power within, between, and among specific trading blocs such as the Economic Union (EU) and the North American Free Trade Agreement (NAFTA).[43] Bilateral trade and investment practices also vary with the practices that evolve in particular trading hubs, such as Hong Kong and Singapore, as each hub seeks to liberalize trade and investment in its own distinctive way.[44]

---

[39] On the debate over the extent to which states, not limited to developing states, protect their agricultural sectors, *see infra* Section III(vi).

[40] *See* Jewswald Salacuse & Nicholas Sullivan, *Do BITs Really Work? An Evaluation of BITs and Their Grand Bargain*, 46 HARV. INT'L L.J. 67 (2005).

[41] *See, e.g.*, Stephan Schill, *Tearing Down The Great Wall—The New Generation Investment Treaties of the People's Republic of China*, 15 CARDOZO J. INT'L & COMP. L. 73. (2007); GERALD CHAN, CHINA'S COMPLIANCE IN GLOBAL AFFAIRS: TRADE, ARMS CONTROL, ENVIRONMENTAL PROTECTION, HUMAN RIGHTS (2006); YONG DENG & FEI-LING, CHINA RISING: POWER AND MOTIVATION IN CHINESE FOREIGN POLICY (2005); PITMAN B. POTTER, THE CHINESE LEGAL SYSTEM: GLOBALIZATION AND LOCAL LEGAL CULTURE (2001).

[42] *See* AIMIN CHEN & SHUNFENG SONG, CHINA'S RURAL ECONOMY AFTER THE WTO: PROBLEMS AND STRATEGIES (2006); DEEPAK BHATTASALI & SHANTONG LI, CHINA AND THE WTO: POLICY AND POVERTY AFTER CHINA'S ACCESSION TO THE WTO (2004). *See also* JIANFU CHEN, CHINESE LAW: CONTEXT AND TRANSFORMATION (2008).

[43] The term "second generation" regional free trade agreements is intended to mean those regional agreements that have arisen over the last two decades under the WTO, notably the North American Free Trade Agreement (NAFTA) as distinguished from "first generation" agreements such as the European Union (EU), which traces back further. We are arguably now in the "third generation" of FTAs and BITs, transcending "second generation' agreements such as the NAFTA. On the history of the EU, *see* CHRISTOPHER STEVENS & JANE KENNAN, POST LOMÉ WTO COMPATIBLE TRADING ARRANGEMENTS, ECONOMIC PAPER 45 (Economic Paper Series, Commonwealth Secretariat, 2002); ERNST-ULRICH PETERSMANN & MARK A. POLLACK, TRANSATLANTIC ECONOMIC DISPUTES: THE EU, THE U.S., AND THE WTO (2003). On investment law in the European Union, *see* ANGELOS DIMOPOULOS, EU FOREIGN INVESTMENT LAW (2011).

[44] *See, e.g.*, L.S. Poulsen, *Are South–South BITs Any Different? A Logistic Regression Analysis of Two Substantive BIT Provisions*, Paper presented at the American Society of International Law Biennial

Whatever the rhetoric—that bilateral trade and investment agreements are used to liberalize trade and investment, or to protect favored or vulnerable industries from competition, most states recognize that the benefits of bilateral trade and investment are inconsistent at best. One can generalize the perceived benefits and disadvantages of free trade zones, such as for the EU or the NAFTA, so long as one considers the exceptions that sometimes disprove the rule.

It is against the background of exceptions that the benefit of bilateral trade and investment should be evaluated. However multifarious bilateral agreements may appear to be, they assuredly satisfy similar economic interests differently and different interests similarly.[45] However distinctive their benefits may be to the bilateral partners and their home and host state investors, pervasive benefits for the multilateral trade community depend upon the social, economic, political, and legal circumstances in which FTAs and BITs arise and to which they are applied.[46] Ascertaining those benefits involves a shift from rhetoric, speculation, and generalizations about the economic rationality of bilateral trade and investment to evidence of identifiable benefits derived from them. It challenges the idealized belief that the liberalization of trade and investment is "good" in itself, and it calls for a demonstration of how bilateral trade and investment agreements actually lead to a greater economic or social "good."

In determining the virtues of FTAs and BITs, it is appropriate to identify the particular obstacles to them, the institutionalized reactions to those obstacles, and the manner in which those reactions have affected trade and investment practice.

IV. CHALLENGES TO FTAS AND BITS

The conduct of bilateral trade and investment is sometimes depicted as a victory for economic and political stability. The rationale is that it leads to more pervasive, effective, reliable, transparent, and predictable trade and investment relations than in

Conference (Nov. 2008); K. Miles, *Imperialism, Eurocentrism and International Investment Law: Whereto from Here for Asia?* Paper presented at the Second Biennial General Conference of the Asian Society of International Law (Aug. 2008); RAMKISHEN S. RAJAN, REZA Y. SIREGAR & RAHUL SEN, SINGAPORE AND FREE TRADE AGREEMENTS: ECONOMIC RELATIONS WITH JAPAN AND THE UNITED STATES (2001); SEN RAHUL, FREE TRADE AGREEMENTS IN SOUTHEAST ASIA (2004); John Ravenhill, *The New Bilateralism in the Asia Pacific*, 24(2) THIRD WORLD Q. 299 (2003).

45 On the significance of complex geopolitical and economic forces within the WTO, *see* JAWARA & KWA, *supra* note 1; Julien Chaisse & Debashis Chakraborty, *Implementing WTO Rules through Negotiations and Sanctions: The Role of Trade Policy Review Mechanism and Dispute Settlement System*, 28 U. PA. J. INT'L ECON. L. 153 (2007).

46 A multilateral trade culture is certainly part of a "legal" culture, but again far from a fixed culture grounded in clear-cut legal principles such as freedom of contract and the binding force of agreements. *See generally* Leon E. Trakman, *Legal Traditions and International Commercial Arbitration*, AM. REV. OF ARBITRATION (Spring 2007), also *available at* http://works.bepress.com/leon_trakman/; Roger Cotterrell, *The Concept of Legal Culture, in* COMPARING LEGAL CULTURES 13–31 (David Nelken ed., 1997); Alan Watson, *Legal Change: Sources of Law and Legal Culture*, 131 U. PA. L. REV. 1121 (1982). *See also* CLIFFORD GEERZ, THE INTERPRETATION OF CULTURES: SELECTED ESSAYS (1973).

centuries past when pirates ravaged and plundered the wealth of targeted states and their subjects.[47] Despite the rhetoric that modern BITs and FTAs stabilize trade and investment, the reality is that modern states sometimes expropriate and confiscate investments,[48] and less self-evidently, that they engage in sanctioned infringements of intellectual property rights.[49] Dominant investors, in turn, exercise quasi-public authority in their sphere of economic influence.

A further challenge to the effective, reliable, and predictable conduct of bilateral trade and investment is in the muting of legal sanctions against states such as in their treatment of home state investors. Not only are states sometimes inefficient in concluding, interpreting, and applying regional or bilateral agreements,[50] but otherwise compliant states resist sanctioning such inefficiency, not least of all to protect their own brand of domestic protectionism.[51] The result is that, however seemingly efficient bilateral trade and investment agreements might have become, they are diffusely construed and applied. The practical reality, too, is that identifying and isolating instances of doubtful state practice is often difficult if states shroud anticompetitive practices

---

47 *See, e.g.*,POWER IN GLOBAL GOVERNANCE 98 (Michael N. Barnett & Raymond Duvall eds., 2005); JAGDISH NATWARLAL BHAGWATI, IN DEFENSE OF GLOBALIZATION (2004); BERNARD M. HOEKMAN & PHILIP AADITYA MATTOO, DEVELOPMENT, TRADE AND THE WTO: A HANDBOOK (2002). On applauding the apparatus supporting the GATT and WTO systems, including the public servants that maintain the offices of multilateral trade institutions, *see* YI CHONG XU & PATRICK WELLER, GOVERNANCE OF WORLD TRADE: INTERNATIONAL CIVIL SERVANTS AND GATT/WTO (2004). *But see* M. Sornarajah, The Clash of Globalizations and the International Law on Foreign Investment, Norman Paterson School of International Affairs Simon Reisman Lecture In International Trade Policy, Ottawa (Sept. 12, 2002), *available at* http://www.carleton.ca/ctpl/pdf/papers/sornarajah.pdf; Robert B. Zoellick, *The WTO And New Global Trade Negotiations: What's at Stake* (Oct. 30, 2001), Council on Foreign Relations, *available at* http://www.cfr.org/world/wto-new-global-trade-negotiations-s-stake/p4149.

48 *See, e.g.*, James E. Anderson & Oriana Bandiera, *Traders, Cops and Robbers*, 70(1) J. INT'L ECON. 197–215 (2006).

49 *See generally* Arthur A. Daemmrich, *Stalemate at the WTO: TRIPS, Agricultural Subsidies, and the Doha Round*, HARVARD BUSINESS SCHOOL BGIE UNIT CASE NO. 711-043, *available at* http://papers.ssrn.com/sol3/papers.cfm?abstract_id=1991981 (Jan. 2012); Matthew Kennedy, *When Will the Protocol Amending the TRIPS Agreement Enter into Force?* 13 J. INT'L ECON. L. 459, 459 (2010); Henning Grosse Ruse-Khan, *Time for a Paradigm Shift? Exploring Maximum Standards in International Intellectual Property Protection*, 1(1) TRADE L. & DEV. 56 (2009); DONALD D. RICHARDS, INTELLECTUAL PROPERTY RIGHTS AND GLOBAL CAPITALISM: THE POLITICAL ECONOMY OF THE TRIPS AGREEMENT (2004); WILL MARTIN & MARI PANGESTU, OPTIONS FOR GLOBAL TRADE REFORM: A VIEW FROM THE ASIA-PACIFIC (2003); *Intellectual Property in the Global Marketplace*, 3(3) ECONOMIC PERSPECTIVES, AN ELECTRONIC JOURNAL OF THE U.S. INFORMATION AGENCY (May 1998); KEITH EUGENE MASKUS, INTELLECTUAL PROPERTY RIGHTS IN THE GLOBAL ECONOMY (2000); MITCHELL B. WALLERSTEIN, MARY ELLEN MOGEE & ROBERTA A. SCHOEN, GLOBAL DIMENSIONS OF INTELLECTUAL PROPERTY RIGHTS IN SCIENCE AND TECHNOLOGY (1993). *See generally* http://www.cid.harvard.edu/cidtrade/issues/ipr.html.

50 For the argument that some developing states have unreliable public institutions, a concept that, in turn, has important implications for the design of monetary policies and institutions, *see* Haizhou Huang & Shang-Jin We, *Monetary Policies for Developing Countries: The Role of Institutional Quality*, 70(1) J. INT'L ECON. 239–52 (2006).

51 It remains to be seen have effectively bilateral agreements can constrain recalcitrant states such as in regard to foreign investment. *But see* Stephan Schill, *International Investment Law and the Host State's Power to Handle Economic Crises*, 24 J. INT'L ARB. 265 (2007). *See also* McMahon, *supra* note 5.

behind the veil of state sovereignty and national interest, in which partner states acquiesce to avoid negative political or economic repercussions.[52]

Finally, any attempt to ensure that bilateral and regional trade and investment agreements are applied in a manner that promotes an idealized "good" practice raises not only the question of what constitutes "bad practice," but the issue of how to identify and regulate "bad" practice. As far as action against allegedly recalcitrant states is concerned, multilateral actions such as was envisaged by Article XXIV of the GATT are difficult to enforce because they require consensus among states to establish principles and guidelines to deal with dubious trade and investment practices.[53] For another thing, the multilateral community may avoid imposing sanctions because the cost of compliance may outweigh the perceived benefit, and because state–investor disputes arising from expropriation as confiscation are considered "private," to be resolved by investment arbitration, not by multilateral state action.[54] The result may well be states that engage in wide-scale confiscation of foreign direct investment are willing to endure trade sanctions, boycotts, and protests from the international community rather than change the way they do business The further prospect is that, however much bilateral trade and investment agreements include provisions that purport to regulate a full spectrum of trade and investment practice, those provisions may be comparatively meaningless if states disregard them, such as by declining to submit to investor–state arbitration.

V. INSTITUTIONAL REMEDIES

An idealized challenge to state practice is to invoke institutional trade and investment remedies to deal with allegedly unfair or unreasonable trade and investment action by states. For example, a global response to alleged infractions of principles of international trade and investment law is to rely on the sanctioning force of the WTO or TRIPS.[55] A regional response is to draw on the agreements and practices that bind the

---

52 Studiously avoiding trade and investment conflict is an old strategy in multilateral trade relationships. For Canadian perspectives including foreign policy on conflict avoidance, *see, e.g.*, PHILIPPE G. LE PRESTRE, ROLE QUESTS IN THE POST–COLD WAR ERA: FOREIGN POLICIES IN TRANSITION (1997); DUNCAN CAMERON, THE FREE TRADE PAPERS (1986). On trading with recalcitrant states, *see, e.g.*, Dilip Das, *Globalization and the Anti-Globalization Lobby: Investigating Two Sides of One Veracity* (Apr. 2005), *available at* http://www.cid.harvard.edu/cidtrade/Papers/das-aaa.pdf.

53 For the reasons the drafts of the GATT included Article XXIV, *see supra* notes 16 and 17. On Article XXIV of the GATT generally, *see* MATHIS, *supra* note 3.

54 *See generally* Susan D. Franck, *The Legitimacy Crisis in Investment Treaty Arbitration: Privatizing Public International Law through Inconsistent Decisions*, 73 FORDHAM L. REV. 1521 (2005); Judith Gill et al., *Contractual Claims and Bilateral Investment Treaties*, 21 J. INT'L ARB. 397 (2004); RUDOLF DOLZER & MARGRETE STEVENS, BILATERAL INVESTMENT TREATIES (1995).

55 *See, e.g.*, POWER IN GLOBAL GOVERNANCE, *supra* note 47; BHAGWATI, *supra* note 47; HOEKMAN & MATTOO, *supra* note 47. On applauding the apparatus supporting the GATT and WTO systems, including the public servants that maintain the offices of multilateral trade institutions, *see* YI CHONG XU & PATRICK WELLER, GOVERNANCE OF WORLD TRADE: INTERNATIONAL CIVIL SERVANTS AND GATT/WTO (2004). *But see* Sornarajah, *supra* note 47; Zoellick, *supra* note 47.

European Union (EU),[56] ASEAN in the Asia Pacific,[57] and the NAFTA in North America.[58] A bilateral response is to rely on trade and investment sanctions within bilateral trade and investment agreements, including remedies available to foreign investors in host states.[59]

However, one should not overemphasize either the authority or the consistency of institutional responses to state action. First, institutions diverge in their responses to aberrant state practice as the institutions themselves change. For example, far from being fixed in its responses to allegedly aberrant state conduct, the global response of the multilateral community has varied markedly from the 1947 General Agreement on Tariffs and Trade (GATT), to the WTO,[60] and from the Uruguay Round in 1994 to Seattle in 1999 to Doha in 2001 to Cancún in 2003 and to Hong Kong in 2005.[61] Regional and bilateral responses to radical shifts in state practices are subject to mass-political change, such as arose out of the democratization of Eastern Europe and China's entry

---

[56] On a history of EU trade policy, *see* STEVENS & KENNAN, *supra* note 43; PETERSMANN & POLLACK, *supra* note 43. *See also* GARY P. SAMPSON & STEPHEN WOOLCOCK, REGIONALISM, MULTILATERALISM, AND ECONOMIC INTEGRATION: THE RECENT EXPERIENCE (2003). *See generally, Symposium on International Investment Law and the European Union, in* YEARBOOK ON INTERNATIONAL INVESTMENT LAW & POLICY 2010–2011 (Karl P. Sauvant ed., 2012).

[57] On the ASEAN Free Trade Area, *see* http://www.us-asean.org/afta.asp; http://www.aseansec.org/economic/afta/afta.htm. *See also* Vinod K. Aggarwal *The Political Economy of a Free Trade Area of the Asia–Pacific*, 14(2) BUS. ASIA (Feb. 2007); Jamus Jerome Lim, *The Dimensions of Regional Trade Integration in Southeast Asia*, 23(3) ASEAN ECON. BULLETIN 395–96 (2006); Vinod K. Aggarwal & Min Gyo Koo, *The Evolution of APEC and ASEM: Implications of the New East Asian Bilateralism*, 4(2) EU. J. EAST ASIAN STUD. 222–64 (2005).

[58] On Article 11 (Investment) of the NAFTA in relation to dispute resolution in particular, *see* T. Weiler, *NAFTA Investment Arbitration and the Growth of International Economic Law*, 36 CAN. BUS. L.J. 405 (2002); C.N. Brower, C.H. Brower II & J.K. Sharpe, *The Coming Crisis in the Global Adjudication System*, 19 ARB. INT'L 415 (2003); TRAKMAN, *supra* note 34. *See also* ANDREW D.M. ANDERSON, SEEKING COMMON GROUND: CANADA–U.S. TRADE DISPUTE SETTLEMENT POLICIES IN THE NINETIES (1995); David A. Gantz, *Resolution of Trade Disputes under NAFTA's Article 19: The Lessons of Extending the Binational Panel Process to Mexico*, 29 LAW & POLICY INT'L. BUS. 3 (1998).

[59] On investor–state arbitration, *see generally* RUDOLF DOLZER & CHRISTOPH SCHREUER, PRINCIPLES OF INTERNATIONAL INVESTMENT LAW (2008); THE OXFORD HANDBOOK OF INTERNATIONAL INVESTMENT LAW (Peter Muchlinski, Federico Ortino & Christoph Schreuer eds., 2008); ANDREW NEWCOMBE & LLUIS PARADELL, LAW AND PRACTICE OF INVESTMENT TREATIES—STANDARDS OF INVESTMENT PROTECTION (2009).On trade and investment remedies, *see* RESOURCE BOOK ON TRIPS AND DEVELOPMENT, UNICTAD-ICTSD STAFF (2005); PANOS KOUTRAKOS, TRADE, FOREIGN POLICY AND DEFENCE IN EU CONSTITUTIONAL LAW (2001).

[60] *See generally* JOHN H. JACKSON, THE JURISPRUDENCE OF GATT AND THE WTO: INSIGHTS ON TREATY LAW AND ECONOMIC RELATIONS (2000); MIKE MOORE, A WORLD WITHOUT WALLS: FREEDOM, DEVELOPMENT, FREE TRADE AND GLOBAL GOVERNANCE (2003); JOHN MICKLETHWAIT & ADRIAN WOOLRIDGE, A FUTURE PERFECT: THE CHALLENGE AND HIDDEN PROMISE OF GLOBALIZATION (2000).

[61] *See* Doha Development Round gateway, *available at* http://www.wto.org/english/tratop_e/dda_e/dda_e.htm; Raj Bhala, *Resurrecting the Doha Round: Devilish Details, Grand Themes, and China Too*, 45 TEX. INT'L L.J. 1, 125 (2009); ANDREW G. BROWN, RELUCTANT PARTNERS: A HISTORY OF MULTILATERAL TRADE COOPERATION, 1850–2000 (2003); BERNARD HOEKMAN & MICHEL KOSTECKI, THE POLITICAL ECONOMY OF THE WORLD TRADING SYSTEM: FROM GATT TO WTO (2001).

to the WTO.[62] Other changes occur gradually but significantly, such as China's gradual realignment of political–economic relations within its neighborhood[63] and commercial hubs such as Singapore imbedding themselves over time as international gateways between East and West.[64]

Nor is it suggested that this realignment of bilateral trade and investment relationships constitutes an insidious plot to shield "bad" practice by states. Using bilateral agreements to support unlawful activity is one thing. States that use bilateral agreements to legitimate self-interested practices that are lawful is another. However much the multilateral community would like to reduce protectionist tariffs, developed and developing states alike are likely to invoke bilateral agreements to expand their exports while also protecting vulnerable industries such as agriculture from foreign trade and investment.[65] The negotiation of selective trade and investment barriers is not per se bad, nor is it akin to unfettered trade reductionism. What is "bad" is the capacity of states to act in flagrant disregard of international instruments and to try to shield themselves from sanction through the protective defense of arbitrary laws disguised as defensible public policies.

---

[62] On China's accession to the WTO, *see* CHINA'S ECONOMIC GLOBALIZATION THROUGH THE WTO (Ding Lu, G.J. Wen & Huizhong Zhou eds., 2003); SHUMING BAO, SHUANGLIN LIN & CHANGWEN ZHAO, THE CHINESE ECONOMY AFTER WTO ACCESSION (2006); GUY LIU SHAOJIA & GUY SHAOJIA LIU, CHINA'S WTO ACCESSION AND THE IMPACT ON ITS LARGE MANUFACTURING ENTERPRISES (2001); CHING CHEONG & CHING HUNG-YEE, HANDBOOK ON CHINA'S WTO ACCESSION AND ITS IMPACTS (2003).

[63] *See, e.g.*, Bruno Cabrillac, *A Bilateral Trade Agreement between Hong Kong And China: CEPA*, 54 CHINA PERSPECTIVES 39 (2004). China's "arrival" in the global trade community is marked by speculation as to how China will change the global trading community, and vice versa. It is also a subject of debate at international conferences. *See, e.g.*, http://www.jurisconferences.com/arbitration.php?id=1&p=1. On China's influence over global trade, *see supra* notes 10, 42, 43, and 62. *See also* Qingjiang Kong, *U.S.–China Bilateral Investment Treaty Negotiations: Context, Focus, and Implications*, 7 ASIAN J. WTO & INT'L HEALTH L. & POL'Y 181 (2012).

[64] *See, e.g.*, R.S. Rajan & R. Sen, *Singapore's New Commercial Trade Strategy: The Pros and Cons of Bilateralism*, *available at* http://scholar.google.com/scholar?hl=en&lr=lang_en&q=cache:_6DNZGy37RMJ:www.adelaide.edu.au/cies/0202.pdf+related:_6DNZGy37RMJ:scholar.google.com/ *Cf.* R.S. Rajan & R. Sen, *Trade Reforms in India Ten Years on: How Has It Fared Compared to Its East Asian Neighbours?*, *available at* http://scholar.google.com/scholar?hl=en&lr=lang_en&q=cache:PZWEzWPPxpkJ:www.adelaide.edu.au/CIES/0147.pdf+related:_6DNZGy37RMJ:scholar.google.com/; Linda Low, *Singapore's Bilateral Free Trade Agreements: Institutional and Architectural Issues* (Apr. 22–23 2003), *available at* http://www.pecc.org/publications/papers/trade-papers/5_CP/3-low.pdf.

[65] *See* STEVE CHARNOTVOTZ, MAPPING THE LAW OF WTO ACCESSION IN THE WTO: GOVERNANCE, DISPUTE STETTLEMENT AND DEVELOPING COUNTRIES CH. 46 (Merit E. Jannow, Victoria Donaldson & Alan Yanovitch eds., 2008), *available at* http://ssrn.com/abstract=957651. On the differential impact welfare and market access has upon tariff structures, *see* James E. Anderson & J. Peter Neary, *Welfare Versus Market Access: The Implications of Tariff Structure for Tariff Reform*, 71(1) J. INT'L ECON. 187 (2007).

VI. PRIVILEGES OF DEVELOPED STATES

It is true that bilateral trade and investment is not conducted on a perfectly level playing field. Some states enjoy a competitive "wealth" advantage over others; sometimes success on the bilateral stage is tinged with a mixture of privilege and opportunism.[66]

On occasions, developing states find themselves in an awkward position. They feel compelled to criticize bilateral trade and investment agreements as generally favoring developed states, while at the same time trying to conclude bilateral agreements with developed states they otherwise would criticize as privileged against them. In trying to win the confidence of international capital markets, some developing states also risk foregoing sensible domestic economic policies in favor of perverse ones.[67] A real hazard is that wealthy developed states may exploit the vulnerabilities of developing states by extracting excessive trade and investment concessions that developing states can ill afford to sustain over the longer term.

Against this background, opponents of bilateral trade and investment agreements worry that FTAs and BITs will fail adequately to redress social and economic deprivation in developing states, and that developed states will turn a blind eye to human rights abuses in developing states as well.[68] A pervasive concern is that, far from liberalizing trade and investment, selectivity in bilateral trade and investment may expand upon the already formidable wealth and investment gap between developing and developed states, institutionalizing the trade and investment advantages of the latter.[69] Coupled with this is the threat of perpetuating a systemic bias in favor of developed states and further marginalizing the competitive disadvantages of developing states, such as in relation to rules of origin.[70]

Accentuating these risks is concern that developing states lack the economic infrastructure to become "equal opportunity" trade and investment partners for developed states and their investors.[71] For example, developing states may feel compelled to

---

66 *See generally* Kyle Bagwell & Robert W. Staiger, *Multilateral Trade Negotiations, Bilateral Opportunism and the Rules of GATT/WTO*, 63(1) J. INT'L ECON. 1–29 (2004).

67 *See* Gea M. Lee & Sharun W. Mukand, *Globalization and the "Confidence Game"*, 70(2) J. INT'L ECON. 406–27 (2006).

68 *See* R.J. Bubb & S. Rose-Ackerman, *BITs and Bargains: Strategic Aspects of Bilateral and Multilateral Regulation of Foreign Direct Investment*, 27 INT'L REV. L. & ECON. 291 (2007); A. Guzman, *Why Developing Countries Sign Treaties That Hurt Them: Explaining the Popularity of BITs*, 38 VA. J. INT'L L. 553 (1998). *See also infra* Section II(iv).

69 Some critics stridently hold this view, and indeed, it forms a core part of their antagonism toward the WTO in general and bilateral trade agreements in particular. *See, e.g., supra* note 9.

70 *See* Won-Mog Choi, *Defragmenting Fragmented Rules of Origin of RTAS: A Building Block to Global Free Trade*, 13 J. INT'L ECON. L. 111, 114–24 (2010). *But see Rules of Origin: Outgoing Chair Says 55% of Rules of Origin Agreed*, WTO: 2010 NEWS ITEMS (Mar. 25, 2010), *available at* http://www.wto.org/english/news_e/news10_e/roi_25mar10_e.htm. *See further infra* Section III(vi).

71 Typical of additional costs to developing states are the communication costs associated with the liberalization of trade, including bilateralism. *See, e.g.*, Carsten Fink, Aaditya Mattoo & Ileana Cristina Neagu, *Assessing the Impact of Communication Costs on International Trade*, 67(2) J. INT'L. ECON. 428 (2005).

comply with international trade and investment standards, including by establishing labor and environment structures at a cost they cannot afford. Typifying this problem, Christian aid agencies claim that the cost of trade and investment to Sub-Saharan Africa comes at the price of US$272 billion in compliance with international standards, in aid, loans, and debt relief. The argument is that such money could be better spent elsewhere, investing in the vaccination of children and providing schooling, shelter, and healthcare.[72] A consequential response is that these standards of healthcare and education are likely to deteriorate further as developing states mollify bilateral trade and investment partners by marginalizing the social cost of such initiatives.[73]

Developing states, as sovereign entities, are free to decline to conclude FTAs and BITs on grounds that doing so conflicts with their collective self-interest.[74] They also have legal remedies if the agreements they conclude are violated, while their home state investors may have the right to bring arbitration claims against dominant host states.[75] However, as a practical matter bilateral trade and investment agreements sometimes resemble adhesion contracts. Powerful states dictate their terms, and dependant states and their investors must either adhere to them or sacrifice the benefits they seek from bilateral trade and investment.[76]

III. Positional Support for Bilateral Trade and Investment

The rationale in support of bilateral trade and investment agreements is grounded in both general and specific arguments. What follows is an articulation of each, followed by a critical reflection.

---

[72] *See* AfricaFocus Bulletin, *Africa: The Cost of Free Trade* (July 5, 2005), *available at* http://www.africafocus.org/docs05/trad0507.php; JOHN HILARY, THE WRONG MODEL: GATS, TRADE LIBERALIZATION AND CHILDREN'S RIGHT TO HEALTH (2000).

[73] On the compliance obligations imposed on developing states, *see, e.g.*, YONG-SHIK LEE, RECLAIMING DEVELOPMENT IN THE WORLD TRADING SYSTEM (2006). *See also* Luis Abugattas Majluf, *Swimming in the Spaghetti Bowl: Challenges for Developing Countries under the "New Regionalism,"* Policy Issues in International Trade and Commodities Study Series No. 27, United National Conference on Trade and Development (New York & Geneva, 2004), *available at* http://scholar.google.com/scholar?hl=en&lr=&q=cache:oQ1Joqun6XcJ:www.unctad.org/en/docs/itcdtab28_en.pdf+.

[74] It is apparent that a number of developing states have opted to enter into bilateral trade agreements. *See* http://www.worldtradelaw.net. At the same time, it is unreasonable to assume that, in doing so, they have somehow leveled the playing field with their developed trade partners.

[75] In addition to their legal remedies for treaty violation, developing states can invoke principles of comity that underscore not only the obligations that are owed to them, but also their historical disadvantages, including in relation to international trade. On arbitral remedies available to foreign direct investors, *see* Trakman, *supra* note 5, at 1. *See* further Section II(ii).

[76] *But see* Gabrielle Marceau, *WTO Dispute Settlement and Human Rights*, 14(4) EUR. J. INT'L. L. 753 (2002), *available at* http://ejil.org/forum_tradehumanrights. On guiding principles of contract law, *see* Leon E. Trakman, *Contracts: Legal, in* INTERNATIONAL ENCYCLOPEDIA OF THE SOCIAL AND BEHAVIORAL SCIENCES, VOL. 3 /8/102 (2001, 2nd ed, 2012 forthcoming).

I. MORE IS BETTER THAN LESS

A simplistic argument in favor of bilateral trade and investment agreements is that, all other things being equal, bilateral trade and investment agreements lead to there being more, and that having more is better than having less. States and their subjects that have more can buy and sell more. Foreign direct investment provides employment and helps to improve standards of living in developing states. Taxes and duties secured from foreign entities enable developing states to extend economic benefits such as social services, healthcare, and education to the less fortunate. Having more allows developing states to share more.[77]

The counter-side to this analysis is that bilateral agreements can cause trade and investment to contract, not expand. For example, the net creation of trade and investment arising from FTAs and BITs can be more than offset by the net diversion of trade and investment to nonparties.[78] Second, bilateral agreements can produce negative trade and investment distortions, as when the benefits of trade and investment in agriculture is diverted from developing states and their investors to developed states and their investors.[79] Third, bilateral agreements may lead to there being more, but not necessarily better results. For example, they may produce greater wealth, but lead to less social justice when developing states decline to provide social services arising from foreign investment and developed states avoid interfering.[80] Indeed, the decline in the colonial dominance of the West has not necessarily led either to mass economic development or to sustained social reform in their once-colonial supplicants.[81] Fourth, the

---

[77] As expressed by the Congressional Budget Office: "Market forces generally ensure that all countries involved in the trade share in the benefits from the increased output." Congressional Budget Office, *The Benefits of Multilateral Trade Liberalization*, *available at* http://www.cbo.gov/showdoc.cfm?index=4458&sequence=0.

[78] *See, e.g.*, T. Hertel, D. Hummels, M. Ivanic & R. Keeney, *How Confident Can We Be in CGE-Based Assessments of Free Trade Agreements?*, Conference Paper, 6th Annual Conference on Global Economic Analysis (The Hague, May 2003), *available at* http://econpapers.repec.org/paper/gtaworkpp/1324.htm; T. Hertel, D. Hummels, M. Ivanic & R. Keeney, *Trade Creation and Trade Diversion in the Canada–United States Free Trade Agreement*, 34(3) CAN. J. ECON. 677 (2001); K. Fukao, T. Okubo & R.M. Stern, *An Econometric Analysis of Trade Diversion under NAFTA*, Discussion Paper 491 (School of Public Policy, Univ. of Michigan: Research Seminar in International Economics, Oct. 30, 2002).

[79] *See* ORGANIZATION FOR ECONOMIC CO-OPERATION AND DEVELOPMENT, AGRICULTURE AND DEVELOPMENT, THE CASE FOR POLICY COHERENCE (2005); WORLD BANK, AGRICULTURE AND THE WTO: CREATING A TRADING SYSTEM FOR DEVELOPMENT (2004); ECONOMIC RESEARCH SERVICE, U.S. DEPARTMENT OF AGRICULTURE, ECONOMIC RATIONALE FOR NONRECIPROCAL PREFERENCES (2006), *available at* http://www.ers.usda.gov/publications/err6/err6b.pdf.

[80] One can also question the extent to which a state's alleged human rights deficiencies are sometimes used as a political weapon directed at embarrassment on the international stage as distinct from a lever directed at social justice reform. *See* UNITED STATES. CONGRESS, HOUSE COMMITTEE ON INTERNATIONAL RELATIONS, SUBCOMMITTEE ON INTERNATIONAL OPERATIONS AND HUMAN RIGHTS, CHINA, THE WTO, AND HUMAN RIGHTS: HEARING BEFORE THE SUBCOMMITTEE ON INTERNATIONAL OPERATIONS AND HUMAN RIGHTS (2000).

[81] *See* James Oliver Gump, *D.K. Fieldhouse's The West and the Third World: Trade, Colonialism, Dependence, and Development* 11(2) J. WORLD HISTORY 396 (Fall 2000) (book review). Nor is economic imperialism

wealth derived from there being more trade and investment may be closely held. For example, corporate investors from wealthy states may distribute the increased profits from bilateral trade and investment primarily to their shareholders to the exclusion of other groups.[82] The net result may be a reduction in the aggregate social services benefits arising from trade and investment between developed and developing states.[83]

II. FTAS AND BITS FILL LACUNAE IN THE MULTILATERAL PROCESS

A similarly superficial argument favoring bilateral trade and investment is grounded in arithmetic. All other factors being constant, bilateral trade and investment negotiation involving a few parties with reconcilable interests is more likely to liberalize trade and investment than multilateral agreements that involve multiple parties with diverse interests that are not readily reconcilable.[84] Instead of requiring the consent of over 150 states with diverse and often conflicting cultural, social, economic, and political priorities, bilateral trade and investment negotiations allow fewer states with fewer differences to reach common ground.[85]

This argument is compelling only in demonstrating that individual states are more likely to reach bilateral than multilateral accord. It does not address the quality of the bilateral agreements actually concluded, as when they provide limited tangible benefits or even disadvantage one party and its investors in favor of the other party and its investors.[86] Negotiating bilateral agreements may also disadvantage parties that negotiate more effectively in larger groups, particularly in dealing with powerful economic blocks such as enjoyed by the EU historically.[87] They may also disadvantage developing states that depend on block support in order to secure trading and investment concessions from developed states generally.[88]

---

confined to colonialism: *see* THE THEORY OF CAPITALIST IMPERIALISM (D.K. Fieldhouse ed., 1967); FREE TRADE AND OTHER FUNDAMENTAL DOCTRINES OF THE MANCHESTER SCHOOL (Francis W. Hirst ed., 1968); P.J. Cain, *J.A. Hobson, Cobdenism, and the Radical Theory of Economic Imperialism, 1898–1914*, 31(4) ECON. HIST. REV. 565 (1978); Michael Freeden, *J.A. Hobson as a New Liberal Theorist: Some Aspects of His Social Thought until 1914*, 34(3) J. HISTORY IDEAS 421 (1973).

82 On trenchant criticism of corporate "abuses" of global trading benefits, *see, e.g.*, LORI WALLACH & MICHELLE SFORZA, THE WTO: FIVE YEARS OF REASONS TO RESIST CORPORATE GLOBALIZATION (2000).

83 Developed states may well provide significant social benefits to developing states, including through bilateral and regional free trade agreements. *See infra* Section III(iv) on the U.S. humanitarian objectives in concluding such agreements with developing states. However, it should not be inferred that such humanitarian ends will trump the primary reasons for such agreements, namely, to build political alliances and to increase trade.

84 For an econometrics analysis of the benefits arising from free trade agreements, *see, e.g.*, Scott L. Baier & Jeffrey H. Bergstrand, *Do Free Trade Agreements Actually Increase Members' International Trade*? 71(1) J. INT'L. ECON. 72–95 (2007).

85 *See, e.g.*, Bagwell & Staiger, *supra* note 66.

86 For a useful site on international trade negotiations, *see* http://www.iht.com/articles/ap/2007/02/23/business/NA-FIN-US-Doha-Talks.php.

87 On the disparities between multilateral and bilateral trade interests, *see* SAMPSON & WOOLCOCK, *supra* note 56.

88 On strategies employed in WTO and related negotiations, *see, e.g.*, POWER IN GLOBAL GOVERNANCE, *supra* note 47; EU TRADE STRATEGIES: BETWEEN REGIONALISM AND GLOBALISM (Vinod K. Aggarwal &

One conclusion might be that, all other factors being constant, bilateral trade and investment agreements are more likely to satisfy the immediate interests of parties than multilateral agreements that usually take longer to conclude and are more complex in nature. Whether the economic and social benefit of these bilateral agreements extends to the multilateral community at large is an aspiration, not a preestablished fact.[89]

III. BILATERAL AGREEMENTS ENRICH MULTILATERAL TRADE AND INVESTMENT

A further quantitative argument favoring bilateral agreements is that the cumulative benefits of a plethora of bilateral agreements constitutes a net gain for the global economy.[90] Illustrating this benefit is the observation that a series of individually negotiated bilateral agreements can overcome obstacles to concluding multilateral trade and investment agreements, such as those relating to multifaceted issues of customs traffic, environment, labor, and electronic trade.[91]

There are benefits to quantifying the costs and benefits of trade and investment agreements in advance in order to reduce barriers to trade and investment between particular parties. Practice in negotiating FTAs and BITs does not make perfect, but it does assist states in avoiding pitfalls. As Daniel Griswald argued, "FTAs can provide useful templates for broader negotiations."[92] The problem is that, absent the capacity to measure the results of such a rationale, it remains speculative. To conclude that bilateral agreements that liberalize trade and investment between particular states encourage other states to follow suit is inspirational only; it does not lead to ensuring beneficial results.

Edward Fogarty eds., 2004); ANDREW G. BROWN, RELUCTANT PARTNERS: A HISTORY OF MULTILATERAL TRADE COOPERATION, 1850–2000 (2003). *See also* NIELS M. BLOKKER, INTERNATIONAL REGULATION OF WORLD TRADE IN TEXTILES: LESSONS FOR PRACTICE, A CONTRIBUTION TO THEORY (1990).

89 On the growing number of bilateral free trade agreements, *see, e.g.*, Global Union Research Network (GURN), *Bilateral and Regional Trade Agreements*, http://www.gurn.info/en/topics/bilateral-and-regional-trade-agreements. On efforts to build a Free Trade Area of the Americas (FTAA), see http://www.ftaa-alca.org/. For an even more comprehensive list of free trade agreements into which the United States has entered, see http://www.cbo.gov/showdoc.cfm?index=4458&sequence=0.

90 *But see* Z. Elkins, A.T. Guzman & B.A. Simmons, *Competing for Capital: The Diffusion of Bilateral Investment Treaties, 1960–2000*, 60 INT'L ORG. 811 (2006); *The Spread of Bilateral and Regional Trade Agreements*, *available at* http://www.gurn.info/topic/trade/.

91 Daniel Griswald proposes that "[n]egotiating with one nation or a small group of like-minded countries can allow more meaningful liberalization.... Those talks can blaze a trail for wider regional and multilateral negotiations." Griswald, *supra* note 13. *See generally* JORGE VIÑUALES, FOREIGN INVESTMENT AND THE ENVIRONMENT IN INTERNATIONAL LAW (2012); PUBLIC HEALTH AND PLAIN PACKAGING OF CIGARETTES: LEGAL ISSUES (Tania Voon et al, eds., 2012).

92 *Id.* The Congressional Economic and Budget Issue brief, *supra* note 13, states that FTAs "also offer a way to continue making headway toward the goal of free trade in the face of difficulties that have slowed progress in the Doha Round of WTO negotiations." *See also supra* note 77.

III. BILATERAL AGREEMENTS CONSOLIDATE REGIONAL ECONOMIES

A related argument is that bilateral trade and investment agreements consolidate the economies of partner states; they also lead to the more efficient production, finance, transportation, and supply of goods and services.[93] Illustrating these efficiencies are regional agreements such as under the NAFTA,[94] and bilateral agreements between a superpower such as the United States and its treaty trade and investment partners in Latin America, Europe, Africa, Asia, and the Middle East.[95]

There is also some evidence of the success of regional integration, including a lengthy literature that lauds the economic growth of the EU[96] and also the NAFTA.[97] There is also recent history of economic integration arising from bilateral trade and investment agreements, but accompanied by growing questions over the utility of such agreements, including in economically dislocated Europe.[98]

However, determining whether and how trade and investment agreements lead to greater efficiency in the production, distribution, and consumption of goods and services hinges upon careful scrutiny of how particular trade and investment agreements impact on specific economic contexts. The conclusion that economic consolidation leads to greater efficiency does not speak for itself.

---

93 For arguments along these lines, *see, e.g.*, SAMPSON & WOOLCOCK, *supra* note 56; International Confederation of Free Trade Unions, *The Spread of Bilateral and Regional Trade Agreements*, *available at* http://www.gurn.info/topic/trade/icftu_0604.pdf.

94 *See, e.g.*, LITAN & HAKIM, *supra* note 34; GARY CLYDE HUFBAUER & JEFFREY J. SCHOTT (assisted by PAUL L.E. GRIECO & YEE WONG), NAFTA REVISITED: ACHIEVEMENTS AND CHALLENGES (2005); JOSEPH A. MCKINNEY, CREATED FROM NAFTA: THE STRUCTURE, FUNCTION, AND SIGNIFICANCE OF THE TREATY'S RELATED INSTITUTIONS (2001); ROBERT A. PASTOR, TOWARD A NORTH AMERICAN COMMUNITY: LESSONS FROM THE OLD WORLD FOR THE NEW (2001).

95 Typifying the growth of bilateral free trade agreements was the push by the George H.W. Bush administration to extend U.S. free trade relationships. Following its FTA with Israel in 1985, the United States concluded ten FTAs: first with Canada, and then with Canada and Mexico under the NAFTA, followed by FTAs with Jordan, Chile, Singapore, Australia, Morocco, El Salvador, Nicaragua, and Honduras, Israel, Costa Rica, Bahrain, the Dominican Republic, Guatemala, Oman, Peru, and Colombia. The United States has also conducted bilateral free trade talks with eleven others, seeking either bilateral agreements or creation of a customs union. The United States has also signaled its intention to negotiate a regional free trade agreement with the thirty-four members of the Free Trade Agreement of the Americas (FTAA), and has engaged in bilateral trade talks with ten members of the Association of Southeast Asian Nations (ASEAN), including Viet Nam. In 2012, the United States and Korea concluded a FTA. Although not all these bilateral and regional agreements are likely to materialize—for example, the FTAA is currently stalled—they do indicate the extent to which a major power that traditionally relied on its muscle at the WTO has now embraced the bilateral trade process.

96 *See supra* note 44.

97 *See supra* notes 44 and 58.

98 On the EU's "commitment to open and fair trade," see http://ec.europa.eu/trade/creating-opportunities/bilateral-relations/. On bilateral trade and investment agreements with Eastern European states, *see* Michele Potestà, *Bilateral Investment Treaties and the European Union: Recent Developments in Arbitration and Before the ECJ* (2009), *available at* http://works.bepress.com/cgi/viewcontent.cgi?article=1000&context=michele_potesta&sei-redir=1#search="bilateral+investment+agreements+Eastern+Europe".

IV. BILATERAL AGREEMENTS AID DEVELOPMENT

The argument in favor of "aid for trade" is that both the state providing the aid for trade or investment and the state receiving that aid benefit in the longer term.[99] Developed states make short-term economic and investment sacrifices in developing states in order to produce a more vibrant trading and investment environment in the future.[100] The anticipated result is growing demand for goods and services and greater access to foreign investment.

The problem is that the rhetoric behind "trade for aid" speaks louder than the practice. For example, nonreciprocal preferences known as "special and differential treatment (SDT)," readily available to developing states under the GATT,[101] have lost much of their moral authority and economic support.[102] The WTO "Aid for Trade" programs that have succeeded SDTs are poorly defined.[103] They also lack the structural support to sustain aid for trade or investment.[104]

Developed states also face the difficult policy choice between promoting social, health, and environmental reform in developing states through trade and investment and protecting local markets from foreign competition, such as lead to declining domestic employment.[105] In the words of U.S. Senator Charles Schumer and Paul Craig Roberts, a former Reagan administration official statement: "Exporting jobs is not free trade."[106]

---

[99] This is the central argument behind "aid for trade." *See, e.g.*, JOSEPH STIGLITZ & ANDREW CHARLTON, FAIR TRADE FOR ALL: HOW TRADE CAN PROMOTE DEVELOPMENT (2005). *See also* E. Neumayer, *Self-Interest, Foreign Need and Good Governance: Are Bilateral Investment Treaty Programs Similar to Aid Allocation?*, 10–11, LSE Research Online (2006), *available at* http://eprints.lse.ac.uk/archive/00000808.

[100] *See* Caroline Dommen, *The WTO, International Trade, and Human Rights, in* MAINSTREAMING HUMAN RIGHTS IN MULTILATERAL INSTITUTIONS (Michael Windfuhr ed., 2004).

[101] For a detailed study on these SDTs, their origins, and how they have fared, *see* Dilip K. Das, *Evolvolution [sic] in the International Trade Regime: Refining and Developing the Special and Differential Treatment, available at* http://www.cid.harvard.edu/cidtrade/Papers/das-emtr.pdf. *See also* Institute for Agriculture and Trade Policy, Trade and Global Governance Program, *Can Aid Fix Trade: Assessing the WTO's Aid for Trade Agenda, available at* http://iatp.org/documents/can-aid-fix-trade-assessing-the-wtos-aid-for-trade-agenda.

[102] On limitations associated with SDTs, *see supra* note 101.

[103] A related problem is that developing countries often lack the resources to evaluate what trade for aid provides them with the most economic benefit. As a result, they sometimes enter into trade-for-aid relationships that fail significantly because the nature of the aid is unsuitable, however laudable the intent. For an interesting discussion on this problem, see http://queriinternational.com/.

[104] *See, e.g.*, *Can Aid Fix Trade?*, *supra* note 101.

[105] *See, e.g.*, Caroline Dommen, *Raising Human Rights Concerns in the World Trade Organization—Actors, Processes and Possible Strategies*, 24 HUMAN RIGHTS Q. 1 (2002); HILARY, *supra* note 72.

[106] *Available at* http://www.iht.com/search/search.php; http://www.brookings.edu/comm/events/20040107.htm. On protectionism arising out of safeguarding measures, *see* M. C.E.J. Bronckers, *Selective Safeguard Measures in Multilateral Trade Relations: Issues of Protectionism in GATT, European Community and United States Law*, 2(4) J. INT'L. ECON. L. 547–66 (1991). On the history of protectionism in relation to textiles, *see* VINOD K. AGGARWAL, LIBERAL PROTECTIONISM: THE INTERNATIONAL POLITICS OF ORGANIZED TEXTILE TRADE (1985).

V. BILATERAL AGREEMENTS PROMOTE FOREIGN POLICY

A related argument to "aid for trade" is that developed states can use bilateral trade and investment agreements to promote their own foreign policy. The rationale is that helping others in order to help oneself is not reprehensible. For example, the United States openly acknowledges its foreign policy goals in concluding both FTAs and BITs.

> Foreign policy constitutes a second reason for the United States to seek FTAs. Because the proposed free-trade agreements would be of substantial benefit to the economies of small developing countries while having little effect on the U.S. economy (and a beneficial effect at that), they provide a relatively easy way for the United States to help such countries.[107]

In concluding bilateral agreements between Middle Eastern states, the United States understandably seeks to promote its foreign policy there, including through aid for development;[108] not unlike BITs concluded between China and African countries.[109]

However, one should not dismiss humanitarian ends that further foreign policy ends. Aid that is good politics is aid all the same.

VI. BILATERAL AGREEMENTS CAN EMPOWER DEVELOPING STATES POLITICALLY

Developing states that conclude FTAs and BITs with one another such as through free trade zones in Africa, Latin America, and Asia are allegedly empowered to conduct trade and investment negotiations in a manner not attainable through multilateral negotiations. They can use bilateral and regional agreements to uplift their fledgling

---

107 *Reasons for and against the Pursuit of Free-Trade Agreements*, in THE PROS AND CONS OF PURSUING FREE-TRADE AGREEMENTS, *available at* http://www.cbo.gov/showdoc.cfm?index=4458&sequence=0. *See also* REVIEW OF THE U.S. MODEL BILATERAL INVESTMENT TREATY: U.S. ADVISORY COMMITTEE ON INTERNATIONAL ECONOMIC POLICY, REPORT OF THE ADVISORY COMMITTEE ON INTERNATIONAL ECONOMIC POLICY REGARDING THE MODEL BILATERAL INVESTMENT TREATY PRESENTED TO: THE DEPARTMENT OF STATE (Sept. 30, 2009), Annex B. *See generally* Kenneth J. Vandevelde, *Model Bilateral Investment Treaties: The Way Forward*, 18 SW. J. INT'L L. 307 (2011).

108 On a proposed U.S.–Middle Eastern Free Trade Area, as articulated by the U.S. Trade Representative, see http://www.ustr.gov/Trade_Agreements/Regional/MEFTA/Section_Index.html. On free trade agreements between the United States and different Middle Eastern countries, see, for example, the U.S.–Oman Free Trade Agreement, *available at* http://www.ustr.gov/assets/Document_Library/Press_Releases/2006/January/asset_upload_file25_8774.pdf. On U.S. policy in which free trade agreements serve political–strategic ends, *see* JEFFRY J. SCHOTT, FREE TRADE AGREEMENTS: U.S. STRATEGIES AND PRIORITIES (2004); ROBERT S. WALTERS, TALKING TRADE: U.S. POLICY IN INTERNATIONAL PERSPECTIVE (1993).

109 On Chinese BITs, *see, e.g.*, http://www.fdi.net/country/sub_index.cfm?countrynum=46; http://www.bilaterals.org/IMG/pdf/Overview.pdf.

economies;[110] to serve as an early warning system of threats to their shared interests;[111] and to provide astute, measured, and robust responses to those threats.[112] One inferred result is that developing states can use such alliances to offset the power of countervailing trading and investment blocks such as the EU and the NAFTA.[113] Another is their capacity to form political alliances around such key issues as agricultural tariffs, as India brokered in the wake of the failed Doha Round.[114]

One should not overstate the capacity of developing states to join forces to offset the power of developed states. First, developed states themselves form powerful countervailing trading and investment alliances, such as through the EU and the NAFTA.[115] Second, developed blocks impose import tariffs to protect their own domestic markets in goods such as agriculture[116] in respect of which some developing states are threatened.[117] Third, even large blocks of developing states are systematically disadvantaged by powerful states that have an expensive infrastructure of health, safety, labor, environmental, and intellectual property requirements that developing states cannot afford.[118] Finally, not only do developed G-33 states fall into

---

110 On global trade negotiations, including strategies by which to protect the interests of developing countries, see Third World Network, *available at* http://www.twnside.org.sg/trade_1.htm.

111 *See, e.g.*, T.N. SRINIVASAN, DEVELOPING COUNTRIES AND THE MULTILATERAL TRADING SYSTEM AFTER DOHA (2002).

112 Even before the Doha Round of trade negotiations, some warned that these issues involving agriculture might well lead to the failure of multilateral negotiations. *See, e.g.*, Tim Gosling, *The WTO Agricultural Negotiations: Progress and Prospects*, *available at* http://www.choicesmagazine.org/2005-2/wto/2005-2-08.htm.

113 *See, e.g.*, the comments of the then U.S. Trade Representative, Susan Schwab, *available at* http://www.iht.com/articles/ap/2007/02/23/business/NA-FIN-US-Doha-Talks.php.

114 *See further* Peter Draper & Razeen Sally, *Developing-Country Coalitions in Multilateral Trade Negotiations*, *available at* http://www.lse.ac.uk/collections/internationalTradePolicyUnit/Razeen_articles/draper-sallyjnu1.doc.

115 The NAFTA is an imperfect example of a free trade zone of developing countries for several reasons. First, unlike the EU, the United States is the dominant party in the NAFTA. Second, although Canada has a developed economy, Mexico has a developing economy. *See generally supra* note 33.

116 Even barriers to trade devised by developed states against one another, such as between the EU and the United States, often gives rise to collateral damage for developing states who are also subject to resulting restrictions in trade and investment. *See, e.g.*, PETERSMANN & POLLACK, *supra* note 43; Vinod K. Aggarwal & Edward Fogarty, *The Limits of Interregionalism: The EU and North America*, 27(3) J. EUR. INTEGRATION, 327–46 (2005).

117 This concern gives rise to related human rights concerns about multilateral trade and investment generally. *See, e.g.*, TOWARDS DEVELOPMENT: HUMAN RIGHTS AND THE WTO AGENDA, Report of a panel discussion held during the WTO Ministerial Conference in Cancún, September 2003, *available at* www.3dthree.org.

118 *See id.* Global trade, understandably, had been oriented in favor of the interests of developed states long before developing states were recognized as players in the global trading community. What is less elucidating is the limited effort by the WTO to activists the resort to FTAs to achieve socioeconomic reform in developing states. Global human rights activist such as Carolyn Dommen clearly do not believe that the WTO has gone far enough in highlighting human rights. *See, e.g.*, Dommen, *supra* note 100. *See generally supra* Section II(vi).

the trap of negotiating themselves into a multilateral impasse: developing states do so as well.[119]

The ongoing fact is that most developing states remain competitively disadvantaged vis-à-vis the developed world. Their disadvantages are borne out by the fact that their average gross domestic production and standards of living are significantly lower than developed states.[120] Take agriculture, the lifeblood of most developing economies: not only must developing states compete among themselves to export their undifferentiated agricultural produce to the developed world, but they also face a formidable array of post-GATT barriers to trade and investment that exclude them from complex markets for high-end agricultural goods that they lack the technological know-how and investment capital to develop themselves.[121]

VII. BILATERAL AGREEMENTS ENCOURAGE HUMAN RIGHTS REFORMS

A final rationale for FTAs and BITs is the assumption that they provide developing states with both the incentive and means to engage in social, economic, and political reform, such as in healthcare, education, and housing.[122] The assumption is that developing states will strive to be socially progressive, especially in regard to human rights, labor, and environmental standards so as to promote trade relations with developed states and attract foreign investors.[123] Whether FTAs and BITs have such an impact depends on the discrete trade and investment context, not on the

---

119 The "success" of trading blocks at negotiating themselves out of deals is the source of extensive debate. *See supra* note 2. *See also* GIOVANNI ANANIA, AGRICULTURAL TRADE CONFLICTS AND GATT: NEW DIMENSIONS IN U.S.–EUROPEAN AGRICULTURAL TRADE RELATIONS (1994).

120 *See, e.g.*, R.C. FEENSTRA & G.H. HANSON, GLOBAL PRODUCTION SHARING AND RISING INEQUALITY: A SURVEY OF TRADE AND WAGES (2001).

121 *See further* BERNARD HOEKMAN & WILL MARTIN, DEVELOPING COUNTRIES AND THE WTO: A PRO-ACTIVE AGENDA (2005); MERLINDA D. INGCO & JOHN D. NASH, AGRICULTURE AND THE WTO: CREATING A TRADING SYSTEM FOR DEVELOPMENT (2004); COMMONWEALTH SECRETARIAT, DEVELOPING COUNTRIES WTO: A COMPELLING CASE FOR FULL PARTICIPATION IN THE NEW ROUND (2002); GIOVANNI ANANIA, AGRICULTURAL TRADE CONFLICTS AND GATT: NEW DIMENSIONS IN U.S.–EUROPEAN AGRICULTURAL TRADE RELATIONS (1994). *See also* Peterson, *supra* note 38, at 17–21.

122 This is the optimistic sentiment of the High Commission for Human Rights. *See* OFFICE OF THE HIGH COMMISSIONER FOR HUMAN RIGHTS (OCHCR), LIBERALIZATION OF TRADE IN SERVICES AND HUMAN RIGHTS—REPORT OF THE HIGH COMMISSIONER, E/CN.4/Sub.2/2002/9, *available at* www.unhchr.ch/huridocda/huridoca.nsf/(Symbol)/E.CN.4.Sub.2.2002.9.En?Opendocument (2002); OHCHR, *Human Rights and Trade*, Paper prepared for the WTO Ministerial Conference in Cancún (2002), *available at* www.unhchr.ch/html/menu2/trade/index.htm.

123 *See, e.g.*, Louis-Pascal Mahe, *Environment and Quality Standards in the WTO: New Protectionism in Agricultural Trade? A European Perspective*, 24 EU. REV. AGRIC. ECON. 480 (1997); K. Bagwell & R.W. Staiger, *The WTO as a Mechanism for Securing Market Access Property Rights: Implications for Global Labor and Environmental Issues*, J. ECON. PERSPECTIVES (May 2001), *available at* http://scholar.google.com/scholar?hl=en&lr=lang_en&q=cache:7ilj73MruewJ:www.ssc.wisc.edu/~rstaiger/jep-standards05072001.pdf+. *See generally* LORENZO COTULA, HUMAN RIGHTS, NATURAL RESOURCE AND INVESTMENT LAW IN A GLOBALISED WORLD: SHADES OF GREY IN THE SHADOW OF THE LAW (2011).

general assumption that developing states will be so impelled in complex global markets.[124]

IV. Reflections

In idealized form, FTAs and BITs facilitate not only the liberalization of trade and investment, but also structural economic, social, and political reform. They benefit transitional economies, such as by responding to divergences in trade and investment cycles over time and contributing to the integration between developed and developing economies.[125] FTAs and BITs also help to reconcile economic and political differences among states and investors that cannot be resolved multilaterally, leading to the expansion of trade and investment and facilitating social reform.[126]

Many states undoubtedly appreciate the virtue of regulating trade and investment in order to produce a global good that is greater than the sum of its bilateral parts. However, for such a global good to occur, states need to arrive at a consensus about the virtue of liberalizing trade and investment and attendant policies of economic rationality and social justice. For some, bilateral agreements will create "systemic problems," subjecting multilateral trade and investment relationships to disparate preferences, inconsistent tariff schedules, and variable rules of origin.[127] For others, bilateral agreements will lead to social transformation within developing states, while yet others will view any such transformation skeptically.[128]

Even states that agree on the liberalization of trade and investment in principle sometimes will consider the combined costs of compliance and enforcement with international measures too great to sustain. Still others will adopt a middle course,

---

124 *See, e.g.*, Kala Krishna & Cemile Yavas, *When Trade Hurts: Consumption Indivisibilities and Labor Market Distortions*, 67(2) J. INT'L ECON. 413 (2005). On the complex apparatus involved in resolving disputes under the WTO, *see* WORLD TRADE ORGANIZATION, WORLD TRADE ORGANIZATION SECRETARIAT, WORLD TRADE ORGANIZATION LEGAL AFFAIRS DIVISION, A HANDBOOK ON THE WTO DISPUTE SETTLEMENT SYSTEM (2004); WORLD TRADE ORGANIZATION, WORLD TRADE ORGANIZATION SECRETARIAT; THE WTO DISPUTE SETTLEMENT PROCEDURES: A COLLECTION OF THE RELEVANT LEGAL TEXTS (2001); ROBERT Z. LAWRENCE, CRIMES & PUNISHMENTS?; RETALIATION UNDER THE WTO (2003).

125 *See* César Calderón, Alberto Chong & Ernesto Stein, *Trade Intensity and Business Cycle Synchronization: Are Developing Countries Any Different?*, 71(1) J. INT'L ECON. 2 (2007). The authors find that differences in the responsiveness of cycle synchronization to trade integration between industrial and developing countries are explained by differences in the patterns of specialization and bilateral trade.

126 On this aspiration, *see, e.g.*, Griswald, *supra* note 13.

127 *See generally Why Asia Must Opt for Open Regionalism on Trade*, FIN. TIMES, Nov. 3, 2006; BHAGWATI, *supra* note 47; JAGDISH BHAGWATI ET AL., THE WIND OF THE 100 DAYS: HOW WASHINGTON MISMANAGED GLOBALIZATION (2001).

128 This is certainly the view of bilateral trade skeptics. *See, e.g.*, Dani Rodrik, *The Global Governance of Trade as if Development Really Mattered* (2001), *available at* http://ksghome.harvard.edu/.drodrik.academic.ksg/UNDPtrade.PDF.

seeking to expand trade and investment only selectively and incrementally.[129] Whether bilateral agreements accomplish some greater good will depend, not on generalities or conjecture, but on how they are concluded and applied in fact.

As an economic reality, bilateral trade and investment agreements can lead to both greater wealth and greater sharing of wealth in general. States may increase their revenues from expanded trade and investment and extend their social services. Corporations that pay lower duties and taxes as a result of bilateral trade and investment can pass on part of their profits to consumers in the form of lower prices.[130] States, multinational corporations, and individuals alike can lever off gains from trade and investment concessions to affirm their commitment to humanitarianism and philanthropy.[131]

However, even if developing states increase revenue streams from bilateral agreements, even if international corporations promote economic development within developing states, and even if bilateral trade and investment leads to lower prices for goods and services, there is still no assurance that these will benefit states' collectivity, nor that state beneficiaries will distribute developments to those in need. Nor do bilateral agreements offer compelling enforcement mechanisms to ensure compliance.[132] However commendable coupling bilateral free trade with "aid for trade" may be, governments may resist social reform.[133] Others may decline to criticize abuse of bilateral agreements by other states because it is impolitic to do so.[134]

Ultimately, the contribution of bilateral trade and investment agreements to multilateral trade and investment depends on whether and how individual states choose to comply with them, and failing that, are compelled to conform to applicable principles

129 Jeffrey J. Schott, Free Trade Agreements: US Strategy and Priorities (2004) (unpublished manuscript, Institute for International Economics, Washington, D.C., cited in Vinod K. Aggarwal *Bilateral Trade Arrangements in the Asia-Pacific: Origins, Evolution, and Implications, available at* http://www.cgp.org/index.php?option=article&task=default&articleid=211). Schott maintains that bilateralism carries not only benefits in fostering trade, but also in helping member countries to reform their legal systems to promote economic development.

130 Part of the argument against a "corporatized" global order is in the extent to which corporations selfishly benefit themselves by exploiting the poor nations of the world, contributing to mass deprivation rather than benefit. *See, e.g.*, WALLACH & SFORZA, *supra* note 82. *See generally* GIORGIO BARBA NAVARETTI & ANTHONY J. VENABLES, MULTINATIONAL FIRMS IN THE WORLD ECONOMY (2004). *But see* J.E. Stiglitz, *Multinational Corporations: Balancing Rights and Responsibilities*, 101 AM. SOC'Y INT'L L. PROC. 3, 4 (2007).

131 In some measure, the philanthropy of multinational corporations has evolved out of the pioneering work of leading foundations and corporations, notably in the United States. *See e.g.*, *Philanthropy at the Carnegie Corporation*, *available at* http://www.carnegie.org/sub/philanthropy/vartan2.html However, philanthropy often is treated as good business practice, indeed as a measure of attracting and satisfying customer needs including in developing countries. *See, e.g.*, *Four Problems: One Solution: Philanthropy*, *available at* http://www.exhibitoronline.com/corpevent/article.asp?ID=1035.

132 On some of these concerns, *see* Jagdish Bhagwati, *U.S. House of Representatives Committee on Financial Services Testimony*, Subcommittee on Domestic and International Monetary Policy, Trade and Technology, Apr. 1, 2003.

133 *See* Roger Normand, *Separate and Unequal: Trade and Human Rights Regimes*, Background Paper for the Human Development Report (2002), *available at* http://hdr.undp.org/publications/papers.cfm.

134 *See* Dani Rodrik, *supra* note 128.

of international law. Given how imperfectly states make choices in international trade and investment, global standards governing the negotiation, performance, and enforcement of bilateral trade and investment agreements are necessary to ensure compliance and offset disparities in powers among negotiating parties, traders, and investors. How to devise such standards will not be easy. States are likely to resist measures that limit their sovereign authority, avoiding reaching multilateral consensus and eluding universal principles governing trade and investment historically ascribed to Article XXIV of the GATT.[135]

[135] For an argument in favor of interaction and coordination between bilateral and multilateral processes in order to enhance the systematic development of international trade policy, *see* Larry Crump, *Global Trade Policy Development in a Two-Track System*, 9 J. INT'L. ECON. L. 487 (2006).

5

NAFTA: AN OVERVIEW

Nicola W. Ranieri

Introduction

Globalization is inexorably compelling the world toward a more interconnected existence and, in the process, altering traditionally held views on international commerce. A notable manifestation of the globalization process is the accelerated rate at which international economic agreements are being concluded. These international economic agreements bespeak the evolving commercial reality.

Trade and investment protocols continue to be the cornerstones of international economic agreements. Trade agreements continue to provide the framework for integrated economic development between nations. Lack of progress on the multilateral front has resulted in countries looking to regional trade agreements as the preferred vehicle for trade liberalization.[1]

[1] The Doha Round, launched in 2001, is the latest round of trade negotiations at the WTO. *See generally*, the Doha Round, *available at* http://www.wto.org. However, although progress in this round has stalled, the explosion in numbers of regional trade agreements continues unabated. The European Union, the NAFTA, the Association of Southeast Asian Nations, the South Asian Association for Regional Cooperation, the Common Market of the South (MERCOSUR), the Australia–New Zealand Closer Economic Relations Agreement, and the CAFTA are among the more notable agreements. As of May 2011, 489 regional trade agreements had been notified to the WTO. Summary tables on WTO figures on RTAs currently in place can be consulted in the RTA database, *available at* http://rtais.wto.org. *See generally* the WTO Committee on Regional Trade Agreements, Basic Information on Regional Trade Agreements, WT/REG/W/)(Feb.7/2002), http://www.wto.org. *See* Jacques Bourgeois, Kamal Dewar and Simon Everett, *A Comparative Analysis of Selected Provisions in Free Trade Agreements* (analyzing the contents of free trade agreements from the European perspective), http://www.scribd.com/doc/50339727/15/annex. *See generally* Claudio Cocuzza & Andrea Forabusco, *Are States Relinquishing Their Sovereignty Rights: The GATT Dispute Settlement Process in a Globalized Economy*, 4 TUL. J. INT'L

More recently, investment protocols have assumed an importance in their own right. Foreign direct investment (FDI) is now considered to be the lifeblood of the global economy, as important to the economic well-being of developing nations as it is to developed nations.[2] Again, the lack of progress on a multilateral investment code has led to an explosion in the number of bilateral investment treaties.[3]

In this context, countries seeking the promise of economic advancement have become more amenable to abandoning the traditional notions of sovereignty in order to participate in bigger and more intricate trade and investment agreements. The inevitable manifestation of concluding more expansive international economic agreements has been the collapsing of domestic policy into foreign policy. The line between what is ruled by sovereign dominion, and what is subject to international agreement, is increasingly obfuscated.

The international commitments taken on by governments inevitably affect the state–citizen relationship. The critics of globalization often allege that governments conclude trade agreements as a justification not to respond to their citizen's concerns. Irrespective of whether such an agenda exists, the new reality has been succinctly stated: "as issues affecting the lives of citizens increasingly evolve outside the domestic sphere, non-state actors' control over their lives diminishes proportionally."[4]

A paradigmatic shift in global economic relations has resulted from this growing body of international economic agreements. The debate over the benefits of trade and investment agreements has evolved beyond a rudimentary focus on jobs and living standards. The debate now focuses on fundamental issues relating to sovereignty, democracy, public regulation, and social well-being. At the heart of the debate lies

---

& COMP. L. 161 (1996). For a perspective, which is less enthusiastic on globalism, *see* PAUL RAULSTON SAUL, THE COLLAPSE OF GLOBALISM AND THE REINVENTION OF THE WORLD (2005).

[2] Calvin A. Hamilton & Paula I. Rochwerger, *Trade and Investment: Foreign Direct Investment through Bilateral and Multilateral Treaties*, 18 N.Y.INT'L L. REV.1 (2005) and BERNARDO CREMADES & DAVID CAIRNS, THE BRAVE NEW WORLD OF GLOBAL ARBITRATION, 3 J. WORLD INV. 173 (2002).

[3] In 1998, the Multilateral Agreement on Investment failed to materialize at the Organization for Economic Development and Cooperation. *See generally* MAI Negotiating Text (Apr. 24, 1998), http://www.oecd.org/daf/cmis/mai/maitext.pdf and Katie Tieleman, *The Failure of the Multilateral Agreement on Investment and the Absence of a Global Public Policy Network* (2000), http.www.gppi.net. There are presently over 2400 BITs, and an increasing number of free trade agreements contain investment provisions. *See, Research Note: Recent Developments in International Investment Agreements*, United Nations Conference on Trade and Development (Aug. 30, 2005) (UNCTAD), http://www.unctad.org.

[4] *See* Noemi Gal-Or, *Private Party Access: A Comparison of the NAFTA and the EU Disciplines*, 21 B.C. INT'L & COMP. L. REV. 1, 2 (1998) (arguing that this democratic deficit results in economic concerns trumping the functioning of representative democratic institutions, and that access to justice is varied among the citizenry of different countries, even though they are all bound by the same treaty). *See also* David Livshiz, *Public Participation in Disputes under Regional Trade Agreements: How Much Is Too Much—The Case for a Limited Right of Intervention*, 61 N.Y.U. ANN. SURV. AM. L. 529 (2005) (arguing that the inclusion of a limited right of intervention in trade agreements would help to legitimize the international trading system by addressing transparency and accountability concerns).

strongly felt notions about the expansion of international commerce on the one hand, and an array of noneconomic concerns on the other.[5]

The neoliberal philosophy, once driving globalization, has given way to a broader social and economic agenda. The powerful engine of rule-based adjudication, once the defining element of cutting-edge trade and investment agreements, has been quieted. Concerns over regulatory sovereignty and the public good now define the contours in the globalization debate. Civil-society influence now permeates global institutions, and these groups have been instrumental in building caucuses to influence governments into shifting positions.[6]

The North American Free Trade Agreement (NAFTA) is a FTA among the United States, Canada, and Mexico[7] that marked an important milestone in the evolution of international economic agreements. When it was concluded, it was hailed as the most modern and advanced FTA ever negotiated, and was looked upon by many as the model for future agreements. In many respects, it established the watershed mark of neoliberal international economic agreements, containing both trade and investment disciplines. Its members effectively created an economic framework for further integration between countries of diverse economic development while relegating noneconomic concerns to amorphous side accords. In other respects, it challenged traditional notions of sovereignty and emboldened the civil-society agenda. In particular, NAFTA's alternative dispute resolution mechanisms made great strides in having the Parties cede sovereignty in traditionally sacrosanct areas and by incorporating private party participation within its dispute resolution processes.

NAFTA's evolution bears witness to a shift in priorities that now transcends purely economic concerns. The United States, Canada, and Mexico have become further integrated into the global partnership and continue dialogue on deeper regional integration. In fact, the NAFTA partners are presently pursuing deeper integration among themselves through the Security and Prosperity Partnership Initiative.[8]

---

5 *See* M. Sornarajah, *The Clash of Globalisations and the International Law of Foreign Investment* (paper presented at a lecture at the Norman Paterson School of International Affairs, Sept. 12, 2002) (copy on file at The Centre for Trade Law and Policy, Carleton University, Ottawa).

6 The growth of civil society activism cannot be turned back. *See* THE FUTURE OF THE WTO: ADDRESSING INSTITUTIONAL CHALLENGES IN THE NEW MILLENNIUM 41 (WTO Report), http://www.wto.org, *and* United Nations Working Papers, http://un.org/issues/civilsociety/index.asp (overview of the role civil society plays in the United Nations). *See also* David Korten, Nicanor Perlas, & Vandana Shila, *Global Society: The Path Ahead,* Discussion Paper, Nov. 20, 2002, http://www.pcdf.org (calling for a more activist role for civil society). *See also* Livshiz, *supra* note 4.

7 North American Free Trade Agreement between the United States, Canada, and Mexico (Dec. 17, 1992. NAFTA entered into force on Jan. 1, 1994 in the United States following the passage of the North American Free Trade Agreement Implementation Act of 1993 on Nov. 20, 1993. *See* Pub. L. No. 103-82, *approved* Dec. 8, 1993, 107 Stat. 2060, *codified* at 19 U.S.C. 3301–3473. Ca.-Mex.-U.S., 32 I.L.M. 289 (NAFTA). *See generally* Daniel Schwanen, *Deeper, Broader: A Road Map for a Treaty with North America*, 10 SPGL & BUS. REV. AM. 345 (Spring 2004).

8 The Security and Prosperity Partnership of North America, http://www.state.gov (the NAFTA partners continue dialogue on a deeper integration within North America, which will cover agreements on continental-wide standards dealing with consumer products, management of industries, law enforcement,

The NAFTA countries have also ventured into broader regional integration by aggressively pursuing FTAs and BITs with various nations and trading blocks. Progress has not, however, been in unison. Political pressures and other noneconomic concerns have precluded the NAFTA nations from pursuing a collective agenda on international economic agreements.

The United States once championed the cause of trade and investment evolution through multilateral *fora*. Seemingly frustrated with the dearth of multilateral progress, it now methodically pursues bilateral or regional international economic agreements.[9] The United States has more recently signed several bilateral agreements and is in regional negotiations with other country blocks, including the Asia–Pacific trade agreement, known as the Trans-Pacific Partnership Agreement.[10]

The NAFTA emboldened Mexico's pursuit of international economic agreements. Mexico abandoned its isolationist economic agenda, based on import substitution, and focused on a "hub and spoke" approach to trade. Since 1994, it signed over fourteen FTAs, which include over Forty countries. The signing of the FTA with the European Union and NAFTA meant that Mexican goods would now receive preferential treatment in some of the biggest and most lucrative markets.[11]

Canada is also a relative latecomer to free trade agreements. Similar to the United States, Canada was traditionally a proponent of multilateral trade liberalization. Again, similar to the U.S. experience, Canadian frustration with the dearth of multilateral trade progress resulted in a relatively recent impetus to conclude bilateral or regional trade agreements. Canada has free trade agreements in place with more than nine

---

and security agencies). *See generally*, Kevin Kennedy, *The First Decade of Free Trade in North America*, *in* THE FIRST DECADE OF NAFTA: THE FUTURE OF FREE TRADE IN NORTH AMERICA (Kevin Kennedy ed., 2004) (providing an overview of the first decade of the NAFTA); Danielle Goldfarb, *The Road to a Canada–U.S. Customs Union: Step-by Step or in a Single Bound*, C.D. Howe Institute Commentary, No. 184, June 2003 (examining the feasibility and desirability of a Canada–U.S. customs union); and BUILDING A NORTH AMERICAN COMMUNITY, Report of an Independent Task Force #53, May 2005, http://www.cfr.org/publications/8102.

[9] For example, in 2002, pressure on Congress led to changes in the president's "Trade Promotion Authority," 19 USC § 3802(b)(3)(2002), which limited the president's ability to negotiate international economic agreements. The changes sought, inter alia, to limit protections offered by these agreements to the types of protections enjoyed by Americans at home, and ironically led the United States to espouse a new permutation of the "Calvo" doctrine, which it had traditionally opposed. The effects of these changes were manifested in the 2004 model BIT and subsequent free trade agreements, which cut back on the sovereignty ceded and the protections available to investors.

[10] The United States has free trade agreements with Australia, Bahrain, Canada, Chile, Costa Rica, Dominican Republic, El Slavador, Guatemala, Honduras, Israel, Jordan, Mexico, Morocco, Nicaragua, Oman, Peru, and Singapore. *See generally* Office of the U.S. Trade Representative Web site, http://www.ustr.gov/trade-agreements/free-trade-agreements.

[11] Mexican FTAs include NAFTA (1994); Colombia and Venezuela (1995); Costa Rica (1995); Bolivia (1995); Nicaragua (1998); Chile (1999); EU (2000); Israel (2000); El Salvador, Guatemala, and Honduras (2001); EFTA (2001); Uruguay (2004); and Japan (2005). Mexico is also in negotiations with Trinidad, Mercosur, Tobago, and Singapore. *See generally* NAFTA Secretariat Web site, http://www.nafta-sec-alena.org. *See generally* Web site of Secretaria de Economia, http://Economia.gob.mx. For an overview of trends relating to Mexican trade policy *see* M. ANGELES VILLAREAL, CONG. RESEARCH SERV., NR 7-5700, R40784, MEXICO'S FREE TRADE AGREEMENTS (2010).

countries and is negotiating with more than fourteen other countries. For example, Canada is in the first round of negotiations with Morocco and in the ninth round with the European Union.[12]

This chapter will review select NAFTA alternative dispute resolution mechanisms. They will be analyzed in terms of structure, effectiveness, and public participation. The case is made that these mechanisms continue to be important milestones in the evolution of international economic agreements.

I. NAFTA'S ADR MECHANISMS

NAFTA promotes the general use of alternative dispute resolution (ADR). The use of ADR, in place of traditional court-based litigation, suggests that the NAFTA Parties not only expected an onslaught of NAFTA-based disputes, but also recognized the limitations of national courts to effectively deal with such controversies. Although questions relating to Mexico's history of confiscation and judicial impartiality may appear to some to have been the more obvious concerns, there is no dispute that the United States was also cognizant of the limitations hindering its own domestic courts. The Foreign Sovereign Immunities Act,[13] Act of State Doctrine, and concepts of comity and other legal barriers have historically precluded U.S. courts from effectively dealing with disputes between private individuals and foreign governments or among governments.[14]

The NAFTA also broke new ground in permitting the public to scrutinize and participate in many of its processes. Although the NAFTA essentially left private commercial ADR to develop on its own,[15] it opened up its processes to citizens, in the context of

---

12 Canada presently has free trade agreements with the United States and Mexico (1994), Panama (2010), Jordan (2009), Colombia (2008), Peru (2009), the European Free Trade Association (2009), Costa Rica (2002), and Chile (1997). Canada also has over twenty-eight operational Foreign Investment Promotion and Protection Agreements with eight more recently negotiated and twelve in ongoing negotiations. *See generally* the Foreign Affairs and International Trade Canada Web site, http://www.international.gc.ca/trade-agreements.

13 Foreign Sovereign Immunities Act of 1976, 28 U.S.C. §§ 1330, 1332, 1391(f), 1441(d), 1602-11.

14 David Gantz, *The United States and NAFTA Dispute Settlement: Ambivalence, Frustration and Occasional Defiance*, *in* THE SWORD AND THE SCALES: THE UNITED STATES AND INTERNATIONAL COURTS AND TRIBUNALS 356 (Cesare Romano ed., 2009) (providing an overview of NAFTA dispute resolution).

15 In terms of private party commercial ADR, the NAFTA institutionalizes the status quo and inadequately provides for the evolution of methods and processes to resolve these disputes. Although the NAFTA devotes several of its chapters to institutionalizing the rights of private parties (both directly and indirectly) to participate in the adjudication of public issues, it deals with the rights of private parties in the resolution of private commercial transaction disputes in only one article. Article 2022 advocates the use of arbitration and other methods of dispute resolution in international trade. It states:

1. Each Party, shall to the maximum extent possible, encourage and facilitate the use of arbitration and other means of alternative dispute resolution for the settlement of international commercial disputes between private parties in the free trade area.
2. To this end, each Party shall provide appropriate procedures to ensure observance of agreements to arbitrate and for the recognition and enforcement of arbitral awards in such disputes.

state-based dispute resolution mechanisms. Private parties may sue, obtain standing, or otherwise participate under many of NAFTA's ADR mechanisms.

Private parties were provided with the mechanisms to participate in the dispute resolution processes and challenge governmental action. These mechanisms were traditionally thought to be in the exclusive domain of the state, and more recently supranational entities. Notwithstanding such progress, the debate on this point remains divided. In answer to those arguing that the NAFTA should be abdicated as a failed experiment, some advocate for the continued development of the NAFTA's ADR models[16], while others argue that the NAFTA should rethink its approach so as to go even further in enhancing the rights of private individuals.[17]

The NAFTA's ADR mechanisms, which involve the state, are intended to give private citizens limited access so they may participate in certain proceedings. These proceedings relate to certain unfair trade practices, investments, and environmental and labor concerns, as well as the interpretation and application of NAFTA. Although these mechanisms may have some common characteristics, they are distinct and call for the application of specific mechanisms to different sectors.

NAFTA's sectoral approach to ADR stands in contrast to other mechanisms. Unlike the other dispute resolution mechanisms found in many treaties and agreements, such as the WTO, which are applied to all disputes in the same way, the NAFTA envisages

---

3. A party shall be deemed to be in compliance with the 1958 United Nations Convention on the Recognition and Enforcement of Foreign Arbitral Awards or the 1975 Inter-American Convention on International Commercial Arbitration.
4. The Commission shall establish an Advisory Committee on Private Commercial Disputes comprising of persons with expertise or experience in the resolution of private international commercial disputes. The committee shall report and provide recommendations to the Commission on general issues referred to it by the Commission respecting the availability, use and effectiveness of arbitration and other procedures for the resolution of such disputes in the free trade area (NAFTA, Article 2022 (1–4)).

This article creates two specific obligations for each of the NAFTA Parties, as well as a collective responsibility. Each country is to encourage and facilitate the use of ADR for commercial disputes between private parties in the NAFTA region. Each Party is also to provide the appropriate procedures for enforcing arbitration agreements and for recognizing and enforcing arbitral awards. Collectively, the NAFTA countries, acting through the FTC, are to establish an Advisory Committee on Private Commercial Disputes to report and provide recommendations, as requested by the Commission, on ADR matters. (NAFTA, Article 2022).

[16] *See* Stephen Powell, *Expanding the NAFTA Chapter 19 Dispute Settlement System: A Way to Declaw Trade Remedy Laws in a Free Trade of the Americas?*, *in* 16(2) NAFTA: L. & BUS. REV, AMERICAS (2010) (arguing that procedural modifications to Chapter 19 in the form of appellate review could provide the practical alternative to negotiating substantive law in the context of the Free Trade agreement of the Americas). *See also* Robert E. Lutz, *Current Developments in the NAFTA: A Guide for Future Economic Integration Efforts*, 18 WHITTIER L. REV. 313 (1997). *See also* Cherie O'Niel Taylor, *Dispute Resolution as a Catalyst for Economic Integration and an Agent for Deepening Integration: NAFTA and MERCOSUR?*, 17 NW. J. INT'L L. BUS. 850 (1996) (discussing the effect of NAFTA's dispute settlement systems on the process of economic integration).

[17] *See* Noemi Gal-Or, *supra* note 4 (arguing that although NAFTA's sectoral approach to private-party participation in ADR mechanisms involving the state recognizes the rights of private participation in the process, it lags behind the EU's institutional and constitutional approach.)

different ADR mechanisms for different situations.[18] The amount of sovereignty that governments are required to cede, and the quality and extent of private party participation, are dependent on the type of dispute and the mechanism available.

NAFTA contains six distinct ADR mechanisms within its framework. Dispute resolution for foreign investment issues is dealt with in Chapter 11, the mechanism for financial services dispute resolution is contained in Chapter 14, unfair trade disputes are handled though Chapter 19, questions relating to the interpretation and application of the NAFTA are handled under Chapter 20, questions relating to the enforcement of environmental law are funneled through the North American Agreement on Environmental Cooperation, and questions relating to labor law enforcement are dealt with in the North American Agreement on Labor Cooperation. The following sections will analyze Chapter 20, Chapter 19, Chapter 11, and then the side accords.

Chapter 20

Chapter 20, a holdover from the Canada–U.S. Free Trade Agreement (CUSFTA), deals with intergovernmental institutional arrangements and dispute settlement procedures.[19] It is designed to foster cooperation between the Parties through the use of ADR. This chapter adopts a three-step sequential process to dispute resolution with respect to issues of interpretation, application of, or alleged breaches of NAFTA.

The first step in the dispute resolution process is for the complaining Party to formally request consultation with the alleged offending Party. ADR processes are heavily relied upon at this juncture, in an attempt to avoid progressively more intrusive steps.[20]

Failing agreement, either Party may make a formal request for a meeting, within thirty days, to the Free Trade Commission (FTC).[21] The FTC must meet within ten days of the request and make a nonbinding recommendation to the Parties suggesting a resolution to the problem.

Finally, if either Party remains dissatisfied with the recommendations of the FTC, it may request the formation of an arbitral panel.[22] Within strict timelines, the Panel will issue an initial report determining the consistency of the impugned matter with the NAFTA, as well as making recommendations for the resolution of the problem.

---

18 *See* Joel Trachtman, *The Domain of WTO Dispute Resolution*, 49 HARV. INT'L L.J. 333 (1999).

19 The Canada-United States Free Trade Agreement (CUSFTA), Chapter 18.

20 William D. Merritt, *Practical Guide to Dispute Resolution under the North American Free Trade Agreement*, 5 NAFTA: L. & BUS. REV. AMERICAS 169, 182 (1999) (arguing that ADR holds the advantages of flexibility, dispensing with complex international legal issues and, most important, approaching the problem from a mutual-interests perspective, rather than from a vindication-of-rights perspective).

21 The FTC is comprised of Cabinet-level representatives of the Parties, or their designees, who are charged with overseeing the implementation and elaboration of NAFTA. *See* NAFTA, ch. 20, art. 2001.

22 This Panel, consisting of five experts in trade or dispute resolution of trade agreements, will review the matter and make findings and determinations. *See id.*

The Parties are allowed to comment on the report, and then the Panel issues its final report. Within thirty days, the Parties are required to agree upon a resolution that eliminates the offending measure and conforms to the Panel's determinations and recommendations. Failing agreement on such a resolution, within thirty days from the release of the final report, the complaining Party may seek suspension of the other Party's equivalent NAFTA benefits.[23]

Systemically, Chapter 20 appears to have worked well as an institutional ADR mechanism to resolve intra-state disputes. It has effectively dealt with the sensitive and politically charged issues that have arisen between the NAFTA trading partners.[24] Moreover, as this chapter does not require that panelists indicate whether they signed on to the majority or dissent, it appears to have functioned without the "nationalistic" overtones found in some Chapter 19 cases.[25] However, its overall effect has been difficult to gauge because although the NAFTA Secretariat tracks the proceedings throughout the three steps, formal recording does not occur until the arbitral stage. It is therefore difficult to know how many Chapter 20 cases not yet at the arbitral stage are ongoing, and, more important, which ones were resolved, as intended, at earlier stages of the proceedings.[26]

The focus on pre-arbitration mechanisms has raised procedural questions with respect to delays and uncertainty. These concerns were highlighted in the cross-border trucking case between the United States and Mexico.[27] Although the issue was resolved, troubling questions linger as to why Mexico delayed the initiation of the arbitral process and why the same issues, which were dealt with in the arbitration, remain unresolved between the Parties.[28]

As the application of this mechanism is limited to intra-state disputes, it does not envision any direct private party participation, either by initiation or access to the process. As such, any issue over the interpretation or application of the NAFTA must be addressed to the panel by the Parties. Further, a NAFTA Party is precluded from authorizing, under its domestic law, a right of action against another NAFTA Party on the ground that it did not properly interpret or apply the NAFTA.[29]

---

[23] NAFTA, ch. 20, arts. 2008–2019.

[24] For example, it was effective in containing the controversy around the Helms-Burton Act. *See* Craig Guieze, *Helms-Burton in Light of the Common Law and Civil Law Traditions: Is Legal Analysis Alone Sufficient to Settle Controversies Arising under International Law on the Eve of the Second Summit of the Americas?*, 32 INT'L L. 51 (analyzing Helms-Burton in accordance with the governing principles of international law and contrasting the civil and common approaches). *See also* Marc Sheer, *Chapter 20 Dispute Resolution under NAFTA: Fact or Fiction?*, 35 GEO. WASH. INT'L L. REV. 1001 (2003).

[25] NAFTA, ch. 20, art. 2017(2)

[26] *See* Merritt, *supra* note 20 (suggesting that more cases have been disposed of in the earlier stages of the proceedings)

[27] *See* Re: Cross Border Trucking, USA-Mex-98-2008-01 (Feb. 16, 2001), NAFTA Secretariat Web site, *supra* note 11.

[28] By definition, free trade agreements should at least permit the free circulation of goods within the Parties' borders.

[29] NAFTA, ch. 20, art. 2021.

These provisions limit private party participation in the process. Although there is no formal role envisaged for private parties in this process, it has been argued that powerful entities might participate indirectly by lobbying their national government to take up their cause.[30] Commentators have noted that this mechanism does little to empower small and medium-sized businesses lacking in sufficient finances, or political clout, to get national governments to rally around their cause.[31]

Chapter 19

The successful conclusion of the CUSFTA hinged on the Parties bridging the divisive issues relating to trade law. The Canadian negotiating position insisted on an exemption from U.S. trade law, which Canada believed to be arbitrary and discriminatory in certain cases.[32] The U.S. position held fast that no exemption from its trade law could exist. During the final hours of President George H.W. Bush's Fast Track Authority to negotiate a free trade deal, the Parties faced the real prospect that years of negotiation and substantial agreement would fade into a nonstarter.

In model negotiations fashion, the Parties agreed to disagree on the development of a harmonized trade code. They referred the harmonization issue on to a committee that could engage in further study and negotiation. However, in order to go forward with the CUSFTA, the Parties agreed to an interim procedural arrangement regarding the resolution of trade disputes. Under this substitute judicial review regime, each country maintained its own trade laws; that is, the importation of goods between the United States and Canada would remain subject to the antidumping and countervailing duty laws of the importing country.[33] This included the substantive and procedural law, as well as the standard of review.[34]

---

30 Noemi Gal-Or, *supra* note 4, at 33.

31 Jonathan I. Miller, *Prospects for Satisfactory Dispute Resolution of Private Commercial Disputes under the North American Free Trade Agreement*, 21 PEPP. L. REV. 1313, 1318–20 (1994).

32 As in every long-standing relationship, trade or otherwise, an overwhelmingly good relationship is often overshadowed by isolated, but prominent irritants. The trade of softwood lumber products between Canada and the United States is an example of a long-standing and festering irritant in an otherwise healthy trade relationship. *See* Eric J. Pan, *Assessing the NAFTA Chapter 19 Binational Panel System: An Experiment in International Adjudication*, 40 HARV. INT'L L.J. 379, 382–83 (1999) (describing the environment between the parties leading up to the establishment of Chapter 19).

33 Antidumping and countervailing duty laws are exceptions to the WTO's fundamental principle of non-discrimination in government measures affecting trade, and although the WTO agreements impose disciplines on the imposition of antidumping and countervailing duties, governments have retained sufficient discretion to "inspire endless litigation" in national courts and WTO dispute settlement procedures, and under NAFTA Chapter 19. See Powell, *supra* note 16, at n.7, referencing SIMON LESTER AND BRYAN MERCURIO, WORLD TRADE LAW: TEXT, MATERIALS AND COMMENTARY CHS. 11–12 (2008).

34 The CUSFTA defined the standard of review in the United States as the standards set forth in Section 516(A) (b) (1) (B) of the Tariff Act of 1930, *as amended*. (Ca.-U.S., 27 I.L.M. 281 (1988), Chapter 19, Article 1911.) That section of the Tariff Act sets forth the standard used by the Court of International Trade (CIT) in its review of agency determinations. The standard is that the court, and the CUSFTA

This substitute judicial review process contained only one level of review. As the process was taken out of the normal judicial review process and its attendant levels of appeals, only one level of review was included.[35] This review was to be provided, upon challenge by one of the Parties, through an Extraordinary Challenge Committee (ECC), made up of three federal judges (or its equivalent in the Canadian context) from both countries. The standard of review for an ECC was limited to taking corrective action upon meeting a three-prong test. The test was whether "the [Chapter 19] Panel manifestly exceeds its power, authority or jurisdiction…, and (b) any of the actions set out in subparagraph (a) has materially affected the Panel's decision and threatens the integrity of the binational panel review process."[36]

In 1994, a more expansive trade agreement was negotiated under the auspices of the NAFTA. It was much more comprehensive and ambitious than its predecessor, but it built upon many of the provisions of the CUSFTA. In particular, Chapter 19 remained intact with few modifications. The temporary substitute judicial review process was retained, but now made permanent. The standard-of-review provisions remained as they were for Chapter 19, but the standard as it applied to Mexican imports was added. The standard of review for an ECC panel was amended to read: "the [Chapter 19] Panel manifestly exceeds its power, authority or jurisdiction set out in this Article, for example by failing to apply the appropriate standard of review and (b) any of the actions set out in subparagraph (a) has materially affected the Panel's decision and threatens the integrity of the binational panel review process."[37]

From a systemic perspective, Chapter 19 has functioned well. It has been used to challenge the decisions of the investigating authority of all three NAFTA countries.[38] Most cases have been decided in a well-reasoned manner benefiting from the binational makeup of the Panel.[39] However, one product in particular—softwood lumber from Canada—continues to be a persistent thorn in Canadian–U.S. trade relations. The Canada–U.S. softwood battles of the past prompted Canada's request for exemption from U.S. law. The softwood battles, in the context of Chapter 19, have provided U.S. critics with the ammunition to call for the repeal of this mechanism.[40] Unlike

---

Chapter 19 Panel, would hold unlawful any determination, finding, or conclusion that is unsupported by substantial evidence on the record or otherwise not in accordance with law.

35 In the case of the United States, an appeal of a decision of the Court of International trade could be made to the Federal Circuit Court of Appeals and then to the U.S. Supreme Court.

36 CUSFTA, art. 1904.13.

37 NAFTA, ch. 19, art. 1904.13.

38 Panel decisions may be consulted at the Web site of the NAFTA Secretariat, *supra* note 11.

39 *See* Eric Pan, *supra* note 32 (arguing that that the Chapter 19 Panel system has worked well and in some respects better than court adjudication).

40 For insight on the Canadian perspective, see C. Gastel & J. Castle, *Should the NAFTA Dispute Settlement Mechanism in Antidumping and Countervailing Duty Cases Be Reformed in Light of Softwood Lumber 111?*, 26 Law & Pol'y Int'l Bus. 823 (1995). For a contrary American perspective *see* G. Carmen, *Resolution of Trade Disputes by Chapter 19 Panels: A Long-Term Solution or Interim Procedure of Dubious Constitutionality?*, 21 Fordham Int'l L.J. 1 (1997).

the great bulk of Chapter 19 cases, one softwood case produced a determination that appeared to follow national lines.[41] This split along national lines appeared to follow the process into the ECC.[42] A subsequent politically charged softwood battle went through the Chapter 19 panel process[43] and was reviewed by the ECC.[44] This latest bout produced similarly divisive reactions, but led to the conclusion of a new memorandum of understanding.[45]

The controversial aspects of Chapter 19 should not prevent it from evolving. [46] Its critics have charged that this constitutionally questionable mechanism has failed to live up to its promise of applying domestic law, especially the standard of review.[47] In so far as Chapter 19 permits private parties to assert their rights and invoke review outside the normal judicial process, it is a positive step in the direction of empowering private party participation in the NAFTA's ADR processes. This process might be further improved by introducing a mandatory mediation process in the system, opening up the appellate process to private party initiation, and permitting third-party or amicus curiae representations.[48] The extra time that such procedures might entail could be offset by stricter timelines in the proceedings, and reduced governmental wrangling and delays in the process, as well as improved institutional support through the NAFTA Secretariat.

---

[41] *See* Re: Softwood, USA-CDA-92-1904-01 (CVD) (May 16, 1993 and Dec. 17, 1993), http:www.nafta-sec-alena.org. However, a closer reading of this case discloses that not all major issues were decided along national lines.

[42] *See* In the Matter of Softwood Lumber Products from Canada (ECC), 1994 WL 405928 (N.A.F.T.A. BINAT. Panel) (the dissent reviews the history of this case and calls for the reversal of the panel, as well as for the repeal of Chapter 19.)

[43] *See* Re: Softwood, USA-CDA-2002—1904-02 (dumping), USA_CDA-2002-1904-03 (CVD), USA-CDA-2002-1904-07 (injury). The decisions are available at the NAFTA Secretariat Web site, *supra* note 11.

[44] In the Matter of Certain Softwood Lumber Products from Canada, Opinion and Order of the Extraordinary Challenge Committee, ECC-2004-1904-01-USA, Aug. 10, 2005, NAFTA Secretariat Web site, *supra* note 8.

[45] *See* CBC Archives, *At Loggerheads: The Canada-US Softwood Lumber Dispute*, http:www.archives.cbc.ca/IDD-1-73-78/politics_economy/softwood (recounting the history of the softwood lumber dispute).

[46] Powell, *supra* note 16 (arguing that the inclusion of an appellate mechanism review mechanism in Chapter 19 would facilitate the adoption of a similar mechanism in the anticipated Free Trade Agreement of the Americas).

[47] *See* Carmen, *supra* note 40; John Ragosta, Harry L.Clark & Latif S. Doman, *Sacrificing the Constitution for Comity? NAFTA Chapter 19 Panels and the U.S. Constitution, in* NUEVOS HORIZONTES 370 (Nick W. Ranieri ed., 1997); and Jennifer Danner Riccardi, *The Failure of Chapter 19 in Design and Practice: An Opportunity for Reform*, 28 OHIO N.U. L. REV. 727 (2002) (arguing that American laws limit the ability of American negotiators to conclude FTAs that require amendment of U.S. law).

[48] *See* Chapter 19 Wheat Opinion, USA-CDA-2003-1904-06, NAFTA Secretatiat Web site, *supra* note 11 (the Panel rejected the Canadian government's request to participate in the hearing on the grounds that it did not participate in the underlying review, and the Canadian government did not request an amicus curiae participation as an alternative.)

Chapter 11

NAFTA's Chapter 11 on investment is more of an evolutionary, rather than a revolutionary development in the area of FDI protocols. That is, although it is in many respects based on evolving concepts known to international law, it also is unique in several ways. To strengthen the increasing trend of modern FDI in the NAFTA region, the NAFTA partners expanded the investment provisions found in the CUSFTA and the various BITs.[49] The result was an investment chapter that bore some resemblance to traditional investment protection mechanisms, but that also broke new ground. It is unique in that, unlike most multilateral agreements, it both regulates investments and calls for compulsory arbitration over the interpretation and application of its substantive provisions between the member states and private investors from other member states. It is unique in that it creates a code of state conduct and calls for the resolution of disputes regarding this conduct to be settled by means of ad hoc, but binding arbitration through different arbitral institutions that utilize different rules. It is unique from most BITs in that it does not compel an investor to choose between the agreement or local remedy.[50] It is unique in the NAFTA context, in that, unlike Chapter 19, it calls for the application of international, rather than domestic law. Perhaps, most important, it is unique in that it represents the first time that this type of investment agreement has been concluded between two highly regulated developed countries and a less-developed country.

It is, perhaps, not so unique from the WTO in that it has become infiltrated by cases with actual or potential environmental and regulatory implications. In fact, many of the known Chapter 11 cases present actual, or potential, regulatory and environmental concerns. Several of the better-known cases involve investments made by waste disposal companies or companies dealing in natural resources. These companies have demanded compensation, alleging, inter alia, that the host government's environmental regulation effectively expropriated their investments.

The NAFTA makes many references to the environment. NAFTA's Preamble states that the Parties resolve to ensure a predictable commercial framework for business planning and investment, in a manner consistent with environmental protection and

---

49 *See* U.S. Statement on Administrative Action, Nov. 1993, and Canada's Statement on Implementation 1994. For an overview of the U.S. S BIT program as well as its negotiating history, see Kenneth J. Vandevelde, *The Bilateral Treaty Program of the United States*, 21 CORNELL INT'L L.J. 201 (1988). *See also* Andrew T. Guzman, *Why LDCS Sign Treaties That Hurt Them: Explaining the Popularity of Bilateral Investment Treaties*, 38 VA. J. INT'L. L. 639 (1998).

50 Most BITs, through the "fork in the road" provisions, restrict investors to pursuing local remedies or the BIT remedy. The more generous NAFTA "waiver" provisions merely restrict investors from pursuing both the NAFTA and local remedy simultaneously. *See generally* Charles Brower, *Investor-State Arbitration under NAFTA's Chapter 11: Where Are We, and Where Are We Going* (paper presented at an ABA Conference, Mar, 19, 1999) (copy on file with author) and Bradford K. Gathright, *A Step in the Wrong Direction: The Lowen Finality Requirement and the Local Remedies Rule in NAFTA Chapter 11*, 54 EMORY L.J. 1093 (2005).

conservation.[51] The NAFTA also contains environmentally related provisions regarding the application of standards.[52] Subject to national treatment and most-favored-nation treatment, Parties are free to apply technology standards to meet environmental regulation requirements.[53] The Parties may adopt or maintain environmental or other measures necessary to protect life, health, or the conservation of living or nonliving exhaustible natural resources.[54] As well, there are references to environmental concerns both in Chapter 11, as well as outside the main NAFTA text, in the NAAEC. [55]

Recognizing the weight of investment pressures, the NAFTA attempts to balance environmental concerns. Chapter 11 does not prevent a NAFTA government from adopting, maintaining, or enforcing any measure that it considers appropriate to ensure that the investment is sensitive to environmental concerns.[56] Moreover, the NAFTA governments have specifically recognized the impropriety of encouraging investment by relaxing domestic health, safety, or environmental measures.[57]

This emphasis on the environment throughout the NAFTA text is instructive. It has led commentators to suggest that it might provide the basis to argue that environmental regulation should get more leeway in the application of Chapter 11 reviews.[58] However, the Chapter 11 cases filed suggest that the line between compensable expropriatory takings and environmental regulation is not universally understood and certainly is open to challenge.[59] The basis of this uncertainty appears to lie with the imprecise, yet potentially broad definition of expropriation in Chapter 11.[60] Article 1110(1) provides that collectively, direct or indirect expropriation, as well as measures tantamount to expropriation, are subject to the compensation requirement. Particularly troubling questions have arisen relating to the scope of indirect expropriation and measures tantamount to expropriation. Do these standards refer to the same governmental actions, or does one build on the other to circumscribe more governmental activity? It is in this context that the NAFTA Investment Chapter, known as Chapter 11, must function.

NAFTA devotes a whole chapter to investment protection.[61] Section A contains an expansive list of investment protection provisions. Section B outlines the procedural

---

51 Dec. 17, 1992, U.S.-Can.-Mex., 32 I.L.M. 289 (chs. 1–9); 32 I.L.M. 605(chs. 10–22) (NAFTA).

52 NAFTA, chs. 7 and 9.

53 NAFTA, art. 1106 (2).

54 NAFTA, art. 1106 (6).

55 North American Agreement on Environmental Cooperation, U.S.-Can.-Mex., 321 L.M. 1482 (NAEEC).

56 NAFTA, art. 1114(1).

57 NAFTA, art. 1114(2).

58 *See* David Gantz, *Potential Conflicts between Investor Rights and Environmental Regulation under NATA Chapter 11*, 33 GEO. WASH. INT'L. L.R. 651 (2001); David Gantz, *Reconciling Environmental Protection and Investor Rights under Chapter 11 of NAFTA*, 31 ENVTL. L. REP. 10646 (2001).

59 *See, e.g.*, the filings in the Metalclad and Ethyl proceedings, NAFTA Claims Web site, *supra* note 62.

60 *See*. J. Martin Wagner, *International Investment, Expropriation and Environmental Protection*, 29 GOLDEN GATE U.L. REV. 465 (1999) (arguing that NAFTA's unclear definition of the actions covered by its expropriation provisions could result in a level of investor protection that goes beyond international and American compensation principles with respect to the economic impact on investments resulting from legitimate environmental regulation).

61 NAFTA, ch. 11

regimes available to investors for the protection of those rights. These safeguards in Chapter 11 constitute a complete investment code that has given NAFTA investors the ability to challenge governmental conduct, which was previously believed to be beyond the purview of litigation. Foreign investors have called into question the ability of sovereigns to claim immunity,[62] regulate natural resources,[63] and permit jury awards.[64] Discussing all the cases that have been filed to date is beyond the parameters of this paper.[65] However, subsequent sections will address select cases that will serve to provide an overview of the themes that have emerged, and the controversies that surround them.

A. SECTION A: SUBSTANTIVE RIGHTS

The substantive provisions of Chapter 11, contained in Section A, are broad. These provisions represent an intricate balance of rights, reservations, and exemptions negotiated by the Parties. Virtually any NAFTA investor is protected with respect to virtually any type of investment in the NAFTA region.[66]

Section A begins by broadly defining the scope and coverage of Chapter 11.[67] Investment is defined to encompass multiple forms. Its coverage extends to an enterprise; an equity security of an enterprise; various debt securities of an enterprise; certain loans to an enterprise; an interest in an enterprise that entitles the owner to share in the assets of that enterprise on dissolution; real estate or other property, tangible or intangible, acquired in the expectation or used for the purpose of economic benefit or other business purposes; and some interests arising from the commitment of capital or other resources in the territory of a Party to economic activity in such territory. Investment of a Party is similarly defined as an investment owned or controlled directly or indirectly by an investor of such Party.[68]

---

62 Mondev International Ltd., a Canadian real estate developer, claimed that the state of Massachusetts's law of sovereign immunity violated NAFTA's investment provisions. Mondev initially sued in a local court and received a substantial jury award against a local development authority. This judgment was eventually overturned on appeal because it was found that the authority enjoyed sovereign immunity. Mondev subsequently initiated NAFTA Chapter 11 proceedings against the United States for the satisfaction of its damages in the amount of fifty million dollars. *See* Chapter 11 claim of Mondev International Ltd. and the United States of America, NAFTA Claims Web site, http:www// naftaclaims.com.

63 Sun Belt Waters Inc., a U.S. company, has sued the Canadian government for damages totaling over ten billion dollars over the province of British Columbia's ban on freshwater exports and the government of British Columbia settled a suit brought by Sunbelt's Canadian joint venture partner. *See* Sun Belt Water, Inc. and the Government of Canada. Documents pertaining to this case are available at the NAFTA Claims Web site, *supra* note 62.

64 Lowen and the United States, documents *available at* NAFTA Claims Web site, *supra* note 62.

65 One of the most comprehensive Web sites containing documents pertaining to Chapter 11 cases is the NAFTA Claims Web site, *supra* note 62.

66 NAFTA Chapter 11, Article 1110(1) broadly defines the scope and coverage of Chapter 11. Article 1139 broadly defines *investor* and *investment*.

67 NAFTA, art. 1101.

68 NAFTA, art. 1139.

The broad scope of Chapter 11 is tempered by a complex balance of reservations, exceptions, limitations, and exclusions. Certain nonconforming measures may be exempted from some of Chapter 11's provisions.[69] These exceptions to Articles 1101–1107 are not blanket ones, but limited in terms of time, application, and conformity.[70] The Parties specifically reserved, exempted, or otherwise made Chapter 11 inapplicable to a variety of activities and sectors. National security, culturally sensitive areas, specific programs, and certain sectors were carefully carved out.[71] However, unless explicitly exempted, Chapter 11 is applicable sectorally throughout the NAFTA.

The NAFTA governments have also carved out various wholesale exceptions to the investor protection provisions of Chapter 11. Politically sensitive sectors, including telecommunications, maritime services, Mexico's petroleum industry, and others have been carefully exempted.[72] The limitations on the scope and coverage of Chapter 11 include certain economic activities reserved to the Parties;[73] measures covered by the Financial Services Chapter, known as Chapter Fourteen;[74] and certain enumerated social services or functions.[75] Interestingly, the enumerated services and functions include health, but not the environment. Moreover, in the event of inconsistency between Chapter 11 and any other chapter, the other chapter will prevail to the extent of the inconsistency.[76]

The Parties also negotiated specific exclusions to Chapter 11. National security measures, taken pursuant to Article 2102, are exempt from Chapter 11 challenge. Furthermore, in the Canadian context, Chapter 11 is not applicable to challenge determinations made pursuant to the Investment Canada Act. In the Mexican context, Chapter 11 is unavailable to challenge decisions of the Comision Nacional de Inversiones Extranjeras (National Commission on Foreign Investment).[77]

NAFTA investors are protected from discrimination in a very comprehensive fashion. Having carved out a broad application, with an equally extensive list of exemptions, Chapter 11 goes on to codify the rights of investors. These rights are substantial and include nondiscrimination through the application of the standards of national treatment and most-favored-nation treatment (MFN).[78] These rights also include a minimum standard of treatment, the prohibition of certain performance requirements, and compensation for certain expropriations.[79] These standards apply to virtually all aspects of the investment, from setting up to its final disposition

69 NAFTA, art. 1108.
70 NAFTA, art. 1108(1–8).
71 NAFTA ch. 11, arts. 1101, 1108, and 1112.
72 NAFTA, annexes 1–VI.
73 NAFTA, art. 1101(2).
74 NAFTA, art. 1101(3).
75 NAFTA, art. 1101(4).
76 NAFTA, art. 1112.
77 NAFTA, art. 1138.
78 NAFTA, arts. 1102, 1103.
79 NAFTA, arts. 1105, 1106, 1101. For a discussion on the relationship between NAFTA's primary five obligations, *see* Todd Wieler, *The Potential for Overlap in NAFTA Chapter 11 Obligations*, *in* THE FIRST

National Treatment

NAFTA investors are protected by national treatment provisions. NAFTA Article 1102 states:

1. Each Party shall accord to investors of another Party treatment no less favorable than it accords, in like circumstances, to its own investors with respect to the establishment acquisition, expansion, management, conduct, operation, and sale or other disposition of investment.
2. Each Party shall accord to investments of investors of another Party treatment no less favorable than it accords, in like circumstances, to investments of its own investors with respect to the establishment, acquisition, expansion, management, conduct, operation, and sale or other disposition of investments.
3. The treatment accorded by a Party under paragraphs 1 and 2 means, with respect to a state or province, treatment no less favorable than the most favorable treatment accorded, in like circumstances, by the state or province to investors, and to investments of investors, of the Party of which it forms a part.[80]

Each Party is obligated to treat investors, and investments, of another NAFTA Party no less favorably than it treats its own investors and their investments. That is, the treatment of NAFTA investors and investments must be no worse than the most favorable treatment that a Party, and its provinces or states, provide local investors, in like circumstances. For greater certainty, the Parties may not impose minimum levels of national equity requirements in an enterprise in its territory, other than nominal qualifying shares for directors or incorporators of corporations. They are further precluded from requiring the disposal of an investment by reason of nationality.[81]

The national treatment analysis is straightforward, consisting of three basic elements. The tribunal will identify the subjects for comparison, consider the relative treatments received, and consider whether any differentiation in treatment is justifiable.[82] The analysis must begin by delineating the universe of comparables to ensure that the balance of the analysis focuses on a proper comparison.[83] The analysis of relative treatments received focuses on the result of the treatment received, and not on whether the treatments appear similar.[84] Once a prima facie case of discrimination has been made, the onus shifts to the government to explain the justification

---

DECADE OF NAFTA: THE FUTURE OF FREE TRADE IN NORTH AMERICA (Kevin Kennedy ed., 2004).

[80] NAFTA, ch.11, arts. 1102 (national treatment), 1103 (most-favored-nation treatment), 1104 (standard of treatment), 1105 (minimum standard of treatment).

[81] NAFTA, art.1102(4).

[82] Pope & Talbot, Final Merits Award, at 9-37, NAFTA Claims Web site, *supra* note 62.

[83] *See* Feldman Award, at 70 and ADF Award, at 72, *available at* the NAFTA Claims Web site, *supra* note 62.

[84] Pope and Talbot, Final Merits Award, at 63 and Myers Award, at 15-15, *available at* the NAFTA Claims Web site, *supra* note 62.

for the dissimilarity in treatment. The measure might be justified if the dissimilarity in treatment results from the local and foreign investor being in dissimilar circumstances.[85]

Most-Favored-Nation Treatment

NAFTA investors are protected by MFN provisions. NAFTA Article 1103, dealing with most MFN, reads:

> 1. Each Party shall accord to investors of another Party treatment no less favorable than it accords, in like circumstances, to investors of any other Party, or of a non-Party with respect to the establishment, acquisition, expansion, management, conduct, operation, and sale or other disposition of investments.
> 2. Each Party shall accord to investments of investors of another Party treatment no less favorable than it accords, in like circumstances, to investments of investors of any other Party, or of a non-Party with respect to the establishment, acquisition, expansion, management, conduct, operation, and sale or other disposition of investments.[86]

MFN treatment protects investors from discrimination. It applies to the establishment, acquisition, expansion, management, conduct, operation, and sale or other disposition of investments. Each Party is obligated to provide NAFTA investors and investments with treatment no less favorable than it gives to investors and investments of any other Party or non-Party, in like circumstances.

The MFN analysis is similar to that used for national treatment. The principles of national treatment and MFN are both comparative standards that are, for the most part identical. The two notable differences include the identity of those making the comparison and the potential scope for application of the comparison. These two principles require a comparative analysis of the treatment received by the investor or investment. However, although the national treatment principle compares the foreign investor with local competitors, the MFN principle compares the foreign investor with similarly situated foreign investors or investments.

At a practical level, the MFN obligation may be given a broader analysis. Article 1103 is subject to the reservations found in Annex IV, and as such the MFN obligation is applied at a broader level than the national treatment obligation. Through Annex IV, the NAFTA Parties have taken reservations for any treaty obligations undertaken by the NAFTA that would result in better treatment being provided to one foreigner over a NAFTA investor. They also took forward-looking reservations for treaties affecting certain business sectors, such as aviation. It has been suggested that the implication of these reservations is that the Parties knew that Article 1103 would require governments

85 Pope and Talbot, Final Merits Award, at 35-6, *available at* the NAFTA Claims Web site, *supra* note 62.

86 NAFTA, art. 1103.

to ensure that NAFTA investors receive no-less-favorable treatment than that promised in any other treaty coming into force after the NAFTA. As there is no national treatment analog, the scope for the comparison of "like" investors or investments can be broader for Article 1103. In the Article 1102 analysis, the indicia of comparison will normally be at the level of industrial sector or narrower.[87]

Standard of Treatment

NAFTA investors and investments are guaranteed the optimal level of protection. Article 1104, dealing with standard of treatment, provides:

Each Party shall accord to investors of another Party and to investments of investors of another Party the better of the treatment required by Articles 1102 and 1103.[88]

Article 1104 includes a mechanism that grants NAFTA investors and investments the best available protection. It establishes a standard of treatment in cases where it is not clear whether national treatment or most-favored-nation treatment would accord NAFTA investors the best treatment. It obligates each Party to accord investors and investments of the other Parties treatment that is the better of the treatment required by national treatment and most-favored-nation treatment.

Minimum Standard of Treatment

The minimum standard of treatment is addressed in MAFTA Article 1105:

1. Each Party shall accord to investments of investors of another Party treatment in accordance with international law, including fair and equitable treatment and full protection and security.
2. Without prejudice to paragraph 1 and notwithstanding Article 1108(7)(b), each Party shall accord to investors of another Party, and to investments of investors of another Party, non-discriminatory treatment with respect to measures it adopts or maintains relating to losses suffered by investments in its territories owing to armed conflict or civil strife.
3. Paragraph 2 does not apply to existing measures relating to subsidies or grants that would be inconsistent with Article 1102 but for Article 1108(7)(b).[89]

Article 1105 establishes specific baselines for the acceptable treatment of NAFTA investors by NAFTA governments. Utilizing a minimum standard of treatment ensures that the Parties will treat each other's nationals with a base level of rights recognized by international law, even if they do not grant the same rights to their own nationals. Each Party shall accord to investments of investors (of another Party) treatment in accordance with international law, including fair and equitable treatment and full

---

[87] Weiler, *supra* note 79, at 326–27.

[88] NAFTA, art. 1104.

[89] NAFTA, art. 1105.

protection and security. With few exceptions, each Party shall provide to investors and their investments (of another Party) nondiscriminatory treatment with respect to measures the Party adopts relating to losses suffered by investments in its territory occasioned by armed conflict or civil strife.[90]

Unlike Articles 1102 and 1103, which are comparative standards, Article 1105 is an absolute standard setting a minimum level of treatment. The content of this minimum standard is context-driven and informed by relevant sources of international law.[91] Treaties, customary international law, and general principles of law, as well as the secondary sources of international law (which include the writings of the most highly qualified publicists and the decisions of international tribunals) might inform the content.[92]

Governmental liability may stem concurrently from various NAFTA provisions. It is possible that certain governmental conduct will be violative of Articles 1102 and 1103, as well as 1105. Cases of discrimination are the ones more likely to violate all these standards because such conduct is prohibited under customary international law as well as the principles of MFN and national treatment.[93]

Performance Requirements

Chapter 11 disciplines performance requirements. NAFTA's Article 1106, dealing with performance requirements, precludes the NAFTA countries from imposing certain performance requirements on investments of an investor of a Party or a non-Party.[94] This follows the practice of BITS to preclude countries from imposing additional requirements that might dilute the value of the investment by requiring decision making to be made on something other than the most-efficient basis.

Article 1106 attempts to keep the investment decision-making power of the investment in the hands of investors. This section has a potentially far-reaching impact because it applies not only to investors from the NAFTA Parties but it may also apply to foreign investors from non-NAFTA countries with investments or holding in the NAFTA region.[95] NAFTA governments are precluded, in seven specific ways, from

---

90 *See* J.C. Thomas, *Reflections on Article 1105 of NAFTA: History, State Practice and the Influence of Commentators*, 17 ICSID Rev.: Foreign Inv. L.J. 21 (2002).

91 ADF Award, ¶¶ 39–89, *available at* the NAFTA Claims Web site, *supra* note 62–89. *See* Todd Weiler, *Nafta Chapter 11 Jurisprudence: Coming Along Nicely*, 9 Sw. J.L. & Trade in the Americas 245 (2003)

92 Statute of the International Court of Justice, [1945], C.T.S. 7, in force Oct. 24, 1945. Article 38(1) contains a definitive list of the sources of international law.

93 For a detailed discussion of overlapping NAFTA obligations *see* Weiler, *supra* note 79 (arguing that the comparative and absolute standards against discrimination share a common objective, but the former focuses on a comparison of the result obtained by the investor and that received by a similarly situated competitor, while the latter focuses on the manner in which the investment has been treated, as compared with the standard required by international law).

94 NAFTA, art. 1106.

95 The Mexican Executive Order creating the Maquiladora Program imposes various export requirements (Sections 1 and II of the Maquildaora Order), which are arguably inconsistent with NAFTA 1106. Similar inconsistencies have been noted with the PITEX Program. *See* Luis F. Martinez, *How to Export*

interfering in the establishment or operation of a NAFTA investment. NAFTA governments cannot: tie sales to foreign exchange earnings; insist that investors buy locally; insist on a minimum amount of local content; request foreign exchange inflows; demand technology transfers, with the exception of corrective anticompetitive measures; demand technology transfers to local companies; demand specific levels of goods or services; or require that foreign markets be supplied from local production.[96] As well, NAFTA governments are required to permit investment transfers to be made freely, and without delay, at prevailing market rates of exchange. This applies to transfers of profits, royalties, sales proceeds, etc.[97]

The NAFTA countries are permitted to undertake certain measures with respect to special formalities and information requirements. These measures are permitted as long as the formalities do not materially impair the protections afforded by a Party to investors of another Party, and the requirements pertain to routine information in the equitable and good faith application of the Party's law.[98] The NAFTA countries are precluded from imposing nationality requirements on senior management positions of an investment of an investor of another Party.[99] However, a NAFTA country may have certain board of director requirements provided that they do not materially impede the ability of the investor to exercise control over its investment.[100]

The NAFTA countries have also agreed not to place transfer restrictions on investments of an investor from another Party.[101] These transfers include any amounts derived from the investment, proceeds of sale, contractual payments, or payments made pursuant to expropriation procedures. Investors are also given the right to make transfers in a freely usable currency at the prevailing market rate.[102] However, the NAFTA countries have reserved for themselves the right to prevent transfers, in limited circumstances, if they employ measures that are equitable, nondiscriminatory, and in good faith application of the country's laws.[103]

Under certain circumstances, the NAFTA countries may deny the benefits of Chapter 11 to a NAFTA investor or investment. This includes circumstances where the enterprise in question is owned, or controlled, by investors of a non-NAFTA government, and the denying NAFTA government does not have diplomatic relations with the non-Party, or adopts measures that prohibit transactions with the enterprise.[104] Furthermore, subject to notification and consultation, a NAFTA country may deny Chapter 11 benefits to an investor of another NAFTA country that is an enterprise

---

Efficiently from Mexico: A Fresh Look at Mexico's Export Incentives, in DOING BUSINESS IN MEXICO (Leon Trakman, Nick Ranieri & Marion Lopez eds., 2006).

96 NAFTA, ch.11, art. 1106(1)(a–g) (performance requirements).

97 NAFTA, ch.11, art. 1109 (transfers).

98 NAFTA, art. 1110(1–2).

99 NAFTA, art. 1107(1).

100 NAFTA, art. 1107(2).

101 NAFTA, art. 1109.

102 NAFTA, art. 1109(2).

103 NAFTA, art. 1109(4–6).

104 NAFTA, art. 1113(1).

lacking substantial business activities in the territory of the NAFTA government under whose laws it is constituted.[105]

Tribunals have shown a propensity to narrowly construe the term "requirement." The majority in *Myers* held that the specific requirements listed in Article 1106 had to be actually imposed for a breach to occur.[106] The *Pope & Talbot* tribunal held that a measure is a "requirement" only if it has a mandatory character that compels the investor's behavior.[107] This narrow construction is not supported by a purposive interpretation of the NAFTA, in light of its liberalizing objectives. Economically inefficient measures that, although not rising to the level of the *de jure* performance requirements listed in Article 1106, constitute *de facto* performance measures should be prohibited. Such an approach is preferable because it is more likely to prevent Article 1106 from being redundant with other provisions. [108]

Expropriation

Chapter 11 also disciplines the Parties' abilities to expropriate. As part of protecting investors from discrimination, Chapter 11 follows the lead of BITs in circumscribing the Parties' ability to expropriate. Article 1110 reads:

> 1. No Party may directly or indirectly nationalize or expropriate an investment of an investor of another Party in its territory or take a measure tantamount to nationalization or expropriation of such an investment ("expropriation"), except:
>
>   a. for a public purpose;
>   b. on a non-discriminatory basis;
>   c. in accordance with due process of law and Article 1105(1); and
>   d. on payment of compensation in accordance with paragraphs 2 through 6.[109]

Compensation shall be paid without delay, and be fully realizable and transferable. This compensation shall be equivalent to the fair market value of the expropriated investment, as determined by the valuation criteria, immediately prior to the expropriation. This compensation shall include interest and be payable in a G-7 currency or, subject to certain provisos, other currency.[110]

---

105 NAFTA, art. 1113(2).

106 Myers, *supra* note 56 (suggesting that this definition is too narrow and does not conform to international jurisprudence).

107 Pope & Talbot, Interim Merits Award, *available at* the NAFTA Claims Web site, *supra* note 62.

108 *See*, Weiler, *supra* note 79, at 337–39, 441 (arguing that when governments impose measures that restrain the normal business decision making of investors for the sake of narrow domestic interests, the investor should be compensated.

109 NAFTA, ch. 11, art. 1110.

110 NAFTA, art. 1110(2–6).

The expropriation provisions have been controversial. In particular, the provisions relating to indirect expropriation, and measures tantamount to expropriation, have raised doubts as to when otherwise-legitimate governmental regulation becomes compensable expropriation. Commentators have noted that these provisions utilize language that is imprecise and susceptible to expansive definitions of compensable expropriation, which may go beyond the takings and expropriations jurisprudence of the Parties and international law.[111] Other commentators have argued that these provisions follow the evolution of takings and expropriations jurisprudence, both domestically and internationally. The argument holds that these provisions are necessary only insofar as governmental regulation is egregious, discriminatory, and unjustified.[112]

The application of the expropriations provisions has also raised concerns. These provisions impose the same standards on three countries. Given the differences in the levels of development, legal traditions, and social philosophies among the NAFTA Parties, the difficulties inherent in applying common standards to a heterogeneous group is certain to raise fairness concerns.

B. SECTION B: PROCEDURAL MECHANISMS

NAFTA's Chapter 11, Section B, spells out the mechanisms available to NAFTA investors to assert their Section A substantive rights. This section adopts the traditional commercial arbitration model, which is essentially private in nature, but does not create any new procedural regimes. Rather, it permits investors from the NAFTA countries to challenge the actions of a host NAFTA country before established international arbitration institutions, rather than before national courts. The purpose of this section is to ensure that NAFTA investors have access to a dispute resolution mechanism that assures equal treatment among the NAFTA investors in accordance with the principles of international reciprocity, and due process before an impartial tribunal.[113]

There are conditions precedent to submitting a claim to arbitration. First, the claim must be founded on a loss occasioned by a breach of a NAFTA provision protecting investors.[114] Second, the investor must consent to arbitration in accordance with the procedures set out in the NAFTA, and waive its rights to litigate in any other administrative tribunal or court.[115] Moreover, the Parties must consent to the submission of a

[111] *See* J. Martin Wagner, *supra* note 60 (arguing that NAFTA's unclear definition of *expropriation* could result in a level of investor protection that goes beyond American and international compensation principles). *See also* William T. Warren, *Paying to Regulate; Guide to* Methanex v. United States *and the NAFTA Investor Rights*, 31 ENV'T. REP. 10986 (2001).

[112] *See* Jason Gudofski, *Shedding Light on Article 1110 of the NAFTA concerning Expropriations: An Environmental Case Study*, 21 N.W.J. INT'L L. & B. 243 (2000). *See also* J. Anthony Van Duzer, NAFTA Chapter 11 to Date: The Progress of a Work in Progress, *in* WHOSE RIGHTS?. THE NAFTA CHAPTER 11 DEBATE (Laura Ritchie Dawson ed., 2002).

[113] NAFTA, art. 1115.

[114] NAFTA, art. 1116–17.

[115] NAFTA, art. 1121.

claim to arbitration, in accordance with the procedures set out in the NAFTA.[116] Third, there is a temporal restriction in that the NAFTA sets a limitation period of three years in which any claim that an investor might have must be made, or it becomes time-barred. The three-year period begins to run from the time that the investor or enterprise knew, or ought to have known, of the alleged breach and subsequent loss.[117]

The disputing parties are encouraged to attempt to resolve their differences through informal methods. The parties should first attempt to settle their differences through consultation or negotiation.[118] The notion that negotiation is the preferred dispute settlement mechanism is reinforced through a mandatory cooling period. The investor is obligated to give the NAFTA host government written notice of its intention to submit a claim to arbitration at least ninety days before the claim is submitted.[119] Moreover, the arbitration claim cannot be submitted until six months have elapsed from the time that the events occurred giving rise to the claim.[120]

Once the mandatory six months and the ninety-day periods have elapsed, the investor is free to decide which arbitral institution to utilize. Chapter 11 provides three options:

1) the Convention on the Settlement of Investment Disputes between States and Nationals of Other States (ICSID)[121]
2) the ICSID Additional Facility;[122]
3) the United Nations Commission on International Trade Law (UNCITRAL)[123]

The ICSID was established in 1965 and is affiliated with the World Bank. The ICSID provides facilities for the conciliation and arbitration of investment disputes between foreign investors and host governments. Arbitrations under ICSID are normally administered through the Centre for the Settlement of International Disputes, located at the World Bank facilities in Washington.

The use of the ICSID has been limited thus far under the NAFTA. The ICSID is available only when the dispute is between a member host government and investors of a member country. When the NAFTA came into force, the United States was its only ICSID member country. As such, the ICSID became a viable option, in the NAFTA context, when Mexico or Canada joined the Convention. Canada signed the ICSID

---

116 NAFTA, art. 1122.

117 NAFTA, arts. 1116(2) and 1117(2).

118 NAFTA, art. 1118.

119 NAFTA, art. 1119.

120 NAFTA, art. 1120(1).

121 ICSID, *supra* note 27. *See generally* Jan Paulson & Georgeos Petrochilos, *Revision of the UNCITRAL Arbitration Rules*, http://www.uncitral.org/pdf/english/news/arbrules_report.pdf.

122 ICSID Additional Facility Rules are available at the World Bank Web site, http:www.worldbank.org/icsid/basic-doc-archive/9.htm.

123 UNCITRAL Arbitration Rules, GA Res.31/98, U.N. UNCITRAL, 99th Plen. Mtg. (Dec.15, 1996) (UNCITRAL Rules), http://www.uncitral.org/pdf/english/texts/arbitrationarb-rules/.pdf.

Convention in the latter part of 2006 and, at this juncture, Mexico remains the only NAFTA country not to sign the ICSID Convention.[124]

The ICSID Additional Facility was established in 1978 as a means to facilitate access to the ICSID dispute resolution system. The ICSID Additional Facility regime has distinct rules from the ICSID, which accommodate disputes where only one of the parties, whether it is the host government or investors from a member country, is a disputant. Given that, until recently, the United States was the only NAFTA country that was a signatory to the ICSID, this regime was only available when the United States, either as the host government or as the investor's government, was involved in the dispute.

The UNCITRAL was established in 1966 as a mechanism to harmonize and unify international trade law. Its principal manner of operation is to establish working groups for specific projects.[125] UNCITRAL's Arbitration Rules were created to assist parties involved in arbitrations by providing a more unified approach to the basic steps in an arbitration. The Rules aim to establish a procedural framework that, if properly carried out, would ensure general international acceptance of the arbitration results.[126] These rules have been adopted, with minor changes, by many international agreements, arbitral institutions, and private parties.[127] Given that the UNCITRAL Rules do not require that the parties be members to any convention as a precondition of their use, the Rules remain completely available for use in the Chapter 11 context.

Chapter 11 permits access to these three arbitral regimes, but then goes on to supplement and modify them.[128] It sets out that a Panel, established under this section, shall decide the issues in dispute in accordance with the NAFTA and the applicable rules of international law.[129] The effect of this modification is to ensure that NAFTA law or international law preempts domestic law.

Chapter 11 also addresses the issues relating to arbitrators. It sets the number of arbitrators at three, unless the parties agree otherwise.[130] It calls for each party to select one arbitrator; the third, who will act as the presiding arbitrator, is selected by agreement of the parties.[131] Notably, the three arbitral regimes do not require that the arbitrators be nationals of the disputing parties, and the NAFTA does not attempt to alter this situation.[132] As such, the possibility exists that all three Chapter 11 arbitrators could be nationals from non-NAFTA countries.

---

[124] Canada signed the ICSID Convention on Dec. 15, 2006.

[125] *See, e.g.*, Report of the Working Group on Arbitration and Conciliation on the work of its forty-second session (New York, Jan. 10–14, 2005), A/CN.9/573, *available at* http://uncitral.org.

[126] Alan Redfern & Martin Hunter, Law and Practice of International Commercial Arbitration 479–80 (2d ed. 1991).

[127] Amanda Debusk, *Investor Dispute Resolution under the NAFTA, in* Nuevos Horizontes 231 (Nick Ranieri ed., 1997).

[128] NAFTA, art. 1120(2).

[129] NAFTA, art. 1131(1).

[130] NAFTA, art. 1123.

[131] *Id.*

[132] *See* Debusk, *supra* note 127.

The NAFTA engrafts the powers of the FTC onto the applicable rules. Chapter 11 ensures that an interpretation of a NAFTA provision by the FTC, established under Article 2001, shall be binding on a tribunal.[133] As the FTC consists of cabinet-level representatives of the NAFTA countries, or their designees, the Parties will be able to exert some control over the process.[134]

The FTC's influence is undeniable. Questions pertaining to the interpretation of indirect expropriation and measures tantamount to expropriation, as well as to the interpretation of the Annexes, could be sent to the FTC for interpretation. For example, questions pertaining to the scope of exceptions or reservations set out in Annex I–IV could be sent by the tribunal, on request of the disputing Party, to the FTC for interpretation.[135] If the FTC agrees on an interpretation of the relevant Annex, it is binding on the tribunal.[136] If the FTC cannot agree on an interpretation within sixty days, the Tribunal shall decide the issue.[137]

The NAFTA further supplements the arbitral regimes by calling for enhanced transparency. Although the NAFTA is, for the most part, silent on the conduct and procedures of the hearings, it does modify the otherwise applicable rules and allows for the Party or the investor to make public an award. This provision overrides the barriers to publication of awards found in the UNCITRAL regime in the case of Canada and the United States. In the case where Canada or the United States is the disputing Party, either the government or the disputing investor may make the award public. In the case where Mexico is the disputing Party, the rules of the arbitral regime control publication.[138]

Chapter 11 specifically reaffirms the power of the panels to call for expert reports and provides for interim measures of protection. The Panel can, at the request of a disputing party or sua sponte, appoint experts to report to it on any factual issue, including environmental or other scientific matters.[139] Subject to certain exceptions, the tribunal may order interim measures of protection. Such measures are intended to preserve the rights of a disputing party, or to ensure that the tribunal's jurisdiction is made fully effective.[140]

Chapter 11 goes on to limit the types of awards that the tribunal may deliver. It permits the tribunal to award, separately or in combination, only monetary damages and interest or restitution. The tribunal may also award costs in accordance with the applicable arbitral rules.[141] However, the disputing Party may pay monetary damages in

133 NAFTA, art. 1131(2).
134 NAFTA, art. 2001(1).
135 NAFTA, art. 1132(1).
136 NAFTA, art. 1132(2).
137 *Id.*
138 NAFTA, art. 1137(4) *and* annex 1137.4.
139 NAFTA, art. 1133.
140 NAFTA, art. 1134.
141 NAFTA, art. 1135(1).

place of complying with a restitution order.[142] A NAFTA country shall not be required to change its laws or pay punitive damages.[143]

The NAFTA provides that, unless the disputing parties agree otherwise, the arbitration shall be held in a country that is signatory to the New York Convention.[144] The New York Convention is a United Nations Convention, signed by over a hundred countries, including Mexico, the United States, and Canada. These countries pledge to recognize and enforce, with limited exceptions and reservations, foreign arbitral awards in their jurisdictions as they would enforce their own domestic judgments. The effect of this provision is to facilitate the enforcement of awards once they are made.

The winning party is precluded from seeking the enforcement of a final award until the required amount of time has elapsed. In the case of a final award under ICSID, a winning party may not seek to enforce the award until 120 days have passed from the date the award was issued, and then only when a revision or an annulment of the award has not been requested, or when revision or annulment proceedings have been completed.[145] In the case of a final award under the ICSID Additional Facility or the UNCITRAL, the winning party is precluded from seeking to enforce the award until three months have passed from the date the award was rendered, and then only when the disputing parties have not commenced proceedings to revise, set aside, or annul the award, or a court has dismissed an application to revise, set aside, or annul the award and there is no further appeal.[146]

In terms of enforcement, Chapter 11 sets out three avenues for compliance. First, it calls for each Party to provide for the enforcement of an award in its territory.[147] Second, it provides that where a disputing Party fails to abide by or comply with a final award, the FTC may, on request of a Party, establish a Panel under Article 2008, which will determine whether the failure to comply or abide by the award is inconsistent with the disputing Party's obligations under the NAFTA and recommend compliance.[148] Third, the winning investor may seek enforcement of the award under the ICSID, the New York Convention, or the Inter-American Convention.[149] The award shall have binding force only as between the disputing parties in the particular case.[150] Subject to certain guidelines, a disputing Party shall abide by and comply with an award without delay.[151]

Although the arbitral regimes are similar, they carry noteworthy differences. The arbitral rules of each regime govern the arbitral proceedings. All three regimes provide

142 NAFTA, art. 1135(1)(b).
143 NAFTA, art. 1135(3).
144 NAFTA, art. 1130.
145 NAFTA, art. 1136(3)(a).
146 NAFTA, art. 1136(3)(b).
147 NAFTA, art. 1136(4).
148 NAFTA, art. 1136(5).
149 NAFTA, art. 1136(6).
150 NAFTA, art. 1136(1).
151 NAFTA, art. 1136(2).

ample discretion to the arbitrators in how they run the arbitral proceedings. The rules provide that arbitral tribunals may conduct the proceedings in the manner they deem appropriate.

The ICSID Additional Facility rules, like the UNCITRAL rules, provide that arbitral tribunals may conduct the proceedings in accordance with their procedural orders. Unlike the UNCITRAL rules, the ICSID Additional Facility rules provide that the tribunal is required to apply the agreement of the parties on procedural matters. Moreover, the UNCITRAL rules provide that the hearings shall be confidential unless the parties agree otherwise.

Interestingly, under the three arbitral regimes, awards are decided by a majority of votes.

The problem that may present itself, at least in the context of UNCITRAL arbitrations, is that although two arbitrators may agree on who the winning party is, they may not agree among themselves as to the quantum. In effect, the arbitrators would have three different decisions and a clear majority, with reference to the quantum of the award, would not result.

Although Chapter 11 places a distinctly NAFTA mark on these arbitral regimes, it falls short of adequately addressing all the areas of concern. These shortcomings have served to compound the legitimacy concerns occasioned by Chapter 11's substantive obligations. As Chapter 11 evolves, it will need to continually reassess itself in light of new developments.

Environmental and Labor Side Agreements

The most comprehensive treatment of the environment in the NAFTA is found in the side agreement, known as the North American Agreement on Environmental Cooperation (NAAEC).[152] The NAAEC deserves credit for breaking new ground in bringing together the trade and environmental communities under the auspices of a FTA.[153] It is also noteworthy for permitting some limited form of private party participation in the NAFTA's ADR processes.

The NAAEC created a Commission for Environmental Cooperation (CEC) with a broad mandate to address environmental concerns in the NAFTA region. A Party who believes that another Party has engaged in a persistent failure to effectively enforce its environmental law may invoke the dispute resolution process. The process is initiated by requesting consultation with the other Party. If negotiations fail, a Party may ask the Council to intervene in resolving the problem.[154] If the Council cannot resolve the

---

152 Ca.-Mex.-U.S., 32 I.L.M. 1480 (1993) (NAAEC). *See generally* Pierre Marc Johnson & Andre Beaulieu, The Environment and NAFTA: Understanding and Implementing the New Continental Law (1996).

153 *See* Daniel Magraw, *NAFTA and the Environment: Substance and Process*, SB79ALI-ABA-117 (1997) (discussing the essential elements of the "NAFTA Package" and the process that led up to it).

154 NAAEC, arts. 22, 23.

problem, it may, by a two-thirds vote, establish an arbitral panel to consider the arguments of the Parties and issue a report.[155]

The process is straightforward. If the Parties cannot reach agreement after reviewing the report, or if one Party believes that the other Party is not satisfactorily implementing the report, the Panel may be asked to impose an action plan, in addition to imposing fines on the recalcitrant Party. If the recalcitrant Party continues, then the other Party may suspend the NAFTA benefits in the cases where the recalcitrant Party is Mexico or the United States. In the case of Canada, the arbitral award may be enforced directly in a Canadian Court.[156]

It might be fairly argued that the NAAEC resembles more of an afterthought than a well-designed environmental code.[157] The NAAEC does not establish a rational mechanism for dealing with more waste, the necessary by-product of more production. It does not require any particular level of environmental quality. Nor does it follow regional and global trends toward the harmonization of environmental standards.[158]

The NAAEC does not provide an effective mechanism for private party ventilation of environmental disputes.[159] Commentators have noted the process is replete with hurdles that might impede public participation.[160] This mechanism is, arguably, Party-driven and susceptible to political negotiation. As well, it has been noted that the enforcement provisions are not as strong as they could have been, and certainly not as strong as the enforcement provisions in other NAFTA sections.[161]

---

155 NAAEC, arts. 24(1), 31, 32.

156 NAAEC, arts 33, 34, 36, and annex 36.

157 It was negotiated by the Clinton administration as a parallel agreement to the main NAFTA text, which was negotiated by the Bush administration. *See* Michael J. Kelly, *Bringing a Complaint under the NAFTA Environmental Side Accord: Difficult Steps under a Procedural Paper Tiger, but Movement in the Right Direction*, 24 PEPP. L. REV. 71, 72–75 (1996). *See also* Kal Raustiala, *The Political Implications of the Enforcement Provisions of the NAFTA Environmental Side Agreement: The CEC as a Model for Future Accords*, 25 ENVT'L L. REP. 31 (1995).

158 It has been suggested that the NAFTA and the Environmental Side Agreement maintain diverging national environmental standards between the countries, thereby repudiating the trend of new regional agreements to harmonize environmental standards. *See* Jeffery Atik, *Environmental Standards within NAFTA: Difference by Design and the Retreat from Harmonization*, 3 IND. J. GLOBAL LEGAL STUD. 81 (1995).

159 *See* Aimee L. Weiss, *An Analysis of the North American Agreement on Environmental Cooperation*, 5 ISA J. INT'L & COMP. L. 185 (1998) (advocating the clarification of vague provisions, providing private parties with a forum to seek damages, and limiting the Council's unfettered powers).

160 *See* Kelly, *supra* note 157 (arguing that although the NAFTA Environmental Side Agreement is a step in the right direction, the political limitations on the complaint process would likely frustrate an NGO complainant who does not have the support of the member government and that the extensive discretion given to the Secretariat, in the context of an inadequate petition process, poses many hurdles for citizen involvement. For a contrary view suggesting optimism, *see* David G. Schiller, *Great Expectations: The North American Commission on Environmental Cooperation Review of the Cozumel Pier Submission*, 28 U. MIAMI INTER-AM. L. REV. 437 (1997).

161 It has been argued that there is a disparity between the strong enforcement mechanisms provided in NAFTA's investment law provisions and the weak enforcement mechanisms provided in the environmental law provisions. *See* Paul Stanton Kibel, *Awkward Evolution: Citizen Enforcement at the North American Environmental Commission*, 32 ENVTL. L. REP. 10769 (2002).

The North American Agreement on Labor Cooperation (NAALC)[162], also known as the labor side agreement, is similarly more of an afterthought than a well-designed code to deal with its subject matter. It is essentially a product of competing business and labor interests. Supporters of the NAALC argue that its true progress is measured in human terms, and not abstract economic indicators.[163] Its detractors have argued that it is an ineffective mechanism designed to appease politically sensitive sectors.[164]

The NAALC is premised on the mutual review of labor matters and labor law in defined areas. The NAALC permits each Party to establish its own labor standards, without setting benchmarks or insisting on harmonization.[165] The NAALC neither creates a new labor enforcement agency nor does it set up a supranational body to adjudicate the merits of complaints lodged against NAFTA employers.[166]

The Parties have established the Commission for Labor Cooperation, which is comprised of a Ministerial Council and Secretariat. The Commission is assisted by the National Administration Office (NAO) of each Party. Each country has set up its own domestic procedures for reviewing complaints.[167]

The NAALC balances a trade and labor perspective in a novel experiment. The core obligation assumed by the NAFTA Parties is the effective enforcement of each Party's own labor laws. Such enforcement is contemplated to occur in a consensual environment where investigation and consultation are the favored means of resolution. It is only in very limited circumstances that a private party may effectively enforce its rights, and then only with its government's support. This preserves sovereignty while creating mutual obligations that combine cooperation and consultation with contentious review, evaluation, and dispute resolution.[168]

The NAO may recommend ministerial consultation with respect to the eleven labor law principles established in the NAALC.[169] Following consultations in any matter, except one arising from the freedom to associate and right to organize, right to bargain collectively, or right to strike, any Party may request the formation of an independent Evaluation Committee (ECE). The formation of an ECE does not require a complaint to have been filed: it can be set up pursuant to a request of any of the Secretaries or Minister of Labor. However, once the request is made, the requesting Party opens up

162 NAALC, 32 I.L.M. 1499 (NAALC).

163 Robert F. Houseman, *The Treatment of Labor and Environmental Issues in Future Western Hemisphere Trade Liberalization Efforts*, 10 CONN. J. INT'L L. 301, 335 (1995).

164 *See* John P. Isa, *Testing the NAALC's Dispute Resolution System: A Case Study*, 7 AM. U.J. GENDER SOC. POL'Y & L. 179 (1999).

165 NAALC, art. 2.

166 NAALC, art. 42.

167 NAALC, Part Three: Commission for Labor Cooperation.

168 Lance Compa, NAFTA'S LABOR SIDE ACCORD: A THREE-YEAR ACCOUNTING, 3-SUM NAFTA: L. & REV. AM. 6, 22 (1997).

169 They include: freedom to associate and organize, right to bargain collectively, right to strike, prohibition of forced labor, labor protection for the young, minimum employment standards, elimination of employment discrimination, equal pay, prevention of occupational injury and illness, compensation for occupational injury and illness, and protection of migrant workers. *See*, NAALC, annex 1.

its own record of enforcement in the area to scrutiny by the ECE on the basis of technical labor standards.[170] Subsequent to the ECE Report, if a Party believes that another country is in a persistent pattern of failure to effectively enforce its occupational safety and health, child labor, or minimum wage technical standards, it may request the establishment of an independent arbitral tribunal.[171]

As the dispute escalates up through the different stages, the review process is narrowed and public participation is further limited. The initial review by the NAO and ministerial consultations constitute the widest mandate of the process. The review and consultations deal with a wide-ranging area of discussion on any matter. Additionally, failure to enforce domestic law is not a precondition for NAO review.[172] The NAO review also does not contain any standing requirement to file a complaint. Therefore, any citizen or organization of any country, alone or in alliance, may file the complaint. Although the NAO need not review the complaint, it must supply written reasons for not doing so.[173]

Subsequent to the NAO review, the process is further narrowed and government-driven. Only the NAO may recommend ministerial consultations, and only a Minister or Secretary may accept the recommendation and request consultations. Moreover, only a Minister or Secretary may initiate the formation of an ECE, whereas two of them must agree to initiate an arbitral panel.[174] As well, two new elements are imposed on the complaint to bring it within the jurisdiction of the ECE. First, the matter must be trade-related, and second, the matter must be covered by "mutually recognized labor laws."

As the matter moves into arbitration, the scope for review is again further constrained. At the arbitral stage, the tribunal is limited to looking at only "alleged persistent pattern of failure to effectively enforce occupational safety and health, child labor or minimum wage technical standards." At this juncture, only three labor principles are susceptible to dispute resolution. Moreover, they must be shown to be the subject of a persistent pattern of failure to effectively enforce labor standards.[175]

The whole process is not meant to be adversarial, punish governments, or give citizens a platform to assert their interests. The decision to accept the complaint in discretionary and subject to a two-thirds council vote. The Parties are given multiple opportunities throughout the process to consult, and the Panels are required to grant the Parties broad discretion. The Panel may not find against a country if the action or inaction in question results from the reasonable exercise of official discretion, or a bona fide decision to allocate resources to enforcement in respect of other labor matters determined to have higher priorities. After the final decision is issued, the panel may reconsider its findings in light of any written responses received from the

---

170 NAALC, arts. 22–23.

171 NAALC, art. 27.

172 *See* Compa, *supra* note 168, at 10–11.

173 *Id.* at 12–14

174 *Id.* at 10–11.

175 *Id.* at 12.

disputing Parties. Lobbying skills and political pressure are essential for private parties to push their complaints forward through the process.[176]

Enforcement initially falls on the disputing Parties to come up with a remedying action plan. The Panel will step in only if the Parties cannot agree.[177] If this action plan is not implemented, the Arbitral Panel may fine the offending Party. These fines are to be used to improve labor enforcement in the offending country. If the fines are not paid, trade sanctions may be applied.[178]

The NAALC opens the door to a limited form of enhanced private party participation. However, it falls short of providing private parties with an effective mechanism to enforce their rights and play a direct and meaningful role in the evolution of labor standards. The dispute resolution process has been called "complex, confusing and elaborate."[179] The NAALC dispute resolution process is potentially subject to abuse because it does not provide guidelines or timetables to regulate cooperative activities. It may take upwards of 1225 days from the date of the decision to accept a complaint for sanctions to be issued for noncompliance.

This process is further compromised through Party autonomy. The Parties can avoid accountability through several listed exceptions, and there is broad discretion at all stages, from the accepting of a complaint to deciding whether the Parties followed a persistent pattern on nonenforcement. In addition, because only governments, and not private parties, can advance the process, it is subject to political negotiation. Furthermore, a loophole to avoid enforcement is found in the provisions stipulating that a Party is not deemed to have failed to comply if the governmental inaction is the result of "discretion or *bona-fides*."[180]

CONCLUSIONS

Where once the NAFTA was hailed as the blueprint for further economic integration, recent history suggests that it might have been the high-water mark of the neoliberal approach to negotiating international economic agreements. More recent agreements suggest that governments may now be more cautious with respect to ceding sovereignty in such agreements, and that civil society groups are more active with respect to ensuring that their concerns are acknowledged by such agreements.

Notwithstanding the criticisms leveled at the NAFTA in general, and its ADR mechanisms in particular, these mechanisms continue to be important milestones and instructive benchmarks. NAFTA's ADR mechanisms were breakthrough mechanisms, which facilitated the conclusion of an important international economic agreement

176 *Id.* at 11.

177 Betty Southard Murphy, *NAFTA'S North American Agreement on Labor Cooperation:The Present and the Future*, 10 CONN. J. INT'L. L. 403, 410–15 (1995).

178 NAALC, arts. 38–41.

179 Isa, *supra* note 164, at 211.

180 *Id.* at 194–213 (discussing the NAALC's Article 40).

when the political will to negotiate substantive positions was lacking. Given the documented experiences of these mechanisms, new international economic agreements continue to routinely be analyzed in reference to the NAFTA.

The relevant question is not whether the NAFTA is a harbinger for future agreements or a failed relic of the twentieth century. The more appropriate question is: how can the NAFTA's ADR mechanisms be recalibrated to facilitate the evolution of international economic agreements?

6

THE LEGAL FRAMEWORK FOR FOREIGN INVESTMENTS IN THE EU: THE EU INTERNAL MARKET FREEDOMS, THE DESTINY OF MEMBER STATES' BITS, AND FUTURE EUROPEAN AGREEMENTS ON PROTECTION OF FOREIGN INVESTMENTS

Anna De Luca

Introduction

The present chapter will provide an overview of the legal framework for foreign investments in the European Union and its Member States. Section A will first focus on the EU internal market freedoms, more specifically the right of establishment, right to provide services within the EU, free circulation of capital, and their aim and scope of application, as elaborated in EU case law.[1] The aforementioned EU internal market freedoms concern the exercise of economic activities within the EU. The EU internal market freedoms grant and protect the exercise of economic activities in cross-border situations just in respect to nationals of Member States (Section B.1 of this chapter), with the exception of free movement of capital, which applies also to movements of capital between Member States and third countries, as outlined in Section B.3. Nevertheless, the right of establishment and right to provide services also apply to foreign investors when they operate their investments in the EU through a company

[1] This chapter will not deal with the free circulation of workers within the EU (Articles 45–48 TFEU) because this internal market freedom concerns the exercise of employed economic activities and regards natural persons holding the nationality of Member States.

vehicle incorporated in a Member State (Section B.2). Because foreign investors can benefit from the internal market freedoms, conditions and limits of applicability of EU law to foreign investors are considered in Section B.2.1 (with reference to the right of establishment and right to provide services) and Section B.3.1 (with reference to free circulation of capital). The conclusion that it is likely that the EU, which has pursued an open door policy toward foreign investment until now, will adopt sectoral harmonized rules limiting the access of foreign investors to the EU market (possibly incorporating a principle of reciprocity) in the future is drawn in Section B.4. Section C will deal with the destiny of BITs between Member States and third countries in the light of the text of the Regulation establishing a transitional regime for bilateral investment agreements between Member States and third countries, recently agreed on between the Council and the European Parliament. Section D will deal with the level of protection that EU stakeholders are envisaging for EU national investors abroad and foreign investors in the EU and its Member States under future European agreements, considering that the EU Commission is currently negotiating Chapters on investment protection to be included in the EU free trade agreements with Canada, India, and Singapore. Some observations on the current discussion on the content and scope of EU investment policy will conclude this chapter.

A. The EU Market Freedoms: Their Aim and Scope of Application

The EU rules on the right of establishment (Articles 49–55 TFEU) and freedom to provide services within the EU (Articles 56–62 TFEU) concern the exercise of economic activities, irrespective of the sector in which they are carried out, and cover industrial activities, commercial activities, activities of craftsmen, and activities of professions as listed in Article 57 TFEU, as well as any self-employed activity performed against remuneration as clarified by the CJEU's case law.[2] The right of establishment entails the right of nationals of a Member State to carry out their economic activities on a stable and permanent basis in another Member State.[3] Under the Treaty EU nationals (both natural persons holding the nationality of a Member State and EU companies as defined in Article 54 TFEU) are entitled to exercise two forms of establishment in

[2] In this respect, see Case C-268/99, Jany and others v. Staatssecretaris van Justitie, 2001 E.C.R. I-8615, at 32–50, where the CJEU held that prostitution can be regarded as a self-employed activity for the purpose of the treaty; in the same direction Case-327/02, Panayotova and others, 2004 E.C.R. I-11055. With regard to the broad concept of economic activity adopted by the CJEU for the purpose of the Treaty, see also Case 196/87, Steymann v. Staatssecretaris van Justitie, 1988 *E.C.R.* 6159; Case C-456/02, Trojani v. CPAS, 2004 E.C.R. 1-7573.

[3] Case C-55/94, Gebhard v. Consiglio dell'Ordine degli Avvocati e Procuratori di Milano, 1995 E.C.R. I-4165, at 25, stating that "[T]he concept of establishment within the meaning of the Treaty is therefore a very broad one, allowing a Community national to participate, on a stable and continuous basis, in the economic life of a Member State other than his/her State of origin and to profit therefrom, so contributing to economic and social interpenetration within the Community in the sphere of activities as self-employed persons (see, to this effect, Case 2/74 Reyners v. Belgium [1974] ECR 631, paragraph 21)."

the territory of a Member State different from the Member State of origin. Article 49 TFEU grants nationals of a Member State "the right to take up and pursue activities as self-employed persons and to set up and manage undertakings, in particular companies or firms within the meaning of the second paragraph of Article 54" (primary establishment), and the right to set up and manage agencies, branches, and subsidiaries in the territory of another Member State (secondary establishment).[4] The freedom to provide services covers the right of nationals of Member States, who are established in a given Member State, to carry out their economic activities in another Member State on a temporary basis. The Treaty Chapters on establishment and services prohibit any restrictions on EU nationals' right of establishment and right to provide services within the EU.

As one can infer from EU case law and EU secondary legislations the above-mentioned internal market freedoms as well as the free circulation of capital, which will be analyzed in Section C, have a twofold purpose. They are aimed at granting to economic operators from a Member State nondiscriminatory conditions of operation within the other Member States and more effective access to the market of the other Member States, with the view to strengthening European integration and promoting legislative and regulatory approximation and harmonization within the EU.[5]

As is well known, Member States' measures that are discriminatory in fact or in law, directly or indirectly, against EU nationals are considered by the CJEU as restrictions under EU law because they have the actual effects of preventing EU nationals from the exercise of internal market freedoms. This is an application of the so-called nondiscrimination test based on nationality. Because EU law goes beyond the elimination of all discrimination on the grounds of nationality, by applying the so-called non-hindrance test the Court has also considered Member States' regulatory measures that apply without distinction as restrictions when they have the (potential)

---

[4] Article 49 TFEU provides that "Within the framework of the provisions set out below, restrictions on the freedom of establishment of nationals of a Member State in the territory of another Member State shall be prohibited. Such prohibition shall also apply to restrictions on the setting-up of agencies, branches or subsidiaries by nationals of any Member State established in the territory of any Member State.

Freedom of establishment shall include the right to take up and pursue activities as self-employed persons and to set up and manage undertakings, in particular companies or firms within the meaning of the second paragraph of Article 54, under the conditions laid down for its own nationals by the law of the country where such establishment is effected, subject to the provisions of the Chapter relating to capital."

[5] In this respect, see Directive 2006/123/EC of the European Parliament and of the Council (Dec. 12, 2006), On services in the internal market, OJ L 376 (Dec. 27, 2006), at 36–68. The Directive established a legal framework aimed at eliminating the obstacles to the freedom of establishment and right to provide services for economic operators of Member States. The legal framework set out in the Directive "is based on a dynamic and selective approach consisting in the removal, as a matter of priority, of barriers which may be dismantled quickly and, for the others, the launching of a process of evaluation, consultation and complementary harmonisation of specific issues, which will make possible the progressive and coordinated modernisation of national regulatory systems for service activities…" (Preamble of the Directive, seventh sentence).

effect of hindering EU nationals from exercising internal market freedoms.[6] The case *Caixa-Bank France v Ministère de l'Économie, des Finances et de l'Industrie* is worthy of mention as an example.[7] In this case the Court clarifies the scope of application to be given to the right of (secondary) establishment[8] as well as the purpose of the non-hindrance test in connection therewith. In evaluating the compatibility of a French law applicable without distinction (i.e., a law preventing banks from paying interest on sight accounts) with the right of secondary establishment the Court states as follows: "A prohibition on the remuneration of sight accounts such as that laid down by the French legislation constitutes, for companies from Member States other than the French Republic, a serious obstacle to the pursuit of their activities via a subsidiary in the latter Member State, affecting their access to the market. That prohibition is therefore to be regarded as a restriction within the meaning of Article 43 EC. That prohibition hinders credit institutions which are subsidiaries of foreign companies in raising capital from the public, by depriving them of the possibility of competing more effectively, by paying remuneration on sight accounts, with the credit institutions traditionally established in the Member State of establishment, which have an extensive network of branches and therefore greater opportunities than those subsidiaries for raising capital from the public. Where credit institutions which are subsidiaries of foreign companies seek to enter the market of a Member State, competing by means of the rate of remuneration paid on sight accounts constitutes one of the most effective methods to that end. Access to the market by those establishments is thus made more difficult by such a prohibition."[9]

The so-called non-hindrance test, as above characterized, has been developed by the CJEU with the aims of achieving a more effective market integration within the EU, and has been applied in respect to all the freedoms in the internal market.[10]

---

[6] The CJEU initially developed and applied the non-hindrance test in respect to the free circulation of services and then extended its scope of application to the other internal market freedoms; see the case law *infra* note 10.

[7] Case C-442/02, Caixa-Bank France v Ministère de l'Économie, des Finances et de l'Industrie, 2004 E.C.R. I-8961.

[8] *Id.* at 11 stating that "Art. 43 EC requires the elimination of restrictions on the freedom of establishment. All measures which prohibit, impede or render less attractive the exercise of that freedom must be regarded as such restrictions (see, inter alia, Case C-55/94 Gebhard [1995] ECR I-4165, paragraph 37, Case C-108/96 Mac Quen and Others [2001] ECR I-837, paragraph 26, and Case C-79/01 Payroll and Others [2002] ECR I-8923, paragraph 26)."

[9] *Id.* at 12—14.

[10] As to the freedom to provide services see, *inter alia*, Case C-205/99, Asociación Profesional de Empresas Navieras de Líneas Regulares (Analir) and Others v. Administración General del Estado, 2001 E.C.R. I-1271, at 21, stating that "It is settled case-law that freedom to provide services requires not only the elimination of all discrimination on grounds of nationality against providers of services who are established in another Member State, but also the abolition of any restriction, even if it applies without distinction to national providers of services and to those of other Member States, which is liable to prohibit, impede or render less attractive the activities of a provider of services established in another Member State where he lawfully provides similar services (see, in particular, Case C-76/90 Säger [1991] ECR I-4221, paragraph 12; Case C-43/93 Vander Elst [1994] ECR I-3803, paragraph 14; Case C-272/94 Guiot [1996] ECR I-1905, paragraph 10; Case C-266/96 Corsica Ferries France [1998] ECR I-3949, paragraph 56;

1. THE SO-CALLED NON-HINDRANCE TEST AND THE (NON)COMPATIBILITY OF MEMBER STATES' MEASURES OF GENERAL APPLICATION WITH THE INTERNAL MARKET FREEDOMS

The application of the non-hindrance test in connection with the EU internal market freedoms affects Member States' competence to adopt legislative measures of general application as concerns the subjects affected. In this respect, the principle of the neutrality of the Treaty as regards Member States' systems of property ownership, enshrined

and Joined Cases C-369/96 and C-376/96 Arblade and Others [1999] ECR I-8453, paragraph 33)." As to free movement of capital, see Case C-367/98, Commission of the European Communities v. Portuguese Republic, 2002 E.C.R. I-4731, at 44 stating that the prohibition of restrictions on free movement of capital "goes beyond the mere elimination of unequal treatment, on grounds of nationality, as between operators on the financial markets," and at 45. It is the position of the Court that a state measure that applies without distinction but is liable to deter, limit, or discourage operators from other Member States from investing or making investments in undertakings of the Member State whose measure is at stake or is liable to make less attractive investments in such undertakings is to be considered as a restriction on free circulation of capital. In this respect, Case C-543/08 European Commission v. Portuguese Republic (Judgment of Nov. 11, 2010), 2010 E.C.R. I-0000, at 47 where, with regards to both direct and portfolio investments, the Court states that "national measures must be regarded as 'restrictions' within the meaning of Art. 56(1) EC if they are liable to prevent or limit the acquisition of shares in the undertakings concerned or to deter investors of other Member States from investing in their capital." *See also* Case C-483/99, Commission of the European Communities v. Republic of France, 2002 E.C.R. I-4781, at 40; Case C-463/00, Commission of the European Communities v. Kingdom of Spain, 2003 E.C.R. I-4581, at 61 and 62; Case C-98/01, Commission of the European Communities v. United Kingdom, 2003 E.C.R. I-4641, at 47 and 49; Case C-174/04, Commission of the European Communities v. Italian Republic, 2005 E.C.R. I-4933, at 30 and 31; Joined Cases C-282/04 and C-283/04, Commission of the European Communities v. Kingdom of the Netherlands, 2006 E.C.R. I-9141, at 20; Case C-112/05, Commission of the European Communities v. Federal Republic of Germany, 2007 E.C.R. I-8995, at 19; and Case C-171/08, European Commission v. Portuguese Republic, 2010 E.C.R. I-0000, at 50, 54, and 56–57. The Court held that "although the relevant restrictions on investment operations apply without distinction to both residents and non-residents, it must nonetheless be held that they affect the position of a person acquiring a shareholding as such and are thus liable to deter investors from other Member States from making such investments and, consequently, affect access to the market." (Case C-463/00, Commission of the European Communities v. Kingdom of Spain, cit., at 61 referring to Case C-98/01, Commission of the European Communities v. United Kingdom, cit., at 47). As to the right of establishment (besides Case C-442/02, Caixa-Bank France v Ministère de l'Économie, des Finances et de l'Industrie, and references therein, *supra* note 7) see, *inter alia*, Joined Cases C-171/07 and C-172/07, Apothekerkammer des Saarlandes and others v. Saarland, Ministerium für Justiz, Gesundheit und Soziales, 2009 E.C.R. I-4171, at 22: ("According to settled case-law, Art. 43 EC precludes any national measure which, even though it is applicable without discrimination on grounds of nationality, is liable to hinder or render less attractive the exercise by Community nationals of the freedom of establishment that is guaranteed by the Treaty (see, in particular, Case C-19/92 Kraus [1993] ECR I-1663, paragraph 32, and Case C-299/02 Commission v. Netherlands [2004] ECR I-9761, paragraph 15"). In legal literature see MASSIMO CONDINANZI, ALESSANDRA LANG, & BRUNO NASCIMBENE, CITIZENSHIP OF THE UNION AND FREEDOM OF MOVEMENT OF PERSONS 130–31 (2008), with reference to the application of the non-hindrance approach in the ambit of the right of establishment (also observing that the approach "has not yet been sufficiently confirmed" in respect of the right of establishment); STEFFEN HINDELANG, THE FREE MOVEMENT OF CAPITAL AND FOREIGN DIRECT INVESTMENT 119 ff. (2009), with reference to the application of the approach in the ambit of free movement of capital.

in Article 345 TFEU (ex–Article 295 TEC),[11] cannot have the effect of shielding such national measures from the application of the fundamental freedoms. It is the Court's view that "[t]hat article does not have the effect of exempting the Member States' systems of property ownership from the fundamental rules of the Treaty."[12] This notwithstanding, the minimum supply of energy resources and goods essential to the public as a whole, the continuity of public service, national defense, the protection of public policy, and public security and health emergencies, act as legitimate interests capable of justifying national restrictions on the fundamental freedoms of the EU market, provided that the general principle of proportionality is respected.[13] As an example, with regard to undertakings operating in the oil, telecommunications, and electricity industries, in the CJEU's view "the object of ensuring a secure supply of such services in the case of a crisis in the territory of the Member State concerned may constitute a reason of public security and, therefore, justify a restriction of a fundamental freedom."[14] Moreover, it is well established under CJEU case law that derogations from internal market freedoms must be interpreted strictly.[15]

The non-hindrance test is seen by the Court as an instrument to grant to economic operators from a Member State more effective access to the market of the other Member States, and its application gives such an overreaching scope of application to the EU freedoms (particularly freedoms of establishment and circulation of capital) so as to "capture" practically any Member State's domestic regulatory measure.

For this reason, the non-hindrance test has been the object of criticism even in the limited context of intra-Community investments and cross-border economic activities within the EU.[16]

---

[11] Art. 345 TFEU (ex–Art. 295 TEC) provides that: "[t]he Treaties shall in no way prejudice the rules in Member States governing the system of property ownership."

[12] Case C-463/00, Commission of the European Communities v. Kingdom of Spain, *supra* note 10, at 67; Case C-367/98, Commission of the European Communities v. Portuguese Republic, *supra* note 10, at 48; Case C-483/99, Commission of the European Communities v. Republic of France, *supra* note 10, at 44, and Case C-503/99 Commission of the European Communities v. Kingdom of Belgium, 2002 E.C.R. I-4809, at 44.

[13] In this respect see Case C-326/07, Commission of the European Communities v. Italian Republic 2009 E.C.R. I-2291, at 45 ("The pursuit of such interests may, subject to observance of the principle of proportionality, warrant certain restrictions of the exercise of fundamental freedoms (see, *inter alia*, judgment of February 2008 in Case C-274/06 Commission v. Spain, paragraph 38)."

[14] *See* Case C-326/07, Commission of the European Communities v. Italian Republic, *supra* note 13, at 69, with reference to Case C-274/06, Commission of the European Communities v. Kingdom of Spain, 2008 E.C.R. I-26, at 71.

[15] As to derogations from free circulation of capital see Case C-543/08, European Commission v. Portuguese Republic, *supra* note 10, at 85 referring to Case C-54/99, Association Eglise de scientologie de Paris and Scientology International Reserves Trust v. The Prime Minister, 2000 E.C.R. I-1335, at 17, and Case C-171/08, European Commission v. Portuguese Republic, *supra* note 10, at 73, where the Court states that: "requirements of public security must, in particular as a derogation from the fundamental principle of the free movement of capital, be interpreted strictly [. . .]."

[16] On the debate on discrimination test versus non-hindrance test see, *inter alia*, DAMIAN CHALMERS, GARETH DAVIES, & GIORGIO MONTI, EUROPEAN UNION LAW: CASES & MATERIALS 678–80 (2010), also referring to the opposite positions of Advocate General Maduro and Advocate General Jacobs.

In the first place, the applicability of the non-hindrance test and its expansive effect on the scope of application of the freedoms has been reappraised by the Court itself with the development of the so-called *Keck* formula and the recent application of the margin-of-appreciation doctrine at the level of grounds of justification for restrictions on internal market freedoms.[17] First, under the *Keck* formula, Member States' regulatory measures might be shielded from the scope of application of the EU freedoms so far as they do not substantially and directly impede market access and are not discriminatory in fact and in law.[18] Second, the Court has recently adopted the margin-of-appreciation doctrine in cases where it has to evaluate whether Member States' regulatory measures applied without distinction (regarded as restrictions because of their effects of hindering EU nationals from the exercise of internal market freedoms) may be justified by overriding reasons in the general interest. In these cases, on the one hand, the Court restates that, in accordance with a well-established principle, such restrictions are compatible with EU law when they are "appropriate for securing attainment of the objective pursued and do not go beyond what is necessary for attaining that objective";[19] on the other, the Court appears to relax the above test of proportionality, allowing Member States to retain "a definite margin of discretion" in determining the level of protection of the general and legitimate interest they intend to protect as well as the way in which that level is to be achieved.[20] In the Court's view, the margin of discretion that has to be left to Member States depends on the fact that the

---

17 For a recent discussion of the issue, see Ilaria Angela Anrò, *Il margine di apprezzamento nella giurisprudenza della Corte di giustizia dell'Unione europea e della Corte europea dei diritti dell'uomo*, in ALBERTO ODDENINO, ELISA RUOZZI, ANNAMARIA VITERBO, FRANCESCO COSTAMAGNA, LORENZA MOLA, & LUDOVICA POLI, *LA FUNZIONE GIURISDIZIONALE NELL'ORDINAMENTO INTERNAZIONALE E NELL'ORDINAMENTO COMUNITARIO* 7 ff (2010).

18 The formula was developed by the Court in the context of free movement of goods. In this regard, see Joined Cases C-267/91 and C-268/91, Criminal proceedings against Bernard Keck and Daniel Mithouard 1993 E.C.R. I-6097 at 16, where the Court states that "... contrary to what has previously been decided, the application to products from other Member States of national provisions restricting or prohibiting certain selling arrangements is not such as to hinder directly or indirectly, actually or potentially, trade between Member States within the meaning of the Dassonville judgment (Case 8/74 [1974] ECR 837), so long as those provisions apply to all relevant traders operating within the national territory and so long as they affect in the same manner, in law and in fact, the marketing of domestic products and of those from other Member States."

19 Joined Cases C-171/07 and C-172/07, Apothekerkammer des Saarlandes and others v Saarland, Ministerium für Justiz, Gesundheit und Soziales, *supra* note 10, at 25.

20 In this regard, see Case C-244/06, Dynamic Medien Vertriebs GmbH v. Avides Media AG, 2008 E.C.R. I-505 at 44; Joined Cases C-171/07 and C-172/07, Apothekerkammer des Saarlandes and others v. Saarland, Ministerium für Justiz, Gesundheit und Soziales, *supra* note 10, at 19. ("When assessing whether that obligation has been complied with, account must be taken of the fact that the health and life of humans rank foremost among the assets and interests protected by the Treaty and that it is for the Member States to determine the level of protection which they wish to afford to public health and the way in which that level is to be achieved. Since the level may vary from one Member State to another, Member States must be allowed discretion (see, to this effect, Case C-322/01 Deutscher Apothekerverband [2003] ECR I-14887, paragraph 103; Case C-141/07 Commission v. Germany [2008] ECR I-0000, paragraph 51; and Hartlauer, paragraph 30)"); C-531/06, Commission of the European Communities v. Italian Republic, 2009 E.C.R. I-4103, at 36, 63.

level of protection of the general interest concerned may vary from one Member State to another.[21] Furthermore, Member States' discretion may be wider in the absence of harmonization measures at the EU level. Therefore it appears that in the absence of an approximation of domestic legislations at the EU level Member States maintain a certain margin of discretion as far as concerns the protection of general and legitimate interests even in the context of the European integration.

In the second place, the applicability of the non-hindrance test as well as the over-reaching scope of application it gives to the EU internal market freedoms has been reconsidered by the EU legislators themselves in respect of the freedom of establishment and right to provide services, when adopting Directive 2006/123/EC on services in the internal market. The Directive is aimed at eliminating the obstacles to the freedom of establishment and right to provide services for economic operators of Member States in the services sector by removing national requirements that affect the access to, or the exercise of, self-employed economic activities. The Directive required Member States to amend their domestic regulations so as to remove the prohibited requirements listed in Article 14 and Article 16(2) concerning the right of establishment and the right to provide services, respectively. Furthermore, it imposed on Member States the obligation to revise their domestic regulations so as to evaluate whether their regulations contain the other requirements laid down in Article 15 (as to the freedom of establishment) and Article 16(1) (as to the right to provide services) and whether these requirements, when existing in their domestic regulations, were compatible with the criteria of nondiscrimination, necessity, and proportionality.[22] In the Preamble, the Directive, echoing the *Keck* formula, clarified that it "applies only to requirements which affect the access to, or the exercise of, a service activity" and does not apply to Member States' rules "which do not specifically regulate or specifically affect the service activity but have to be respected by providers in the course of carrying out their economic activity in the same way as by individuals acting in their private capacity."[23]

Notwithstanding that the debate on the scope of application to be given to the EU freedoms and permissible and legitimate derogations therefrom is still open, as pointed

---

[21] In this respect see also the leading-case C-36/02, Omega Spielhallen-und Automatenaufstellungs-Gmb v. Oberbürgermeisterin der Bundesstadt Bonn, 2004 E.C.R. I-9609, at 31, 37, and 38. For a critical review of this case, see CONDINANZI ET AL., *supra* note 10, at 181, observing that "[t]he judgment in Omega marks a retrograde step in Community case-law as far as the identification of a common concept of public policy is concerned [...]."

[22] Nondiscrimination, proportionality, and necessity are the principles applied by the CJEU in evaluating whether a Member State measure, which would be otherwise in contrast with one of the EU internal market freedoms, falls under one of the public interest objective derogations from the Treaty rules provided under EU law.

[23] Preamble of Directive 2006/123/EC of the European Parliament and of the Council (Dec. 12, 2006), On services in the internal market, *supra* note 5, see the ninth sentence, which mentions "road traffic rules, rules concerning the development or use of land, town and country planning, building standards" among Member States' rules that do not specifically regulate or specifically affect the service activity.

out above, at the moment it remains the case that EU law protects very broadly the free exercise of economic activities within the EU.

B. The EU Market Freedoms and Foreign Investors

1. EU NATIONALS AS BENEFICIARIES OF THE RIGHT OF ESTABLISHMENT AND TO PROVIDE SERVICES

As results from the Treaty and clearly established by the Court, "[c]ontrary to the chapter of the Treaty concerning the free movement of capital, the chapter regulating the freedom to provide services does not contain any provision which enables service providers in non-member countries and established outside the European Union to rely on those provisions."[24] The same holds true in respect of the freedom of establishment.[25] Therefore companies established in third countries cannot rely on the Treaty rules on the right of establishment and right to provide services. As stated by the Court in its Opinion 1/94, "the sole objective of those chapters [i.e., the chapters on the right of establishment and on freedom to provide services] is to secure the right of establishment and freedom to provide services for nationals of Member States. They contain no provisions on the problem of the first establishment of nationals of non-member countries and the rules governing their access to self-employed activities."[26]

In 1994 this led the Court to find that the EC did not have an exclusive competence to conclude GATS.[27] Issues concerning initial establishment of non-EU undertakings pursuing their economic activities in the services sector, as well as in other sectors, fell within the joint competence of the EC and its Member States. According to the Court, this principle was also applicable to issues concerning the conditions for the participation of foreign-controlled undertakings in the internal economic life of the Member States in which they operate.[28] Conversely, according to the CJEU, an exclusive compe-

---

[24] Case C-452/04, Fidium Finanz AG v. Bundesanstalt für Finanzdienstleistungsaufsicht, 2006 E.C.R. I-9521, at 25, with reference to CJEU, Opinion 1/94, Competence of the Community to conclude international agreements concerning services and the protection of intellectual property, 1994 E.C.R. I-5267 ["As the Court found in its Opinion of November 15, 1994, Opinion 1/94 [1994] ECR I-5267, paragraph 81, the objective of the latter chapter is to secure the right to provide services for nationals of Member States. Therefore, Article 49 EC *et seq.* cannot be relied on by a company established in a non-member country."]

[25] Case C-351/08, Christian Grimme v Deutsche Angestellten-Krankenkasse, 2009 E.C.R. I-10777, at 33–34.

[26] CJEU, Opinion 1/94, Competence of the Community to conclude international agreements concerning services and the protection of intellectual property, *supra* note 24, at 81.

[27] *Id.* at 81 where the Court states that "One cannot therefore infer from those chapters that the Community has exclusive competence to conclude an agreement with non-member countries to liberalize first establishment and access to service markets, other than those which are the subject of cross-border supplies within the meaning of GATS, which are covered by Article 113."

[28] *See* CJEU, Opinion 2/94, Competence of the Community or one of its institutions to participate in the Third Revised Decision of the OECD on national treatment, 1995 E.C.R. I-521, section IV, 4–8 with reference to national treatment rule provided for by the Third Revised Decision.

tence of the EC could be inferred from an EC legislative act authorizing the EC to negotiate an international agreement with a third country or an EC legislative act including provisions relating to the treatment of nationals of non-member countries.[29] The same rule applied in the case that a complete harmonization of the rules governing access to a certain self-employed activity occurred at the EC level.[30]

The situation above described has changed, however, due to the subsequent revisions of the Treaties. More specifically, the scope of the Common Commercial Policy was extended by the Treaty of Nice to foreign direct investments by service providers[31] and then by the Treaty of Lisbon to foreign direct investments by all companies,[32] as specified below in Section B.4.

2. NON-EU UNDERTAKINGS AS BENEFICIARIES OF THE RIGHT OF SECONDARY ESTABLISHMENT AND FREEDOM TO PROVIDE SERVICES WITHIN THE EU UNDER THE TREATY

Notwithstanding Member States' competence on first establishment of non-EU undertakings in the absence of harmonization at the EU level, internal market freedoms also

---

29 CJEU, Opinion 1/94, *supra* note 24, at 95.

30 *Id.* at 96, where the Court states that: "The same applies in any event, even in the absence of any express provision authorizing its institutions to negotiate with non-member countries, where the Community has achieved complete harmonization of the rules governing access to a self-employed activity, because the common rules thus adopted could be affected within the meaning of the AETR judgment if the Member States retained freedom to negotiate with non-member countries."

31 In this respect, see CJEU, Opinion 1/08, Community Competence to Conclude with Certain Member States of the WTO Agreements Modifying Schedules of Specific Commitments of the Community and its Member States under the GATS, 2009 E.C.R. I-0000, interpreting the amendments introduced by the Treaty of Nice to the EC Treaty's rules on Common Commercial Policy and, more specifically, Art. 133 TEC. The CJEU held at 119 that under Art. 133(5) TEC, which was introduced by the Treaty of Nice: "[...] the Community is now also competent to conclude, under the common commercial policy, international agreements relating to trade in services supplied under modes 2 to 4. Such modes of supply of services, which the GATS refers to as 'consumption abroad', 'commercial presence' and 'presence of natural persons' respectively and which were formerly outside the sphere of the common commercial policy (see Opinion 1/94, paragraph 47), now fall within it on the conditions laid down in Article 133(5) and (6) EC." That said, the CJEU went on to observe that under Art. 133(5) and (6) TEC "agreements relating to trade in cultural and audiovisual services, educational services, and social and human health services, shall fall within the shared competence of the Community and its Member States" in accordance with the text of Art. 133(6), second paragraph TEC (at 132–35). According to the CJEU, this holds true even in the case that international agreements on trade in services do not "exclusively and predominantly" concern trade in services in the sensitive sectors listed above, namely cultural and audiovisual sectors, the educational sector, and the social and human health sector (at 137–40). On CJEU Opinion 1/08, see Alberto Alemanno, *Opinion 1/08, Community Competence to Conclude with Certain Members of the World Trade Organization Agreements Modifying the Schedules of Specific Commitments of the Community and Its Member States under the General Agreement on Trade in Services*, 104 AM. J. INT'L L. 467 (2010).

32 For a more extensive analysis, see Anna De Luca, *New Developments on the Scope of the EU Common Commercial Policy under the Lisbon Treaty, Investment Liberalization vs. Investment Protection?*, in YEARBOOK ON INTERNATIONAL INVESTMENT LAW & POLICY 2010/2011 ch. 5, 165–215 (Karl P. Sauvant ed., 2012).

applied (and still apply), to a certain extent, to foreign undertakings as far as they can be regarded as EU nationals under Article 54 TFEU (ex–Article 48 ECT).

In accordance with Article 54 TFEU (ex–Article 48 TEC), companies "formed in accordance with the law of a Member State and having their registered office, central administration or principal place of business within the Union" are for the purpose of the Treaty equated to natural persons having a Member State's nationality. The above three connecting links are alternative and not cumulative, and indicate that at least one factual connection with the legal system of a Member State is required. In this respect, it is worth noting that according to the Court, "a situation in which a company formed in accordance with the law of a Member State in which it has its registered office desires to set up a branch in another Member State falls within the scope of Community law. In that regard, it is immaterial that the company was formed in the first Member State only for the purpose of establishing itself in the second, where its main, or indeed entire, business is to be conducted."[33] Similarly, ownership or control by third country's nationals is immaterial in principle.[34] The case *Commission of the European Communities v. Kingdom of the Netherlands*[35] illustrates the point. In this case the Court analyzes the compatibility with the right of establishment of a Dutch law that required shipping companies of a Member State or of a State Party to the Agreement on the European Economic Area (EEA) to be owned and controlled by natural persons having EU or EEA nationality by at least a two-thirds shareholdings in order to be able to register a ship in the Netherlands.[36] By applying the non-hindrance test, already discussed above in Section A, and recalling that, pursuant to Article 54 TFEU, the right to freedom of establishment is guaranteed also to companies "formed in accordance with the law of a Member State and having their registered office, central administration or

[33] Case C-212/97, Centros Ltd v. Erhvervsog Selskabsstyrelsen, 1999 E.C.R. I-1459, at 17, referring to Case 79/85, Segers v. Bedrijfsvereniging voor Bank- en Verzekeringswegen, Groothandel en Vrije Beroepen, 1986 E.C.R. 2375, at 16. In this regard see also Case C-167/01, Kamer van Koophandel en Fabrieken voor Amsterdam, v. Inspire Art Ltd, 2003 E.C.R. I-10155, at 95 and Case C-208/00, Überseering BV v. Nordic Contsruction Company Baumangagement GmBH (NCC), 2002 E.C.R. I-9919. In legal literature, see CONDINANZI ET AL., *supra* note 10, at 122–26.

[34] In this respect, see General Programme for the abolition of restrictions on freedom of establishment (OJ (1962) 36) and General Programme for the abolition of restrictions on freedom to provide services (OJ (1962) 35). The two documents listed the beneficiaries of the two freedoms of circulation. Among these are companies formed in accordance with the law of a Member State and having only their registered office within the Community, "provided that, where only the seat prescribed by their statutes is situated within the Community or in an overseas country or territory, their activity shows a real and continuous link with the economy of a Member State. . . ." To this end "such link shall not be one of nationality, whether of the members of the company or firm, or of the persons holding managerial or supervisory posts therein, or of the holders of the capital."

[35] Case C-299/02, Commission of the European Communities v. Kingdom of the Netherlands, 2004 E.C.R. I-9761.

[36] *Id.* at 4. The same law imposed on shipping companies of a Member State or a State Party to the EEA two other conditions to be fulfilled in order to operate their business in the Netherlands: their directors and local representatives should be natural persons having the nationality of a Member State or State Party to the EEA.

principal place of business within the Union,"[37] the Court found that the Dutch law at stake was incompatible with EU law because of its effect of restricting the freedom of secondary establishment of shipping companies.[38] More important, the Court explicitly rejected the argument put forward by the Netherlands government that a condition requiring undertakings primarily established in other Member States to be owned and controlled by natural persons, holding a nationality of a Member State or EEA nationality, cannot amount to a restriction on the right of establishment, as opposed to a condition requiring the nationality of the host Member State or a given Member State. It was the view of the Court that "In the absence of a harmonised rule valid for the entire Community, a condition of Community or EEA nationality, like a condition of nationality of a specific Member State, may constitute an obstacle to freedom of establishment."[39]

Consequently, a company owned or controlled by non-EU nationals, that is incorporated (and therefore primarily established) in a Member State, is granted the right of secondary establishment, which entails the setting up of agencies, branches, or subsidiaries, and freedom to provide services (Article 54 TFEU) in another Member State under the same conditions provided for by the law of that Member State for its own nationals.

This case law on EU rules on establishment shows the irrelevance of an effective primary establishment in the Member State of incorporation in order for companies (non–EU-owned or controlled companies included)[40] to take advantage of the right of secondary establishment and freedom of circulation of services. Furthermore, it shows that Member States cannot, unilaterally, lay down requirements based on ownership and/or control by Member States' nationals in order to limit business operations of companies lawfully incorporated and primarily established in other Member States. Following this case law, it would be sufficient for companies based outside the Community to incorporate a subsidiary in a Member State and to have the subsidiary's registered office there in order to benefit from the right of secondary establishment

---

[37] *Id.* at 15 and 16, respectively.

[38] *Id*, at 19, where the Court states: "In this case, the ship registration scheme has the effect of restricting the freedom of establishment of shipowners. When shipowner companies wishing to register their ships in the Netherlands do not satisfy the conditions in issue, their only course of action is to alter the structure of their share capital or of their boards of directors; and such changes may entail serious disruption within a company and also require the completion of numerous formalities which have financial consequences. Likewise, shipowners must adjust their recruitment policies in order to ensure that their local representatives are not nationals of a State which is not a Member State of the Community or of the EEA."

[39] *Id.* at 20.

[40] This holds true due to the general propositions made by the CJEU in its rulings on the matter, even if Case C-212/97 Centros, *supra* note 33, clearly involves EU-nationals (see at 3) and Case C-167/01, Inspire Art, *supra* note 33, regards economic activities already carried out in a Member State other than that of primary establishment.

and freedom to provide services in other Member States, even in those laying down restrictions against the establishment of foreign-controlled companies.[41]

This is true, of course, provided that there are not specific sectoral restrictions or limitations on access and operation of non-EU undertakings set out in EU legislations. Avoiding extending EU internal market freedoms to non-EU investments in Member States' services of general interest or strategic sectors appears to have led the EU to adopt legislative acts imposing restrictions on access of non-EU undertakings to the internal market. Three recent EU legislative acts are worthy of mention, as examples of the harmonized rules valid for the entire Union to which the Court refers to in the above-quoted case *Commission of the European Communities v. Kingdom of the Netherlands*.

First, among these are Directive 2009/72/EC and Directive 2009/73/EC, regulating electricity and natural gas sectors respectively.[42] The two directives, adopted on the basis of the Treaty's Chapters on the right of establishment and freedom to provide services and Article 95 TEC (now Article 114 TFEU), limit investment operations by non-EU operators in electricity and sectors in the EU market. Article 11 of Directive 2009/72/EC and Article 11 of Directive 2009/73/EC set out restrictions on electricity and gas transmission operations, respectively, by undertakings that are controlled by a person or persons from a third country or third countries[43] unless some requirements are met.[44] Among these are the compliance by undertakings controlled by non-EU persons with the requirements of effective separation of transmission activities from activities of generation and supply (the so-called unbundling of transmission systems and transmission system operators as provided for by Article 9 of both Directives) that apply inside the Community,[45] and the requirements that the security of the energy

[41] This possibility was envisaged even before the EU case law of notes 33 and 35; in this regard see HANS SMIT & PETER HERZOG, THE LAW OF THE EUROPEAN ECONOMIC COMMUNITY, A COMMENTARY ON THE EEC TREATY, Vol. 2 (1976) on Article 58 of the Treaty of Rome (p. 645) where it was observed at that moment that it would be sufficient for companies based outside the Community to incorporate a subsidiary in a Member State and to have the subsidiary's registered office there, in order to benefit from the right of secondary establishment and freedom to provide services in other Member States, even in those laying down restrictions against the establishment of foreign-controlled companies.

[42] Art. 11 of Directive 2009/72/EC of the European Parliament and of the Council (July 13, 2009), Concerning common rules for the internal market in electricity, OJ L 211/51 (Aug. 14, 2009), and Art. 11 of Directive 2009/73/EC of the European Parliament and of the Council (July 13, 2009), Concerning common rules for the internal market in natural gas, OJ L 211/94 (Aug. 14, 2009).

[43] According to Art. 2(35) Directive 2009/72/EC, *supra* note 42, "'control' means rights, contracts or any other means which, either separately or in combination and having regard to the considerations of fact or law involved, confer the possibility of exercising decisive influence on an undertaking, in particular by: (a) ownership or the right to use all or part of the assets of an undertaking; (b) rights or contracts which confer decisive influence on the composition, voting or decisions of the organs of an undertaking." In identical terms, Art. 2(36) Directive 2009/73/EC, *supra* note 42.

[44] Preamble of Directive 2009/72/EC, *supra* note 42, twenty-fifth sentence and Preamble of Directive 2009/73/EC, *supra* note 42, twenty-second sentence.

[45] Art. 11(3)(a) Directive 2009/72/EC, *supra* note 42, and Art. 11(3)(a) Directive 2009/73/EC, *supra* note 42.

supply of the Member State and the Community will not be jeopardized.[46] Second, Regulation (EC) No. 1008/2008 of the European Parliament and of the Council[47] provides some restrictions on non-EU investors operating air services within the EU. The above-mentioned Regulation regulates EU air carriers as to their licensing and their right to operate air services within the EU. Article 4 of the Regulation lists the requirements that a Community air carrier has to meet in order to obtain an operating license. Among these are: (1) the principal place of business of the undertaking interested in taking the operating license is located in the Member State releasing the license; and (2) "Member States and/or nationals of Member States own more than 50% of the undertaking and effectively control it, whether directly or indirectly through one or more intermediate undertakings, except as provided for in an agreement with a third country to which the Community is a party." (Article 4(a) and (f), respectively.)[48]

2.1 Is the "Real/Effective and Continuous Link with the Economy of a Member State" Requirement Still Relevant for Companies to Be Considered EU Nationals under Article 54 TFEU?

Certain elements point, however, to the continuous relevance of the "real and continuous link with the economy of a Member State" requirement, notwithstanding the meaning of the requirement has never been conclusively clarified, as outlined below. First of all, during the initial stage of the realization of the European integration, the EC Council referred to this prerequisite of the "real and continuous link with the economy of a Member State" in its General Programmes for the abolition of restrictions on freedom of establishment and freedom to provide services.[49] Second, some scholars[50] and the EU's international practice still emphasize the "real and continuous link with the economy of a Member State" requirement. With regard to the EU's international practice, the Declaration made by the European Communities and their Member States with respect to Article 25 of the Energy Charter Treaty and EU–Korea FTA's definition of "juridical person of a Party" for the purpose of the agreement are relevant in this respect. According to the Declaration with regard to Article 25 of the Energy Charter Treaty, "The European Communities and their Member States recall that, in accordance with Article 58 of the Treaty establishing the European Community [now Article 54 TFEU]: a) companies or firms formed in accordance with the law of a Member State and having their registered office, central administration or principal place of business

---

[46] Art. 11(3)(b) Directive 2009/72/EC, *supra* note 42, and Art. 11(3)(b) Directive 2009/73/EC, *supra* note 42.

[47] Regulation (EC) 1008/2008 of the European Parliament and of the Council (Sept. 24, 2008), On common rules for the operation of air services in the Community, OJ L 293 (Oct. 31, 2008), 3–20.

[48] According to Art. 2 of Regulation 1008/2008, *supra* note 47, "principal place of business" means the head office or registered office of a Community air carrier in the Member State within which the principal financial functions and operational control, including continued airworthiness management, of the Community air carrier are exercised.

[49] *See supra* note 34.

[50] *See, e.g.*, GIUSEPPE TESAURO, DIRITTO DELL'UNIONE EUROPEA 532, 580 (2010).

within the Community shall, for the right of establishment pursuant to Part Three, Title III, Chapter 2 of the Treaty establishing the European Community, be treated in the same way as natural persons who are nationals of Member States; companies or firms which only have their registered office within the Community must, for this purpose, have an effective and continuous link with the economy of one of the Member States [. . .]."[51] According to Article 7.2(f)(i) of the Free Trade Agreement between the European Union and its Member States, on the one side, and the Republic of Korea, on the other side,[52] "juridical person of a Party" means a juridical person established "in accordance with the laws of one of the Member States or of Korea, and having its registered office, central administration or principal place of business" in the territory of the Union or of Korea, respectively. The above definition is identical to the definition of EU companies contained in Article 54 TFEU. Nevertheless, pursuant to Article 7.2(f)(i) of the EU–South Korea FTA, when the juridical person above defined has only its registered office or central administration in the territory of the EU or of Korea, it cannot be considered as a juridical person of the EU or of Korea, respectively, "unless it engages substantive business operations" in the territory of the EU or of Korea, respectively.[53] In turn, Article 7.2(f)(i), footnote 6[54] recalled that, in accordance with the notification of the Treaty establishing the European Community to the WTO, the "effective and continuous link" requirement with the economy of a Member State has to be understood as a concept equivalent to the concept of "substantive business

---

[51] The Declaration made by the European Communities and their Member States with respect to Article 25 of the Energy Charter Treaty, ENERGY CHARTER SECRETARIAT, THE ENERGY CHARTER TREATY AND RELATED DOCUMENTS, A LEGAL FRAMEWORK FOR INTERNATIONAL ENERGY COOPERATION 32 (2004). (*See also* Decision by the European Energy Charter Conference with respect to Articles 24(4)(a) and 25, Energy Charter Secretariat, The Energy Charter Treaty and Related Documents, A Legal Framework for International Energy Cooperation 137 (2004), *available at*: http://www.ena.lt/pdfai/Treaty.pdf (last visited: April 4, 2011).

[52] Free Trade Agreement between the European Union and its Member States, of the one part, and the Republic of Korea, of the other part, of Oct. 6, 2010, OJ L 127/6 (May 14, 2011) [hereinafter EU–Korea FTA].

[53] *Id.* Art. 7.2(f)(i) states as follows: "(i) a juridical person set up in accordance with the laws of one of the Member States of the European Union or of Korea respectively, and having its registered office, central administration or principal place of business in the territory to which the Treaty on European Union and the Treaty on the Functioning of the European Union apply, or of Korea respectively. Should the juridical person have only its registered office or central administration in the territory to which the Treaty on European Union and the Treaty on the Functioning of the European Union apply or of Korea, it shall not be considered as a juridical person of the European Union or of Korea respectively, unless it engages in substantive business operations in the territory to which the Treaty on European Union and the Treaty on the Functioning of the European Union apply or of Korea respectively."

[54] *Id.* Art. 7.2(f)(i), footnote 6 provides that: "In line with its notification of the Treaty establishing the European Community to the WTO (WT/REG39/1), the EU Party understands the concept of 'effective and continuous link' with the economy of a Member State of the European Union enshrined in Article 48 of the Treaty as equivalent to the concept of 'substantive business operations' provided for in paragraph 6 of Article V of the GATS. Accordingly, for a juridical person set up in accordance with the laws of Korea and having only its registered office or central administration in the territory of Korea, the EU Party shall only extend the benefits of this Agreement if that juridical person possesses an effective and continuous link with the economy of Korea."

operations" set out in Article V, paragraph 6 of the GATS.[55] The latter concept is unexplored under WTO case law. It is worth noting that the EU FTA with Korea deals also with trade in services and establishment, although its provisions do have not direct effect and cannot be directly invoked by individuals before Union or Member State courts and tribunals.[56] Article 7.2(f)(ii) identifies two categories of beneficiaries of the establishment provided for in Article 7.9(a), namely the juridical persons as defined above and juridical persons owned or controlled by natural persons of the Parties.[57]

Although the above-mentioned references to the "effective and continuous link" requirement (as well as its declared equivalence to the concept of "substantive business operations" under WTO law) do not shed any particular light on its interpretation, some indications might be inferred from Directive 2006/123/EC on services in the internal market.[58] On the one hand, the Directive does not cover external aspects[59] and applies just to providers established in a Member State (Article 1(2)) (i.e., any natural person who is a national of a Member State or any legal person engaged in a service activity in a Member State); on the other hand, as specified by the Preamble of the Directive, "the concept of a provider should not cover the case of branches in a Member State of companies from third countries because, under Article 48 of the Treaty [now Article 54 TFEU], the freedom of establishment and free movement of services may benefit only companies constituted in accordance with the laws of a Member State and having their registered office, central administration or principal place of business within the Community."[60] The Directive does not define the term "branches." Nor does the Treaty, which refers to the terms "agencies, branches or subsidiaries" in connection with the right of secondary establishment (Article 49(1) TFEU), include such a definition. Nevertheless, other EU acts contain a definition of "branches," though it is to be applied to different contexts from the one discussed here. Article 7.9(a) of the EU FTA with Korea includes a definition of establishment that means "the constitution, acquisition or maintenance of a juridical person" ("capital participation in a juridical

55 According to Article V, paragraph 6 of the GATS a service supplier of any other Member that is a juridical person constituted under the laws of a party to an economic integration agreement referred to in paragraph 1 "shall be entitled to treatment granted under such agreement, provided that it engages in substantive business operations in the territory of the parties to such agreement."

56 Art. 8 Council Decision 2011/265/EU, On the signing of EU–Korea FTA, *supra* note 52, stating that: "The Agreement shall not be construed as conferring rights or imposing obligations which can be directly invoked before Union or Member State courts and tribunals."

57 Art. 7.2(f)(ii), points (i)–(iii) of EU–Korea FTA, *supra* note 52, lists the criteria on the basis of which a given juridical person has to be considered as owned or controlled by natural persons of the EU Party or of Korea, respectively.

58 Directive 2006/123/EC of the European Parliament and of the Council (Dec. 12, 2006), On services in the internal market, *supra* note 5.

59 *Id.*, Preamble, sixteenth sentence stating that "[T]his Directive concerns only providers established in a Member State and does not cover external aspects. It does not concern negotiations within international organisations on trade in services, in particular in the framework of the General Agreement on Trade in Services (GATS)."

60 *Id.* Preamble, thirty-sixth sentence.

person with a view of establishing or maintaining lasting economic links" included)[61] and "the creation or maintenance of a branch or a representative office" within the territory of a Party in order to carry out an economic activities. Pursuant to Article 7.9(e) of the FTA, the term "branch" means "a place of business not having legal personality which has the appearance of permanency, such as the extension of a parent body, has a management and is materially equipped to negotiate business with third parties so that the latter, although knowing that there will, if necessary, be a legal link with the parent body, the head office of which is abroad, do not have to deal directly with such parent body but may transact business at the place of business constituting the extension." In turn, this definition replicates the meaning given by the Court to a similar expression ("the operations of branch, agency or other establishment") contained in the Brussels Convention of September 27, 1968, on jurisdiction and the enforcement of judgments in civil and commercial matters (now Council Regulation (EC) No 44/2001 of December 22, 2000, on jurisdiction and the recognition and enforcement of judgments in civil and commercial matters).[62]

Summing up, on the one hand, EU case law appears to hold that a mere factual link with a Member State's legal system (for example the incorporation and registered office therein only) is sufficient for non-EU undertakings to meet the "real and continuous link with the economy of a Member State" requirement, unless expressly required otherwise by the legislation of the Member State of primary establishment or EU legislative acts, such as the acts discussed above in Section B.2.[63] In this respect, although pursuant to Article 54(2) TFEU just "legal persons" are equated to natural persons holding the nationality of a Member State for the purpose of the Treaty, a broad interpretation of the term, so as to include also collective entities not having legal personality under Member States' domestic laws, had prevailed over a literal interpretation of the provision.[64] On the other hand, the afore-mentioned acts of the EU state that branches in a Member State of companies from third countries have to be excluded from the benefit of the right of establishment and right to provide service under the Treaty, because they would not meet the effective and continuous requirement with the economy of a Member State. In this respect, the above statement does not seem to reflect the status of EU case law at the moment.

In conclusion, the liberal approach resulting from the aforementioned Court's caselaw on the right of establishment has minimized the potential negative effects of

---

61 Article 7.9(a)(i) and footnote 12 EU–Korea FTA, *supra* note 52.

62 Council Regulation (EC) No 44/2001, On jurisdiction and the recognition and enforcement of judgments in civil and commercial matters (Dec. 22, 2000), OJ L 12 (Jan. 16, 2001), 1–23, Article 5(5). According to the Court, "the concept of branch, agency or other establishment implies a place of business which has the appearance of permanency, such as the extension of a parent body, has a management and is materially equipped to negotiate business with third parties so that the latter, although knowing that there will if necessary be a legal link with the parent body, the head office of which is abroad, do not have to deal directly with such parent body but may transact business at the place of business constituting the extension." (See Case 33/78, Somafer SA v. Saar-Ferngas AG, 1978 E.C.R. 2183, at 12)

63 In this respect, see SMIT & HERZOG, *supra* note 41, at 645–46.

64 In legal literature, see CONDINANZI ET AL., *supra* note 10, at 114–15.

Member States' competence on primary establishment of non-EU nationals and their different policies on access of foreign direct investments in general (discussed below in Section B.3) on the overall degree of openness of the internal market to foreign direct investments in the absence of a complete harmonization at EU level, except when the matter is covered by agreements between the EU and third countries, such as a EU Association Agreement.[65]

3. FREE MOVEMENT OF CAPITAL VIS-À-VIS THIRD COUNTRIES UNDER THE TREATY

Looking at the pre–Lisbon Treaty, it appeared that under the chapter on capital movements (Article 56 et seq. TEC), these were unconditionally liberalized not only in an intra-Community context but also in a third country context. The freedom of capital movement became effective as to capital movements between Member States and third countries as of the entry into force of the Treaty of Amsterdam.[66] Apparently, Article 56(1) TEC realized a unilateral and unconditional liberalization of movements of capital (direct investment included) *erga omnes*.[67] The concept of capital movements includes both direct investments and portfolio investments. Under EU law, direct investment includes any type of investment that serves to establish or to maintain lasting and direct links with an undertaking to which the capital is made available in order to carry on an economic activity, and direct investment in the form of participation in an undertaking "is characterized, in particular, by the possibility of participating effectively in the management of a company or in its control."[68] Conversely, any other form of investment, which does not give the holder the possibility to participate effectively in the management of a company or in its control, should be considered as a portfolio investment. It is well established under CJEU's case law that direct investment constitutes a subcategory of capital under the Treaty.[69]

---

[65] As to establishment of companies see *id.* at 115–18.

[66] Art. 63(1) TFEU reproduces verbatim Art. 56(1) TEC and states that "all restrictions on the movement of capital between Member States and between Member States and third countries shall be prohibited."

[67] In this respect, see HINDELANG, *supra* note 10, discussing also the contrary view.

[68] The same definition of direct investment is contained in the European Commission's Communication, *Towards a Comprehensive European International Investment Policy* [hereinafter the Communication]. European Commission, Communication from the Commission to the European Parliament, The Council, the European Economic and Social Committee and the Committee of the Regions, *Towards a Comprehensive European International Investment Policy*, COM(2010)343 final, pp. 2–3, *available at*: http://trade.ec.europa.eu/doclib/docs/2011/may/tradoc_147884.pdf (last visited Sept. 10, 2012).

[69] In this respect, see Council Directive 88/361/EEC (June 24, 1988), For the implementation of Art. 67 of the Treaty, OJ L 178 (July 8, 1988), which completed the realization of the internal market and introduced a complete liberalization of capital movements between Member States. Directive 88/361 covered direct investments that are defined in Annex I under Heading I as "1. Establishment and extension of branches or new undertakings belonging solely to the person providing the capital, and the acquisition in full of existing undertakings. 2. Participation in new or existing undertaking with a view to establishing or maintaining lasting economic links. 3. Long-term loans with a view to establishing or maintaining lasting economic links. 4. Reinvestment of profits with a view to maintaining lasting economic links." In the Explanatory Notes of Annex I, it was further explained that for the purposes of the Directive and Nomenclature annexed thereto only, direct investments mean: "Investments of all kinds

This unilateral and unconditional liberalization of capital vis-à-vis third countries was (and still is) undermined in practice from various directions, as outlined below.

Contrary to the free movement of capital in an intra-Community context, free movement of capital vis-à-vis third countries was (and still is) subject to the so-called grandfather clause of Article 57(1) TEC (now Article 64.1 TFEU).[70] According to Article 57(1), Member States had the right to maintain any restrictions vis-à-vis third countries existing as of December 31, 1993, under their national law in respect of the movement of capital to or from third countries involving direct investment (including in real estate), establishment, the provision of financial services, or the admission of securities to capital markets.[71] The same provision covered restrictions existing as of the same date under Community law. This provision allowed each Member State to maintain its restrictions on market access by foreign direct investments as well as less severe restrictions that discriminate against non-EU undertakings, irrespective of whether these restrictions under national law address directly or indirectly foreign investments.[72] Moreover, this provision has been liberally construed by the CJEU,

---

by natural persons or commercial, industrial or financial undertakings, and which serve to establish or to maintain lasting and direct links between the person providing the capital and the entrepreneur to whom or the undertaking to which the capital is made available in order to carry on an economic activity. This concept must therefore be understood in its widest sense." EC Treaty as amended by the Amsterdam Treaty substantially reproduced the contents of Art. 1 of Directive 88/361 and extended the freedom to capital movements between Member States and third countries. In any case, under the CJEU's case law it is well established that the nomenclature annexed to Directive 88/361 "still has the indicative value, for the purposes of defining the notion of capital movements" under the Treaty (Case C-222/97, Trummer and Mayer, 1999 E.C.R. I-1661 at 20 and 21 and, *inter alia*, Case C-483/99, Commission of the European Communities v. Republic of France, *supra* note 10, at 36). As to direct investments as included in the material scope of application of the freedom of capital movement see, *inter alia*, Case C-54/99, Association Eglise de scientologie de Paris and Scientology International Reserves Trust v. The Prime Minister, *supra* note 15, at 14; Case C-483/99, Commission of the European Communities v. Republic of France, *supra* note 10, at 37 ("Points I and III in the nomenclature set out in Annex I to Directive 88/361, and the explanatory notes appearing in that annex, indicate that direct investment in the form of participation in an undertaking by means of a shareholding or the acquisition of securities on the capital market constitute capital movements within the meaning of Art. 73b of the Treaty. The explanatory notes state that direct investment is characterized, in particular, by the possibility of participating effectively in the management of a company or in its control."); Joined Cases C-463/04 and C-464/04 Federconsumatori and Others v. Comune di Milano, 2007 E.C.R. I-10419, at 20. In legal literature, see HINDELANG, *supra* note 10, at 66–74.

70 Art. 64(1) TFEU reproduces verbatim Art. 57(1) TEC.

71 As to restrictions on movements of capital between Estonia and Hungary and third countries, the relevant date is December 31, 1999.

72 HINDELANG, *supra* note 10, at 277 indicating the protection of "a certain degree of Member State control on the system of property ownership in those States" as the rationale underlying the grandfather clause. The present author doubts that this was (and still is) the rationale underlying the clause. First, if this were to be considered the rationale of the clause, in any case there would be another provision of the Treaty more appropriate for the above purpose, namely Art. 295 TEC (now Art. 344 TFEU). Putting pressure on third countries to open up their markets could be regarded as a rationale of the so-called grandfather clause, if one reads the latter clause together with the other safeguard clauses and derogations that apply to free movements of capital between Member States and third countries only. It is worth noting, however, the CJEU considered a similar argument put forward by Germany and The Netherlands to support their position that the concept of restrictions under Art. 57(1) has to

in favor of Member States.[73] There is no obligation on Member States to notify the Commission of their restrictions under Article 64(1) TFEU (ex–Article 57(1) TEC). To conclude, as observed by the Commission in 2003, "[a]t national level there is a fairly large number of third-country restrictions remaining."[74]

Under the Treaty, Member States were therefore able to pursue their own policies on market access by foreign direct investments and establishment of non-EU undertakings. Some Member States adopted "open door" policies toward inward direct investments,[75] while others adopted more restrictive regimes, as one can infer from national reservations to the OECD Code of Liberalization of Capital Movements[76] as well as from liberalization commitments under the GATS. In this respect, the Commission observed in 2003 that "as indicated in the Community position under the GATS, the lack of liberalization commitments for some important economic sectors (notably rail, space, and pipeline transport, and postal, courier and audiovisual services) reveal some Member States' reluctance to accept significant third-country presence in these areas, and most probably the existence of third-country restrictions at national level (although the situation can be contrasted between Member States)."[77]

3.1. The CJEU's Case Law on Free Circulation of Capital and Its Relationship with the Other Internal Market Freedoms

Free circulation of capital movements overlaps with the freedom of establishment (and free circulation of services in certain instances)[78] because the two freedoms have partially the same material scope, at least with regard to direct investments.[79] The exact delimitation of the material scope of application of the freedom of capital movement with respect to the right of establishment and to provide services is not a theoretical issue but a practical one, if one adopts the point of view of a foreign investor seeking to invest in the EU. This is considering that the freedom of circulation of capital is the only internal market freedom having a third-country dimension. However, the Court

---

be interpreted differently as it is interpreted in an intra-Community context as not decisive (see Case C-101/05, Skatterverket v. A, 2007 E.C.R. I-11531, at 38).

73 In this respect, HINDELANG, *supra* note 10, at 276–91 (critically) reviewing CJEU's case law. In case law see, *inter alia*, Case C-101/05, Skatterverket v. A, *supra* note 72.

74 *See* European Commission, The EU Economy: 2003 Review, *European Economy*, No. 6/2003 (Brussels: European Communities, 2004), p. 328, ***available at:*** http://ec.europa.eu/internal_market/capital/docs/europeaneconomy_en.pdf (last visited Sept. 27, 2012).

75 This is the case of the UK that has adopted such an "open door" policy since the 1980s. In this regard, see PETER MUCHLINSKI, MULTINATIONAL ENTERPRISES AND THE LAW 216–18 (2007).

76 For example, compare Austria's List A (OECD Code of Liberalization of Capital Movements, 2010, p. 47) to United Kingdom's List A (OECD Code of Liberalization of Capital Movements, 2010, p. 135).

77 European Commission, *supra* note 74, at 328.

78 For some examples of overlaps between free movement of capital and free circulations of services, see John A. Usher, *EMU and Financial Services*," *in* EUROPEAN UNION LAW FOR THE TWENTY-FIRST CENTURY 73, 80–81 (Takis Tridimas & Paolisa Nebbia eds., 2004), referring to C-222/97 Trummer and Mayer, *supra* note 69, and C-410/96, Andre Ambry, 1998 E.C.R. I-7875. For a more recent example, see *infra* note 87.

79 In this respect, see HINDELANG, *supra* note 10, at 82–88.

had not clearly distinguished the material scope of application of each freedom with respect to the others for a long time. There are different views in the literature as to the relationship between free circulation of capital, on the one side, and the right of establishment and freedom to provide services on the other.[80] These different views can be summarized in the following terms. According to one view,[81] the freedom of circulation of capital is closely related to the actual exercise of the other freedoms and, more specifically, to the freedom of establishment. The latter freedom should be regarded in any case as prevalent over free circulation of capital when the acquisition of shares give to the shareholder concerned a "definite control" over a company's decisions and the possibility of determining its activity (as in the case of a direct investment).[82] As a result, restrictions on free movement of capital are possible when they are the result of a legitimate restriction on the exercise of one of the other freedoms.[83] Furthermore, these restrictions are irrelevant for EU law when the competing freedoms (i.e., right of establishment and free circulation of services) are not applicable because the factual situation at stake is considered as purely internal.[84] According to the opposite view, free movement of capital and the freedom of establishment have to be applied in parallel with respect to direct investments with the result that "the facts of a given case must be measured against the background of both freedoms."[85] The question whether the relationship between the two freedoms has to be regarded as exclusive or the two freedoms can be applied in parallel, which is of limited importance in respect of intra-Community investments, is decisive with regards to foreign direct investments, taking into account that right of establishment (as well as the freedom to provide services) applies only to EU nationals. In fact, natural persons holding a Member State's nationality and EU undertakings as defined above[86] can invoke the right of establishment and freedom to

80 The same is true also in respect of potential overlaps between free movement of capital and free movement of services.

81 For example, see Tesauro, *supra* note 50, at 623–24; Arie Landsmeer, *Movement of Capital and Other Freedoms*, 28(1) LEGAL ISSUES ECON. INTEGRATION 57 (2001), pp. 67–69; HINDELANG, *supra* note 10, pp. 108–10, referring to German scholars who endorse the exclusivity approach.

82 *See* AG Colomer Opinion (Feb. 6, 2003), C-463/00, Commission of the European Communities v. Kingdom of Spain, 2003 E.C.R. I-4581; and C-98/01 Commission of the European Communities v. United Kingdom, 2003 E.C.R. I-4641, at 36, stating that the appropriate framework within which to evaluate "golden shares" is freedom of establishment.

83 *See* Tesauro, *supra* note 50, at 623–24, referring to C-204/90 Bachmann v. Belgian State, 1992 E.C.R. I-249, at 34 ("It need merely be observed in that regard, first, that Art. 67 does not prohibit restrictions which do not relate to the movement of capital but which result indirectly from restrictions on other fundamental freedoms, and, secondly, that provisions such as those at issue before the national court preclude neither the payment of insurance contributions to insurers established in another Member State nor their payment in the currency of the Member State in which the insurer is established.")

84 AG Tesauro Opinion (Nov. 18, 1992), Case C-148/91, Vereniging Veronica Omroep Organisatie v Commissariaat voor de Media, 1993 E.C.R. I-487, at 8 and 10.

85 HINDELANG, *supra* note 10, at 110; Leo Flynn, *Coming of Age: The Free Movement of Capital Case-Law 1993–2002*, 39 COMMON MKT. L. REV. 773, 787 (2002).

86 It is worthy of note that, in accordance with Art. 56(1) TFEU (ex–Art. 49(1) TEC), nationals of Member States have to be "established in a Member States other than that of the person for whom the services are intended" in order to rely on the freedom to provide services. The personal scope of this freedom

provide services before Member States' judges. Conversely, the two freedoms cannot be successfully invoked by non-EU nationals before Member State national judges, as already outlined above.[87]

If one focuses on the case law, some indications, although not conclusive, as to the relationship between the freedom of capital movement and right of establishment can be inferred when the factual situation at stake involves a direct investment.[88]

It is the Court's view that, where a national measure affects more than one freedom, "the Court will, in principle, examine it in relation to just one of those two fundamental freedoms if it is clear that, in the circumstances of the case, one of those freedoms is entirely secondary in relation to the other and may be attached to it."[89] This approach is the so-called "center of gravity" approach. More specifically, the Court has applied the "center of gravity" approach to Member States' measures affecting both freedom to provide services and free movement of capital in a third country context and then extended it to the relationship between the right of establishment and free circulation of capital. According to the Court, where freedom to provide services (or right of establishment) competes with free circulation of capital, it is necessary in principle to "examine the measure in dispute in relation to only one of those two freedoms if it appears, in the circumstances of the case, that one of them is entirely secondary in relation to the other and may be considered together with it."[90] The purpose of the regulatory measure at stake is taken by the Court as a decisive element in order to draw a distinction between the material scope of the competing freedoms. As pointed out in

---

is generally limited to nationals of Member States already established within the EU and does not extend to nationals of third countries established within the EU, unless provided otherwise in EU legislative acts. In accordance with Art. 56(2) TFEU (ex-Art. 49(2) TEC), "The European Parliament and the Council, acting in accordance with the ordinary legislative procedure, may extend the provisions of the Chapter to nationals of a third country who provide services and who are established within the Union." In any case, these two requirements (i.e., nationality of a Member State and establishment within the EU) are more burdensome for physical persons than for EU undertakings.

87 *See*, with regard to the right to provide services, Case C-452/04, Fidium Finanz AG v. Bundesanstalt für Finanzdienstleistungsaufsicht, *supra* note 24, at 25; with regard to the right of establishment Case C-351/08, Grimme v. Deutsche Angestellten-Krankenkasse, *supra* note 25, at 33–34.

88 For an in-depth analysis see De Luca, *supra* note 32, at 182–95.

89 Case C-36/02, Omega Spielhallen- und Automatenaufstellungs-GmbH v. Oberbürgermeisterin der Bundesstadt Bonn, *supra* note 21, at 26 on a national measure that affects both freedom to provide services and free movement of goods. *See also* Case C-275/92 H.M. Customs and Excise v. Schindler, 1994 E.C.R. I-1039, at 22; Case C-390/99, Canal Satélite Digital SL v. Administración General del Estate, 2002 E.C.R. I-607, at 31; Case C-71/02, Herbert Karner Industrie- Auktionen GmbH v. Troostwijk GmbH, 2004 E.C.R. 1-3025, at 46.

90 Case C-452/04, Fidium Finanz AG v. Bundesanstalt für Finanzdienstleistungsaufsicht, *supra* note 24, at 34. With regards to the relationship between the freedom of establishment and free movement of capital in a third country context see Case C-524/04, Test Claimants in the Thin Cap Group Litigation v. Commissioners of Inland Revenue, 2006 E.C.R. I-2107, at 33, 38; more recently C-157/05, Winfried L. Holböck v. Finanzamt Salzburg-Land, 2007 E.C.R. I-4051, at 28, referring to Case C-102/05 Skatteverket v. A, *supra* note 63, at 28 ("However, the chapter of the Treaty concerning the right of establishment does not include any provision extending its application to situations which involve the establishment in a non-member country of a Member State national or of a company incorporated under the legislation of a Member State").

legal literature, " [...] the Court places emphasis on the final encroachments intended by the national measure on the movement, charactering factual effects as 'unavoidable consequences' and thus masking them out; however, it reserved itself a loophole by defining the purpose of the national measure and what constitutes an 'unavoidable consequences.'"[91]

The Court further deepens the "center of gravity" approach, merging it with the exclusivity approach in case of direct investments, while it does not exclude the parallel application of right of establishment and free circulation of capital in case of portfolio investments. It is the Court's view that "if the legislation under examination concerns a stake which gives its holder definite influence over the decisions of the company concerned and allows him to determine its activities, it is the provisions relating to freedom of establishment which are applicable."[92] On the contrary, "if that legislation is not intended to apply only to stakes which enable the holder to have a definite influence on a company's decisions and to determine the company's activities, it should be examined in relation to both Article 43 EC and Article 56 EC."[93] At the same time, the Court reserves itself a wide margin of discretion in determining whether a certain national legislation falls within the ambit of one or other of those fundamental freedoms by recalling that to this end "it is clear from well established case-law that the purpose of the legislation concerned must be taken into consideration."[94]

In light of the above analysis of the CJEU's case law, both right of establishment and freedom to provide services and their limitations take precedence over free circulation of capital, particularly in the third country context. Furthermore, there are also clear signals of this prevalence in EU legislation. This is the case with Directive 2009/72/EC and Directive 2009/73/EC,[95] setting out restrictions on electricity and gas transmission operations, respectively, by undertakings that are controlled by a person or persons from a third country or third countries.

It is worthy of note that the two directives have been adopted on the basis of the Treaty's Chapters on the right of establishment and freedom to provide services and Article 95 TEC (now Article 114 TFEU). The latter provision is the legal basis for the Council and the European Parliament to adopt measures "for the approximation of the provisions laid down by law, regulation or administrative action in Member States

[91] HINDELANG, *supra* note 10, at 100.

[92] Case C-531/06, Commission of the European Communities v. Italian Republic, *supra* note 20, at 40 referring to Case C-251/98, Baars, 2000 E.C.R. I-2787, at 21–22, and Case C-436/00, X, Y v. Riksskatteverket, 2002 E.C.R. I-10829, at 37 and 66–68; Case C-543/08, European Commission v. Portuguese Republic, *supra* note 10, at 41 referring to Case C-251/98, Baars, cit., at 22 and Case C-326/07, Commission of the European Communities v. Italian Republic, *supra* note 13, at 34–35 and at 42, referring to Case C-112/05, Commission of the European Communities v. Federal Republic of Germany, *supra* note 10, at 18.

[93] Case C-531/06, Commission of the European Communities v. Italian Republic, *supra* note 20, at 40 referring to C-446/04, Test Claimants in the FII Group Litigation, 2006 E.C.R. I-11753, at 36 and 38, and Case C-157/05, Winfried L. Holböck v. Finanzamt Salzburg-Land, *supra* note 90, at 23 and 25; Case C-543/08, European Commission v. Portuguese Republic, *supra* note 10, at 43.

[94] Case C-543/08, European Commission v. Portuguese Republic, *supra* note 10, at 40.

[95] Directive 2009/72/EC, *supra* note 42, and Directive 2009/73/EC, *supra* note 42.

which have as their object the establishment and functioning of the internal market." Neither the Preamble of the two directives nor the text thereof refers to the free movement of capital and the CJEU's case law thereon. This supports the position that both right of establishment and freedom to provide services and their limitations take precedence over free circulation of capital.

With regard to the material scope of application of free circulation of capital, the Court has made application of the so-called non-hindrance test also in respect to free circulation of capital, as already pointed out above. It is the CJEU's position, as it results from its case law on "golden shares," that a State measure that applies without distinction but is liable to deter, limit, or discourage operators from other Member States from investing or making investments in undertakings of the Member State whose measure is at stake or is liable to make less attractive investments in such undertakings is to be considered as a restriction on free circulation of capital.[96] The CJEU's case law on "golden shares" affects Member States' competence to adopt legislative measures of general application as concerns the subjects affected. By applying the non-hindrance test, the Court held that "although the relevant restrictions on investment operations apply without distinction to both residents and non-residents, it must nonetheless be held that they affect the position of a person acquiring a shareholding as such and are thus liable to deter investors from other Member States from making such investments and, consequently, affect access to the market."[97]

As already observed above, the application of the non-hindrance test gives such an overreaching scope of application to the EU freedoms so as to "capture" practically any Member State's domestic regulatory measure. In this respect, it is worth recalling that the Court's case law on "golden shares" and the scope of prohibition of restrictions on free movement of capital given by the Court thereunder has been developed by the Court in respect of investments made in an intra-Community context only and that, as pointed out by the Court, "movement of capital to or from third countries takes place in different legal context from that which occurs within the Community."[98] If we take into account that the non-hindrance test is aimed at strengthening European integration by granting economic operators from a Member State more effective access to the market of the other Member States, its applicability in respect of free circulation of capital in a third-country context appears to be quite uncertain.

The principles developed by the CJEU in its case law on "golden shares" cannot be generally exported to a third country context, as indeed international practice shows. In this regard, it is worth noting that state measures such as "licensing requirements and other domestic regulations and internal arrangements such as 'golden shares'" are not considered in principle as restrictions under Article 1 of the OECD *Code of*

---

96 *See* the CJEU's case law on free circulation of capital, *supra* note 10.

97 Case C-463/00, Commission of the European Communities v. Kingdom of Spain, *supra* note 10, at 61 referring to Case C-98/01, Commission of the European Communities v. United Kingdom, *supra* note 10, at 47.

98 Case C-101/05, Skatterverket v. A, *supra* note 72, at 36.

Liberalization of Capital Movements and *Code of Liberalization of Current Invisible Operations*, notwithstanding their possible economic impact on operations governed by the Codes.[99]

Summing up, first neither CJEU's case law on free circulation of capital and its relationship with the other freedoms nor the chapter on free movements of capital suggests an unconditional liberalization of capital vis-à-vis third countries.[100] To the contrary, CJEU's case law appears at the moment to point in the opposite direction. This outcome results from the application by the Court of the "center of gravity" and exclusivity approaches mingled together as well as from the grandfather clause of Article 64(1) TFEU as liberally interpreted in favor of Member States. Furthermore, there is actually no evidence in the Court's case law that the principles developed by the CJEU in its case law on "golden shares" (namely, the non-hindrance test and the interpretation of the principle of neutrality of the Treaty as described above) are to be applied within the ambit of free circulation of capital vis-à-vis third countries. The Treaty of Lisbon not only upheld the restrictions and exceptions already provided by the preceding Treaty, but also added new potential restrictions on foreign investments.[101]

According to some authors, the approach of the Court, which gives prevalence to the right of establishment (or right to provide services) over free movements of capital, would leave a third-country direct investment without protection and "would lead to the odd result that the protection enjoyed by an investor would be inversely proportionate to the size of his holdings."[102] This critical observation does not appear to be totally convincing, considering the liberal approach followed by the Court in connection with the right of secondary establishment. As far as foreign investors, seeking to make a direct investment in the EU internal market, will use a corporate vehicle incorporated in a Member State (which adopts an open door policy toward foreign investments), they will enjoy the benefits of the right of secondary establishment and right to provide services as EU undertakings under Article 54 TFEU. More specifically, the liberal approach on the right of establishment (described above in Section B.2),

---

[99] *See* OECD, OECD CODES OF LIBERALISATION USER'S GUIDE 2008 AT 23–24 (2008), *available at*: http://www.oecd.org/dataoecd/21/23/38072327.pdf (last visited Sept. 10, 2012); OECD, OECD CODE OF LIBERALIZATION OF CAPITAL MOVEMENTS (2010), *available at* http://www.oecd.org/dataoecd/10/62/39664826.pdf (last visited Sept. 10, 2012); OECD, CODE OF LIBERALIZATION OF CURRENT INVISIBLE OPERATIONS (2010), *available at*: http://www.oecd.org/dataoecd/41/21/2030182.pdf (last visited Sept. 10, 2012).

[100] In this regard, see also Usher, *supra* note 78, at 73, 74–75.

[101] Art. 65(4) TFEU states as follows: "In the absence of measures pursuant to Art. 64(3), the Commission or, in the absence of a Commission decision within three months from the request of the Member State concerned, the Council, may adopt a decision stating that restrictive tax measures adopted by a Member State concerning one or more third countries are to be considered compatible with the Treaties in so far as they are justified by one of the objectives of the Union and compatible with the proper functioning of the internal market. The Council shall act unanimously on application by a Member State."

[102] *See* Steffen Hindelang & Niklas Maydell, *The EU's Common Investment Policy—Connecting the Dots*, *in* INTERNATIONAL INVESTMENT LAW AND EU LAW 4, 6 (Marc Bungenberg, Jörn Griebel, & Steffen Hindelang, eds. 2011).

together with the case law where the Court has given precedence to both right of establishment and freedom to provide services and their limitations over free circulation of capital, in case of direct investment (discussed in Section B.3.1), has neutralized the specific sectoral restrictions or limitations on access and operation of non-EU undertakings set out in Member States' laws, covered by the so-called grandfather clause of Article 64(1) TFEU (ex-57(1) TEC), included in the Treaty's Chapter on free movement of capital.[103]

4. CONCLUDING REMARKS

Until the entry into force of the Treaty of Lisbon, and in the absence of harmonized company law rules at the EU level, Member States were able to pursue their own policies on market access by foreign direct investments and first establishment of non-EU undertakings. However, distortion of competition within the internal market or disturbance to the functioning thereof arose from Member States' different policies on first establishment of foreign-controlled undertakings. Some Member States adopted "open door" policies toward inward direct investments,[104] while others adopted more restrictive regimes, as one can infer from national reservations to the OECD Code of Liberalization of Capital Movements.[105] As pointed out in legal literature, the unity of the internal market has been undermined by Member States' different policies on access of foreign direct investment by service providers.[106]

The situation above described has changed, however, due to the subsequent revisions of the Treaties. The successive revisions introduced by the Nice and Lisbon Treaties were aimed at overcoming the problems resulting from the shared competence between Member States and the EU over initial establishment of non-EU companies that, as argued by the Commission,[107] undermined the EU's unity of action vis-à-vis the rest of the world as well as, to a certain extent, the unity of the internal market, and weakened EU's negotiating power in the international scene and, more specifically, in the WTO's context. The scope of the Common Commercial Policy was, therefore, extended by the Treaty of Nice to foreign direct investments by service providers and then by the Treaty of Lisbon to foreign direct investments by all companies. The post-Lisbon rules on the Common Commercial Policy indicate that the EU's exclusive competency includes the admission and establishment of foreign direct investments. As rightly pointed out by the Commission, with regard to market access "the Union

[103] Art. 64(1) TFEU reproduces verbatim Art. 57(1) TEC.

[104] *See supra* note 75.

[105] *See supra* note 76.

[106] In this regard, see Piet Eeckhout, External Relations of the European Union, Legal and Constitutional Foundations 30–31 (2004), in reviewing Opinion 1/94, *supra* note 24. The author observes that "[...] the Opinion does not refer to the unity of the internal market. [...] For example, in an integrated and liberalized internal financial services market, different policies by Member States' on access and treatment of foreign financial services companies seeking to operate on that market are just as much likely to distort competition as are different policies on imports of goods."

[107] Opinion 1/94, *supra* note 24, at 78.

has exclusive competence to autonomously legislate on FDI, as in the other areas of the common commercial policy, such as the import and export regulation."[108] As a consequence, after the entry into force of the Treaty of Lisbon, Member States cannot pursue their own autonomous policies toward inward foreign investments.

This notwithstanding, there is still a strong need to ensure the coherence between the functioning of the internal market and each Member State's own national policy on the admission and initial establishment of foreign investors, on the one side, and the external action of the EU in eliminating restrictions on foreign direct investment, on the other side. To ensure the coherence and consistency between the functioning of the internal market and the external action of the EU appears to be necessary in order to strengthen the EU's power in negotiating market access commitments with third parties. Although the EU market is quite foreign investor–friendly and open toward foreign investments, as outlined above, many other countries and, more specifically, emerging economies such as China, Brazil, and India are less open to foreign investments, and in particular EU investments. Therefore it cannot be excluded that the EU will adopt in the future sectoral harmonized rules limiting the access of foreign investors to the EU market (possibly incorporating a principle of reciprocity) in order to push unwilling commercial partners to open their markets to EU investors and conclude international agreements, including market access commitments to the benefit of EU investors.

The Draft Regulation on the access of third-country goods and services to the Union's internal market in public procurement and procedures supporting negotiations on access of Union goods and services to the public procurement markets of third countries, proposed by the Commission on March 26, 2012,[109] illustrates the point. The draft regulation, as proposed by the Commission, is a measure based on Article 207 TFEU and is to be taken within the framework of the exclusive external competence of the EU in the area of the Common Commercial Policy, as extended by the Treaty of Lisbon to include the liberalization of restrictions on foreign direct investment (Article 206 TFEU).[110] The Draft Regulation on the access of third-country goods and services to the Union's internal market in public procurement mainly aims at regulating and limiting, under certain conditions, the access of foreign goods, services, and suppliers to EU public procurement markets with the view to strengthening the position of the EU in negotiating substantive market access commitments with third countries at the international level.[111] As explained by the Commission in the Explanatory Memorandum,

---

108 The Communication, *supra* note 68, at 5, n.14.

109 European Commission, *Proposal for a Regulation of the European Parliament and of the Council on the access of third-country goods and services to the Union's internal market in public procurement and procedures supporting negotiations on access of Union goods and services to the public procurement markets of third countries*, COM(2012) 124 final [hereinafter Draft Regulation on Access], *available at* http://trade.ec.europa.eu/doclib/docs/2012/march/tradoc_149243.pdf (last visited Sept. 10, 2012).

110 Preamble of the Draft Regulation on Access, *supra* note 109, second sentence.

111 A further and secondary aim of the Draft Regulation on Access is to ensure the effective enforcement of the international market access commitments undertaken by the EU and its Member States vis-à-

the closeness of third countries' public procurement markets toward EU operators and the increasing adoption of protectionist measures by emerging economies, as opposed to the openness of the EU public procurement market toward foreign economic operators, are the grounds on which the proposal is rooted. In fact, the absence of a level playing field to the detriment of EU economic operators and the lack of leverage that can allow the EU in its negotiations with third countries "to redress the imbalance and to gain substantial market access commitments for the benefit of EU business" are the problems the Draft Regulation on the access of third-country goods and services to the Union's internal market in public procurement that the draft Regulation is intended to respond to.[112] In order to foster the leverage of the EU in international negotiations on market access, the said draft regulation sets out two mechanisms possibly leading to exclude from procedures for the award of contracts with a value equal or above EUR 5.000.000, tenders that comprise "non-covered goods and services" for a value exceeding 50 percent of the total value of the goods and services that are the object of the tender. Pursuant to Article 1(e) of the Draft Regulation on the access of third-country goods and services to the Union's internal market in public procurement, "non-covered goods and services" are goods and services originating in third countries with which the EU has not concluded international agreements, including market access commitments in the field of public procurement, or with which the EU has concluded such agreements in the case that these agreements do not apply. The draft regulation provides for the rules of origin applicable for determining whether goods and services are covered by international commitments of the EU. With regard to the origin of goods, Article 3.1 refers to the nonpreferential rules of origin for goods contained in Regulation (EC) No 2913/92 establishing the Community Customs Code.[113] With regard to the determination of the origin of services, reference is made to the origin of service providers on the basis of the Treaty's rules on the right of establishment as well as the definitions contained in Article XXVII of the GATS (Article 3.2). More specifically, under Article 3.2(a) of the Draft Regulation on the access of third-country goods and services to the Union's internal market in public procurement, the country of origin of a service provider (natural person), is the country of which he or she is a national or where he or she has a right of permanent residence. Article 3.2(b) of the Draft Regulation on the access of third-country goods and services to the Union's internal market in public procurement provides for two alternative criteria for determining the origin of services providers, legal persons, which are more complicated than the rule applied in the case the provider is a natural person. Pursuant to Article 3.2(b)(1), the country of origin of a legal person, supplying the service by modes other than a commercial presence within the EU, is "the country where the juridical person is constituted or otherwise organised under the laws of that country and in

vis third countries. (Preamble of the Draft Regulation on Access, *supra* note 109, ninth sentence).

[112] *Id.*, sixth sentence and Explanatory Memorandum thereto, p. 2.

[113] Regulation (EC) No 2913/92 of the European Parliament and the Council (Oct. 12, 1992), Establishing the Community Customs Code, OJ L302 (Oct. 19, 1992), at 1–50.

the territory of which the legal person is engaged in substantive business operations." Alternatively, "if the service is provided through a commercial presence within the Union," the country of origin of the service is "the Member State where the legal person is established and in which territory it is engaged in substantive business operations such that it has a direct and effective link with the economy of a Member State concerned." Furthermore, the same article specifies that: "For the purposes of point (2) if the legal person is not engaged in substantive business operations such that it has a direct and effective link with the economy of a Member State concerned," the origin of the natural or legal persons that own, or control the juridical person providing the service, becomes relevant in order to determine the origin of the service.[114] The Draft Regulation on the access of third-country goods and services to the Union's internal market in public procurement sets out two mechanisms enabling the Commission to limit the access of noncovered goods, services and suppliers to the EU public procurement market by adopting restrictive measures. First, under Article 6, Member States' contracting authorities and entities may exclude tenders that comprise "non-covered goods and services" for a value exceeding 50 percent of the total value of the goods and services that are the object of the tender, upon the approval of the Commission. The Commission approves the intended exclusion, among other cases, when an international agreement containing market access commitments between the EU and the third country in which the goods and/or the service originate does not exist and the third country maintains restrictive measures "leading to a lack of substantial reciprocity in market opening between the Union and the third country concerned" (Article 6.4(b)). Second, under Article 8 the Commission may start an investigation into restrictive procurement measures of third countries, on its own initiative or upon application of interested EU companies (as defined in Article 54 TFEU)[115] or a Member State. Pursuant to Article 10, when following the investigation it is found that the third country has adopted or maintains restrictive measures leading to a lack of substantial reciprocity in market opening between the Union and the third country concerned, and the consultation mechanism with the third country concerned, set out in Article 9, has failed to result in the removal of the restrictive measures on the part of the third country concerned (by means of the undertaking of international market access commitments or adoption of corrective measures), the Commission may adopt measures limiting the access of noncovered goods and services, originating in the targeted country, to

[114] Article 3.2(b) of the Draft Regulation on Access, *supra* note 109, goes on to state: "The legal person providing the service shall be considered to be: 'owned' by persons of a given country if more than 50% of the equity interest in it is beneficially owned by persons of that country and 'controlled' by persons of a given country if such persons have the power to name a majority of its directors or otherwise to legally direct its actions."

[115] Pursuant to Art. 1(g) of the Draft Regulation on Access, *supra* note 109, "'interested parties' means a company or firm formed in accordance with the law of a Member State and having its registered office, central administration or principal place of business within the Union, directly concerned by the production of goods or the provision of services which are the subject of restrictive procurement measures of third countries."

the EU procurement market. These restrictive measures may consist in the exclusion of tenders made up for more than 50 percent of goods and services originated in the country concerned or a mandatory price penalty on the part of the tender comprising goods and services originating in the third country.

The Draft Regulation on the access of third-country goods and services to the Union's internal market in public procurement has met with strong opposition from some of the EU's Northern Member States, such as the UK, Finland, and Germany, which judge the Draft Regulation as a protectionist measure. On the contrary, some other Member States, such as Italy and France, welcome the proposal by the Commission. The current discussion on the Draft Regulation on the access of third-country goods and services to the Union's internal market in public procurement shows, on the one hand, that harmonized measures on access of foreign investors to the Union's internal market as well as conditions of operation of foreign investors therewithin at the EU level are also necessary for the EU to exercise its new competence on liberalization of restrictions on foreign direct investments with a real prospect of achieving substantial results. On the other hand, it shows how adopting such harmonized measures by EU institutions can be difficult due to Member States' resistances.

C. The Destiny of Member States' BITs: The Transitional Regime for BITs between Member States and Third Countries

The Draft Regulation establishing a transitional regime for BITs between Member States and third countries, proposed by the EU Commission in July 2010 and strongly opposed by the Council,[116] has been amended by the European Parliament (EP) during the first reading on May 10, 2011 and transmitted to the Council, which intended to seek a negotiated agreement with the EP with the view to allowing the Regulation to enter into force as soon as possible. Since the approval by the Permanent Representatives Committee of the negotiating mandate in June 2011, a number of informal meetings have been held with the EP, the latest on February 28, 2012.[117] During their informal meetings, the Council and the EP reached an agreement on the changes to be introduced to the text of the Regulation. The Council adopted its position at first reading on October 4, 2012 and transmitted the text of the Regulation to the EP. The text of the Regulation, agreed between the Council and the EP, is expected to be adopted by the

---

[116] European Commission, *Proposal for a Regulation of the European Parliament and of the Council establishing transitional arrangements for bilateral investment agreements between Member States and third countries*, COM(2010)344 final [hereinafter the Draft Regulation Establishing Transitional Arrangements), *available at*: http://trade.ec.europa.eu/doclib/docs/2010/july/tradoc_146308.pdf (last visited Sept. 13, 2012).

[117] On the current status of the legislative procedure, see http://www.europarl.europa.eu/oeil/popups/ficheprocedure.do?lang=en&reference=2010/0197(COD)—keyEvents (last visited Sept. 15, 2012).

Plenary Assembly of the EP without amendments at its second reading. Therefore the agreed text is highly likely to be the final and definitive text of the Regulation.

The present section will provide an overview of the transitional regime for Member States' BITs, contained in the text of the Regulation, agreed on between the Council and the EP.[118]

In the first place, existing BITs between Member States and third countries, signed before the entry into force of the Treaty of Lisbon (December 1, 2009) (or for new Member States the date of their accession to the EU) and notified by Member States to the Commission within thirty days from the entry into force of the Regulation, can be maintained into force (or enter into force) until their replacement with an investment agreement between the same third country and the EU (Article 3). The text of the Regulation, agreed between the Council and the EP, should enable Member States to maintain into force their BITs with third countries signed before December 1, 2009, without any authorization by the Commission. This is in line with the position, taken by EU Council in its Conclusions on a comprehensive European international investment policy of October 25, 2010,[119] that BITs concluded by Member States with third countries should remain effective until "they are replaced by at least equally effective EU agreements."[120] Conversely, under the Draft Regulation proposed by the Commission in July 2010, Member States would need explicit authorization by the Commission not only to amend their BITs with third countries or to conclude new BITs ,but also to maintain existing BITs.[121] The Commission would not grant (and would be able to withdraw) the authorization necessary for a Member State to maintain an existing BIT if certain circumstances occur.[122]

Under the text of the Regulation agreed between the Council and the EP, a cooperation mechanism should replace the authorization mechanism envisaged by the Commission in its initial proposal. The cooperation mechanism included in the agreed

---

118 The text of the Regulation agreed between the Council and the EP has been released and made available to the public in October 2012 (**Position (EU) No. 11/2012 of the Council at first reading with a view to the adoption of a Regulation of the European Parliament and of the Council establishing transitional arrangements for bilateral investment agreements between Member States and third countries (Oct. 4, 2012), OJ C 352 E/23 (Nov. 23, 2012)**).

119 *See*: http://www.consilium.europa.eu/uedocs/cms_data/docs/pressdata/EN/foraff/117328.pdf (last visited Sept. 5, 2012).

120 *See* Council of the European Union, Conclusions on a comprehensive European international investment policy (Oct. 25, 2010), at 9, *available at* http://www.consilium.europa.eu/uedocs/cms_data/docs/pressdata/EN/foraff/117328.pdf (last visited Sept. 5, 2012).

121 Article 3 Draft Regulation, *supra* note 116. For a more extensive discussion of the text of the Draft Regulation initially proposed by the Commission, see De Luca, *supra* note 32, at 171–73; Colin Brown & Maria Alcover-Llubià, *The External Investment Policy of the European Union in the Light of the Entry into Force of the Treaty of Lisbon*, in YEARBOOK ON INTERNATIONAL INVESTMENT LAW & POLICY 2010/2011, 149–58 (Karl P. Sauvant ed., 2012).

122 Article 5 (on the review by the Commission of existing Member States' BIT) and Article 6 (on the ground that would lead the Commission to withdraw the authorization required for a Member State BIT to remain in force) of the Draft Regulation, *supra* note 116.

text of the Regulation is modeled on the provisions of Article 351 TFEU,[123] as interpreted by the CJEU in its case law on BIT clauses on transfer of funds.[124] On the one hand, BITs between Member States and third countries, signed before December 1, 2009, remain effective as a general rule. On the other, under the cooperation mechanism, set out in Article 6, the Member States have a duty to take any measures necessary to ensure that their BITs do not constitute a serious obstacle to the negotiation or conclusion of bilateral investment agreements with third countries by the EU, in view of their progressive replacement. Furthermore, the Commission may evaluate whether BITs contain provisions that constitute a serious obstacle to the negotiation or conclusion of bilateral investment agreements with third countries by the EU, in view of their progressive replacement (Article 5). If the Commission finds that this is the case, a consultation phase between the Commission and the Member State concerned, lasting no longer than ninety days, is open, and the Commission and the Member State have to cooperate in order to identify the appropriate actions to be taken in order to remove the obstacle. At the end of the consultations, if the matter has not been resolved otherwise, the Commission may indicate the appropriate measures and actions to be taken by the Member State. The text of the Regulation imposes upon the Member States an *obligation de résultat*, namely an obligation to remove the obstacles with any available means. Among these are the suspension and denunciation of the BIT, in line with the case law of the CJEU on Article 351 TFEU.[125]

In the second place, the text of the Regulation, agreed by the Council and the EP, sets out a two-step authorization mechanism allowing Member States to amend existing

[123] In accordance with Article 351(1) TFEU, the TEU and TFEU do not (and cannot) affect the rights and obligations arising from agreements concluded by Member States before January 1, 1958 or, for acceding states, before the date of their accession, with third countries. However, according to Article 351(2) "[t]o the extent that such agreements are not compatible with the Treaties, the Member State or States concerned shall take all appropriate steps to eliminate the incompatibilities established. Member States shall, where necessary, assist each other to this end and shall, where appropriate, adopt a common attitude."

[124] Case C-249/06, Commission of the European Communities v. Kingdom of Sweden, 2009 E.C.R. I-1335, at 34–35, 44; Case C-205/06, Commission of the European Communities v. Republic of Austria, 2009 E.C.R. I-1301, at 33–34, 44; and Case C-118/07, Commission of the European Communities v. Republic of Finland, 2009 E.C.R. I-10889, at 27–28, 35.

[125] In this respect, see the case law *supra* note 124. The three cases concern the incompatibility of the clauses on funds transfer contained in some BITs concluded between Finland, Sweden, and Austria and certain third countries with the pre-Lisbon Treaty rules on free movement of capital and payments allowing the Council to unilaterally adopt measures restricting movement of capital and payments. It is the Court's position that, although being in principle in line with free circulation of capital (Case C-249/06, Commission of the European Communities v. Kingdom of Sweden, *supra* note 124, at 27; Case C-205/06, Commission of the European Communities v. Republic of Austria, *supra* note 124, at 26; and Case C-118/07, Commission of the European Communities v. Republic of Finland, *supra* note 124, at 20), BIT clauses on funds transfer are, however, not in line with the Treaty's chapter on free movement of capital and payments as far as they do not expressly safeguard the above powers of the Council (Case C-249/06, Commission of the European Communities v. Kingdom of Sweden, *supra* note 124, at 38; Case C-205/06, Commission of the European Communities v. Republic of Austria, *supra* note 124, at 37; and Case C-118/07, Commission of the European Communities v. Republic of Finland, *supra* note 124, at 31).

BITs or to conclude new ones. As a first step, Member States notify the Commission of their intentions to open negotiations with a given third country in order to amend an existing BIT or to conclude a new one. The Commission authorizes the opening of negotiations unless one of the following four circumstances occurs. First, the opening of negotiations is in conflict with EU law other than the incompatibilities resulting from the appropriate allocation of competences between the Union and Member States. Second, the opening of negotiations is incompatible with the EU's principles and objectives under Articles 21–22 of the Treaty on European Union. Third, the opening of negotiations is superfluous because the Commission has submitted or decided to submit to the Council a recommendation to open negotiations with the third country concerned. Fourth, the opening of negotiations constitutes a serious obstacle to the negotiation or conclusion of bilateral investment agreements with third countries by the EU. Furthermore, the Commission may require Member States to include in or remove from negotiations or future agreements any clauses aimed at ensuring compatibility with EU law or consistency with the investment policy of the EU. The Commission makes its decision on the authorization within ninety days from the notification by the Member State. The Committee for the Investment Agreements, made up of representatives of the Member States, takes part in the authorization procedure, delivering an advisory opinion, pursuant to Article 4 of Regulation (EU) No 182/2011 of the European Parliament and of the Council of February 16, 2011.[126] In accordance with Article 4(2) of Regulation No 182/2011, the Commission shall decide on the authorization "taking the utmost account of the conclusions drawn from the discussions within the committee and of the opinion delivered." In the case that the authorization is not granted, the Commission issues a decision addressed to the Member State concerned, possibly subject to the CJEU's judicial review. As a second step, following the closure of negotiations, Member States notify the Commission of the text of the BIT agreed to with the third country concerned, in order to obtain the authorization by the Commission to sign and conclude the BIT. The authorization to conclude the BIT is granted unless the Commission finds one of the grounds for a refusal to authorize the opening of negotiations (already listed above) exists. The decisions authorizing Member States to sign or conclude a BIT are taken by the Commission with the participation of the Committee for the Investment Agreements, pursuant to the advisory procedure laid down in Article 4 of Regulation No 182/2011. In the case that the Commission decides to refuse an authorization, it issues a decision addressed to the Member State concerned, possibly subject to the CJEU's judicial review.

In the third place, the text of the Regulation, as agreed between the Council and the EP, establishes a transitional regime for BITs signed by Member States between the entry into force of the Treaty of Lisbon (December 1, 2009) and the entry into force of the Regulation. These BITs can be maintained in force or entered into force

---

126 Regulation (EU) No 182/2011 of the European Parliament and of the Council (Feb. 16, 2011), Laying down the rules and general principles concerning mechanisms for control by Member States of the Commission's exercise of implementing powers, OJ L 55 (Feb. 28, 2001), at 13–18.

upon explicit authorization by the Commission. The authorization mechanism, to which Member States are subject to in this respect, is similar to the authorization mechanism allowing Member States to amend their existing BITs and to conclude new ones.

Finally, the agreed text of the Regulation regulates the conduct of Member States with regard to their BITs in identical terms to those provided for in Article 13 of the Draft Regulation, proposed by the Commission. The Member States must inform the Commission of any request for arbitration against them under a BIT, and the Commission and Member States shall fully cooperate in order to prepare an effective defense. To this end, the Commission reserves the right to participate in an arbitration procedure.[127] Similarly, the Member States must inform the Commission of all meetings that take place under their BITs, as well as all issues under discussion. The Commission can require Member States to take a particular position when an issue under discussion might affect the implementation of investment policies of the EU. Furthermore, the Member States must seek the agreement of the Commission before commencing any dispute settlement proceedings against a third country under the BIT, and commence such proceedings when the Commission so requires.

To conclude, looking at the text of the Regulation, agreed on between the Council and the EP, it can be expected that existing Member States' BITs with third countries will remain effective for a long time to the benefit of EU investors abroad and foreign investors in the EU, because their replacement with bilateral investment agreements of the EU in the short term seems to be highly unlikely. Furthermore, the text agreed on between the Council and the EP seems to be more neutral than the Draft Regulation, initially proposed by the Commission, as to the question of the exact scope of the exclusive external competence of the EU in investment matters. It is the Commission's view that the exclusive competence of the EU, as extended by the Treaty of Lisbon to include foreign direct investment, would concern the admission of foreign direct investments, as well as all aspects of treatment and protection of foreign investments. Furthermore, it is the Commission's position that, besides the new rules on Common Commercial Policy, the Chapter on capital and payments (Articles 63–66 TFEU) would also imply the exclusive competence of the EU to conclude international agreements on the protection of investments in general, portfolio investments included, to the extent that international agreements on investment affect the scope of the common rules set by the Treaty's chapter on capitals and payments.[128] Consequently, because future EU agreements on investment protection will include investor–State dispute settlement clauses, in line with Member States' BITs with third countries,[129] in the context of treaty-based

---

[127] *See* Article 13(2) of the Draft Regulation Establishing Transitional Arrangements, *supra* note 116.

[128] *See* the Communication, *supra* note 68, at 8, with reference to Article 3(2) TFEU. This provision states that "the Union shall also have exclusive competence for the conclusion of an international agreement when its conclusion is provided for in a legislative act of the Union or is necessary to enable the Union to exercise its internal competence, or in so far as its conclusion may affect common rules or alter their scope."

[129] *Id.* at 10.

arbitration proceedings, according to the Commission, there is no need to distinguish between actions and measures taken by EU institutions and those taken by Member States for the purpose of international responsibility. As explained by the Commission in its Communication: "[T]he European Union, represented by the Commission, will defend all actions of EU institutions. Given the exclusive external competence, the Commission takes the view that the European Union will also be the sole defendant regarding any measure taken by a Member State which affects investments by third country nationals or companies falling within the scope of the agreement concerned."[130] As is well-known, some Member States (such as France, Germany, and the Netherlands) strongly oppose the far-reaching scope of EU exclusive competence over foreign investments claimed by the Commission.[131] The exact scope of EU competence in investment matters is still an unresolved issue. In this respect, it is worth noting that the text of the Regulation, agreed on between the Council and the EP, abandons the premise on which the Commission's initial proposal was based, that Member States' BITs would not be compatible with EU law due to the new allocation of competence between Member States and the EU over foreign investments. In other terms, the agreed text does not prejudge the question of the correct allocation of competences between the EU and its Member States over foreign investments under the Treaty.

D. Future European Agreements on Protection of Foreign Investments

The present section will provide an overview of the level of investment protection (substantive protection and procedural protection) that future EU agreements should include. This overview will be based on the general indications given by the Commission, the Council, and the EP in their official documents available to the public at the moment. These documents are the Commission's Communication, *Towards a Comprehensive European International Investment Policy*, of July 2010[132] Council's Conclusions on a comprehensive European investment policy of October 25, 2010,[133] and European Parliament's Resolution on the future European international investment policy.[134] First, the positions of the Commission, the Council, and the EP will be

130 *Id.*

131 The Commission has restated its position that "the Union has exclusive competence to conclude agreements covering all matters relating to foreign investment, that is both foreign direct investment and portfolio investment" in its *Proposal for a Regulation of the European Parliament and of the Council establishing a framework for managing financial responsibility linked to investor-state dispute settlement tribunals established by international agreements to which the European Union is party*, COM(2012)335 final, at 3 where the citation appears and 4–5. The Commission's proposal is available at http://trade.ec.europa.eu/doclib/docs/2012/june/tradoc_149567.pdf (last visited Sept. 15, 2012).

132 The Communication, *supra* note 68.

133 Council of the European Union, Conclusions on a comprehensive European international investment policy (Oct. 25, 2010), *supra* note 120.

134 European Parliament, Resolution of Apr. 6, 2011, *On the future European international investment policy, 2010/2203(INI)*, *available at*: http://www.europarl.europa.eu/sides/getDoc.do?type=TA&reference=P7-

considered separately. Second, the section will deal with the latest developments as to the level of protection to be granted to protected investors and the related issue of balancing non-trade values protection and investment protection. These latest developments are the guidelines given by the Council to the EU Commission in the negotiating mandate for the Chapters on investment protection in FTAs of the EU with Canada, India, and Singapore.[135]

Finally, the section will conclude with some indications on the possible basic elements of future chapters on investment protection that will be included in EU FTAs with Singapore, Canada, and India.

As to the position of the Commission, the Communication contains the Commission's view as to the core elements of the oncoming European international investment policy. The Communication has great significance in elucidating the European Commission's view as to the scope and level of protection for EU investors as well as the balancing between investment protection and non-trade values protection. As to the scope and level of protection for EU investors, according to the Commission, future European agreements will cover both direct investment and portfolio investments and will include all aspects of treatment and protection of foreign investments with which Member States' BITs deal. These aspects encompass, not only the relative standards of treatment (namely, the national treatment and most-favored-nation (MFN) standards), but also the absolute standards to be applied at the post-entry stage set out in Member States' bilateral investment treaties (BITs). These standards are the fair and equitable treatment standard; full protection and security; and protection from expropriation, nationalization, and equivalent measures, as well as protection of contractual rights granted by the host state to foreign investors (namely, the so-called umbrella clauses) and clauses on free transfer of funds.[136] Moreover, future EU agreements on investment protection will include investor–State dispute settlement clauses, in line with Member States' BITs with third countries.

The inclusion of the above core elements in the oncoming EU investment policy, as envisaged by the Commission, is coherent and in line with Member States' international practices on the protection of their investors abroad, generally speaking of course.[137] As observed in legal literature, the main purpose of Member States' BITs "was historically that of protecting investments from industrialized party into the developing one, thereby (hopefully) attracting capital into the latter's economy."[138] The

TA-2011-0141&language=EN (last visited Sept. 14, 2012).

135 Council of the European Union, Negotiating mandates for investment protection chapters in free trade agreements of the EU with Canada, India, and Singapore, *available at*: http://www.bilaterals.org/spip.php?article20272&lang=en (last visited Sept. 14, 2012).

136 The Communication, *supra* note 68, at 8.

137 This is because not all clauses, listed by the Commission in its Communication, can be considered as standard clauses in respect of all European models of BIT. For instance, this is the case with the so-called umbrella clause and the full protection and security standard clause.

138 Giorgio Sacerdoti, *Bilateral Treaties and Multilateral Instruments on Investment Protection*, 269 Recueil des Cours 251, 327, 328 (1997). In this respect, see also Patrick Juillard, *Freedom of Establishment,*

great majority of Member States still stick to the above traditional purpose of BITs. Member States' BITs aim to provide the highest possible level of protection to their nationals' economic interests abroad.

In this regard, it is the view of the Commission that the investment policy of the EU should be based on Member State best practices. Moreover, the Union's action should be aimed at achieving better results than those that have been obtained or could have been obtained by Member States individually.[139] This implies that, when negotiating new international investment agreements (IIAs) with any given third country, the EU has to consider the level of protection already granted to EU investors by Member States' BITs. In other terms, the protection under future EU agreements should be above or at least equivalent to the overall level of protection granted by Member States BITs to EU investors.

With regard to non-trade values protection and investment protection and their balancing, the Commission refers to two issues. The first concerns the protection of state freedom of action in regulating in the interest of non-trade values, such as health, safety, or environmental concerns. The second issue concerns the need to take into account the promotion of non-trade values such as the rule of law, human rights, environment, and sustainable development in elaborating the investment policy of the EU.

As to the first issue, namely the safeguarding of host states' regulatory space for regulation in the public interest, it is the Commission's view that the common investment policy has to "continue to allow the Union, and the Member States to adopt and enforce measures necessary to pursue public policy objectives."[140] As to the type of regulatory interests deserving protection, in its Communication the Commission explicitly mentions the protection of the environment, decent work, health and safety at work, consumer protection, cultural diversity, development policy, and competition policy.[141] In this respect, it is worth noting that the Commission does not specify the means through which the right of parties to EU investment agreements to adopt and enforce regulatory measures will be concretely safeguarded in future investment agreements.

As to the second issue, namely the promotion of the rule of law, human rights, environment, and sustainable development, the Commission explicitly makes reference to the OECD Guidelines for Multinational Enterprises as an important instrument as to balancing investors' rights and responsibilities.[142] The Commission paves the way for a possible inclusion of a reference to the Guidelines in future investment agreements or chapters on investment protection in its FTAs.

Freedom of Capital Movements, and Freedom of Investment, 15 ICSID Rev.—For. Inv. L.J. 322, 328 (2000).

139 The Communication, *supra* note 68, at 6.

140 *Id.* at 9.

141 *Id.*

142 *Id.* at 9.

In its Conclusions on a comprehensive European international investment policy of October 25, 2010, the Council took its position on the core elements of EU's investment policy as envisaged by the Commission.

As far as regards the level of protection for EU investors, it is sufficient to say that the position of the Council is close to the position of the Commission.

With regard to non-trade values protection and investment protection and their balancing, the Council emphasized that "in keeping with existing practices by Member States" and in accordance with Article 205 TFEU and Article 21 TEU, the European policy in investment matters should be guided by principles such as the rule of law, human rights, and sustainable development.[143] Apparently, the Council's position is that a European investment policy, elaborated on the basis of Member States' BITs, will continue to allow the EU and Member States to pursue public policy objectives as do Member States' BITs. It is the position of some Member States that BITs foster the economic development of contracting parties by promoting the rule of law. The principal aim of Member States' BITs is the protection of investments. Nevertheless, in providing high standards of protection of foreign investors against the arbitrary conduct of host states, BITs have the further effect of generally promoting the rule of law, which is also in the interest of national investors.[144] In turn, the promotion of the rule of law has been argued as a means of (indirectly) fostering economic development.[145]

Contrary to the position of the Commission on the OECD Guidelines for Multinational Enterprises, the Council does not consider a reference to such Guidelines in an investment protection context as appropriate. The Council makes it clear that "the main focus of international investment agreements should continue to be effective and ambitious investment protection and market access."[146]

Although the Commission and the Council seem to have quite converging views regarding the level of substantive and procedural protection to be granted to EU investors under future EU investment agreements as well as the balancing between investment protection and states' right to regulate in the public interest, a divergent view has been expressed by the EP in its Resolution of April 6, 2011 on the future European international investment policy.[147]

---

[143] Council of the European Union, Conclusions on a comprehensive European international investment policy (Oct. 25, 2010), *supra* note 127, at 17.

[144] In this respect, see Roberto Echandi, *What Do Developing Countries Expect from the International Investment Regime?*, *in* THE EVOLVING INTERNATIONAL INVESTMENT REGIME: EXPECTATIONS, REALITIES, OPTIONS 3 ff., 13–14 (José E. Alvarez, Karl P. Sauvant, Kamil Gérard Ahmed & Gabriela del P. Vizcaíno eds., 2011).

[145] In this respect, see Thomas W. Wälde, *Improving the Mechanisms for Treaty Negotiation and Investment Disputes, Competition and Choice as the Path to Quality and Legitimacy*, *in* YEARBOOK ON INTERNATIONAL INVESTMENT LAW AND POLICY, 2008–2009, at 505 ff., 513–14 (Karl P. Sauvant ed., 2009).

[146] Council of the European Union, Conclusions on a comprehensive European international investment policy (Oct. 25, 2010), *supra* note 127, at 16.

[147] European Parliament, Resolution of Apr. 6, 2011, *On the future European international investment policy*, *supra* note 141.

In its Resolution, the EP first emphasizes the need to protect the right to regulate in the public interest in new investment agreements,[148] based on the assumption that BITs of Member States with third countries are too one-sided in favor of investors and a too investor-oriented arbitral practice interpreting and applying the fair and equitable treatment standard exists at the moment.[149] In this respect, a clear (although implicit) reference is made by the EP to the first generation of decisions concerning Argentina's emergency measures.[150]

Given the above considerations, according to the EP, future European agreements should include not all standards listed by the Commission and Council, but only non-discrimination standards drafted so as to include the "in like circumstances" requirement, a fair and equitable treatment standard with an express linkage to customary international law (namely, the international minimum standard of treatment) and protection against direct and indirect expropriation provided that a definition that balances (in a clear and fair manner) public welfare objectives and investors' interests is given.[151]

In order to safeguard host states' regulatory space in the public interest, according to the EP, all EU agreements have to include specific clauses on the right of Contracting States to regulate in the public interest.[152] Among the type of regulatory interests mentioned are the protection of national security, environment, public health, workers' and consumers' rights, industrial policy, and cultural diversity.[153] Furthermore, the EP refers to the inclusion of sector-specific reservations/exceptions and carve-out clauses concerning "sensitive sectors such as culture, education, public health and those sectors which are strategically important for national defence."[154] Finally, the EP "strongly support[s]" the inclusion in all European agreements of a reference to the OECD Guidelines for Multinational Enterprises[155] as well as the inclusion of the corporate social responsibility clauses, and effective social and environmental clauses.[156] In this respect, the EP draws the attention of the Commission to the clauses that prevent the watering-down of social and environmental legislation in order to attract investment contained in some recent investment agreements,[157] such

---

148 *Id.* at 6, 17, 23 and 25.

149 *Id.* at G and 24.

150 CMS Gas Transmission Company v. Argentina, ICSID Case No. ARB/01/8, *award* (May 12, 2005); Sempra Energy International v. The Argentine Republic, ICSID Case No. ARB/02/16, *annulment decision* (June 19, 2010); Enron Corporation and Ponderosa Assets, L.P v. Argentine Republic, ICSID Case No. ARB/01/3, *annulment decision* (July 30, 2010), at 367–95).

151 European Parliament, Resolution of Apr. 6, 2011, *On the future European international investment policy*, *supra* note 141, at 19.

152 *Id.* at 25.

153 *Id.*

154 *Id.* at 26.

155 *Id.* at 27.

156 *Id.* at 28.

157 *Id.* at 30.

as the U.S.–Panama Trade Promotion Agreement,[158] the U.S. BIT model of 2012,[159] and the EU–South Korea FTA.[160]

In the latest developments, in September 2011, the Council authorized the Commission to negotiate investment protection chapters in EU FTAs with Canada, India, and Singapore.[161]

Pursuant to the mandate, the general objective of the Commission in negotiating the Chapters on investment protection with Canada, India, and Singapore should be to obtain the highest possible level of legal protection and certainty for EU investors. The provisions of the new Chapters should preserve the right of the EU and the Member States to adopt and enforce measures necessary to pursue legitimate public policy objectives in a nondiscriminatory manner. As to the type of regulatory interests, the mandate lists social and environmental security, public health and safety, and cultural diversity. The Chapters should include broad definitions of both "covered investors" and "investments."

The new Chapters should provide investors with all standards of protection listed by the Commission and the Council in their Communication and Conclusions, respectively.

State-to-state dispute settlement clauses will be included in the Chapters but will not interfere with the right of investors to pursue international arbitration directly against the host state. This in an important indication, indeed. The Council excludes that the new Chapters will include clauses that allow Contracting Parties to stop investment arbitration proceedings commenced by investors or influence the final outcomes of arbitral tribunals with their binding decisions, such as the clauses on prudential measures in financial services and tax matters included in the U.S. BIT models of 2004 and 2012.[162]

The Chapters will include just post-establishment standards of treatment and protection. As a rule, market access commitments should be excluded from the scope of investor–state dispute settlement clauses. Once again this is in line with Member States' BITs, which do not include commitments on admission and initial establishment of foreign investors and investments, generally speaking of course.[163]

Finally, the mandate of the Council to the Commission does not make any reference to investors' responsibilities or to OECD Guidelines.

Let us conclude with some indications on the possible basic elements of the Chapters on investment protection, which the Commission is currently negotiating: it

---

[158] Chapter Sixteen (Labor) and Chapter Seventeen (Environment) U.S.–Panama Trade Promotion Agreement of June 28, 2007.

[159] Art. 12 (Investment and Environment) and Art. 13 (Investment and Labor) U.S. BIT Model of 2012.

[160] Art. 13.3, Art. 13.4.3, and Art. 13.7 EU–South Korea FTA.

[161] The text of the negotiating mandates approved by the General Affairs Council for investment protection chapters in free trade agreements of the EU with Canada, India, and Singapore is available at: http://www.bilaterals.org/spip.php?article20272&lang=en (last visited Sept. 15, 2012).

[162] Art. 20 and Art. 21 U.S. BIT Models of 2004 and 2012.

[163] For example, the 2003 Italy BIT model is worthy of mention as an exception.

is likely that the new Chapters will include "in accordance with host State's laws" provisions[164] that preserve the sovereign rights of each party to the agreement to regulate the admission and the initial establishment of covered investments.[165] In fact, following the indication of the Council in the mandate, market access commitments should be excluded from the scope of investor–state dispute settlement clauses. Conversely, these commitments will be enforceable under state-to-state dispute settlement mechanisms only.

Following the indications given by both the Council and the Commission, it is likely that EU FTAs' chapters on investment protection will include a definition of covered investments similar to the asset-based definition of covered investments contained in the great majority of Member State BITs. As to the definition of covered investors, it is likely that the new chapters will recall the definition of "juridical persons" included in Article 7.2(f)(i) of the EU–South Korea FTA, already reported in Section B.2.1. Because the definition of "juridical persons" included in Article 7.2(f)(i) of the EU–South Korea FTA does not cover juridical persons incorporated in the host state of the investment, even if controlled and/or owned by foreign investors, a definition to include juridical persons incorporated and established in the host party but owned or controlled by natural or juridical persons of the other party will be added for the purpose of investor–state arbitration.

Finally, it is likely that the Chapters on investment protection will safeguard expressly the right of Contracting Parties to regulate in the public interest. That said, it is unclear how the safeguarding of such a right will be achieved. There are at least three possible means in this respect. First, the Parties' right to regulate in the public interest could be mentioned in the Preamble of the agreement, following the recent practice of the EU in these matters. In this respect, the Preamble of the EU–South Korea FTA is worthy of mention. In the Preamble of the EU–South Korea FTA, the Parties recognize "the right of the Parties to take measures necessary to achieve legitimate public policy objectives on the basis of the level of protection that they deem appropriate, provided that such measures do not constitute a means of unjustifiable discrimination or a disguised restriction on international trade, as reflected in this Agreement."[166] This sentence concerning the right of the Parties to regulate in the public interest is clearly modelled on the text of Article XX of the General Agreement

---

164 For example, see Article 2(1) 2008 Germany Model BIT, which provides that "[e]ach Contracting State shall in its territory promote as far as possible investments by investors of the other Contracting State and admit such investments *in accordance with its legislation*" (emphasis added). With similar wording, Article 2 of the 2006 France Model BIT provides that: "[e]ach Contracting Party shall promote and admit on its territory and in its maritime area, *in accordance with its legislation* and with the provisions of this Agreement, investments made by nationals or companies of the other Contracting Party" and Article 2(1) of the 2005 UK. Model BIT provides that: "[e]ach Contracting Party shall encourage and create favourable conditions for nationals and companies of the other Contracting Party to invest capital in its territory, and, subject to its right to exercise powers conferred by its laws, shall admit such capital" (emphasis added).

165 In this respect, see De Luca, *supra* note 32, at 203–11 and references cited there.

166 EU–Korea FTA, *supra* note 52, sixth sentence.

on tariffs and trade. Second, Contracting Parties' regulatory powers could be made the object of a specific and autonomous clause of a general character, following the indications of the EP. A clause worded in similar terms to those of Article 7.1(4) EU–Korea FTA might be included. Article 7.1(4), which is among the general provisions opening the Chapter governing trade in services, establishment, and electronic commerce, provides that "[c]onsistent with this Chapter, each Party retains the right to regulate and to introduce new regulations to meet legitimate policy objectives." Third, a reference to the Parties' right to regulate in the public interest could be included in the clauses on the standards of protection and treatment or in an interpretative Annex to the Chapters.

Conclusions

The need to better protect EU investors' interests abroad, possibly integrating investment liberalization and investment protection, brought about the extension of the EU external competence to include foreign direct investment. The Treaty of Lisbon extended the EU's exclusive competence on Common Commercial Policy to foreign direct investments with the purpose of strengthening the role of the EU on the international scene as an economic actor in competition with NAFTA signatories and Japan, as well as new and emerging players such as China. The extension of the EU external competence over investment matters is mainly aimed at strengthening the EU's power in negotiating market access commitments with third parties. Nevertheless, the external action of the EU in eliminating restrictions on foreign direct investment might prove less effective than expected unless European harmonized rules on access and conditions of operation of foreign investors are adopted. Furthermore, the "old" problem of the exact scope of EU exclusive competence over investments is still open, and new issues, such the protection of the right of contracting parties to investment agreements to regulate in the public interest (at least as far as concerns some Member States' BIT models), and the consistency between the FTAs' chapters on trade in services and establishment, on the one side, and the FTAs' chapters on investment protection, on the other, has emerged from the discussion between Member States and the Commission on the chapters on investment protection that the EU is currently negotiating with third parties. It can be expected that the next years will be decisive in delineating a clearer framework for foreign investment in the EU.

7

THE EFFECT OF SURVIVAL AND WITHDRAWAL CLAUSES IN INVESTMENT TREATIES: PROTECTION OF INVESTMENTS IN LATIN AMERICA

Gisela Bolívar

I. Introduction

As a result of trade opening in recent years, Latin American countries have faced the need to comply with international treaties and, in tandem, the need to attract Foreign Direct Investment (FDI) in harmony with domestic legislation and their international obligations.

Analyzing the treaties that protect FDI, especially those clauses that determine its benefits and its permanence, such as the survival and withdrawal clauses, it is an important task to better understand the impact of international obligations, vis-à-vis national legislations, particularly in countries where investors' rights have been jeopardized.

There are several cases where countries have decided not to comply with their international obligations in order to gain political support from some social sectors. It is worthy to mention as examples among Latin American countries, Venezuela,[1]

[1] Since Hugo Chávez has been in power, there have been several state actions against companies that invested through FDI in Venezuelan territory. This chapter intends to analyze the effects of those actions against one particular company; irrespective to that case, more than twenty other cases have been filed against Venezuela before the International Centre for Settlement of Investment Disputes (ICSID). Most of those cases are still pending resolution. It is noteworthy to report that on January 24, 2012, the Venezuelan government denounced the ICSID Convention. For other cases filed before the

Argentina,[2] and Bolivia,[3] where their governments have decided to nationalize some important sectors of their industry, as well as apply denunciation clauses to avoid continuing respecting their international obligations through treaties.

Statistics show that one of the principal benefits created by free trade zones[4] is growth in investments, particularly in FDI. According to several publications that reflect the impact of FDI on development: "Beyond the initial macroeconomic stimulus from the actual investment, FDI influences growth by raising total factor productivity and, more generally, the efficiency of resource use in the recipient economy. This works through three channels: the linkages between FDI and foreign trade flows, the spillovers and other externalities vis-à-vis the host country business sector, and the direct impact on structural factors in the host economy."[5]

Although it is true that a variety of economic theories have explained the need for international trade to exist worldwide,[6] it is also true that the reasons behind the existence of FDI do not necessarily stem from the creation of free trade zones, although these do benefit FDI by providing clear rules that give security and legal certainty to investors through free trade agreements (FTAs), and in particular through bilateral investment treaties (BITs).

ICSID against the Venezuelan government, please refer to: http://icsid.worldbank.org/ICSID/Index.jsp, and for the denunciation of Venezuela of the ICSID to: http://icsid.worldbank.org/ICSID/FrontServlet?requestType=CasesRH&actionVal=OpenPage&PageType=AnnouncementsFrame&FromPage=Announcements&pageName=Announcement100.

[2] In April 2012, the Argentinian president took over the management of a shareholder Spanish oil company, "Repsol," and nationalized most of its assets without paying the corresponding market price. Argentina has also faced several cases before the ICSID related to its nationalization policy. Please refer to: http://icsid.worldbank.org/ICSID/Index.jsp.

[3] Since 2007, the Bolivian government has denounced the ICSID Convention, followed in 2009 by Ecuador, with the main aim of avoiding compliance with international obligations derived therefrom. Among other publications, please refer to: http://www.iisd.org/itn/2012/04/13/venezuelas-withdrawal-from-icsid-what-it-does-and-does-not-achieve/.

[4] Free trade zones are considered the second level among the traditional forms of integration—a step more developed than preferential tariff areas, because they seek to eliminate tariff and nontariff barriers. But in addition opening up of trade in goods and services has affected other sectors that have shown clear and substantial benefits, such as foreign direct and indirect investments.

[5] "Foreign Direct Investments for Development. Maximising Benefits, Minimising Costs. Overview." OECD 2002, *available at* http://www.oecd.org/dataoecd/47/51/1959815.pdf.

[6] Note the evolution of economic theories beginning with Adam Smith, David Ricardo, and Heckscher-Ohlin, and passing through the Product Life-Cycle Theory of the 1960s, the New Trade Theory of the 1970s that included such concepts as economies of scale and "first mover advantages" as well as Porter's Diamond and National Competitive Advantage, arriving at today's theories, among which the most noteworthy were developed by Paul Krugman on imperfect competition and the international economy. For a summary of these subjects refer to E. HELPMAN & P. KRUGMAN, MARKET STRUCTURE AND FOREIGN TRADE: INCREASING RETURNS, IMPERFECT COMPETITION, AND THE INTERNATIONAL ECONOMY (1985). *See also* P. Krugman, *Does the New Trade Theory Require a New Trade Policy?*, 15(4) WORLD ECON. 423–41 (1992).

There are also theories[7] that have tried to explain the FDI phenomenon, especially from an economic point of view. These theories have focused on the reasons companies and/or investors prefer to make an investment acquiring assets in a foreign country in order to manage these assets, independently of the economic, legal, and social costs[8] that this implies.

One of the countries that has experienced greater development of FDI around the world has been the United States,[9] which since the end of World War II has been the country with the highest level of FDI, a ranking that it maintained until the end of the twentieth century. Another five countries that have traditionally represented an important source for generating FDI are Great Britain, France, Germany, Holland, and Japan.[10] Given those countries' experience with FDI, they have more-developed legislation on this subject, and their experience is also evident from their signing of various bilateral investment treaties.

However, worldwide interest has arisen in the existence of foreign investment in specific nations' territories, as in the outstanding case of China, a nation that has even created modern legal models that ensure assistance to foreign investors and thereby encourage FDI.[11]

---

[7] *See, e.g.*, S.H. HYMER, *The International Operations of National Firms: A Study of Direct Foreign Investment* (1976); A.M. RUGMAN, INSIDE THE MULTINATIONALS: THE ECNOMICS OF INTERNAL MARKETS (1981).

[8] It is worth mentioning (as an example of the variety of problems faced by companies) the solution to practical problems of adaption, such as different consumer tastes, which depend on—among other things—their customs. This creates, for example, product *tropicalization*, or adaption to different legal and economic systems, that most of the time result in an increase of costs of production.

[9] However, in some sectors, such as communications, the United States has maintained certain protective rules for its domestic investors by imposing more requirements for compliance on foreign investors, such as limits on the percentage of participation.

[10] *See* UNITED NATIONS, WORLD INVESTMENT REPORT, 2006 (2006). Cited by CHARLES W. L. HILL, INTERNATIONAL BUSINESS: COMPETING IN THE GLOBAL MARKET PLACE 247 (7th ed. 2009).

[11] China's FDI legislation presents a special case and includes a variety of examples of how this type of investment has been fostered. Since the early 1980s, China reformed its tax system by promulgating several tax laws to attract FDI; these caused foreign companies to enjoy preferential tax treatment vis à vis domestic companies. After that, in 1994, the Chinese government implemented a simplified tax system that also benefitted foreign companies. More recently, since 2008, Chinese tax legislation has been equalized between local companies and foreign companies, leading that regime into a more modernized and fairer system. The development of the Chinese tax regime shows a modern way, first to improve FDI to grant access to new technology, and then to promote a strong growth in quality among competitors. The new tax regulation in addition to the entry to the World Trade Organization, made China to progress in the facilitation of the FDI during the Tenth Five Year Plan period (such periods are set up by the Chinese government as an organization plan), which started in 2001. During that period, FDI grew by more than 34%. All this new income tax and foreign investment regulation has made China an important production base. This has signified a total success for China attracting FDI. *See* Suwina Cheng & Shanshan Shi, *The Impact of New Income Tax on Foreign Invested Enterprises in China*, 38(1) INT'L TAX J. 17–48, 10P (2012); Hui Huang, *The Regulation of Foreign Investment in Post-WTO China: A Political Economy Analysis*, 23(1) COL. J. ASIAN L. 185–215, 31P (2009) ; Invest in China, available at: http://www.fdi.gov.cn/pub/FDI_EN/Economy/Investment%20Environment/default.htm; for further analysis on the effects of Investment Law in China, please refer to: Wenhau Shan, "China and International Investment Law," Chapter 9 in the present volume.

As part of fostering the FDI that countries seek, we observe the signing of more than two thousand bilateral investment treaties. These treaties ensure, among other things, the permanence of FDI in the country of one party, and provides investors with the certainty and legal security necessary to maintain their investments, particularly through respect for the principle of nondiscrimination that is safeguarded by the concepts of national treatment and most-favored-nation status, as well as by dispute settlement mechanisms such as arbitration that are contained in these treaties.

Nevertheless, not all nations receiving investments have sought to encourage FDI. Several examples to the contrary demonstrate obstacles that impede investors from beginning projects, and some policies that actually provide disincentives for FDI and international trade.[12]

The latter countries include Venezuela, a country that changed its international trade policy when Hugo Chavez rose to power, placing major restrictions on FDI development, especially for those companies where the government has had a special interest, owing to the economic income that they represent for the Venezuelan state.

During the 1990s Venezuela had been characterized by its intent to open its market to a broader panorama, as evidenced by the signing of a variety of trade treaties. It was in this era—a little after its adherence to GATT, on August 31, 1990, and after becoming a member of the WTO in 1995—when like several other Latin American countries it began its process of trade liberalization.

Venezuela signed several treaties, including, among others, the Free Trade Agreement with Mexico, Colombia, and Venezuela (G3); the Bilateral Investment Treaty with the Netherlands (BIT); and the Convention on the Settlement of Investment Disputes between States and Nationals of Other States (the ICSID Convention[13]), among others.

On January 1, 1995,[14] the G3 came into effect. This treaty contained the rules that were to govern international trade between the three member nations. It also regulated investments and defined what was considered an investment and an investor of another Party. It also established the dispute settlement mechanism applicable to

---

[12] It bears mention that in fact many countries that have traditionally promoted FDI have as a means of protecting their national industry also occasionally implemented policies to discourage this type of investment.

[13] International Centre for Settlement of Investment Disputes. According to what is stated on the ICSID's own Web page: "ICSID is an autonomous international institution established under the Convention on the Settlement of Investment Disputes between States and Nationals of Other States (the ICSID or the Washington Convention) with over one hundred and forty member States. The Convention sets forth ICSID's mandate, organization and core functions. The primary purpose of ICSID is to provide facilities for conciliation and arbitration of international investment disputes. The ICSID Convention is a multilateral treaty formulated by the Executive Directors of the International Bank for Reconstruction and Development (the World Bank). It was opened for signature on March 18, 1965 and entered into force on October 14, 1966."; *available at* http://icsid.worldbank.org/ICSID/FrontServlet?requestType=CasesRH&actionVal=ShowHome&pageName=AboutICSID_Home.

[14] *See* Decree Promulgating the G3, published in Mexico's *Diario Oficial de la Federación* on Jan. 9, 1995, Article 23-04.

conflicts that arise regarding the one company's or person's investment in another Party-State.

One of the G3's primary goals—in addition to establishing clear rules for the three countries' international trade—was to fix a predictable framework for trade that allowed planning productive activities and investment,[15] as well as to generate more businesses that would foster development of their economies.

For its part, the Bilateral Investment Treaty (BIT) with the Netherlands ensured nondiscriminatory fair treatment for investments from member countries and provided clear rules to protect investors' interests.

As for the ICSID Convention, it gave security in case of disputes and provided that Venezuela would use the dispute settlement mechanisms set forth in this treaty.

Because of both the economic and the legal importance of FDI issues in less-developed countries, and because of its repercussions in areas such as Latin America, we will take a "case study" approach to analyzing the FDI issues involving the company Cementos Mexicanos (CEMEX) in Venezuela, vis à vis the treaties protecting investment that Venezuela had signed. We will also analyze the effects of the survival and denunciation or withdrawal clauses in the treaties that protect FDI and investor interests.

II. Cemex and Venezuela

CEMEX[16] is a Mexican company that currently produces one-third of all cement and ranks third in cement sales worldwide. It has a presence in more than fifty countries and operates on five continents: North America, South America, Europe, Asia and Africa. It is one of the leading companies in the sector around the world.

The cement company first began its expansion in Mexico by acquiring and setting up several plants, then began its international expansion at the beginning of the 1990s.

Its first acquisition abroad took place in Spain. In Latin America, it bought producing cement plants established in Venezuela, Panama, the Dominican Republic, Colombia, and Costa Rica. It also made investments in the Philippines and in Egypt.

Owing to its rapid and accelerating expansion, CEMEX has had to seek out legal formulas that ensure the success and permanence of its investments, precisely because of the different positions countries have taken with regard to FDI.

Therefore, when it decided to invest in Venezuela, and foresaw possible future disputes, CEMEX decided to make this investment on the basis of the Netherlands' legislation. That is, CEMEX bought shares in Venezuela as a company constituted under Dutch law.

15 *Id.* at 3.

16 Company information was obtained from the Web page: www.cemex.com.

Up until the beginning of 1998, Venezuela had sought to expand its economy using a neoliberal policy that led to signing trade treaties and bilateral investment treaties with a variety of countries.[17]

According to the Annual worldwide Cemex Report, on 1997, Venezuela enjoyed a very strong year under economic terms. Construction activity increased 13 percent in 1997, and domestic cement demand grew 16 percent. The Report stated that such growth was driven by the private sector, mainly the petroleum industry, while public sector construction activity remained relatively flat. The same Report states that cement sales volume grew 15 percent compared to the previous year, due to a rising domestic demand and increased in capacity utilization. During that year the company increased its facilities and foresaw a significant growth for the upcoming years.[18]

Irrespective to the growth of economic participation of several foreign companies, including CEMEX, Venezuela's trade relations with other countries—and above all trade relations with investors from other countries investing in Venezuela—have been seriously impaired since Chavez came to power in 1998/[19] In several cases the Venezuelan government has invoked the application of domestic legislation under which it has revoked permits and has even expropriated goods for state ownership.

Protectionist measures have caused companies that were already established in Venezuela to move elsewhere (in the best of cases), to accept some payment agreement from the Venezuelan government that has become the majority shareholder or the owner of the company, or—as is the case with CEMEX—to initiate international legal proceedings against measures imposed by the Venezuelan government because the company considers these measures as violating trade treaties or bilateral trade agreements.[20]

---

[17] Venezuela has signed almost thirty different BITs since 1993. Even after 1998, the Venezuelan government signed some BITs. *See* http·//unctad.org/Sections/dite_pcbb/docs/bits_venezuela.pdf.

[18] http://www.cemex.com/InvestorCenter/files/1997/Ar97full.pdf, at 18.

[19] Venezuelan domestic legislation, and in particular the Venezuelan Constitution, has been amended on several occasions since Chavez came to power; these changes include, among other things, allowing the president to remove and appoint Supreme Court judges, as well as to extend the term of office of the serving president. Those changes implied a stronger individual power for Chavez, who in other words is allowed to act without legal restrictions in various sectors. For additional information on the history and political evolution of *Chavismo* in Venezuela, see sources such as RICHARD GOTT, HUGO CHAVEZ AND THE BOLIVARIAN REVOLUTION: THE BOLIVARIAN REVOLUTION IN VENEZUELA (2005); JORGE JORQUERA, VENEZUELA: THE REVOLUTION UNFOLDING IN LATIN AMERICA (2005); ENRIQUE KRAUZE, *El Poder Y El Delirio* (2008).

[20] Venezuela has been the respondent in a variety of cases before the ICSID for several years. The claimants are companies of various nationalities that have invested in Venezuela, and some are even companies constituted under Venezuelan law. Among other cases, there is that of the Mobil Corporation in the energy sector, Mobil Corp. and Others v. Bolivarian Republic of Venezuela, ICSID Case No. ARB/07/27. *See* the list of cases at http://icsid.worldbank.org/ICSID/FrontServlet.

III. The Effects of Denunciation or Withdrawal in the Treaties that Protect Investments and in the G3

After the signing of the G3, trade relations between Mexico and Venezuela took a turn for the better, and several Mexican companies were interested in investing in Venezuela.[21] The treaty came into effect beginning in 1995, but once Chavez was in power, he withdrew from the treaty on May 22, 2006, on the basis of its Article 23-08.

The denunciation of or withdrawal from treaties is done through a unilateral state declaration and is an example of the exercise of sovereignty by states in addressing international treaties. Although that is the consensus interpretation, from our point of view, the negative impact of a withdrawal on the other Parties should be taken into account and consequently, those rights that have already been exercised in application of the treaty in question, before the withdrawal, should be legally ensured.

The denunciation should not proceed if the other Parties to the treaty can allege an adverse effect deriving directly from the denunciation: for example, if one of the Parties has failed to comply in a way that could affect the future development of transactions carried out before the denunciation (derived from the application of the treaty), and if the damage caused by such violation is difficult to resolve or remedy owing to the denunciation's effects. In the case of trade treaties these violations could, for example, be related to failure to comply with the decisions of the dispute settlement mechanisms or failure to comply with tariff reduction periods, and, in regard to investments specifically, include violations that could impair investments that have already been made.

This is precisely the reason there is a survival clause in a variety of bilateral investment treaties. A survival clause extends the mandatory applicability of a treaty for a sufficient period of time after the withdrawal is made by one of the Parties so that those affected can take corresponding action to ensure the protection of their investment rights acquired as part of the treaty provisions.

The foregoing notwithstanding, in a general sense we understand that states must be able to maintain intact their sovereignty both for signing treaties and for withdrawing from them or ceasing to be part of them. That is the reason the Vienna Convention on the Law of Treaties (known as the Vienna Convention)[22] established the following as a general rule on denunciation in its Article 56:

Article 56 Denunciation of or withdrawal from a treaty containing no provision regarding termination, denunciation or withdrawal

---

[21] In the first ten years that the G3 was in effect, trade among the three countries was 132% greater than in the year before the treaty went into effect. According to international figures, in 2008 trade between Mexico and Venezuela reached US$3.08 billion. GUSTAVO VEGA CÁNOVAS, *El Tratado De Libre Comercio En América Del Norte. Visión Retrospectiva Y Retos Al Futuro.* EL COLEGIO DE MÉXICO 377 (2010).

[22] Done at Vienna on May 23, 1969. Entered into force on Jan. 27, 1980. United Nations, *Treaty Series*, Vol. 1155, p. 331, *available at* http://untreaty.un.org/ilc/texts/instruments/english/conventions/1_1_1969.pdf

1. A treaty which contains no provision regarding its termination and which does not provide for denunciation or withdrawal ***is not subject to denunciation or withdrawal unless***:

(*a*) it is established that the parties intended to admit the possibility of denunciation or withdrawal; or (*b*) a right of denunciation or withdrawal may be implied by the nature of the treaty.

2. A party shall give not less than twelve months' notice of its intention to denounce or withdraw from a treaty under paragraph 1."

(emphasis added)

In other words, the Vienna Convention as an exception has established the denunciation. The foregoing reaffirms that one of the main objectives of the member country signatories to the Vienna Convention was to establish the rules for compliance as well as the mandatory nature of treaties and consequences in cases of treaty violations.

Nonetheless, as in any other international agreement provision, it is impossible to determine the different scenarios that one Party may face. Therefore, we do consider that it would be advisable to give to the other involved Parties the opportunity to analyze what consequences a denunciation may cause among them, and particularly, where investments are involved, the effects on their investors.

As the nature of investment treaties is to protect investors' rights along with creating jobs, infrastructure, and economic growth, a survival clause ensures that any investment made before a denunciation takes place is protected.

Although in the G3 text there is no obligation to establish the reasons for denunciation, Venezuela withdrew arguing supposedly negative economic effects on population that were caused not only by companies such as CEMEX in its territory, but also by many other foreign companies. What had actually happened was that these companies had helped to develop industries that until such FDI was made had not been competitive in the Venezuelan market, much less in the world market.

In the case of the G3, the withdrawal from the treaty was set forth in Article 23-08 under the following terms:

"Article 23-08: Denunciation

1. ***Any Party may withdraw from this Treaty.*** This denunciation will take effect 180 days after being communicated to the other Parties and after communicating the withdrawal to the Secretary General's Office of the Latin American Integration Association, without prejudice to the Parties' ability to agree on a different time period.

2. The withdrawal from this Treaty by one Party does not affect its being in force among the other Parties." (emphasis added)

The treaty text does not include an obligation for the Party that is withdrawing to allege any type of violation or failure to comply with the treaty, but contains the obligation to give notice of said denunciation and the obligation to comply with the time period that must elapse for it to come into effect (six months). We view this as a measure that ensures "mitigation" for the remaining Parties of possible ownership impairment derived from the withdrawal,[23] however this is not mitigation that is sufficient to compensate for the effects.

There are some treaties that extend the time period after which the effects of a denunciation come into force. For example, the Treaty on Patent Rights, which was adopted by the June 1, 2000, Diplomatic Conference,[24] establishes that once a Party carries out a denunciation, it shall come into effect one year after the date on which the General Director has received notification. In addition, it stipulates that a withdrawal will not affect patents in force or any request being processed with respect to the withdrawing Party, making it evident that patents remain protected indefinitely. We believe that the same type of measures should be adopted in relation to investments by a Party or a national of a Party that have already been made before the withdrawal so that they may remain protected indefinitely, regardless of the denunciation.

The survivorship clause may be subject to qualitative restrictions, on the one hand a limitation to investments that can be proved were made while the Treaty was in effect and, on the other hand, when a state can demonstrate a serious and ongoing harm to its economy caused by that survivorship, due to an investment, it may only take measures that counters the effects: based in the public interest, under due process of law, on a nondiscriminatory basis, respecting any undertaking previously agreed by the affected state and against a just compensation.[25]

Going back to the effects in the G3 in our particular analysis and based upon the definitions of *investment* and *investor* contained in Article 17-01 of the G3, the CEMEX company established in Venezuela should be considered an investor of another Party if it is considered a subsidiary company or a branch of a headquarters company established in Mexico or, in any case, if the nationality of the individual who established the company is taken into account.

Once the withdrawal from the G3 took place, the direct consequence was that the Mexican companies that had made investments in Venezuelan territory lost their right to petition for the establishment of dispute settlement mechanisms contained in the G3[26] in protest of actions carried out by the Venezuelan government. Evidently

---

23 Later in this same chapter we will analyze the consequences of the withdrawal from the G3 with regard to CEMEX's FDI in Venezuela.

24 http://www.wipo.int/treaties/es/ip/plt/trtdocs_wo038.html.

25 Please refer to Article 6 of the BIT between Holland and Venezuela cited below. This clause it is always included in BIT's.

26 Unless these mechanisms were made effective during the grace period for handling the effects of the withdrawal—six months after the notice—for which in any case some Venezuelan government action of complaint against the legal interests of the companies was required.

to bring these settlement mechanisms into effect, it was necessary to be credited as an investor from a Party, which meant that even though the cement company set up in Venezuela was considered a Mexican company, because it was constituted under Dutch law it was possible it could not have used those benefits.

In this regard it bears mention that there have been some decisions issued by arbitration tribunals through which they have defined local corporations, in other words, which corporations are treated equally under the concept of investment when they are *effectively controlled* by investors from another Party. Mutatis mutandi, in this case Cemex Caracas could be considered a corporation whose effective control rests in Cemex Mexico's hands.[27]

Under the provisions of the G3's Chapter XVIII, the procedure for resolving controversies is to resort to ICSID arbitration, using this mechanism to recognize the decisions handed down by said Center are mandatory for the Parties involved in the dispute. The foregoing would apply to the case of conflicts arising from investments made between investors of one Party in another Party. However, because Chavez withdrew from the treaty, that possibility for resolution was lost.

As we have expressed, the actual reasons for the denunciation were in fact that the Venezuelan government wanted to take control of the companies that had managed to be very successful in competing both nationally and internationally, and, of course, to benefit from the investments already made by those companies, without having to pay them the corresponding legal and fair indemnification. Thus, a denunciation of the G3 treaty fitted into noncompliance with international obligations vis à vis other Parties to the Treaty, irrespective of the real economic costs[28].

The G3 Article 17-08 prohibits the governments of member nations from carrying out expropriations, unless these actions are undertaken to serve the public interest (in which case it must be legally justified through a corresponding decree), and unless there is a corresponding fair payment (that is, market price) for the purpose of expropriation. This argumentation could have been used by the cement company, in conjunction with the participation of the Mexican government, if the Venezuelan government had not withdrawn from the G3.

After the Chavez government announced these first actions in May 2008, it continued with other actions that implied the takeover[29] of plants and even closing plants without legally notifying the affected companies.

---

[27] *See, inter alia*, the judgment of the ICSID tribunals of Feb. 21, 1997, in the matter of American Manufacturing & Trading, Inc. (AMT) c. Zaire, and of Sept. 2, 1998, in the matter of Antoine Goetz et Consorts c. République du Burundi.

[28] According to several economists who have recently studied the situation, the cost of the expropriations has even left a deficit balance for Venezuela: "The government spent between 2007 and 2009, more funds to pay for expropriations and nationalizations than the production of PDVSA state oil company (U.S. $23,377 million versus U.S. $21,931 million)." *See, inter alia*: Juan Paullier, *Venezuela: Expropriations on Red Numbers* (Aug. 16, 2011), article published by BBC MUNDO VENEZUELA and others, *available at* http://www.bbc.co.uk/mundo/noticias/2011/08/110812_venezuela_economia_expropiaciones_empresas_jp.shtml.

[29] The legal term of "taking over" for purposes of this article is the act to expropriate or nationalize productive plants, in order to give the government the administration of such plants.

Before beginning this expropriation procedure (which was not permitted by the G3 without proper legal compliance), and possibly before even knowing the legal structure of CEMEX in Venezuela, Chavez—foreseeing the legal and international actions that the cement company might resort to, either directly or with the support of its government—decided to withdraw from the G3 in anticipation of such actions to thereby free himself from the dispute resolution mechanisms agreed on in the treaty being invoked and to put the cement company in an unprotected position.

What would have happened had Chavez not withdrawn from the G3? The immediate consequence would have been that both CEMEX and the Mexican government would have requested an arbitration process set up under the Rules of the ICSID, alleging a violation of the G3 Chapter XVII, which would have given CEMEX and the Mexican government not only legal indemnification payment consistent with the market price, but also the power to apply economic retaliation measures if a favorable outcome for CEMEX were not duly carried out.

What then were the consequences of the Chavez denunciation of the G3 to the detriment of CEMEX and the Mexican government? The immediate result was that both the company and the government were left without legal recourse to this mechanism under the provisions established in the G3, thus losing any potential for either negotiation with the Chavez government or for recovering the FDI money invested by the company.

However, what Chavez did not know was that the company was constituted under Dutch law. Or, what Chavez wanted to get off his back were the possible effects of applying a trade treaty in addition to the effects of the content of a bilateral investment treaty.

On the basis of what is stated here, the impact of Chavez's early withdrawal from the G3 and his failure to comply with the protective subsequent time period provided by the survival clause left CEMEX unable to defend itself using the dispute resolution mechanisms provided under the terms of the G3 treaty. That would not happened if all investment treaties or treaties that include investment provisions (such as trade treaties) had an extended survival clause.

IV. The Effects of the Survival Clause in Bilateral Investment Treaties (BITs)

During the 1990s, Venezuela signed various bilateral investment treaties.[30] Among these was the Agreement on Encouragement and Reciprocal Protection of Investments between the Kingdom of the Netherlands and the Republic of Venezuela (BIT), which

[30] Please refer to *supra* note 21.

was signed on October 22, 1991, and went into effect in 1993 for an initial period of fifteen years.[31, 32]

During this period many Latin American countries signed various regional trade treaties and also signed BITs, primarily in order to make FDI more secure in their countries, as well as to establish clear rules for the permanence of their own investors in other nations[33].

Article 6 of the BIT between Holland and Venezuela established that:

> Neither Contracting Party shall take any measures to expropriate or nationalise investments of nationals of the other Contracting Party or take measures having an effect equivalent to nationalisation or expropriation with regard to such investments, unless the following conditions are complied with:
>
> (a) the measures are taken in the public interest and under due process of law;
>
> (b) the measures are not discriminatory or contrary to any undertaking which the Contracting Party taking such measures may have given;
>
> (c) the measures are taken against just compensation. Such compensation shall represent the market value of the investments affected immediately before the measures were taken or the impending measures became public knowledge, whichever is the earlier, it shall include interest at a normal commercial rate until the date of payment and shall, in order to be effective for the claimants, be paid and made transferable, without undue delay, to the country designated by the claimants concerned and in the currency of the country of which the claimants are nationals or in any freely convertible currency accepted by the claimants.[34]

In other words, the potential for signatory states to conduct expropriation or nationalization—unless the state complies with the requirements described therein—are limited. This was evidently done based on the desire to protect investments and investors of each Party.

In addition, Article 9 established the dispute resolution mechanism. In case of a conflict, these provisions indicate that Venezuela should participate using the Rules of the ICSID, because consistent with the ICSID Convention Venezuela had accepted the obligation to use the ICSID's rules in writing in conjunction with its own domestic legislation on investments.

---

31 http://www.unctad.org/sections/dite/iia/docs/bits/netherlands_venezuela.pdf.

32 As we will see later under the heading "The Case of CEMEX's FDI in Venezuela," CEMEX Caracas was constituted under Dutch law and therefore enjoyed the protection of the BIT, owing to its survival clause.

33 From 1990 to 2003, the number of BITs signed worldwide increased from almost 400 to more than 2,299 treaties involving 176 nations: http://www.unctadxi.org/templates/Page____1007.aspx.

34 http://www.unctad.org/sections/dite/iia/docs/bits/netherlands_venezuela.pdf.

Nevertheless, in April 2008, Chavez sent notification of BIT nonrenewal to the Dutch authorities. That notification had the same effects as the denunciation; the BIT expired in November of that year and under Article 14, section 2, a Party had to send this notification before the conclusion of the treaty period or else it would automatically renew for ten additional years; as the BIT was not renewed, the effects of withdrawal were brought into play.

Similarly, BIT Article 14, section 3 included a "survival clause" under which if one of the Parties withdrew from the treaty, all investments made up to the time of the withdrawal would remain protected by the Treaty and its provisions for up to fifteen years after the formal announcement of denunciation.

> Article 14:
>
> ...3) In respect of investments made before the date of the termination of the present Agreement the foregoing Articles thereof shall continue to be effective for a further period of fifteen years from that date.

It is precisely this "survival clause" that has enabled various foreign investors affected by measures Chavez has imposed to see that their companies and investments have remained protected, or at least they have received compensation as a result of arbitration, even after expropriations and nationalizations have been conducted by the Venezuelan government.[35]

In addition, BIT Article 3, among others, included some interesting postulates that developed the principles of nondiscrimination, national treatment, and most-favored-nation status.[36] In particular, Article 3 established that each Party must ensure fair and equitable treatment for investors of another Party and not hinder through arbitrary or discriminatory measures the administration, management, use, enjoyment, and so forth of their investments.

---

35 *See*, among other materials, the article *Of 44 Expropriated Companies 9 Have Received Indemnification*, GUIA DE VENEZUELA, Sept. 21, 2010, *available at* http://www.guia.com.ve/noti/67040/de-44-empresas-expropiadas-9-han-recibido-indemnizacion. This article also mentions the Venezuelan–American Chamber of Commerce and Industry's concern for the impact that the Chavez government's policy has had on investments, which have fallen until they "are almost at zero."

36 (a) National treatment: "Treating foreigners and locals equally.... This principle of 'national treatment' (giving others the same treatment as one's own nationals)" is found in the three main World Trade Organization (WTO) agreements (Article 3 of GATT, Article 17 of GATS and Article 3 of TRIPS), and it is applied in the basic concepts of Trade Related Investment Measures of Annex 1A of Multilateral Agreements on Trade in Goods of the WTO. This principle has been developed and used in Investment Treaties, where a national of one Party should receive the same treatment as a national of another Party.

(b) Most-Favored-Nation (MFN) "treating other people equally. Under the WTO agreements, countries cannot normally discriminate between their trading partners. Grant someone a special favour (such as a lower customs duty rate for one of their products) and you have to do the same for all other WTO members." *See* UNDERSTANDING THE WTO: BASICS: *Principles of the Trading System. Trade without discrimination*, *available at* http://www.wto.org/english/thewto_e/whatis_e/tif_e/fact2_e.htm.

Each Party must provide legal certainty, protection, and equal treatment that is no less than that provided for its own citizens (national treatment) or to the nationals of third parties if their status were that of most favored nation. The latter applies with exceptions regarding agreements made with third parties derived from customs unions, regional blocs, or similar institutions.[37]

Finally, this article established the formula for making effective any either domestic or international legislative changes that occurred after the BIT was signed that would benefit the Parties, for which purpose they committed to making the corresponding extension.

The content of BITs is usually similar. The content ensures protection for an investment made by an investor from one Party in the territory of another Party; this is through fair and equitable treatment, the right to receive the same treatment as national investors, the right to receive compensation if expropriation occurs, the right to free transfer of profits, and the right to receive the same treatment afforded investments from third countries not a Party to the BIT.

These measures provided certainty for the foreign investor that the propositions contained therein, such as enjoyment of extended benefits, especially under the "survival clause" that protected those investments made under the terms of the BIT in force at the time that the respective investment was made, and they assured there would be an extended compliance period even after a potential withdrawal.

In other words, the effects of the survival clause are to extend the protection of investments even after withdrawal from a treaty. It has been discussed that this protection includes those investments made between the denunciation and the survival clause extension time period (this has not been defined). However, it is our opinion that the extended period of protection should be indefinite for those investments made up until the time of the denunciation of the treaty, for example as is the case for patent subjects.[38] By establishing this indefinite measure, investments would enjoy effective protection that would prevent government abuses and would drive FDI growth in signatory nations.

---

[37] In the same way that the WTO establishes this by applying GATT Article XXIV to exceptions allowed for establishing regional blocs.

[38] *See, e.g.*, the Treaty on Patent Rights of June 1, 2000, in which a specific provision establishes (just as in other treaties dealing with patents) the validity of patents even after denunciation of or withdrawal from a treaty, such that they are protected. We believe this provision should be included for similar purposes in BITs to ensure effective protection for investments.

V. The Convention on the Settlement of Disputes Related to Investments Between States and Nationals of Other States: "The ICSID Convention" and ICSID[39]

As stated in the ICSID Regulations:

> The International Centre for Settlement of Investment Disputes (ICSID or the Centre) is established by the Convention on the Settlement of Investment Disputes between States and Nationals of Other States (the ICSID Convention or the Convention). The Convention was formulated by the Executive Directors of the International Bank for Reconstruction and Development (the World Bank). On March 18, 1965, the Executive Directors submitted the Convention, with an accompanying Report, to member governments of the World Bank for their consideration of the Convention with a view to its signature and ratification. The Convention entered into force on October 14, 1966, when it had been ratified by 20 countries. As of April 10, 2006, 143 countries have ratified the Convention to become Contracting States.[40]

The purpose of the ICSID is to establish a reconciliation and arbitration procedure consistent with the Convention's provisions so that the Convention's Member Parties can resolve disputes involving investments. The Parties must always submit themselves in writing to ICSID jurisdiction.

Venezuela signed the ICSID Convention with a view to assuring investors that should conflicts arise from investments made in Venezuela, they could rely on clearly defined mechanisms, but particularly on internationally recognized mechanisms—not those recognized at a national level only—in order to settle such controversies.

The ICSID Convention signatory Parties must submit voluntarily to the mechanisms, bodies, and procedures contained in that agreement to settle controversies involving investments. As compliance for this mandate, both the G3 and the BIT referred to the dispute resolution mechanism contained in the ICSID Convention.

The stipulations of international treaties are not the only documents to refer to the dispute settlement procedures. The Venezuelan Constitution[41] itself in its Articles 253 and 258 expressly establishes recognition of alternative means for dispute resolu-

---

39 Venezuela signed the ICSID Convention on Aug. 8, 1993; it filed the ratifying document on May 2, 1995, and the agreement went into force on June 1, 1995. On Jan. 24, 2012, Venezuela denounced the ICSID Convention before the World Bank. In accordance with the ICSID Convention, this denunciation will take place six months after reception of Venezuela's notice.

40 Please refer to *supra* note 15, Introduction part, http://icsid.worldbank.org/ICSID/ICSID/RulesMain.jsp.

41 On the Venezuelan Constitution, published in the Official Extraordinary Gazette Number 5453 of the Venezuelan Bolivarian Republic. Caracas, Mar. 24, 2000. The original text in Spanish can be retrieved from: http://www.tsj.gov.ve/legislacion/constitucion1999.htm.

tion as ways to settle conflicts, indicating that the laws shall promote these methods. In other words, the importance of protection for investments, as well as the submission to dispute settlement mechanisms for these matters, is recognized within the Venezuelan legal system itself.

Why are countries interested in maintaining a safety net that includes clear guidelines and internationally mandatory (*jus cogens*)[42] multilateral mechanisms to resolve any conflicts that should arise regarding FDI? The immediate answer would be because of the economic income that FDI represents in the economies of these countries, and, as a result, because of their interest in not losing the investors in their nations and in not becoming a country with a negative rating.[43]

Venezuela was legally obligated under the mechanisms established in the various treaties (G3, BIT, and the ICSID Convention), as well as under its own domestic legislation, to follow the applicable rules regarding investments and arbitration. Therefore, despite Chavez's premature denunciation of the G3, "Cemex Caracas" investments were protected under the terms of the BIT, the ICSID Convention, and Venezuelan legislation.

VI. The Case of Cemex in Venezuela's FDI and the Proceedings Before the ICSID

The companies Cemex Caracas Investments B.V. and Cemex Caracas II Investments B.V. ("Cemex Caracas") were constituted in the Netherlands under the laws in force at the time. These companies began operation on Venezuelan territory through the purchase of shares in the form of FDI before 1998.

On April 30, 2008, Venezuela withdrew from the BIT between Venezuela and the Netherlands.[44]

---

[42] *Jus cogens* is a "compelling law" that must be followed by all countries. This principle has been recognized by the Vienna Convention on the Law of Treaties in its Article 53 that states: "A treaty is void, if, at the time of its conclusion, it conflicts with a peremptory norm of general international law."

[43] As for use of the term "rated," we are referring to the evaluation that rating agencies make of "country risk" to express positive or negative opinions about whether to invest in a country based on its economic and social policies, among other factors. The agencies that made these qualifications are known as credit rating agencies. The "big three" agencies are Standard & Poor's, Moody's Investor Services, and Fitch Ratings. Kevin Voigt & Paul Armstrong, *Explainer: The Power of Credit Rating Agencies,* CNN ONLINE, June 22, 2012, http://edition.cnn.com/2012/06/22/business/credit-ratings-agencies-explained/index.html.

[44] Could Chavez not have been notified until this time that the company was legally a Dutch corporation? Or were there many other cases of foreign companies that had protected themselves through the Venezuelan–Netherlands' BIT or other BITs, which made the Venezuelan government withdraw from that treaty? As it can be checked in the ICSID registration of cases, there were other companies that before CEMEX had requested an arbitration process within the framework of the BIT between Venezuela and the Netherlands, due to an expropriation done by Chavez.

Cemex Caracas was notified of the takeover of its plants' operations in this South American country by a communication from Petróleos de Venezuela, S.A. (PDVSA).[45] The Organic Law on the Regulation of Cement Producing Companies in Venezuela[46] went into force on June 18, 2008. Under this law, the Venezuelan government sought control of the cement industry by owning at least a 60 percent share of each company. This enabled the government to maintain operational and administrative control of the companies and thereby meet the country's domestic demand.

Chavez expropriated the Mexican cement company through decrees on May 27, 2008, August 15, 2008, and August 19, 2008, and had the Venezuelan Armed Forces occupy the Cemex plants.[47] He ordered the conversion of Cemex Venezuela, S.A.C.A., Holcim Venezuela, C.A. y C.A. (a Swiss company), and Fábrica Nacional de Cementos S.A.C.A. (Grupo Lafarge de Venezuela—a French company) into Venezuelan state enterprises.

As a result of the expropriation, the Cemex Caracas companies filed with the ICSID on October 16, 2008 a Petition for Arbitration against Venezuela.[48]

Cemex Caracas filed this request as a company constituted under the laws of the Netherlands and because of the existence of a BIT between Venezuela and the Netherlands. The group of arbitrators constituted consistent with ICSID rules was requested to study if the expropriation decreed by the Chavez government was a violation of the rights acquired by Cemex Caracas as a foreign investor in Venezuelan territory.

For its part the Venezuelan government argued that the company was a subsidiary of a headquarters company constituted in Spain, and therefore the arbitration group did not have jurisdiction to hear this dispute, because the BIT between Venezuela and the Netherlands was not applicable.

An Arbitration Tribunal was established to solve this petition. On the basis of ICSID Convention Article 41, which stipulates that the arbitration tribunal itself shall decide if it has jurisdiction, as well as on the basis of the BIT and the Venezuelan investment law, on December 30, 2010, the Arbitration Tribunal issued a decision on jurisdiction to hear the matter.[49] On the basis of that decision the Tribunal continued to study the

---

45 The National Oil Company of Venezuela. In the 1970s the Venezuelan oil industry had been nationalized by decree; later, in the 1990s, with trade liberalization greater domestic and international private sector participation in that industry was permitted. When the Chavez government took over, the legal structure was again changed to prohibit any type of private investment in this sector. The most recent changes in the law were made in 2010. For further information, see the Petroleos de Venezuela Web page: www.pdvsa.com.

46 Published on the Official Gazette on June 18, 2008. Extraordinary Number 5886. The original text in Spanish can be retrieved from the Web page: http://es.scribd.com/doc/3893782/Ley-Organica-de-Ordenacion-de-las-Empresas-Productoras-de-Cemento.

47 *See* ICSID Case No. ARB/08/15. "B. The Claimants' Counter-Memorial on Jurisdiction" Number 29, Ruling on Jurisdiction, p. 9 in: http://icsid.worldbank.org/ICSID/FrontServlet.

48 *Id.* "I. Procedure" Number 1.

49 The same tribunal has issued other decisions in this same case, one on provisional measures requested by the claimant Party, and another on a motion to disqualify an arbitrator within the arbitration proceedings in question. However, because that is not within the scope of this analysis, we will not refer

case because it determined that it was competent to do so under the BIT. The Tribunal ruled that the claimants have *jus standi*[50] in this case.

As regards jurisdiction, the Arbitration Tribunal set forth that it did not base its decision on the contents of Article 22 of the Venezuelan Law on Investments, because of its obscure wording that did not clearly establish unilaterally Venezuela's consent to use the ICSID forum, but nevertheless it did determine the ICSID's jurisdiction based on the BIT.

Investments are safeguarded under the principle of nondiscrimination established in the BIT, which is also reflected in the shielding concepts of national treatment and most-favored-nation status. It is noteworthy that this same nondiscrimination principle is set forth in Articles 7, 8, and 9 of the Venezuelan Law on Investments. This is what provided the claimants with the legal basis for their argument that the treatment received was discriminatory, because in expropriating Cemex Caracas and other foreign companies, the government did not also expropriate other Venezuelan companies.

The Venezuelan government also violated the principles of fair and equitable treatment contained both in the BIT and the Venezuelan Law on Investments, because no payment that could realistically be considered fair or equitable was made in conducting the expropriation.

Protection for the investments is manifest in the existence of the survival clause, and specifically in the time period for protection after withdrawal from a treaty, which provides for the opportunity of invoking the dispute resolution mechanisms. These mechanisms have the objective not only of mitigating conflicts that arise between the investors of one Party and the measures of another Party, but also have demonstrated that they are an *effective negotiating tool that makes it possible to protect the investors' interests.*

On February 15, 2012, the Tribunal issued an order taking note of the discontinuance of the proceeding pursuant to Rule 43(1) of the ICSID.[51] This order was issued on the basis of the settlement that was started between CEMEX and the Venezuelan government. Although the Tribunal did not issue a final order resolving the dispute among the parties, the international mechanism established on the ICSID Convention served as a negotiating tool.

VII. Conclusion

In recent years Venezuela has become a country that has gradually closed its economy to foreign investments, especially by failing to comply with the international treaties that Venezuela has signed, and by failing to comply with its own local laws, which

to those decisions in this chapter. *See* ICSID Case No. ARB/08/15, Decisions and Awards. http://icsid.worldbank.org/ICSID/FrontServlet.

50 The right to be heard before a Court, in this case before the Arbitration Tribunal.

51 *See* ICSID Case No. ARB/08/15. Procedural Details. http://icsid.worldbank.org/ICSID/FrontServlet.

has had an adverse impact on the development of its economy. It is well known that President Chávez does not respect the legislative and judicial branches of government in any way, such that when a company is involved in a domestic legal proceeding within the Venezuelan system, it means the company is acting "against" the interests of the Chávez government and will lose its assets to the state. In other words, it is a system in which foreign investors have no protection at all.

We must take into account the fact that one of the advantages of international agreements with regard to the dispute resolution mechanisms that these treaties contain is that there is always the potential—before requesting the establishment of a mechanism of this kind—for the parties to negotiate among themselves to try to reach an agreement. This is impaired by premature withdrawal, because when this occurs, the parties do not have the opportunity to negotiate. In other words, the denunciation impedes the treaty's applicability with respect to the possibility of successful negotiations that prevent a dispute resolution procedure from being invoked because the Party withdrawing tacitly expresses its position of not wanting to negotiate with the other Parties to the treaty.

The law applicable to the dispute is another aspect affected by a withdrawal. Although the majority of BITs provide that the applicable law will be international law, when reference is made—for example to the mechanisms established consistent with ICSID—it is also the case that the withdrawing Party is tacitly expressing its position that the applicable law should no longer be that contained in the corresponding agreement, nor, therefore, in other agreements to which the corresponding agreement refers.

What consequences await a country that does not respect signed international treaties? On one hand, this creates a lack of confidence, and on the other, isolation in terms of financial, legal, and development matters that imply for the country's future separation from the international arena.

As for the consequences of Venezuela denouncing the ICSID Convention, it is enough to say that because the ICSID is a Centre that has a close relationship with the World Bank, withdrawing from this accord could mean that Venezuela would have a poor relationship with a world financial institution on which economic decisions of developing countries are highly dependent.

From another perspective, what result can be expected in the instance that there is an unlimited extension period for protection of investments from a treaty? This covers those investments made by investors under the protection of such treaties to ensure the legal rescue of their assets through dispute resolution mechanisms that also provide an efficient tool for negotiation.

We therefore suggest that any treaty addressing investments contain an unlimited time period for protection of investments made between the time the treaty comes into effect and the time it is terminated, thereby extending its benefits to all those investments made during the life of the treaty, and not allowing a unilateral declaration to impair the development of those investments. Accordingly, it is suggested that bilateral treaties dealing with investment and trade contain survival clauses of unlimited duration, subject only to quality restrictions.

The immediate practical and economic consequence of a failure to comply with international trade treaties addressing investments of a bilateral nature, as well as the premature withdrawal from these treaties—without a survival clause that extends protection for investments for an unlimited time period—is that foreign investors avoid or reduce investment in countries that do not assure secure treatment for that investment. The foregoing is further accentuated by the lack of compliance with dispute resolution mechanisms and failure to abide by the decisions handed down in the different forums constituted to settle the differences among member countries.

The effect of the unlimited survival clause will be to counteract the negative effects of denunciation, to protect FDI, and to serve as a negotiating tool.

8

ASEAN: THE LIBERALIZATION OF INVESTMENT THROUGH REGIONAL AGREEMENTS

Vivienne Bath[1]

I. Introduction

This chapter looks at developments in international investment law and practice of the Association of Southeast Asian Nations (ASEAN), focusing on the ASEAN Comprehensive Investment Agreement (ACIA),[2] which came into effect on Jan. 1, 2010,[3] and the investment agreements that ASEAN has entered into with a number of the countries surrounding it, particularly China, Korea, Australia, and New Zealand.[4] The

1 Professor of Chinese and International Business Law, University of Sydney. This chapter draws on a presentation given by the author, Vivienne Bath, Consolidation of International Investment Agreements: Disentangling the Spaghetti Bowl? UNCTAD Ad Hoc Experts Meeting (Sept. 8, 2011). Some of the issues discussed in this chapter are also addressed by Bath and Nottage in *The ASEAN Comprehensive Investment Agreement and "ASEAN Plus"—The Australia–New Zealand Free Trade Area (AANZFTA) and the PRC–ASEAN Investment Agreement, in* INTERNATIONAL INVESTMENT LAW (Marc Bungenberg, Jörn Griebel, Stephen Hobe & August Reinish eds., forthcoming, 2013).

2 ASEAN Comprehensive Investment Agreement, Feb. 26, 2009, Association of Southeast Asian Nations, *Agreements and Declarations*, http://www.asean.org/22244.htm.

3 Association of Southeast Asian Nations, *Table of ASEAN Treaties/Agreements and Ratification as of June 2012*, http://www.aseansec.org/document/Table%20of%20Agreement%20and%20Ratification%20as%20of%20June%202012.pdf (hereinafter "Table of ASEAN Treaties").

4 Agreement on Investment of the Framework Agreement on Comprehensive Economic Co-Operation between China and ASEAN, Aug. 15, 2009, China FTA Network, *China's Free Trade Agreements, China–ASEAN Free Trade Agreement*, http://fta.mofcom.gov.cn/topic/chinaasean.shtml [hereinafter PRC–ASEAN Agreement], effective as of January 1 2010 among Brunei Darussalam, Cambodia, Indonesia, Malaysia, Philippines, and China, National University of Singapore, Centre for International Law, *CIL Treaty States Database*, http://www.cil.nus.edu.sg/treaty-status-database, made pursuant to the

chapter focuses on the liberalization objectives of ASEAN in relation to market access for foreign investment, the way in which these objectives are implemented through the ACIA and its predecessor agreements, and the extent to which these liberalization objectives are reflected in agreements between ASEAN and its regional neighbors. It concludes that although ASEAN has had considerable success in obtaining agreement to the concept of investment liberalization within ASEAN, it has had less success in implementing its agenda through regional agreements. The content of the ACIA and of ASEAN's regional agreements suggest that although it may be possible to achieve a degree of investment liberalization within the jurisdiction of a strong regional organization such as ASEAN, the degree to which investment liberalization can generally be achieved through bilateral and plurilateral agreements is likely to be limited.[5]

Although geographically close, the ASEAN nations are in many ways quite dissimilar—in population size, level of development, government structure, historical background, and legal systems. Singapore, Malaysia, and Brunei have legal systems based on the common law. Malaysia, Brunei, and Indonesia (the largest country in ASEAN, with a population in 2010 of almost 238 million people)[6] are predominantly Islamic countries. Vietnam, Cambodia, and Lao PDR share a communist background and are, together with Myanmar, the poorest countries in ASEAN.[7] Together, the ASEAN nations have a population of approximately 590 million people[8] and a GDP (in 2010)

Framework Agreement on Comprehensive Economic Co-Operation between ASEAN and the People's Republic of China, Nov. 4, 2002, Association of Southeast Asian Nations, *Framework Agreement on Comprehensive Economic Co-Operation between ASEAN and the People's Republic of China, Phnom Penh, 4 November 2002*, http://www.aseansec.org/13196.htm; Agreement Establishing the ASEAN-Australia-New Zealand Free Trade Area, Feb. 27, 2009, 2010 Austl. T.S. No. 1, Chapter 11 [hereinafter ASEAN–ANZ Agreement]; Agreement on Investment under the Framework Agreement on Comprehensive Economic Cooperation among the Governments of the Member Countries of the Association of Southeast Asian Nations and the Republic of Korea, June 2, 2009, Association of Southeast Asian Nations, http://www.aseansec.org/22973.pdf [hereinafter ASEAN–Korea Agreement], ratified by all parties, Table of ASEAN Treaties, *supra* note 3, and effective Sept. 1, 2009, Association of Southeast Asian Nations, http://www.aseansec.org/7672.htm. All parties to the ASEAN–Korea Agreement had lodged notifications by the end of Oct. 2010. However, most of the substantive provisions of this agreement are subject to further agreement pursuant to a five-year program of work. *See* ASEAN–Korea Agreement, Art. 27; Table of ASEAN Treaties, *supra* note 3, at 18–19. With the entry into force for Indonesia on Jan. 10, 2012, the ASEAN–ANZ Agreement is now in force for all ten ASEAN countries, as well as Australia and New Zealand. See Australian Government, Department of Foreign Affairs and Trade, *ASEAN-Australia-New Zealand FTA (AANFTA) Enters into Force for Indonesia* (undated), http://www.dfat.gov.au/fta/aanzfta/index.html, under "News."

[5] I do not attempt in this chapter to provide a definition of what constitutes the Asian region. There are numerous different initiatives aimed at consolidating or integrating different "Asian" communities, which are covered in more detail elsewhere. See AUSTRALIAN GOVERNMENT, PRODUCTIVITY COMMISSION, BILATERAL AND REGIONAL TRADE AGREEMENTS 202 (2010).

[6] Badan Pusat Statistik Republik Indonesia (Indonesia statistics) (undated) http://dds.bps.go.id/eng/tab_sub/view.php?tabel=1&daftar=1&id_subyek=12&notab=1.

[7] Association of Southeast Asian Nations, ASEAN COMMUNITY IN FIGURES, ACIF, 2010, at 7 (2011).

[8] *Id.*

in excess of US$1800 billion.[9] Despite their different backgrounds and cultures, and their sometimes conflicting territorial claims, their geographical situation gives them a common interest in that they are surrounded by countries that are larger, stronger, wealthier or all three.[10] To the north are the economic giants of Japan, China, and Korea. India, with its large, well-educated population and rapid growth rate, is to the southwest, and the small but wealthy countries of Australia and New Zealand are to the south.

The Association of Southeast Asian Nations was established in 1967 by Indonesia, Malaysia, Philippines, Singapore, and Thailand pursuant to the ASEAN Declaration.[11] Brunei Darussalam became a party in 1984, followed by Vietnam in 1995, Lao PDR and Myanmar in 1997, and Cambodia in 1999.[12] As set out in the ASEAN Declaration, the aims and purposes of ASEAN were both economic and political:

> the countries of South East Asia share a primary responsibility for strengthening the economic and social stability of the region and ensuring their peaceful and progressive national development, and.... they are determined to ensure their stability and security from external interference in any form or manifestation in order to preserve their national identities in accordance with the ideals and aspirations of their peoples.[13]

In 1976, the Treaty of Amity and Cooperation[14] set out the principles of non-interference by ASEAN States in each other's internal affairs and peaceful settlement of disputes. ASEAN has traditionally operated as a much looser confederation of nations than the European Union,[15] subject to efforts since its establishment to integrate and cooperate particularly in relation to trade and investment.

In the twenty-first century, the members of ASEAN have moved toward the establishment of a more cohesive and tighter form of cooperation, with the decision in 2003 to establish the "ASEAN Community."[16] The ASEAN Charter was finalized in 2007,

---

9 ASEAN-Australia-New Zealand Free Trade Area, *Key Statistics on AANZ*, http://www.aanzfta.asean.org/index.php?page=key-statistics-on-aanz, as of Sept. 2011, based on ASEANstats and IMF WEO Database.

10 Vivienne Bath & Luke Nottage, *Foreign Investment and Dispute Resolution Law and Practice in Asia: An Overview, in* FOREIGN INVESTMENT AND DISPUTE RESOLUTION LAW AND PRACTICE IN ASIA (Vivienne Bath & Luke Nottage eds., 2011).

11 ASEAN Declaration (Bangkok Declaration) (Aug. 8, 1967) [hereinafter ASEAN Declaration], Association of Southeast Asian Nations, *The ASEAN Declaration*, http://www.asean.org/1212.htm .

12 Association of Southeast Asian Nations, *Overview, Introduction* (undated) http://www.asean.org/about_ASEAN.html (last visited Mar. 25, 2012).

13 ASEAN Declaration, *supra* note 11, fourth preamble.

14 Association of Southeast Asian Nations, *Treaty of Amity and Cooperation in Southeast Asia, Indonesia, 24 February 1976*, http://www.asean.org/1217.htm. In addition to the ASEAN states, eighteen other states have acceded to a form of this treaty. *See* Table of ASEAN Treaties, *supra* note 3, at 91–92.

15 Amitav Acharya, *Asian Regional Institutions and the Possibilities for Socializing the Behavior of States* (ADB Working Paper Series on Regional Economic Integration, No. 82, 2011).

16 Resolved by the ASEAN Leaders at the 9th ASEAN Summit (2003) *supra* note 12.

and entered into effect on December 15, 2008.[17] The ASEAN Charter, while reiterating the cooperative principles set out in the earlier ASEAN documents, created a new, tighter legal framework for ASEAN and, in particular, established ASEAN as an international organization with legal personality.[18] Structurally, the ASEAN Charter reflects the decision of the member nations to create a distinct ASEAN Community through the establishment of three different cooperative community councils—the ASEAN Political–Security Community Council, the ASEAN Economic Community Council, and the ASEAN Socio-Cultural Community Council.[19]

The ASEAN Economic Community has had a long-standing goal of achieving regional economic integration, dating back to the launch of the ASEAN Free Trade Area in 1992,[20] with the objective of transforming ASEAN "into a region with free movement of goods, services, investment, skilled labor, and freer flow of capital."[21] The Blueprint for the ASEAN Economic Community[22] contemplated the review of the existing agreements relating to investment in order to enhance ASEAN's ability to attract foreign direct investment (FDI) from outside ASEAN and to facilitate and increase investment within ASEAN. The reasoning for this was that "[s]ustained inflows of new investments and reinvestments will promote and ensure dynamic development of ASEAN economies."[23]

The concept of cooperation and liberalization in relation to investment within ASEAN pursues objectives laid out in existing ASEAN agreements—the 1987 ASEAN Agreement for the Promotion and Protection of Investments (IGA)[24] and the 1998 Framework Agreement on the ASEAN Investment Area (AIA).[25] The content of these agreements was reviewed and revised, resulting in the 2009 ACIA, which incorporates much of the material from the previous agreements, but also establishes what is intended to be a comprehensive investment regime, reflecting "international best practice."[26] After a considerable delay, the ACIA finally took effect on March 29, 2012

[17] Charter of the Association of Southeast Asian Nations, Nov. 20, 2007, Association of Southeast Asian Nations, http://www.asean.sec/publications/ASEAN-Charter.pdf.

[18] *Id.* at Article 3.

[19] *Id.* at Article 9.

[20] *See* Masahiro Kawai & Ganeshan Wignaraja, Regionalism as an Engine of Multilateralism: A Case for a Single East Asian FTA (ADB Working Paper Series on Regional Economic Integration, No. 14, 2008).

[21]. Declaration on the ASEAN Economic Community Blueprint adopting the ASEAN Economic Community Blueprint (Nov. 20, 2007) [hereinafter Blueprint], Association of Southeast Asian Nations, http://www.aseansec.org/5187-10.pdf at Article I(4).

[22] *Id.*

[23] *Id.*, at Article 23.

[24] Agreement for the Promotion and Protection of Investments, Nov. 15, 1987, Association of Southeast Asian Nations, *Agreement among the Government of Brunei Darussalam, the Republic of Indonesia, Malaysia, the Republic of the Philippines, the Republic of Singapore, and the Kingdom of Thailand for the Promotion and Protection of Investments, Manila, December 15, 1987*, http://www.asean.org/6464.htm.

[25] Framework Agreement on the ASEAN Investment Area, Oct. 7, 1998, Association of Southeast Asian Nations, http://www.asean.org/7994.pdf.

[26] ASEAN, *Highlights of the ASEAN Comprehensive Investment Agreement (ACIA)* (Aug. 26, 2008), http://www.asean.org/21885.ppt, slide 5. "International best practice" was taken to include the 2004 U.S. Model Investment Text; the North America Free Trade Area agreements; the OECD Guidelines for

and now constitutes the basic document between all of the ASEAN states relating to the liberalization and promotion of intra-ASEAN investment.[27]

The history of the individual ASEAN States in attracting investment is variable, although the trend since 1990 has been generally upward. As noted above, the population size, economic strength, and level of development varies considerably across ASEAN, and this is reflected in the figures relating both to FDI into the ASEAN countries and in the investments made by ASEAN countries in other ASEAN states and outside ASEAN.

TABLE 1
ASEAN COUNTRIES: INBOUND FDI IN 1990, 2000, AND 2011; STOCKS OF INBOUND FDI IN 2011

Country	1990	2000	2011	Stocks 2011
ASEAN	$12,821	$22,696	$116,539	$1,077,284
Brunei Darussalam	$7	$550	$1,208	$12,452
Cambodia	0	$149	$892	$6,850
Indonesia	$1,092[28]	-$4,495	$18,906	$173,064
Lao PDR	$6	$34	$450	$2,521
Malaysia	$2,611	$3,788	$1,966	$114,555
Myanmar	$225	$208	$850	$9,123
Philippines	$550	$2,240	$1,262	$27,581
Singapore	$5,575	$15,515	$64,003	$518,625
Thailand	$2,575	$3,410	$9,572	$139,735
Vietnam	$180	$1,298	$7,430	$72,778

In millions in United States Dollars. Based on "Inward and outward foreign direct investment flows, annual, 1970–2011," http://unctadstat.unctad.org/TableViewer/tableView.aspx?ReportId=88, and "Inward and outward foreign direct investment stock, annual, 1980–2011," http://unctadstat.unctad.org/TableViewer/tableView.aspx?ReportId=89 (last visited Oct.4, 2012).

Table 1 reflects the strength of Singapore, Malaysia, Indonesia, and Thailand in attracting FDI. It also indicates that—in most cases—there has been a steady increase in FDI into ASEAN since 1990.

Notwithstanding the existence of the IGA and the AIA, investment within ASEAN has constituted a relatively low proportion of total inbound FDI. In 2010, intra-ASEAN investment constituted 16.1 percent of total incoming FDI in ASEAN,[29] whereas

Multinational Enterprises; the drafts of the Free Trade Agreements then being negotiated with China, Korea, Australia, and New Zealand (see text *infra*); and the United Nations Commission on Trade and Development's assessments on international investment agreements.

27 *See supra* notes 2 and 3.

28 Statistics for 1990 and 2000 include East Timor.

29 Association of Southeast Asian Nations, *ASEANstats*, http://www.aseansec.org/stat/Table25.pdf (as of Feb. 15, 2012).

investment from outside ASEAN constituted 83.9 percent.[30] The more developed countries of Indonesia, Malaysia, Philippines, Singapore, and Thailand (the "ASEAN 5") received 83.3 percent of the intra-ASEAN investment and 87.3 percent of the extra-ASEAN investment.[31] Only in the case of Cambodia, Indonesia, and Lao PDR did the percentage of investment from inside ASEAN constitute a substantial percentage (that is, more than 40 percent) of received investment, and in no case did investment from within ASEAN constitute more than half of a country's inflow of FDI.[32]

FDI from outside ASEAN comes from a variety of sources. In 2010[33] the European Union contributed 20.6 percent of total FDI, the United States 10.1 percent, Japan 10.1 percent, China 5.3 percent, Cayman Islands 4.4 percent, Korea 4.3 percent, India 2.5 percent, Australia 2.1 percent and Canada 1.7 percent.[34]

ASEAN countries have traditionally been recipients of FDI rather than investor countries. This is, however, beginning to change. Singapore and Malaysia are the largest investors overseas by a considerable margin, but there is generally a trend upward in terms of outbound investment by other ASEAN nations since 1990, and particularly from 2000, although investment stocks are still low, as set out on Table 2.

TABLE 2

OUTBOUND FDI FROM ASEAN COUNTRIES IN 1990, 2000, AND 2011; STOCKS IN 2011

Country	1990	2000	2011	Stocks 2011
ASEAN	$2,328	$8,978	$59,890	$495,704
Brunei Darussalam	0	$30	$10	$691
Cambodia	0	$7	$24	$377
Indonesia	-$11[35]	$150	$7,771	$9,502
Lao PDR	0	$10	$7	$6
Malaysia	$129	$2,026	$12,258	$106,217-
Myanmar	-	-	-	-
Philippines	$22	$125	$9	$6,590
Singapore	$2,034	$6,650	$25,227	$339,095
Thailand	$154	-$20	$10,634	$33,226
Vietnam	0	0	$950	-

In millions in United States Dollars. Based on "Inward and outward foreign direct investment flows, annual, 1970–2011," http://unctadstat.unctad.org/TableViewer/tableView.aspx?ReportId=88, and "Inward and outward foreign direct investment stock, annual, 1980–2011," http://unctadstat.unctad.org/TableViewer/tableView.aspx?ReportId=89 and http://unctadstat.unctad.org/TableViewer/tableView.aspx (last visited Oct. 4, 2012).

30 *Id.*

31 *Id.*

32 *Id.*

33 Association of Southeast Asian Nations, *ASEANstats*, http://www.aseansec.org/stat/Table27.pdf (as of Feb. 21, 2012).

34 *Id.* The sources of investments made through the Cayman Islands are unclear, but presumably reflect investments by third-country investors made through Cayman Islands entities.

35 Statistics for 1990 and 2000 include East Timor.

Singapore invests mainly in China, the British Virgin Islands (presumably as a conduit for investment in China and elsewhere), the United Kingdom, and Malaysia.[36] Malaysian investment abroad is diverse and includes investments in India, Indonesia, Egypt, and Nigeria.[37]

Each of the ASEAN countries has entered into a number of bilateral investment treaties (BITs) for the purpose of promoting and protecting investment, although some ASEAN countries have been significantly more active than others in negotiating and subsequently ratifying BITs. Reflecting their interest in investing in other countries in the region and the amount of investment that flows from sources outside the region, bilateral investment agreements entered into by ASEAN states do not necessarily include all of their ASEAN neighbors. In some cases, agreements that have been entered into have never entered into force. Nothing in the IGA, AIA, and ACIA precludes ASEAN countries from entering into other bilateral or plurilateral arrangements, either with each other or with other countries. However, the different levels of activity relating to investment treaties suggest differences of view between the ASEAN nations as to the importance of entering into bilateral arrangements that may complement intra-ASEAN investment agreements.[38] This can be seen from Table 3:

TABLE 3

BILATERAL INVESTMENT TREATIES TO WHICH ASEAN COUNTRIES ARE PARTIES

Country	BITS signed	BITS in force	ASEAN (in force)	ASEAN (not in force)
Brunei Darussalam	6	3	0	0
Cambodia	21	11	2 (Singapore, Thailand)	5 (Indonesia, Lao PDR, Malaysia, Philippines, Vietnam)
Indonesia	63	45	5 (Lao PDR, Malaysia, Singapore, Thailand, Vietnam)	2 (Cambodia, Philippines)
Lao PDR	23	19	4 (Indonesia, Singapore, Thailand, Vietnam)	3 (Cambodia, Malaysia, Myanmar)
Malaysia	68	49	2 (Indonesia, Vietnam)	2 (Cambodia, Lao PDR)
Myanmar	6	3	1 (Philippines)	3 (Lao PDR, Thailand, Viet Nam)

36 "The bulk of Singapore's overseas investments were channelled to China ($68 billion), British Virgin Islands ($34 billion), United Kingdom ($32 billion) and Malaysia ($31 billion)." Department of Statistics Singapore, *Educational Corner, FAQ on Direct Foreign Investment and Direct Investment Abroad* (Dec. 30, 2011), http://www.singstat.gov.sg/educorner/faqsinvestment.html#qn7 (figures in Singapore dollars).

37 Summit Level Group of Developing Countries GROUP OF FIFTEEN, A Survey of Foreign Direct Investment in G-15 Countries (Working Paper Series, Volume 7, 2010).

38 FOREIGN INVESTMENT, *supra* note 10, at 11–13.

Country	BITS signed	BITS in force	ASEAN (in force)	ASEAN (not in force)
Philippines	35	30	3 (Myanmar, Thailand, Vietnam)	2 (Cambodia, Indonesia)
Singapore	41	35	4 (Cambodia, Indonesia, Lao PDR, Vietnam)	0
Thailand	40	34	5 (Cambodia, Indonesia, Lao PDR, Philippines, Vietnam)	1 (Myanmar)
Vietnam	58	42	6 (Indonesia, Lao PDR, Malaysia, Philippines, Singapore, Thailand)	2 (Cambodia, Myanmar)

Based on information found on the UNCTAD, Investment Instruments Online, Bilateral Investment Treaties, http://www.unctadxi.org/templates/DocSearch____779.aspx.[39]

Reflecting the fact that most FDI into ASEAN comes from outside ASEAN, all of the ASEAN countries have signed bilateral investment agreements with China, although the Brunei Darussalam treaty, signed in 2000, is not in force.[40] All of the ASEAN countries other than Myanmar have treaties with the Republic of Korea. With the exception of Cambodia and Singapore, all of the ASEAN countries have treaties with India. Japan, even though it has entered into relatively few bilateral investment treaties,[41] has treaties with Cambodia, Lao PDR and Vietnam, as well as comprehensive trade and investment agreements with Brunei, Indonesia, Malaysia, Philippines, Singapore, Thailand, and Vietnam.[42] None of the ASEAN countries has a bilateral investment agreement with the United States, although the United States is one of the major investors in the region. However, Singapore has a free trade agreement with the United States that includes an investment chapter,[43] and the United States has entered into trade and investment framework agreements with ASEAN, Brunei, Cambodia, Indonesia, Malaysia, the Philippines, Thailand, and Vietnam.[44] Indonesia, Lao PDR,

[39] All information is current as of June 1, 2012, except in the case of Brunei Darussalam, which is current as of June 1, 2010.

[40] All information in this paragraph is based on UNCTAD, Investment Instruments Online, *Bilateral Investment Treaties*, http://www.unctadxi.org .

[41] See Shotaro Hamamoto, *A Passive Player in International Investment Law: Typically Japanese, in* FOREIGN INVESTMENT, *supra* note 10, at 53–56.

[42] Ministry of Foreign Affairs of Japan, *Free Trade Agreement (FTA) and Economic Partnership Agreement (EPA)*, http://www.mofa.go.jp/policy/economy/fta/index.html. In relation to Indonesia, *see* discussion in Sita Sitaresmi, *The Japan-Indonesia Economic Partnership Agreement: An Energy Security Perspective, in* FOREIGN INVESTMENT, *supra* note 10, at 135–52.

[43] United States–Singapore Free Trade Agreement, May 6, 2003, Office of the United States Trade Representative, *Singapore FTA*, http://www.ustr.gov/trade-agreements/free-trade-agreements/singapore-fta.

[44] Office of the United States Trade Representative, *Trade & Investment Framework Agreements*, http://www.ustr.gov/trade-agreements/trade-investment-framework-agreements. On the prospects and possible content of a free trade agreement between ASEAN and the United States, see Jordan C. Kahn,

the Philippines, and Vietnam have BITs with Australia. Singapore and Thailand have entered into free trade agreements with Australia, both of which include provisions relating to investment protection and increased access for investors,[45] reflecting a trend toward comprehensive trade and investment arrangements in preference to the more traditional bilateral investment treaty. Despite the substantial number of agreements, therefore, the network of ASEAN BITs is not comprehensive, particularly in relation to major trading and investment partners of ASEAN. The effect of the ACIA in terms of both intra-ASEAN investment and investment between ASEAN countries and the outside world is therefore intended to be significant.

In addition to, and in conjunction with, the program of trade and investment liberalization contemplated in the Blueprint and the efforts by individual countries in ASEAN to improve trade and investment relations with other countries, ASEAN itself has become active in negotiating and signing free trade agreements with other countries in the region for the purpose of establishing free trade and investment areas. These are generally described as the ASEAN-Plus agreements. So far, ASEAN has signed agreements with the People's Republic of China ("China"),[46] Japan,[47] Korea,[48] India,[49] and Australia and New Zealand.[50] Subsequently, and as part of the commitment in these agreements to investment cooperation, China and Korea have signed separate investment agreements with ASEAN,[51] whereas the ASEAN–ANZ Agreement contains a comprehensive investment chapter. However, the substantive investment provisions in both the ASEAN–Korea Agreement and the ASEAN–ANZ Agreement are subject to five-year work programs; the agreement with India does not deal with investment; and the agreement with Japan, which provides for further discussions in

Investment Protection under the Proposed ASEAN–United States Free Trade Agreement, 33 SUFFOLK TRANSNAT'L L. REV. 225 (2010), and Pasha L. Hsieh, *The Roadmap for a Prospective US–ASEAN FTA: Legal and Geopolitical Considerations*, 46(2) J. WORLD TRADE 367–96 (2012).

45 Australian Government, Department of Foreign Affairs and Trade, *Key Outcomes of Thailand–Australia Free Trade Agreement*, http://www.dfat.gov.au/fta/tafta/key-outcomes.html .

46 Framework Agreement on Comprehensive Economic Co-Operation between ASEAN and the People's Republic of China, *see supra* note 4. Annexes and amendments available at Association of Southeast Asian Nations, *ASEAN–China Free Trade Area*, http://www.aseansec.org/19105.htm.

47 Agreement on Comprehensive Economic Partnership among Member States of the Association of Southeast Asian Nations and Japan, Apr. 14, 2008, Ministry of Foreign Affairs of Japan, *Free Trade Agreement (FTA) and Economic Partnership Agreement (EPA)* http://www.mofa.go.jp/policy/economy/fta/asean/agreement.pdf.

48 Framework Agreement on Comprehensive Economic Cooperation among the Governments of the Member Countries of the Association of Southeast Asian Nations and the Republic of Korea, Dec. 13, 2005, Association of Southeast Asian Nations, http://www.aseansec.org/18063.htm. Annexes and amendments available at Association of Southeast Asian Nations, *ASEAN–Republic of Korea Free Trade Area*, http://www.aseansec.org/22557.htm .

49 Framework Agreement on Comprehensive Economic Cooperation between the Republic of India and the Association of Southeast Asian Nations, Oct. 8, 2003, Association of Southeast Asian Nations, http://www.asean.org/15278.htm.

50 *See supra* note 4, at ch. 11.

51 *See supra* note 4.

relation to investment, has not yet resulted in a concrete agreement, although negotiations between the parties are in progress.[52]

As can be expected, the ASEAN-Plus parties have also entered into agreements with individual ASEAN countries and with each other. Australia, New Zealand, Korea, India, and to a lesser extent, Japan, are all active in negotiating free trade agreements and investment agreements.[53] Australia and New Zealand have a long-standing regional relationship covering many aspects of economic cooperation and, most recently, have entered into a protocol relating to investment, which is not yet in force.[54] China has an extensive network of more than 120 international investment agreements, including bilateral investment treaties and free trade agreements, and has recently entered into a trilateral investment agreement with Korea and Japan.[55] Although the focus of investors and states in negotiating free trade agreements is traditionally principally on the benefits to be obtained by liberalizing and reducing tariffs and other imposts on trade in goods and services, recent agreements entered into often incorporate provisions relating to investment, including investment protection and, on some occasions, investment liberalization. China has negotiated a free trade agreement with New Zealand, for example, which includes an investment chapter.[56] In the Australia–U.S. Free Trade Agreement, Australia granted U.S. investors significant concessions in relation to investment access.[57] The Australia–Singapore and Australia–Thailand Free Trade Agreements also contain provisions relating to investment.[58]

II. Intra-ASEAN Investment Agreements—IGA and AIA

The ASEAN states have a relatively long history of attempting to establish comprehensive intra-ASEAN investment arrangements. The IGA was entered into on December 15, 1987, between the governments of Brunei Darussalam, the Republic of Indonesia, Malaysia, the Republic of the Philippines, the Republic of Singapore, and the Kingdom

---

52 ASEAN Secretariat, *ASEAN in the global community*, ANNUAL REPORT 2010–2011 (2011), at 33.

53 FOREIGN INVESTMENT, *see supra* note 10.

54 Protocol on Investment to the Australia–New Zealand Closer Economic Relations Trade Agreement, Feb. 16, 2011, 2011 Aust'l T. N.I.F. 6.

55 *See* NORAH GALLAGHER & WENHUA SHAN, CHINESE INVESTMENT TREATIES: POLICIES AND PRACTICE (2009); Chinese bilateral investment treaties as of June 1, 2012, listed at UNCTAD, Investment Instruments Online, *Bilateral Investment Treaties*, http://www.unctadxi.org; Ministry of Foreign Affairs of Japan, *Agreement Among the Government of Japan, the Government of the Republic of Korea and the Government of the People's Republic of China for the Promotion, Facilitation and Protection of Investment*, http://www.mofa.go.jp/announce/announce/2012/5/0513_01.html, signed May 13, 2012.

56 Free Trade Agreement between the Government of New Zealand and the Government of the People's Republic of China, Oct. 1, 2008, 2008 N.Z. T.S. 19.

57 Australia–United States Free Trade Agreement, May 18, 2004, 2005 Aust'l T.S. 1. See discussion below.

58 Singapore–Australia Free Trade Agreement (Feb. 17, 2003), 2003 Aust'l T.S. 16, at Chapter 8; amended particularly in relation to investment by the Singapore–Australia Free Trade Agreement amendments, July 27, 2009, 2011 Aust'l T.S. 31; Australia–Thailand Free Trade Agreement, July 5, 2004, 2005 Aust'l T.S. 2, at ch. 9.

of Thailand. The stated aim of the IGA was to stimulate the flow of technology and private investment among the signatories. It is described in the Blueprint[59] as an agreement the purpose of which was to provide investment protection (as opposed to the AIA, which is described as an investment cooperation agreement).

The scope of the IGA was ambitious. Although it was expressed as applying to "nationals or companies of any other Contracting Party" (Article II (1)), the definition of "company" in Article I included any entity incorporated or constituted in a Contracting Party "wherein the place of effective management is situated." As long as there was an operational presence in an ASEAN country, therefore, the language of the IGA was wide enough to cover investments that were owned by non-ASEAN nationals. "Investment" was similarly widely defined and included stocks, property, intellectual property, and business concessions. The IGA, although brief, also contained many of the provisions of a BIT in relation to investment protection, and required the signatories to provide investments with full protection in relation to the "management, maintenance, use, enjoyment, extension, disposition or liquidation" of investments and fair and equitable treatment to investments on terms no less favorable than those granted to an "investor of a most-favored-nation" (but not national treatment unless specifically negotiated on a bilateral basis).[60] The IGA also provided for the payment of restitution in case of war or a state of emergency (again on a most-favored-nation basis),[61] free transfer in a convertible currency of capital and other funds relating to an investment,[62] and payment of "adequate compensation" on expropriation.[63] Provision was made for the settlement of disputes by state-to-state discussions (Article IX) or investor–state arbitration (Article X).[64] In 1996 a Protocol[65] acknowledged the accession of Vietnam, and, among other things, added provisions requiring the simplification and streamlining of investment procedures and approvals in order to expedite investment. It also required that signatories provide up-to-date information on laws and regulations relating to investment.

In 1998, the ASEAN states made a further attempt to enter into comprehensive investment relations. The AIA was signed by all of the ASEAN nations other than Cambodia, and in 2001 the AIA was amended by all of the ASEAN States, including Cambodia.[66] The AIA was a more ambitious document than the IGA in that it aimed

59 *See supra* note 21, at Article 24.

60 Article IV(1), (2), and (4).

61 Article IV(3).

62 Article VII.

63 Article VI.

64 Diane A. Desierto, *ASEAN's Constitutionalization of International Law: Challenges to Evolution under the New ASEAN Charter*, 49 COLUM. J. TRANSNAT'L L. 268 (2010–2011).

65 Protocol to Amend the Agreement among the Governments of Brunei Darussalam, the Republic of Indonesia, Malaysia, the Republic of the Philippines, the Republic of Singapore, and the Kingdom of Thailand for the Promotion and Protection of Investments, Sept. 12, 1996, Association of Southeast Asian Nations, http://www.aseansec.org/6465.htm.

66 Protocol to Amend the Framework Agreement on the ASEAN Investment Area, Sept. 14, 2001, Association of Southeast Asian Nations, http://www.aseansec.org/6467.htm.

to achieve an ASEAN-wide liberalization of investment policy and the establishment of a distinct regional investment zone by 2010. In other respects, it was less encompassing but possibly more realistic than the IGA. The concept of liberalization was not defined in the AIA, but, as in the ACIA, was equated with increased market access for investment.[67] The Preamble refers to "joint efforts in liberalizing trade and promoting intra-ASEAN trade and investment flows" and establishing a competitive ASEAN Investment Area "through a more liberal and transparent investment environment." Under Article 2, the scope of industries to be opened up to investment was unlimited, except for portfolio investment, which was not covered, and investments covered by other ASEAN agreements. The 2001 Protocol, however, effectively limited the scope of the agreement by amending Article 2[68] to provide that the AIA covered direct investments, and related services, in manufacturing, agriculture, fishery, forestry, mining, and quarrying and direct investment in such other sectors and services as may be agreed by the member states. Although the signatory states were in principle in favor of the principle of liberalization, it appears that in practice they found it difficult to make a full commitment to the opening up of their economies.[69]

Articles 3 and 4 of the AIA indicated that the purpose of investment liberalization was to increase the flow of investments from sources inside and outside ASEAN. All industries were to be opened up to ASEAN investors by 2010 and to all investors by 2020.[70] Accordingly, Article 5 required that member states begin the process of "facilitation, promotion and liberalisation which would contribute continuously and significantly to achieving the objective of a more liberal and transparent investment environment."[71] Article 6 required the preparation of Action Plans for cooperation and facilitation of investment, promotion, and awareness and investment liberalization. To this end, Article 16 created a formal body, the ASEAN Investment Area Council, of which the members were the Secretary-General of ASEAN and the Ministers responsible for investment in the ASEAN States.

As part of the two-stage process of liberalization, Article 1 created a definition of "ASEAN investor," the purpose of which was to ensure that the benefits of the agreement accrued, at least initially, to investors that were owned within ASEAN. The concept of "ASEAN investor" was therefore tied to the idea of "ASEAN equity." The AIA did not set out a clear test of control or ownership, and in case of doubt Article 1 of the

[67] Darryl S.L. Jarvis, *Foreign Direct Investment and Investment Liberalization in Asia: Assessing ASEAN's Initiatives* (Lee Kuan Yew School of Public Policy Research Paper No. LKYSPP08-002, 2008), http://www.ssrn.com/sol3/papers.cfm?abstract_id=1160074, takes the view that ASEAN's commitment to investment liberalization in the AIA, if realized, should have resulted in progress in for areas: reductions in national autonomy in relation to investment screening and conditionality, increased transparency, enhanced standardization and codification of foreign investment regulatory standards, and enhanced centralized coordination and decision making in respect of corporate governance.

[68] *See supra* note 66, Art. 1.

[69] *See* discussion in Jarvis, *supra* note 67.

[70] Article 4(c).

[71] Article 5(c).

AIA effectively gave to the host state the ability to determine whether an ownership interest should be considered to be ASEAN equity.

Article 7 provided for the immediate opening up of investment to all signatory states and required that member states:

> (b) accord immediately to ASEAN investors and their investments, in respect of all industries and measures affecting investment including but not limited to the admission, establishment, acquisition, expansion, management, operation and disposition of investment, treatment no less favorable than that it accords to its own like investors and investments ("national treatment").

The effect of this potentially wide provision was, however, limited by Article 7(2), which allowed countries to compile Temporary Exclusion Lists and Sensitive Lists setting out exceptions to the opening up of investment.[72] Differential treatment was accorded to the less-developed states in ASEAN (Vietnam, Lao PDF, and Myanmar) in terms of opening up investment markets.[73] Article 8 provided for what was described as most-favored-nation treatment to be accorded by member states—that is, by the grant of "treatment no less favorable than that [Member State] accords to investors and investments *of any other Member State*" [emphasis added] with respect to all investment measures, including admission, establishment, acquisition and expansion. Again, this was qualified by Articles 7 and 9, which allowed a State that was "temporarily not ready to make concessions under Article 7" to delay doing so.

With the exception of the provisions relating to national treatment and most-favored-nation treatment and more detailed requirements relating to transparency obligations set out in Article 12, the AIA did not contain investor protections such as fair and equitable treatment, full protection, or provisions relating to compensation in time of war or emergency or for expropriation. In Article 12, however, the parties reaffirmed "their existing rights and obligations" under the IGA, which did set out such requirements. Article 12 also made clear that provisions of other agreements entered into by ASEAN member states (such as bilateral investment agreements) were not affected by the requirements of the AIA and parties were free to enter into such agreements individually as they considered appropriate.

The drafters of the AIA were much more concerned about protecting the autonomy of states in taking measures in the public interest and in the national interest of states than were the drafters of the IGA. Article 13 of the AIA contained a detailed "General Exceptions" clause making clear that states may, subject to a restriction on the adoption of measures that may constitute arbitrary discrimination or disguised restrictions on investment, adopt measures for the protection of national security, public morals, life or health, legal compliance and collection of taxes even if these measures restrict investment. These provisions follow the content of Article XIV of the General

[72] Article 7(2).

[73] Article 7(3).

Agreement on Trade in Services (GATS) and Article XX of the General Agreement on Tariffs and Trade, and are replicated in the ACIA. In addition, the AIA introduced emergency safeguard measures (Article 14) and provisions designed to allow for the protection of balance of payments (Article 15).

The relationship between the IGA, with its emphasis on investment protection, and the AIA, with its focus on liberalization and more comprehensive and nuanced provisions setting out a balance between the interests of host state and investor, was not clearly spelled out in the AIA. This was highlighted in the investor–State arbitration of *Yaung Chi Oo Trading Pte. Ltd v Government of the Union of Myanmar*,[74] in which the tribunal held that the AIA should be considered to be complementary to the IGA and did not amend its terms. In particular, it did not have the effect of applying the provisions of the IGA (which utilized a wide definition of "investments") to the more limited concept of "ASEAN investments" under the AIA. This decision highlighted the need for an agreement that set out clearly the objectives and agreement of the ASEAN nations in relation to investment as well as integrating the content of the two agreements and standardizing their terms—a purpose ultimately filled by the ACIA.

III. ASEAN Comprehensive Investment Agreement

The ACIA has now replaced the IGA and the AIA, which, upon the entry into force of the ACIA, were terminated pursuant to Article 47(1). The agreement by the ASEAN states that there was a need for a comprehensive new investment agreement reflects the difficulties encountered in effecting the liberalization objectives of the IGA and AIA,[75] as well as the textual and practical problems inherent in attempting to implement the two agreements. The ACIA is also an important part of the plan for the ASEAN Economic Community and the overall plan for closer integration of the ASEAN states. The issues were summarized in the words of the Honorable Dato' Seri Abdullah Ahmad Badawi, prime minister of Malaysia, in his Opening Address at the Opening Ceremony of the 39th ASEAN Ministerial Meeting.[76]

> 4. On the building of the ASEAN Community, he underlined three overarching principles, whereby there should be a universal acceptance that community interests would prevail over national interests on issues affecting the community and that ASEAN has to do better in giving national effect to wider international treaties and conventions, including ASEAN treaties and agreements by putting in place capacities for enforcing community decisions.

---

[74] (2003) 42 I.L.M. 540, ¶ 82.

[75] *See* discussion in Jarvis, *supra* note 67.

[76] Association of Southeast Asian Nations, JOINT COMMUNIQUE OF THE 39TH ASEAN MINISTERIAL MEETING (AMM) KUALA LUMPUR (July 25, 2006), http://www.aseansec.org/18561.htm.

As noted above, the ACIA came into effect on March 1, 2012, at which time the IGA and AIA were terminated pursuant to Article 47(1). The ACIA Reservation List (ACIA Schedule) had not been finalized on that date but was subsequently made available on the ASEAN website.[77]

The stated objective of the ACIA is economic integration, which is to be effected through progressive liberalization of foreign investment, provision of enhanced investment protection for investors of member states and their investments, improved transparency and predictability of investment rules and regulations, joint promotion of the ASEAN area as an integrated investment destination, and cooperation to create favorable conditions for the investment by investors of one member state in another member state (Article 1). The Guiding Principles in Article 2, however, suggest a slightly different set of priorities, and refer to the creation of a "free and open investment environment" and the encouragement of investment generally, while still allowing for preferential treatment between the ASEAN states and the preservation of special and differential treatment for those states that need it. Article 2(e) provides that there shall be no "back-tracking" from the commitments made in the IGA and the AIA.

The substantive provisions of the ACIA indicate that the encouragement of investment is not limited to ASEAN investors, and this wish to create a welcoming investment environment for all investors, not just investors from ASEAN itself, is reflected in the provisions of the ASEAN-Plus agreements. In substance, the ACIA combines the liberalization and encouragement objectives of the AIA with the more traditional investment protection content of the IGA. Its fourfold objectives mean that the ACIA attempts to fill numerous functions—creation of state-to-state agreements on liberalization of investment access, improvement of investment regulatory regimes, facilitation and encouragement of investment, and provision of guarantees of investor protection on which investors can rely and which, if breached, can provide the basis for legal action in the form of investor–state arbitration.

These multiple roles raise the question as to how the ACIA should be construed. Is it primarily a plurilateral investment protection treaty, for example, or does it have a wider scope? In particular, is the liberalization agenda enforceable against states by investors, or is it a component of the state-to-state agreement documented in the ASEAN Charter and its associated documents? Zewei Zhong argues strongly that an appropriate reading of the ACIA, putting it in its context as part of the creation of an ASEAN Community, combined with a textual reading of the document, is that ACIA is in the image of "regionalised governance" rather than an agreement that merely transplants investor-protective rules.[78] Indeed, Zhong ends with the comment that "[It] beggars belief that Member States would, through an RIT embedded within that

---

77 Association of Southeast Asian Nations, *ASEAN Comprehensive Investment Agreement (ACIA) Enters into Force Creating a Stable and Predictable Business Investment Environment* (Apr. 4, 2012), http://www.aseansec.org/26842.htm; Association of Southeast Asian Nations, *ASEAN Comprehensive Investment Agreement Reservation List*, http://www.aseansec.org/20632_a.htm.

78 Zewei Zhong, *The ASEAN Comprehensive Investment Agreement: Realizing a Regional Community*, 6(1) Asian J. Comp. L. 1, 14 (2011).

same regional framework, intentionally cede large amounts of their sovereign rights in regulating foreign investment to the oversight of international arbitrators."[79] As discussed in more detail below, investment liberalization is treated separately from investment protection in the ACIA, which defers to the interests and policies of states in relation to investment access and provides that disputes in relation to liberalization are matters for state-to-state resolution, and are not subject to investor–state arbitration.

The creation of a liberalized ASEAN-wide investment area would be a very significant achievement for this ambitious project. The terms of the ACIA give an indication of the difficulty in balancing the interests and rights of states in relation to the public interest and the domestic ability to determine investment policy with the regional objective of creating an ASEAN investment zone. The practical issues are highlighted by the fact that, during the term of their operation, the IGA and AIA were not successful in creating a fully liberalized investment zone within ASEAN.[80] The considerable time that elapsed between the signing of the ACIA and ratification by Indonesia and Thailand[81] gives some indication of the domestic difficulties encountered by a number of the ASEAN states in agreeing fully (or even partially) to open up their foreign investment regimes as freely as required by the ACIA. These problems arise from the differing approaches of the ASEAN nations to the admission of FDI. Indonesia, for example, has made major improvements in liberalizing its approach to foreign investment in order to attract more FDI, but is nevertheless ranked by the authors of the OECD Restrictiveness Index as a country that maintains a very restrictive investment regime.[82] The ongoing issues for Indonesia are exemplified by the fact that although it has recently ratified both the ACIA and the ASEAN–ANZ Agreement, the Indonesian government has also recently announced legislation providing that all mining investments in Indonesia must be majority Indonesian-owned by the tenth year of operation.[83] Vietnam also maintains a system of strict control over the admission of FDI.[84] These aspects of domestic policy are reflected in the content of the Reservation List.

---

[79] *Id.* at 38–39.

[80] Jarvis, *supra* note 67.

[81] See Edmund Sim, *Wrap-Up of the ASEAN Economic Ministers Retreat* (Mar. 8, 2012), http://www.aseanec.blogspot.com/2012/03/wrap-up-on-asean-economic-ministers.html. Indonesia ratified the ACIA on Aug. 8, 2011. *See* Lubis Ganie Surowidjoj, *Indonesia Ratifies the ASEAN Comprehensive Investment Agreement* (Sept. 2011), http://www.legal500.com/indonesia/developments/15399 (last visited Mar. 21, 2012).

[82] Blanka Kalinova, Angel Palerm & Stephen Thomsen, *OECD's FDI Restrictiveness Index: 2010 Update* (OECD Working Papers on International Investment No. 2010/3, 2010) at Table II.

[83] Robin Brumby, *Jakarta Moves to Limit Foreign Ownership of Mines to 49pc*, AUSTRALIAN, Mar. 8, 2012; Simon Butt & Luke Nottage, *Divestment of Foreign Mining Interests in Indonesia*, EAST ASIA FORUM, May 13, 2012, http://www.eastasiaforum.org/2012/05/13/divestment-of-foreign-mining-interests-in-indonesia/.

[84] *See* Hop Dang, *Legal Issues in Vietnam's FDI Law: Protections under Domestic Law, Bilateral Investment Treaties and Sovereign Guarantees*, in FOREIGN INVESTMENT, *supra* note 10, at 225–42.

The concept of liberalization is not defined in ACIA. Article 30 of the Blueprint, however,[85] states that liberalization of the investment regime in order to achieve "free and open investment by 2015" should involve the following actions: extension of non-discriminatory treatment to investors in ASEAN through the grant of national and most-favored-nation treatment, with minimal exceptions; reduction or elimination of restrictions to entry for investments in the sectors where priority access to goods has been granted; and reduction or elimination of restrictive investment measures, including performance requirements.

Thus, Article 1 of the ACIA refers to the "progressive liberalisation of the investment regimes of member States."[86] The Guiding Principles (Article 2) refer to the "progressive liberalisation of investment with a view towards achieving a free and open investment environment in the region."[87] The right to investment market access created by the ACIA, however, is circumscribed and generally reflects the compromise reached in the Protocol to the AIA. The industries to be liberalized are listed: manufacturing, agriculture, fisheries, forestry and mining and quarrying, and services incidental to these areas, although there is an option for the addition of sectors if so agreed by all of the member states (Article 3). The ACIA, however, sets out clear—and potentially substantial—exceptions to the obligation of states to implement this liberalization policy, which include taxation, subsidies, government procurement, and services provided to government on noncommercial terms (Article 3(4)).

The objective of liberalization through the ACIA is to be achieved by the inclusion of provisions for the grant of national treatment and most-favored-nation treatment for the admission, establishment, and management of investments; the prohibition of restrictive performance requirements in Article 7; and the imposition of limits on nationality requirements for directors and senior managers.[88] Thus Article 5 requires each member state to accord to investors and investments of any other member states:

> treatment no less favorable than that it accords, in like circumstances, to its own investors with respect to the admission, establishment, acquisition, expansion, management, conduct, operation and sale or other disposition of investments in its territory.[89]

Article 6 similarly requires each member state to accord to investors and investment of another member state treatment no less favorable than that accorded, in like circumstances, to investors of either an ASEAN state or a non-ASEAN state with respect to "admission, establishment, acquisition, expansion, management, conduct, operation

---

85 *See supra* note 21.

86 *See supra* note 2, at Article 1(a).

87 *Id.*, at Article 2(b).

88 *Id.* at Article 8.

89 *Id.* at Art 5(1).

and sale or other disposition of investments in its territory" (subject to exceptions for sub-regional arrangements and the 1966 Treaty of Amity and Economic Relations between Thailand and the United States).[90]

Unlike the AIA, the ACIA potentially extends benefits in relation to investment liberalization and protection to corporations or persons from outside ASEAN. Article 19 allows a member state to deny the benefits of the Agreement to an investor only where the investor is owned or controlled by a person from a non–member state and where there are no "substantive business operations in the territory" of the member state where it is established, or to an investor that is actually owned or controlled by investors from the member state in which it sets up operations or which comes from a state with which the host state has no diplomatic relations. Any other investor, no matter where it is owned and controlled, is entitled to enjoy the benefits of the ACIA, including the right to bring an investor–state arbitration against the host State, as long as it has substantial business operations located in the territory of a member state.[91] The purpose of this is to effect the goal of encouraging investment from outside ASEAN. It has the potential advantage of allowing investors the benefits of investment liberalization negotiated under the ACIA. It has the potential disadvantage of causing ASEAN states to weigh carefully the extent to which they are prepared to modify their investment policies because the benefits will be accorded to all investors, not merely to investors owned or controlled within other ASEAN states.

However, the provisions relating to national treatment (Article 5) and to senior management and boards of directors (Article 8) are subject to any existing measure maintained by a level of government of a member state and included on its Reservation List (a negative list approach). A substantial period of grace for the modification of commitments under the Reservation List is given under Article 10. Article 10 also allows states to modify their commitments subsequently, subject to provisions protecting investments existing at the time of the change. Pursuant to Article 9(4) of the ACIA, member states should reduce or eliminate the reservations in the Reservations List in accordance with the Strategic Schedule of the Blueprint, which provides for the realization of a free and open investment regime by 2015.[92]

The adoption of a negative list structure in the ACIA, and of the Strategic Schedule, suggests a rigorous approach to the adoption by member states of regulatory restrictions relating to investment. Certainly, from the point of view of investors, the ACIA Reservation List provides a number of significant advantages in terms of transparency and clarity. The use of a negative list requires states to set out clearly exactly all restrictions on foreign investment. The Reservation List not only itemizes each reservation by a state and its content, but also sets out the legislation that is the basis for the measure

[90] *Id.* at Article 6(3)(b), n.6.

[91] Note, however, that Thailand does not extend the benefits of the ACIA to investors of other Members owned or controlled by nationals of a non-Member State, a provision that is subject to annual review by the AIA Council. *See supra* note 77, Reservation List, Headnote, Art. 8.

[92] *See supra* note 21.

limiting the implementation of the particular obligation. As noted above, however, the Reservation List under the ACIA may be modified if states change their policies toward investment. In addition, the existence of a negative list does not necessarily result in the reduction of impediments to foreign investment or the improvement of the foreign investment environment. The content of the Reservation List makes clear that the ASEAN states continue to maintain their own priorities in relation to the admission and operation of FDI in their territory. Indonesia's lengthy schedule, for example, sets out thirty-five pages of limitations and restrictions.[93]

Notwithstanding its liberalization objectives, the ACIA is protective of the autonomy of states in relation to policy on the admission of investment generally, as well as the admission of individual investments. The ACIA endeavors to provide clarity in relation to what constitutes an investment by making clear that "the characteristics of an investment include the commitment of capital, the expectation of gain or profit, or the assumption of risk."[94] The requirement that investments be admitted in accordance with "laws, regulations and national policies"[95] potentially gives states the right to impose restrictions on the admission of investment and the establishment of new investment entities notwithstanding the liberalization objectives of the ACIA.

Similarly, the definition of "covered investment" in Article 4 states that an investment in a state must "be admitted according to its laws, regulations and national policies, and, where applicable, specifically approved in writing by the competent authority of a Member State..." Annex I clarifies the provisions of the previous agreements in relation to approvals in writing (where such approvals are required for the admission of investment) by setting out requirements for the creation of a transparent process where approvals in writing are necessary, including a requirement for the provision of reasons.[96] A further clarification of the scope of the national treatment and most-favored-nation treatment provisions is set out in Article 20 of the ACIA, which states that nothing in Articles 5 or 6 "shall be construed to prevent a Member State from adopting or maintaining a measure that prescribes special formalities in connection with investments, including a requirement that investments be legally constituted or assume a certain legal form under the laws or regulations with the Member State and compliance with registration requirements..." provided that the requirements do not "materially impair the rights afforded by a Member State to investors of another Member State."

The description of the investor's right to initiate investor–state arbitration in the ACIA is carefully drafted to ensure that it does not extend to claims against states in respect of their commitments on investment liberalization. First, the right to bring a claim is restricted to claims for breach of specified obligations—namely, those relating

93 *See supra* note 77.
94 *Id.* at Article 4(c), definition of "investment," footnote 2.
95 ACIA, *see supra* note 2, at Article 4(c), definition of "investment."
96 Michael Ewing-Chow & G.R. Fischer, *ASEAN IIAs: Conserving Regulatory Sovereignty While Promoting the Rule of Law?* 8(5) Transnat'l Dispute Management J. 6 (2011).

to national treatment; most-favored-nation treatment; nationality of senior management and board of directors; treatment of investment; and compensation in cases of strife, transfers, and expropriation.[97] General commitments related to investment liberalization, disclosure, transparency, investment facilitation, and so on are not covered. Second, there is no right to bring action in relation to the "admission, establishment, acquisition or expansion of an investment." Arbitration may be brought only in respect of a breach "relating to the management, conduct, operation or sale or other disposition of a covered investment."[98] Third, the disputing investor must be able to show loss or damage in relation to the investment and arising out of the breach.[99] As a consequence, claims by investors in relation to market access commitments are effectively barred under the ACIA—a dispute about contravention of any of these requirements must be brought on a state-to-state basis.

Like the AIA, the ACIA contains provisions relating to General Exceptions and Security Exceptions,[100] which have a similarly broad scope of application. Article 17 in particular makes clear that, subject to the requirement that measures are not applied "in a manner which would constitute a means of arbitrary or unjustifiable discrimination between Member States or their investors where like conditions prevail, or a disguised restriction on investors of any other Member States and their investors," states can adopt measures affecting investors or investments on a variety of grounds—to protect public morals or public order, protect life, secure compliance with laws, collect taxes, protect national treasures, and conserve natural resources (if similar domestic measures are taken). Annex 2, which deals with expropriation, similarly makes clear that nondiscriminatory measures designed to protect public health, safety, and the environment do not constitute a form of indirect expropriation for which compensation must be paid.

In summary, although the ACIA sets out ambitious objectives in relation to the liberalization or opening up of market access to FDI, it reflects a carefully struck balance between the rights of states to determine their own investment policies and the liberalization across the region of investment market access. States may exercise significant control over the admission of FDI through the maintenance of rules regulating establishment and admission. States may exempt sectors or types of investment through the Reservation List. Even though the concept underlying the ACIA is that the reservations should be phased out, Article 10 allows for future modifications to be made as long as existing investments are not affected. Above all, the ACIA ensures that disputes relating to the implementation of market access commitments are a matter for state-to-state resolution rather than investor–state arbitration.

At a practical level, the ASEAN states are well aware of the issues relating to implementation of the ambitious ASEAN Community goals and, in addition to ongoing

---

[97] ACIA, *see supra* note 2, at Article 32(a).

[98] *Id.*

[99] *Id,* at Article 32(b).

[100] *Id.* at Articles 17 and 18.

work programs, the ASEAN Secretariat publishes a scorecard setting out the degree to which goals relating to the ASEAN Economic Community have been satisfied. In the scorecard published in March 2012, slightly fewer than half of the goals relating to the flow of investment had been satisfied in the 2010–2011 period.[101] This ongoing work program, and the related internal pressure within ASEAN, which is applied to ASEAN states to bring themselves into compliance with the objectives of the ASEAN Charter, are features that distinguish the ACIA from other bilateral or plurilateral investment treaties such as the ASEAN-Plus treaties that do not have a similar mechanism creating an impetus for parties to continue working toward compliance.

IV. ASEAN-Plus Agreements and Liberalization of Investment

As noted above, the ASEAN states and ASEAN itself have negotiated and signed a considerable number of bilateral or plurilateral agreements designed to facilitate both trade and investment. In particular, ASEAN has entered into a series of free trade arrangements with countries in the region. Increasingly, these cover investment. The importance of investment as part of the ASEAN view of its regional trade arrangements is reflected in the draft ASEAN Framework for a Comprehensive Regional Partnership,[102] which sets out a framework for future free trade agreement negotiations by ASEAN and reportedly makes clear that investment is regarded by ASEAN as a fundamental part of its free trade negotiations. This is reflected in the PRC–ASEAN Agreement, the ASEAN–Korea Agreement, and Chapter 11 of the ASEAN–ANZ Agreement.

The ASEAN-Plus agreements were drafted concurrently with the ACIA and they reflect many of the principles set out in the ACIA. In particular, each of them refers to some, if not all, of the ACIA's objectives—that is, the liberalization and facilitation of trade in goods and services, the creation of a favorable investment environment,[103] the liberalization of investment regimes,[104] the protection of cooperation between the state and investor,[105] the promotion of the transparency of investment rules,[106] and the grant of special and differential treatment to the less-developed states in the ASEAN

---

101 ASEAN Secretariat, *ASEAN Economic Community Scorecard, Charting Progress towards Regional Economic Integration* (Mar. 2012), http://www.aseansec.org/documents/scorecard_final.pdf. The Scorecard indicates that the ASEAN states "have developed a modality to further eliminate investment restrictions and impediments and improve investment regulations" (at 6). As Sim comments, however, the quantitative measures used in the Scorecard are not finely tuned and, in particular, do not assess the standard of domestic compliance with treaties that states have ratified. Grading the ASEAN Economic Community Scorecard (May 25, 2012), http://aseanec.blogspot.com.au/2012/05/grading-asean-economic-community.html.

102 Edmund Sim, *ASEAN Economic Ministers Lay Down a Marker for FTA Negotiations* (Oct. 18, 2011), http://aseanec.blogspot.com.au/2011/10/asean-economic-ministers-lay-down.html.

103 ASEAN–ANZ Agreement, *supra* note 4, Chapter 11, Article 1(c).

104 PRC–ASEAN Agreement, *supra* note 4, Preamble, second paragraph.

105 ASEAN–ANZ Agreement, *supra* note 4, Chapter 11, Article 1(d).

106 See discussion *infra*.

region.[107] In particular, the PRC–ASEAN Agreement refers specifically to the liberalization of investment as one of its objectives,[108] whereas the ASEAN–Korea Investment Agreement and Chapter 11 of the ASEAN–ANZFTA provide for a program of work the purpose of which is to liberalize investment between the contracting states.[109]

It is questionable, however, to what extent the objective of liberalization, in the sense of wider market access for foreign investors, is actually achieved in any of these agreements. The strong impetus behind the ASEAN-Plus free trade agreements is to liberalize the market for trade in goods and services, increase market access, and improve transparency. For example, the New Zealand National Interest Analysis sets out seven reasons supporting New Zealand's decision to become a party to the ASEAN–ANZ Agreement, but only one relates to investment—a statement that the agreement will provide greater security for New Zealand investors in ASEAN markets, including through recourse to binding investor–state arbitration.[110]

Despite its reference to investment liberalization, the PRC–ASEAN Agreement actually contains few substantive commitments relating to wider market access for investors. The ASEAN–ANZ Agreement provides for a five-year work program relating to the preparation of reservation lists in relation to the grant of national treatment and the possibility of granting most-favored-nation treatment, but, as noted in the New Zealand National Interest Analysis, it does not contain any upfront commitments.[111] Indeed, New Zealand was recently moved to complain publicly about additional restrictions imposed by Indonesia on imports and investment that have a potentially adverse effect on New Zealand companies.[112]

Liberalization in the ASEAN-Plus agreements is dealt with mainly through provisions relating to the grant of national treatment or most-favored-nation treatment in relation to the admission or establishment of investment. As in the ACIA, the effect of such a provision is to allow foreign investors opportunities in relation to the entry of investments, through establishment of a new entity or by acquisition, which are no less favorable than those accorded nationals of the host state or to nationals of any other country. Clearly, the optimal position is to be accorded the same treatment as nationals who, presumably, have wider access to domestic investment opportunities. As discussed above, this is reflected in the ACIA, which accords both national and most-favored-nation treatment in relation

[107] ASEAN–ANZ Agreement, *supra* note 4, Chapter 11, Article 15; PRC–ASEAN Agreement, *supra* note 4, Preamble, third paragraph; ASEAN–Korea Agreement, *supra* note 4, Article 16.

[108] PRC–ASEAN Agreement, *supra* note 4, at Article 2(a).

[109] ASEAN–Korea Agreement, *supra* note 4, Articles 26 and 27; ASEAN-ANZ Agreement, *supra* note 4, Chapter 11, Article 16.

[110] Ministry of Foreign Affairs and Trade, New Zealand, *Agreement Establishing the ASEAN-Australia-New Zealand Free Trade Area (and associated instruments), National Interest Analysis*, http://www.asean.fta.govt.nz/assets/Downloads/asean-national-interest-analysis-2.pdf, at 3–4.

[111] *Id.* at 30.

[112] Linda Yulisman, *Trade and Investment Climate Needs Improvement: New Zealand* (Feb. 2, 2012), http://www.asianewsnet.net/home/news.php?id=27363&sec=2.

to establishment, admission, acquisition and expansion, of investments of eligible investors—although subject to the provisions of the Reservation List.

The PRC–ASEAN agreement provides for national treatment, but this does not extend to the admission or establishment of investments. This agreement does accord most-favored-nation treatment in relation to "admission, establishment, acquisition, expansion" of investment.[113] This is, however, subject to Article 5(2), which states that a Party which in the future grants preferential treatment to another state is not required to accord the benefits of this treatment to the Parties to the treaty. Article 5(3) provides another exception for preferential treatment accorded pursuant to any existing "bilateral, regional or international" agreement or other form of cooperation with a non-Party or any agreement among the ASEAN member states. Article 6 provides that neither national treatment nor most-favored-nation treatment provisions override any existing or new nonconforming measures although there is a rather general requirement in Article 6(2) that "Parties will endeavor to progressively remove the non-conforming measures." Similarly, under Article 6(3), the Parties should enter into discussions to further the liberalization and transparency objectives set out in Article 2. As in the ACIA, the investor–state arbitration clause is limited to claims for breach causing loss or damage to an investor "in relation to its investment with respect to the management, conduct, operation, or sale or other disposition of an investment."[114] Disputes relating to admission, establishment, acquisition, and expansion are not covered.

The ASEAN–Korea Agreement, by contrast, notionally provides for the grant of national treatment and most-favored-nation treatment in respect of the "establishment, admission, acquisition, expansion" of investment.[115] However, the grant of national treatment, along with provisions relating to reservations, performance requirements, Annexes on expropriation and dispute resolution, and other major substantive issues is subject to conclusion of a work program that must be completed within five years from the date on which the agreement comes into effect.[116] Articles 3 and 4, together with various other important provisions, do not come into effect until that time.[117] The agreement follows the PRC–ASEAN Agreement in providing that most-favored-nation treatment does not apply in the case of any existing preferential arrangements provided pursuant to bilateral, regional, or international agreements or other forms of cooperation or any existing or future treatment accorded pursuant to agreements between ASEAN states. Similarly, a Party may negotiate more favorable treatment with any other state, and is not required to grant the benefits of that treatment to parties under this agreement.[118] Again, investor–state arbitration is not available in respect

[113] PRC–ASEAN Agreement, *supra* note 4, at Articles 4 and 5(1).

[114] PRC–ASEAN Agreement, *supra* note 4, at Article 14(1).

[115] ASEAN–Korea Agreement, *supra* note 4, Articles 3 and 4.

[116] *Id.* Article 27.

[117] *Id.* Article 27(4).

[118] *Id.* Article 4(3) and (4).

of a claim that national treatment and most-favored-nation treatment have not been accorded in the case of establishment or admission of investment.[119]

The ASEAN–ANZ Agreement takes a different approach, although the end result in relation to liberalization is similar. First, Article 4 of Chapter 11 provides for national treatment for the "establishment, acquisition, expansion" and so on of investments.[120] Article 4 does not enter into force until the conclusion of the discussions to be undertaken pursuant to the Work Programme outlined in Article 16 relating to the schedule of reservations and treatment of investment in services. Chapter 11 does not include a provision in relation to most-favored-nation treatment, although as part of the Work Programme the parties are also required to enter into discussions "with a view to agreeing on" the application of most-favored-nation treatment to future investments.[121] Article 20, which deals with claims by an investor of a party, allows claims in respect of a breach of an obligation of a state "relating to the management, conduct, operation or sale or other disposition of a covered investment" but does not extend to claims in respect of the establishment, expansion, or acquisition of an investment. Although all parties have now ratified the ASEAN–ANZ Agreement,[122] it is therefore not clear at this stage to what extent, if any, this program will result in significant liberalization. In summary, the ASEAN–ANZ Agreement and the ASEAN–Korea Agreement provide for the possibility of liberalized terms of investment—subject to negotiations as to the exact nature of any commitments relating to liberalization. The PRC–ASEAN Agreement, although already effective, is very limited in its terms.[123]

The ASEAN-Plus agreements reiterate a number of provisions in the ACIA in relation to the admission of investment. The PRC–ASEAN Agreement[124] provides in relation to the definition of "investment" that this means an asset invested "in accordance with the relevant laws, regulations and policies" of the host state. A footnote explains that "policies" refer to "those affecting investment that are endorsed and announced by the Government of a Party, and made publicly available in a written form."[125] The ASEAN–ANZ Agreement provides that a covered investment means an investment "which, where applicable, has been admitted by the host Party, subject to its relevant laws, regulations and policies ..."[126] The ASEAN–Korea Agreement does not contain a provision of this kind, but the footnote to the definition of "investor of a Party" states

---

119 *Id.*, Article 14(1).

120 There is no reference to "admission." The same language is used in relation to Performance Requirements (Article 5), which refers to "establishment, acquisition, management" and so on.

121 ASEAN–ANZ Agreement, *supra* note 4, Chapter 11, Article 16(2).

122 *See supra* note 4.

123 *See also* Xiao, Jun, The ASEAN-China Investment Agreement: A Regionalization of Chinese New BITs (June 23, 2010). Society of International Economic Law (SIEL), Second Biennial Global Conference, University of Barcelona, July 8–10, 2010. Available at SSRN: http://ssrn.com/abstract=1629202, who reviews China's agreements with individual ASEAN states and concludes that China is not prepared to undertake new liberalization objectives in its free trade agreements.

124 PRC–ASEAN Agreement, *supra* note 4, Article 1.

125 *Id.* n.1.

126 ASEAN–ANZ Agreement, *supra* note 4, Chapter 11, Article 2(a).

that a person who is seeking to make an investment includes an investor who has taken active steps to initiate a notification or approval process, where applicable.[127] Both the PRC–ASEAN Agreement and the ASEAN–ANZ Agreement provide that protection will be accorded only to investments that have satisfied the requirements of certain states that they be formally approved in writing.[128] Article 15 of the ASEAN–Korea Agreement provides that Article 3 (National Treatment) should not be construed to prevent a Party from "adopting or maintaining a measure that prescribes special formalities in connection with the establishment of investment by investors of any other Party..."[129]

Thus, in a similar fashion to the ACIA, the right of the host state to impose requirements relating to the admission of investment is recognized. Where national treatment or most-favored-nation treatment is to be granted to admission or establishment of investments, the relevant provision is either hedged around with qualifications or implementation is subject to a lengthy negotiation process. The fact that investor–state arbitration does not cover admission or establishment of investment also reflects the balance that is struck in the ACIA between the right of the host state to control both policy and individual cases in relation to admission and the general principle of granting investors rights against the host state in relation to a breach of the offered investment protection. In summary, the stated objective of liberalization insofar as it relates to market access is carefully limited and controlled by the terms of the ASEAN-Plus Agreements.

V. Discussion

The content of the ACIA and the ASEAN-Plus agreements raise a number of questions in relation to the objective of achieving investment liberalization through bilateral and plurilateral regional agreements. The scope of the ACIA is ambitious, and indicates a collective intention of the ASEAN states to press forward with regional investment liberalization in the areas specified in the ACIA while at the same time preserving domestic state autonomy over investment admission. This does not mean, however, that implementation of the ACIA will automatically result in widespread intra-ASEAN investment liberalization. The practical difficulty of achieving implementation of the agenda set out in the ACIA is indicated by the delay in the ACIA coming into effect and by a review of the content of the Reservation List. Nevertheless, the ACIA is supported by the agreement of the ASEAN states to set up the ASEAN Communities and by the ASEAN Secretariat and administrative infrastructure, which works to achieve the goals of the ASEAN Charter.

---

127 ASEAN–Korea Agreement, *supra* note 4, Article 1(k).

128 PRC–ASEAN Agreement, *supra* note 4, Article 3(3) in relation to Thailand.

129 ASEAN–Korea Agreement, *supra* note 4, Article 15(1).

Achieving investment liberalization through the medium of the ASEAN-Plus agreements is considerably more problematic, even though ASEAN's regional neighbors appear to acknowledge in the agreements the desirability of, and their intention to engage in, a process of regional liberalization. A number of issues arise here. First is the question of the role played by multiple bilateral and plurilateral investment agreements in relation to investment liberalization. Second, and related to this, is the issue of domestic policy relating to inbound investment and the relationship between domestic policy, international commitments and investment treaties.

It is clear from the text of the ACIA and the ASEAN-Plus agreements that there is no expectation that these agreements will replace bilateral free trade agreements or investment treaties or other regional or sub-regional treaty arrangements that individual parties may be able to negotiate on more favorable terms. Chapter 18.2 of the ASEAN–ANZ Agreement provides that the treaty does not derogate from any other agreement to which the states may be parties, particularly agreements between ASEAN states and agreements between an ASEAN state and Australia or New Zealand. As a result, "the provisions of AANZFTA ensure that it can have no impact on those existing FTAs."[130] The PRC–ASEAN Agreement allows a party to enter into future preferential arrangements in the future without granting those preferences to other parties to the PRC–ASEAN Agreement, although there is an obligation to inform other parties of any arrangement that grants preferential treatment and to give them an adequate opportunity to negotiate similar terms.[131] The ACIA's most-favored-nation clause (Article 6), in marked contrast, extends to all parties preferential treatment accorded to investments from both ASEAN and non-ASEAN states, with the exception of sub-regional arrangements and existing arrangements notified to the AIA Council under the AIA.

Individual ASEAN States and their regional neighbors, as discussed in more detail above, have entered into a wide range of agreements with an impact on trade and investment. In addition to the significant number of bilateral investment treaties, Asian states generally have entered into and continue to negotiate a large number of free trade agreements, which cover trade and may also cover investment. It is reported, for example, that in mid-2009, East Asia had 109 free trade agreements at various stages of signing, effectiveness, and negotiation.[132] The consequences in relation to provisions on investment and investment protection, as the discussion of the terms of the ASEAN-Plus agreements shows, is that there will be inconsistencies, and, in some cases, serious inconsistencies, between the terms of these agreements. Although this is particularly the case in relation to trade, these inconsistencies also potentially arise in relation to investment, including in provisions that grant concessions and

---

130 Australian Government, Department of Foreign Affairs and Trade, The ASEAN-Australia-New Zealand Free Trade Agreement, Fast Facts about ASEAN-Australia-New Zealand FTA (undated), http://www.draft.gov.au/aanzfta/fast-facts.html.

131 PRC–ASEAN Agreement, *supra* note 4, Articles 5(2) and 19(d).

132 Masahiro Kawai & Ganeshan Wignaraja, *The Asian "Noodle Bowl": Is It Serious for Business?* (ADBI Working Papers Series, No. 136, 2009), at 4, n.2.

preferences in relation to the admission and establishment of investments—that is, liberalization of market access.[133] The terms of the ASEAN-Plus Agreements, however, indicate that outside ASEAN, states are generally cautious in agreeing to provisions on national and most-favored-nation treatment relating to market access, notwithstanding general commitments to the concept of liberalization.

A major issue in relation to bilateral and plurilateral liberalization of investment, as opposed to trade in goods and services, is the question of consistency in relation to inbound investment. In addition, domestic politics and domestic concerns relating to inbound investment play a significant role in investment policy, and thus have a direct impact on decisions relating to liberalization of market access. The approaches taken by China and Australia in their various investment and free trade agreements provide some insight on the issues that may arise.

China maintains a tightly regulated series of laws and policies relating to admission of investment, and with the exception of some concessions made under agreements with those areas that it considers to be part of China (i.e., Hong Kong, Macao, and Taiwan), China is generally not prepared to give preferential treatment in relation to the admission of investment, nor is it prepared to surrender its ability to control the admission of investment.[134] In its bilateral investment treaties, it has accordingly been reluctant to grant concessions in relation to national treatment, particularly in the preestablishment stage.[135] The terms of the PRC–ASEAN Agreement are entirely consistent with this approach. There is no grant of national treatment for admission or establishment under Article 4 of that agreement. Because China takes an evenhanded approach to the regulation of the admission of foreign investment, the grant of most-favored-nation treatment in relation to admission and establishment is not a major concession, and it appears in the PRC–ASEAN Agreement, although, as discussed above, hedged around with restrictions designed to preserve each state's ability to enter into other agreements on different or more-preferential terms.[136]

China's approach is, however, not completely uniform. Most-favored-nation treatment in relation to the preestablishment phase of investment also appears in the New Zealand China Free Trade Agreement.[137] Unlike the PRC–ASEAN Agreement, however, Article 139 of the New Zealand China Free Trade Agreement restricts the right of the parties subsequently to grant more preferential treatment without also

133 *See also* the discussion in Tubagus Feridhanusetyawan, *Preferential Trade Agreements in the Asia–Pacific Region* (IMF Working Paper WP/05/149, 2005), particularly at 23, Table 6, Services and Investment Liberalization in Selected Asia–Pacific PTAs.

134 Vivienne Bath, *The Quandary for Chinese Investors: Controlling the Flow of Investment into and out of China, in* Foreign Investment, *supra* note 10, at 69 to 73.

135 Congyuan Cai, *China–US BIT Negotiations and the Future of Investment Treaty Regime: A Grand Bilateral Bargain with Multilateral Implications,* 12(2) J. Int'l Econ. L. 457, 469 (2009).

136 PRC–ASEAN Agreement, *supra* note 4, Article 5.

137 Free Trade Agreement between New Zealand and China (Apr. 7, 2008), 2008 N.Z. T.S. 19, Chapter 11, Art 139(1).

providing this treatment to investors under the New Zealand–China agreement.[138] In Article 4 of the recently signed trilateral investment agreement between China, Korea and Japan,[139] the parties agreed to accord most-favored nation treatment to investors and investments, including in relation to admission of investment (subject to the right of the admitting party to exercise powers in relation to admission, including in relation to "foreign ownership and control").[140] Although there are exceptions set out in Article 492) with regard to customs unions, agreements on small-scale border trade, and agreements relating to aviation, fishery, and maritime matters involving salvage, Article 4 contains no provision in relation to nonconforming measures, or future nonconforming measures.

Again, in contrast to the PRC–ASEAN Agreement, the dispute resolution clause in the New Zealand–China agreement applies to all "legal disputes" between an investor of one party and the other party "directly concerning an investment," with no exception for disputes relating to establishment of investments.[141] Footnotes 9 and 11 to this chapter, however, make clear that rights relating to establishment of investment are included only in Articles 139 and 142 (transfers of funds) and that the right to transfer funds to establish or expand an investment applies only after "successful completion of the approval procedures for inward investment." Article 14 of the investment agreement between Japan, Korea and China similarly does not exempt disputes relating to the admission of investment under Article 4(1) from investor–state dispute resolution.

Australia's position in relation to investment liberalization has not been as consistent as China's and the agreements that Australia has entered into illustrate some of the issues that arise when states agree to increased market access on different terms in bilateral or plurilateral agreements. As discussed above, the ASEAN–ANZ Agreement, which provides for a five-year program of work in relation to national treatment (including in relation to establishment, but not admission, of investments) and the possible grant of most-favored-nation treatment for investments, provides the potential for liberalization rather than concrete commitments. In the Australia–United States Free Trade Agreement,[142] however, Australia agreed to accord national treatment, most-favored-nation treatment, and prohibition of performance requirements in relation to the "establishment, expansion, management" and so on of covered investments.

[138] In contrast to the PRC–ASEAN Agreement, Article 5(2) of which allows a Party to enter into more favorable agreements without according the benefit to other States, Article 139 of the New Zealand–China FTA allows only for more favorable treatment accorded under existing free trade agreements or multilateral international agreements, and for future agreements relating to fisheries and maritime matters. As in the case of the ACIA and ASEAN-plus agreements, Article 139(2) makes clear that most-favored-nation treatment does not extend to dispute resolution procedures. *See also* ACIA, n.1, Article 6, footnote 4; PRC–ASEAN Agreement, *supra* note 4, Article 5(4).

[139] *See supra* note 55.

[140] *Id.* at Article 2(2). Pursuant to the Protocol to the agreement, Article 4(1) does not apply to the acquisition of land property.

[141] *See supra* note 137, Article 152.

[142] *See supra* note 57.

Exceptions to Australia's obligations in relation to investments were set out in Annex 1 and Annex 2, in relation to exceptions for existing nonconforming measures and measures in sectors that were scheduled.[143] In particular, Australia agreed that investments made by U.S. investors would not be subject to notification and screening by the Australian Foreign Investment Review Board unless they were in a sensitive sector or exceeded a specified amount—an amount that was significantly larger than the amount at which all other investments into Australia became subject to screening.[144] The benefit of these significant concessions will be extended to New Zealand when the Protocol on Investment to the Australia–New Zealand Closer Economic Relations Trade Agreement takes effect.[145] They are not, however, available to investors from other countries. Significantly, in neither case are these market access commitments subject to investor–state arbitration, as neither the Australia–U.S. agreement[146] nor the Protocol provide for it.[147]

Australia's commitments in other free trade agreements demonstrate different approaches. The free trade agreement with Singapore, which was amended in 2009 (effective in 2011), has a negative list of reservations to the grant of national treatment in relation to the "establishment, acquisition, expansion" and so on of investments, but does not provide for most-favored-nation treatment.[148] The free trade agreement with Thailand provides for national treatment in respect of the establishment and acquisition of investments in its territory in the sectors set out in Annex 8, but otherwise provides only for national treatment in relation to "management, conduct, operation and sale or other disposition of covered investments."[149] The most-favored-nation treatment clause refers only to investors and investment.[150] In both cases, the Australian lists reflect Australian investment policy at the date of signing.

The Australian experience highlights the issues for a state in agreeing to investment liberalization in different terms in different agreements. Australia's agreements with the United States and New Zealand in relation to the liberalization of access make it difficult for Australia to give most-favored-nation treatment to other countries in relation to the establishment of investment unless it is willing to lift the limits for

143 *See supra* note 57, Articles 11.3, 11.4, 11.9, and 11.13.

144 *See supra* note 57, Annexes I and II. *See also* Foreign Acquisitions and Takeovers Act 1975, ss.17B and 17E; Foreign Acquisitions and Takeovers Regulations 1989, reg. 2AB, 6 and 9.

145 Protocol on Investment to the Australia–New Zealand Closer Economic Relations Trade Agreement (Feb. 16, 2011), 2011 Aust'l T. N. I. F. S. No.6, Schedule.

146 *See supra* note 57, Article 11.16 provides that a party may request consultations on investor–state arbitration.

147 *See supra* note 145. Article 6 makes clear that most-favored nation treatment does not apply to dispute settlement.

148 *See supra* note 58. Article 17 provides for the opportunity of a review of this position if a party enters into an agreement with another party relating to investment.

149 *See supra* note 58, Articles 904 and 907.

150 *Id.*, Article 910. For a comparison of the investment provisions in Australia's free trade agreements with New Zealand, the United States, Chile, Singapore (prior to the amendments) and Thailand, see Kristen Bondietti, Inconsistencies in Treatment of Foreign Investment in Trade Agreements (AOIF Paper 5, 2008) at 10.

investment review for investors from a larger number of countries, which so far it has not been. With these exceptions, Australia's overall approach is reflected in the Productivity Commission Research Report on Bilateral and Regional Trade Agreements to the effect that Australian practice has generally been to bind current arrangements and provide protection against future policy changes.[151]

The Australian example also illustrates a significant issue in relation to investment liberalization. In contrast to commitments on protection of investments, which become most controversial when a dispute arises, foreign acquisition of local assets is often most controversial domestically when it is proposed. Recent debates in Australia, which is traditionally a major recipient of FDI, in relation to foreign ownership policy, in relation to investments in Australia by Chinese state-owned enterprises, the proposed merger of the Singapore Stock Exchange with the Australian Stock Exchange (notwithstanding the free trade agreement between Australia and Singapore),[152] changes in Indonesian law relating to ownership of mining operations,[153] and the institution by the Chinese government in 2011 of a national security review process for the acquisition by foreigners of a controlling interest in a wide range of industries[154] are just a few examples of the conflicts that can arise between domestic politics and policy and international treaty negotiations and commitments. A survey of the Australian public in 2008, for example, indicated that 90 percent of Australians considered that the Australian government should ensure that major Australian companies were kept under Australian control, although Australians were at the same time overwhelmingly conscious of the advantages of globalization.[155] A survey in 2012, which shows overwhelming opposition to foreign acquisition of Australian farm land and a strong feeling that there is too much Chinese investment in Australia, demonstrates the need for politicians to tread carefully.[156]

Do the ACIA and the ASEAN-Plus Agreements have a liberalizing effect, and what does this say about the prospects for achieving investment liberalization through bilateral and regional agreements, at least in the Asian region?

First, a distinction needs to be drawn between the ACIA and the ASEAN-Plus Agreements in terms of both content and progress toward implementation, despite their similarities and the general commitment to liberalization set out in these agreements. The ACIA is a sincere attempt by ASEAN to promote an agenda of investment

---

[151] *See supra* note 5, Finding 6.4, at 78.

[152] Lanai Vasek, *Abbott Hardens Coalition Stance on Foreign Investment amid Liberal, Nationals Tensions*, AUSTRALIAN, Mar. 25, 2012. Geoff Kitney, *China Demand Could Disrupt Trade Talks*, AUST'L FIN. REV., May 21, 2012; Eric Johnston, *Singapore Finally Walks from ASX Bid*, SYDNEY MORNING HERALD, Apr. 8, 2011; Ticky Fullerton, *Cubbie Conundrums: the Foreign Investment Debate*, DRUM, Oct. 2, 2012, http://www.abc.net.au/news/2012-10-01/fullerton-cubbie-conundrums/4288350.

[153] *See supra* note 83.

[154] *See* Vivienne Bath, *Foreign Investment, the National Interest and National Security—Foreign Direct Investment in Australia and China*, 34(1) SYDNEY L. REV. 5–34 (2012).

[155] Tom Switzer, *Public Attitudes towards Foreign Investment* (AIOF paper No. 6, 2008).

[156] Fergus Hanson, *The Lowy Institute Poll 2012: Public Opinion and Foreign Policy* (June 5, 2012), http://www.lowyinstitute.org/publications/lowy-institute-poll-2012-public-opinion-and-foreign-policy.

liberalization by balancing the objective of liberalization of market access with provisions designed to protect the autonomy of states to control admission and to ensure that disputes are handled on a state-to-state basis. The determination of ASEAN to create the ASEAN communities and to proceed with the internal liberalization agenda, as well as pursuing investment liberalization and facilitation through the medium of the ASEAN-Plus agreements, has had the effect of putting not just investment cooperation but investment liberalization on the ASEAN and the regional agenda.

Although the ACIA came into effect well behind schedule, it has now come into force with ratifications from all parties, and the Reservation List has been finalized. It represents an important and carefully negotiated commitment by all of the ASEAN states in relation to investment liberalization, and constitutes part of an ambitious plan to achieve coherence and integration within ASEAN, a community of states united primarily by geography. The incorporation of the ACIA within the overall ASEAN plan to build its various communities also means that there will be continued pressure within ASEAN for progress to be made under the ACIA. This does not necessarily mean that the ACIA will ultimately succeed in its objectives. The success of the IGA and AIA was limited. The fact that the ACIA is intended not just to liberalize investment within ASEAN but also to offer additional opportunities to investors from outside ASEAN may have an inhibiting effect on the willingness of the ASEAN states to open up investment opportunities more widely than they would be prepared to do on a unilateral basis. The list of reservations in the Reservation List is formidable, and the task of negotiating modifications and further liberalization of inbound investment policy by the ASEAN states is substantial. The fact that the ASEAN states have committed to the ASEAN Charter project and have ratified the ACIA, however, gives the ACIA a considerable chance of success in achieving a significant degree of investment liberalization within the ASEAN region.

The ASEAN-Plus Agreements, however, indicate that it may be difficult to extend this liberalization project further, at least through the medium of bilateral or plurilateral investment agreements. On their face, the ASEAN-Plus Agreements show considerable consistency with the ACIA. In particular, the parties agree on the principle of balancing respect for the host state's domestic policies and practices on admission of investment with liberalization and on the concept that disputes relating to admission and liberalization are matters for state-to-state discussion rather than investor–state arbitration. In substance, however, liberalization commitments by the various states are relatively weak. The PRC–ASEAN Agreement came into effect in relation to a number of ASEAN states relatively promptly after signature, but the lack of new parties and the generality of its contents suggest that the agreement does not have, and is not currently intended to have, a significantly liberalizing effect, at least in relation to market access. The ASEAN–Korea Agreement and the ASEAN–ANZ Agreement ostensibly indicate commitment by the parties to the concept of investment liberalization, but the fact that substantive commitments are subject to five-year work programs suggests that without any strong impetus for the parties to make concessions, it is unlikely that major investment liberalization initiatives will result from these treaties.

Although the content of these agreements indicates interest by the parties in a more liberal regime, the fact that further lengthy negotiations are required suggests that no firm commitment on this aspect has really been made by the contracting states.

Thus, the ACIA represents a genuine attempt to provide the framework and the means to implement a more liberal investment regime for the benefit of ASEAN states as recipients and sources of investment, and for foreign investors through a cohesive and well-organized regional community. The terms of the ASEAN-Plus agreements, however, set out a commitment to the principles of consistency and liberalization but at the same time reflect the difficulty of obtaining agreement on substantive issues of investment liberalization through the medium of bilateral or plurilateral agreements. The multiplicity of bilateral investment agreements, free trade agreements, and related investment arrangements in the Asian region potentially increases the problems for host states in adopting a consistent approach to inbound investment and makes it less likely that liberalization will be achieved through bilateral or plurilateral arrangements other than as part of regional arrangements such as ASEAN or the Australia–New Zealand Closer Economic Relations.

9

CHINA AND INTERNATIONAL INVESTMENT LAW[1]

Wenhua Shan

I. Introduction

China's success in attracting foreign direct investment (FDI) is undisputed and unprecedented. It now ranks second in the world in attracting FDI inflows and fifth in exporting foreign investment. This success is driven primarily by China's significant economic progress but has been facilitated by China's effort in streamlining the legal framework, including the establishment of the world's second-largest network of bilateral investment treaties (BITs).

This chapter attempts to analyze the role of law in China's international investment activities. After an introduction regarding the historical development of FDI both in China and out of China, the chapter explores the legal framework governing such investments. It then moves on to analyze the most important legal issues involved in international investment, namely the admission regime, the general standards of treatment, expropriation and compensation, transfer, and dispute resolution. The chapter discusses the interaction between China's international and domestic norms in regulating foreign investment activities. It also demonstrates whether and to what extent the European-styled BIT prototype has been revised to fit "Chinese characteristics."

The chapter concludes that although the extensive regulatory framework has contributed to China's success in foreign investment activities, China has to do more to

[1] This chapter is written based on several previously published works including in particular the books CHINESE INVESTMENT TREATIES: POLICIES AND PRACTICE (Norah Gallagher & Wenhua Shan eds., 2009) and WENHUA SHAN, THE LEGAL FRAMEWORK OF EU–CHINA INVESTMENT RELATIONS: A CRITICAL APPRAISAL (2005), and the chapter on China in COMMENTARIES ON SELECTED MODEL INVESTMENT TREATIES (Chester Brown & Devashish Krishan eds., forthcoming).

further strengthen the framework and be fully prepared for the change of role from a participant to a leader in international investment activities.

1. China, International Investment, and the Law

I. CHINA'S INTERNATIONAL INVESTMENT AND THE ROLE OF LAW

a. FDI in China

As the second largest FDI recipient since 1992,[2] China presents a great success story in attracting FDI inflows.[3] However, China had been very hostile to FDI from its foundation in 1949 to the late 1970s, during which period many foreign enterprises in China were expropriated.[4] This situation was, nevertheless, changed in 1979 when the open-up policy was adopted to restore the collapsing economy after ten years of social disorder caused by the "Great Proletarian Cultural Revolution" (1966–1976). As an important part of the open-up policy, attracting FDI became the focus of work of the government, and numerous FDI-friendly measures at both international and national levels were adopted to create a competitive and attractive foreign investment environment.

As illustrated in Chart 1, FDI in China had been steadily increasing since the late 1970s until the early 1990s, when it experienced the first surge after Deng Xiaoping pronounced that China was to establish a "Socialist Market Economy." A second surge happened in the early twenty-first century mainly due to China's accession to the WTO in 2001. The chart also shows that China has generally maintained a high speed of growth in FDI inflow despite the global financial crisis, except for a slight drop in 2009. In 2010 China experienced a 17 percent increase in FDI inflow, proof of China's rapid recovery from the global crisis.

It can be expected that China will keep its position as a most popular FDI destination in the future. A series of UNCTAD surveys reveal that China is the top destination for FDI in 2010–2012 for transnational corporations (TNCs).[5] Moreover, a survey held by the American Chamber of Commerce confirms that U.S. companies remain optimistic about their China outlook in the medium term.[6]

---

[2] UNCTAD, *World Investment Report 2010: Investing in a Low-Carbon Economy* 4 (WIR series, United Nations, New York and Geneva 2010).

[3] UNCTAD, *World Investment Report 2011: Non-Equity Modes of International Production and Development* 4 (WIR series, United Nations, New York and Geneva 2010).

[4] *See* CHINESE INVESTMENT TREATIES, *supra* note 1, at 4–5.

[5] UNCATD, *supra* note 2, at 25.

[6] AMCHAM-CHINA, 2010 CHINA BUSINESS CLIMATE SURVEY REPORT 3 (2011), http://www.amchamchina.org/upload/cmsfile/2011/03/22/efb2ab9d3806269fc343f640cb33baf9.pdf (last visited Nov. 8, 2011). It is pointed out that 91% of the respondent companies reported their business outlook in China is "slightly optimistic" or "optimistic." *Id.*

CHART 1: FDI in China 1979–2010
(Unit: US$ 100 million)

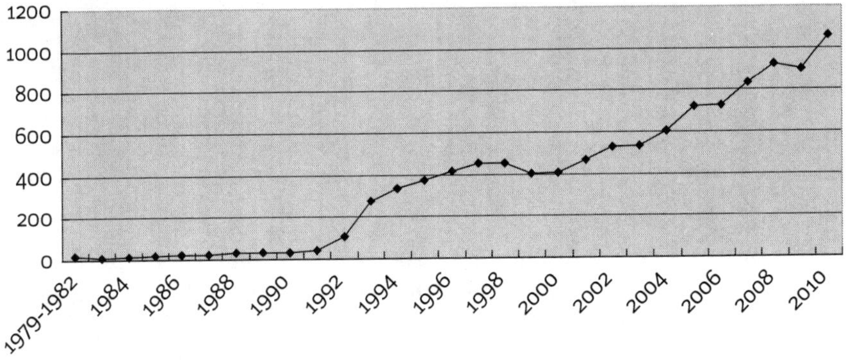

(Source: compiled by the author in accordance with data from China's official FDI Web site: www.fdi.gov.cn)

b. ODI from China

China's performance in stimulating outward direct investment (ODI) in recent years is equally if not even more spectacular. According to UNCTAD, investors from South, East, and Southeast Asia and Latin America were the major contributors to the strong growth in global FDI outflows.[7] In 2010, outflows from China reached their historical high of $68 billion, and China has overtaken Japan in total outward FDI to become the fifth-largest home economy.[8]

As demonstrated in Chart 2, before 2000, Chinese outward investment was insignificant, despite a perceivable increase in the early 1990s following the announcement of the "Socialist Market Economy." In contrast, there has been a steep increase in ODI from China since 2000 when the "going abroad" policy was pronounced.[9] According to the recently published statistics, the ODI from China has been rapidly increasing in the last nine years with an average growth rate of 49.9 percent. By the end of 2010, more than 13,000 domestic entities had established around 16,000 overseas enterprises, covering 178 countries/regions.[10]

---

[7] UNCTAD, *supra* note 3, at 7.

[8] *Id.* at 7–9.

[9] The "going abroad" policy was first proposed in 1998, which aimed to explore international market and take advantage of resources abroad. This strategy was written in the Outline of the Tenth Five-Year Plan for National Economy and Social Development in 2001. Accordingly, the Chinese government took various measures to promote ODI. For details, please see Cai Congyan, *Outward Foreign Direct Investment Protection and the Effectiveness of Chinese BIT Practice*, 7 J. WORLD INV. & TRADE 621, 627–31 (2006).

[10] Ministry of Commerce, *2010 Statistical Bulletin of China's Outward Foreign Direct Investment* (2011), http://hzs.mofcom.gov.cn/accessory/201109/1316069658609.pdf (last visited Nov. 8, 2011). Some scholars, however, questioned the accuracy of China's ODI date and pointed out that there were some

CHART 2: ODI from China 1990–2010
(Unit: US$ 100 million)

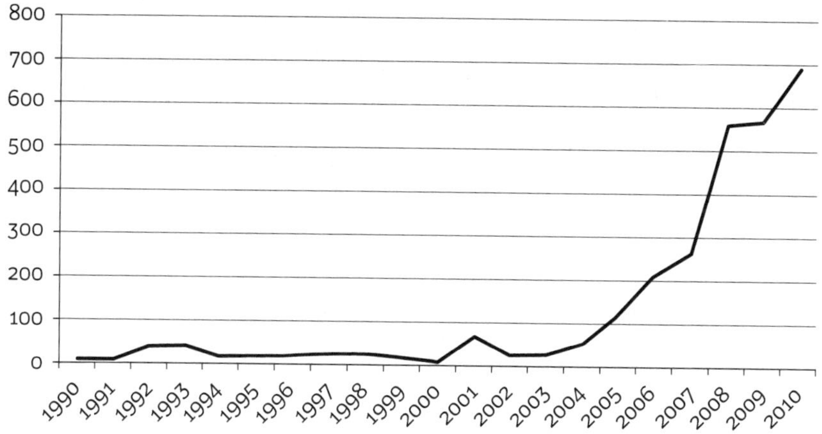

(Source: compiled by the author in accordance with data from China's official FDI Web site: www.fdi.gov.cn)

c. Role of Law in Attracting FDI to China: Empirical Evidences

It is generally believed that law, among other things such as economic determinants and business facilitation, has contributed to China's success in attracting FDI and promoting ODI, especially after China's accession into the WTO.[11] However, empirical studies on the extent to which the law has played a role are rare. To fill the gap, the author conducted two empirical studies in 2001 and 2008. The first one aimed to study the role of law in EU investors' decisions as to whether to invest in China,[12] whereas the

distortions, though they admitted that China's ODI has reached significant levels commercially and geoeconomically and has begun to challenge international investment norms and affect international relations. *See* Daniel H. Rosen & Thilo Hanemann, *China's Changing Outbound Foreign Direct Investment Profile: Drivers and Policy Implications, Policy Brief of Peterson Institute for International Economics* 2–7 (June 2009), http://www.iie.com/publications/pb/pb09-14.pdf (last visited Nov. 8, 2011).

[11] *See, e.g.*, Hui Huang, *The Regulation of Foreign Investment in Post-WTO China: A Political Economy Analysis*, 23 COL. J. ASIAN L,, 185 (Fall 2009); Stephan W. Schill, *Tearing Down the Great Wall: The New Generation Investment Treaties of the People's Republic of China*, 15 CORDOZO J. INT'L & COMP. L. 73 (2007); Jessica Zoe Renwald, *Foreign Investment Law in the People's Republic of China: What to Expect from Enterprise Establishment to Dispute Resolution*, 16 IND. INT'L & COMP. L. REV. 453 (2006); Shaukat Ali & Wei Guo, *Determinants of FDI in China*, 1(2) J. GLOBAL BUS. & TECH. 21 (Fall 2005); Qun Li, *Tax Incentive Policies for Foreign-Invested Enterprises in China and Their Influence on Foreign Investment*, 18(1) REVENUE L.J., Article 5 (2008); Chen Yongmei, *The Legal Climate for Foreign Investment in China after Its WTO Accession*, 20(1) BOND L. REV., Article 2 (2008); Jordan Brandt, *Comparing Foreign Investment in China, Post-WTO Accession, with Foreign Investment in the United States, Post-9/11*, 16 PACIFIC RIM L. & POL. J. 285 (Mar. 2007).

[12] Comprehensive analysis of this investigation may be found in SHAN, THE LEGAL FRAMEWORK OF EU–CHINA INVESTMENT RELATIONS, *supra* NOTE 1, at 247–64; Wenhua Shan, *Law and Foreign Investment in China: General Role of Law and Substantive Issues*, 2(3) MANCHESTER J. INT'L ECON. L. 41

second one was conducted in the SuZhou Industrial Park (SIP)[13] to investigate the role of law in foreign investment activities in the SIP. Both of the surveys have confirmed that the law has played an increasingly important role when the investment decisions were made. Specifically, the 2001 survey shows that 83 percent of the investors saw the legal framework as an element of substantial importance,[14] and in a 2008 survey this number rose to 88 percent.[15]

II. THE REGULATORY FRAMEWORK

a. The Framework

The general regulatory framework concerning FDI in China is composed of both domestic and international laws. Between them Chinese domestic laws and regulations constitute the most important source of law because these lay down the basic conditions for the entry and operation of FDI in China. Until now, there has not been a unified FDI code in China. Foreign investors have to refer to a series of national and subnational laws and regulations that apply to FDI activities, which together constitute the domestic FDI legal system.

The other source is international law, which serves to protect and promote foreign investment. China has the second-largest BIT network in the world and has sought to participate in regional economic integration arrangements since the beginning of the twenty-first century. China currently has entered into nine FTAs, including two Closer Economic Partnership Arrangements (2003) signed separately with Hong Kong and Macao. The remaining seven FTAs each have an investment chapter.[16] China is also in ongoing FTA negotiations with the Gulf Cooperation Council, Australia, Iceland, Norway, and the Southern African Customs Union. Feasibility studies are being conducted with India, Korea, Japan, and Switzerland on potential FTAs. On the other hand, China has signed more than ninety Double Taxation

(2005); Wenhua Shan, *Law and Foreign Investment in China: Effectiveness of the Chinese FDI Legal System*, 3(1) MANCHESTER J. INT'L ECON. L. 51 (2006).

13 Though all of the respondent companies are from the Suzhou Industrial Park, they represent almost all the companies investing in Mainland China. For details, please see Wenhua Shan & Sheng Zhang, *FDI in China and the Role of Law: An Empirical Approach*, 12 J. WORLD INV. & TRADE 457 (2011).

14 SHAN, LEGAL FRAMEWORK OF EU–CHINA INVESTMENT RELATIONS, *supra* note 1, at 248.

15 Wenhua Shan & Sheng Zhang, *supra* note 13.

16 China–Costa Rica FTA (2010) Chapter 9; China–New Zealand FTA (2008) Chapter 11; China–Pakistan FTA (2006) Chapter IX; China–Peru FTA (2010) Chapter 10; China–Singapore FTA (2008) Chapter 10. The China–ASEAN FTA has an entire agreement on investment signed in 2009. Full texts are available online at http://fta.mofcom.gov.cn/english/index.shtml (last visited Nov. 8, 2011). The China–Chile FTA (2005) has an article on the promotion of investment and a commitment to negotiation of a future agreement on trade in services and investment. The supplementary Agreement on Trade in Service was signed with Chile in 2008; the negotiations on investment are pending. The China–Singapore FTA chapter on investment does not contain any provisions but confirms that the ASEAN China Investment Agreement will be incorporated into the FTA.

Avoidance Treaties (DTTS),[17] and is also a contracting party to relevant multilateral treaties such as the ICSID Convention (the Convention on the Settlement of Investment Disputes between States and Nationals of Other States), the Convention on Multilateral Insurance Guaranty Agency (MIGA), and the WTO agreements. This following section provides some further discussions on these elements of the regulatory framework.

b. Interaction between the International and Domestic Norms[18]

No constitutional rules in China have been enacted as yet to govern the relationship between international treaties and domestic law. The Chinese constitution merely provides for general rules on treaty making and ratification[19] but is silent on these treaties'their legal status within the municipal legal system. Numerous laws and regulations do however provide that in case of conflict between international treaty and domestic law, international treaty provisions shall prevail. Thus the General Principles of Civil Law (GPCL) stipulates that:

> If an international treaty concluded or acceded to by the PRC contains provisions differing from those in the civil laws of the PRC, the provisions of the international treaty shall apply, unless the provisions are ones on which the PRC has made reservations thereon.[20]

Similar provisions can be found in as many as seventy laws and regulations, ranging from civil law and civil procedures law to administrative procedures law, patent law, wildlife preservation law, and postal administration.[21] The Regulations on Some Issues in Handling Foreign-Related Cases, jointly promulgated in August 1987 by the Ministry of Foreign Affairs, the Supreme People's Court, the Supreme People's Procuratorate,

---

[17] As of May 2011, China has signed ninety-six DTTs, ninety of which have entered into force. A list of these DTTs may be found on the following Web site of the State Administration of Taxation of China, http://www.chinatax.gov.cn/n8136506/n8136593/n8137537/n8687294/8688432.html (last visited Nov. 8, 2011).

[18] SHAN, THE LEGAL FRAMEWORK OF EU–CHINA INVESTMENT RELATIONS, *supra* note 1, pp. 106–08.

[19] The Chinese Constitution provides that the State Council shall sign treaties and agreements with other countries, while the Standing Committee of the National People's Congress (SCNPC) shall decide to ratify or abolish these treaties and agreements, and the Head of State shall approve or abolish these treaties and agreements in line with the decisions of the SCNPC. The treaty-making procedure is similar to the procedure for domestic legislation. Such similarity suggests that international treaties have the same legal effect as domestic legislation. *See* Articles 89, 67, and 81, the Constitution of the People's Republic of China. *See also* judge TIEYA WANG, INTERNATIONAL LAW 33 (1995) 33; Lingliang Zeng, *Application of WTO Agreements in China and a Revolution of China's Legal Construction*, 6 CHINESE LEGAL SCI. [*Zhongguo Faxue*] 42 (2000).

[20] Article 142, General Principles of Civil Law.

[21] Hanfeng Chen, Weiguo Zhou & Jao Jiang Hao, *The Relationship between International Treaties and Municipal Law and the Practices of China*, 2 TRIBUNE POLITICAL SCI. & L. 122 [*Zhengfa Luntan*] (2000); WANG, *supra* note 19, at 33.

the Ministry of Public Security, Ministry of State Security and the Ministry of Justice, provide that:

> When domestic legislation or internal regulations are in conflict with obligations undertaken by China under an international treaty, rules of the international treaty shall be applied. Provisions of domestic legislation shall not be invoked as justification for the refusal to perform the obligations undertaken by China under the international treaty.

These provisions have been cited as evidence that China has already accepted the superiority of treaties over all municipal laws and regulations,[22] but most Chinese international lawyers believe that such provisions are merely an expression of China's willingness to accept the superiority of treaties within the legal hierarchy in specific areas, such as foreign-related civil and commercial, civil procedural, and administrative procedural areas rather than over the entirety of Chinese law.[23] As a result it is unclear whether the overriding effect of international treaties over domestic law can be maintained in the absence of further constitutional clarification.[24]

Whether the aforementioned investment-related multilateral and bilateral agreements (hereinafter "investment treaties") override domestic law is accordingly debatable. As a matter of fact, all major Chinese laws and regulations on foreign trade and FDI do not mention the status of international treaties vis-à-vis domestic law. Scholarly debates about the application of the WTO agreement in China have suggested that certain issues in the WTO Agreement relating to tariffs, antidumping, market access of financial services, and trade-related investment measures are not subject to the principle of the superiority of international treaties over national law.[25] With regard to the general status of the WTO Agreement within the Chinese legal system, Xiaoyong has argued that the place of WTO agreements should be equal to laws made by the Standing Committee of the National People's Congress (SCNPC)—that is, higher within the overall legal hierarchy than administrative regulations and local regulations but lower than the constitution and basic laws made by the National People's Congress (NPC).[26] Lingliang Zeng has further argued that should conflicts arise between WTO agreements and Laws, the principles of *lex posterior derogate priori* or *lex speciali derogate generalis* ought to apply.[27]

---

22 *See, e.g.*, Xiaoyong He, *On the Application of WTO Agreements in Chinese Courts*, 3 J. INT'L TRADE 50 [*Guoji Maoyi* Went] (2001).

23 *See, e.g.*, WANG, *supra* note 19, at 33; Zeng, *supra* note 19, at 45; Chen et al., *supra* note 21, at 122.

24 It has been further pointed out that, given that the right to interpret rules on applicable laws rests in the hands of the Standing Committee of the National People's Congress (SCNPC), the general binding effect of the Regulations is debatable. *See* He, *supra* note 22.

25 *Id.*

26 *Id.* at 50–51.

27 Zeng, *supra* note 19, at 45; *see also* He, *supra* note 22, at. 51.

Indeed, under international law and as restated in the Vienna Convention on the Law of Treaties,[28] China may not "invoke the provisions of its internal law as justification for its failure to carry out an international agreement."[29] In other words China must guarantee that the treaties and agreements it concludes or to which it accedes have binding force in China. Furthermore as observed by Judge Tieya Wang, the sheer fact that a series of laws covering a wide range of areas has adopted the principle of superiority of international treaties over domestic law indicates a clear legislative policy trend and has made it possible for the principle to become a general principle of law in China.[30]

However, this does not mean that international treaty provisions can be directly applied before Chinese courts (or have "direct effect" in an EU law term). According to a recent regulation stipulated by the Supreme People's Court (SPC)[31], when adjudicating administrative cases involving international trade, Chinese courts should apply only Chinese national and local laws and regulations.[32] The authority's explanations of the regulation clarify that this regulation also applies to international investment administrative cases.[33] Such a regulation is said to be compatible with the commitments that China made in the course of WTO accession negotiations.[34] It is therefore clear that, at least from a judicial point of view, international trade and investment agreements to which China is a party must be transformed into Chinese law before they can be applied and implemented. Nonetheless the regulation also requires that the domestic laws and regulations implementing international trade and investment treaties should be interpreted in a manner consistent with international treaties if there should be more than one interpretation of any specific provision of those domestic laws and regulations.[35]

c. Multilateral Agreements

As mentioned above, China is concurrently a member state of the ICSID Convention, MIGA Convention, and WTO Agreement. These multilateral agreements play an increasingly important role in China's international investment activities, in particular given the increasing use of the ICSID and WTO dispute settlement systems.

---

[28] According to the Chinese Ministry of Foreign Affairs, China deposited the protocol of accession on Sept. 3, 1997, which took effect in China on Oct. 3, 1997.

[29] Article 26, Vienna Convention on the Law of Treaties.

[30] WANG, *supra* note 19, at 33.

[31] The Provisions on Some Issues on the Adjudication of Administrative Cases Concerning International Trade (The Trade Cases Provisions), promulgated by the SPC on Aug. 29, 2002.

[32] *Id.* Articles 7 and 8.

[33] Ji Tian & Zhi Lin, *Judicial Review of Administrative Actions Involving International Trade*, PEOPLE'S DAILY (overseas edition), Sept. 7, 2002, at 3.

[34] *Id.*

[35] Article 9, the Trade Cases Provisions, *supra* note 31.

i. ICSID Convention

The ICSID Convention was signed in 1965 under the auspices of the World Bank. The Convention was signed to remove major impediments to the free international flows of private investment posed by noncommercial risks against the absence of specialized international methods for investment dispute settlement. The International Centre for the Settlement of Investment Disputes (ICSID), which was created in accordance with the ICSID Convention, is an autonomous institution with 140 member states now, and is the leading international arbitration institution in investor–state dispute settlement.

China signed the convention in February 1990, and this Convention has been effective in China since February 1993. Before the signature, there were fierce debates over whether China should enter into the ICSID Convention.[36] Chinese traditional skepticism toward international law made China become very cautious on such an international commitment. However, the references to ICSID arbitration were already provided in some Chinese BITs before China entered into the ICSID Convention. Article 6 of the Protocol of the China-Belgian-Luxembourg BIT, for example, provides that international tribunals may use, as a guideline, the arbitral rules of the ICSID mechanism. The MoU (Memorandum of Understanding) of the China–Malaysia BIT (1988) also provides that the contracting parties should hold negotiations on the enlargements of the extent of the investor–state disputes submitted to the ICSID provided both of the contracting parties become members of the ICSID Convention. Nevertheless it was not possible to allow investor–state disputes to be referred to the ICSID for resolution until the convention became applicable to China in 1993. Recent years have witnessed increasing use of the ICSID mechanism by foreign and Chinese investors. So far the first and only case against the Chinese government registered at the ICSID was *Ekran Berhad v. China*,[37] which is suspended at the moment. Earlier on a Hong Kong investor successfully made use of the Convention and the China–Peru BIT to sue the Peruvian government at the ICSID.[38] In September 2012, another case initiated by an Insurance Company of China, Ping An Life Insurance Company, against the Republic of Belgium was registered by ICSID.[39]

ii. MIGA Convention

The Convention Establishing the Multilateral Insurance Guaranty Agency (MIGA Convention) was signed in October 1985 and entered into force in 1988. The MIGA created by the MIGA Convention aims to promote the flows of FDI to and among

36 For details, please see COMMENTS ON ICSID (Chen An ed., 1990).

37 Ekran Berhad v. People's Republic of China (ICSID Case No. ARB/11/15).

38 Tza Yap Shum v. Republic of Peru (ICSID Case No. ARB/07/6).

39 Ping An Life Insurance Company of China, Limited and Ping An Insurance (Group) Company of China, Limited v. Kingdom of Belgium (ICSID Case No. ARB/12/29)

developing countries by providing political risk insurance to foreign private investors against the risks of expropriation, transfer restriction, breach of contract, and war and civil disturbance. As of September 2011, the MIGA has 175 member countries, among which 25 are industrial countries while the rest of the 150 are developing countries.[40]

From the beginning China has taken a positive attitude toward MIGA. It signed and ratified the Convention as early as 1988. China is the fifth-largest shareholder in MIGA, and the largest shareholder among developing states.[41] As a developing state, China is an eligible host state under MIGA Convention. Until now MIGA has issued about forty guarantees for investment in China from 1993. Currently, ten investment projects are under MIGA guarantee with a total limit of liability of about US$ 240 million.[42] Moreover, MIGA is closely cooperating with China to facilitate Chinese ODI. It is reported that in June 2005, MIGA signed a Memorandum of Understanding with China's only policy-related insurance company, China Export & Credit Insurance Corporation (Sinosure), on cooperation in marketing and coinsurance of Chinese outward investment.[43]

iii. WTO Agreements

Most of the WTO agreements are the result of the General Agreement on Tariff and Trade (GATT) Uruguay Round negotiations, and were signed at the Marrakesh ministerial meeting in April 1994. Developed from the GATT system, the WTO system was mainly intended to cover intentional trade. However, much effort has been made to include the investment issue within the framework of the multilateral trade system because of the close link between trade and investment.[44] Among various WTO agreements, the Agreement on Trade-Related Investment Measures (the TRIMs Agreement) and the General Agreement on Trade in Service (GATS) are the prominent ones for investment. Some other WTO agreements, for instance, the Agreement on Subsidies and Countervailing Measures (SCM Agreement) and the Agreement on Trade-Related Aspects of Intellectual Property Rights (TRIPS) are also closely related to investment activities.

China was officially accepted as a WTO member on December 1, 2001. In order to comply with various WTO obligations, China made great efforts to reform its FDI regime. After its accession, China has been active in the participation in the Working Group on the Relationship between Trade and Investment, and China has

---

[40] MIGA, MIGA Member Countries, http://www.miga.org/whoweare/index.cfm?stid=1789, (last visited Nov. 8, 2011).

[41] Shan, THE LEGAL FRAMEWORK OF EU–CHINA INVESTMENT RELATIONS, *supra* note 1, at 100.

[42] MIGA, Projects in Asia and the Pacific, http://www.miga.org/projects/advsearchresults.cfm?srch=s&hctry=2r&hregioncode=2&dispset=10&sortorder=asc&sortby=hctry&srow=11&erow=20 (last visited Nov. 8 , 2011).

[43] Actually this MOU is designed to deepen the cooperation. The former one was signed in Beijing on August 27, 2002. For details, please see Highbeam Business, *Sinosure Signs Cooperation MOU with MIGA*, June 13, 2005, http://business.highbeam.com/436093/article-1G1-133188796/sinosure-signs-cooperation-mou-miga (last visited Nov. 8, 2011).

[44] SHAN, THE LEGAL FRAMEWORK OF EU-CHINA INVESTMENT RELATIONS, *supra* note 1, at 103.

proposed at least two Communications of the potential multilateral framework of investment (MFI).[45]

d. Bilateral Investment Treaties (BITs)

Since the first BIT with Sweden in 1982, China has signed 130 BITs, among which 100 have entered into effect.[46] These BITs cover most of the developed states except the United States, and Ireland. Currently China is negotiating BITs with the United States.[47] The China–Canada BIT was signed in September 2012, ending a long negotiation spanning eighteen years since 1994. In July 2011, it was reported that China and the European Union (EU) had agreed to negotiate a BIT,[48] which was regarded as signaling a redirection of foreign investment to Europe.[49]

Generally Chinese BIT practice can be divided into two phases. The first phase of BITs was signed with major European states. Admittedly China also signed BITs with other developing states and transition economies, but such BITs were signed more for diplomatic purposes than for investment protection because the Chinese economy was not strong enough to invest abroad.[50] The contents of the BITs signed during that period were accordingly rather conservative: only disputes concerning the amount of compensation for expropriation were allowed to be submitted for arbitration, while no substantial national treatment was committed.[51] It is therefore clear that the investment policy orientation of Chinese BITs at that time was to promote inward foreign investment rather than protect outward investment.

This policy orientation changed in 1998 when the Chinese government decided to implement a "Going Abroad" strategy focusing on investing abroad. In 2001, the "Going Abroad" strategy for the first time was written in the Outline of the Tenth Five-Year Plan

---

45 WTO Working Group on the Relationship between Trade and Investment, Communication from China, WT/WGTI/W/159, Apr. 15, 2003; Communication from China, Cuba, India, Kenya, Pakistan and Zimbabwe, WT/WGTI/W/152, Nov. 19, 2002.

46 Ling Li, *Chinese Bilateral Investment Treaties: Practice and Challenges* (2010) 17 J. INT'L ECON. L. [in Chinese] 1, 2 (2010).

47 The U.S.–China BIT negotiation may be dated back to as early as the 1980s. However, the first round of negotiation ended with no result because of disputes over the core issues such as national treatment and the investor–state disputes settlement mechanism. The second round of negotiation was launched in 2008, After exchanging their drafts in 2010, China and the United States formally pronounced the launching of the BIT negotiation in the 4th Strategic and Economic Dialogue held in May 2012. For more about China–U.S. BIT negotiations, see Cai Congyan, *China–US BIT Negotiations and the Future of Investment Treaty Regime about China–Canada BIT negotiations—A Grand Bilateral Bargain with Multilateral Implications"* (2009) 12 J. INT'L ECON. L. 457 (2009).

48 CHINADAILY, *China, EU to Seek Bilateral Investment Treaty*, July 14, 2011, http://www.chinadaily.com.cn/china/2011-07/14/content_12906429.htm (last visited Nov. 8, 2011).

49 Michael S. Snarr, *Europe Leaps Ahead of United States in Bilateral Investment Treaty Negotiations with China*, July 20, 2011, http://www.chinaustradelawblog.com/tags/bilateral-investment-treaty/ (last visited Nov. 8, 2011).

50 *See, e.g.*, the Chinese BITs with Romania (1983), Thailand (1985), Sri Lanka (1986), and Poland (1988). Ling Li, Chinese BIT Practice and Challenges, Address before the 2010 Chinese Society of International Economic Law Annual Conference, Oct. 16, Nanjing, China.

51 Li, *id*.

for National Economy and Social Development. Various measures were accordingly implemented.[52] Against this background, a more liberal BIT regime was adopted by China beginning in 1998, which notably included access to (ICSID) arbitration for all investor–state disputes and a substantial national treatment commitment.[53] Clearly the new BIT policy is geared to the promotion and protection of both inward and outward investments.

e. Domestic Laws

The Chinese domestic legal system governing FDI has three distinct features, namely foreign-oriented, enterprise-focused, and unsystematic. It is "foreign-oriented" because it is a system that is generally separated from the legal regime governing domestic investments. Its rules primarily address issues of foreign invested enterprises, and hence are "enterprise-focused." Finally, it is unsystematic because its rules are found in numerous laws and regulations, and there is no general FDI code to hold them together. This long-established and relatively well-developed distinct legal regime for FIEs has its historical and political reasons.[54]

Specifically the FDI legal system consists of a series of national and local laws. Among the national legislation, the constitution is the highest. Since 1982, China amended its constitution to allow for FDI. Article 18 of the constitution stipulates that China "permits foreign enterprises, other foreign economic organizations and individual foreigners to invest in China and to enter into various forms of economic cooperation with Chinese enterprises and other Chinese economic organizations in accordance with the law of the People's Republic of China," and that the lawful rights and interests of foreign enterprises, other foreign economic organizations as well as Chinese-foreign joint ventures "are protected by Chinese law."

Apart from the constitution, China has enacted a number of laws and regulations exclusively applicable to FDI. Among them some are "Laws" (*Falu*), which are enacted by the National People's Congress (NPC) (including its Standing Committee). The most important among them include (1) the Chinese–Foreign Equity joint venture Law (EJVL), which was first adopted in 1979 and has been amended several times afterwards; (2) the Chinese–Foreign Contractual Joint Venture Law (CJVL), which was first adopted on April 13, 1988 (hereinafter referred to as "CJVL"); (3) the Wholly Foreign Owned Enterprises Law, which was first adopted on April 12, 1986 (hereinafter referred to as "WFEL"); (4) Income Tax for Foreign Invested Enterprises and Foreign Enterprises, which was adopted on April 9, 1991 but was replaced by Enterprise Income Tax (hereinafter referred to as "Enterprise Income Tax Law 2007") in 2007 implementing an equal tax regime on both domestic and foreign invested enterprises. Such laws are considered the basic laws for FDI activities in China.

---

52 See Cai, *supra* note 9.

53 Details can be found in CHINESE INVESTMENT TREATIES, *supra* note 1, ¶¶ 1.77–1.82.

54 Huang, *supra* note 11, at 202–03.

Apart from these basic laws, there are more general laws adopted by the NPC that apply to FDI in the same way as they do to domestic investments. In other words, they apply to FDI on a nonexclusive basis. They include for instance the Foreign Trade Law 1995, Contract Law 1999, Negotiable Instrument Law 1995, Insurance Law 1995, Guarantee Law 1995, Maritime Law 1992, Customs Law 1987, and so forth. Below these NPC legislations, the Central government (the State Council) promulgates "Administrative Regulations" (*Xinzhen Fagui*), which provide more detailed rules on FDI activities, some of which are in the form of implementing regulations of the basic FIE laws. The most important ones include Implementing Regulations for EJVL 1979, first adopted on September 20, 1983; Implementing Regulation for CJVL 1988, first adopted in August 1995; Implementing Regulation for WFEL 1986, first adopted in October 1990; State Council Provisions for Encouraging Foreign Investment, adopted in October 1986; and Provision on Guidance on the Direction of Foreign Investment, adopted in February 2002.

Still lower on the hierarchy than national legislation are the rules issued by various departments of the State Council, which are named as "Department Rules" (*Bumen Guizhang*) in the Chinese legal system. They mainly include: Interim Provisions on the Takeover of Domestic Enterprises by Foreign Investors (August 2008);[55] Measures for Strategic Investment by Foreign Investors upon Listed Companies (January 2006);[56] Provisions Concerning the Administration of Foreign-Funded Venture Enterprises (January 2003);[57] Interim Provisions on the Merger and Acquisition (M&A) of Domestic Enterprises by Foreign Investors (March 2003, hereinafter referred to as "M&A Provisions 2003");[58] Interim Provisions on Restructuring State-Owned Enterprises with Foreign Investment (November 2002);[59] and Tentative Provisions on Guidance on the Direction of Foreign Investment (hereinafter referred to as "Investment Guidance 1995") (June 1995).[60]

---

55 It was co-adopted by the Ministry of Commerce (MOFCOM), State Assets Supervision and Administration Commission of the State Council (SASAC), State Administration of Taxation (SAT), State Administration for Industry and Commerce (SAIC), China Securities Regulatory Commission (CSRC), and State Administration of Foreign Exchange (SAFE).

56 It was co-adopted by the Ministry of Commerce (MOFCOM), China Securities Regulatory Commission (CSRC), State Taxation Administration (STA), State Administration of Industry and Commerce (SAIC), and State Administration of Foreign Exchange (SAFE).

57 It was co-promulgated by the Ministry of Foreign Trade and Economic Cooperation (now MOFCOM) JMinistry of Science and Technology (MOST), State Administration for Industry and Commerce (SAIC), State Administration of Taxation (SAT), and State Administration of Foreign Exchange (SAFE).

58 It was co-promulgated by the Ministry of Foreign Trade and Economic Cooperation (MOFTEC, now MOFCOM), State Administration of Taxation (SAT), State Administration of Industry and Commerce (SAIC), and the State Administration of Foreign Exchange (SAFE).

59 It was co-promulgated by State Economic and Trade Commission, China (SETC), Ministry of Finance (MOF), State Administration for Industry and Commerce (SAIC), and State Administration of Foreign Exchange (SAFE).

60 It is jointly issued by the State Planning Commission (SPC), State Economic and Trade Commission (SETC), and Ministry of Foreign Trade and Economic Cooperation (MOFTEC, now MOFCOM).

In addition, there are two special catalogs (i.e., the Catalogue of Encourage Industries for Foreign Investment in the Middle and Western Areas, which is aimed to promote investment in the middle and western areas of China, and the Catalogue of Encouraged High-Tech Products for Foreign Investment).

According to the Law on Legislation 2000, some local governments and local People's Congresses are authorized to enact laws applicable at the local level, known in the Chinese legal system respectively as "Local Regulations" (*Difang Fagui*) and "Local Governmental Rules" (*Difang Zhengfu Guizhang*).[61] For instance, governments of provinces, Minority Autonomous Areas (MMAs), and Special Economic Zones (SEZ) may enact Local Regulations (*Difang Fagui*). Although these local laws, according to the Law on Legislation 2000, are required to conform to "Law" (*Falu*) by the NPC and "Administrative Regulation" (*Xinzhen Fagui*) by the State Council,[62] in some cases they might actually deviate from these national laws and regulations.[63]

There is therefore a sophisticated and multitiered domestic law regulating foreign investment in China. The types of foreign investment permitted are clearly defined, and once approved would then qualify as a covered investment for the purposes of applicable laws and regulations.

II. Admission

1. UNDER MULTILATERAL AGREEMENT

Under the scheme of the WTO Agreement, both the TRIMS Agreement and GATS include admission-related provisions. The TRIMS Agreement eliminates some Performance Requirements (PRs), and the GATS provides the admission of investment in services sectors in the attachment of "specific commitments" on "market access."

Article 2 of the TRIMS Agreement requires that members not apply any Trade-Related Investment Measures (TRIMS) that are inconsistent with the principles of "national treatment" and "the general elimination of quantitative restrictions" of GATT. Article 5 also requires each member to notify the Council of Trade in Goods under the Agreement of all their TRIMS within ninety days of the Agreement's entry into force, and eliminate them within a certain period of time. The TRIMS Agreement provides an illustrative list of restrictive measures that "are mandatory or enforceable under domestic law or under administrative rulings or with which it is necessary to comply for advantage" in its annex, and these include the local content requirement, trade-balancing requirement, general and trade-balancing importation restriction, forex (foreign exchange) balancing requirement, and exportation restriction.[64] According to the Protocol on the Accession of the People's Republic of China, China not only undertakes to comply with the TRIMS Agreement without any transnational arrangement, but also goes beyond to undertake to abolish the export or performance requirements besides these require-

[61] Law on Legislation 2000, articles 63, 65, 66, 73.

[62] *See, e.g.*, Law on Legislation 2000, article 63.

[63] SHAN, THE LEGAL FRAMEWORK OF EU–CHINA INVESTMENT RELATIONS, *supra* note 1, at 36.

[64] See Annex: Illustrative List, to the TRIMS Agreement.

ments provided in the illustrative list. Moreover, China modified its FDI laws and regulations to ensure compatibility with the TRIMS Agreement.[65]

GATS is considered to be a set of "Rules for Growth and Investment" or "investor's agreement."[66] According to this agreement, investment is also stipulated because one of the four modes of trade in service in through "commercial presence," and this includes "any type of business or professional establishment" either in the form of a judicial person, or a branch or representative office. The GATS substantive rules may be divided into three parts. The first part provides the "general obligations and disciplines," including MFN, transparency, a number of traditional GATT-type exceptions, competition, business practices, and government procurement. The second part is provided in the "specific commitments," and it establishes the framework for a schedule of commitments from each member; three categories of commitments are included: limitations on market access, limitations on national treatment and additional commitments. The third part includes several articles on "progressive liberalization," and it mainly deals with further negotiations on the various specific commitments to be included in the schedules. The "specific commitments" provided in the second part on market access for admission of investment in the services sectors are of vital importance for investors. China makes "horizontal commitments" and "specific commitments" in the Schedule of Specific Commitments on Services as Part II of the Report of the Working Party on the Accession of China. The horizontal commitments apply to all sectors included in the schedule,[67] whereas the specific commitments apply to the specific sectors or subsectors that they address.[68] As with its compliance with the TRIMS Agreement, China also amended its domestic laws and made numerous new regulations to implement its "specific commitments" on market access in services sectors.[69]

II. UNDER BITS

General international law does not compel states to admit foreign investment. Territorial sovereignty entitles the governments to decide whether to close the national economy to foreign investors or whether to open it up, fully or with restrictions.[70] In

---

65 SHAN, THE LEGAL FRAMEWORK OF EU-CHINA INVESTMENT RELATIONS, *supra* note 1, at 119–21.

66 WORLD TRADE ORGANIZATION: TRADING INTO THE FUTURE 21 (2d ed. 1998).

67 It specifically covers forms of investment, term limitations on land use, and entry and staying of key personnel with a service presence in China. *See* Schedule CLII-The People's Republic of China Part II—Schedule of Specific Commitments on Service, List of Article II MFN Exemptions, WT/ACC/CHN/49/Add.2, at 2–4.

68 Specific commitments cover professional services, computing and related services, real estate services, other business services, communication services, construction and related engineering services, distribution, educational services, environmental services, financial services, tourism and travel-related services, and transport services. Several annexes on basic telecommunication, distribution services, and insurance services are also included. *Id.* at 5–48.

69 For more, please see SHAN, THE LEGAL FRAMEWORK OF EU–CHINA INVESTMENT RELATIONS, *supra* note 1, at 121–23.

70 RUDOLF DOLZER & CHRISOPH SCHREUER, PRINCIPLES OF INTERNATIONAL INVESTMENT LAW 79–80 (2008).

BIT practice, there are basically two different approaches to dealing with admission and establishment. Thus BITs concluded by European countries tend to maintain the traditional sovereignty right of the host state concerning admission. A typical clause provides that each contracting state shall in its territory promote as far as possible investments by investors of the other contracting state and admit such investments in accordance with its legislation. This type of admission clause does not expose the host state to any substantive obligation to revise its domestic laws of admission after the ratification of the BIT.[71] However, the BITs negotiated by the United States, Canada, and Japan, to some extent, impose market access obligations, and these obligations are combined with most-favored-nation (MFN) and national treatment (NT) clauses.[72] The Chinese BITs have generally followed the European prototype leaving control and protection of the admission stage to the discretion of the host country.[73] This is largely due to the fact that BITs were not originally crafted as "market access" treaties but rather to protect investments once they had been made in the host state. Under Chinese BITs, foreign investments are encouraged and admitted in accordance with the laws and regulations of the host state.[74] They also require that, subject to its laws and regulations, the contracting parties must facilitate the obtaining of visas and working permits for personnel engaging in investment-related activities.[75]

III. UNDER CHINESE LAW

China still implements a "one-by-one" approval system on foreign direct investment admission, which requires each and every foreign investment project to be approved by relevant authorities before it can be established. Two instruments are most important to ascertain whether a particular investment project is permitted in China, namely (1) the Guidance on the Direction of Foreign Investment (Investment Guidance),[76] and (2) the attached Guiding Catalogue of Industries for Foreign Investment (Guiding Catalogue).[77] The Chinese government first issued the Investment Guidance and the Guiding Catalogue in 1995, which adopted the "negative list" approach. Both regulations are subject to periodic revisions. The Guidance has so far only been revised once, in 2002, soon after China's WTO accession. The Catalogue, however, has been subject to frequent revisions, and the latest version was published in December 2011.

---

71 *Id.* at 81.

72 *Id.*

73 The U.S. BITs, notably, do impose obligations on investment admission by the combination of the MFN and national treatment clauses. *See* RUDOLF DOLZER & MARGRETE STEVENS, BILATERAL INVESTMENT TREATIES 49 (1995). *See also* UNCTAD, Key Issue I, at 143–44.

74 *See, e.g.*, China–Germany BIT 1983, Article 2; China–Switzerland BIT, Article 2. For details of investment admission under Chinese law, see SHAN, THE LEGAL FRAMEWORK OF EU–CHINA INVESTMENT RELATIONS, *supra* note 1, ch. 4 (Admission and Establishment).

75 *See, e.g.*, China–Russia BIT, Article 2(3).

76 Guidance on the Direction of Foreign Investment (Investment Guidance, promulgated by the State Council Decree No. 346 on Feb. 21, 2002 and entered into force on Apr. 1, 2002).

77 Guiding Catalogue of Industries for Foreign Investment ("Guiding Catalogue," first promulgated in 2002, latest revision took place in 2007 and entered into force on Dec. 1, 2007).

The Guidance and the Catalogue classify all the foreign investment projects (FIPs) into four sub-catalogues: Encouraged, Restricted, Prohibited, and Permitted. The Encouraged, Restricted, and Prohibited industries are specifically defined while all others are classified as Permitted industries by default. FIPs in the Encouraged Catalogue enjoy certain special incentives, such as tax incentives. FIPs in the Restricted Catalogue are, on the contrary, subject to certain restrictions. Some of the restrictions are linked to the modes of investment. Basically there are three modes of foreign investment in China: EJVs (Equity Joint Ventures), CJVs (Contractual Joint Ventures), and WFEs (Wholly Foreign Owned Enterprises). The Catalogue, however, requires some FIPs take the form of either the CJV or EJV, not the WFE. Some FIPs are subject to more stringent conditions requiring "Chinese Partners Equity Control" (CPEC), or "Chinese Partners Relative Equity Control" (CPREC). The former requires that all Chinese partners taken together control 51 percent or more of the total equity of the FIE, whereas the latter only requires all the Chinese partners taken together to have more equity than any one of the foreign investors.[78] Such restrictions also apply to foreign invested merger and acquisition (M&A) activities.[79] In accordance with Article 4 of the 2006 Provisions of Merger and Acquisition of Domestic Enterprises by Foreign Investors, in sectors that require "JV only," or CPEC or CPREC, the enterprises should maintain their status as a JV, CPEC, or CPREC after such M&A takes place. Likewise, in sectors where foreign investments are prohibited, foreign investors are not allowed to conduct M&A activities.

In this connection, it should be noted that, in addition to the general Catalogue, China has also adopted a Catalogue of Encouraged Industries for Foreign Investment in the Middle and Western Areas ("Western Catalogue")[80] and a Catalogue of Encouraged High-Tech Products for Foreign Investment ("High-Tech Catalogue").[81] The High-Tech Catalogue has been integrated into the general Catalogue, though the Western Catalogue continues to take effect.

Recent years have witnessed China's effort to ensure the security of M&A activities by foreign investors. Alongside the antimonopoly review provided in the above-mentioned 2006 Provisions on M&A, China adopted the Antimonopoly Law in August 2007. Accompanied this law, Provisions on the Criteria for Reporting Concentration of Undertakings was issued by the State Council on August 2008. In February 2011, the State Council issued the Notice of the General Office of the State Council concerning

78 The Guidance on the Direction of Foreign Investment (Investment Guidance), Article 8.

79 Article 4, Provisions of Merger and Acquisition of Domestic Enterprises by Foreign Investors (published jointly by MOFCOM and six other ministries in August 2006), which entered into force on Sept. 8, 2006). This regulation was drafted on the basis of the Provisional Regulations on Mergers and Acquisitions of Domestic Enterprises by Foreign Investors promulgated on Mar. 7, 2003. The revised regulation provides detailed guidelines on the requirements and the application process for foreign companies wishing to engage in M&A of China's domestic enterprises.

80 This Catalogue was first published in June 2000 jointly by the former State Economic and Commerce Commission, the State Planning Commission, and the Ministry of Foreign Trade and Economic Cooperation (MOFTEC). It was revised in July 2004 by the SDRC, and has been in force since Sept. 1, 2004.

81 This Catalogue was originally promulgated in July 2003 jointly by the MOFCOM and the Ministry of Science and Technology (MOST). The recent revision was issued on Dec. 31, 2006.

Security Review of Mergers and Acquisitions of Domestic Enterprises by Foreign Investors, which takes a rather broad definition of covered sectors.[82] To implement the Notice, the Ministry of Commerce accordingly issued its Provisions on Implementing a Security Review System for Mergers and Acquisitions of Domestic Enterprises by Foreign Investors. After the entry into force of the above-mentioned Provisions in September 2011, China has formally established its security review system to review M&A activities by foreign investors.[83]

III. General Standards of Treatment

General standards of treatment are often found in China's international investment treaties. Some of them are also stipulated in Chinese legislation. The most common standards include fair and equitable treatment (FET), national treatment (NT), and most-favored-nation treatment (MFN). Together they define the general level of treatment foreign investors and their investment may receive in China.

1. FAIR AND EQUITABLE TREATMENT

Fair and Equitable Treatment (FET) has been the most commonly used standard of treatment under BITs, and is the most frequently invoked standard in investment disputes.[84] The content and nature of the FET remains difficult to define despite the fact that it is included in most investment treaties.[85] It is reported by the UNCTAD that at least four approaches were taken in defining the concept of FET.[86]

FET is also the most commonly used substantive protection in Chinese BITs.[87] All three versions of the Model BIT contain this standard, accompanied by the provision of "protection" or "constant protection and security." The effect of the FET may differ according to its location in the BIT. It is believed that it may have only a hortatory effect and not create concrete legal obligations if appears only in the preamble,[88] as it does in the first BIT with Sweden.

---

[82] European Union Chamber of Commerce in China, European Chamber Comments on State Council's Notice on Mergers and Acquisitions, Feb. 16, 2011, http://www.europeanchamber.com.cn/view/media/fullview?cid=8000 (last visited Nov. 8, 2011).

[83] Wenhua Shan, Norah Gallagher & Sheng Zhang, *National Treatment for Foreign Investment in China: A Changing Landscape*, 27(1) ICSID REV. 120 (2012); *see also* Sheng Zhang, *The Energy Charter Treaty: Member or Bystander?*, 13(4) J. WORLD INV. & TRADE 597, 612 (2012).

[84] DOLZER & SCHREUER, *supra* note 70, at 119.

[85] *See, e.g.*, DOLZER & STEVENS, *supra* note 73, at 58–61.

[86] UNCTAD, Fair and Equitable Treatment, UNCTAD Series on issues in international investment agreements, UNCTAD/ITE/IIT/11 (Vol. III), United Nations, New York, and Geneva, 1999, at 1–2.

[87] CHINESE INVESTMENT TREATIES, *supra* note 1, at 126. Some Chinese BITs, such as the BITs with Japan, former Czechoslovakia, Romania (both 1983 and 1994 versions) and Belarus, however, do not include FET.

[88] *Id.* at 127.

Some earlier Chinese BITs incorporate it with both the MFN and national treatment standards,[89] or with at least one of the latter standards.[90] An UNCTAD study considers that such provision provided foreign investors with both noncontingent and contingent forms of protection. Under such provision, national and MFN treatment protect each beneficiary of those standards by ensuring equality or nondiscrimination for that beneficiary vis-à-vis other investments.[91] Other Chinese BITs however do not make express reference to a particular body of law or other standards. In such cases, the FET provision should first be considered against other explicit provisions of the treaty, then general international law and/or domestic law of the host state.[92] In applying general/customary international law, it should be taken into account that many principles of general/customary international law emerged and were developed in the context of Europe and among developed states, with little or no participation at all of China in the process.[93] It is therefore unsurprising that there has been only a limited familiarity with and consequently a certain degree of resistance to such principles by China.

Indeed, some earlier writings by eminent Chinese scholars have flatly denied the existence and the applicability of international law/minimum standard. Meizhen Yao, for instance, wrote that the international (law/minimum) standard "is essentially an imperialist and colonialist theory, and does not conform to contemporary international law," and therefore "cannot be accepted either in theory or in practice."[94] Accordingly, earlier Chinese BITs have tried as far as possible to avoid any reference to "international law," either as the law for the interpretation of FET, or the applicable law for the settlement of investment disputes. In the rare cases when reference is made, it is substantially qualified by confining such international law to be only those that have been "generally recognised" and that have also been "accepted" by both contracting parties.[95] Acceptance of such principles without qualifications did not appear in Chinese BITs until recent years. Therefore, it can be expected that there will be disagreements between China and its counterparts as to the exact scope and contents of "general/customary international law," even though the concept has been accepted. China's more recent treaties have included express reference to general principles of international law; for example, Article 9(7) China–Cyprus BIT (2001) refers to the "applicable principles of international law."[96] Article 9(5) of the China–Czech Republic

89 *See, e.g.*, the China–Morocco BIT, Art 3(1) and the China–Yemen BIT, Art 2(2).

90 Art 3 (2) of the China–Poland BIT, for instance, incorporates FET with MFN. The China–Syria BIT is a little interesting because it uses the MFN standard for China and NT standard for Syria when defining the minimum threshold for the FET.

91 UNCTAD, *supra* note 86, at 15–16.

92 CHINESE INVESTMENT TREATIES, *supra* note 1, at 108–10.

93 For an overview of China's changing attitude to international law, see Junwu Pan, *Chinese Philosophy and International Law*, 1 ASIAN J. INT'L L. 233 (2010).

94 MEIZHEN YAO, INTERNATIONAL INVESTMENT LAW 334–38 [in Chinese] (1987).

95 *See, e.g.*, China–BLEU BIT 1984, Article 7 of the Protocol.

96 Other treaties refer to "principles of international law recognised by both Contracting Parties." Article 8(5) China–Germany BIT (2003).

BIT (2005) refers to the "general principles of international law," indicating a shift over the years in China's approach to the application of these principles.

More states have incorporated qualifications into their treaties in particular relating to this standard of protection. The United States as a direct result of its experience under NAFTA has done so in its Model BIT.[97] More recently China in the BIT with Mexico also incorporated qualifying language similar to that of the NAFTA Free Trade Commission at Article 5(2). It confirms that the fair and equitable treatment does not require anything "in addition to or beyond that which is required by the international law minimum standard of treatment of aliens . . . "[98] Thereby it acknowledges the international minimum standard for the fair and equitable treatment provision.

II. NATIONAL TREATMENT

National treatment (NT) is the other main standard that underpins the principle of nondiscrimination under investment treaties.[99] The purpose of this clause is to oblige a host state to make no negative differentiation between foreign and national investors.[100] However, the NT clause is not as common as the MFN clause in the BITs. In China's 130 BITs, for example, less than half of them have an NT provision. However, given that all the Chinese BITs contain a MFN clause, the investors and investments covered by a BIT without an NT clause may be entitled to NT by virtue of the MFN clause.[101]

a. Under BITs

Due to the planned economy legacy in China, the National Treatment (NT) standard has not been widely used in Chinese BIT practice. It is worth noting that the OECD Draft Convention 1967 did not contain a NT provision either.[102] China did not accept NT in its BIT practice until 1986 when the China–UK BIT 1986 was signed including a "best endeavours" NT provision. Among the three Model BITs, the first version did not have such a clause at all. The second version contained only a "best endeavors" or soft NT provision, whereas the third subjects the NT to local laws and regulations. However, a qualification in Version III subjecting NT to domestic laws and regulations

---

[97] Article 5(2) U.S. Model BIT (2004).

[98] Article 5(2) China–Mexico BIT (2008). No such qualifying language appears in the investment Chapter 11 of the China–New Zealand FTA (2008) (see Article 143) or in the China–ASEAN Investment Agreement (2009) although both treaties do include what a breach of fair and equitable treatment means. Article 7(2) (a) of the China–ASEAN Investment Agreement confirms that "fair and equitable treatment refers to the obligation of each Party not to deny justice in any legal or administrative proceedings."

[99] CHINESE INVESTMENT TREATIES, *supra* note 1, at 157.

[100] DOLZER & SCHREUER, *supra* note 70, at 178.

[101] CHINESE INVESTMENT TREATIES, *supra* note 1, at 157.

[102] In the 1960s there was no consistent or "typical" format of NT; *see* K.J. VANDEVELDE, BILATERAL INVESTMENT TREATIES: HISTORY, POLICY AND INTERPRETATION 374 (2010).

has been modified by some recent BITs.[103] These BITs removed the "domestic laws and regulations" qualification from the treaty text, but retain a "grandfather provision" or "freezing clause" in their Protocols applicable to China, allowing it to maintain and modify existing nonconforming measures inconsistent with the NT standard, as long as this will not increase the general level of inconsistency. China also agrees in these BITs to gradually phase out such inconsistent measures.[104] The national treatment provision was one of the stumbling blocks for the failed BIT negotiations between the United States and China in the 1980s.[105] This may not be such an issue in the resumed talks on a BIT with the United States as China, since 2008, has shown its willingness to accept national treatment protections.

b. Under Chinese Law

NT is generally an inherent element of the market economy. This treatment is, nevertheless, unfeasible under the Planned Economy system that used to be implemented in China. During that period, foreign investors in China were accorded "inferior" NT in some respects, while they enjoyed "superior" NT in some other aspects such as tax and other preferential measures. This situation changed when China began to develop its market economy system in the early 1990s. With its economic growth and enormous achievements in the past two decades, China gradually has made efforts to provide a level playing field for both domestic and foreign investors. Affirmative evidence is the enactment of the Enterprise Income Tax Law 2007, which unifies the tax burden between domestic investors and foreign investors. The Property Law adopted in 2007 also provides that "equal legal status and the right to development of all market subjects shall be protected."[106] In 2010, Premier Jiabao Wen also said that China will make institutional agreements to provide a "fair playing ground" for foreign investors and grant them "national treatment."[107]

III. MOST-FAVORED-NATION TREATMENT

The most-favored-nation (MFN) standard of treatment is the most commonly adopted standard in investment treaties. Under such a standard, the relevant parties undertake to treat each other in a manner that is at least as favorable as they treat third parties. The purpose of this standard therefore is to create a level playing field among different foreign states by prohibiting discrimination on the basis of different foreign nationalities.[108] The

103 *See, e.g.*, Articles 3(1) of the China–Bosnia and Herzegovina BIT 2002, 2(2) of the China–Germany BIT 2003, and 3(2) of the China–Finland BIT 2004.

104 For further details, please see CHINESE INVESTMENT TREATIES, *supra* note 1, ¶¶ 4.65–4.90.

105 *See* T.A. Steinert, *If the BIT Fits: The Proposed Bilateral Investment Treaty between the United States and the People's Republic of China*, 2 J. ASIAN L. 405 (2008).

106 Property Law 2007, article 3(3).

107 Xinhua Press, *Wen Promises to Grant Foreign Enterprises "National Treatment"*, Mar. 14, 2010, http://www.china.org.cn/china/NPC_CPPCC_2010/2010-03/14/content_19606081.htm (last visited Nov. 8, 2011).

108 CHINESE INVESTMENT TREATIES, *supra* note 1, at 140.

MFN treatment in most of the BITs and FTAs is restricted to the post-establishment phase of an investment. However, in the recent BIT practice by the United States and Canada, this treatment is extended to cover the establishment stage of foreign investment.[109]

i. Under BITs

Unlike the NT standard, MFN treatment is common in all Chinese BITs. This is perhaps not surprising given the long history of the MFN provision in treaties.[110] Some of China's earlier BITs are limited in scope and cover only investments in their MFN clause, without direct reference to "investment-related activities."[111] All three Model BITs, however, have a similar MFN clause covering both investments and investment-related activities. Unlike many other Model BITs, the Chinese BITs do not cover both investors and investments in separate provisions. This may begin to change as the China–Mexico BIT does expressly refer to both protection of investors and investments in Article 4(1) and (2) respectively. It is not clear yet whether this is a new trend for China or a concession made to Mexico as the language is similar to that of Article 1105 of the NAFTA. Chapter 11 of the China–New Zealand FTA (2008) does not have a separate provision in Article 139, nor does the China–ASEAN Investment Agreement (2009) in Article 5. The MFN provision requires foreign investments to be treated no worse than investments made by investors from any other country, thereby preventing discrimination on the ground of nationality.[112]

Most Chinese BITs have not included the "in like circumstances" wording in the MFN provision, yet this is appearing in the more recent treaties signed by China; see for example Article 4 of the China–Mexico BIT (2008). Preadmission activities are covered by MFN clauses in some recent BITs, for example the China–Finland BIT (2004). As is typical in most MFN provisions, there are certain important exceptions. For example, the China–Germany BIT (2003) does not apply to any membership of customs unions, free trade zones, economic unions, or common markets, or to any double taxation agreements.[113] The MFN clause does not expressly refer to dispute resolution, as is made clear, for example, in the UK Model BIT. It is not certain whether the MFN provision in China's current Model BIT could therefore be extended to refer to substantive as well as procedural rights of the treaty. In light of the recent changes made

---

[109] Article 4 "most-favored-nation treatment" of the U.S. Model BIT 2004 provides that "Each Party shall accord to investors of the other Party treatment no less favorable than it accords, in like circumstances, to investors of any non-Party with respect to the establishment, acquisition, expansion, management, conduct, operation, and sale or other disposition of investments in its territory." Article 4 of the Canada Model BIT 2004 has almost the same stipulation with that of the United States.

[110] For a discussion of the origins of MFN protection, see VANDEVELDE, *supra* note 102, at 352–57. The MFN standard has been included in "virtually all investment treaties"; DOLZER & SCHREUER, *supra* note 70, at 186. *See also* ILC Draft Article on Most-Favoured-Nation Clauses 2(2) Y.B. ILC (1978) and C. MCLACHLAN, L. SHORE & M. WEINIGER, INTERNATIONAL INVESTMENT ARBITRATION: SUBSTANTIVE PRINCIPLES 254–57 (2007).

[111] *See, e.g.*, Article 2(2) of the China–Sweden BIT 1982.

[112] Article 3(3) of the current Model BIT.

[113] Article 3(4) of the China–Germany BIT 2003.

to the dispute resolution provisions in Chinese BITs that now permit resort to ICSID arbitration for investor–state disputes, the exact scope and application of the MFN clause has significance for foreign investors in China.[114]

The tribunal in *Tza Yap Shum v Peru,* the first tribunal dealing with the interpretation of a Chinese BIT, considered the claimant's assertion that it could invoke the MFN in the China–Peru BIT to rely on Article 12 of the Peru–Colombia BIT to extend the scope of its ICSID claim. The tribunal ultimately rejected the claimant's argument, finding that "Article 3 cannot be interpreted so as to extend the jurisdiction of the Centre as a basis for an independent source of competence of the Tribunal."[115] There are other Chinese treaties that also include this provision, thus broadly limiting the application of the MFN clause.[116] This outcome in *Tza Yap Shum* would not necessarily preclude a tribunal from adopting the broader application of the MFN provision in China's treaties that do not contain this additional language. In its more recent treaties, China has been including an express provision excluding the application of the MFN provision to dispute resolution provisions. The China–ASEAN Investment Agreement (2009), for example, provides at Article 5(4) that:

> For greater certainty, the obligation in this Article does not encompass a requirement for a Party to extend to investors of another Party dispute resolution procedures other than those set out in this Agreement.[117]

IV. Expropriation and Compensation

Expropriation has long been of central concern to foreign investors because it is the most severe form of interference with property.[118] Hence modern international law

---

114 For further details see CHINESE INVESTMENT TREATIES, *supra* note 1, at 145–57.

115 Tza Yap Shum v Peru, ICSID Case No. ARB/07/6 ¶ 220 (unofficial translation). *See also* Plama Consortium Ltd. v Bulgaria, ICSID Case No. ARB/03/24 Award on Jurisdiction, Feb. 8, 2005, Berschader v. Russia, SCC Case No. 080/2004 Award, Apr. 21, 2006 and Telenor Mobile Commc'ns A.S. v. Republic of Hungary ICSID Case No. ARB/04/15.

116 *See, e.g.*, Article 10(2) China–Greek BIT (1992). *See, e.g.*, a broader application of the MFN provision in Maffezini v. Spain, ICSID Case No. ARB/97/7 Award on Jurisdiction, Jan. 25, 2000 and Gas Natural SDG SA v. Argentina, ICSID Case No. ARB/03/10, Award on Jurisdiction, June 17, 2005 and commentary in UNCTAD Series II MFN, at 66–92.

117 *See also* Article 139(2) of the China–New Zealand FTA (2008), which also includes an express exclusion of procedural rights in similar terms. It provides: "For greater certainty, the obligation in this Article does not encompass a requirement to extend to investors of the other Party dispute resolution procedures other than those set out in this Chapter."

118 DOLZER & SCHREUER, *supra* note 70, at 89. For a general statement on expropriation, please see VANDEVELDE, *supra* note 102, at 271; J.W. SALACUSE, THE LAW OF INVESTMENT TREATIES CH. 12 (2010); A. Reinisch, *Expropriation, in* THE OXFORD HANDBOOK OF INTERNATIONAL INVESTMENT LAW 408 (P. Muchlinski, F. Ortino & C. Schreuer eds., 2008); MCLACHLAN ET AL., *supra* note 110, at 265. *See, e.g.*, Art 4(1) of the China–Poland BIT (1988).

does not prevent a state from expropriating property of foreign investors located within its territory.[119] Expropriation per se is not illegal so long as certain requirements are fulfilled. Under customary international law and typical international investment agreements, four principal requirements need to be considered to determine whether expropriation is lawful: public purpose, due process of law, nondiscrimination, and against compensation. In practice, it is difficult to differentiate expropriation from legitimate regulation in the context of international investment law. Its conclusions can be assessed and the quantum debated, but whether an expropriation exists at all will be decided case by case.[120]

I. UNDER BITS

Expropriation constitutes perhaps the most controversial part of the Chinese attitude toward foreign investment.[121] All Chinese BITs include a clause regarding expropriation. It is also not surprising that all three of China's Model BITs have such a clause. The expropriation clause in earlier Chinese BITs is rather simple. The China–UK BIT (1986), for example, provides only two paragraphs on the subject. Most BITs stipulate only that each Contracting Party may nationalize, expropriate, or take similar measures against investments of investors of the other Contracting Party, but the BITS lack a definition of expropriation. In particular, indirect expropriation is not explicitly mentioned in the traditional investment treaties. The China–India BIT (2006) for the first time sought to clarify indirect expropriation.[122] A close examination of the

---

119 DOLZER & SCHREUER, *supra* note 70, at 89.

120 CHINESE INVESTMENT TREATIES, *supra* note 1, at 253–54.

121 Qingjiang Kong, *Bilateral Investment Treaties: The Chinese Approach and Practice*, 8 ASIAN Y.B. INT'L L. 106, 125 (1998–99).

122 The Protocol of the China–India BIT provides:

> With regard to the interpretation of expropriation under Article 5, the Contracting Parties confirm their shared understanding that:
>
> 1. A measure of expropriation includes, apart from direct expropriation or nationalization through formal transfer of title or outright seizure, a measure or series of measures taken intentionally by a Party to create a situation whereby the investment of an investor may be rendered substantially unproductive and incapable of yielding a return without a formal transfer of title or outright seizure.
> 2. The determination of whether a measure or a series of measures of a Party in a specific situation, constitute measures as outlined in paragraph 1 above requires a case by case, fact based inquiry that considers, among other factors:
>   i. the economic impact of the measure or a series of measures, although the fact that a measure or series of measures by a Party has an adverse effect on the economic value of an investment, standing alone, does not establish that expropriation or nationalization, has occurred;
>   ii. the extent to which the measures are discriminatory either in scope or in application with respect to a Party or an investor or an enterprise;
>   iii. the extent to which the measures or series of measures interfere with distinct, reasonable, investment-backed expectations;
>   iv. the character and intent of the measures or series of measures, whether they are for bona fide public interest purposes or not and whether there is a reasonable nexus between them and the intention to expropriate.

definition included in this BIT reveals that it largely resumes the provision included in the 2004 U.S. Model BIT,[123] but only makes some modifications to make this provision more predictable. A definition of indirect expropriation may also be found in the China–New Zealand FTA (2008), along with a list of some circumstances where indirect expropriation most probably occurs.[124]

With respect to the conditions to be satisfied, most Chinese BITs follow the typical international practice and provide the above-mentioned four conditions. However, there are some slight changes. For instance, most Chinese BITs refer to "due process of domestic law," but not "due process of law" or "legal order."[125] It is said that the "due process of law" might be interpreted as "due process of international law," which is considered fairer than "due process of domestic law" because there are a few international conventions concerning judicial procedure.[126] It is not clear whether this would result in any significant difference were a case to arise as the domestic law in China relating to expropriation does require that the same conditions be met. Expropriations have occurred in China as evidenced by the takings in the early years after the establishment of the People's Republic of China.[127] Investor disputes and disagreements also arose,[128] but none that have resulted in an international award against China. To date,

---

3. Except in rare circumstances, non-discriminatory regulatory measures adopted by a Contracting Party in pursuit of public interest, including measures pursuant to awards of general application rendered by judicial bodies, do not constitute indirect expropriation or nationalization.

[123] *See* U.S. 2004 BIT Model, Annex B.

[124] Annex 13 "Expropriation" of this FTA provides that:

3. In order to constitute indirect expropriation, the state's deprivation of the investor's property must be:
   (a) either severe or for an indefinite period; and
   (b) disproportionate to the public purpose.
4. A deprivation of property shall be particularly likely to constitute indirect expropriation where it is either:
   (a) discriminatory in its effect, either as against the particular investor or against a class of which the investor forms part; or
   (b) in breach of the state's prior binding written commitment to the investor, whether by contract, licence, or other legal document.

[125] *See, e.g.*, China–Yemen BIT, article 4(1); China–Ukraine BIT, article 4(1).

[126] These international conventions especially include the relevant human rights conventions, for example International Covenant on Civil and Political Rights(General Assembly resolution 2200A (XXI) of Dec. 16, 1966). According to article 14 of the Convention, all persons shall be equal before the courts and tribunals and everyone shall be entitled to a fair and public hearing by a competent, independent and impartial tribunal established by law. Dolzer and Stevens also suggested that domestic law not be accepted as an ultimate standard of the legality of expropriation because "the lack of reference to domestic law reflects the very purpose of BIT." DOLZER & STEVENS, *supra* note 73, at 106.

[127] P.K. Chew, *Political Risk and U.S. Investment in China: Chimera of Protection and Predictability?*, 34 VA. J. INT'L L. 615, 626 (1994), where it states that "China began a 'slow motion nationalization' program resulting in the virtual termination of all direct foreign investment by 1957." *See generally* SHAN, THE LEGAL FRAMEWORK OF EU–CHINA INVESTMENT RELATIONS, *supra* note 1, at 8; LianLian Lin & John R. Allison, *An Analysis of Expropriation and Nationalization Risk in China*, 19 YALE J. INT'L L. 135 (1994); A. JEROME & H. CHIU, PEOPLE'S CHINA AND INTERNATIONAL LAW 686 (1974).

[128] For example, the *Changchun Huijin* case; *see* CHINESE INVESTMENT TREATIES, *supra* note 1, ch. 8, ¶¶ 168–71. *See also* the *Huang Qiao* case mentioned in SHOUSHUANG LI, THE LEGAL ENVIRONMENT AND

ICSID has rendered its award in *Tza Yap Shum v. Peru* in July 2011, in which the tribunal ruled that it was not the audit taken by the Peruvian tax authority but the imposition of interim measures that constituted an indirect expropriation.[129] This is the first public award concerning the expropriation clause included in a Chinese BIT.

As to standard of compensation for expropriation, China has traditionally rejected using the Hull rule (i.e., prompt, adequate, and effective compensation). Occasionally Chinese BITs refer to concepts such as "fair and equitable compensation,"[130] "fair, effective and non-discriminatory compensation,"[131] and "fair and reasonable compensation."[132] In terms of calculating the damages payable, some of China's BITs refer to the "real," "actual," or "market" value. Arbitral tribunals have interpreted these terms to mean the "fair market value" of the investment.

Nevertheless, in practical terms, Chinese BITs do not depart significantly from general BIT practice. First, on the amount of compensation, although they do not refer to "adequate" or "full" compensation, they require it to be "equivalent to the value of the expropriated investments,"[133] or calculated on the basis of "market value."[134] Such value shall be determined in accordance with "generally recognized principles of valuation,"[135] such as capital invested, depreciation, capital repatriated, replacement value, and other relevant elements.[136] This standard of compensation is not substantially different from the "adequate" compensation requirement under the "Hull formula." Second, with regard to the time and method of payment, Chinese BITs require compensation to be made "without delay, be effectively realizable and freely transferable," which is not that different from the "prompt" and "effective" compensation required under the "Hull formula." Although most of China's BITs require expropriation to be carried out in accordance with the host state laws, there are few if any additional limitations under China's law. On balance, it seems that China's position on expropriation and the laws that an international tribunal would apply are not so different as compared to most other states.[137]

It is worth pointing out that some Chinese BITs contain a provision at the end of the expropriation section confirming that the contracting parties agree to provide MFN

RISKS FOR FOREIGN INVESTMENT IN CHINA 115 (2007).

[129] International Arbitration Case Law, Summary of the award of Tza Yap Shum v. Republic of Peru (ICSID Case No. ARB/07/6), case report by Kenneth Juan Figueroa, at 5–6, http://italaw.com/documents/TzaYapShumAwardIACLSummary.pdf (last visited Nov. 8, 2011). The final award on Merits (in Spanish) was rendered on July 7, 2011.

[130] *E.g.*, Article 5(1) of the China–India BIT 2006.

[131] *E.g.*, Article 6(1) of the China–EAU BIT.

[132] *E.g.*, Article 5(1) of the China–Kuwait BIT 1985.

[133] Art 4(2) of the third version of the Chinese Model BIT.

[134] Art 4(2) of the second version of the Chinese Model BIT.

[135] Art 4(2) of the third version of the Chinese Model BIT.

[136] Art 4(2) of the second version of the Chinese Model BIT.

[137] For further details, see CHINESE INVESTMENT TREATIES, *supra* note 1, ch. 7.

treatment relating to the expropriation provisions specifically.[138] Article 4(4) of the China–Italy BIT (1985), for instance, provides that:

> Nationals or companies of either Contracting Party shall enjoy *most favoured-nation treatment* in the territory of the other Contracting Party in respect of the matters provided for in the present Article. (emphasis added)

In *Tza Yap Shum*, the tribunal also took the opportunity to interpret the meaning of "appropriate compensation" included in the China–Peru BIT. In the view of the tribunal, appropriate compensation means the amount needed should place the claimant in the same position he or she would have been without the act of expropriation.[139] Finally, the tribunal rejected the request proposed by the claimant that damages should be based on the discounted cash flow, but adopted the respondent's position that appropriate compensation should be based on the adjusted book value.[140]

II. UNDER CHINESE LAW

China was relatively slow in enacting legislation on expropriation and compensation. The Law of Legislation provides that the expropriation of non–state-owned properties must be laid down in the form of "Law" (*Falu*),[141] which means it must be formulated by the National People's Congress or its Standing Committee.[142] When the EJVL was adopted back in 1979, it was silent on expropriation. In the REOFF for offshore exploitation concessions, China included a limited right to expropriate in the event of war or other emergency.[143] It was only over twenty years ago that China first introduced a specific expropriation provision in the WFEL. Article 5 confirms that:

> China does not carry out expropriations or nationalisations of WFE's. Under special circumstances, in the public interest, WFEs can be expropriated in accordance with legal procedures and appropriate compensation will be provided.

This provision was followed in subsequent legislation relating to FIEs except the CJVL.[144] It is not very prescriptive other than to confirm the general position against expropriation. It leaves open the question of what "special circumstances" means. Other than that, it contains three of the four conditions commonly found in China's

---

138 *Id.* at 286.

139 Figueroa, *supra* note 129, at 8.

140 *Id.*

141 Article 8, the *Law of Legislation*, passed on Mar. 15, 2000 by the National People's Congress.

142 Article 7, the *Law of Legislation*.

143 Article 26, REOFF. The article reads:

> In the course of war, threat of war or other emergencies, the Chinese Government has the right to requisition or expropriate a part or all of the oil that the foreign contractors earn or buy.

144 *See* Article 2(3) EJVL as amended in 1990.

BITs: expropriation must be in the public interest, it must be in accordance with legal procedures, and payment of appropriate compensation is required.

A key concept here is "appropriate compensation," which again is not further defined in Chinese law. A reasonable interpretation of this standard may be twofold: if there is an applicable BIT to the expropriation, the standard of compensation should be compatible with that stipulated in the BIT; in other cases, "appropriate compensation" requires the amount of compensation to be determined, taking into account "all circumstances" that are "pertinent."[145] As a result, the actual compensation may or may not be equivalent to the "Hull Formula" standard of compensation traditionally asserted by some Western countries.[146] Chinese foreign investment laws do not go any further in defining expropriation, its conditions, or the standard of compensation.

The 2007 Property Law, which applies to both public and private properties, sets forth general principles on the issue of expropriation of collectively owned land, premises of enterprises and individuals, and other immovable properties.[147] The law requires that expropriation of such properties take place for public interests and in accordance with the procedures stipulated under the law.[148] The law points out the general scope of compensation for the expropriation of such properties, without giving any further details as to the specific standards of compensation.[149] Such standards are said to be laid down in other more specific laws and regulations.[150] Reference must therefore be made to applicable BITs to find a clearer answer on the matter of calculation of compensation on expropriation.

V. Transfer

The ability to freely transfer capital and profits is central to the investment protection paradigm as "an investor expects to be able to repatriate his capital and his profits."[151] It is unlikely an investor would risk making an investment if a profit could not be

---

145 Such circumstances may include, as Judge Aréchaga has once suggested, "Whether the initial investment has been recovered, whether there has been undue enrichment as a result of the colonial situation, whether the profits obtained have been excessive, the contribution of the enterprise to the economic and social development of the country, its respect for labour laws and its investment policies." *See* Eduardo Jiménez de Aréchaga, *State Responsibility for the Nationalisation of Foreign Owned Property*, 11 N.Y.U. J. INT'L L. & POLITICS 179, 185 (1978).

146 For instance, the United States voted in favor of UN Res. 1803 and asserted that in its view the "appropriate compensation" therein was equivalent to the "Hull Formula" (namely "prompt, adequate and effective" compensation) it had advocated since 1938. *See* 2 RESTATEMENT (THIRD) OF THE FOREIGN RELATIONS LAW OF THE UNITED STATES § 206 (1986).

147 According to Article 4, the law protects properties of the state, collectives, individuals, and other proprietors. *See* Property Law of the People's Republic of China (adopted at the 5th session of the Tenth National People's Congress on Mar. 16, 2007). The expropriation clause is located in Article 42.

148 *Id.*, Article 42, ¶ 1.

149 *Id.*, Article 42, ¶¶ 2–4.

150 XINHUANET, *Protecting the Rights of the Expropriated, the Property Law Detailed Rules on Expropriation*, Mar. 8, 2007, http://news.xinhuanet.com/misc/2007-03/08/content_5819987.htm (last visited Nov. 8, 2011).

151 F.A. Mann, *British Treaties for the Promotion and Protection of Investments*, 52 BRIT. Y.B. INT'L L. 241, 243 (1981).

generated and freely transferred without undue exchange control restrictions, taxes, or additional permissions being imposed. The balancing interest is that of the host state in controlling and protecting its currency and foreign reserves.[152]

I. UNDER BITS

As with the expropriation clause, all the Chinese BITs contain a provision on free transfers. Earlier Chinese BITs provide that free transfer is "subject to its laws and regulations…"[153] to allow for China's foreign exchange controls. However, some of China's more recent treaties, such as China–Germany BIT (2003), have not referred to this restriction.[154] The Protocol to China–Germany BIT (2003) however contains a clarification with regard to China only that transfer of funds under Article 6(1)(c) is allowed so long as it complies "with the relevant formalities stipulated by the present Chinese laws and regulations relating to exchange control."[155] Besides, all Chinese treaties provide that the transfer shall be "fully convertible"[156] under the "prevailing make rate of exchange."[157]

Some of China's BITs include not just a list of the types of payments that are freely transferable, but also specific exclusions where transfer can be prevented or delayed. One of the more detailed transfer provisions is the ASEAN–China Investment Agreement (2009), which permits a state to prevent a transfer if applying in a fair way its laws relating to:

> (a) bankruptcy, loss of ability or capacity to make payments, or protection of the right of creditors;
> (b) non-fulfilment of the host Party's transfer requirements in respect of trading or dealing in securities, futures, options or derivatives;
> (c) non-fulfilment of tax obligations…[158]

Some recent BITs also include a provision on the "balance of payments." Article 8(3) of the Mexico BIT, for example, provides:

> In case of a serious balance of payments difficulty or of a threat thereof, each Contracting Party may temporarily restrict transfers provided that such a

---

152 K.J. VANDEVELDE, UNITED STATES INVESTMENT TREATIES: POLICY AND PRACTICE 143 (1992). *See also generally* UNCTAD, TRANSFER OF FUNDS (2000) and UNCTAD, INTERNATIONAL INVESTMENT AGREEMENTS: KEY ISSUES 257 (2004); DOLZER & STEVENS, *supra* note 73, at 85.

153 *See, e.g.*, Art. 6 of the China–Italy BIT (1985).

154 Article 6(1) Germany BIT (2003). *See also* Article 6 Finland BIT (2004).

155 German BIT (2003) Protocol Ad Article 5; *see also* Finland BIT (2004) Ad Article 6.

156 *See, e.g.*, 2003 China BIT Model, Article 6(3).

157 *See, e.g.*, 2003 China BIT Model, Article 6(3). If a market rate of exchange does exist, the rate of exchange shall correspond to the cross rate obtained from those rates, which would be applied by the IMF; *see, i.e.*, China–Portugal BIT, Article 6, ¶ 2.

158 Article 10(3)(a)–(h) China–ASEAN Investment Agreement (2009). *See also* Article 8(3) Mexico BIT (2008). *See also* A. Kolo & T. Wälde, *Capital Transfer Restrictions under Modern Investment Treaties*, *in* STANDARDS OF INVESTMENT PROTECTION 205 (A. Reinish ed., 2008).

Contracting Party implements measures or a program in accordance with international standards. These restrictions should be imposed on an equitable, non-discriminatory and in good faith basis.[159]

Despite the significance of the transfer provisions, they have still not featured much in the cases after the global economic crisis when restrictions on capital flows would have been expected. However, these provisions did receive some attention since the European Commission successfully took proceedings against Austria, Finland, and Sweden under Article 226 EC Treaty as some of their BITs (predating accession to the EU) were incompatible with the EC Treaty as they did not have an express carve-out for restrictions that might be imposed by the European Council on free movement of capital. The Commission was concerned that the treaties might limit the powers of the EU Council to impose restrictions on the free movement of capital. The infringement proceedings under Article 226 were successful from the Commission's point of view as the European Court of Justice found the countries had failed to comply with their obligation under Article 307. This required the states to take appropriate steps to remove any incompatibilities from preexisting treaties once those states become members of the EU.[160] The ECJ found a breach in all three cases, and the member states must now take appropriate action, either by entering a new treaty or revising the existing ones, to comply with their EU obligations. The ECJ "added that, as follows from the judgment delivered today in Case C-205/06 *Commission v Austria* [2009] ECR I-0000, the incompatibilities with the Treaty to which the investment agreements with third countries give rise and which militate against the application of the restrictions on movement of capital and on payments which the Council may adopt under Articles 57(2) EC, 59 EC and 60(1) EC are not limited to the Member State which is the defendant in the present case."[161] China will now have to engage with these states as their European counterparts seek to comply with these obligations. This may result in a revised version of the transfer provisions in China's next Model BIT.

II. UNDER CHINESE LAW

China has taken an increasingly liberal approach toward the issue of monetary transfer. Nowadays the RMB, the Chinese currency, is fully convertible under current

---

159 *See also* Protocol to Slovakia BIT, Article 7(4); Uganda BIT (2004), Article 8(3); Sri Lanka BIT (1986).

160 Commission v. Austria Case C-205/06, Judgment of Mar. 3, 2009 [2009] ECR I-01303, Commission v. Sweden, Case C-249/06, Judgment of Mar. 3, 2009 and Commission v. Republic of Finland, Case C-118/07 Judgment of Nov. 19, 2009. *See* E. Denza, *Bilateral Investment Treaties and EU Rules on Free Transfer: Comment on Commission v Austria, Commission v. Sweden and Commission v. Finland*, 35(2) Eur. L. Rev. 263 (2010).

161 *Id.* C-249/06 ¶ 43. See also C-205/06 ¶¶ 43 and C-118/07 ¶ 34 where the ECJ noted that its findings in the earlier cases were not limited to the defendant member state. For consideration of the extra- and intra-EU BIT obligations, see Eureko BV v Slovakia, PCA Case No. 2008-13, UNCITRAL Award on Jurisdiction, Oct. 23, 2010, ¶¶ 57–83.

transactions,[162] though not under capital transactions. In this respect, foreign exchange transactions on China's capital account require a case-by-case review.

All the basic FIE laws and regulations have general guarantees on the rights of repatriation of investments and returns. Article 11 of the EJVL, for example, provides that foreign joint ventures' net profit and other funds may be remitted abroad in accordance with the foreign exchange regulations and in the currency specified in the joint venture contract. Likewise, article 12 of the EJVL also allows foreign employees of an FIE to remit their salary and other legitimate incomes out of China. Moreover, since 1996 FIEs were allowed to open forex accounts to hold foreign-invested capital and sell from these accounts upon the approval of SAFE. FIEs may also borrow forex directly from domestic and overseas banks provided that they shall register with SAFE afterwards and obtain approval for debt repayment and services. Upon approval by SAFE, FIEs could make payments from their forex accounts or in forex purchased from designated forex banks after liquidation.[163]

Nowadays, there is a strong recommendation that China need to further liberalize monetary transfer rules to fully facilitate FDI activities. In this connection, it is noted that Yi Gang, head of the State Administration of Foreign Exchanges, mentioned in early 2011 that China would progressively make its currency, RMB, convertible on the capital account in the next five years as China pushes for deeper internationalization of the currency.[164]

VI. Settlement of Disputes

The greatest breakthrough in the area of international investment law is the creation of an investor–state dispute settlement mechanism enabling foreign investors to sue the host government. Without a fair and effective dispute settlement mechanism, the substantive provisions of a BIT would be meaningless.[165]

---

162 Official RMB exchange rates were unified with the market rates in 1994, and since then China has adopted a single and managed floating exchange rate regime based on market. China formally undertook the IMF obligations in 1996, thus making RMB fully convertible on current accounts. On Jan. 1, 1994, official RMB exchange rates were unified with the market rates and thereby China had adopted a single and managed floating exchange rate regime based on supply and demand. On Dec. 1, 1996, China formally accepted the obligations of Article VIII of the IMF's Articles of Agreement, making RMB fully convertible on current accounts. *See* Congyan Cai. *Jurisdictional Report of China*, *in* The Legal Protection of Foreign Investment: A Comparative Study 243–86. (Wenhua Shan ed., 2005).

163 WTO, Report of the Working Party on the Accession of China, WT/ACC/CHN/49, Oct. 1, 2001, ¶ 33.

164 *See* China Daily, *China to Make RMB Convertible on Capital Account in 5 Years*, Jan. 19, 2011, http://www.chinadaily.com.cn/bizchina/2011-01/19/content_11878739.htm (last visited Nov. 8, 2011).

165 Steinert, *supra* note 105, at 405.

I. UNDER BITS

The investor–state dispute resolution provisions in China's BITs have generated much debate and speculation over the years. This is largely due to China's initial reluctance to accept international arbitration as a means of settling investment disputes. Earlier Chinese BITs, especially those signed before 1998, provide for "disputes involving the amount of compensation for expropriation" to be referred to ad hoc arbitration comprised of a three-member tribunal.[166] Originally it was assumed that this wording would preclude a tribunal from deciding whether an actual expropriation had occurred and limit its remit to questions of quantum only.[167]

Yet recent jurisprudence indicates that this is not the case. In the *Tza Yap Shum* matter the Chinese investor persuaded the tribunal, relying on earlier cases, that this same wording in the Peru BIT did allow it not only to "determine the amount but also any other issues normally inherent to an expropriation, including whether the property was actually expropriated in accordance with the BIT provisions and requirements, as well as the determination of the amount of compensation due…"[168] The tribunal felt to decide otherwise would render obsolete the last sentence of Article 8(3)—the fork-in-the-road provision confirming that if a party refers a dispute to the national courts, the arbitration provision does not apply. Presumably the tribunal felt that if the investor had referred the dispute on whether an expropriation had in fact occurred to the local courts of China, but not the question of quantum, this would activate the final sentence of Article 3 and exclude arbitration altogether. Another possible interpretation is that the final sentence relates only to the question of quantum; if the claimant had argued the damages before the national courts, it could not do so before an investment tribunal at a later time.

Some BITs also provide that "other disputes shall be submitted to ICSID on agreement between the parties."[169] This additional wording relating to "other disputes" (meaning other than involving compensation) appears in a significant number of China's treaties, and also appeared in the China–Peru BIT in the *Tza Yap Shum* case. The tribunal in that matter rejected the submission of the claimant that he could rely on the MFN provision to extend the scope of the arbitration clause by invok-

166 *See, e.g.*, Article 8(3) Mongolia BIT. Other examples include: Article 8(3) Argentina BIT (1992); Article IX(3) Indonesia BIT (1994); Article 13(3) Sri Lanka BIT (1986); Article 8(3) Lebanon BIT (1996); Article 9(3) Syria BIT (1996), Article 9(3) Cambodia BIT (1996).

167 Kong, *supra* note 121, at 130. *See also* M.C.E. Heymann, *International Law and the Settlement of Investment Disputes relating to China*, 11 J. INT'L ECON. L. 507, 515 (2008); T.G. Nielson, *Investor State Arbitration and Investment Treaty Protection: The South-East Asian Angle*, 28 Australian Res. & Energy L.J. 213 (2009). *See generally* on investor–state arbitration VANDEVELDE, *supra* note 102, ch. 15; DOLZER & SCHREUER, *supra* note 70, chs. X and C; MCLACHLAN ET AL., *supra* note 110, ch. 3.

168 Tza Yap Shum v Peru ICSID Case No. ARB/07/6, Award on Jurisdiction, June 19, 2009 ¶ 188 (unofficial translation). *See also* decision of the English Court in European Media Ventures v Czech Republic [2007] EWHC 2851 upholding a similar finding of the tribunal that it did have jurisdiction to decide on expropriation even though the BIT referred to disputes "concerning compensation."

169 *See, e.g.*, Art 11(2) of the China–Japan BIT (1988).

ing Article 12 of the Peru–Columbia BIT. The claimant wanted the tribunal to have jurisdiction to consider other breaches of the treaty, for example fair and equitable treatment and full protection. The tribunal noted that the application of the MFN is one of the "*quaestiones vexatae*" of investment arbitration. After reviewing the numerous conflicting awards on this issue, the tribunal concluded that Article 8(3) of the China–Peru BIT was restricted in nature. The parties had agreed to two things; that expropriate matters would be arbitrated, and that other disputes could—if agreed upon—be referred to ICSID. In accordance with Article 31 of the Vienna Convention, the tribunal held the correct interpretation was that this specific agreement should prevail over the more general language in the MFN clause. The tribunal "does not accept the arguments presented by the Claimant relating to the interpretation of the MFN clause in the BIT (Article 3)." The tribunal "finds that Article 3 can not be interpreted to extend the jurisdiction of the Centre or as an independent source of competence for the Tribunal."[170] It is not certain given the existing divergent jurisprudence whether a future tribunal would also refuse to apply the MFN in the face of the additional wording on future disputes.

It is only in the last decade that China has included a broad or expansive investor state dispute resolution option. These third-generation BITs cover "all disputes" or all "disputes relating to an investment" and are consistent with global BIT practice. This shift in modern BITs only really started in earnest in the early 1980s. The Protocol to China's first BIT with Sweden refers to ICSID and the possibility of reaching agreement on mandatory arbitration in the future. The Finland BIT (2004) is an example of this new wording in the current Model BIT providing at Article 9(1) "Any dispute arising out of an investment between one Contracting Party and an investor of the other Contracting..." can, at the investor's choice, be referred to international arbitration (ICSID or ad hoc). Other treaties such as the Uganda BIT (2004) provides for "Any legal dispute...in connection with an investment"[171] The Mexico BIT has one of the most detailed investor–state dispute resolution provision in Section III, which is based more on NAFTA Chapter 11 than the China Model BIT. Article 13 covers any alleged breach of obligation in Chapter II, the substantive protections.[172] These third-generation treaties do as does the Model BIT include a provision, either in the clause itself or in a Protocol, that the investor "shall go through the domestic administrative review procedures as specified by the laws and regulations of the disputing Contracting Party

---

170 Tza Yap Shum v Peru, Award on Jurisdiction, ¶ 220: the tribunal specifically endorses the approach in Plama v. Bulgaria. ICSID Case No. ARB/03/24, noting that in *Plama* "they actually took into account the warnings set out in paragraph 63 of the Award in *Maffezini*."[unofficial translation] *See generally* P.J. Turner & M. Mangan, *China's Investment Treaties: Substantive and Procedural Rights*, ASIAN COUNSEL (May 2007) and Y. Radi, *The Application of the Most-Favoured-Nation Clause to the Dispute Settlement Provisions of Bilateral Investment Treaties: Domesticating the "Trojan Horse"*, 18 EUR. J. INT' LAW 757 (2007).

171 Article 8(1); *see also* Article 10(1) Jordan BIT (2005). There are now close to forty BITs that China has signed that contain these expansive dispute resolution provisions.

172 Article 13 (1) Mexico BIT(2008); *see also* Article 14(4) China–ASEAN Investment Agreement (2009).

before the submission to international arbitration..."[173] There is often a time limit within which to pursue this domestic administrative review; for example, no more than three months in the Finland BIT and four months in the Mexico version. A tribunal might be persuaded to forgo this requirement as in *Maffezini*, although this is not certain.[174] There is also a question of whether a future tribunal would apply the MFN clause to extend the scope of a restrictive Chinese BIT to the broader one in the third-generation treaties. Clearly this could only happen now if there was no specific wording in the principle treaty investment-dispute clause relating to "other disputes" as in *Tza Yap Shum*.

China became a contracting state of the ICSID Convention in 1993, and so it is not surprising the reference in the first two Model BITs was to ad hoc arbitration. They both do, however refer to ICSID as the appointing authority if the tribunal has not been constituted within four months from the notice of application. China when it ratified the ICSID Convention filed a notification under Article 25(4) of the Convention confirming that:

> Pursuant to Article 25(4) of the Convention, the Chinese Government would only consider submitting to the jurisdiction of the International Centre for Settlement of Investment Disputes disputes over compensation resulting from expropriation and nationalization.[175]

This notification does not amount to a consent (or lack thereof) for the purposes of ICSID jurisdiction, nor does it prevent a state from consenting to ICSID arbitration subsequent to the notification. China did so for the first time when it consented to arbitrate all disputes in its BIT with Barbados in 1998. The significance now of the notification made by China appears to have limited if any impact although it has been suggested that if a consent to arbitrate was unclear, it might be "interpreted by reference to a prior notification of classes of disputes in respect of which the host State has expressed its intentions."[176] There would be a presumption that the state intended to stay within the confines of the notification. China has also entered into BITs that provide for ICSID Additional Facility, for example with India, not yet a signatory to the ICSID Convention. There are also references to the UNCITRAL Arbitration Rules and the Stockholm Chamber of Commerce as an appointing authority.[177]

---

[173] Annex C to Article 13(5) Mexico BIT (2008). Other examples include the Protocol to the Finland and Germany BITs.

[174] In Maffezini v Spain, ICSID Case No. ARB/97/7, Award on Jurisdiction, Oct. 28, 1999, the tribunal applied the MFN to permit the claimant to proceed directly to international arbitration without having to attempt to resolve the dispute in the local courts for eighteen months as stipulated in the basic treaty. In contrast, the opposite finding was made in Wintershall v Argentina, ICSID Case No. ARB/04/14, Award, Dec. 8, 2009.

[175] Notification of China, Jan. 7 January, 1993, www.worldbank.org/icsid (last visited Nov. 8, 2011).

[176] C.H. Schreuer, Loretta Malintoppi, August Reinisch, & Anthony Sinclair, The ICSID Convention: A Commentary (2009) (discussion re: Article 25).

[177] *See* BITs with Cuba, Kuwait, Norway (Protocol), and Austria (Protocol).

On May 24, 2011, ICSID registered a case initiated by a Malaysian investor against China. This case, *Ekran Berhad v. People's Republic of China* (ICSID Case No. ARB/11/15) is the first one ever filed before the ICSID against the Chinese government. The dispute concerns rights to a leasehold over land in the Province of Hainan held by a subsidiary of Erkan Berhad, Sino Malaysia Art & Culture, and revoked by the local authorities in Hainan. However, according to ICSID, the proceeding was suspended pursuant to the parties' agreement on July 22, 2011 even before the constitution of the tribunal.[178]

II. UNDER CHINESE LAW

Chinese law regarding dispute settlement, particularly its administrative procedures, plays a very important role in settling investment disputes.[179] Normally Chinese BITs may require an administrative review process before a party may resort to international arbitration.[180] In China, state–investor disputes are normally handled through administrative channels, namely "administrative review" (*Xingzheng Fuyi*) and/or "administrative litigation" (*Xingzheng Susong*).[181]

The most relevant procedure to Chinese BIT is the "administrative review" because it is imposed in almost every new-generation BIT as the only local control over investor–state disputes. It is a hierarchical supervision mechanism within the administrative system permitting administrative organs of a higher level to review any specific administrative acts of lower-level organs for legality and propriety, upon request by any citizens, legal persons, and other organizations. The Chinese NPC adopted the Administrative Review Law of the People's Republic of China ("Administrative Review Law of 1999") on April 29, 1999, which replaced the Administrative Review Regulations of 1990. Article 6 of the Administrative Review Law lists a series of "specific administrative acts" under review. Moreover, administrative review may also be conducted against "provisions" (guiding) adopted by lower-level administrative authorities, if they are the basis of a specific administrative act in question. These provisions are provided in Article 7. In this respect, it can be seen that the scope of review is relatively wide, covering not only "specific administrative acts," but also "abstract administrative acts." Again, the threshold for review is also relatively high, as it not only reviews "illegal" acts but also "improper" ones. The time limit for administrative review is normally sixty days, with ninety days as the maximum time allowed. This is probably the

---

178 http://icsid.worldbank.org/ICSID/FrontServlet (last visited Nov. 8, 2011).

179 SHAN, THE LEGAL FRAMEWORK OF EU–CHINA INVESTMENT RELATIONS, *supra* note 1, at 223.

180 For instance, Article 6 of the Protocol of the China–Germany BIT (2003) provides:

> With respect to investments in the People's Republic of China an investor of the Federal Republic of Germany may submit a dispute for arbitration under the following conditions only: (a) the investor has referred the issue to an administrative review procedure according to Chinese law, (b) the dispute still exists three months after he has brought the issue to the review procedure, and (c) in case the issue has been brought to a Chinese court, it can be withdrawn by the investor according to Chinese law.

Similar content can also be found in the Protocol of the China/Finland BIT (2005).

181 CHINESE INVESTMENT TREATIES, *supra* note 1, at 367.

ground for China's insistence on the three-month, or ninety-day, maximum administrative review time limit in its BITs. An administrative review decision, however, may be challenged by bringing an administrative lawsuit to a Chinese court, unless otherwise stipulated by the law. Further details with regard to the implementation of the law are contained in the Implementing Regulations for the Administrative Review Law adopted in 2007.[182]

On the other hand, the administrative litigation procedure will also apply because Chinese courts are the default remedy for most investor–state disputes in China under Chinese BITs. Unlike administrative review, which is essentially an internal supervision mechanism conducted within the administrative system, an administrative process, or remedy, administrative litigation is conducted within the general judicial system and is therefore part of the formal judicial process. Since 1989, the promulgation of the Administrative Procedures Law (APL) has made it possible for all citizens, juridical persons, and other organizations to bring an action before a court against "specific administrative acts" by administrative authorities. Such acts are rather broadly defined in Article 11 to cover all "specific" regulatory activities by the government authorities on foreign investment. However, *abstract administrative acts* such as administrative regulations, rules, or decisions and orders with general binding force formulated by administrative organs, including provisions that may be reviewed under the administrative review process, are not subject to administrative proceedings.[183]

Many Chinese BITs have a fork-in-the-road provision requiring a choice between domestic court and international arbitration. Some BITs, such as the China–Germany BIT (2003), allow for further flexibility by permitting submission to international arbitration after a case has been submitted to a local court, provided that the investor withdraws the case from such court procedures before submitting it to international arbitration. However, if the local court procedures have been completed and a final ruling has been made, the investor cannot resort to international arbitration.[184]

III. CALVO IN CHINA?

The Calvo Doctrine is a foreign policy doctrine that arose from the idea of Carlos Calvo, an Argentine jurist. The essence of this doctrine is "anti–super-national-treatment," which focuses on the opposition and rejection of any discriminatory treatment by Western powers against weak, developing host states and their nationals, as compared to the treatment those Western powers accord each other and demand for their citizens in these host states.[185]The "anti–super-national-treatment" approach is reified in

---

[182] CHINESE INVESTMENT TREATIES, *supra* note 1, at 367–69.

[183] *Id.* at 369–70.

[184] *Id.* at 391.

[185] Wenhua Shan, *Is Calvo Dead?*, 55 AM. J. COMP. L. 123, 124 (2007).

the widely used "Calvo Clauses" in domestic constitutions and laws, and in bilateral and regional treaties.[186] In context, such clauses often highlight that the treatment of foreigners and foreign investors should be "no more favorable than" that accorded to nationals and national investors.[187] The Calvo Doctrine was enthusiastically received by Latin American states, and these states refer to the Calvo Clause to enforce this doctrine as a countermeasure to the rejection of the doctrine by Western powers.[188]

Though first embraced by Latin American states, after World War II the influence of this doctrine has gone well beyond them to be accepted by other states, such as a number of new ones that have emerged in Asia and Africa as the result of the decolonization process. A Calvo Clause was also included in the United Nations General Assembly resolutions when the New International Economic Order movement reached its summit.[189] In the 1990s, the "imminent death" of this doctrine was declared due to changing attitudes in Latin American states toward foreign investment as witnessed in their international and domestic lawmaking practice.[190] However, although Calvo is not completely dead, it has largely been deactivated. It is still alive respecting rejection of diplomatic protection, yet in others ways it is greatly transformed.[191]

As with the Latin American States, China traditionally accepted the Calvo Doctrine. China was also actively participated in establishing the "New International Economic Order" that emphasized state sovereignty over natural resources and denied any substantial protection of foreign investment under international law.[192] During the period before 1979, China's foreign policy was characterized by the "Five Principles of Peaceful Co-Existence," a set of principles similar to the Calvo Doctrine.[193] "Five Principles of Peaceful Co-Existence" consist of "mutual respect for each other's sovereignty and territorial integrity, mutual non-aggression, non-interference in each other's internal affairs, equality and mutual benefit and peaceful coexistence."[194] In the sphere of foreign investment, these five principles were specified to have the following requirements: (1) states have the sovereign right to control the entry of FDI and to regulate the activities of foreign investors in their territory; (2) the right of the state to nationalize foreign property is an inherent attribute of national territorial sovereignty, and the exercise of this fundamental right is not subject to any precondition such as: public interest, due process of law, nondiscrimination, and against compensation; (3) state contracts or concessions are to be observed, subject to the sovereign power of host

186 *Id.* at 125.

187 *Id.*

188 *Id.* at 127.

189 *Id.* at 129.

190 Denise Manning-Cabrol, *The Imminent Death of the Calvo Clause and the Rebirth of the Calvo Principle: Equality of Foreign and National Investors*, 26 L. & POL'Y INT'L BUS. 1169 (1995).

191 For more, please see Shan, *supra* note 185.

192 Schill, *supra* note 11, at 78.

193 *Id.*

194 Kong, *supra* note 121, at 109.

countries to mandate renegotiation, revision, or even unilateral modification on the basis of changed circumstances or public interests.[195]

However, China's attitude toward FDI has been changed fundamentally since its open-up policy. China's notion of sovereignty changed with its attempt to attract FDI. Nowadays, a more liberal approach is taken by China in negotiating BITs, evidenced by the inclusion of national treatment and full access to ICSID arbitration. Its domestic laws and regulations have also changed, especially after its access to the WTO. In general, the Calvo Doctrine and the Calvo Clause are derogated in China, yet they still have some place in China's FDI legal framework.

In China's domestic law, there is still a "Calvo Clause" in its law dealing with the foreign-related contracts since 1989, and as it stands today. It is provided that all Sino–foreign equity joint venture contracts, Sino–foreign cooperative joint venture contracts, and Sino–foreign contacts for the joint exploration and development of natural resources shall be governed by Chinese law and subject to the exclusive jurisdiction of Chinese courts.[196]

When it comes to Chinese BIT practice, the situation is a little complicated. According to Schreuer, the exhaustion of local remedies is taken as Calvo's children and grandchildren.[197] As mentioned above, among Chinese investment treaties allowing all invest disputes to be submitted to international arbitration, a few investment treaties authorize China as host country can demand that foreign investors seek a local remedy (e.g., administrative review procedure) before resorting to international arbitration. On the other hand, some Chinese BITs with the inclusion of full access to international arbitration have a "fork-in-the road" clause, which aims to preclude an investor from commencing other legal remedies having been chosen. Article 9(3) of the Sino–Russia BIT, for instance, provides:

> Once the investor has submitted the dispute to the competent court of the concerned Contracting Party or to the Centre or to the ad hoc arbitration court, the choice of one of the three procedures shall be final.

Therefore, if an investor decides to resort to legal remedies in China, he or she may not be able to submit an investment dispute to international arbitration.[198]

---

195 *Id. See also* Schill, *supra* note 11, at 78.

196 Article 126 of the Contract Law of the People's Republic of China provides that such contracts should be governed only by Chinese law, and Article 246 of the Civil Procedure Law of the People's Republic of China states that any disputes arising out of such contracts should be subject only to the jurisdiction of Chinese courts.

197 Christoph Schreuer, *Calvo's Grandchildren: The Return of Local Remedies in Investment Arbitration*, 1 L. & PRAC. INT'L CTS. & TRIBS. 1, 3 (2005).

198 It should be admitted that the "fork-in-the road" clause appears not to prevent investors from resorting to international arbitration even though the investor has chosen national court proceeding. *See, e.g.*, Alex Genin, Eastern Credit Limited, Inc. and A.S. Baltoil v. The Republic of Estonia, ICSID Case No. ARB/99/2.

VII. Conclusion

China's success in attracting FDI is undisputed and unprecedented, partly owing to its efforts in strengthening the legal framework, both international and domestic. Recent years have witnessed some significant changes in both China's domestic FDI law and BITs practice. In the sphere of domestic law, a unified and balanced approach is taking shape. The enactment of the Enterprise Tax Law 2007 and the application of the company law system to FIEs[199] illustrate a move toward convergence of the long-established dual systems of enterprise regulation. However, the establishment of the security review system further confirms that China is moving forward from its single focus on the amount of FDI to emphasizing both the quantity and the quality of FDI, trying to achieve a sustainable development of the economy. On the international stage, China is beginning to challenge existing international investment norms.[200] Its role has been developing from a participant to a leader in the world economy in general, and in international investment in particular.[201]

Yet China needs to do more to be fully prepared for the change in its role. On the one hand, the domestic legal framework relating to FDI is not sufficient to be effective.[202] On the other hand, China's success in attracting FDI is likely to result in the proliferation of FDI disputes between international investors and local governments, in addition to disputes involving China's central government. Given the magnitude of the FDI and the scale of investments in China, the ability to effectively deal with these disputes will not only affect China's ability to keep attracting and regulating FDI, but will also impact on the growing interconnection between the Chinese and the global economies. The future of China's investment program will depend not only on continuing adjustment of the notions of sovereignty and its actual exercise, but also on whether and how China may continue to cede control over aspects of its social and economic programs in order to continue attracting FDI in an increasingly interdependent world.

---

199 Article 218 of the Company Law of the People's Republic of China (revised in 2005) provides that "The limited liability companies and joint stock limited companies invested by foreign investors shall be governed by the present Law. Where there are otherwise different provisions in any law regarding foreign investment, such provisions shall prevail."

200 Rosen & Hanemann, *supra* note 10.

201 Guiguo Wang, *China's Practice in International Investment Law: From Participation to Leadership in the World Economy*, 34 YALE J. INT'L L. 575 (2009).

202 Shan & Zhang, *supra* note 13.

10

THE ICSID AND INVESTOR–STATE ARBITRATION

Leon E. Trakman[*]

"RIGHTS-BASED PROCESSES, including binding arbitration and traditional court trials, have limited remedies and may not address the full range of interests and needs that the parties may have. Disputes resolved on the basis of power (e.g. through gunboat diplomacy, or at the extreme, violence and war) weight the outcome in favor of the party with the most leverage, status and resources, but this may be costly on the relationships involved and may result in failure to vindicate rights."[1]

I. INTRODUCTION

In the wake of the global financial crisis, 2009 was a bad year for the International Centre for the Settlement of Investment Disputes (ICSID). In May of that year, the president of Ecuador, Raphael Correa, denounced the ICSID. He proclaimed that his country's withdrawal from the ICSID was necessary for "the liberation of our countries

[*] Professor of Law & Immediate Past Dean, Faculty of Law, University of New South Wales, Sydney, Australia; B.Com. LL.B. (Cape Town), LL.M., S.J.D. (Harvard). The author is indebted to Susan Francks, Mark Kantor, Luke Nottage, and Luke Peterson for their comments, to the participants at the International Investment Workshop and Roundtable on the "ICSID" held at Xi'an Jiaotong University, July 25–30, 2012 for their insights, and to Kunal Sharma for his research assistance. Thanks are also owed to the Social Sciences and Humanities Research Council of Canada for its research support and the University of New South Wales in Sydney, Australia, for study leave to complete it. A modified version of this chapter entitled *The ICSID under Siege* will appear in 45(3) Cornell, etc Int'l L.J. (forthcoming 2012).

[1] U.N. CONFERENCE ON TRADE & DEV., UNCTAD SERIES ON INT'L INV. POLICIES FOR DEV.: INVESTOR–STATE DISPUTES: PREVENTION AND ALTERNATIVES TO ARBITRATION, at xvi, U.N. Sales No. E.10.II.D.11 (2009). *See also* O. Thomas Johnson, Jr. & Jonathan Gimblett, *From Gunboats to BITs: The Evolution of Modern International Investment Law*, *in* YEARBOOK ON INTERNATIONAL INVESTMENT LAW & POLICY 2010–2011 (Karl P. Sauvant ed., 2012).

because [it] signifies colonialism, slavery with respect to transnationals, with respect to Washington, with respect to the World Bank."[2] This public representation was followed by a challenge to the ICSID by the presidents of Bolivia and Ecuador at a UN conference in June 2009 where they declared that the ICSID should be disbanded.[3] Although those events occurred over three years ago, the debate has continued with Venezuela recently withdrawing from the ICSID Convention.[4]

These withdrawals from the ICSID raise some challenging questions. Is the ICSID ideologically, structurally, procedurally, or functionally deficient? Are those deficiencies ascribed to the ICSID by President Hugo Chavez Frias of Venezuela and President Raphael Correa of Ecuador justified, and if so, why? Are these concerns confined to several Latin American countries? Are there cogent reasons to the contrary? Is the alternative to have resort to another international investment alternative, or to rely on domestic courts to resolve investment disputes previously submitted to the ICSID, as Australia announced in 2011? Why have major economies and destinations for foreign investment in Asia, varying from Vietnam to India, never acceded to the ICSID?[5] Why has Brazil declined to sign the ICSID Convention? These questions are economically, politically, and socially important. If neither country to an investment treaty is a party to the ICSID Convention, or if their investment treaty provides for investor–state ad hoc arbitration under the rules of another organization, such as the United Nations Commission on International Trade Law (UNCITRAL Rules), domestic courts can review the award if the investor seeks enforcement in a host state. However, if domestic courts have the final word on state–investment arbitration, domestic laws and interests are likely to further dilute international investment law and practice.

---

2 *See ICSID in Crisis: Straight-Jacket or Investment Protection?*, BRETTON WOODS PROJECT (July 10, 2009), http://www.brettonwoodsproject.org/art-564878 (alterations in original); *see generally* Antonios Tzanakopoulos, *Denunciation of the ICSID Convention under the General International Law of Treaties*, *in* INTERNATIONAL INVESTMENT LAW AND GENERAL INTERNATIONAL LAW: FROM CLINICAL ISOLATION TO SYSTEMIC INTEGRATION? (Rainer Hofmann & Christian J. Tams eds., 2011); MICHAEL WAIBEL ET AL., THE BACKLASH AGAINST INVESTMENT ARBITRATION (2010); Karsten Nowrot, *International Investment Law and the Republic of Ecuador: From Arbitral Bilateralism to Judicial Regionalism*, 96 BEITRAGE ZUM TRANSNATIONALEM WIRTSCHAFSRECHT 5–52 (May 2010); Tor Krever, *The Legal Turn in Late Development Theory: The Rule of Law and the World Bank's Development Model*, 52 HARV. INT'L L.J. 287 (2011); Ignacio A. Vincentelli, *The Uncertain Future of ICSID in Latin America*, 16 LAW & BUS. REV. AM. 409 (2010); UNCTAD, *Denunciation of the ICSID Convention and BITs: Impact on Investor–State Claims*, IIA Issues Note No. 2 (Dec. 2010), http://www.unctad.org/diae.

3 *See ICSID in Crisis*, *supra* note 2.

4 *See, e.g.*, *Venezuela Submits a Notice under Article 71 of the ICSID Convention*, ICSID (Jan. 26, 2012), http://icsid.worldbank.org/ICSID/FrontServlet?requestType=CasesRH&actionVal=OpenPage&PageType=AnnouncementsFrame&FromPage=Announcements&pageName=Announcement100. *See also* Luis Britta Garcia, *We Have to Get Out of the ICSID*, *available at* http://venezuelanalysis.com/analysis/6766 (in which Hugo Chavez Frias, president of Venezuela, stated on January 24, 2012, "'We have to get out of ICSID").

5 *See, e.g.*, *List of Contracting States and Other Signatories of the Convention* (as of April 18, 2012), ICSID, http://icsid.worldbank.org/ICSID/FrontServlet?requestType=ICSIDDocRH&actionVal=ShowDocument&language=English (last visited June 17, 2012).

This chapter evaluates the criticisms leveled at the ICSID in five particular respects. First, it considers the perceived bias of the ICSID toward wealthy Western states and their investors as an ideological and normative proposition. Second, it evaluates the extent to which the processes of the ICSID incorporate this perceived bias into its institutional mechanisms. Third, it considers whether ICSID arbitration is a viable alternative to domestic courts resolving investment disputes between states and foreign investors. Fourth, it proposes ways in which the ICSID can become more transparent as a mechanism for resolving investment disputes in the face of criticism that it suffers from ideological, structural, and functional myopia. Fifth, it reflects on dispute avoidance alternatives to both arbitration and national courts in resolving investment disputes.[6]

A contrite and diffident defense of the ICSID is that its problems can be ascribed to the complexity of the multiple layers of investment law, that many of these layers are outside of its control, and that the ICSID has attempted to redress those complexities that are within its control.[7] The purpose of this chapter is not to identify the heroes and villains in investment law and practice, but to resolve real conflicts with real human, social, and political potency. In this respect, ICSID arbitration is one among other means of resolving such conflicts. It is not an end in itself, nor should it be so construed.

II. CHALLENGES TO THE ICSID

Whether international arbitration jurisprudence in general can evolve into commonly accepted principles of international investment law is open to debate.[8] Arguably, the failure of the global community of states to reach a multilateral investment accord in the past demonstrates the difficulty for states in finding common ground on the treatment of foreign investment, including institutions and processes for dispute resolution.[9] In dispute is whether investment rights ought to be determined by general

[6] For general information on the ICSID and investment treaties, see generally RUDOLF DOLZER & CHRISTOPH SCHREUER, PRINCIPLES OF INTERNATIONAL INVESTMENT LAW (2008) (investment treaties); RUDOLF DOLZER & MARGRETE STEVENS, BILATERAL INVESTMENT TREATIES (1995); CHRISTOPH H. SCHREUER, THE ICSID CONVENTION: A COMMENTARY 89–91 (2001) (ICSID).

[7] *See, e.g.*, WAIBEL ET AL., *supra* note 2 (defending ICSID). *See also* EVOLUTION IN INVESTMENT TREATY LAW AND ARBITRATION (Chester Brown & Kate Miles eds., 2011); LUCY REED ET AL., GUIDE TO ICSID ARBITRATION, at ix (2004); MAKING TRANSNATIONAL LAW WORK IN THE GLOBAL ECONOMY: ESSAYS IN HONOUR OF DETLEV VAGTS (Pieter Bekker, Rudolf Dolzer & Michael Waibel eds., 2010).

[8] *See generally* STEPHAN W. SCHILL, THE MULTILATERALIZATION OF INTERNATIONAL INVESTMENT LAW, at VI–VII (2009) (discussing non-ICSID methods of multilateralization and investment jurisprudence); Steffen Hindelang, *Bilateral Investment Treaties, Custom and a Healthy Investment Climate—The Question of Whether BITs Influence Customary International Law Revisited*, 5 J. WORLD INV. & TRADE 789 (2004); Jeswald W. Salacuse, *The Treatification of International Investment Law*, 13 LAW & BUS. REV. AM. 155 (2007).

[9] *See* ORGANISATION FOR ECONOMIC CO-OPERATION AND DEVELOPMENT, *The Multilateral Agreement on Investment Negotiating Text* (Apr. 24, 1998), *available at* http://italaw.com/documents/MAIDraftText.pdf;

principles of investment law, or more truly by geopolitical and economic interests that circumscribe those principles.[10] Also in contention is whether arbitration processes that are ad hoc in nature and sometimes closed to public scrutiny are sufficiently transparent to transcend the political context in which ICSID awards are reached.[11]

A. IDEOLOGY

An underlying concern among some developing states, most vividly expressed in 2009 by President Raphael Correa of Ecuador, is that the ICSID was established by, and arguably in the interest of, wealthy countries and their investors abroad.[12] A related concern is that ICSID arbitration has done more to protect capital exporter states and the "equitable" interests of their investors than address the fledgling economies and social plight of capital importer states in Africa, Asia, and Latin America that historically were economically exploited by colonial powers and their investors.[13] These concerns of developing states are reflected in their collective attempts to protect "their" New International Economic Order through the General Assembly of the United States, a Charter of Economic Rights and Duties of States, and a Declaration on the Permanent Sovereignty of States over Natural Resources.[14]

Human rights challenges to international investment law and investor–state arbitration in particular also reflect the attacks by developing states on economic exploitation imputed to investors from wealthy developed states. The accusation of developing states is that principles of investment law are espoused through selective privileging under a rule-of-law regime devised by Old World powers at the expense of the new developing world order.[15] Proponents of this view argue that, whereas international

---

Katia Tieleman, *The Failure of the Multilateral Agreement on Investment (MAI) and the Absence of a Global Public Policy Network*, GLOBAL PUBLIC POLICY INSTITUTE 17–20 (2000), *available at* http://www.gppi.net/fileadmin/gppi/Tieleman_MAI_GPP_Network.pdf (last visited June 17, 2012).

10 By far the most dominant view is that investment law is based on determinative principles. *See, e.g.*, DOLZER & SCHREUER, *supra* note 6, ch. 1; *see also* M. Sornarajah, Chapter 16 of the current book (providing a critique of this "principled" approach).

11 *See generally* Jason W. Yackee & Jarrod Wong, *The 2006 Procedural and Transparency-Related Amendments to the ICSID Arbitration Rules: Model Intentions, Moderate Proposals, and Modest Returns*, *in* THE YEARBOOK ON INTERNATIONAL INVESTMENT LAW & POLICY 2009–2010 (Karl P. Sauvant ed., 2010) (discussing transparency in international investment arbitration); Cornel Marian, *Balancing Transparency: The Value of Administrative Law and Mathews-Balancing to Investment Treaty Arbitrations*, 10 PEPP. DISP. RESOL. L.J. 275 (2010) (discussing transparency in international investment arbitration).

12 *See generally ICSID in Crisis, supra* note 2.

13 *See* M. SORNARAJAH, THE INTERNATIONAL LAW ON FOREIGN INVESTMENT 142–45 (2d ed. 2004) (outlinines the history of this division between capital exporter and importer states).

14 *See* G.A. Res. 3281(xxix), U.N. GAOR, 29th Sess., Supp. No. 3150, UN Doc. A/9631 (Dec. 12, 1974) (Charter of Economic Rights and Duties of States); G.A. Res. 3201 (S-VI), U.N. Doc. A/res/S-6/3201 (May 1, 1974) (New International Economic Order). *See also* NICO SCHRIJVER, SOVEREIGNTY OVER NATURAL RESOURCES: BALANCING RIGHTS AND DUTIES (1997); Leon E. Trakman, *Foreign Direct Investment: Hazard or Opportunity?*, 41 GEO. WASH. INT'L. L. REV. 1, 15–16, 20 (2010).

15 *See* Ibrahim F.I. Shihata, *Towards a Greater Depoliticization of Investment Disputes: The Roles of ICSID and MIGA*, *in* INVESTING WITH CONFIDENCE: UNDERSTANDING POLITICAL RISK MANAGEMENT IN THE

human rights are based on universal norms of fair treatment, the "fair and equitable" treatment of foreign investors is grounded in self-serving norms directed at the market efficiency of capital flows.[16] Underpinning this rationale is the insinuation that the de-politicization of international investment is code for economic rationalism by which wealthy transnational corporations pontificate profit-maximizing outcomes that ultimately favor them over developing states and their citizenry.[17] The alleged enemy is a superpower such as the United States with an Alien Tort Claims process by which non-U.S. citizens can be held liable in any U.S. civil court for transforming the United States into a universal international law jurisdiction. The limit on this power is perceived as minimal at best, as the defendant must merely be in the United States in order to be subject to a subpoena,[18] although the Alien Act is ordinarily only applied in cases involving the allegation of serious crimes.

Developing states sometimes also decry the shift in the "regime theory" by which powerful countries in the West have invoked customary law and treaty defenses, such as the defense of necessity to foreign investors from developing states,[19] even though those same Western states denounced those defenses when they were capital

---

21ST CENTURY 2–35 (Kevin W. Lu et al. eds., 2009) (discussing risk management from the perspective of established developed countries); Susan D. Franck, *Foreign Direct Investment, Investment Treaty Arbitration, and the Rule of Law* 19 PAC. MCGEORGE GLOBAL BUS. & DEV. L. J. 337 (2007) (analyzing different views of the rule of law).

16 *See* Moshe Hirsch, *The Interaction between International Investment Law and Human Rights Treaties: A Sociological Perspective, in* MULTI-SOURCED EQUIVALENT NORMS IN INTERNATIONAL LAW 211–14 (Tomer Broude & Yuval Shany eds., 2011); Sara L. Seck, *Conceptualizing the Home State Duty to Protect Human Rights, in* CORPORATE SOCIAL AND HUMAN RIGHTS RESPONSIBILITIES: GLOBAL LEGAL AND MANAGEMENT PERSPECTIVES 34 (Karin Buhmann et al. eds., 2011).

17 *See* U.N. Secretary-General, *Protect, Respect, and Remedy: A Framework for Business and Human Rights:* Special Rep. of the Sec'y Gen., U.N. Doc. A/HRC/8/5 (Apr. 7, 2008) (by Professor John Ruggie) (discussing alleged human rights abuses by transnational corporations). *See generally* Rachel J. Anderson, *Reimagining Human Rights Law: Toward Global Regulation of Transnational Corporations,* 88 DENV. U. L. REV. 183 (2010); LORENZO COTULA, HUMAN RIGHTS, NATURAL RESOURCE AND INVESTMENT LAW IN A GLOBALISED WORLD: SHADES OF GREY IN THE SHADOW OF THE LAW (2011).

18 *See* U.S. Catholic Conference v. Abortion Rights Mobilization, Inc., 487 U.S. 72, 76 (1988) ("[T]he subpoena power of a court cannot be more extensive than its jurisdiction."). *But see* Fred L. Morrison, *The Protection of Foreign Investment in the United States of America,* 58 AM. J. COMP. L. 437 (2010). *See generally,* The Kiobel Symposium, *available at* SCOTUSBLOG.COM. http://www.scotusblog.com/category/special-features/kiobel-symposium/.

19 *See generally* Andrea K. Bjorklund, *Emergency Exceptions: State of Necessity and* Force Majeure, *in* THE OXFORD HANDBOOK OF INTERNATIONAL INVESTMENT LAW 474–99 (Peter Muchlinski et al. eds., 2008) (discussing the necessity defense); Alberto Alvarez-Jiménez, *Foreign Investment Protection and Regulatory Failures as States' Contribution to the State of Necessity under Customary International Law,* 27 J. INT'L ARB. 141 (2010) (discussing the necessity defense in investment arbitration, including under customary investment law); Nicholas Song, *Between Scylla and Charydbis: Can a Plea of Necessity Offer Safe Passage to States in Responding to an Economic Crisis without Incurring Liability to Foreign Investors?,* 19 AM. REV. INT'L ARB. 235 (2008) (discussing the necessity defense as a solution to the "conundrum" caused when a country faces an economic crisis but still must satisfy its BIT obligations); *Panel Discussion: Is There a Need for the Necessity Defense for Investment Law?, in* INVESTMENT TREATY ARBITRATION AND INTERNATIONAL LAW 189 (T.J. Grierson Weiler ed., 2008); *see also infra* notes 34, 57 and 58. *See generally* SANTIAGO MONTT, STATE LIABILITY IN INVESTMENT TREATY ARBITRATION: GLOBAL CONSTITUTIONAL AND ADMINISTRATIVE LAW IN THE BIT GENERATION (2009).

exporters.[20] Coupled with these concerns is disquiet about developed states crafting reservations and exceptions in investment treaties to service their national security, public health, labor, and environmental safety interests.[21] Furthermore, a countervailing concern is that developing states such as South Africa are more willing to conclude bilateral investment agreements providing for investor–state arbitration with capital-exporting than capital-importing countries.[22] The signing of bilateral investment agreements incorporating investor–state arbitration is therefore not simply about developed states imposing their will on developing states. Rather, these agreements are strategically important, and states elect among them in a calculated manner according to the perceived benefits arising from prospective investment flows.[23]

The fact that the choice of bilateral investment agreements and investor–state arbitration is strategic still does not contradict the argument by some developing states that they lack the array of strategic options that are available to powerful developed states. From this perspective, the ICSID is a vehicle by which wealthy developed states have manicured investment law, and through it investor–state arbitration, into a self-serving *ius cogens* to suit themselves and their investors abroad.[24] Here, the inference is not that ICSID arbitrators have acquiesced formally to the power of developed states and their investors, or that ICSID arbitrators happily do their bidding. Instead, it is supposed that, if a bilateral investment treaty is devised by a capital exporter, ICSID arbitrators who are trained predominantly as civil and common lawyers are likely to construe that already one-sided treaty textually in favor of that capital exporter.[25] Added to this is the concern that ICSID arbitrators, who are usually commercial and not public lawyers, will pay less attention to the public policy ,"environmental and public health" consequences of their awards for developing states than to the plain words of treaties devised by dominant treaty parties.[26]

Over its forty-year history, the ICSID has acquired many more signatories than the original elite twenty. New members emanate from Africa, Latin America, Eastern Europe, and Asia among others.[27] However, the perception is that, in interpreting

---

20 *See generally* REGIME THEORY AND INTERNATIONAL RELATIONS (Volker Rittburger ed., 1993) (discussing international regime theory).

21 On such criticism, see SORNARAJAH, *supra* note 13, at chs. 7–8.

22 *See* Luke Eric Peterson, South Africa Pushes Phase-Out of Early Bilateral Investment Treaties after at Least Two Separate Brushes with Investor–State Arbitration, INV. ARB. REPORTER, Sept. 23, 2012. *See generally,* David A. Gantz, *Investor–State Arbitration under ICSID, the ICSID Additional Facility and the UNCTAD Arbitral Rules* (U.S.-Vietnam Trade Council Education Forum, Aug. 17, 2004), http://www.usvtc.org/trade/other/Gantz/Gantz_ICSID.pdf, at 1: "Presumably, the explosion of BITs means that many developing nations believe that the existence of BITs with capital exporting countries is a factor in encouraging foreign investment."

23 *See* Gantz, *supra* note 22.

24 *See* M. Sornarajah, Chapter 16 of the current book.

25 *See, e.g.*, JESWALD W. SALACUSE, THE LAW OF INVESTMENT TREATIES 111–137 (2010)

26 *See* INTERNATIONAL INVESTMENT LAW AND COMPARATIVE PUBLIC LAW (Stephan W. Schill ed., 2010); GUS VAN HARTEN, INVESTMENT TREATY ARBITRATION AND PUBLIC LAW, 122–51 (2007).

27 *See generally* LORENZO COTULA, LAW AND POWER IN FOREIGN INVESTMENT IN AFRICA—SHADES OF GREY IN THE SHADOW OF THE LAW (2011); A.A. Agyemang, *African States and ICSID Arbitration*, 21

investment treaties literally, ICSID arbitrators have continued to service developed states by applying regulatory defenses crafted by developed states in the interests of those states.[28] This concern gives rise to the inference that investment arbitrators have devised a self-serving *ius cogens* through interpretative practices that perpetuate the status quo.[29] In particular, they have recognized international investment laws, not limited to investment treaties, that protect the property of transnational corporations from expropriation by developing states.[30] Furthermore, investment arbitrators allegedly have failed adequately to address the tension between protecting private property and promoting international investment on the uneven investor–state platform of multistate relations.[31]

A related dilemma is that, with new super–economic powers such as China extending the scope of dispute resolution by treaty beyond expropriation, ICSID arbitrators are likely to construe those treaties purposively, consistent with China's treaty purpose of protecting its national interests such as in its rural areas from foreign investors while also defending the interests of its investors abroad.[32] China is also likely to follow the direction of the Supreme People's Court, which commentators perceive, correctly or otherwise, to be protectionist.[33] The feared result of these trends is another New International Economic Order, following the recession of 2008, in which economically powerful states, now including China and possibly India, replicate the empowerment previously limited to the United States and Western European states. There is worry about increases in investment awards in favor of states, not limited to developed states that invoke the defense of necessity, couched as the national interest in a recession, to defend against investor claims of unjust expropriation.[34] The related concern is that

---

CILSA 177 (1988) (discussing the African signatories, particularly their consent to jurisdiction, their position in the ICSID, and the appointment of African arbitrators); Alec R. Johnson, *Comment: Rethinking Bilateral Investment Treaties in Sub-Saharan Africa*, 59 EMORY L.J. 919 (2010) (discussing BITs in relation to African countries).

28 *See, e.g.*, Stephen Schwebel, *The Influence of Bilateral Investment Treaties on Customary International Law*, TRANSNAT'L DISP. MGMT, 1, 28 (Nov. 2005) (discussing the allegedly customary roots of international law). For a rejection of the proposition that BITs represent customary law, see Patrick Dumberry, *Are BITs Representing "the New" Customary International Law in International Investment Law?*, 28 PENN. ST. INT'L L. REV. 675, 681–82, 684 (2010) ("BITs are missing the two necessary elements of Custom.").

29 *See* Campbell McLachlan, *Investment Treaties and General International Law*, 57 INT'L & COMP. L.Q. 361, 361 (2008); *see generally* Margrete Stevens, *The ICSID Convention and the Origins of Investment Treaty Arbitration, in* 50 YEARS OF THE NEW YORK CONVENTION (Albert Van Den Berg ed., 2009) (describing international investment law as a coherent system since the inception of the ICSID Convention).

30 *See* McLachlan, *supra* note 29, at 394.

31 *See, e.g.*, DOLZER & SCHREUER, *supra* note 6, chs. 1–2 (discussing the alleged foundations of investment law in contract and property).

32 *See, e.g.*, Lutz-Christian Wolff, *Pathological Foreign Investment Projects in China: Patchwork or Trendsetting by the Supreme People's Court?* 44 INT'L LAW. 1001, 1003 (2010) (noting China's protectionism)

33 *See, e.g.*, *id.* at 1003, 1010–11; *see also* Wei Shen, Case Note, *Beyond the Scope of "Investor" and "Investment": Who Can Make an Arbitration Claim under a Chinese BIT?—Some Implications from a Recent ICSID Case*, 6 ASIAN INT'L ARB. J. 164, 183–85 (2010) (discussing limits placed on complainants under bilateral investment agreements with China).

34 *See* JOSEPH STIGLITZ, FREEFALL: AMERICA, FREE MARKETS, AND THE SINKING OF THE WORLD ECONOMY (2010) (providing an account of these recessionary forces and their global consequences). On

these defenses will assume ever-newer forms. An example of these newer forms is the bilateral investment agreements of some Asian countries that limit investment protection to investments "approved in writing"[35] or made in "accordance with the laws and regulations from time to time in being."[36] These stipulations empower signatory countries to deny foreign investor rights by withholding written approval to such investments, or by changing laws and regulations that deny protection previously granted to foreign investors.[37]

To these concerns, supporters of investor–state arbitration and the ICSID in particular respond that, whatever the ills of arbitration may be, the ICSID is not to blame. Rather, the ICSID merely facilitates the resolution of investment disputes through the ICSID Convention and Rules. Furthermore, independent arbitration panels decide those disputes.[38] In effect, the ICSID "provides the institutional and procedural framework for independent conciliation commissions and arbitral tribunals constituted in each case to resolve the dispute."[39] In fulfilling this facilitative function, the ICSID operates comparably to private arbitration associations such as the International Center for Dispute Resolution of the American Arbitration Association (ICDR) and the International Chamber of Commerce (ICC).[40] It provides rules of operation to govern the appointment of arbitrators, the conduct of arbitral proceedings, and the rendering of awards, but It does not decide, or influence, substantive awards in particular cases.[41]

A further defense of ICSID arbitration is that attacks by countries such as Ecuador upon an ICSID process or award reflect an individual net cost–benefit analysis for that

---

the necessity defense, *see* José E. Alvarez & Tegan Brink, *Revisiting the Necessity Defense: Continental Casualty v. Argentina*, *in* YEARBOOK ON INTERNATIONAL INVESTMENT LAW & POLICY 2010–2011 (Karl P. Sauvant ed., 2012); Alberto Alvarez-Jiménez, *The Interpretation of Necessity Clauses in Bilateral Investment Treaties after the Recent ICSID Annulment Decisions*, *in* YEARBOOK ON INTERNATIONAL INVESTMENT LAW & POLICY 2010–2011 (Karl P. Sauvant ed., 2012).

35 On such clauses in BITs, *see, e.g.*, Philippe Gruslin v. Malaysia, ICSID Case No. ARB/94/1 (Apr. 24, 1996), 5 ICSID Rep. 483 (2000); Yaung Chi Oo Trading Pte Ltd. v. Gov't of the Union of Myan., 42 I.L.M. 540, 551 (2003).

36 *See* Fraport AG Frankfurt Airport Serv. Worldwide v. Rep. of the Phil., ICSID Case No. ARB/03/25 (Aug. 16, 2007) (providing such phraseology in an investment agreement with the Philippines).

37 *See supra* notes 33 and 35.

38 *See* Convention on the Settlement of Investment Disputes between States and Nationals of Other States § 14(1), INTERNATIONAL CENTRE FOR SETTLEMENT OF INVESTMENT DISPUTES, *available at* http://icsid.worldbank.org/ICSID/FrontServlet?requestType=CasesRH&actionVal=ShowHome&pageName=Rules_Home.

39 *See ICSID Dispute Settlement Facilities*, INTERNATIONAL CENTRE FOR SETTLEMENT OF INVESTMENT DISPUTES, http://icsid.worldbank.org/ICSID/FrontServlet?requestType=CasesRH&actionVal=RightFrame&FromPage=Dispute Settlement Facilities&pageName=Disp_settl_facilities (last visited June 17, 2012).

40 *See* ICDR, http://www.adr.org/icdr (last visited June 17, 2012); ICC, http://www.iccwbo.org (last visited June 17, 2012); Leon E. Trakman, *Legal Traditions and International Commercial Arbitration*, 17 AM. REV. INT'L. ARB. 1, 19–20, 26–28 (2006) (discussing private international commercial arbitration associations).

41 *See ICSID Dispute Settlement Facilities*, *supra* note 39.

state.[42] They do not reflect a systemic bias in ICSID proceedings or awards against developing states and their investors in general. Furthermore, the loss of an ICSID investor–state dispute by one developing state does not translate into a net loss for developing countries as a class.[43]

These defenses do not respond to the underlying assault on the ICSID, based on the perception that institutionalized arbitration, exemplified by the ICSID, protects the interests of developed states and their investors systemically, structurally, and, ultimately, functionally.

B. IMPACT OF IDEOLOGY ON ICSID ARBITRATION

The perception that ICSID arbitration empowers both old and new wealthy countries at the expense of poorer countries is supported by the criticism that the ICSID is a witting or unwitting party to a world order dominated by institutions and processes that are directed at wealth enhancement, not wealth sharing. Typifying this criticism is the fact that the ICSID is part of the World Bank Group. As such, it allegedly acts as a proxy for affluent investors from the United States and prosperous Western European countries and, in the long term, wealthy countries in general that can afford its services.[44] Although the ICSID's homepage presents the ICSID as an "autonomous international institution,"[45] member countries are members of the World Bank.[46] The governor of the Bank is an ex officio member of the ICSID's governing body, the Administrative

[42] On how different investment policies can influence investment law, see generally Andreas von Staden, *Towards Greater Doctrinal Clarity in Investor–State Arbitration: The CMS, Enron, and Sempra Annulment Decisions*, 2 CZECH Y.B. INT'L L. 207 (2011).

[43] *See* Susan D. Franck, *The ICSID Effect? Considering Potential Variations in Arbitration Awards* (2011) 51 VA. J. INT'L L. 977 (2011). Franck undertakes a quantative analysis of awards with Latin American countries as parties, and finds that "on the whole, . . . ICSID arbitration awards were not statistically different from other arbitral processes, which is preliminary evidence that ICSID arbitration was not necessarily biased or that investment arbitration operated in reasonably equivalent ways across forums." *See also id.* at 898 onward.

[44] *Cf. id. But see* http://www.ase.tufts.edu/gdae/Pubs/wp/11-01TreatyArbitrationReappraisal.pdf. *See also ICSID—International Centre for Settlement of Investment Disputes* (July 14, 2009), *available at* http://www.brettonwoodsproject.org/item.shtml?x=537853. "Reasons for the vocal and mounting critiques against ICSID peg around its governance, its biasness in favour of rich countries and its role in crisis."

[45] This self-description appears on the ICSID's home page, *available at* http://icsid.worldbank.org/ICSID/Index.jsp (last visited June 17, 2012).

[46] *Compare List of Contracting States and Other Signatories to the Convention*, INTERNATIONAL CENTRE FOR SETTLEMENT OF INVESTMENT DISPUTES, http://icsid.worldbank.org/ICSID/FrontServlet?requestType=ICSIDDocRH&actionVal=ContractingStates&ReqFrom=Main (last visited June 17, 2012), *with Member Countries*, WORLD BANK, http://web.worldbank.org/WBSITE/EXTERNAL/EXTABOUTUS/0,contentMDK:22427666~menuPK:8336899~pagePK:51123644~piPK:329829~theSitePK:29708,00.html (last visited June 17, 2012).

Council.[47] The chair of the Administrative Council is the president of the World Bank.[48] The annual meeting of the World Bank and its Fund coincides with the annual meeting of the Administrative Council of the ICSID.[49] Not insignificantly, the World Bank funds the ICSID Secretariat.[50] The Secretary General of the ICSID has the authority to appoint arbitrators to resolve investment disputes, and, given the limited number of qualified candidates, the balance of the appointment process allegedly favors developed countries.[51] ICSID hearings are often held in Washington, D.C., but also in expensive cities such as London and Paris; these locations are convenient for and affordable to wealthy investors, but not for more distant and poorer developing states, their investors, and civic groups in their countries.[52]

A further contention against investor–state arbitration under the ICSID is that international principles of investment law that require developing states to pay "prompt, fair and effective" compensation for expropriation bypass the fact that many developing states lack the resources to compensate foreign investors according to such an international "fair and equitable" standard.[53] As a result, "prompt, fair and effective" compensation for a foreign investor from a developed state may "unfairly" cripple a developing country by perpetuating a history of dominant foreign states and their investors dispossessing it of its natural resources.[54] Conversely, new investment

---

47 *See Organizational Structure of ICSID*, International Centre for Settlement of Investment Disputes, http://icsid.worldbank.org/ICSID/FrontServlet?requestType=CasesRH&actionVal=RightFrame&FromPage=Organization%20and%20Structure&pageName=Organization (last visited June 17, 2012).

48 *See id.*

49 *See id.*

50 *See id.*

51 This challenge to the authority of the Secretary General arose in arbitration against Gambia in which the Tribunal upheld his authority. *See Co-Arbitrators in Mining Dispute Rule That ICSID Acted within Its Authority When It Nominated an Arbitrator after Gambia Failed to Do so within Prescribed Time Limit*, Investment Reporter, May 20, 2011, *available at* http://www.iareporter.com; *see also Effort to Disqualify Arbitrator in Venezuelan Oil Case Unsuccessful; Adjudicators Acknowledge That Multiple Arbitral Appointments Can Be a Concern*, Investment Reporter, May 20, 2011, *available at* http://www.iareporter.com/articles/20110520.

52 For more on the ICSID's organizational structure and the role of the World Bank, Administrative Council, and Secretariat, see *Organizational Structure*, *supra* note 47.

53 On the dominance of developed states over trade and investment and challenges by developing states, see generally D.K. Fieldhouse, The Theory of Capitalist Imperialism (1967) (discussing imperialism); Free Trade and Other Fundamental Doctrines of the Manchester School (Francis W. Hirst ed., 1968) (providing a collection of speeches from the nineteenth century considering the development of free trade); P.J. Cain, *J.A. Hobson, Cobdenism, and the Radical Theory of Economic Imperialism, 1898–1914*, 31 Econ. Hist. Rev. 565, 576–80 (1978); Michael Freeden, *J. A. Hobson as a New Liberal Theorist: Some Aspects of His Social Thought until 1914*, 34 J. Hist. Ideas 421 (1973); James Oliver Gump, *The West and the Third World: Trade, Colonialism, Dependence, and Development*, 11 J. World Hist. 396 (2000) (book review). On the choice between compensation or restitution, *see* Borzu Sabahi, Compensation and Restitution in Investor–State Arbitration: Principles and Practice (2011).

54 On the "fair and equitable" treatment standard in investment treaties, see, for example, Christoph Schreuer, *Fair and Equitable Treatment in Arbitral Practice*, 6 J. World Inv. & Trade 357 (2005). *See generally* Roland Kläger, Fair and Equitable Treatment in International Investment Law

treaties devised by developed states that are now capital importers may artfully invoke such defenses as necessity, national security, health, safety, and the protection of the environment to deny "fair and equitable" treatment to investors from developed and developing countries alike.[55] Here, the inference is that successful arbitration awards favoring wealthy investors sometimes undermine the reasonable expectations, not of investors, but of developing states seeking to protect their fledgling economies from a litany of exploitative foreign investors.[56]

A related criticism is that in ICSID investor-state arbitration in particular, host state defenses such as necessity may trump the claims to "fair and equitable" treatment by foreign investors. Although expansive defenses of necessity were upheld in *LG&E v. Argentine Republic*[57] and *Continental Casualty Company v. Argentine Republic*,[58] this is not necessarily so. In contrast, the arbitral panel in the NAFTA case of *Pope and Talbot v. Government of Canada* administered by the UNCITRAL concluded that it was not limited under NAFTA Article 1005 to the "international minimum standard of treatment," even though Canada won the case.[59] However, minimalist standards of treatment are

---

(2011); Hussein Haeri, *A Tale of Two Standards: "Fair and Equitable Treatment" and the Minimum Standard in International Law,* 27 ARB. INT'L 27 (2011); Andrew P. Tuck, *The "Fair and Equitable Treatment" Standard Pursuant to the Investment Provisions of the U.S. Free Trade Agreements with Peru, Colombia and Panama,* 16 LAW & BUS. REV. AM. 385 (2010); Kenneth J. Vandevelde, *A Unified Theory of Fair and Equitable Treatment,* 43 N.Y.U. J. INT'L L. & POL. 43 (2010).

55 *See Trade and Investment for Growth,* DEP'T FOR BUS. SKILLS & GROWTH, http://www.bis.gov.uk/assets/biscore/international-trade-investment-and-development/docs/t/11-717-trade-investment-for-growth.pdf (last visited June 19, 2012) (discussing the UK's defense of its international trade and investment after the 2008 recession in a White Paper presented to the Parliament in February 2011). *But see* P.P. CRAIG, ADMINISTRATIVE LAW 639–56 (5th ed. 2005); Francisco Orrego-Vicuña, *Foreign Investment Law: How Customary Is Custom?,* 99 PROCEEDINGS OF THE ANNUAL MEETING (AM. SOC'Y OF INT'L L.) 98, 99 (2005) ("[F]air and equitable treatment is not really different from the legitimate expectations doctrine as developed, for example by the English courts and also recently by the World Bank Administrative Tribunal.").

56 *See* KYLA TIENHAARA, THE EXPROPRIATION OF ENVIRONMENTAL GOVERNANCE: PROTECTING FOREIGN INVESTORS AT THE EXPENSE OF PUBLIC POLICY 152–57 (2009); *see also Submission of Phillip Morris International in Response to the Request for Comments Concerning the Proposed Trans-Pacific Partnership Trade Agreement, available at* http://www.regulations.gov/#!documentDetail;D=USTR-2009-0041-0016;oldLink=false (last visited June 19, 2012).

57 *See* ICSID Case No. ARB/02/1, ¶¶ 2–3 (July 25, 2007), http://icsid.worldbank.org/ICSID/FrontServlet?requestType=CasesRH&actionVal=showDoc&docId=DC786_En&caseId=C208.

58 ICSID Case No. ARB/03/9, ¶ 28 (Sept. 5, 2008). *See also* Eric David Kasenetz, *Desperate Times Call for Desperate Measures: The Aftermath of Argentina's State of Necessity and the Current Fight in the ICSID,* 41 GEO. WASH. INT'L L. REV. 709, 721–23 (2010); Antoine Martin, *International Investment Disputes, Nationality and Corporate Veil: Some Insights from Tokios Tokelés and TSA Spectrum De Argentina,* 8 TRANSNAT'L DISP. MGMT 1 (2011); José E. Alvarez & Tegan Brink, *Revisiting the Necessity Defense: Continental Casualty v. Argentina* 6–11 (Int'l Law & Justice Working Paper No. 2010/3, 2010), *available at* http://www.iilj.org/publications/documents/2010-3.Alvarez-Brink.pdf; Tarcisio Gazzini, *Necessity in International Investment Law: Some Critical Remarks on* CMS v. Argentina, 26 J. ENERGY & NAT. RESOURCES L. 450, 452–53 (2008); José Rosell, *The CMS Case: A Lesson for the Future?,* 25 J. INT'L ARB. 493 (2008).

59 *See* Pope & Talbot Inc. v. Can., Award, Part III. (Apr. 10, 2001) (UNCITRAL AWARD). *See also* Pope & Talbot Inc. v. Gov't of Canada, FOREIGN AFFAIRS & INT'L TRADE CANADA, http://www.international.gc.ca/trade-agreements-accords-commerciaux/disp-diff/pope.aspx?lang=en (last visited June 19, 2012).

applied to a variety of specific defenses in the U.S. and Canadian Model Investment Treaties.[60]

A further criticism leveled against investor–state arbitration is that substantive defenses invoked by developed states in foreign investor claims have grown exponentially. This is typified in the NAFTA case, *Methanex v. United States of America*,[61] the U.S. and Canadian Model Treaties,[62] and the India–Singapore Economic Cooperation Agreement.[63] In particular, each treaty includes defenses to investor claims on such grounds as health, public morality, social welfare, and sustainable development.[64] ICSID tribunals have accommodated these defenses.[65] They have also rejected investor claims that such defenses deny foreign investors "fair and equitable treatment," or that a signatory state has exceeded the limits of the "margin of appreciation" doctrine in protecting its public interests over the investment interests of foreign investors.[66]

---

60 *See* Patrick Dumberry, *The Quest to Define "Fair and Equitable Treatment" for Investors under International Law: The Case of the NAFTA Chapter 11 Pope & Talbot Awards*, 3 J. World Inv. 657, 663 (2002). *See also* Directorate for Financial and Enterprise Affairs, *Fair and Equitable Treatment Standard in International Investment Law* 11–12 (Organisation for Economic Co-operation and Development, Working Paper No. 2004/3, 2004), *available at* http://www.oecd.org/dataoecd/22/53/33776498.pdf.

61 *See* Methanex Co. v. US, Final Award, (Aug. 7, 2005), http://www.state.gov/documents/organization/51052.pdf, (2005) (Rowley, Reisman, & Vedeer, Arbs.); *see also Methanex Corporation and the United States of America*, NAFTA Claims, http://www.naftaclaims.com/disputes_us_6.htm (last visited June 19, 2012); Courtney Kirkman, *Fair and Equitable Treatment:* Methanex v. United States *and the Narrowing Scope of NAFTA Article 1105*, 34 Law & Pol'y Int'l Bus. 343 (2002).

62 *See* Treaty between the Government of the United States of America and the Government of [Country] Concerning the Encouragement and Reciprocal Protection of Investment, http://www.state.gov/documents/organization/117601.pdf (American 2004 Model Bilateral Investment Treaty); *see also* Andrew Newcombe, *Canada's New Model Foreign Investment Protection Agreement*, Investment Treaty Arbitration (2004), *available at* http://ita.law.uvic.ca/documents/CanadianFIPA.pdf (Canadian Model Bilateral Investment Treaty). *But see* United States Trade Representative, 2012 U.S. Model Bilateral Investment Agreement, *available at* http://www.ustr.gov/sites/default/files/BIT%20text%20for%20ACIEP%20Meeting.pdf.

63 *See* Comprehensive Economic Cooperation Agreement between the Republic of India and the Republic of Singapore, *available at* http://commerce.nic.in/ceca/toc.htm.

64 *See* Andrew Newcombe, *General Exceptions in International Investment Agreements* at 4 (BIICL Eighth Annual WTO Conference Draft Discussion Paper, May 13 and 14, 2008), *available at* http://www.biicl.org/files/3866_andrew_newcombe.pdf.

65 A series of cases illustrate these variable conceptions of "fair and equitable" treatment. *See* Maffezini.v Kingdom of Spain, ICSID Case No. ARB/97/7, Award on the Merits, ¶ 64 (Nov. 13, 2000), http://italaw.com/documents/Maffezini-Award-English.pdf; MTD Equity Sdn Bhd & MTD Chile SA v. Chile, ICSID Case No. ARB/01/7, ¶ 178 (May 25, 2004), http://italaw.com/documents/MTD-Award.pdf; Ian A Laird, *MTD Equity Sdn Bhd and MTD Chile SA v. Republic of Chile—Recent Developments in the Fair and Equitable Treatment Standard*, Transnat'l Disp. Mgmt (Oct. 2004).

66 *See generally* R. St. J. Macdonald, *The Margin of Appreciation, in* The European System for the Protection of Human Rights 83 (R. St. J. Macdonald et al. eds., 1993); Onder Bakircioglu, *The Application of the Margin of Appreciation Doctrine in Freedom of Expression and Public Morality Cases*, 8 German L. J. 711 (2007); Yuval Shany, *Toward a General Margin of Appreciation Doctrine in International Law?*, 16 Eur. J. Int'l L. 907 (2005); Eyal Benvenisti, *Margin of Appreciation, Consensus, and Universal Standards* 31 N.Y.U. J. Int'l L. & Pol. 843 (1999).

These objections are directed at more than treaty exceptions to standards of treatment accorded to investors from wealthy countries.[67] More accurately, the objection is that wealthy countries are able to impose their model codes and treaties on developing states, along with self-serving substantive intellectual property and other laws.[68] The further objection is that investment arbitrators, in construing those treaties literally, are likely to perpetuate an unequal playing field for investors from poor and lower middle-income states. The result is the protection of the "legitimate expectations" of investors from wealthy states at the expense of the even more legitimate needs of developing states and their subjects.[69]

C. COMPLEXITY AND COST

A functional challenge to ICSID arbitration is the sheer cost and complexity of ICSID proceedings.[70] In addition, arbitration proceedings are also perceived to be dilatory, difficult to manage, disruptive, unpredictable, and not subject to appeal.[71] Coupled with these challenges is the observation that low-income countries lack the resources to bear the legal fees and related costs of defending against well-resourced transnational corporations.[72] Moreover, these countries lack the econometric data

---

67 *See generally* M. Sornarajah, The Norman Paterson School of International Affairs Simon Reisman Lecture in International Trade Policy: The Clash of Globalizations and the International Law on Foreign Investment (Sept. 12, 2002), *as reprinted in* 10 CANADIAN FOREIGN POL'Y 1 (2003) (discussing limitations associated with traditional "international" principles of compensation for expropriation, particularly in relation to developing countries).

68 *See* SUSAN SELL, PRIVATE POWER, PUBLIC LAW: THE GLOBALIZATION OF INTELLECTUAL PROPERTY RIGHTS, ch. 5 (2008).

69 *See, e.g.*, Saluka Inv. BV (Neth) v. Czech, Partial Award, ¶ 304 (Mar. 17, 2006), http://italaw.com/documents/Saluka-PartialawardFinal.pdf (arbitration under the UNCITRAL rules) (noting the "legitimate expectations"); Waste Mgmt, Inc. v. The United Mexican States, ICSID Case No. ARB(AF)/00/3, Final Award, ¶ 98 (NAFTA) (Apr. 30, 2004), http://italaw.com/documents/laudo_ingles.pdf; Int'l Thunderbird Gaming Corp, v. Mex., Award, ¶ 147 (Jan. 26, 2006), http://italaw.com/documents/ThunderbirdAward.pdf (arbitration under the UNCITRAL rules); GAMI Inv. Inc. v. Gov't of the United Mexican States, Final Award, ¶ 100 (Nov. 15, 2004), http://www.state.gov/documents/organization/38789.pdf (Arbitration under the UNCITRAL Rules). *See also* G. C. Christie, *What Constitutes a Taking of Property under International Law?* 38 BRIT Y.B. INT'L L 307, 321–23 (1962); John Herz, *Expropriation of Foreign Property*, 35 AM. J. INT'L L. 243, 251 (1941) (discussing the history of expropriation in international law); Patrick M. Norton, *A Law of the Future or a Law of the Past? Modern Tribunals and the International Law of Expropriation*, 85 AM J. INT'L L. 474, 493 (1991) (discussing also the history of expropriation in international law).

70 *See Schedule of Fees*, INTERNATIONAL CENTRE FOR SETTLEMENT OF INVESTMENT DISPUTES (Jan. 1, 2012), http://icsid.worldbank.org/ICSID/FrontServlet?requestType=ICSIDDocRH&actionVal=scheduledFees&reqFrom=Main (indicating the cost of ICSID arbitration).

71 On the absence of an appeal in ICSID arbitration, see Convention on the Settlement of Investment Disputes between States and Nationals of Other States, Art. 53(1), Apr. 2006, ICSID/15 ("The award . . . shall not be subject to any appeal or to any other remedy except those provided for in this Convention."). The most significant remedy under the ICSID is the annulment of an award under Article 53.

72 See *Schedule of Fees*, *supra* note 70. *See also Memorandum on the Fees and Expenses of ICSID Arbitrators*, INTERNATIONAL CENTRE FOR SETTLEMENT OF INVESTMENT DISPUTES (July 6, 2005), http://icsid.worldbank.org/ICSID/FrontServlet?requestType=ICSIDDocRH&actionVal=Memorandum.

to verify the adverse impact of foreign investment upon their local economies, such as upon the environment.[73]

What developing countries require is the capacity to identify, explore, and verify complex socioeconomic data to defend against the claims of investors from wealthy states. They need to be able to assess dispassionately the net cost and benefit to them of investor–state arbitration, as well as to discrete sectors of their economies. They also need to ascribe costs and benefits to normative values, such as to the political value of adapting their legal systems to the rule-of-law expectations of developed states and their investors. However, trying to generate such complex economic data places developing countries at a comparative disadvantage to developed countries and their investors that have ready access to such data, including from private sector sources. Developing countries are further disadvantaged in utilizing incomplete econometric measures to weigh competing policies in regulating direct foreign investment and in order to defend against foreign investor claims. Finally, yet another disadvantage is that investors from developed countries use precisely such deficiencies in considering whether to mount investor–state arbitration against targeted developing countries.[74]

Concerns about the high costs of investor–state arbitration are not entirely partisan or isolated. The cost hurdles of arbitration are also not limited to developing states and their investors. In fact, studies on conflict resolution in international investor–state arbitration, including by the United Nations Conference on Trade and Development (UNCTAD), level criticism at both investor–state arbitration and litigation on economic grounds, including the high cost of managing disputes generally:

> ... [T]he financial amounts at stake in investor–State disputes are often very high. Resulting from these unique attributes, the disadvantages of international trade and investment arbitration are found to be the large costs involved, the increase in the time frame for claims to be settled, the fact that ISDS cases are increasingly difficult to manage, the fears about frivolous and vexatious claims,

---

73 *See, e.g.*, Hillary French, *Capital Flows and the Environment*, 3(22) Foreign Policy in Focus (Aug. 1998): "As investors search the globe for the highest returns, they are often drawn to places endowed with bountiful natural resources but are handicapped by weak or ineffective environmental laws. Many people and communities are harmed as the environment that sustains them is damaged or destroyed—villages are displaced by the large construction projects, for example, and indigenous people watch their homelands disappear as timber companies level old-growth forests. Foreign investment-fed growth also promotes western-style consumerism, boosting car ownership, paper use, and Big Mac consumption rates towards the untenable levels found in the United States—with grave potential consequences for the health of the natural world, and the stability of the earth's climate, and the security of food supplies." *See also* Economic Watch, *Disadvantages of Foreign Direct Investment* (June 30, 2010), *available at* http://www.economywatch.com/foreign-direct-investment/disadvantages.html.

74 *See also* Andreas von Staden, *Towards Greater Doctrinal Clarity in Investor–State Arbitration: The CMS, Enron and Sempra Annulment Decisions*, 2 Czech Y.B. Int'l L. 207 (2011) (discussing how different investment policies can influence investment law); Susan D. Franck, *Rationalizing Costs in Investment Treaty Arbitration*, 88 Wash. U. L. Rev. 769, 789, 815–16 (2011), *available at* http://papers.ssrn.com/sol3/papers.cfm?abstract_id=1781844 (providing an economic rationalization of the costs of arbitration under investment treaties).

> the general concerns about the legitimacy of the system of investment arbitration as it affects measures of a sovereign State, and the fact that arbitration is focused entirely on the payment of compensation and not on maintaining a working relationship between the parties.[75]

However plausible these concerns may be, the actual cost of an ICSID arbitration is sometimes hard to fathom with accuracy. Some costs are known. For example, the ICSID's memorandum of the fees and expenses of ICSID arbitrators are specified, as of July 6, 2005, on the ICSID Web site. The new Schedule of ICSID Fees came into effect on January 1, 2012.[76] However, the length and complexity of ICSID hearings that have cost implications are usually not known in advance, other than as macro statistics.[77] Similarly the fees of party representatives, primarily lawyers, that may include contingency fees, are often not known.[78] In addition, losing parties, including losing states, sometimes resist publicizing both the costs and results of ICSID awards for fear of diminishing their stature in the global community.[79] Added to this is the tendency of some poorer countries that depend on foreign investment to deflect concerns about the social costs of adverse foreign investments on their domestic economies as they wish to be perceived as being economically and politically stable.[80] Although civic groups from such countries can help to demonstrate the social cost of adverse

---

[75] INVESTOR–STATE DISPUTES: PREVENTION AND ALTERNATIVES TO ARBITRATION, *supra* note 1, at xxiii; *see also* U.N. Conference on Trade & Dev., *Latest Developments in Investor–State Dispute Settlement*, UNCTAD/WEB/DIAE/IA/2010/3 (Mar. 2011), *available at* http://www.unctad.org/en/docs/webdiaeia20113_en.pdf.

[76] *See supra* note 72 (providing further information on costs and fees).

[77] *See, e.g.*, Anthony Sinclair et al., *ICSID Arbitration: How Long Does It Take?* in 4(5) GLOBAL ARB. REV., *available at* http://www.goldreserveinc.com/documents/ICSID%20arbitration%20%20How%20long%20does%20it%20take.pdf.

[78] *See, e.g.*, Hugo Perezcano, *ICSID Arbitrator Fees: Some Pratical Considerations*, *in* TRANSNAT'L DISP. MGMT., *available at* http://www.transnational-dispute-management.com/article.asp?key=674.

[79] In some respects, this is the dilemma of El Salvador in the ongoing case Pacific Rim Cayman LLC v. Republic of El Salvador (ICSID Case No. ARB/09/12). On the one hand, El Salvador seeks to demonstrate a strong interest in denying mining rights to Pacific Rim, notably on grounds of health hazards from mining operations. On the other hand, El Salvador has an interest in presenting itself as a self-determining state that is capable of protecting and sustaining its own public interests. The result is strong public interventions in support of El Salvador, including entreaties to states such as the United States, to pressurize Pacific Rim to withdraw its Claim. This reaction is tempered by caution by El Salvador not to compromise its position as Respondent in the case, and not to undermine its status as a self-determining state. *See, e.g.*, *Voices from El Salvador, available at* http://voiceselsalvador.wordpress.com/2010/05/31/summary-of-day-1-in-the-pacific-rim-v-el-salvador-preliminary-hearings-at-icsid/; *El Salvador Mining Case Could Affect Business in Central America*, INSIDE COUNSEL, Sept. 1, 2011, *available at* http://www.insidecounsel.com/2011/09/01/el-salvador-mining-case-could-affect-business-in-c; *World Bank Tribunal Ruling in El Salvador Mining Case Undermines Democracy*, NETWORK FOR JUSTICE IN GLOBAL INVESTMENT, June 2, 2012, *available at* http://justinvestment.org/2012/06/world-bank-tribunal-ruling-in-el-salvador-mining-case-undermines-democracy/.

[80] *See, e.g.*, Torbjörn Fredriksson, *Forty Years of UNCTAD research on FDI*, 12(3) TRANSNAT'L CORPS. 2003, *available at* http://biblioteca.hegoa.ehu.es/system/ebooks/14053/original/Forty_Years_of_Unctad_Research_on_FDI.pdf.

determinations against their countries, those groups can do so only if they are privy to cost data, only if they can afford to petition to be heard, and only if their petitions are granted.[81]

What are available are rough empirical assertions about the wealth of state parties to ICSID arbitration and foreign investors, albeit with inadequately defined terms and the lack of a detailed and explanatory methodology. For example, 2007 data supposedly evinces that 1.4 percent of all arbitration cases were filed against G8 countries. However, U.S. investors reportedly filed each of those cases. According to the data, investors brought 74 percent of all ICSID cases against so-called middle-income states, while low-income states accounted for 17 percent of ICSID cases.

Evidencing the extent to which large corporations invoked the ICSID was the statement that 20 percent of investors that brought ICSID cases were Fortune 500 companies globally. Seven of these corporate investors were reported as having revenues exceeding the gross national production of the country against which they proceeded, while 48 percent of ICSID/ICSID Additional Facility decisions favored foreign investors.[82]

One can draw equally broad, albeit not necessarily reliable, inferences from this macro data. For example, one inference is that middle-income and, relative to their economic wealth, poorer countries bear the brunt of ICSID arbitration. Furthermore, investors mounting successful claims include a disproportionate number of wealthy transnational corporations. However, that data does not take into account developing countries that settle disputes in advance of investor–state arbitration because they cannot afford the cost or publicity of fending off investor attacks.

The perception of developing countries capitulating to investor demands is not peculiar to investor–state arbitration. For instance, developing countries may also succumb to foreign investor demands because of the cost and reputational damage arising from such arbitration.[83] What is distinctive about investor–state arbitration is that such capitulation can occur in many different ways in investment practice, much of which is difficult to detect in the absence of a public claim or other publicity. All this

[81] *See infra* Section IV(iii) (discussing the plight of civic groups seeking status to file amicus curiae briefs); Stavros Brekoulakis, Third Parties in International Commercial Arbitration (2011) (discussing third parties in international commercial arbitration).

[82] *See, e.g.*, ICSID, Bretton Woods Project (July 14, 2009), *available at* http://www.brettonwoodsproject.org/item.shtml?x=537853. On ICSID's figures, including that investors won 48% of ICSID/Additional Facility cases, see Chart 9 on p. 13 of The ICSID Caseload – Statistics (Issue 2012-2), *available at* http://icsid.worldbank.org/ICSID/FrontServlet?requestType=ICSIDDocRH&actionVal=CaseLoadStatistics. Based on Chart 12 in the same document, ICSID appears to have issued 150 awards in the aggregate. For an empirical analysis of the costs of ISA arbitration, see Susan D. Franck, *Rationalizing Costs in Investment Treaty Arbitration*, *supra* note 74, 769, 789, 815–16 (2011).

[83] *See, e.g.*, Borzu Sabahi, Compensation and Restitution in Investor–State Arbitration: Principles and Practice 143 (2011), discussing arbitration in which Turkey alleged damage to its international reputation as a result of the "jurisdictionally baseless claim asserted in bad faith." http://books.google.com.au/books?id=IP5yMH3IquQC&pg=PA137&lpg=PA137&dq=damage+from+reputation+from+investor+state+arbitration&source=bl&ots=SUXy-r6Hr6&sig=oCK92HXKh5lFFFTC5n-3Xr2CBZw&hl=pt&sa=X&ei=MtT1T4juJ4mroQXcqciqBw&ved=0CEIQ6AEwAA#v=onepage&q=damage%20fr.

makes it more difficult to determine the actual extent of costs, including the social costs of dispute settlement.

In addition, there is no suitable macro data that satisfactorily identifies when and to what extent third parties are involved in investment arbitration proceedings. What is needed, at the outset, is comprehensive information on: the nature of petitions by third parties to participate in ICSID proceedings, when these parties constitute public interest groups in developing countries, the success or failure of their petitions, the reasons provided for that success or failure, and the transparency of the proceedings in which those determinations are reached. Such information could further assist in allaying concerns about biases in arbitration proceedings against developing countries and public interests being represented in those countries.

In contrast, the statistics provided by ICSID on caseload leads to more value-neutral inferences about the nature and significance of its caseload.[84] For example, the ICSID Web site shows the growth of bilateral investment agreements, from the 1959 agreement between West Germany and Pakistan to over 3,000 anticipated by the end of 2012. Foreign direct investment, in turn, has grown geometrically since 1970, exceeding US$1,400 billion in 2009. Developing countries account for a disproportionate share of that growth. The ICSID statistics also demonstrate that ICSID cases arising from the consent of the parties include 63 percent brought under bilateral investment agreements, with 20 percent arising from investor–state agreements.[85]

The ICSID caseload has also grown geometrically, from a single case in 1972 to approximately ten cases in 1990, to thirty-eight new cases filed so far in 2012 alone. However, despite the growth in ICSID cases, the absolute number of ICSID cases is limited compared to international commercial arbitration cases, such as 1,435 claims filed with the China International Economic and Trade Arbitration Commission (CIETAC), 994 cases filed with the International Center for Dispute Resolution (ICDR) of the American Arbitration Centre (AAA), and 795 cases filed with the International Chamber of Commerce (ICC).[86]

Regarding winners and losers in investor–state disputes, the ICSID statistics reveal that 61 percent of cases filed with the ICSID are decided by arbitration tribunal, while 39 percent are settled or otherwise discontinued. In addition, states win ICSID investor–state disputes approximately half of the time. ICSID tribunals dismiss 53 percent of the cases, primarily on jurisdictional grounds. They uphold 46 percent of investor claims in whole or part.[87]

These statistics do not clarify the number of investor claims cases brought by foreign investors from developed countries against less-developed or developing states. Nor do the ICSID statistics establish the extent to which claims for compensation are

---

[84] *See The ICSID Caseload*, available at http://icsid.worldbank.org/ICSID/FrontServlet?requestType=ICSIDDocRH&actionVal=CaseLoadStatistics.

[85] *Id. See also* Andrea M. Steingruber, Consent in International Arbitration (2012).

[86] *Id.*

[87] *Id.*

successful or not. However, it is not reasonable to expect the ICSID to provide such information, given the somewhat arbitrary classification among the wealth of investors on the one hand, and the distinction among developed, developing, and less-developed states on the other hand.

D. THE PUBLIC-PRIVATE NATURE OF ICSID ARBITRATION

A further critique is specific to investor–state arbitration in particular. Investment arbitration, not limited to ICSID, is modeled somewhat on "private" commercial arbitration.[88] Investment arbitrators are ad hoc appointees, not domestic judges holding permanent office.[89] ICSID hearings are often conducted privately.[90] Third parties including civic interest groups are permitted to participate in proceedings only if the disputing parties consent.[91] Arbitration awards are published, again only if the parties agree, or if the applicable investment treaty so provides, such as in U.S. BITs after 2002. However, the ICSID Arbitration Rules do state that "the Centre shall, however, promptly include in its publications excerpts of the legal reasoning of the Tribunal."[92] A review committee with limited authority, which includes no right to overturn an ICSID award on the merits, may review ICSID decisions.[93] A less-than-heartening observation is that annulment proceedings are "not designed to bring about consistency in the interpretation and application of international investment law."[94]

One consequence of private hearings and ad hoc awards is that there is only limited public understanding of the processes through which arbitration institutions such as the ICSID function.[95] There is uncertainty over the limits of investor rights and state

---

[88] *See Rules*, INTERNATIONAL CENTRE FOR SETTLEMENT OF INVESTMENT DISPUTES, http://icsid.worldbank.org/ICSID/FrontServlet?requestType=CasesRH&actionVal=ShowHome&pageName=Rules_Home (last visited June 19, 2012).

[89] *See id.* at Art. 5(3).

[90] *See id.* at Art. 63(a).

[91] *See id.* at Art. 34(2).

[92] *Compare Rules, supra* note 38, Art. 48(4), *with ICSID Additional Facility Arbitration Rules*, Art. 53(3), *available at* http://icsid.worldbank.org/ICSID/ICSID/AdditionalFacilityRules.jsp (last visited June 19, 2012) (almost identical text). *See also* Susan D. Franck, *The Legitimacy Crisis in Investment Treaty Arbitration: Privatizing Public International Law through Inconsistent Decisions*, 73 FORDHAM L. REV. 1521, 1616 (2004–05); Julie A. Maupin, *MFN-Based Jurisdiction in Investor–State Arbitration: Is There Any Hope for a Consistent Approach?*, 14 J. INT'L ECON. L. 157, 162 (2011).

[93] *See, e.g.*, K.V.S.K. NATHAN, THE LAW OF THE INTERNATIONAL CENTRE FOR SETTLEMENT OF INVESTMENT DISPUTES 94 (2000).

[94] *See* M.C.I. Power Grp. L.C. & New Turbine, Inc. v. Ecuador, ICSID Case No. ARB/03/6, Annulment Decision, ¶ 24 (Oct. 19, 2009); *see also* Hochtief AG v. Arg., ICSID Case No. ARB/07/31 (Oct. 7, 2011) (providing in the dissent of Christopher Thomas, Q.C., different interpretations of a treaty in the same case). *See generally* Sergio Puig & Meg Kinnear, *NAFTA Chapter Eleven at Fifteen: Contributions to a Systemic Approach in Investment Arbitration*, 25 ICSID L. REV. 225 (2010) (providing a systematic approach toward investment arbitration through the prism of Chapter 11 of the NAFTA).

[95] For a general discussion, see LUCY REED ET AL. GUIDE TO ICSID ARBITRATION (2004). Preview: http://books.google.pt/books?id=p5KY-Y7jwr4C&printsec=frontcover&hl=pt-PT&source=gbs_ge_summary_r&cad=0#v=onepage&q=understanding&f=false.

powers, and significant variations in the compensation and other remedies that ICSID tribunals award for an expropriation,[96] coupled with uncertain enforcement mechanisms.[97] A related consequence is that ad hoc arbitration processes, deliberations, and determinations are unlikely to lead to uniform investment jurisprudence. It also follows that, absent full access to the records of investment arbitration case documentation and testimony, it is sometimes difficult to draw conclusions about the issues, how they are presented, or how arbitrators construe them. Nor do the ICSID's internal procedures adequately address these issues. ICSID procedures require the Secretary General "to make public, information on the registration of all requests for conciliation or arbitration and to indicate in due course the date and method of the termination of each proceeding."[98] However, the procedures only require the Secretary General to publish reports of conciliation commissions or awards rendered by arbitral tribunals in ICSID proceedings "with the consent of both disputing parties."[99] Similarly, the ICSID procedural rules provide for the manner in which third parties may apply to file amicus curiae briefs, but whether they are permitted to file them in the first place again rests with the disputing parties.[100]

Concern over the uncertain public access to ICSID deliberations is typified in the 2002 ICSID arbitration of *Aguas del Tunari, S.A. v. Republic of Bolivia.*[101] In that case, 300 representatives of social organizations across and beyond Bolivia sought the right to file amicus curiae briefs, as well as to secure access to prosecution and defense statements.[102] They argued that ICSID hearings should be public, and that the arbitrators should visit Cochabamba, Bolivia, where the alleged impact of the investment in dis-

---

96 See Patrick Dumberry, *Satisfaction as a Form of Reparation for Moral Damages Suffered by Investors and Respondent States in Investor–State Arbitration Disputes*, J. Int'l Disp. Settlement 1 (2012), *available at* http://papers.ssrn.com/sol3/papers.cfm?abstract_id=1996500; Patrick Dunaud & Maria Kostytska, *Declaratory Relief in International Arbitration*, 29(1) J. Int'l Arb. 18 (2012); Yaraslau Kryvoi, *Counterclaims in Investor–State Arbitration* 21 Minn. J. Int'l L. (2012), http://papers.ssrn.com/sol3/papers.cfm?abstract_id=1993116.

97 The lack of enforcement mechanisms under the ICSID has given rise to a renewed interest in diplomatic intervention following ICSID awards. *See, e.g.*, Victorino J. Tejera Pérez, *Diplomatic Protection Revival for Failure to Comply with Investment Arbitration Awards*, 10 J. Int'l Disp. Resolution 1093 (2012).

98 *See ICSID Cases*, International Centre for Settlement of Investment Disputes, http://icsid.worldbank.org/ICSID/FrontServlet?requestType=CasesRH&actionVal=ShowHome&pageName=Cases_Home. *See also infra* note 197 (ICSID's procedural Order of Feb. 2, 2011, inviting third parties to apply to submit *amici curiae* briefs under ICSID Arbitration Rule 37(2)).

99 *See* ICSID Rule 27, ICSID Convention, Regulation and Rules, *available at* http://icsid.worldbank.org/ICSID/StaticFiles/basicdoc/CRR_English-final.pdf. On the application of this rule by the ICSID to various awards, see http://icsid.worldbank.org/ICSID/FrontServlet?requestType=CasesRH&actionVal=ShowHome&pageName=Cases_Home

100 *See infra* notes 105–06.

101 *See* Aguas del Tunari, S.A. v. Bol., ICSID Case No. ARB/02/3 (Oct. 21, 2005), *available at* http://ita.law.uvic.ca/documents/AguasdelTunari-jurisdiction-eng_000.pdf.

102 *See id.*

pute was most profound.[103] Six months later, the ICSID Tribunal responded that it lacked authority to decide such matters, which rested with the parties.[104]

A comparable result occurred in 2005 when a coalition of organizations from Argentina sought information about, and the right to participate in, the ICSID arbitration in *Suez, Sociedad General de Aguas de Barcelona S.A., and Vivendi Universal S.A. v. Republic of Argentina*.[105] In responding to that petition, the Tribunal acknowledged that the case "potentially involved matters of public interest and human rights" and that the public access "would have the additional desirable consequence of increasing the transparency of investor–state arbitration."[106] However, the petition was denied because the corporate complainant refused access, although the government of Argentina clearly would have allowed it.[107]

One result of the public–private nature of ICSID awards is that, despite an increase in the number of published ICSID awards, the right to deny public access to them still rests significantly with the parties, not with the ICSID or the presiding arbitrators.[108] ICSID parties may have good reason to deny public access to awards[109] and whether those reasons are in the public interest is open to debate in discrete cases. The winds of change are nevertheless blowing. In October 2003, the NAFTA Free Trade Commission issued an Interpretative Statement saying "no provision of the North American Free Trade Agreement limits a Tribunal's discretion to accept written submissions from a person or entity that is not a disputing party."[110] Given that investor–state arbitration under the

---

[103] *See id.*

[104] *See generally* Alexandre de Gramont, *After the Water War: The Battle for Jurisdiction in* Aguas Del Tunari, S.A. v. Republic of Bolivia, TRANSNAT'L DISP. MGMT. (Dec. 2006); Kenneth J. Vandevelde, *Aguas del Tunari, S.A. v. Republic of Bolivia*, 101 AM J. INT'L. L. 179 (2007).

[105] *See* Suez v. Arg., ICSID Case No. ARB/03/19, Order in Response to a Petition by Five Non-Governmental Organizations for Permission to Make an Amicus Curiae Submission (Feb. 12, 2007). The petition challenged the decision by the government of Argentina to accede to the ICSID treaty, on grounds that it violates the constitutional guarantees of citizens of Argentina to participate in proceedings. Although the government of Argentina was willing to hear the petition, the complainant company was not. However, the attorney general of Argentina published on the Internet the information in his possession on the related cases. *See generally* Carlos E. Alfaro & Pedro M. Lorenti, *The Growing Opposition of Argentina to ICSID Arbitral Tribunals: A Conflict between International and Domestic Law?*, 6 J. WORLD INV. & TRADE 417 (2005)

[106] *See* Suez v. Arg., ICSID Case No. ARB/03/19, Order in Response to a Petition for Transparency and Participation as *Amicus Curiae*, ¶¶ 19, 22 (May 19, 2005).

[107] *See* Suez v. Arg., ICSID Case No ARB/03/19, Order in Response to a Petition by Five Non-Governmental Organizations for Permission to Make an Amicus Curiae Submission (Feb. 12, 2007).

[108] *See, e.g., supra* note 91.

[109] *See infra* Part IV(ii).

[110] *See Statement of the Free Trade Commission on Non-Disputing Party Participation*, NAFTA FREE TRADE COMMISSION (Oct. 7, 2003), *available at* http://www.international.gc.ca/trade-agreements-accords-commerciaux/assets/pdfs/Nondisputing-en.pdf. For different reactions to "requests" by civic interest groups to submit public interest briefs, see, e.g., GEA Grp. Aktiengesellschaft v. Ukr., ICSID Case No. ARB/08/16, Award (Mar. 31, 2011), http://icsid.worldbank.org/ICSID/FrontServlet?requestType=CasesRH&actionVal=showDoc&docId=DC2131_En&caseId=C440; Talsud, S.A. v. Mex., ICSID Case No. ARB(AF)/04/4, Award (June 16, 2010), http://icsid.worldbank.org/ICSID/FrontServlet?requestType=CasesRH&actionVal=showDoc&docId=DC2112_En&caseId=C41; Gemplus, S.A. v. Mex., ICSID Case No. ARB(AF)/04/3, Award (June 16, 2010), http://icsid.worldbank.org/ICSID/FrontServlet?requestType=CasesRH&actionVal=showDoc&docId=DC2112_En&caseId=C41.

NAFTA is sometimes conducted under the ICSID's auspices, this development is of some significance. Furthermore, in 2006, the ICSID adopted a new Rule 37 that provides tribunals with at least some discretion to admit third party submissions.[111] In addition, the admission of amicus curiae briefs is increasingly endorsed within new bilateral investment agreements.[112] These developments will be discussed in Sections IV and V below.

E. LOOKING AHEAD

It may be observed that wealthy developed countries are conceivably less directly interested in the transparency of ICSID proceedings and the publicity of awards than poorer countries because wealthy countries are less frequently the defending parties in ICSID proceedings.[113] An opposing observation is that wealthy countries have credible reasons to support transparent ICSID proceedings, if only to avoid the criticism that they have sought to perpetuate the ICSID in their own image.[114] A mediated proposition is that wealthy countries are likely to adopt double standards in regard to ICSID arbitration. On the one hand, they favor arbitration to restrain "interference" by foreign governments with private investment. On the other hand, they disfavor ICSID arbitration filed against them.[115] A sobering observation is that academic and NGO speculation about the positions taken by various types of states on transparency issues is often greatly at odds with actual positions publicly taken by states, casting doubt on some of the arguments above.[116]

The view of the ICSID as an instrument of prosperous nations of the North exploiting the poorer nations of the South is offset by at least two related developments in the global economic order. First, investors from some developing countries, such as China and India as growing capital exporters, have increasing economic incentives to mount ICSID claims including against developed countries that are now capital importers. This developed is evident in the recent ICSID claim filed by China's second largest life insurance company, Ping An, against Belgium for US$2.2 billion arising from Ping An's investment in the failed Belgo-Dutch bank, Fortis.[117] The result is that wealthy

---

111 *See* Convention on the Settlement of Investment Disputes between States and Nationals of Other States, Rules of Procedure for Arbitration Proceedings (Arbitration Rules), Rule 37, Apr. 2006, ICSID/15, *available at* http://icsid.worldbank.org/ICSID/StaticFiles/basicdoc/CRR_English-final.pdf (Visits and Inquiries; Submissions of Non-Disputing Parties).

112 *See infra* Section VI.

113 See *ICSID—International Centre for Settlement of Investment Disputes* (July 14, 2009), *available at* http://www.brettonwoodsproject.org/item.shtml?x=537853.

114 *See* SORNARAJAH, *supra* note 13, ch. 2 (arguing that the primary interests of wealthy developed states are economic and less about perception of bullying).

115 *See* Guillermo Aguilar Alvarez & William W. Park, *The New Face of Investment Arbitration: NAFTA Chapter 11*, 28 YALE J. INT'L L. 365, 368–69 (2003) (discussing the U.S. alleged double standard in favor ing resorting to arbitration to restrain interference by foreign governments with private investment while disfavoring arbitration filed against the U.S. government).

116 See Mark Kantor, *The Transparency Agenda for UNCITRAL Investment Arbitrations: Looking in All the Wrong Places*, *available at* http://www.iilj.org/research/documents/IF2010-11.Kantor.pdf.

117 See Ping An Life Insurance Company of China, Limited and Ping An Insurance (Group) Company of China, Limited v. Kingdom of Belgium (ICSID Case No. ARB/12/29). China is a clear example of a capital

developed countries that are more dependent on imported capital investments are increasingly likely to be the subject of ICSID claims.[118] Second, investors from developing countries are ever more likely to file investment claims against other developing countries, given the divergence in their economic, political, and social stature and the prospect of adversarial investor–state relationships. Such changes in the new global economic order are likely to evolve slowly. However, it is notable that the first such ICSID arbitration was filed by a Malaysian construction company against China in May 2011,[119] but suspended on July 22, 2011, pursuant to an agreement between the parties.[120] This case is further evidence that foreign investors from developing countries are willing to mount investor–state claims against economically powerful countries such as China. However, the strong reaction of China to that claim and the circumstances surrounding its withdrawal suggest that claims against states such as China are likely to encounter strenuous resistance.[121]

A further challenge for the ICSID is that investor–state disputes that are submitted to it will decline due to the consolidation of bilateral investment treaties, possibly leading to a reduction in the number of ICSID disputes. This challenge could result from a recent recommendation by the Commission of the European Union that only the EU, and not individual EU Member States, can conclude bilateral treaties with non-EU countries.[122] Given that the EU itself cannot submit disputes to the ICSID because the EU is not a Member State, claims against the EU brought by foreign investors cannot be submitted to the ICSID. Given the further fact that Germany, Switzerland, and France have concluded more bilateral investment treaties individually with non-EU states than

---

importer that is increasingly a capital exporter. *See, e.g.*, Ted Planfker, *Doing Business in China: How to Profit in the World's Fastest Growing Market* (2008), *available at* http://www.amazon.com/s/?url=search-alias=stripbooks&field-keywords=044669696X&tag=technicalibra-0&link_code=wql&camp=212361&creative=380601&_encoding=UTF-8; Li Yong & Jonathan Reuvid, *Doing Business with China* (GMB Pub., 2006), *available at* http://www.amazon.com/Doing-Business-China-Lord-Brittan/dp/1905050089/ref=sr_1_1?s=books&ie=UTF8&qid=1341704036&sr=1-1&keywords=1905050089#reader_B0015T65F4.

118 For example, the United States and the European Union, once predominantly capital exporters, are increasingly capital importers. China, once a significant capital importer, is now a significant capital exporter as well. *See* QingJiang Kong, *U.S.-China Bilateral Investment Treaty Negotiations: Context, Focus, and Implications,* 7 Asian J. WTO & Int'l Health L. & Pol'y 18 (2012). *See generally* Lauge N. Skovgaard Poulsen, *Investment Treaties and the Globalisation of State Capitalism: Opportunities and Constraints for Host States, in* Prospects in International Investment Law and Policy (R. Echandi & P. Sauvé, eds. 2012), *available at* http://papers.ssrn.com/sol3/papers.cfm?abstract_id=2050919.

119 *See* Ekran Berhad v. People's Republic of China, ICSID Case No. ARB/11/15 (May 24, 2011), http://icsid.worldbank.org/ICSID/FrontServlet?requestType=CasesRH&reqFrom=ListCases&caseId=C1600&actionVal=viewCase.

120 *See* http://icsid.worldbank.org/ICSID/FrontServlet?requestType=CasesRH&reqFrom=ListCases&caseId=C1600&actionVal=viewCase.

121 *See further* Leon E. Trakman, *China and State-Investor Arbitration, available at* SSRN, http://papers.ssrn.com/sol3/papers.cfm?abstract_id=2157387

122 On these recent developments, see European Commission, *Proposal for a Regulation of the European Parliament and of the Council, Establishing a Framework for Managing Financial Responsibility Linked to Investor–State Dispute Settlement Tribunals Established by International Agreements to which the European Union Is Party* (Brussels, Belgium, 21/06/2012), *available at* http://trade.ec.europa.eu/doclib/docs/2012/june/tradoc_149567.pdfBrussels, 21.6.2012.

any other country, except for China, and that the EU may prohibit such treaties in the future, this could cause a decline in investor–state claims against individual EU members submitted to the ICSID. A presumed incidental beneficiary of this decline in ICSID cases is likely to be the UNCITRAL because it does not require that the respondent in investor–state disputes be states.[123] It is too early to predict with conviction that these results will eventuate in fact. In particular, the EU Commission's report is a recommendation to the EU Council, which consists of all the members of the EU; it is apparent that a number of EU Members are opposed to the EU having exclusive authority to negotiate investment treaties with non-EU members. It is also possible that the EU will reach a compromise in which the EU and individual countries jointly conclude investment treaties with non-EU countries. Finally, these developments do not ordinarily preclude a foreign investor from making a claim against a state party to an enforceable investment treaty, including between a EU Member State and a non-EU state.

III. A FUNCTIONAL DEFENSE OF THE ICSID

A defense of investor–state arbitration under the ICSID is that, although not giving rise to judicial precedent, ICSID jurisprudence is nevertheless more certain and more stable than a myriad of national courts applying divergent domestic laws to investor–state disputes. Importantly, investor–state arbitration can help to produce a body of international investment law that is more coherent than the judicial endorsement of investment laws that diverge from one national legal system to the next.[124]

A further defense is that the ICSID is not the archetype villain that surreptitiously protects investors from wealthy countries at the expense of poorer developing countries with impoverished populations. Developing countries presumably enter into investment agreements that include arbitration by taking the calculated risk that the economic and social benefits of such agreements outweigh their costs. In doing so, they weigh the competing options, such as not entering into investment agreements, or entering into such agreements with dispute prevention and avoidance options and/or resorting to domestic courts to resolve investor–state disputes.[125] However, whether

---

[123] On the distinctive attributes of the investment arbitration under the UNCITRAL Rules, including that member states need not be parties to UNCITRAL proceedings, *see* 2010 UNCITRAL Rules on Arbitration, *available at* http://www.uncitral.org/uncitral/uncitral_texts/arbitration/2010Arbitration_rules.html. *See also* Claudia M. Gross, *Current Work of UNCITRAL on Transparency in Treaty-Based Investor–State Arbitration*, *available at* http://www.oecd.org/dataoecd/14/5/46770295.pdf.

[124] Kenneth Vandevelde writes that in 1969 there were only seventy-five BITs. During the 1970s, nine BITs were negotiated each year; that rate doubled in the 1980s and increased significantly in the 1990s. However, it has slowed in the last five years, but with noticeable growth in 2012. *See* Kenneth Vandevelde, *A Brief History of International Investment Agreements*, 12 U.C. DAVIS J. INT'L L & POL'Y 157, 172 (2005). *See also* U.N. Conference on Trade & Dev. *Recent Developments in International Investment Agreements*, U.N. Doc. UNCTAD/WEB/ITE/IIT/2005/1 (Aug. 30, 2005).

[125] *See infra* Section VI (discussing dispute prevention and avoidance options, propagated by the UNCTAD).

developing countries, unlike developed countries such as Australia,[126] have the political and economic influence to negotiate agreements in which domestic courts resolve investor–state disputes is not self-evident. Indeed, for some developing countries, concluding bilateral investment treaties is a means of economic survival, not a dispensable luxury.[127]

A countervailing macro argument is that developing states have contributed to their own economic disadvantages. According to this argument, they have concluded bilateral investment treaties ill-advisedly, on terms that privilege their investment partners.[128] They have also failed to protect themselves en masse against the institutional and structural biases that inhere in bilateral investment agreements that incorporate investor–state arbitration. Moreover, they have acted unilaterally when they should have devised a multilateral strategy to thwart these structural biases. These criticisms are harsh. A willingness to enter into bilateral investment agreements is not in itself cogent evidence of complicity by developing states in perpetuating their or their investors' economic disadvantages. Rather, for many developing countries, succumbing to the demands of a dominant treaty partner is preferable, on balance, to concluding no treaty at all.

Further, it must be acknowledged that an ever-growing number of ICSID members are from developing countries.[129] ICSID members also conclude second- and third-generation bilateral investment agreements in which newly prosperous developing countries, such as China, not only include ICSID arbitration in their bilateral investment agreements, but also affirm their commitment to the rule of law in relation to the

126 The Australian government is the first developed state to openly declare that it will no longer agree to the adoption of arbitration within its bilateral trade and investment treaties, and that, henceforth, it will negotiate that investment disputes with foreign investors be heard by domestic courts of law. *See* Dept. of Foreign Affairs and Trade, Austl. Gov't, *Gillard Government Trade Policy Statement: Trading Our Way to More Jobs and Prosperity*, 14 (Apr. 12, 2011), *available at* http://www.dfat.gov.au/publications/trade/trading-our-way-to-more-jobs-and-prosperity.pdf#investor-state [hereinafter Policy]. *See also* Luke Peterson, *Australia Rejects Investor–State Arbitration Provision in Trade Agreements*, Don't Trade Our Lives Away (Apr. 19, 2011), *available at* http://donttradeourlivesaway.wordpress.com/2011/04/19/australia-rejects-investor-state-arbitration-provision-in-trade-agreements/ (providing an incisive commentary on the Australian government's Policy announced in April 2011); Leon E. Trakman, *Investor State Arbitration or Local Courts: Will Australia Set a New Trend?*, 46 J. World Trade 83 (2012).

127 Such dependence includes the need to attract foreign investment to sustain economic growth in, among other sectors, essential social services and programs. *See* Leon E. Trakman, *Foreign Direct Investment: Hazard or Opportunity?*, 41 Geo. Wash. Int'l. L. Rev. 1 (2010).

128 *See, e.g.*, http://www.downtoearth.org.in/content/secretive-tribunals-hidden-damages. Here, Van Harten observes that developing countries sometimes are the target of treaties directed at enhancing opportunities for foreign investors from other states, on occasion leading to significant losses for those target countries.

129 *See* U.N. Conference on Trade & Dev, World Investment Report 2010, at xxv, U.N. Doc. UNCTAD/WIR/2010, U.N. Sales No. E.10.II.D.2 (2010) [hereinafter World Investment Report 2010]; *see also* Stanimir A. Alexandrov, *The "Baby Boom" of Treaty-Based Arbitrations and the Jurisdiction of ICSID Tribunals: Shareholders as "Investors" and Jurisdiction* Ratione Temporis, 4 Law & Prac. Int'l Courts & Tribunals 19, 19–20, 58 (2005).

rights of foreign traders and investors.[130] Developing countries are also increasingly parties to bilateral investment treaties: the total number of international investment agreements has grown to more than 3,000 today.[131] In addition, ICSID has expanded geometrically from 20 members in 1966 to 158 members today that, again, now include most developing countries.[132] Furthermore, ICSID annual revenues arising in part from disputes between member states and investors have increased from $2,270,000 in 2000 to over $25 million in 2010;[133] two-thirds of these revenues derive from investment arbitration disputes that, again, include developing countries.[134]

The problem with these arguments is that the political impetus for entering into bilateral free trade and investment agreements still lies significantly more with developed than developing states. Dissatisfaction among developed states with multilateral trade and investment initiatives, notably expressed in the World Trade Organization (WTO), somewhat fuel that impetus. Developed countries discernibly conclude bilateral trade and investment agreements outside the WTO fabric to avoid a multilateral trade and investment regime in which developing states have the numerical superiority, the will, and sometimes the capacity, to exercise their power collectively.[135]

It is not fitting to blame the ICSID for the development of bilateral investment treaties between state parties that include both developed and developing countries, as the ICSID is not itself a party to such treaties. It is also not entirely reasonable to accuse foreign investors that proceed against "home" states of unbridled opportunism when they rely on treaties between "home" and developing "host" states in conducting their trade and investment abroad. For one thing, foreign investors from developed countries are not uniformly prosperous any more than investors from developing states are uniformly underprivileged. In addition, home states do not ordinarily collude with their small and medium scale investors abroad in order to secure a political or economic advantage for those investors in host states. Home states often have both a political and an economic incentive not to become unduly embroiled in individual investor claims against host states. The political incentive is for states, both developed and developing, to avoid alienating host states by supporting claims by home state

---

130 *See* Randall Peerenboom, China's Long March toward Rule of Law 450 (2002) (arguing that "[o]ne of the main motivating forces behind China's turn toward rule of law has been the belief that legal reforms are necessary for economic development.").

131 *See* World Investment Report 2010, *supra* note 129, at xxv.

132 *See Member States*, International Centre for Settlement of Investment Disputes, http://icsid.worldbank.org/ICSID/FrontServlet?requestType=CasesRH&actionVal=ShowHome&pageName=MemberStates_Home (last visited June 19, 2012) (current membership).

133 *See ICSID Annual Report*, International Centre for Settlement of Investment Disputes, http://icsid.worldbank.org/ICSID/FrontServlet?requestType=ICSIDPublicationsRH&actionVal=ViewAnnualReports (last visited June 19, 2012).

134 *See The ICSID Caseload—Statistics*, International Centre for Settlement of Investment Disputes, http://icsid.worldbank.org/ICSID/FrontServlet?requestType=ICSIDDocRH&actionVal=CaseLoadStatistics (last visited June 19, 2011) (illustrating the proportion of arbitration disputes that include developing countries).

135 *See* Leon E. Trakman, *The Proliferation of Free Trade Agreements: Bane or Beauty?* 42 J. World Trade 367, 378, 385–86 (2008).

investors. The economic incentive for host states to avoid intervening on behalf of its foreign investors is to limit the political risks as well as the administrative costs of such intervention.[136]

It is also not reasonable to blame the ICSID for all the ills imputed to the operation of investment arbitration generally. This is because the ICSID's formal function is to provide a process by which to resolve investment disputes between signatory states to the ICSID Convention and foreign investors from other signatory states. The result is that the ICSID operates within the radar of its administrative council, and it does not impose itself on those members.[137]

The law of the ICSID, arguably, is also not profoundly out of step with the law applied to investment disputes generally. Notwithstanding variations among investment treaties and differences in investment jurisprudence itself, the ICSID has contributed to a body of investment law that includes established standards of treatment that are applied to foreign investors.[138] However, although these standards are sometimes fragmented and it is difficult to derive cohesive principles from ad hoc and unpublished ICSID awards, an international investment jurisprudence does exist.[139] Even though the ICSID has had to deal with a plethora of bilateral investment agreements, it has helped to resolve complex investor–state disputes arising from investment treaties.[140] Nor should the ICSID Secretariat be blamed when ICSID proceedings are not transparent and awards are not published.[141] After all, ICSID members that are and represent nation states approve the rules governing ICSID procedures. It is also unfair to accuse the ICSID of inconsistencies in reasoning and determinations reached by ICSID arbitrators who, although assisted by the ICSID, reach decisions independently of it.[142]

---

136 *But see* Pérez, *supra* note 97 on the probable increase in diplomatic intervention by home states on behalf of their foreign investors in dealing with host states.

137 *See* Structure of the ICSID Administrative Council, ICSID Web site, *available at* http://icsid.worldbank.org/ICSID/FrontServlet?requestType=CasesRH&actionVal=RightFrame&FromPage=Organization%20and%20Structure&pageName=Organization.

138 This contribution of the ICSID to international investment law is apparent from the ICSID REVIEW—FOREIGN INVESTMENT LAW JOURNAL, available on the ICSID Web site at http://icsid.worldbank.org/ICSID/FrontServlet?requestType=ICSIDBibliographyRH&actionVal=IcsidReview.

139 *See, e.g.*, TRAKMAN & RANIERI, *supra* note 2; SORNARAJAH, *supra* note 13; SCHILL, *supra* note 8, at VII. *See generally* DOLZER & SCHREUER, *supra* note 6; Wenhua Shan & Sheng Zhang, *The Treaty of Lisbon: Half Way toward a Common Investment Policy*, 21 EUR. J. INT. L. 1049 (2010).

140 *See, e.g.*, Aurélia Antonietti, *The 2006 Amendments of the ICSID Rules and Regulations and the Additional Facility Rules*, 21 ICSID REV.— FOR. INV. L.J. 427 (2006) (discussing how various arbitration tribunals have resolved complex issues).

141 *See generally* James Harrison, *Recent Developments to Promote Transparency and Public Participation in Investment Treaty Arbitration* (University of Edinburgh Law School Working Paper No. 2011/01, 2011), *available at* http://papers.ssrn.com/sol3/papers.cfm?abstract_id=1739181 (providing a balanced defense of transparency in ICSID proceedings).

142 On consistency in international investment arbitration, see INTERNATIONAL INVESTMENT LAW AND GENERAL INTERNATIONAL LAW: FROM CLINICAL ISOLATION TO SYSTEMIC INTEGRATION? (Rainer Hofmann & Christian Tams eds., 2011); Jan Paulsson, *International Arbitration and the Generation of Legal Norms: Treaty Arbitration and International Law*, *in* INTERNATIONAL ARBITRATION 2006: BACK TO BASICS? (International Council for Commercial Arbitration Congress Series No. 13) 879 (Albert Jan van den Berg ed., 2007). On the critique of allegedly inconsistent ICSID decisions in a series of

This is not to suggest that ICSID operations are beyond reproach. Specifically, although not a party to bilateral investment agreements, the ICSID may nevertheless be an instrument that dominant treaty parties try to utilize to perpetuate their control over investment markets.[143] However, railing against the ICSID as a prop for capitalist excesses makes it harder to repair those parts of it that are in need of repair while leaving intact those parts that work fairly and well.

Further, potential divisions among developing states in treaty making and the interpretation of these treaties by ICSID tribunals are not issues to be ignored. A challenge ahead for ICSID tribunals is in reconciling the traditional liberty of states to conclude treaties with their obligation to protect private property in the face of emerging global powers such as China whose full endorsement of those liberties is sometimes questioned. However much China has embarked along the road to the rule of law, investment tribunals may still diverge over the significanceof that passage in particular cases. In addition, it is harder to categorize China as a typical developing state in light of its enormous economic resources and global political power. Further, China's defense of social programs, such as protecting its rural sectors from foreign investment, is not wholly distinct from American and European protection of sectors that those countries regard as vulnerable.[144] Comparable issues may well arise in relation to India as it shifts from being a capital importer to a global capital exporter.[145]

IV. REFORMING THE ICSID FROM WITHIN

Concerns about the ICSID's operations are sporadic, uneven in gravity, and lack a unified voice. Governments are understandably cautious about taking critical positions against institutions such as the ICSID, in part because they cannot be sure when they may become embroiled, directly or indirectly, in an investment dispute before the ICSID. Moreover, developed and developing governments, ICSID Administrative Council members, and ICSID officials do not ordinarily retain office sufficiently long to both initiate and effectuate ICSID reform. The nature of reforming the ICSID is also subject to debate including whether the ICSID has the moral authority and collective will to produce those changes.

---

investment claims against Argentina, commencing with the *CMS*, *Enron*, and *Sempra* cases, see *infra* notes 216–218.

143 *See supra* Part II(i).

144 *See* Karl P. Sauvant, Lisa Sachs, Ken Davies & Ruben Zandvliet Vale, *FDI Perspectives: Issues in International Investment*, Part 2 (Vale Columbia Center on Sustainable International Investment, Jan. 2011), *available at* http://www.vcc.columbia.edu/files/vale/content/PerspectivesEbook.pdf; Olivier De Schutter & Peter Rosenblum, *Large-Scale Investments in Farmland: The Regulatory Challenge*, *in* YEARBOOK ON INTERNATIONAL INVESTMENT LAW & POLICY 2010–2011 (Karl P. Sauvant ed., 2012).

145 *See generally* PEERENBOOM, *supra* note 130, chs. 6, 10 (discussing China's progression toward the rule of law).

A. ICSID SECRETARIAT DISCUSSION PAPER

Internally generated reforms of the ICSID began in October 2004 with a discussion paper prepared by the ICSID Secretariat, entitled *Possible Improvements of the Framework for ICSID Arbitration*.[146] The Secretariat then presented its paper for response to the Administrative Council of the ICSID, to investment arbitrators, selected investors, and an undefined number of groups within civil society.[147]

The rationale behind the discussion paper was that the ICSID Secretariat, an expert body, should assume a leadership role in reforming the structure and operation of the ICSID and in rendering it more transparent, consultative, and effective.[148]

The paper identified two overriding issues: a lack of transparency in ICSID proceedings and a lack of public participation in and access to ICSID awards. It also dealt with disclosure requirements for arbitrators and with arbitrators' fees.[149] The paper's key proposals included: encouraging the endorsement of amicus curiae briefs being admitted into arbitral proceedings and promoting the publication of arbitral awards.[150] These proposals implicitly addressed the lack of transparency and publicity in prior cases such as *Aguas del Tunari S.A. v. Republic of Bolivia* in which the Tribunal denied third party participation in ICSID proceedings, primarily on public interest grounds.[151]

The responses to the proposals at the time were uneven at best. Neither developed or developing countries, nor investor constituencies adopted unified positions to address them.[152]

Notwithstanding the expectation that key developed states might oppose the Report, the United States and Canada supported it, although few other developed states did so as well. Of note, a think tank on trade and investment in Canada, the International Institute for Sustainable Development (IISD), supported it.[153] IISD favored wider public participation in ICSID proceedings through the admission of amicus briefs and

---

146 *See* International Centre for Settlement of Investment Disputes, *Suggested Changes to the ICSID Rules and Regulations* (ICSID Secretariat Working Paper, 2005), *available at* http://icsid.worldbank.org/ICSID/FrontServlet?requestType=ICSIDPublicationsRH&actionVal=ViewAnnouncePDF&AnnouncementType=archive&AnnounceNo=22_1.pdf [hereinafter Working Paper].

147 *See id.* at 3.

148 For critical but also supportive reflections on how the ICSID Secretariat's framed its proposals, notably in relation to sustainable development, see Howard Mann, Aaron Cosbey, Luke Peterson & Konrad von Moltke, Comments on ICSID Discussion Paper *Possible Improvements of the Framework for ICSID Arbitration, International Institute for Sustainable Development* (Dec. 2004), *available at* http://www.iisd.org/pdf/2004/investment_icsid_response.pdf. The ICSID Working Paper nevertheless uses fairness neutrally without reference to the systemic disadvantage of developing state parties. It provides for participation of third parties if the Tribunal is satisfied that the "non-disputing party has a significant interest in the dispute and that this would not disrupt the proceeding or unfairly burden either party." *See* Working Paper at 11.

149 *See id.* at 10–11 (Access to Third Parties), 12–13 (Publication of Awards).

150 *See id.* at 9, 11.

151 *See* Aguas del Tunari, S.A. v. Bol., ICSID Case No. ARB/02/3, *supra* notes 101–104.

152 *See* text immediately below. For criticism of the Report, *see infra* notes 157-161.

153 *See* Mann et al., *supra* note 148 (generally supporting the suggestions).

argued that doing so would benefit disputing parties in general, and would not be cost prohibitive for civic groups of member states.[154] It further proposed that the ICSID would benefit from public participation arising from amicus briefs, and that this would promote transparent and cost-effective proceedings.[155] It also noted that public participation in WTO proceedings had not led to any significant increase in the costs or administrative superstructure of the WTO.[156]

Furthermore, despite the prospect that developing states would support the Secretariat's proposals favoring more transparent proceedings, the South Centre, an intergovernmental organization of developing states in Geneva, initially argued that the ICSID Secretariat lacked the authority to reach such determinations.[157] It observed that transparent ICSID proceedings would advantage developed states and their investors who had more resources to participate in proceedings than developing states and their investors.[158] The South Centre also suggested that some developing states would prefer private to public arbitration proceedings, presumably for varied and not necessarily consistent reasons.[159] Interestingly, the South Centre did not persist with its objections, but the sting of its initial onslaught on the proposed reform of the ICSID remained.[160] One inference from these reactions to the ICSID Secretariat's proposals is that it is difficult to please everyone all the time. A more troubling reaction is that the resistance to public interest interventions are not limited to foreign investors that wish to exclude third parties for commercial "in confidence" reasons. Despite strong public interest grounds favoring amicus curiae briefs in support of respondent developing states, those states sometimes have countervailing interests to exclude third party testimony that bolsters the claims of foreign investor claimants.[161]

However seemingly irreconcilable some of these reactions are to the ICSID proposals, they underlie a deeper problem. Specifically, the ICSID Secretariat lacks the legal authority to initiate substantial reform.[162] First, it cannot promise authoritative time-

[154] *See id.* at 8–10.

[155] *See id.* at 8.

[156] *See id.* at 9.

[157] *See* South Centre, *South Centre Analytical Note: Developments on Discussions for the Improvement of the Framework for ICSID Arbitration and the Participation of Developing Countries* 5–7 (Feb. 2005), *available at* http://www.southcentre.org/index.php?option=com_content&view=article&id=387%3Adevelopments-on-discussions-for-the-improvement-of-the-framework-for-icsid-arbitration-and-the-participation-of-developing-countries&catid=68%3Ainternational-taxation-investment-a-financing-for&Itemid=67&lang=es.

[158] *Id.* at 11–12.

[159] *Id.* at 13.

[160] *See, e.g.*, Mark Kantor, *Criticism of ICSID Reform Proposals by South Centre*, Transnational 3 Dispute Management (2005), *available at* http://www.transnational-dispute-management.com/article.asp?key=439.

[161] This objection to third-party interventions is reflected in the initial attack by the South Centre, representing developing countries, to the reforms proposed by the ICSID, including in support of third-party interventions. *See supra* note 157.

[162] *See* functions of the ICSID Secretariat: http://icsid.worldbank.org/ICSID/FrontServlet. There is no indication of any such legal authority inhering in the ICSID. Its role is supportive and facultative. *See further* http://icsid.worldbank.org/ICSID/FrontServlet?requestType=CasesRH&actionVal=Right

lines and procedures for the implementation of reforms, let alone promise reform.[163] Second, a practical limitation is that ICSID officials who championed the proposals were not in office sufficiently long to shepherd them to fruition.[164] A debatable inference perhaps is that the Secretariat did not adequately cultivate the ICSID Council's support or distribute its report sufficiently widely to public interest groups.[165]

However, the recommendations of the ICSID Secretariat did not go entirely unheeded. In 2006, the ICSID added a new Rule 37 to its Rules of Procedure.[166] That Rule provided that a tribunal may admit the brief of a non-disputing party (after consulting the direct parties) that addresses "a matter within the scope of the dispute."[167]

Nevertheless, the discretion the ICSID accorded to a tribunal is decidedly limited. In considering whether to admit the brief of a non-disputing party, Rule 37(2) stipulates that the Tribunal must consider, among other factors, the extent to which:

(a) the non-disputing party submission would assist the Tribunal in the determination of a factual or legal issue related to the proceeding by bringing a perspective, particular knowledge or insight that is different from that of the disputing parties; (b) the non-disputing party submission would address a matter within the scope of the dispute; (c) the non-disputing party has a significant interest in the proceeding.[168] As a further qualification, Rule 37 requires that the Tribunal "shall ensure that the non-disputing party submission does not disrupt the proceeding or unduly burden or unfairly prejudice either party, and that both parties are given an opportunity to present their observations on the non-disputing party submission."[169]

This 2006 Rule 37(2) on the Submissions of Non-Disputing Parties is limited in key respects. First, tribunals are likely to construe the need for a non-disputing party to have a "sufficient interest" as requiring it to demonstrate that it has a "public interest." The alternative that a non-disputing party need only have a "sufficient" interest to participate in ICSID proceedings could lead to a floodgate of interpleader claims by private parties asserting that an investor–state dispute has or will have a direct impact

---

Frame&FromPage=Organization%20and%20Structure&pageName=Organization. *But cf* the authority of the Secretary General of the ICSID to decline to register a request for arbitration. *See* Sergio Puig & Chester W. Brown, THE SECRETARY-GENERAL'S POWER TO REFUSE TO REGISTER A REQUEST FOR ARBITRATION UNDER THE ICSID CONVENTION, ICSID REV.—FOR. INV. L.J. (2012), *available at* http://papers.ssrn.com/sol3/papers.cfm?abstract_id=2045645.

163 At the level of policy, such responsibilities rest with the Administrative Council of the ICSID. Applying such policy rests with ICSID arbitration tribunals. See *Organizational Structure of ICSID*, INTERNATIONAL CENTRE FOR SETTLEMENT OF INVESTMENT DISPUTES, http://icsid.worldbank.org/ICSID/FrontServlet?requestType=CasesRH&actionVal=RightFrame&FromPage=Organization%20and%20Structure&pageName=Organization.

164 Of note, a particularly vocal supporter of reform of the ICSID, Antonio Parra, vacated his office as Deputy Secretary-General of the ICSID shortly after the Secretariat proposed the reforms.

165 *See* Kantor, *supra* note 160. *See also supra* note 47 (ICSID's organizational chart).

166 *See ICSID Rules of Procedure for Arbitration Proceedings*, at 117, ICSID/15 (Apr. 2006), *available at* http://icsid.worldbank.org/ICSID/StaticFiles/basicdoc/CRR_English-final.pdf.

167 *See id.* Rule 37(2)(a)(c).

168 *See id.*

169 *See id.*

upon their particular commercial or other interests. However, requiring that a non-disputing party to investor–state arbitration have a "public interest" poses its own difficulties. In particular, investor–state arbitration often involves significantly private interests, not unlike international commercial arbitration. The fact that one party is a state does not necessarily render that dispute pervasively "public." Indeed, states are frequently parties to private commercial litigation. Nor are ICSID tribunals likely to conclude that public interests are sufficiently "public" to justify admitting non-disputing parties, unless those interests are both predominant and the non-disputing party can establish them at the outset in order to gain admission to proceedings.[170]

Second, the requirement that a third party must bring "a perspective, particular knowledge[,] or insight that is different from that of the disputing parties" is also likely to discourage tribunals from admitting third parties to proceedings. After all, employees, suppliers, debtors, creditors, and insurers, among others, are often materially affected by investor–state arbitration. That impact does not constitute a principled basis for arbitral tribunals to admit them into proceedings, as this would often be perceived as violating the autonomy of the disputing parties.[171]

Even if an ICSID tribunal allows third parties to participate in proceedings under Rule 37, that still does not render those proceedings "public" in the sense of being transparent. Specifically, a tribunal may limit both the kind and extent of third party participation, varying from participating at a particular stage during proceedings, to having a limited function such as presenting a brief, stipulating arguments, and responding to questions. In addition, a tribunal may admit evidence by a third party, but decline to provide it with the full record of proceedings. For example, it may deny requested information on grounds that the third party has failed to justify why it should receive that information, that it is already publicly available, or that it is privileged.[172] Furthermore, even if a tribunal provides a third party with requested information, it may still place a gag on that party, prohibiting it through a confidentiality order from making public disclosures. The result is that, despite third parties participating in ICSID proceedings, the proceedings may still be shrouded from public gaze.[173]

---

170 *See, e.g.*, Methanex Corp. v. U.S., Decision of the Tribunal on Petitions from Third Persons to Intervene as *Amici Curiae*, ¶ 49 (Jan.15, 2001), *available at* http://naftaclaims.com/Disputes/USA/Methanex/MethanexDecisionReAuthorityAmicus.pdf. (Arbitration under Chapter 11 of the NAFTA and the UNCITRAL Arbitration Rules) ("[T]here are of course disputes involving States which are of no greater general public importance than a dispute between private persons."); *see also* Suez v. Arg., ICSID Case No. ARB/03/19, Order in Response to a Petition for Transparency and Participation as *Amicus Curiae*, ¶ 19 (May 19, 2005).

171 *See* Leon E. Trakman, *The Twenty-First Century Law Merchant*, 48 AM. BUS. L. J. 775, 800–03 (2011).

172 *See* Glamis Gold, Ltd. v. U.S., Award, 106, 121 (June 8, 2009) *available at* http://www.state.gov/s/l/c10986.htm (Arbitration under the UNCITRAL Arbitration Rules). *See also* Suez v. Arg., ICSID Case No. ARB/03/19, Order in Response to a Petition for Transparency and Participation as *Amicus Curiae*, ¶ 24 (May 19, 2005) (denying third party access to documentation); Biwater Gauff (Tanz.) Ltd. v. Tanz., ICSID Case No. ARB/05/22, Procedural Order concerning a petition for *Amicus Curiae* Status, at 30 (Feb. 2, 2007).

173 This is implicit in the fact that tribunals, with the consent of the direct parties to the dispute, may grant third parties intervener status for only limited purposes, and insofar as those parties have

Finally, and most lethally, Rule 37's requirement that a third party not "disrupt the proceeding" or "unduly burden or unfairly prejudice either party" is an understandable reason for a tribunal not to admit third parties to proceedings. There are reasonable grounds for a tribunal not to admit such parties, not least of all to avoid a subsequent annulment procedure. Among other concerns, permitting third party intervention will inevitably "burden" or "prejudice" at least one of the disputing parties. Requiring a tribunal to decide at the outset whether admitting that third party will cause "undue" prejudice or unfairness to a disputing party may itself be hazardous as this is something that is often difficult to determine confidently at that early stage. Whether admitting a third party will disrupt ensuing proceedings is equally speculative.

Given these risks, an investment tribunal has a number of reasons not to admit a third party to proceedings under Rule 37 of the ICSID Rules, if not in the interests of the disputing parties, then in its own interests. The core problem lies in Rule 37 itself. Specifically, in granting qualified arbitral discretion, it exposes the tribunal to subsequent attack for failing to comply with those qualifications. Adding to this concern is Rule 37's description of third parties as "non-disputing parties."[174] A practical inference for a tribunal to draw from this is that, if third parties are not "disputing parties," they should not participate in proceedings.

An alternative is for the ICSID to grant intervener standing to third parties based on whether they can demonstrate a material public interest in the proceedings. Particularly, third parties may better inform the tribunal and the parties about the investment issues in dispute, they may facilitate greater transparency in proceedings, they may add to rather than disrupt hearings, and they may assist tribunals to reach determinations with greater confidence and erudition. Nevertheless, this claim for intervener status should not be overstated. First, amicus curiae briefs are peculiar to common law systems; they are virtually unknown in civil law. Second, common law courts generally do not grant intervener status on such expansive "public interest" grounds as are proposed for investor–state arbitration proceedings. Third, if NGOs are granted the right to intervene, arguably they may also be forced by direct parties to participate in arbitration proceedings.[175]

Certainly investment tribunals could avoid these problems by excluding third parties in general from participating in proceedings, something they could not do in respect of disputing parties. Should tribunals admit third parties into proceedings, they would also need to consider the fairness of doing so, particularly given that most third parties seek intervention, not on neutral grounds, but in support of one party, usually the state party to an investor–state dispute. Such decisions further complicate the ultimate question of whether the public interest in allowing non-disputing parties

---

access to confidential information, require them to maintain confidentiality. *See* ICSID Rule 37, ICSID Convention, Regulation and Rules, *available at* http://icsid.worldbank.org/ICSID/StaticFiles/basicdoc/CRR_English-final.pdf.

174 *See* The ICSID Convention, Regulation and Rules, *available at* http://icsid.worldbank.org/ICSID/StaticFiles/basicdoc/CRR_English-final.pdf, at 22.

175 *See* Kantor, *supra* note 116, at p. 18.

to participate in proceedings outweighs the procedural efficiency attained by excluding them. It also does not answer the question why "public interest" NGOs should get better treatment in investor–state arbitration than before their own national courts.

B. SECRECY IN ICSID PROCEEDINGS

Redressing the secrecy of ICSID proceedings poses its own challenges. International commercial arbitration, to which investor–state arbitration is related, was traditionally conceived as a confidential process between disputing parties and distinct from a public hearing.[176] A further attribute of commercial arbitration is that it reflects the autonomy of the disputing parties. Any change in proceedings, such as the admission of public interpleading, traditionally required the parties' consent, which is now subject to ICSID Rule 37 permitting tribunals to admit third parties to proceedings within confined limits.[177] Even though investor–state arbitration takes place between states and private parties under the ICSID, rather than between private parties, it is arguably arbitration all the same. As such, like commercial arbitration, ICSID arbitration is likely to be praised for preserving confidentiality, however much it is condemned for being secretive.[178]

This is not to claim that investor–state arbitration is inevitably or totally secret. In fact, the conduct of investor–state arbitration proceedings is often public and awards are published, as under Chapter 11 on investment under the North American Free Trade Agreement.[179] All that is asserted is that the private attributes of investor–state arbitration are derived somewhat from international commercial arbitration and that the drafters of the ICSID Convention ought not to be condemned for having adapted that institutional and functional heritage at the outset. What the ICSID Convention did, in part, was take cognizance of different models of arbitration, including international commercial arbitration in the latter half of the twentieth century, in formulating dispute resolution in the ICSID Rules.[180] Principal among its similarities to commercial

---

176 *See* Leon E. Trakman, *Confidentiality in International Commercial Arbitration*, 18 ARB. INT'L 1–18 (2002).

177 ICSID tribunals began to allow third-party interventions in 2007, after the ICSID's new rules came into force. See, e.g., Biwater Gauff (Tanzania) Ltd. v. United Republic of Tanzania, ICSID Case No. ARB/05/22 (Feb. 2, 2007); Suez, Sociedad General de Aguas de Barcelona, S.A., and Vivendi Universal S.A. v. The Argentine Republic, ICSID Case No. ARB/03/19 (Feb. 12, 2007). On Rule 37, *see supra* note 173.

178 *See* Trakman, *supra* note 176 (discussing confidentiality in international commercial arbitration and its relationship to investment arbitration).

179 *See* Settlement of Disputes between a Party and an Investor of Another Party: Transparency, NAFTA Chapter 11—Investment, NAFTA Secretatiat, Canada, *available at* http://www.international.gc.ca/trade-agreements-accords-commerciaux/disp-diff/nafta-transparency-alena-transparence.aspx?lang=en&view=d.

180 *See generally* VAN HARTEN, *supra* note 26, at 121 (noting the influence of commercial law, as distinct from public international law, on the development of investment law); Leon E. Trakman, *Arbitrating Investment Disputes under Chapter 11 of the NAFTA*, 18 J. INT'L. ARB. 385 (2001) (discussing investment arbitration under Chapter 11 of the NAFTA).

arbitration is the right of investor–state parties to require proceedings and awards to be private in a manner that judicial proceedings ordinarily are not.[181]

Nevertheless, investor–state arbitration under the ICSID is distinct from private arbitration in key respects. First, it derives from an agreement between or among states, beyond any contractual or other relationship between a signatory state and an investor from another state.[182] As such, investor–state disputes are subject to the accord of state parties that conclude regional and bilateral investment agreements to which foreign investors are not parties.[183]

Second, ICSID arbitration often involves public interest considerations that transcend the ordinary commercial interests of private parties, such as the public interests of economically fragile developing countries and vulnerable sectors of their economies.[184] This is not to assert that private arbitration outside the ICSID, including between states and foreign investors, cannot have similar public interest ramifications, such as claims by developing countries in Latin America that they were economically exploited by transnational corporations. The difference is that modern bilateral investment agreements increasingly imbed these social and economic consequences in the structure of investor–state arbitration provisions, rather than treat them as a coincidental by-product of such arbitration.[185]

Third, if one accepts that public participation in ICSID arbitrations is desirable, there are both institutional and practical objections to achieving that result. The institutional objection is the arbitral preference for requiring that disputing parties consent to public participation insofar as protected information may arise during proceedings, notwithstanding the authority of tribunals to admit third party evidence under Rule 37 after consulting with the disputing parties.[186] However, this concern over the limits of party consent is endemic to investor–state arbitration in general, not to public interest participation in it in particular. Arbitrators can impose restrictions on access

---

181 *See generally* KYRIAKI NOUSSIA, CONFIDENTIALITY IN INTERNATIONAL COMMERCIAL ARBITRATION 37–41 (2010) (discussing confidentiality requirements); Trakman, *supra* note 176 (discussing confidentiality requirements).

182 *See* DOLZER & SCHREUER, *supra* note 6, chs. 1.2–1.3.

183 On the tension between the law governing treaties and investor-state disputes, *see* DOLZER & SCHREUER, *supra* note 6, at chs.1.2-1.3; SCHREUER, *supra* note 6, at 346-48; SCHILL, *supra* note 6, at VI.

184 *See supra* text following note 156.

185 *See, e.g.*, Franck, *supra* note 92.

186 It is potentially difficult for an investment tribunal to determine, when admitting third party briefs or testimony, whether, when and how confidential information may arise subsequently during the course of deliberations. This factor is a significant reason for tribunals to constrain the participation of third parties a priori, or to exclude such participation *ex posteriori* if and when confidentiality is raised by direct parties to the dispute. *See* Katia Fach Gómez, *Rethinking the Role of Amicus Curiae in International Investment Arbitration: How to Draw the Line Favorably for the Public Interest,* 35 FORDHAM INT'L L.J. 510 (2012).

to and disclosure of such information upon public interest participants, as they do upon investor–state parties.[187]

Fourth, significant practical obstacles to public interest participation in ICSID arbitration are the prohibitive costs, not least of all the costs of travelling from afar to participate at venues such as Washington D.C., Paris, and London, all of which are high-cost cities.[188] In addition, there are further costs to the ICSID and World Bank in institutionalizing such participation in arbitration proceedings. These costs vary from accommodating third party participants at arbitration venues to managing the submission of amicus curiae briefs and ensuring hearings in which civic interest groups participate.[189] Finally, there are also the management and publicity costs associated with third party representation in ICSID proceedings.[190]

C. THE BOUNDARIES OF PARTY AUTONOMY

The prospect of ICSID parties disagreeing over the nature and extent of public participation in arbitration, which has often been the case historically, may also lead to burdensome consequences for investor–state parties, tribunals, and the ICSID. For example, investment arbitrators advised by the ICSID Secretariat may be expected to resolve differences between the parties in determining when to admit evidence from third parties in proceedings and, conceivably, when to permit an award to be published in whole or part.[191]

More controversial still is whether and how arbitrators, acting independently or in consultation with the ICSID Secretariat, should rule on the nature of public participation in particular cases.[192] One issue is whether the exercise of that discretion explicitly or implicitly violates the autonomy ascribed to parties to arbitration in general, as distinct from protected information in particular.[193] Another issue is whether admitting third-party briefs and testimony will lead to annulment proceedings.[194] Yet another

---

[187] On the tension between private and public interests in investor–state arbitration in regard to the publication of awards, see Joshua D. H. Karton, *A Conflict of Interests: Seeking a Way Forward on Publication of International Arbitral Awards*, 28 ARB. INT'L (2012), *available at* http://papers.ssrn.com/sol3/papers.cfm?abstract_id=2030948. On the public interest rationale for amicus curiae interventions, see Eric De Brabandere, *NGOs and the "Public Interest": The Legality and Rationale of Amicus Curiae Interventions in International Economic and Investment Disputes*, 12(1) CHIC. J. INT'L L. 85 (2011).

[188] The precise extent to which these costs inhibit participation by public interest groups is speculative, except that they seldom have deep pockets comparable to many international corporate parties to investor–state disputes. *See* Aguas del Tunari, S.A. v. Bol., ICSID Case No. ARB/02/3, *supra* notes 101–04.

[189] *See* De Brabandere, *supra* note 187. On the time and costs associated with international commercial arbitration, *see* Antonio Hierro, *Reducing Time and Costs in ICC International Arbitration Excess Time and Costs of Arbitration: An Incurable Disease?*, 12–13 SPAIN ARB. REV. 37 (2012);

[190] *See supra* note 72 (discussing such costs).

[191] *See generally* Harrison, *supra* note 141 (discussing transparency in arbitration).

[192] *See generally* on this issue, De Brabandere, *supra* note 187; *See* Trakman, *supra* note 171 (discussing autonomy of medieval and modern law merchants, including arbitration); Gómez, *supra* note 186.

[193] *See* Gómez *supra* note 186.

[194] *Id.*

issue is whether admitting civic interest groups in principle will prejudice those third parties that cannot afford the direct or indirect costs of such participation.[195]

Robust challenges to investment arbitrators' appointment or continuance, not least of all arising from a conflict of interest, further complicates the thorny issue of whether investment arbitrators ought to have some latitude in deciding whether and how to admit third parties.[196]

The historical response to third-party participation in investor–state arbitration is not altogether comforting. If ICSID proceedings are to involve greater public participation, ICSID members ought to agree to such a process collectively or through individual bilateral investment agreements. Fortunately, the ICSID Rules already include a foundation for such collective agreement. A tribunal can invoke ICSID Arbitration Rule 37 to invite any person or entity that is not a Disputing Party in arbitration proceedings to make a written application to the Tribunal for permission to submit an amicus curiae brief.[197] Moreover, a Procedural Order of the ICSID of February 2, 2011, also provides a process by which non-disputing parties can file such briefs.[198] This practice of inviting third parties to file amicus briefs is also replicated in arbitration clauses in various free trade agreements, such as under Article 10.20.3 of the Dominican Republic–Central America–United States Free Trade Agreement, which was applied in a recent case involving third-party participation in investment proceedings.[199] Consequently, it is arguable that the ICSID has done enough to facilitate public participation in its proceedings.

---

195 *Id.*

196 *See* Lise Johnson, *Annulment of ICSID Awards: Recent Developments* (Fourth Annual Forum for Developing Country Investment Negotiators, New Delhi, Background Papers, Oct. 27–29, 2010), *available at* http://www.iisd.org/publications/pub.aspx?id=1423 (providing recent decisions on parties' applications for and grounds of annulment of ICSID awards). *See also* Universal Compression Int'l Holdings, S.L.U. v. Ven., ICSID Case No. ARB/10/9 (May 20, 2011), *available at* http://italaw.com/documents/UniversalCompressionDecisiononDisqualification.pdf (challenges to ICSID arbitrators). *See generally* Robin Hansen, *Parallel Proceedings in Investor–State Treaty Arbitration: Responses for Treaty-Drafters, Arbitrators and Parties,* 73 MODERN L. REV. 523 (2010); Daphna Kapeliuk, *The Repeat Appointment Factor: Exploring Decision Patterns of Elite Investment Arbitrators,* 96 CORNELL L. REV. 47 (2010); William W. Park, *Arbitrator Integrity: The Transient and the Permanent,* 46 SAN DIEGO L. REV. 629, 657–61 (2009); Jan Paulsson, *Moral Hazard in International Dispute Resolution,* 25 ICSID L. REV 339 (2010); Leon E. Trakman, *The IBA Guidelines on Conflict of Interest in International Commercial Arbitration,* 10 INT'L ARB. L. REV. 124 (2007).

197 *See Chapter IV: Written and Oral Procedures,* INTERNATIONAL CENTRE FOR THE SETTLEMENT OF INVESTMENT DISPUTES, *available at* http://icsid.worldbank.org/ICSID/StaticFiles/basicdoc/partF-chap04.htm#r37 (last visited June 19, 2012) (providing the language for Rule 37).

198 *See Procedural Order Regarding* Amici Curiae, INTERNATIONAL CENTRE FOR SETTLEMENT OF INVESTMENT DISPUTES (Feb. 2, 2011), http://icsid.worldbank.org/ICSID/FrontServlet?requestType=CasesRH&actionVal=OpenPage&PageType=AnnouncementsFrame&FromPage=Announcements&pageName=Announcement81 (noting developments in relation to the ICSID).

199 On March 2, 2011, a coalition of community organizations, research institutes, and environmental, human rights, and faith-based nonprofit organizations filed an application to submit an amicus brief in the ongoing ICSID dispute between Pac Rim Cayman LLC and the Republic of El Salvador. *See* Pac. Rim. LLC v. El. Sal., ICSID Case No. ARB/09/12, Registered (June 15, 2009). *Cf* Glamis Gold, Ltd. v. U.S., Award (June 8, 2009), *available at* http://www.state.gov/s/l/c10986.htm (arbitration under the UNCITRAL Arbitration Rules).

The cost of public participation in investor–state proceedings is a further concern. In effect, the benefit of encouraging public participation in ICSID proceedings, including by civic groups from developing countries, is counterbalanced by the risk of third parties with identifiable public interests not being able to fund that participation adequately.[200] If such groups are to have a voice that is heard, the case for funding their participation is greater.[201] However, if public participation is to be subsidized, it ought to be based on evenhanded policies such as to redress systemic disadvantage, not unlike defense or aid funds for needy litigants. Moreover, subsidization ought also to be based on verifiable data, such as confirmation of limited funding to participate in proceedings.[202]

The question of determining when to admit or deny third–party participation in ICSID proceedings is difficult to answer in principle. A complicating factor is that ICSID arbitration is essentially ad hoc.[203] As such, principles governing the conduct of international investment law are the product not only of an evolving consensus "among states" but also of dissension over the nature and application of those principles to specific cases.[204] Should ICSID arbitrators have discretion in principle to admit third-party briefs or oral testimony, the difficult question is in determining the authoritative source of that discretion. The most authoritative source is for ICSID to stipulate that arbitrators are so empowered as a condition of their appointment to which the ICSID Administrative Council, consisting of member states, is unlikely to agree.[205] Alternatively, a more cautious approach is for the ICSID to endorse the arbitration provisions contained in the applicable bilateral investment agreement, conceivably based on the model bilateral investment agreements adopted by the United States and Canada.[206] The problem here is that despite the fact that bilateral

---

200 *Id.*

201 *Id.* The rationale is that public interest groups may have a voice, but lack the resources to be heard. That lack of resources may vary from the prohibitive costs of securing qualified counsel to represent them at ICSID hearings to being unable to fund ongoing public interest participation at lengthy hearings.

202 *See* Nigel Blackaby, *Public Interest and Investment Treaty Arbitration, in* INTERNATIONAL COMMERCIAL ARBITRATION: IMPORTANT CONTEMPORARY QUESTIONS 355 (Albert Jan van den Berg ed., 2003) (discussing public interest in investment arbitration); *see generally* Maciej Zachariasiewicz, *Amicus Curiae in International Investment Arbitration: Can It Enhance the Transparency of Investment Dispute Resolution?*, 29(2) J. INT'L ARB. 205 (2012).

203 Investor–state arbitration is ad hoc in that each decision binds the parties, but does not serve as an arbitral precedent, as common lawyers conceive of precedent. *See generally* Tony Cole, *Non-Binding Documents and Literature, in International Investment Law: Sources of Rights and Obligations* (Tarcisio Gazzini & Eric De Brabandere, eds., 2012).

204 On variable principles of international investment law, see RUDOLF DOLZER & CHRISTOPH SCHREUER, PRINCIPLES OF INTERNATIONAL INVESTMENT LAW (2d ed. 2012); SURYA P. SUBEDI, INTERNATIONAL INVESTMENT LAW: RECONCILING POLICY AND PRINCIPLE (2d ed. 2012).

205 In the author's view, the Council is unlikely to so agree due to concerns among member states over the negative impact the exercise of arbitral discretion could have over the public interest of respondent states in subsequent ICSID proceedings.

206 *See, e.g.*, Central American Free Trade Agreement, Dispute Resolution, signed Aug. 5, 2004 (entered into force Aug. 2, 2005 (United States), Mar. 1, 2006, (El Salvador), Apr. 1, 2006, (Honduras and Nicaragua), July 1, 2006 (Guatemala), Mar. 1, 2007 (Dominican Republic), Jan. 1, 2009 (Costa Rica)) especially

investment agreements increasingly define complex concepts, such an expropriation, and the nature of "most favored nation treatment" and "national treatment," the specific nature and scope of such agreements remain distinctly variable.[207]

None of this addresses resistance that investor–state arbitrators face when deciding in practice whether to allow third parties to participate in proceedings. A principled objection is the perceived ingrained right of disputing parties to deny consent to third-party participation.[208] The practical difficulty is in arbitrators ameliorating public and private tensions within investor–state arbitration. This includes: providing public access to the expropriation practices of states while avoiding the public disclosure of sensitive state or investor information, requiring that a state demonstrate that its expropriation is for a public purpose without publicly victimizing the state; and complying with the rules of the ICSID and the applicable investment treaty in reaching such determinations.[209]

Arbitrators need not make these determinations in a vacuum. Indeed, investment arbitration may entail consultative expectations, such as arbitrators conferring with the ICSID Secretariat and the investor–state parties in determining whether and how to admit third-party briefs or testimony. In answering these questions, the ICSID and its arbitrators can also draw from experience in commercial arbitration, such as the practices used in ICC and ICDR arbitration.[210]

What is evident, too, is that these formal and informal methods of redressing public–private tensions are already in use in investor–state arbitration, such as the NAFTA, and in more recent regional and bilateral investment agreements such as the

---

Article 21-22 [hereinafter CAFTA]. *See also* Model United States BIT (2004) art. 29, "Transparency of Arbitral Proceedings," *available at* http://www.state.gov/documents/organization/117601.pdf; Peru Trade Promotion Agreement, U.S.–Peru, signed Apr. 12, 2006 (entered into force Feb. 1, 2009) art. 10.21; Free Trade Agreement, U.S.–Colombia, signed Nov. 22, 2006 (anticipated entry into force, 2012) art. 10.21, Free Trade Agreement, Korea–U.S., signed June 30, 2007 (Approved by Congress Oct. 12, 2011) art. 11.21 [hereinafter Korea–U.S. FTA]. *See also* Model Canadian Foreign Investment Promotion and Protection Agreement (2003) art. 38(1) (providing for "open hearings" but also stating that "the Tribunal may hold portions of hearings *in camera*"). *See also* 2012 Model United States Bilateral Investment Treaty, *available at* http://www.ustr.gov/sites/default/files/BIT%20text%20for%20ACIEP%20Meeting.pdf; Kenneth J. Vandevelde, *Model Bilateral Investment Treaties: The Way Forward,* 18 Sw. J. Int'l L. 307 (2011).

207 *See e.g.*, Clint Peinhardt & Todd Allee, *Devil in the Details? The Investment Effects of Dispute Settlement Variation in BITs, in* Yearbook on International Investment Law & Policy 2010–2011 (Karl P. Sauvant ed., 2012).

208 This right is preserved in the ICSID Convention, Regulations and Rules, including in Rules 27, 35–37, *available at* http://icsid.worldbank.org/ICSID/StaticFiles/basicdoc/CRR_English-final.pdf.

209 On this public–private tension, see generally Alvarez & Park, *supra* note 115; Franck, *supra* note 92; Alex Mills, *The Public–Private Dualities of International Investment Law and Arbitration, in* Evolution in Investment Treaty Law and Arbitration 97–116 (Chester Brown & Kate Miles eds., 2011); Catherine A. Rogers, *International Arbitration's Public Realm, in* Contemporary Issues in International Arbitration and Mediation: The Fordham Papers (2010).

210 *See generally* Martin F. Gusy et al., A Guide to the ICDR International Arbitration Rules (2011); Tony Cole & Anuj Kumar Vaksha, *Power-Conferring Treaties: The Meaning of "Investment" in the ICSID Convention,* 24 Leiden J. Int'l L. 305 (2011); *supra* note 39.

Central American Free Trade Agreement (CAFTA).[211] The telling issue is in how the ICSID investor–state arbitrators can open the door to public participation in otherwise protected arbitration proceedings in a fluid and sometimes unstable investment climate.

D. INCONSISTENT DECISIONS

A particular critique of international investment arbitration generally is that arbitrators will reach different determinations in otherwise comparable cases. This criticism can be directed against any form of decision making involving discretion, where decision makers do not treat like cases alike.[212] However, ICSID arbitrators have the additional burden of having to interpret differently worded treaties and applying variable conceptions such as direct and indirect expropriation, as well as fair and equitable treatment, to distinct cases.[213] Added to these interpretative and substantive difficulties facing investment arbitrators are dissimilar practices among arbitral tribunals on how to hear a case, how to address past decisions that are not formally precedents but nevertheless influential, and how to write arbitral awards.[214]

Illustrating inconsistent methods of construing international investment law are six investor claims against the Republic of Argentina. All of the cases dealt with the defense of necessity against an expropriation arising from the alleged severity of Argentina's economic crisis primarily in late 2001 and early 2002, and its rescue package that foreign investors alleged was unfair to them.[215] Three of the cases, *CMS, Enron,* and *Sempra*, were all decided by tribunals with the same president, they each employed different methods of interpretation, and they reached different conclusions.[216] Specifically, *CMS* and *Sempra* rejected Argentina's pleas under both treaty and customary law and found

---

[211] *See, e.g.*, CAFTA, signed Aug. 5, 2004 (entered into force Aug. 2, 2005 (United States), Mar. 1, 2006 (El Salvador), Apr. 1, 2006 (Honduras and Nicaragua), July 1, 2006 (Guatemala), Mar. 1, 2007 (Dominican Republic), Jan. 1, 2009 (Costa Rica)) art. 10.21 (Transparency of Arbitral Proceedings).

[212] This is the case in civil law systems generally in which courts are not bound by judicial precedent, but whose decisions collectively constitute part of an *opinio juris*, or opinion of jurists. *See, e.g*, the Web site, Opinio Juris, http://opiniojuris.org/tag/ats/.

[213] On differently worded bilateral investment treaties giving rise to different interpretations, see Peinhardt & Allee, *supra* note 207; J. ROMESH WEERAMANTRY, TREATY INTERPRETATION IN INVESTMENT ARBITRATION (2012).

[214] *See* Jurgen Kurtz, *Adjudging the Exceptional at International Investment Law: Security, Public Order, and Financial Crisis,* 59 INT'L. COMP. L.Q. 325, 329 (2010) (noting such differences in interpretation and identifying three methodologies of interpretation).

[215] *See infra* cases cited in notes 216–218.

[216] CMS Gas Transmission Co. v. Arg., ICSID Case No. ARB/01/8, Award May 12, 2005); Enron Corp. Ponderosa Assets, L.P. v. Argentine, ICSID Case No. ARB/01/3, Award (May 22, 2007); Sempra Energy Int'l v. Arg., ICSID Case No. ARB/02/16, Award (Sept. 28, 2007). *See generally* August Reinisch, *Necessity in International Investment Arbitration—An Unnecessary Split of Opinions in Recent ICSID Cases? Comments on* CMS v. Argentina *and* LG&E v. Argentina, 8 J. WORLD INV. & TRADE 191 (2007); Stephan W. Schill, *International Investment Law and the Host State's Power to Handle Economic Crises: Comment on the ICSID Decision in* LG&E v. Argentina, 24 J. INT'L ARB. 265 (2007); Michael Waibel, *Two Worlds of Necessity in ICSID Arbitration*: CMS and LG&E, 20 LEIDEN J. INT'L L. 637 (2007).

Argentina responsible for causing damage to foreign investors that required compensation.[217] In comparison, the tribunals in *Continental Casualty, LG&E,* and *Metalpar* decided in favor of the Republic of Argentina, absolving it from the responsibility to compensate foreign investors for any damage suffered.[218] An Annulment Tribunal following *CMS* held that the investment tribunal had interpreted the Treaty incorrectly because it construed its provision for necessity in the same manner as customary investment law as stated in Article 25 of the International Law Commission (ILC) Code on State Responsibility.[219] *Enron* and *Sempra* were also annulled.

The problem of arbitrators reaching inconsistent decisions in seemingly similar cases is not entirely one that investor–state arbitrators can resolve. Furthermore, the problem of inconsistency is not limited to investor–state arbitration. Indeed, judicial precedent is a common law, not a civil law concept. Similarly, international law, including the International Court of Justice, does not adhere to case precedent.[220] Further limiting the potential ambit of precedent in investor–state arbitration is the observation that awards are case-specific and bind only the disputing parties.[221] In addition, the uniform interpretation of investment treaties is also likely to be elusive when the wording of treaties differ and when customary investment laws and practices diverge.[222] Further undermining the prospects of investment arbitrators reaching

---

217 *See* CMS Gas Transmission Co. v. Arg., ICSID Case No. ARB/01/8, Award (May 12, 2005); Enron Corp. Ponderosa Assets, L.P. v. Arg., ICSID Case No. ARB/01/3, Award (May 22, 2007); Sempra Energy Int'l v. Arg., ICSID Case No. ARB/02/16, Award (Sept. 28, 2007).

218 *See* Cont'l Cas. Co. v. Arg., ICSID Case No. ARB/03/9, Award (Sept. 5, 2008); LG&E Energy Corp. v. Arg., ICSID Case No. ARB/02/1, Decision on Liability (Oct. 3, 2006; Award, July 25, 2007); Metalpar S.A. v. Arg., ICSID Case No. ARB/03/5, Award, ¶¶ 208–13 (June 6, 2008).

219 *See* International Law Commission, Draft Articles on Responsibility of States for Internationally Wrongful Acts with Commentaries, U.N. GAOR, 56th Sess., at ch. 4, U.N. Doc. A/56/10 (2001). *See also* Responsibility of States for Internationally Wrongful Acts, G.A. Res. 56/83, U.N. Doc. A/56/49(Vol. I)/Corr.4 (Dec. 12, 2001) Article 25 provides:

> 1. Necessity may not be invoked by a State as a ground for precluding the wrongfulness of an act not in conformity with an international obligation of that State unless the act: (a) is the only way for the State to safeguard an essential interest against a grave and imminent peril; and (b) does not seriously impair an essential interest of the State or States towards which the obligation exists, or of the international community as a whole. 2. In any case, necessity may not be invoked by a State as a ground for precluding wrongfulness if: (a) the international obligation in question excludes the possibility of invoking necessity; or (b) the State has contributed to the situation of necessity.

But see Matthew Parish, *On Necessity*, 11 J. WORLD INV. & TRADE 169, 173 (2010).

220 Gilbert Guillaume, *The Use of Precedent by International Judges and Arbitrators*, 2(1) J. INT'L DISP. DISPUTE SETTLEMENT 5–13 (2011), available at http://intl-jids.oxfordjournals.org/content/2/1/5.full.

221 The binding force of arbitral awards, including investor–state arbitration, is a contentious topic. *See, e.g.*, Christoph Schreuer & Matthew Weiniger, *A Doctrine of Precedent?*, *in* THE OXFORD HANDBOOK OF INTERNATIONAL INVESTMENT LAW 1188 (Peter Muchlinski et al. eds., 2008) (discussing the absence of binding precedents, at least in principle, in international investment law); Andrea K. Bjorklund, *Investment Treaty Arbitral Decisions as* Jurisprudence Constante, *in* INTERNATIONAL ECONOMIC LAW: THE STATE AND FUTURE OF THE DISCIPLINE 265 (Colin Picker et al. eds., 2008).

222 *See* Kurtz, *supra* note 214, at 392 (noting three different methods of interpreting investment treaties); William W. Burke-White & Andreas von Staden, *Investment Protection in Extraordinary Times: The*

uniform awards is the realization that international investment law focuses on the expropriation of property. This is significant because the law of property varies from jurisdiction to jurisdiction and there is no truly pervasive body of international law of property governing investment.[223] Not only are investment arbitrators under the ICSID called upon to interpret complex property concepts, they also must reach decisions based on divergent conceptions of property in otherwise similar cases.[224] Against such a background, investment arbitrators understandably struggle to reach decisions that, with the benefit of hindsight, appear confusing or at worst wrong in subsequent annulment proceedings.[225]

E. GREASING THE SQUEAKY WHEEL

The ICSID Secretariat's recommendations relating to public participation in proceedings and the publication of awards are not as intensely under the public microscope today as they were when the Secretariat proposed them. That is partly the consequence of the new Rule 37, which goes some of the way to accommodate the Secretariat's recommendations. Nevertheless, the recommendations have had an incremental political and jurisprudential influence in providing greater transparency and publicity to arbitration hearings, including a shift in political will favoring public proceedings and published results as well as the formal adoption of new Rule 37 evidencing that shift. This shift toward greater transparency is also attributable in part to the growth of informed investment reporter services on ICSID developments including arbitration awards. Particularly, ever readier and cheaper access to information makes it difficult to shroud ICSID hearings or awards in secrecy.[226] In addition, the Internet provides

---

Interpretation and Application of Non-Precluded Measures Provisions in Bilateral Investment Treaties, 48 VA. J. INT'L L. 307, 340 (2008) (discussing "nuances of state intent").

[223] On different conceptions of property rights, see Frank Michelman, *Property, Utility, and Fairness: Comments on the Ethical Foundations of "Just Compensation" Law*, 80 HARV. L. REV. 1165 (1967); J.E. PENNER, THE IDEA OF PROPERTY IN LAW (1997); Felix Cohen, *Dialogue on Private Property*, 9 RUTGERS L. REV., 357 (1954). On different conceptions of property rights in international investment law, see, for example, Salini Costruttori SpA v. Morocco, Decision on Jurisdiction (July 23, 2001); 42 I.L.M. 609 (2003). *See also* MONIQUE SASSON, SUBSTANTIVE LAW IN INVESTMENT TREATY ARBITRATION: THE UNSETTLED RELATIONSHIP BETWEEN INTERNATIONAL AND MUNICIPAL LAW, *see especially* ch. 4 (2010). On the requisites that must be met to invoke the ICSID's jurisdiction, *see* SCHREEUER, *supra* note B, at 89-91 and Omar E. García-Bolívar, *Protected Investments and Protected Investors: The Outer Limits of ICSID's Reach*, 2 TRADE L. & DEV. 145, 147 (2010) (discussing requisites that must be met to invoke the ICSID's jurisdiction).

[224] *See generally* Luzius Wildhaber & Isabelle Wildhaber, *Recent Case Law on the Protection of Property in the European Convention on Human Rights*, *in* INTERNATIONAL INVESTMENT LAW FOR THE 21ST CENTURY: ESSAYS IN HONOUR OF CHRISTOPH SCHREUER 657 (Christina Binder et al. eds., 2009) (discussing the European Convention of Human Rights).

[225] *See supra* Section IV(iv) (articulating this interpretative confusion in the trilogy of investment claims against the government of Argentina).

[226] Online reporting services that are easily accessible through conventional search engines illustrate this ready access to information on developments in international investment law. See further note 227 immediately below.

foreign investors with ready access to databases of arbitration cases and commentaries that demystify complex property concepts, among others, in particular cases.[227] Furthermore, there are, of course, information leaks.[228]

Indeed, in the Argentine case of *Aguas Argentinas S.A., Suez Sociedad General de Aguas de Barcelona S.A., Vivendi Universal S.A. v. Republic of Argentina*, the attorney general of the Republic of Argentina published the relevant arbitration proceedings along with the reasons the Tribunal denied the petition of civic groups in Argentina.[229] In contrast, the 2006 ICSID case of *Biwater Gauff (Tanzania) Ltd v. Tanzania* saw lukewarm support for the publication of investment arbitration awards.[230]

However, attitudes, including among ICSID members and foreign investors, have changed to accept that greater openness, or at least the appearance of it in ICSID proceedings, is often appropriate.[231] In particular, a debatable but nevertheless identifiable attitudinal change is the 2006 ICSID Rule 37 providing for submissions of non-disputing parties subject to limiting guidelines.[232] Added to this change is the wider availability of investor–state awards on the ICSID Web site, along with references to academic and professional commentaries on ICSID cases.[233] These attitudinal changes do not in themselves simplify the complexity of international investment law and investor–state arbitration in particular. In fact, notwithstanding Arbitration Rules 35 and 36 providing for expert witnesses,[234] expert testimony on the significance of conflicting conceptions of contract and property law can complicate as much as it clarifies such differences.[235] Moreover investor–state parties have uneven access to such evidence, and it is difficult to ensure that such evidence is heard and understood.[236]

---

227 *See generally* THE INVESTMENT REPORTER, http://www.investmentreporter.com/ (last visited June 19, 2012); *World Investment Report*, UNITED NATIONS CONFERENCE ON TRADE AND DEVELOPMENT, http://www.unctad.org/Templates/Page.asp?intItemID=1465 (last visited June 19, 2012).

228 For a classical ICSID case involving such "leaks," see the text immediately below and *infra* note 233.

229 ICSID Case No ARB/03/19. *See further supra* note 105 and the accompanying text.

230 ICSID Case No ARB/05/22, Procedural Order No. 3 (Sept. 29, 2006). The tribunal permitted a disputing party to "engage in general discussion about the case in public, provided that any such public discussion is restricted to what is necessary, and is not used as an instrument to antagonise the parties, exacerbate their differences, unduly pressure one of them, or render the resolution of the dispute potentially more difficult." *See id.*; *see also* SCHREUER, *supra* note 6, at 822 (contending that a party to an ICSID arbitration can publish the award).

231 It is a virtual certainty that the reasons as to why investors and sometimes states sought to avoid third party interventions, public hearings and the publication of awards, remain. What has changed is the fact that these aspirations are more difficult to justify in the face of growing transparency requirements, and public expectations.

232 *See supra* Section IV(i) (discussing amended Rule 37 of the ICSID Arbitration Rules). *See also supra* notes 165.

233 *See ICSID Cases*, INTERNATIONAL CENTRE FOR SETTLEMENT OF INVESTMENT DISPUTES, http://icsid.worldbank.org/ICSID/FrontServlet?requestType=CasesRH&actionVal=ShowHome&pageName=Cases_Home (last visited June 19, 2012).

234 *See ICSID Arbitration Rules*, *supra* note 33.

235 On the difficulties arising in interpreting different conceptions of property, *see supra* note 118–124.

236 *See supra* Section II(iii).

The status of investor–state awards is also changing, albeit incrementally. Regional and bilateral agreements sometimes entitle disputing parties to make arbitration awards public, such as Annex 1137.4 of the NAFTA, which stipulates that, where the United States or Canada is the disputing party, either party to the arbitration may make the award public.[237] This practice has been affirmed by the NAFTA Free Trade Commission; and by individual statements by the U.S. and Canada in 2003 and ultimately by Mexico in 2004 issuing individual statements consenting to open hearings for all of their own cases under Chapter 11 of the NAFTA.[238]

Regional and bilateral treaties also reflect these changes, notably in the CAFTA, which requires public access to arbitration proceedings and which does not allow a disputing party to object.[239] Further illustrating the publicity of investor–state proceedings and awards is the CAFTA arbitration, *Commerce Group Corporation and San Sebastian Gold Mines v. Republic of El Salvador*, decided by the ICSID.[240] The *Commerce Group* proceedings were broadcast live on the World Wide Web, and both the proceedings and award are available on the ICSID Web site.[241]

What does all this mean for the operation of the ICSID? From a systemic perspective, comprehensive institutional reforms of the ICSID are realistic only if signatory states to the ICSID Convention so agree. It also anticipates signatory states agreeing upon criteria on how the ICSID Secretariat and investment arbitrators ought to direct or guide such participation, including the protection of sensitive information from public disclosure. In the absence of such support, and even with it, much depends on how individual states provide for public participation in bilateral or investor–state agreements, the substantive laws states invoke to govern such participation, and the

237 NAFTA Article 1137 and its Annex 1137.4, provides that either party may publish the award, which includes not only the final award but also preliminary awards. On the text of this Article and Annex, *see* SICE, Foreign Trade and Information Service, available at http://www.sice.oas.org/trade/nafta/chap-112.asp.

238 On public access to Chapter 11 proceedings under the NAFTA, *see* NAFTA Free Trade Commission, *Notes of Interpretation of Certain Chapter 11 Provisions* (July 31, 2001), *available at* http://www.international.gc.ca/trade-agreements-accords-commerciaux/disp-diff/nafta-interpr.aspx?lang=en&view=d. On public statements by the NAFTA parties on open hearings, see NAFTA—Chapter 11—Investment Settlement of Disputes between a Party and an Investor of Another Party, Transparency, http://www.international.gc.ca/trade-agreements-accords-commerciaux/disp-diff/nafta-transparency-alena-transparence.aspx?lang=en&view=d. This commitment to open hearings is further reflected in the interpretation of Chapter 11 by the Free Trade Commission, confirming the decision in *Metalclad v. Mexico* that "Nothing in the NAFTA imposes a general duty of confidentiality on the disputing parties to a Chapter Eleven arbitration": *id.*

239 *See* CAFTA, arts.i 10.21(2) & (5) (Transparency of Arbitral Proceedings). The CAFTA-DR extends beyond the NAFTA by requiring explicitly that proceedings take place in public.

240 See Commerce Grp, Corp. v. El Sal., ICSID Case No. ARB/09/17, Award (Mar. 14, 2011) (available on the ICSID Web site at Commerce Group, Corp. v. El Sal., ICSID Case No. ARB/09/17, Award (Mar. 14, 2011); Commerce Grp, Corp. v. El Sal. Public Hearing, Nov. 15, 2010, INTERNATIONAL CENTER FOR SETTLEMENT OF INVESTMENT DISPUTES (Nov. 17, 2010), http://icsid.worldbank.org/ICSID/FrontServlet?requestType=CasesRH&actionVal=OpenPage&PageType=AnnouncementsFrame&FromPage=Announcements&pageName=Announcement71.

241 *Id.*

prospect of investor–state arbitration being subject to inconsistent constitutional laws of state parties.

From the perspective of risks, the ICSID like any other international organization faces the risk that disenchanted member states will desert it if its structure is not reformed, while others will leave if its structure is reformed. If member states contemplate changes to the transparency and publicity of ICSID arbitration, the World Bank conceivably may establish block grants to subsidize developing countries and particularly civic groups that qualify for subsidization, subject to prescribed terms of reference. On the other hand, levies on wealthier countries may also be needed to subsidize the costs of public participation by civic groups, which are not necessarily limited to poorer countries. It is unlikely that wealthier countries would agree to such a grant scheme in the absence of constrained terms of reference governing both the availability and quantum of those grants. However they may agree to subsidize such participation in order to diffuse the hostility of some developing countries toward investment arbitration and the ICSID.

Another prickly issue in the process of ICSID reform is in signatory parties agreeing on a threshold at which parties to ICSID disputes ought not unreasonably to resist third-party participation and the publication of investment awards. Agreement by ICSID members on these issues is unlikely unless and until there is a persistent groundswell of support arising from crises of confidence in the delivery of investor–state arbitration, not limited to the ICSID. However, if such a groundswell does not eventuate, the tendency will be to grease the squeaky wheel, not change it.

A more invasive approach is for the ICSID to consider the practice adopted by the NAFTA Free Trade Commission. In October 2003, that Commission issued an interpretative statement specifying that "[n]o provision of the North American Free Trade Agreement [] limits a tribunal's discretion to accept written submissions from a person or entity that is not a disputing party."[242] The Trade Commission's interpretation is distinctive in two respects. First, the NAFTA is silent on amicus curiae briefs. Second, its interpretation establishes a procedure to which a non-disputing party must adhere in applying for leave to file a submission in arbitration.[243] The Trade Commission's interpretative statement is also not isolated. Indeed, the U.S. Trade Act of 2002 already required that trade negotiators establish "a mechanism for acceptance of amicus curiae submissions from businesses, unions, and nongovernmental organizations."[244] Similarly, these developments under the NAFTA and the CAFTA are not isolation. This is evident in more recent investment agreements, such as the Korea–U.S. Free

---

[242] *See Statement of the Free Trade Commission on Non-Disputing Party Participation*, NAFTA Free Trade Comm'n (Oct. 7, 2003), available at http://www.international.gc.ca/trade-agreements-accords-commerciaux/assets/pdfs/Nondisputing-en.pdf.

[243] *Id. See also* Nathalie Bernasconi-Osterwalder & Lise Johnson, Int'l Inst. for Sustainable Dev., *Transparency in the Dispute Settlement Process: Country Best* Practices 9 (Best Practices Series, Bulletin No. 2, Feb. 2011), *available at* http://www.iisd.org/pdf/2011/transparency_dispute_settlement_processes.pdf.

[244] *See* Trade Act 2002, Pub. L. No. 107-210, 116 Stat 933, 995 (2002) § 2102(b)(3)(H)(iii).

Trade Agreement and some model bilateral investment agreements that provide for the admission of amicus briefs. These agreements highlight three criteria: "(a) the appropriateness of the subject matter of the case, (b) the suitability of a given non[-] party to act as amicus curiae in that case, and (c) the procedure by which the amicus submission is made and considered." [245] These criteria, in the main, provide a reasonable basis upon which investor–state arbitrators can choose whether and how to admit "non-parties" to assume amicus curiae roles. If anything, each of these developments provides some fortitude to the ICSID in deciding how it wishes to proceed on the issue of transparency of proceedings, such as under Rule 37.

V. DOMESTIC COURTS OR ICSID ARBITRATORS?

An alternative to investor–state arbitration, not limited to the ICSID, is that foreign investors, like domestic investors, ought to be subject to the territorial sovereignty of the state in which they invest, including to the jurisdiction of domestic courts.[246] Arguably, domestic courts, not ICSID tribunals, are the appropriate bodies to resolve investment disputes between domestic states and foreign investors, in the same manner as domestic courts decide "other" domestic disputes.[247] Here, the inference is that domestic courts can ensure that foreign and domestic investors receive comparable rights and are subject to comparable duties.[248] As the Australian Government contended in its Policy Statement in April 2011, "dispute settlement processes should not afford foreign investors in Australia with access to litigation options not normally afforded to local investors."[249] The intention is to ensure that investor–state parties

---

245 *See* Free Trade Agreement, Korea–U.S., art. 11.20, signed June 30, 2007 (Approved by Congress Oct. 12, 2011) (Korea–U.S. FTA). *See also* Free Trade Agreement, Canada–Colombia, art. 831, signed Nov. 11, 2008 (entered into force Aug. 15, 2011); Model Canadian Foreign Investment Promotion and Protection Agreement (2003) art. 39.

246 *See, e.g.*, REDEFINING SOVEREIGNTY IN INTERNATIONAL ECONOMIC LAW, Part Four (Wenhua Shan et al. eds., 2008) (providing commentary on the complexity of sovereignty in international investment law); Robert Stumberg, *Sovereignty by Subtraction: The Multilateral Agreement on Investment*, 31 CORNELL INT'L L. J. 491, 503–04, 523–25 (1998) (discussing sovereignty). *See also* INTERNATIONAL ECONOMIC LAW AND NATIONAL AUTONOMY (Meredith Kolsky Lewis & Susy Frankel eds., 2010); ROBERT H. JACKSON, QUASI-STATES: SOVEREIGNTY, INTERNATIONAL RELATIONS AND THE THIRD WORLD (1990); JOHN H. JACKSON, THE JURISPRUDENCE OF GATT AND THE WTO: INSIGHTS ON TREATY LAW AND ECONOMIC RELATIONS, ch. 18 (2000); Michael Reisman, *International Arbitration and Sovereignty*, 18 ARB. INT'L (LCIA) 231 (2002); OPPENHEIM'S INTERNATIONAL LAW 927 (Sir Robert Jennings & Sir Arthur Watts eds., 1992).

247 *See generally* Leon E. Trakman, *Investor State Arbitration or Local Courts: Will Australia Set a New Trend?*, 46 J. WORLD TRADE 83 (2012); Leon E. Trakman, *Foreign Direct Investment: An Australian Perspective*, 13 INT'L TRADE & BUS L. REV. 31, 48–53 (2010).

248 *See* Trakman, *Foreign Direct Investment*, *supra* note 247, at 48–49 (discussing these arguments buttressing the dispute resolution mechanisms adopted under the Australia–United States Free Trade Agreements).

249 *See* Productivity Commission, *Bilateral and Regional Trade Agreements* (Draft Research Report, July 16, 2010) [hereinafter Productivity Commission]; *see also* Patricia Ranald & Harvey Purse, *Supplementary*

resolve their investment disputes in a transparent, public, and cost-effective manner before duly appointed domestic courts that also consider domestic public policies. Included among the rights of foreign investors is their right to natural justice or due process before domestic courts, offset by the power of that state to restrict private investor rights on public policy grounds, such as to ensure that foreign investors do not receive advantages not availed to local investors, and to protect public health, welfare, and the environment.[250]

This development in Australia is not entirely novel. Specifically, the *Calvo Doctrine* that was enunciated in Latin America decades before had a comparable focus, albeit reflecting the perspective of developing, not developed, countries.[251] Under the Australian approach, national law should govern the rights of foreign investors, particularly foreign investors filing claims against the Australian government, and the authority of domestic courts should prevail over other options, including resort to diplomatic channels.[252] The jurisdictional rationale for this proposition is that investment disputes ought to be decided by the domestic courts of host states, not international tribunals.[253] The substantive rationale is that domestic courts ought to confer only national treatment on foreign investors, there being no better treatment than is accorded to local investors.[254] The equitable inference from these rationales is that, were investor–state arbitration to privilege foreign investors, it would not serve the national interest, and if it fails to service the national interest, domestic courts ought to replace it.

A. THE CASE FOR AND AGAINST DOMESTIC COURTS

There are several related arguments in support of domestic courts deciding investment disputes. First, domestic courts decide cases according to domestic laws that include the interpretation of bilateral investment treaties between host and home states.[255] Second, domestic courts are subject to established procedural and evidential

---

Submission on behalf of the Australian Fair Trade and Investment Network (AFTINET) to the Productivity Commission Review into Bilateral and Regional Trade Agreements, *available at* http://www.pc.gov.au/__data/assets/pdf_file/0015/102525/subdr068.pdf (last visited June 20, 2012) (making a supplementary submission to the Productivity Commission in response to the Commission's request for comments); Australian Government's Trade Policy, *supra* note 126, 4–15 (emphasizing the importance of investment for Australia's economy); Trakman, *Foreign Direct Investment*, *supra* note 247, at 31.

250 *See* DAVID SCHNEIDERMAN, CONSTITUTIONALIZING ECONOMIC GLOBALIZATION: INVESTMENT RULES AND DEMOCRACY'S PROMISE, chs. 2, 6 (2008).

251 *See id.* at 59–60.

252 *See generally* Wenhua Shan, *From "North-South Divide" to "Private–Public Debate": Revival of the Calvo Doctrine and the Changing Landscape in International Investment Law*, 27 NW. J. INT'L. L. & BUS. 631 (2007); Bernardo Cremades, *Resurgence of the Calvo Doctrine in Latin America*, 7 BUS. L. INT'L 53 (2006).

253 *See, e.g.*, SCHNEIDERMAN, *supra* note 250, at 59; Cremades, *supra* note 252, at 59.

254 *See* SCHNEIDERMAN, supra note 250, at 59.

255 On the jurisdiction of domestic state courts over international investment disputes under Chapter 11 of the NAFTA, see Mondev Int'l Ltd. v. U.S., ICSID Case No. ARB(AF)/99/2, Award (Oct. 11, 2002); The Loewen Grp., Inc. v. U.S., ICSID Case No. ARB(AF)/98/3, Award (June 26, 2003).

constraints in deciding cases. Third, domestic courts are required to protect the rights of foreign investors while also taking into account the applicable public policy of the forum.[256] Finally, decisions by domestic courts are subject to appeal.

In addition, based on several indices, many domestic judicial systems are not reliable in resolving investor–state disputes based. Approximately 76 percent of the cases in which investment treaty awards were rendered up to June 2006 involved states that fell at or below Number 50 on the Transparency International's 2008 Corruption Perception Index. That number increased to 84 percent when cases involving the United States and Canada were excluded. Over 69 percent involved states that fell at or below Number 70 on that Corruption Index.[257] The World Bank's Worldwide Governance Indicators produced similar results. Its Indicator demonstrated that 68 percent of those states were in the bottom 60 percent of the World Bank's WGI index for the "rule of law."[258]

In further support of domestic courts deciding investor–state disputes, ICSID arbitration is subject to ICSID Rules that are broadly framed and less contestable than domestic law. For example, ICSID awards are subject to annulment procedures that are limited predominantly to jurisdictional grounds.[259] Either party can request an annulment, in which case an annulment committee is set up for that purpose, with the power to modify or nullify an award on restrictive grounds under Article 75 of the ICSID Convention.[260] These grounds include: (1) that the ICSID tribunal was not properly constituted; (2) that the tribunal manifestly exceeded its powers; (3) that there was corruption on the part of a tribunal member; (4) that there was a serious departure from a fundamental rule of procedure; or (5) that the award failed to state the reasons on which it was based.[261] ICSID Annulment Committees historically have interpreted these grounds expansively. However, resort to a domestic court is not considered an option under the ICSID Rules.[262]

---

256 *See* Loewen Group, *supra* note 255, at 436.

257 *See* Kantor, *supra* note 116, at p. 10. Kantor based this information on the list of states in Annex 1 to Susan Franck, *Empirically Ealuating Claims about Investment Treaty Arbitration*, 86 N.C. L.Rev, 1 (2007) [information provided to the author by Mark Kantor on July 3, 2012].

258 *Available at* http://info.worldbank.org/governance/wgi/index.asp,

259 *See* Convention on the Settlement of Investment Disputes between States and Nationals of Other States, ICSID/15, Art. 52 (Apr. 2006), *available at* http://www.icsid.worldbank.org/ICSID/StaticFiles/basicdoc/CRR_English-final.pdf (last visited June 13, 2012). *See generally* http://www.worldbank.org/icsid (last visited June 13, 2012) (ISCID documents); James Crawford & Karen Lee, 6 ICSID Reports 192 (2004) (analyzing the *Mondev International* award); http://icsid.worldbank.org/ICSID/ICSID/AdditionalFacilityRules.jsp (last visited June 13, 2012) (ISCID additional facility rules).

260 *See* Convention on the Settlement of Investment Disputes between States and Nationals of Other States, *supra* note 259, Art. 52(1) and (3).

261 *See id.*, Art. 52(1).

262 *See supra* note 71. *See also* Art. 53(1), *supra* note 259 (stating that an ICSID award is binding and shall not be subject to an appeal or any other remedy except those provided in the convention). Remedies under the convention consist of Art. 51 (revision by the Secretary-General) or Art. 52 (annulment); Andrea K. Bjorklund, *The Continuing Appeal of Annulment: Lessons from* Amco Asia *and* CME, *in* International Investment Law and Arbitration: Leading Cases from the ICSID, NAFTA, Bilateral Treaties and Customary International Law 471, 479 (Todd Weiler ed., 2005).

Support for domestic courts over arbitrators deciding investor–state disputes is also grounded in economic efficiency. For example, Australia's Productivity Commission expressed concern that investor–state arbitration exposes Australia to costly, fractious, and dysfunctional disputes with foreign investors, such as Philip Morris Australia, that have deep pockets.[263] In criticizing investor–state arbitration, the Commission contended: "At a minimum, the economic value of Australia's preferential BRTAs has been oversold."[264] Notwithstanding the contention that litigation is often more fractious and costly than other modes of dispute avoidance, the Commission asserted that Australian courts are more fitting bodies to preside over such investor–state disputes than arbitrators.[265] However, what was not adequately addressed is the often dilatory nature of judicial procedures, the unfamiliarity of foreign investors with domestic law, the cost and protraction of proceeding before some domestic courts, and the potential unfairness of applying that law to investor–state disputes.[266]

A possible motivation, albeit not comprehensively addressed in either the Productivity Commission's Research Report or the Australian government's Policy, is trepidation that foreign investors from other developed states might invoke investor–state arbitration to attack the social and economic policies of Australia. In particular, there is some concern that foreign investors from the United States could mount investment claims against the Australian government that would erode the autonomy of the Australian government in devising policies, such as regulating cigarette advertising, on public health, safety, and environmental grounds. Here, a probable inference is that Australian courts are more likely than investment arbitrators to identify the public health risks of cigarette advertising with violations of Australian public policy.

A further assumption in favor of litigation over investor–state arbitration is that a domestic appeals process is more likely to be robust than an ICSID annulment procedure. First, the grounds for an appeal are ordinarily not only jurisdictional, but also on the merits. Second, appeal courts are subject to prescribed rules of proce-

---

263 *See* Leon E. Trakman, *Investor State Arbitration or Local Courts: Will Australia Set a New Trend?* 46 J. WORLD TRADE 83 (2012); Luke R. Nottage, *Consumer Product Safety Regulation and Investor–State Arbitration Policy and Practice after* Philip Morris Asia v Australia, 22(1 & 2) AUSTRALIAN PROD. LIAB. R. 154 (2011), also available at http://papers.ssrn.com/sol3/papers.cfm?abstract_id=2041680 (updated and expanded as ch 15 of this volume).

264 *See* Productivity Commission, *supra* note 249 at XXVIII.

265 *See* Trakman, *supra* note 263, at 86–89 (2012); *but see Tobacco Company Files Claim against Uruguay over Labeling Laws*, INTERNATIONAL CENTRE FOR TRADE AND SUSTAINABLE DEVELOPMENT (Mar. 10, 2010), http://ictsd.org/i/news/bridgesweekly/71988/. *See also* Jurgen Kurtz, *The Australian Trade Policy Statement on Investor State Dispute Settlement*, 15(2) INSIGHT (American Society of International Law Newsletter (Aug. 2, 2011) (noting that the Productivity Commission's Report, while offering a rigorous quantitative analysis of the net economic benefits of BITs, fails to take into account the dynamism of international law, as "critical barriers to foreign investment do not usually take the form of simple border measures whose effects are easily quantifiable").

266 *See* Leon E.Trakman, *Investor State Arbitration or Local Courts: Will Australia Set a New Trend?*, 46 J. WORLD TRADE 83 (2012) (discussing these deficiencies in relying on domestic courts to resolve investor–state disputes).

dure on the record. Finally, both trial and appeal courts are bound by the applicable substantive law.

The choice of domestic litigation over investor–state arbitration nevertheless is not compelling, beyond the concern that investor–state arbitration is more likely than reliance on domestic courts to favor foreign investors over states.[267] The virtue of each is contingent on the value preferences its proponents ascribe to it. The proposition that domestic courts are subject to tried-and-tested domestic rules of evidence and procedure is offset by the fact that ICSID arbitration is guided by rules of procedure that seek to ensure that arbitration procedures are clear in nature and that an ICSID arbitrator's failure to apply them fairly can lead to annulment for noncompliance.[268] Further, the rationale that domestic courts ought to accord no more than national treatment to foreign investors is countered by the argument that investment arbitrators are equally capable of subscribing to comparable standards of national treatment , subject to the terms of an applicable investment treaty or agreement.[269] The supposed insularity of ICSID arbitration from domestic law and procedure is also disputable on the grounds that ICSID arbitrators cannot summarily disregard domestic law if a bilateral investment agreement that refers disputes to the ICSID chooses that law, or that law applied by investor–state agreement to disputes.[270]

Ultimately, parties must make a choice. An appeal to a domestic court is desirable if the party seeks a final determination on jurisdictional and substantive grounds. An annulment procedure on narrow jurisdictional grounds under Article 75 of the ICSID Convention is preferable if the claimant considers those grounds suitable. Beauty lies in the eyes of the beholder.

B. ADDRESSING THE DILEMMA

A formal way to resolve the dilemma between domestic courts and ICSID arbitration is to hold that domestic litigation ought to prevail over ICSID arbitration as a principle of state sovereignty. However, that principle alone is hardly supportable when states repeatedly surrender their sovereignty under both customary international and treaty law to international institutions. Nor is it credible to respond that a multilateral investment accord amounts at least to the sum total of sovereignty surrendered by signatory nation states. The contrary may be true: the result may be "sovereignty

267 For an open letter by prominent jurists objecting to the incorporation of investor–state arbitration into the Trans-Pacific Partnership Agreement, see Trans-Pacific Partnership Agreement Digest, *available at* http://tppdigest.org/index.php?option=com_content&view=article&id=303:news-1105-jurists-write-open-letter-objecting-to-lack-of-tpp-transparency-and-opposing-investor-state-clauses-chile-make-equivocal-noises-about-signing-final-agreement-anti-tpp-animated-video-hits-the-net-&catid=1:latest-news.

268 *See supra* notes 6 and 45 (providing information on the ISCID).

269 This proposition is complicated, particularly by the fact that different national legal systems have incorporated investment law differently. *See especially* Sornarajah, Chapter 16 of the current book.

270 *See, e.g.*, Schreuer, *supra* note 54, at 357.

by subtraction,"[271] which arguably is one reason states failed to arrive at a multilateral investment accord in the first place. [272]

A notable argument in favor of choosing ICSID arbitration over domestic courts is that ICSID arbitrators are ordinarily experts in international investment law while domestic courts are not. At best, domestic judges sit as courts of general commercial jurisdiction and are not particularly experienced in international investment disputes.[273] However, this reasoning, holding that ICSID arbitrators are specialized tribunals as distinct from national judges that operate as courts of general jurisdiction, is contestable. Indeed, the ICSID does not ensure that arbitration is delivered expertly. Further, evidence of an expropriation calls for reasonable judgment about the nature and effect of that expropriation. Moreover, full-time national court judges arguably often have as much, if not more, experience in exercising reasonable judgment as part-time and disparately trained and experienced ICSID arbitrators. Finally, elected judges also sometimes have incentives to thoroughly consider applicable public policies governing expropriation, not least of all if judicious decision making is a credible basis for judicial reelection in jurisdictions in which judges are elected, not nominated.

In contrast, if a judgment about the virtue of ICSID arbitration depends on a study of ICSID jurisprudence, there are only a limited number of ICSID arbitration cases to review.[274] If a judgment about the virtue of ICSID arbitration is about effectiveness, decisions are likely to vary over the nature and extent of that effectiveness. If the inquiry about imperfections in ICSID arbitration is that its social costs exceed the costs of litigation, there is limited experience of investment treaties opting for domestic courts over investor–state arbitration. There is, therefore, limited evidence by which to assess the costs of investment litigation and even less evidence of the comparative social costs of resorting to domestic courts rather than investment arbitration. Only rarely do treaties refer investment disputes to domestic courts, such

---

271 *See* Stumberg, *supra* note 246. *See also* Kevin Kennedy, *A WTO Agreement on Investment: A Solution in Search of a Problem?* 24 U. PA. J. INT'L ECON. L. 77, 87, 152–54, 179–80 (2003) (considering sovereignty concerns). On the prospective impact of the Doha round of multilateral negotiations on Chapter 11 of the NAFTA, *see* Bryan Schwartz, *The Doha Round and Investment: Lessons from Chapter 11 of NAFTA*, 3 ASPER REV. INT'L BUS. & TRADE L. 1 (2003).

272 *See* Katia Tieleman, *The Failure of the Multilateral Agreement on Investment [MAI] and the Absence of a Global Public Policy Network, Global Public Policy Network, available at* http://www.gppi.net/fileadmin/gppi/Tieleman_MAI_GPP_Network.pdf.

273 On the case for investor–state arbitration, see generally OXFORD HANDBOOK ON INTERNATIONAL INVESTMENT LAW (Peter Muchlinski et al. eds., 2008); CAMPBELL MCLACHLAN ET AL., INTERNATIONAL INVESTMENT ARBITRATION: SUBSTANTIVE PRINCIPLES (2007); NEW ASPECTS OF INTERNATIONAL INVESTMENT LAW (Philippe Kahn & Thomas W. Walde eds., 2007); VAN HARTEN, *supra* note 26; R. DOAK BISHOP ET AL., FOREIGN INVESTMENT DISPUTES: CASES, MATERIALS AND COMMENTARY (2005); INTERNATIONAL INVESTMENT LAW AND ARBITRATION: LEADING CASES FROM THE ICSID, NAFTA, BILATERAL TREATIES AND CUSTOMARY INTERNATIONAL LAW (Todd Weiler ed., 2005); ARBITRATING FOREIGN INVESTMENT DISPUTES (Norbert Horn & Stefan Kroll eds., 2004).

274 *See generally Concluded Cases*, INTERNATIONAL CENTRE FOR SETTLEMENT OF INVESTMENT DISPUTES, http://icsid.worldbank.org/ICSID/FrontServlet?requestType=GenCaseDtlsRH&actionVal=ListConcluded (last visited June 20, 2012) (listing 238 concluded cases as of June 20, 2012).

as under the U.S.-Australia Free Trade Agreement.[275] The choice of investor–state arbitration by treaty is the pervasive norm, and ICSID jurisprudence also extends beyond investment treaties between states. A further issue is whether principles of international investment law applied by investment arbitrators, such as the "fair and equitable" standard, require that a foreign investor receive a minimum standard of treatment, or treatment according to the "reasonable expectations" of those investors. A further problem arises if the "reasonable expectations" of foreign investors are deemed to encompass rights not available to domestic investors and extending beyond "national treatment." A related concern is in ensuring, as far as possible, a conception of "fair and reasonable" treatment that is clear, consistent, and predictable, as well as effectively applied to investors and states.[276]

It may well be that the Australian government's choice of domestic courts over arbitration in its recent investment policy reflects its expectation that Australian investors abroad will secure their own protection against political and economic risks, such as through the Multilateral Investment Guarantee Agency (MIGA) and the Export Finance and *Insurance* Corporation (EFIC) for Australian investors abroad, the Overseas Private Investment Corporation (OPIC) available to U.S. investors, and the Export Credits Guarantee Department (ECGD) available to British investors. How investors choose among risk insurance options, if at all, is likely to reflect how they arrive at the best risk–reward ratio. The fact that Australian investors may rely on private insurance still does not preclude their residual reliance on the Australian government to provide de facto insurance against political risks, or to intervene diplomatically. Indeed, they may factor in government intervention in calculating the best risk–reward ratio.

---

275 *See generally* Trakman, *Foreign Direct Investment*, *supra* note 247, at 79–81; Westcott, *supra* note 244; *see generally* Drusilla K. Brown et al., *Computational Analysis of the US FTAs with Central America, Australia and Morocco*, 28 WORLD ECON. 1441 (2005) (discussing the U.S.–Australia Free Trade Agreement); Philippa Dee, *The Australia–US Free Trade Agreement: An Assessment*, 345 PAC. ECON. PAPERS (2005) (Paper prepared for the Senate Select Committee on the Free Trade Agreement between Australia and the United States of America, June 2004); *Free Trade Agreements with Australia*, OFFICE OF THE U.S. TRADE REP., http://www.ustr.gov/trade-agreements/free-trade-agreements/australian-fta (last visited June 13, 2012).

276 *See generally* Thomas Westcott, *Recent Practice on Fair and Equitable Treatment*, 8 J. WORLD INV. & TRADE 409, 425 (2007); 35 ILA International Law on Foreign Investment Committee, International Law on Foreign Investment: *First Report of the International Law Association*, 16. 36 (2006); Catherine Yannaca-Small, *Fair and Equitable Treatment Standard in International Investment Law*, 26 (OECD Working Papers on International Investment, 2004) (referring to the state's duty to treat foreign investors reasonably and equitably including the obligation of vigilance and protection; due process including non-denial of justice and lack of arbitrariness, transparency, and good faith, which could cover transparency and lack of arbitrariness). *See also* Peter Behrens, *Towards the Constitutionalization of International Investment Protection* 45 ARCHIV DES VÖLKERRECHTS 153, 175 (2007) (listing good faith, nondiscrimination, lack of arbitrariness, due process, transparency, consistency, and proportionality as the key requirements of fair and equitable treatment); Michael Muse-Fisher, *CAFTA-DR and the Iterative Process of Bilateral Investment Treaty Making: Towards a United States Takings Framework for Analyzing International Expropriation Claims,* 19 PAC. MCGEORGE GLOBAL BUS. & DEV. L.J. 495, 518–19 (2007) (discussing the minimum standard of fair and equitable treatment).

C. LIMITATIONS IN POLITICAL RISK INSURANCE

Political risk insurance (PRI) is far from a panacea. In particular, the foreign investor is seldom able to secure full PRI coverage against risks to a foreign investment. Some risks are not covered by PRI. In addition, the insured is often required to self-insure in respect of part of the risk.

In addition, PRI covers only expropriation, political violence, and foreign exchange (FX) payments/transfers restrictions and, in some specifically negotiated PRI policies, breach of contract or refusal to honor an arbitral award by a state entity. Conduct by a host state constituting a denial of justice, breach of international minimum standards of treatment, unfair and inequitable and improper discrimination under international law are not ordinarily covered, save for a substantial expropriation such as deprivation of the full value of an investment.

From the perspective of the host state, lodging a PRI claim does not eliminate an insurance claim: it merely transfers it from the investor to the insurer, who then pursues it in its own name.[277]

There are also significant limits on PRI. First, PRI ordinarily is subject to a ceiling above which the investor is self-insured. Second, the OECD rules for PRI insurance require public insurers to impose 15 percent risk sharing on the insured. As a result, the investor ordinarily is a self-insurer for at least 15 percent of the risk in addition to any excess above the PRI ceiling. Finally, most PRI pay only the accounting book value (i.e., the net invested capital). Any market value in excess of book value is not covered. Again, an investor in a successful venture is a self-insurer for the excess of market value over accounting book value.

Finally, it is important to differentiate PRI from access to a dispute resolution forum. PRI consists of a contractual undertaking by a third-party insurer to make a payment in the specified circumstances above to the foreign investor, in effect adding that protection to the credit of the primary obligor. In contrast, investor–state arbitration provides the foreign investors with an independent forum in which to proceed against a host state, and if that investor is successful, an award. Nor is an award to a foreign investor anything like an insurance payment. The foreign investor can ordinarily only enforce the arbitration award against a state by invoking national court proceedings. That investor is then subject to the defenses of sovereign immunity from execution against state assets. The investor also faces the practical problem arising from most states placing their commercial assets into separately incorporated state enterprises that are not parties to the arbitration and are therefore not subject to attachment in the enforcement of an award.

---

277 On the example of the Patuha/Himpurna arbitration and OPIC insurance, see Mark Kantor, *Political Risk Insurance and Investment Arbitration*, TDM 3 (2005), *available at* http://www.transnational-dispute-management.com/article.asp?key=441,

D. ARRIVING AT A BALANCE

ICSID arbitration is not an elixir of perfection that ought to be perpetuated as of right. Like all institutions, it has its beauty spots and warts. What can be said is that a shift toward domestic courts resolving investment disputes is one alternative dispute resolution option, not limited to arbitration under the ICSID. Were that choice to be based solely on the perceived quality of decision making, one could attribute particular normative qualities to the effective and fair use of judicial or arbitral processes in discrete cases. However, ascribing normative values to decision-making processes is unavoidably subjective. Specifically, an assessment of the economic rationale favoring domestic litigation over ICSID arbitration reflects self-interested propositions, such as the perceived benefit of one's foreign investors succeeding before a foreign court compared to before an ICSID tribunal. Moreover, the political reality is that, in exercising preferences, countries are more likely to trust the domestic courts of other countries with which they share common social and economic traditions than those with which they do not.[278] Countries are also readier to endorse a "rule-of-law" culture with which they identify than a culture with which they do not.[279]

Given these imponderables, the result may be that the choice between ICSID or some other form of investor–state arbitration and litigation before domestic courts should be pragmatically determined on the basis of preexisting experience, including prior cases. However, it is too early to arrive at a pragmatic conclusion about domestic judges deciding investment cases, except to acknowledge a shift to domestic courts deciding investment disputes, which began decades ago in Latin America with the once-disavowed and now-resurrected *Calvo Doctrine*.[280] The reasons for this more recent shift toward domestic courts by a developed state such as Australia are complex and potentially contradictory, but that shift could gain momentum in responding to dissatisfaction with investor–state arbitration including under the ICSID. Whatever the institution adopted to resolve investor–state disputes, not limited to litigation or

[278] These observations are exemplified in Chapter 11 jurisprudence under the NAFTA. *See, e.g.*, Mondev Int'l Ltd. v. U.S., ICSID Case No ARB(AF)/99/2, Award, ¶ 159 (Oct. 11, 2002); Loewen Grp., Inc. v. U.S., ICSID Case No. ARB(AF)/98/3, Award (June 26, 2003); William Dodge, *Loewen v. United States: Trials and Errors under NAFTA Chapter 11*, 52 DEPAUL L. REV. 563(2002); Bradford K. Gathright, *A Step in the Wrong Direction: The Loewen Finality Requirement and the Local Remedies Rule in NAFTA Chapter Eleven*, 54 EMORY L.J. 1093 (2005) (discussing the judicial review of the Loewen Chapter 11 decision); Dana Krueger, *The Combat Zone:* Mondev International, Ltd v. United States *and the Backlash against NAFTA Chapter 11*, 21 B.U. INT'L L.J. 399 (2003) (arguing that, but for a technical time bar, two tribunal decisions—*Mondev* and *Loewen*—might have prevailed over U.S. judicial decisions). For a discussion on the judicial review of the *Loewen* Chapter 11 decision, see Trakman, *Foreign Direct Investment, supra* note 247, at 52.

[279] The United States–Australia Free Trade Agreement empowers domestic courts in each signatory state to resolve investor–state disputes, rather than rely on investor–state arbitration. One of the rationales for this position was that the United States and Australia share a common "rule of law" tradition. *See further* Leon E. Trakman, *Foreign Direct Investment: Hazard or Opportunity?*, 41 GEO. WASH. INT'L. L. Rev. 1 (2010).

[280] *See supra* note 252 (discussing the Calvo doctrine).

arbitration, the imponderable is in determining how the rule of law should be defined, applied, and enforced in relation to such disputes.[281] There are no fixed or infallible answers to these intertwined questions.

VI. DISPUTE PREVENTION AND AVOIDANCE

Neither litigation nor investor–state arbitration is an exclusive means of resolving investor–state disputes. For example, dispute prevention and avoidance options are potentially low-cost, informal, expeditious, party-friendly, private, and nondisruptive ways in which foreign investors and host states can resolve differences while continuing their relationships with minimal disruption. Indeed, the UNCTAD has proposed a series of dispute prevention and avoidance remedies as conceivable alternatives to investor–state arbitration and litigation, namely, conciliation, direct negotiation, and dispute prevention and avoidance.[282]

None of these "alternatives" to arbitration and litigation is startling in itself. Negotiation and conciliation are invariably options available to states and investors, regardless of whether they are provided for by treaty or contract. In addition, such measures do not preclude parties from resorting to either arbitration or litigation should negotiation or conciliation fail. In addition, bilateral investment agreements and investor–state contracts that provide for, or even mandate conflict-avoidance options, invite lip service to such options as much as the serious pursuit of them by one or both parties. Going through the motions of conflict avoidance, intent on arbitrating or litigating, is ultimately costly and dilatory for at least one party to such machinations.

Nevertheless, the institutional adoption of dispute prevention and avoidance mechanisms is a way in which investor–state parties can ameliorate their differences before they grow into conflicts. Should states endorse dispute avoidance measures by treaty, as the UNCTAD proposes, it could lead to the wider use of such measures, and it could promote innovation in reconciling differences between states and foreign investors. Such adoption could redress the effect of high cost and often complex arbitration and litigation proceedings, and it could also encourage local, regional, and global institutions to adopt innovative processes to prevent or avoid disputes. In particular, states could be relied on to incorporate negotiation or conciliation into their investment

[281] *See, e.g.*, Charles Brower & Lee Steven, *NAFTA Chapter 11: Who Then Should Judge? Developing the International Rule of Law under NAFTA Chapter 11*, 2 CHI. J. INT'L L. 193, 193–95 (2001); Jack J. Coe, Jr., *Domestic Court Control of Investment Awards: Necessary Evil or Achilles Heel within NAFTA and the Proposed FTAA*, 19 J. INT'L. ARB. 185 (2002); David A. Gantz, *An Appellate Mechanism for Review of Arbitral Decisions in Investor–State Disputes: Prospects and Challenges*, 39 VAND. J. TRANSNAT'L L. 39, 43–44 (2006); Gary R. Saxonhouse, *Dispute Settlement at the WTO and the Dole Commission: USTR Resources and Success*, *in* ISSUES AND OPTIONS FOR U.S.–JAPAN TRADE POLICIES 363 (Robert M. Stern ed., 2002).

[282] *See generally* INVESTOR–STATE DISPUTES, *supra* note 1.

treaties as requirements prior to investors initiating arbitration or litigation proceedings. Furthermore, states could also construct restrictive dispute resolution clauses in their investment agreements, including requiring mandatory mediation.[283]

Although it is preferable to avoid investor–state conflicts rather than resort to litigation or arbitration, there is no assurance that negotiation, conciliation, mediation, or some other variant of managed conflict prevention will avoid or resolve conflicts in investment disputes with states.[284] Indeed, a systemic problem is that investment disputes often arise in arms-length as distinct from informal investor–state relationships. Specifically, investors interact impersonally with government bureaucracies, and informal methods of dispute avoidance often are ill-suited to resolving disputes that are formally dealt with by legal departments within those bureaucracies. This absence of a preexisting culture of cooperation between states and foreign investors, especially when investors are ill-attuned to cultural dynamics within the forum, makes dispute avoidance measures harder to implement.[285]

Nevertheless, there may be distinct advantages in states endorsing mandatory conflict prevention measures that are reinforced by international protocols. For example, states may agree multilaterally or bilaterally to intergovernmental mechanisms by which to redress investor–state disputes. These mechanisms may vary from diplomatic measures, such as under reconstituted treaties of peace, friendship, commerce, and navigation, to formal mechanisms for intergovernmental consultations, such as under Chapter 20 of the NAFTA.[286]

Foreign investors may also benefit from established guidelines and processes governing foreign investment in host states including: clear and transparent licensing requirements, methods of securing such licenses, time lines within which to secure regulatory approval, facilitative meetings between investors and host states, contact persons to consult in complying with those regulations, warnings for noncompliance

---

283 *See* August Reinisch, *How Narrow Are Narrow Dispute Settlement Clauses in Investment Treaties?*, 2 J. INT'L DISP. SETTLEMENT 115 (2011) (discussing the restrictive construction of investment agreements). Such adoptions may be comparable to states acceding to international conventions, such as the UNCITRAL's Model Law on International Commercial Conciliation (2002) and its Model Law on International Commercial Arbitration (1985, as amended 2006). *See International Commercial Arbitration & Conciliation*, U.N. COMM'N ON INT'L TRADE LAW, http://www.uncitral.org/uncitral/en/uncitral_texts/arbitration.html (last visited June 19, 2012). *See also* Leon E. Trakman, *International Investment Law*, *in* INTERNATIONAL BUSINESS LAW 443–49 (arbitrating investment disputes), 427–36 (BITs, FTAs and multilateral agreements) (Bryan Mercurio et al. eds., 2010).

284 *See* Mark Kantor, *Negotiated Settlement of Public Infrastructure Disputes*, *in* NEW DIRECTIONS IN INTERNATIONAL ECONOMIC LAW: IN MEMORIAM THOMAS WÄLDE (Todd Weiler & Freya Baetens eds., 2011).

285 *See generally* Colin B. Picker, *International Investment Law: Some Legal Cultural Insights*, *in* INTERNATIONAL INVESTMENT LAW, *supra* note 2, ch.6 (discussing the influence of legal cultures and traditions on investment law); Trakman, *Legal Traditions and International Commercial Arbitration*, *supra* note 40 (noting the influence of legal traditions on international commercial arbitration).

286 On governmental bureaucracies faced by foreign investors in Asia, in particular in China and Australia, *see* Vivienne Bath, *Foreign Investment, the National Interest and National Security—Foreign Direct Investment in Australia and China*, 34 SYDNEY L. REV. 5 (2012), also *available at* http://papers.ssrn.com/sol3/papers.cfm?abstract_id=2042318.

by investors, and procedures for curing such noncompliance. The guidelines may also provide for the appointment of conciliators or mediators, including applicable terms of reference, should investor–state disputes eventuate.

At their best, these dispute prevention and avoidance mechanisms may discourage parties from resorting to fractious, costly, and disruptive arbitration or litigation. At their worst, however, they may protract investor–state conflict, delay dispute resolution, and increase its costs. Institutionalized dispute resolution options that are incorporated into bilateral investment treaties may avert litigation or arbitration, or they may simply delay it. Conciliation may fail because one party objects to the appointment of a facilitator, or, on appointment, that facilitator may fail to secure investor–state cooperation in managing a conflict, such as by a party declining to allow consultation with nongovernmental agencies.

The inference is not that dispute prevention and avoidance measures are ill-fitting to international investment. Insofar as states and foreign investors have economic and political incentives to prevent and avoid disputes, these measures may well carry the day. Indeed, dispute prevention and avoidance mechanisms may both anticipate and resolve investor–state differences before they regress into costly and dilatory disputes. However, construing such measures as salutary cures to differences between investors and states amounts, at best, to wishful thinking.

VII. RECOMMENDATIONS

The recommendations below are made in light of positive and reinforcing developments in ICSID investor–state arbitration in recent years. In particular, investment treaties in their genesis and earlier development included scant detail about dispute resolution, including investor–state arbitration. More recent treaties, starting with Chapter 11 of the NAFTA, include reservations and exclusions. They define an "expropriation," "most favored nation," and "national treatment" that was largely undefined in earlier investment treaties. A greater proportion of investor–state disputes in recent years are also settled or otherwise discontinued. Dispute avoidance, arguably, is also being used, less as an instrument to secure pre-disclosure and increasingly in a genuine attempt by investor–state parties to resolve disputes. In addition, a body of international investment jurisprudence is developing around such concepts as "most favored nation" and "national treatment", a regulatory expropriation, "local content" requirements, and "fair and equitable" treatment.[287]

The following are recommendations for the amendment, directly or indirectly, of the ICSID rules and procedures based on the discussion in this chapter and in light of the positive developments above. Indirect measures for amending the ICSID Rules

---

287 *See generally* UNCTAD, How to Prevent and Manage Investor–State Disputes: Lessons from Peru (UNCTAD, Feb. 3, 2012), *available at* http://archive.unctad.org/templates/Page.asp?intItemID=3666&lang=1.

include provision in BITs which regulate the manner in which investor–state arbitration is conducted, including but not limited to ICSID proceedings.

The first four recommendations below include measures that are more appropriately addressed in BITs and in most cases, are already reflected in BIT practice. The remaining recommendations are directed more specifically at the ICSID.

First, guidelines are needed to discourage premature, opportunistic, and pernicious claims from being brought by adventitious investors against vulnerable host states. Among others, and reflected in BIT practice, these guidelines should require that investors initiate mediation or conciliation proceedings in good faith and within specified time limits, without which investor–state arbitration should not be permitted.

Second, guidelines are needed to further delineate when host states have excluded their liability to foreign investor claimants on overbroad grounds such as in relation to natural resources, agriculture, and financial markets. Guidelines are also required to further determine when host states have discriminated unfairly against foreign investors on overextended grounds of essential security, national identity, public health, and environmental safety. These guidelines should take account of provisions in existing BITs and FTAs that address these issues.

Third, rules are needed that define an expropriation more clearly, including by distinguishing between a direct and an indirect expropriation, and by differentiating more clearly between a legitimate and an illegitimate government taking.

Fourth, procedural rules should require disputing parties to resort to negotiation or conciliation prior to initiating investor–state arbitration. This requirement, often adopted in BITs, reaffirms the importance in principle Fourth, procedural rules should require disputing parties to resort to negotiation or cooperation among investor–state parties, especially because investor–state arbitration is often costly and time-consuming, and such disputes sometimes have devastating economic consequences for investors and drastic social and economic impacts upon host states.

The further recommendations and proposed guidelines below are directed more specifically at the ICSID.

First, the ICSID needs standing panels to interpret ICSID rules as they apply to often complex investor–state arbitration cases.

Second, consistent with the development of ICSID Rule 34, rules are needed to ensure that arbitration proceedings are transparent, while still preserving confidential information in the public or commercial interests of one or both direct parties to an investor–state dispute. Efforts at greater transparency should encompass greater public access to arbitration proceedings. Provision should be made for the publication of tribunal reasons for admitting or denying admission to proceedings by third parties, whether in whole or part. *Amici curiae* briefs; social, economic, and environmental impact reports; and arbitration awards should be publicly available, subject to excluding confidential parts as recommended above. These recommendations are consistent with the public–private, as distinct from a wholly commercial, nature of investor–state arbitration. They distinguish investor–state arbitration appropriately from international commercial arbitration. They also reflect developments in BITs and

FTAs providing for public interest participation in arbitration proceedings and the publication of awards, notably under Chapter 11 of the NAFTA.

Third, ICSID needs further guidelines to govern conflicts of interest and duties of disclosure by arbitrators to redress the perception that a small number of arbitrators are repeatedly subject to challenges.[288]

Fourth, guidelines are needed that strike a balance between restricting the capacity of arbitrators to act as legal counsel and provide expert opinions in other investor–state arbitration disputes and enabling parties in such other cases to secure the most informed and expert advice. An issue for the ICSID is determining when arbitrators engaging in such multiple functions are in a position unduly to influence the functioning of investor–state arbitration on account of their standing, directly or otherwise, as ICSID arbitrators.

Fifth, ICSID needs more diverse sitting arbitrators who represent more developing member states and include more women.[289] The nomination of seventy-two arbitrators to the ICSID list in 2011 is limited in light of the growth in ICSID cases in recent years. Such action would also help to redress the impression that a small number of arbitrators preside over a growing number of panels.[290]

Sixth, more explicit provision is needed for interim measures to inhibit host states from initiating regulations that unreasonably interfere with investor claims. Such interim measures would be appropriate, for example, to inhibit the Australian government from implementing fast track tobacco legislation to sidetrack arbitration initiated against it by Philip Morris. Conversely, interim measures should discourage claimants, such as Philip Morris, from protracting investment arbitration in order to delay the implementation of such regulations.

Seventh, rules are needed to regulate how arbitral decisions are reached. In particular, arbitration tribunals should make awards by a majority on all issues, without the chair enjoying a casting vote.

Eighth, a challenge committee should be instituted to decide any challenges to an arbitrator. This challenge committee should also exclude arbitrators sitting on the same tribunal as the challenged arbitrator.

Ninth, guidelines are needed to regulate, and also reduce legal costs generally. Such measures should regulate the use of contingency fees, place ad valorem caps on the fees of the arbitrator; and regulate the allocation of costs among the parties. Arbitrators may be requested at the commencement of arbitration to provide the parties with a

---

288 *See also* Daphna Kapeliuk, *Collegial Games: Analyzing the Effect of Panel Composition on Outcome in Investment Arbitration*, 31 REV. LITIG. 267 (2012).

289 *See also* Gus Van Harten, *The (Lack of) Women Arbitrators in Investment Treaty Arbitration*. FDI Perspectives (Feb. 2012), *available at* http://papers.ssrn.com/sol3/papers.cfm?abstract_id=2005336. On the distributional inequality of women in corporations engaged in foreign direct investment more generally, *see* Rachel J. Anderson, *Promoting Distributional Equality for Women: Some Thoughts on Gender and Global Corporate Citizenship in Foreign Direct Investment*, 32 WOMEN'S RIGHTS L.R. 1. (2010).

290 *See* the ICSID Caseload, *available at* http://icsid.worldbank.org/ICSID/FrontServlet?requestType=ICSIDDocRH&actionVal=CaseLoadStatistics.

nonbinding estimate of costs based on the anticipated nature, complexity, and length of proceedings.

Tenth, ICSID rules should require parties to register claims and counterclaims within prescribed time limits, to clarify their availability in advance of hearings, and to be available prior to and directly after hearings, such as a day before and remain a day after hearings.

Eleventh, guidelines are needed by which arbitrators can encourage investor–state parties to settle their disputes during the course of proceedings, without mandating such action.

Twelfth, the ICSID arguably needs an appellate body. An appellate body with a wider mandate than annulment could expand the grounds of an appeal and consider remedies beyond annulment. It could also help render ICSID jurisprudence more consistent in nature. It is noteworthy that, of the total number of ICSID awards in the 1990s (namely eighteen), there was only one annulment, while there were ninety-six awards in the 2000s and eight annulments. Thus, despite an increase in the number of annulments relative to awards, annulment proceedings are occasional and seldom successful.[291]

Finally, ICSID needs a process for the ongoing scrutiny of proposals such as those above, directed at implementing new or modified rules to redress problems relating to investor–state arbitration.

In defense of the ICSID and its Secretariat, although the ICSID can regulate investor–state arbitration procedurally, it cannot adopt substantive law requirements. For example, the ICSID cannot determine how the defense of necessity ought to apply in particular cases, or how to construe intellectual property rights. These are matters for arbitration tribunals to decide.

A further defense of the ICSID is that, even in devising procedural rules to govern investor–state arbitration, the ICSID cannot require states to adopt particular dispute resolution clauses by treaty, or investor–state parties to adopt them by agreement. These are matters to be determined by host and home states, and by host states and foreign investors respectively.

VIII. CONCLUSION

A state that foreign investors consider unattractive may lose not only stature in the global community of states and investors, but also credibility in the eyes of its domestic constituents. As the history of ICSID arbitration has demonstrated, debate about the value of international institutions such as the ICSID is significantly about perceived political and economic costs and benefits to social interests groups not limited to states and investors. A state that identifies a benefit in becoming a signatory to an

[291] *See id.*

international investment convention such as the ICSID may as a consequence of losing a case quickly shift to condemning ICSID arbitration, and, with it, lose stature both domestically and in the international community. Bad experiences that states have with ICSID arbitration is one factor in periodic attacks on it, such as Latin American governments asserting that ICSID proceedings perpetuate systemic inequalities in favor of investors from wealthy Northern countries at the expense of their Southern neighbors.

These criticisms notwithstanding, the ICSID is unlikely to be overhauled institutionally in the absence of widely endorsed motivations for such reform. Simmering resentment about secrecy in investor–state arbitration, explosive challenges to the appointment of ICSID arbitrators, and adverse awards in particular cases will not be enough to incite the radical transformation of international investment law. If a body, such as the ICSID Secretariat, that is best able to evaluate the efficient operation of ICSID arbitration is unable to further instigate institutional reform leading to greater transparency in proceedings and publicity in awards, the prospects for such reform recede further.

However, the ICSID Secretariat should not be expected to be the center of gravity for reforms to the structure and operation of the ICSID. The Secretariat does not have the authority to reform ICSID rules: it is not the ICSID's governing body, and it, unavoidably, lacks the gravitas among its membership to spearhead change. It is also unfair to blame the ICSID Secretariat for failing to effectuate reforms that, realistically, are beyond its grasp. Indeed, proposals for reform of the ICSID rules require the support of the ICSID signatory states, which is dependent on these states being able to reconcile their often inconsistent political and economic agendas.

On the other hand, it is unlikely that ICSID member states will agree that domestic courts resolve investor–state disputes as an alternative to investor–state arbitration. Notwithstanding Australia's stand-alone commitment to forsake arbitration in favor of domestic courts, few states are likely to follow suit due to concerns about national biases among national courts and confusion over disparate domestic systems of law, among other factors.

States may incorporate dispute prevention and avoidance provisions into investment treaties as plausible ways to dissipate conflict. However, such measures may represent preliminary steps leading to investor–state arbitration or litigation. They may also delay and increase the cost of an investor–state conflict.

However, the greatest threat to the ICSID is not about the availability of alternatives to investor–state arbitration. Rather, the greatest threat is one of perception about how it ought to operate, and who it ought to and does in fact benefit. That threat to the ICSID is most strongly articulated by some developing states, not limited to Latin America. Their perception is that the track record of investor–state arbitration reflects a history of servicing developed states and their investors above developing states and their civic interests. A further perception among some developing states is that ICSID proceedings lack transparency; ICSID arbitrators sometimes fail to make material disclosures or are otherwise in a conflict of interest; ICSID arbitrators reach inconsistent decisions in seemingly similar cases; and the costs of ICSID proceedings are sometimes prohibitive for governments, investors, and civic interest groups from poorer countries.

However, the problem with any assault on the ICSID is in failing to recognize that the ICSID is the supplicant of its signatories. The ICSID did not create itself, but rather member states created it. Blaming ICSID for a myriad of ills is to forget that, insofar as it is a singer, the song was scripted by member states that now include the vast majority of developed and developing states.

Nor should the sufficiency of the ICSID depend on a tally of states, investors, and public interest groups that favor it juxtaposed against a tally of those that do not. Indeed, the sufficiency of the ICSID depends on whether competing interests favoring or opposing it can be reconciled. Consequently, mediating among such competing interests will be a key determinant of the future of investor–state arbitration and the ICSID in particular.

Short of a robust account of the capacity of the ICSID to satisfy a plurality of competing interests, systematic reform of ICSID principles and rules of operation is unlikely to materialize. Conversely, inertia in the face of concerted attacks on the ICSID's credibility is likely to undermine its stature among states, investors, and public interest groups that distrust it, however much they use its services. If investors see that the ICSID takes on these challenges but still fails sufficiently to redress them, it will be perceived as being as being paralyzed and unable to progress beyond the status quo.

The stakes are high for states, foreign investors, and public interest groups. Should stakeholders push for reform now and fail, they may undermine confidence in international investment law and practice, beyond the perceived failings of investor–state arbitration. On the other hand, should stakeholders wait patiently for the next rampage of crises of confidence in investor–state arbitration to materialize, they may make it harder to declare that these crises were unprecedented and unavoidable. In truth, we have all been warned.

11

THE LAW OF INDIRECT EXPROPRIATION AND THE IRAN–UNITED STATES CLAIMS TRIBUNAL'S ROLE IN ITS DEVELOPMENT

Romesh Weeramantry

1. INTRODUCTION

The burgeoning mass of contemporary investment arbitration awards has provided a wealth of jurisprudence on the law of indirect expropriation. Prior to this recent deluge of case law, the largest body of international awards on expropriation was issued by the Iran–U.S. Claims Tribunal (hereafter the "Tribunal"). Before the Tribunal was established, international tribunal decisions on indirect expropriation were few and far between.[1]

This chapter focuses not on direct expropriation but rather on indirect expropriation. The latter type of expropriation has been chosen as the subject matter of examination because investment treaty arbitrations infrequently deal with direct expropriations.[2]

[1] *See, e.g.*, CHARLES N. BROWER & JASON D. BRUESCHKE, THE IRAN-UNITED STATES CLAIMS TRIBUNAL 440 (1998) (stating that "the awards of the Tribunal constitute a significant body of precedent and an important addition to the relatively few decisions of international tribunals on the subject of what constitutes and expropriation.").

[2] *See* August Reinisch, *Expropriation*, *in* PETER MUCHLINSKI, FEDERICO ORTINO & CHRISTOPH SCHREUER, THE OXFORD HANDBOOK OF INTERNATIONAL INVESTMENT LAW 408 (2008); and RUDOLF DOLZER & CHRISTOPH SCHREUER, PRINCIPLES OF INTERNATIONAL INVESTMENT LAW 92 (2008). However, the Iran–U.S. Claims Tribunal has issued a number of awards that dealt with claims of direct expropriation. *See, e.g.*, *American International Group, Inc. v Iran*, Award No. 93-2-3 (Dec. 13, 1983), 4 Iran–U.S. Cl. Trib. Rep. 96, and *INA Corporation v Iran*, Award 184-161-1 (Aug. 13, 1985), 8 Iran–U.S. Cl. Trib. Rep. 373 (both cases concerned a 1979 Iranian law nationalizing all insurance companies operating in Iran); and *Malek v. Iran*, Award No. 534-193-3 (Aug. 11, 1992), 28 Iran–U.S. Cl. Trib. Rep. 246 (concerning the 1979 Iranian law nationalizing all Iranian banks). On the difference between nationalization and expropriation, see *Lauder v. Czech Republic*, UNCITRAL, Award (Final), Sept. 3, 2001, at

The chapter seeks to highlight the international law attributes of current investment treaty law on indirect expropriation by exploring references in investment treaty jurisprudence to Tribunal case law.

After providing a brief factual background on the historical events in Iran that led to the establishment of the Tribunal, the chapter will survey the Tribunal's formation, jurisdiction, and core functions. Tribunal awards pertaining to indirect expropriation and the international sources upon which they are based will then be reviewed. The chapter then turns to investigate the role played by Tribunal jurisprudence in investment law by examining references to Tribunal cases in major investment law commentaries that address the subject of expropriation. Thereafter, a number of investment arbitration awards that involve determinations on indirect expropriation will be considered, with a focus on how those awards utilize the case law of the Tribunal. Next, Tribunal awards on "other measures affecting property rights" are discussed, and the question of whether these awards are a type of *lex specialis* that are inappropriate for use in investment arbitration will be explored. The concluding section will briefly discuss the future role of Tribunal awards in investment law.

2. REVOLUTION IN IRAN

Iran, with its vast oil resources, was a significant beneficiary of the 1970s' oil boom. For petroleum-exporting nations, the financial prosperity created during that period was unprecedented. On the back of this boom, Iran's then- Shah set the country on a course of major economic and military development. This intended growth and expansion caused hundreds of American corporations to become associated with business ventures in Iran, and generated an inflow into Iran of billions of U.S. dollars in private capital from the United States. As a consequence, 45,000 Americans are estimated to have lived and worked in Iran at the end of the 1970s.[3]

Notwithstanding this seemingly boundless cauldron of wealth and inward foreign investment, disenchantment and revolutionary zeal spread within segments of Iranian society. The stirrings of revolution gained considerable momentum in late 1978, and by January 1979 the Shah had fled Iran. The Islamic Republic of Iran was proclaimed on February 11, 1979 and a measure of normality was established in the summer of that year. The tipping point for the United States occurred in November 1979 after the seizure of its embassy and personnel in Tehran by protestors, who demanded that the United States return the Shah, who was receiving surgical treatment in the United

para. 200 ("expropriation means the coercive appropriation by the State of private property, usually by means of individual administrative measures. Nationalization involves large-scale takings on the basis of an executive or legislative act for the purpose of transferring property or interests into the public domain."). For a rare example of direct expropriation in investment arbitration, see *Sedelmayer v Russian Federation*, International Court of Arbitration at the Chamber of Commerce in Stockholm, Award, July 7, 1998.

3 BROWER & BRUESCHKE, *supra* note 1, at 1–4.

States. The U.S. response was to prohibit oil imports from Iran and to freeze approximately US$8 billion in Iranian assets held in the United States and with American financial institutions located abroad.[4]

Unwilling to negotiate directly, the United States and Iran discussed their differences through the good offices of Algeria. Eventually, a suite of declarations and agreements was concluded, commonly referred to as the "Algiers Accords." Pursuant to these documents, Iran released the U.S. embassy hostages and the United States unfroze the US$8 billion of Iranian assets. Most important for the purpose of this chapter, a tribunal to hear and adjudicate (1) claims between the two disputing states, (2) claims of U.S. nationals against Iran, and (3) claims of Iranian nationals against the United States was established pursuant to a "Claims Settlement Declaration" made by Algeria.[5]

3. CLAIMS SETTLEMENT DECLARATION

The Claims Settlement Declaration is the Tribunal's foundation document. Although made by Algeria, both Iran and the United States undertook to adhere to its terms. Pursuant to the Declaration, both countries agreed to promote the settlement of claims listed in Article II therein. Any such claims not settled within six months were to be submitted for binding third-party arbitration. In furtherance of this objective, Article II provides that "[a]n international arbitral tribunal (the Iran–United States Claims Tribunal) is hereby established for the purpose of deciding [those] claims."

The jurisdictional provision of signal importance to this chapter is Article II(1) of the Claims Settlement Declaration, which provides that the Tribunal was

> established for the purpose of deciding claims of nationals of the United States against Iran and claims of nationals of Iran against the United States, and any counterclaim . . . if such claims and counterclaims are outstanding at the date of this Agreement . . . and arise out of debts, contracts . . . expropriations or other measures affecting property rights . . .[6]

[4] George H. Aldrich, The Jurisprudence of the Iran–United States Claims Tribunal 4 (1996). *See also* Nils Mangard, *The Hostage Crisis, the Algiers Accords, and the Iran–U.S. Claims Tribunal*, *in* Festschrift Till Lars Hjerner, Studies in International Law 363 (1990).

[5] Declaration of the Government of the Democratic and Popular Republic of Algeria concerning the Settlement of Claims by the Government of the United States of America and the Government of the Islamic Republic of Iran, Jan. 19, 1981 [hereinafter Claims Settlement Declaration], *reprinted in* 1 Iran-U.S. Cl. Trib. Rep. 13 and also *in* Aldrich, *supra* note 4, at Annex I.

[6] *See* Claims Settlement Declaration, Article II(1).

The Declaration avoided the requirement of exhaustion of local remedies by expressly stating that jurisdiction was granted over outstanding claims "whether or not filed with any court."[7]

The definition of "nationals" who may make claims and issues pertaining to the nationality of their "claims" is contained in Article VII. The Declaration also addresses, among other things, the composition of the Tribunal (Article III), the finality and enforcement of its awards (Article IV), the law to be applied by it (Article V), its seat (Article VI(1))[8], payment of its expenses (Article VI(3)), and the mechanism to resolve disputes as to the interpretation of the Declaration (Article VI(4)).

4. THE IRAN–U.S. CLAIMS TRIBUNAL

The Tribunal was established in July 1981 pursuant to the Claims Settlement Declaration. As of September 30, 2011, the Tribunal has resolved almost 4,000 cases. During this process, the Tribunal has issued over 800 awards and decisions, which comprise 601 awards (including partial and agreed terms awards), over 80 interlocutory and interim awards and over 130 decisions.[9] Given these extraordinary statistics, it is not surprising that the Tribunal has been described as the busiest-ever single arbitration tribunal.[10] As of September 2011, the total amount awarded by the Tribunal to U.S. parties has been in excess of US$2.1 billion, of which US$1.6 billion resulted from awards on agreed terms.[11]

The Tribunal is different from arbitral institutions such as, for example, the International Centre for the Settlement of Investment Disputes (ICSID) in many fundamental ways. The Tribunal is a "one-stop-shop." It operates out of one dedicated premises at Parkweg 13, The Hague. The property houses the Tribunal's registry and the offices of the Tribunal's staff (including legal assistants and translators). Nine full-time arbitrators work at the Tribunal (see below), who, for the most part, review written submissions, hear cases, deliberate, and draft awards at Parkweg 13.[12] ICSID, in contrast, is an institution—not a tribunal. It administers and supports the dozens of individual tribunals that are established and operate under its auspices. Arbitrators

---

[7] Claims Settlement Declaration, Article II(1). *See also* ALDRICH, *supra* note 4, at 173.

[8] The seat of the Tribunal is The Hague, the Netherlands.

[9] Iran–United States Claims Tribunal, *Communiqué No. 11/4* (Oct. 6, 2011), *available at* http://www.iusct.org/communique-english.pdf (last visited Dec. 19, 2011). *See also* CS Gibson & CR Drahozal, *Iran–United States Claims Tribunal Precedent in Investor–State Arbitration*, 23(6) J. INT'L ARB. 521, 521 (2006).

[10] SIMON GREENBERG, CHRISTOPHER KEE & J. ROMESH WEERAMANTRY, INTERNATIONAL COMMERCIAL ARBITRATION: AN ASIA–PACIFIC PERSPECTIVE 15 (2011). As to the extraordinary number of prominent international arbitration lawyers who have been involved with or started their arbitration careers at the Tribunal, see Sebastian Perry, *Children of the Revolution*, GLOBAL ARB. REV., Apr. 27, 2012.

[11] Iran–United States Claims Tribunal, *Communiqué No. 11/4* (Oct. 6, 2011), *available at* http://www.iusct.org/communique-english.pdf (last visited Dec. 19, 2011).

[12] For large cases, sometimes the hearing facilities of the Permanent Court of Arbitration in The Hague's Peace Palace are used.

sitting on ICSID tribunals do not work at ICSID on a full-time basis but are appointed for each individual case. Their ICSID mandate expires once the respective tribunal has issued its final award.[13]

Another noteworthy difference between the Tribunal and ICSID (and almost all other ad hoc international tribunals for that matter) is that the Tribunal has a direct payment method of enforcing its pecuniary awards against Iran. The ICSID Convention contains provisions designed to facilitate enforcement in ways more efficient than those found under the 1958 New York Convention on the Enforcement of Foreign Arbitral Awards. However, direct enforcement is not possible under the ICSID Convention. Moreover, objections based on state immunity may be raised in domestic court enforcement actions relating to ICSID awards, and a number of its decisions remain unpaid.[14]

In contrast, monetary awards made by the Tribunal against Iran are paid from an escrow account established and funded by Iran for that specific purpose. Iran was obligated under its adherence to the Declaration of the Government of the Democratic and Popular Republic of Algeria of January 19, 1981 (also referred to as the "General Declaration") initially to pay US$1 billion into that account.[15] According to paragraph 6 of the General Declaration, should the balance of the escrow account fall below US$500 million, Iran is obliged to make new deposits to maintain a minimum balance of US$500 million. Once the Tribunal issues a monetary award against Iran, it simply notifies the bank at which the escrow account is held to pay the awarded amount directly to the claimant. The transfer is then executed and no state immunity issues are involved. This mechanism constitutes one of the most effective enforcement systems in the history of international arbitration.

On the groundbreaking nature of the Tribunal, Professor Richard Lillich spoke of the Tribunal at the American Society of International Law annual conference in 1982 in the following terms:

> The current effort in The Hague is the most significant international arbitration in history. It dwarfs such earlier landmarks as the Jay Treaty Commissions and the *Alabama Claims Arbitration*. If not in number of claims, then certainly in amount of money and complexity of issues involved, it far exceeds its predecessors—including the U.S.–German and U.S.–Mexican Claims Commissions of the 1920s and 1930s—whose decisions still fill the pages of the leading international law

---

13 Well over one hundred different arbitrators have been appointed in different ICSID arbitrations over the years. *See, e.g.*, Jeffery Commission, *A Snapshot of ICSID Arbitrators in Pending Cases*, KLUWER ARBITRATION BLOG, Sept. 4, 2009.

14 Argentina, for example, has not yet paid any ICSID awards under which it has been required to pay compensation. *See, e.g.*, Lucy Reed, *Scorecard of Investment Treaty Cases against Argentina since 2001*, KLUWER ARBITRATION BLOG, Mar. 2, 2009. On the enforcement of ICSID awards generally, see GREENBERG, KEE & WEERAMANTRY, *supra* note 10, at 503–04.

15 Declaration of the Government of the Democratic and Popular Republic of Algeria, *reprinted in* 1 Iran-U.S. Cl. Trib. Rep. 3 and also *in* ALDRICH, *supra* note 4, at Annex I. This document, also known as the "General Declaration," should not be confused with the Claims Settlement Declaration.

> casebooks 50 years later. The largest and most important international arbitration to date, it surely will influence the development of the law of international claims well into the coming century.[16]

The awards and decisions of the Tribunal have so far been reported in thirty-eight volumes of the *Iran–US Claims Tribunal Reports*.[17] The considerable scale of its output has given rise to the observation that the Tribunal has "contributed the largest single corpus of precedent in public international law, and also in commercial law, produced by any international claims body."[18] In more qualitative terms, the Tribunal's awards have been regarded as the "most important body of international arbitration jurisprudence" and that the "significance of these decisions as persuasive authority is second to none."[19] On a substantive level, in addition to its jurisprudence on indirect expropriation (which will be discussed in detail later) the jurisprudence of the Tribunal is well-known for providing valuable insights into the application of the UNCITRAL Arbitration Rules and has contributed significantly to the growth and advancement of international commercial law or *lex mercatoria*.[20] Frequent reference is also made to Tribunal awards in discussions on valuation in international arbitration. In Marboe's book on calculating damages in investment law, for example, reference has been made to approximately seventy Tribunal awards.[21]

However, the favorable facts and opinions set out above need to be evaluated in the light of some circumspect views about the Tribunal. Brower and Brueschke have helpfully summarized these more cautious positions as follows:

> Loosely grouped, there are four main criticisms of the Tribunal as a potential source of public international law jurisprudence: the awards constitute *lex specialis* and therefore are not relevant beyond the Tribunal itself; at times the hostile nature of the relationship between the United States and Iran has so politicized the Tribunal that its decisions are suspect; the third-country Chairmen have been subjected, and have improperly yielded, to intense forms of pressure exerted by the State Party–appointed Members; and finally, the awards of the Tribunal are

---

[16] Richard Lillich, *Iran/United States Claims Tribunal: Remarks*, 76 AM. SOC. INT'L L. PROCEEDINGS 1, 5 (1982).

[17] Published by Cambridge University Press. The awards and decisions of the Tribunal are also available on Westlaw.

[18] BROWER & BRUESCHKE, *supra* note 1, at 669.

[19] Rodger P. Alford, *The American Influence on International Arbitration*, 19 OHIO ST. J. DISP. RESOLUTION 69, 86 (2003).

[20] BROWER & BRUESCHKE, *supra* note 1, at 669. *See also* the list of issues and facts that have been addressed by the Tribunal as set out in Christopher R. Drahozal & Christopher S. Gibson, *Iran-U.S. Claims Tribunal Precedent in Investor–State Arbitration*, *in* THE IRAN–U.S. CLAIMS TRIBUNAL AT 25: THE CASES EVERYONE NEEDS TO KNOW FOR INVESTOR–STATE & INTERNATIONAL ARBITRATION 1, 13 (Christopher R. Drahozal & Christopher S. Gibson eds., 2007).

[21] IRMGARD MARBOE, CALCULATION OF COMPENSATION AND DAMAGES IN INTERNATIONAL INVESTMENT LAW (2009).

merely decisions in cases and therefore not worthy of being afforded any significant persuasive weight in international law.[22]

In one critique, Joelson has commented that "a number of important Tribunal decisions were adopted which did not reflect a fair and reasonable application of settled international law to the facts adduced in the case."[23] He attributes this perceived flaw largely to the political nature of the Tribunal. Nonetheless, Brower and Brueschke, as well as Joelson, still see value in the case law produced by the Tribunal. The former authors comment that despite the criticisms "the decisions of the Tribunal do constitute a very significant source of jurisprudential development of public international law."[24] Joelson, despite his concerns, still states that "the Tribunal has made many significant and valid contributions to the international jurisprudence on state responsibility."[25]

For the purpose of this chapter, the question as to whether the Tribunal's awards have generally contributed to the development of international investment law needs to be addressed. Scholarly literature has already examined this issue. Drahozal and Gibson, in a volume titled *The Iran-U.S. Claims Tribunal at 25: The Cases Everyone Needs to Know for Investor–State & International Arbitration* have taken the view that the Tribunal's awards are "an essential source for lawyers and parties involved in investor-State disputes."[26] As discussed below, investment law literature frequently contains citations to Tribunal awards. In this regard, the late Thomas Wälde was prescient when he commented in 2003 that the sheer number of Tribunal cases and their public accessibility "is likely to make them as a first port of call when the very open-ended articles of modern bilateral and multilateral investment treaties, including their recourse to customary international law standards, are to be interpreted."[27]

In an attempt to measure empirically the reliance on Tribunal decisions in investment arbitration, Drahozal and Gibson examined eighty-one ICSID awards and decisions and found that twenty-six of them (or 32 percent) cited Tribunal precedent.[28] From another perspective, the study revealed that Tribunal precedent was cited in 45 percent of ICSID awards that considered the merits and only 20 percent of ICSID awards that related to jurisdiction.[29] This suggests that ICSID tribunals refer to the Tribunal's findings on substantive issues more often than procedural ones. That same study also analyzed party submissions in sixteen NAFTA arbitrations and concluded

---

22 BROWER & BRUESCHKE, *supra* note 1, at 644.

23 Mark R. Joelson, *The Contributions of the Iran–U.S. Claims Tribunal to the International Law on Expropriation*, *in* THE IRAN-U.S. CLAIMS TRIBUNAL AT 25, *supra* note 20, at 216.

24 BROWER & BRUESCHKE, *supra* note 1, at 655.

25 Joelson, *supra* note 23, at 216.

26 Christopher R. Drahozal & Christopher S. Gibson, *Preface*, *in* THE IRAN-U.S. CLAIMS TRIBUNAL AT 25, *supra* note 20, at viii.

27 Thomas W. Wälde, *Book Review: The US–Iran Claims Tribunal*, 1 OIL, GAS & ENERGY LAW (2003), www.ogel.org, quoted in Drahozal & Gibson, *supra* note 26, at viii.

28 Drahozal & Gibson, *supra* note 20, at 22.

29 *Id.* at 27.

that Tribunal precedent was cited in fourteen (or 87.5 percent) of those cases.[30] This statistic on party (as opposed to tribunal) use indicates that Tribunal jurisprudence is a commonly consulted source by parties when pleading their cases.

Now that this general background on the significance of the Tribunal and its case law has been provided, it merits note that the Tribunal's jurisprudence on expropriation has been described as the area in which it has "made perhaps its greatest contribution to the public international law."[31] We now proceed to look at this question more specifically, and examine the role the Tribunal has played in the development of expropriation law in the relatively nascent field of international investment law.

5. IRAN–UNITED STATES CLAIMS TRIBUNAL JURISPRUDENCE ON INDIRECT EXPROPRIATION

Before delving deeper into international investment law, the Tribunal's jurisprudence on indirect expropriation requires examination. The Tribunal has rendered approximately sixty awards on expropriation.[32] A number of these awards deal with investment law–related issues such as whether certain unofficial interferences with property could also be attributable to a government or how to calculate compensation for expropriated assets.[33] These issues are not the focus of this chapter. The Tribunal awards that are of primary concern for this chapter are those that have been required to define indirect expropriation. Based on the research conducted for this chapter, the Tribunal awards referred to most frequently for guidance on the definition of indirect expropriation are *Starrett Housing Corporation v. Iran*,[34] and *Tippetts, Abbett, McCarthy, Stratton v. TAMS-AFFA Consulting Engineers of Iran*.[35] They will be addressed below in chronological sequence. However, before turning our attention to these awards, it is worthwhile to consider antecedent Tribunal awards that dealt with expropriation.

Harza Engineering Company v. Iran,[36] issued in December 1982, is the earliest award in which the Tribunal casts light on the circumstances that would constitute

30 *Id.* at 25.

31 BROWER & BRUESCHKE, *supra* note 1, at 370.

32 *See* Maurizio Brunetti, *Indirect Expropriation in International Law*, 5 INTERNATIONAL LAW FORUM DU DROIT INTERNATIONAL 150, 152 (2003).

33 *See also* Veijo Heiskanen, *The Contribution of the Iran–United States Claims Tribunal to the Development of the Doctrine of Indirect Expropriation*, 5 INTERNATIONAL LAW FORUM DU DROIT INTERNATIONAL 176, 187 (2003) (stating that the Tribunal found that nationalizations and expropriations "trigger the host State's liability and give rise to a right to compensation under international law, whether or not the measures are taken for a *prima facie* legitimate public purpose and whether or not they are discriminatory. The possible lawfulness of such measures under international law or under the law of the host State does not really matter; even if the measure were considered lawful, a right to compensation would still arise. Confirming this rule is one of the most important contributions made by the Iran–United States Claims Tribunal to international investment law." (footnote omitted)).

34 Interlocutory Award No. ITL 32-24-1 (Dec. 19, 1983), *reprinted in* 4 Iran–U.S. Cl. Trib. Rep. 122.

35 Award No. 141-7-2 (June 29, 1984), *reprinted in* 6 Iran–U.S. Cl. Trib. Rep. 219.

36 Award No. 19-98-2 (Dec. 30, 1982), *reprinted in* 1 Iran–U.S. Cl. Trib. Rep. 499.

indirect expropriation. But despite being first in time, *Harza* is not often referred to in investment arbitration awards. In *Harza*, Chamber One observed that "a taking of property may occur under international law, even in the absence of a formal nationalization or expropriation, if a government has interfered unreasonably with the use of property."[37] The proposition was buttressed with a footnote citing, inter alia, (i) Professor Christie's seminal article "What Constitutes a Taking of Property Under International Law";[38] (ii) Article 10(3) of the Harvard Draft Convention on the International Responsibility of States for Injuries to Aliens;[39] and (iii) Whiteman's *Digest*.[40] However, the Chamber considered that it need not decide "how unreasonable the interference must be to constitute a taking of property" because the claimant failed to prove that the alleged acts of expropriation (in relation to bank account funds) amounted to unreasonable interference.[41] The *Harza* award's requirement of an "unreasonable interference" to be present for expropriation to take place mirrors the wording of Article 10(3) of the Harvard Draft Convention (extracted below). The position of *Harza* in relation to expropriation was expressly adopted three months later by Chamber Two in *Golpira v. Iran*.[42]

The next decision of significance was the *ITT Industries, Inc. v. Iran* award issued in May 1983.[43] The circumstances surrounding this award are noteworthy. Thirty minutes prior to its signature by Chamber Two, the arbitrators were informed that the parties had settled the matter. George Aldrich, the U.S. arbitrator in Chamber Two, has written that he believed that someone in the Tribunal had passed on to Iran information about the draft award in that case. As a result, he filed a Concurring Opinion to the Award on Agreed Terms. He states that his Opinion was essentially the draft award that Chamber Two would have issued had no settlement occurred.[44] The relevant part of the Concurring Opinion stated as follows:

> Property may be taken under international law through interference by a state in the use of that property or with the enjoyment of its benefits, even where legal title to the property is not affected. See 8 Whiteman, *Digest of International Law* 1006–20; Christie, *What Constitutes a Taking under International Law?* 38 Brit. Y.B. Int'l. Law 307 (1962); *Harvard Draft Convention on the International Responsibility of States for Injuries to the Economic Interests of Aliens*, articles 3 and 38, *reprinted in* 55 Am. J. Int'l Law 545 (1961); the *Lena Goldfield's Case*, *reprinted in* Nussbaum,

[37] 1 Iran–U.S. Cl. Trib. Rep. 499, at 504.

[38] G.C. Christie, *What Constitutes a Taking of Property under International Law*, *in* 38 BRITISH YEAR BOOK OF INTERNATIONAL LAW 307 (1962).

[39] Louis B. Sohn & R.R. Baxter, *Responsibility of States for Injuries to the Economic Interests of Aliens*, 55 AM. J. INT'L L. 545, 553 (1961).

[40] MARJORIE WHITEMAN, DIGEST OF INTERNATIONAL LAW, Vol. VIII, at 1006–20 (1967).

[41] Award No. 19-98-2 (Dec. 30, 1982), *reprinted in* 1 Iran–U.S. Cl. Trib. Rep. 499, at 499–500.

[42] Award No. 32-211-2 (Mar. 29, 1983), *reprinted in* 2 Iran–U.S. Cl. Trib. Rep. 171, at 177.

[43] Award on Agreed Terms No. 47-156-2 (May 26, 1983), *reprinted in* 2 Iran–U.S. Cl. Trib. Rep. 348.

[44] ALDRICH, *supra* note 4, at 175.

> *The Arbitration Between the Lena Goldfields, Ltd. and the Soviet Government*, 36 Cornell L.Q. 31 (1950).
>
> These authorities indicate that, while assumption of control over property by a government does not automatically and immediately justify a conclusion that the property has been taken by the government, thus requiring compensation under international law, such a conclusion is warranted whenever events demonstrate that the owner was deprived of fundamental rights of ownership and it appears that this deprivation is not merely ephemeral. The intent of the government is less important than the effects of the measures on the owner, and the form of the measures of control or interference is less important than the reality of their impact.[45]

It was only after the awards mentioned above were issued that Chamber One made its decision on expropriation in the *Starrett* proceedings.

5.1 *STARRETT HOUSING CORPORATION V. IRAN*

In its interlocutory award of December 19, 1983 in *Starrett*, Chamber One held that the government of Iran had taken the claimants' physical assets as well as its contractual rights to construct and manage a large housing project in Iran. It so held even though Iran had not issued any law or decree under which the project was expressly expropriated. In stating its reasons for its findings, Chamber One observed:

> it is recognized in international law that measures taken by a State can interfere with property rights to such an extent that these rights are rendered so useless that they must be deemed to have been expropriated, even though the State does not purport to have expropriated them and the legal title to the property formally remains with the original owner.[46]

This finding (hereafter the "*Starrett* finding"), along with the *Tippetts* case decision as noted below, has been one of the most frequently quoted passages of the Tribunal on the subject of expropriation. Although the Tribunal refers to "international law" as recognizing the position the award takes on expropriation, no specific instances of such "law" are set out. The details of the "law" to which the Tribunal appears to have made reference is set out in the Concurring Opinion of Howard M. Holtzmann. He extracts the above passage from the *Starrett* finding and comments that it represents "well-settled principles of international law," adding that those principles were stated

---

[45] Concurring Opinion of George H. Aldrich in ITT Industries, Inc v Iran, Award on Agreed Terms No. 47-156-2 (May 26, 1983), *reprinted in* 2 Iran–U.S. Cl. Trib. Rep. 348, at 351.

[46] Interlocutory Award No. ITL 32-24-1 (Dec. 19, 1983), *reprinted in* 4 Iran–U.S. Cl. Trib. Rep. 122, at 154.

in the 1961 Harvard Draft Convention.[47] Particular reference is made to Article 10(3)(a) of that instrument, which states:

> A "taking of property" includes not only an outright taking of property but also any such unreasonable interference with the use, enjoyment or disposal of property as to justify an interference that the owner thereof will not be able to use, enjoy, or dispose of the property within a reasonable period of time after the inception of such interference.[48]

Judge Holtzmann then proceeds to state that "[t]his concept has firm roots in the decisions of international tribunals,"[49] and cites as supporting authority the *Chorzow Factory*[50] and the *Norwegian Shipowners'* cases[51] These well-known cases involved the taking of physical property as well as contractual rights connected with that property. Next, he quotes the following passage from Professor Christies' *British Year Book of International Law*, article which established from the *Chorzow Factory* and *Norwegian Shipowners'* cases that

> a State may expropriate property, where it interferes with it, even though the State expressly disclaims any such intention. More important, the two cases [i.e., *Chorzow Factory* and *Norwegian Shipowners'*] taken together illustrate that even though a State may not purport to interfere with rights to property, it may, by its actions, render those rights so useless that it will be deemed to have expropriated them.[52]

Judge Holtzmann concludes his discussion of the law on expropriation by referring with approval to the pronouncements on expropriation in *Harza* and *ITT Industries*, as mentioned above.[53]

---

47 Concurring Opinion of Howard M. Holtzman in Starrett Housing Corporation v Iran, Interlocutory Award No. ITL 32-24-1 (Dec. 19, 1983), *reprinted in* 4 Iran–U.S. Cl. Trib. Rep. 122, at 162.

48 Sohn & Baxter, *supra* note 39, at 553. The commentary to the Draft Articles provide the following general guidance on what is meant by unreasonable interference: "The unreasonableness of an interference with the use, enjoyment, or disposal of property must be determined in conformity with the general principles of law recognized by the principal legal systems of the world. No attempt has been made to particularize on the expression used in the text, since the matter seems one best worked out by international tribunals." *Id.* at 559. Perhaps in this way, much discretion was left to a body such as the Tribunal to articulate the concept of expropriation and define what type of conduct transgressed reasonable levels of interference.

49 Concurring Opinion of Howard M. Holtzman in Starrett Housing Corporation v Iran, Interlocutory Award No. ITL 32-24-1 (Dec. 19, 1983), *reprinted in* 4 Iran–U.S. Cl. Trib. Rep. 122, at 163.

50 *Certain German Interests in Polish Upper Silesia* (Ger. v Pol.), 1926 P.C.I.J. ser. A, No. 7, at 14-45 (Judgment of May 25, 1926).

51 Norwegian Shipowners' Claims (Nor. v. U.S.) Award (Oct. 13, 1922), 1 Reports of International Arbitral Awards 307.

52 Christie, *supra* note 38, at 311.

53 Concurring Opinion of Howard M. Holtzman in Starrett Housing Corporation v Iran, Interlocutory Award No. ITL 32-24-1 (Dec. 19, 1983), *reprinted in* 4 Iran–U.S. Cl. Trib. Rep. 122, at 163–64.

5.2 *TIPPETTS, ABBETT, MCCARTHY, STRATTON V. TAMS-AFFA CONSULTING ENGINEERS*

Six months after the *Starrett Housing* case, the award in *Tippetts* was issued. This case related to architectural and engineering services for the Tehran International Airport. In finding that the claimant was deprived of its property interests, Chamber Two reasoned as follows (hereafter the "*Tippetts* finding"):

> The Claimant is entitled under international law and general principles of law to compensation for the full value of the property which was deprived. The Tribunal prefers the term "deprivation" to the term "taking", although they are largely synonymous, because the latter may be understood to imply that the Government has acquired something of value, which is not required.
>
> A deprivation or taking of property may occur under international law through interference by a state in the use of that property or with the enjoyment of its benefits, even where legal title to the property is not affected.
>
> While assumption of control over property by a government does not automatically and immediately justify a conclusion that the property has been taken by the government, thus requiring compensation under international law, such a conclusion is warranted whenever events demonstrate that the owner was deprived of fundamental rights of ownership and it appears that this deprivation is not merely ephemeral. The intent of the government is less important than the effects of the measures on the owner, and the form of the measures of control or interference is less important than the reality of their impact.[54]

The position that a taking or deprivation may occur even when title has not been affected was supported in the award by a footnote reference to three sources: Whiteman's *Digest*,[55] Professor Christie's *British Year Book* article on expropriation,[56] and the *Lena Goldfields* case.[57] A similarity is clearly evident between these references and those set forth in both George Aldrich's Concurring Opinion in *ITT Industries* and Howard Holtzman's Concurring Opinion in *Starrett*.

---

[54] Award No. 141-7-2 (June 29, 1984), *reprinted in* 6 Iran–U.S. Cl. Trib. Rep. 219, at 225–26 (footnotes omitted).

[55] WHITEMAN, *supra* note 40.

[56] Christie, *supra* note 38.

[57] Lena Goldfields, Ltd. v USSR, Award (Sept. 3, 1930), *reprinted in* 5 ANNUAL DIGEST 3 (1930); Arthur Nussbaum, *The Arbitration between the Lena Goldfields, Ltd. and the Soviet Government*, 36 CORNELL L.Q. 31, 42 (1950).

5.3 SOURCES USED IN *TIPPETTS* AND *STARRETT*

Apparent from the above review of the Tribunal cases on indirect expropriation is that most of the supportive jurisprudence relied upon is common to most awards. Christie's article (which relies on the *Chorzow Factory* and *Norwegian Shipowners'* cases), Whiteman's *Digest*, the Harvard Draft Convention, and the *Lena Goldfields* case are recurring references. These materials fall under Article 38(1)(d) of the Statute of the International Court of Justice, which allows "judicial decisions and the teachings of the most highly qualified publicists" to be used as "subsidiary means for the determination of rules of law." These are not of themselves "sources" of international law but are materials that may be used to identify or indicate the content of international law. The Tribunal awards discussed above take this approach in that they do not appear to regard the materials as "sources of law" but "documentary sources" that cast light on what the law is.[58] Having identified the law, the Tribunal in effect incorporates that law into its awards.[59] In this regard, Rubins and Kinsella have commented that "[s]ome of the decisions of the Iran–U.S. Claims Tribunal are also evidence of the state of the international law of expropriation."[60]

An example of the general recognition of some of the authorities cited by the Tribunal is found in Rudolf Dolzer's entry on "Expropriation and Nationalization" in the *Encyclopedia of Public International Law*, which refers to the *Chorzow Factory*, *Norwegian Shipowners'*, and *Lena Goldfields* cases as particularly relevant decisions on the subject.[61] The *Chorzow Factory* case in particular is considered a seminal case in international law on the law of expropriation.[62] In relation to the Harvard Draft, it is the work of two distinguished Harvard law professors and can be classified without much doubt as the product of eminently qualified publicists. Article 10(3) of that draft is, for example, the first reference quoted in "The nature of expropriation" section in Malcolm Shaw's well-regarded work, *International Law*,[63] and the Explanatory Note to Article 10 is quoted at length in David Harris' *Cases and Materials on International Law*.[64] Additionally, the general principles on indirect expropriation formulated by

---

58 On this aspect of the Statute of the ICJ, see J.R. WEERAMANTRY, TREATY INTERPRETATION IN INVESTMENT ARBITRATION 125–26 (2012).

59 *See, e.g.*, W. Michael Reisman & Robert D. Sloane, *Indirect Expropriation and Its Valuation in the BIT Generation*, *in* 74 BRITISH YEAR BOOK OF INTERNATIONAL LAW 115, 120 (2004).

60 NOAH RUBINS & N. STEPHAN KINSELLA, INTERNATIONAL INVESTMENT, POLITICAL RISK AND DISPUTE RESOLUTION: A PRACTITIONER'S GUIDE 168 (2005).

61 Rudolf Dolzer, *Expropriation and Nationalization*, *in* ENCYCLOPEDIA OF PUBLIC INTERNATIONAL LAW Vol. 2, at 320, 322 (Rudolf Bernhardt ed., 1995). In particular regard to the *Lena Goldfields* case, *see also* V.V. Veeder, *The Lena Goldfields Arbitration: The Historical Roots of Three Ideas*, 47 I.C.L.Q. 47 (1998).

62 See, *e.g.*, RUBINS & KINSELLA, *supra* note 60, at 155.

63 MALCOLM SHAW, INTERNATIONAL LAW 830 (6th ed. 2008).

64 DAVID HARRIS, CASES AND MATERIALS ON INTERNATIONAL LAW 480 (7th ed. 2010).

Professor Christie have been approved by numerous scholars and international law materials.[65]

The general conclusion that can be drawn from the above is that the determinations on expropriation made by the *Tippetts* and *Starrett* awards have as their underlying basis a solid body of well-recognized or authoritative international law.

5.4 TRIBUNAL CASES SUBSEQUENT TO *TIPPETTS* AND *STARRETT*

The initial Tribunal decisions described above set the basis for the law on expropriation that the Tribunal would adopt in future cases. A good example is *Phillips Petroleum Company Iran v. Iran*,[66] which in the Gibson–Drahozal study was (along with *Amoco International Finance Corporation v. Iran*[67]) the most frequently cited Tribunal case in ICSID arbitration awards.[68] In that case the claimant asserted that Iran expropriated the claimant's contractual rights to explore and exploit petroleum resources in the Persian Gulf. Chamber Two dealt with this issue by stating the following proposition as to what type of acts constitute expropriation, which was supported by a list of prior cases starting with *Starrett* and *Tippetts*:

> As the Tribunal has held in a number of cases, expropriation by or attributable to a State of the property of an alien gives rise under international law to liability for compensation, and this is so whether the expropriation is formal or de facto and whether the property is tangible, such as real estate or a factory, or intangible, such as the contract rights involved in the present Case. See, e.g., *Starrett Housing Corporation and The Government of the Islamic Republic of Iran*, Interlocutory Award No. ITL 32-24-1 (19 December 1983), reprinted in 4 Iran–U.S. C.T.R. 122, and Award No. 314-24-1 (14 August 1987), reprinted in 16 Iran–U.S. C.T.R. 112, *Tippetts, Abbett, McCarthy, Stratton and TAMS-AFFA Consulting Engineers of Iran*, Award No. 141-7-2 (29 June 1984), reprinted in 6 Iran-U.S. C.T.R. 219, *Phelps Dodge Corp. and Overseas Private Investment Corp. and The Islamic Republic of Iran*, Award No. 217-99-2 (19 March 1986), reprinted in 10 Iran–U.S. C.T.R. 121, and *SEDCO, Inc. and National Iranian Oil Company*, Interlocutory Award No. ITL 55-129-3 (28 October 1985), reprinted in 9 Iran–U.S. C.T.R. 248 and Award No. 309-129-3 (7 July 1987), reprinted in 15 Iran-U.S. C.T.R. 23.[69]

---

[65] *See, e.g.*, Reisman & Sloane, *supra* note 59, at 119–21; and Rosalyn Higgins, *The Taking of Property by the State: Recent Developments in International Law*, 176 Recueil des Cours 259, 322–24 (1982-III).

[66] Award No. 425-39-2 (June 29, 1989), *reprinted in* 21 Iran–U.S. Cl. Trib. Rep. 79.

[67] Award No. 310-56-3 (July 14, 1987), *reprinted in* 15 Iran–U.S. Cl. Trib. Rep. 189.

[68] Drahozal & Gibson, *supra* note 20, at 23.

[69] Phillips Petroleum Company Iran v Iran, 21 Iran–U.S. Cl. Trib. Rep. 79, at 120–121.

6. INVESTMENT LAW JURISPRUDENCE

Two of the main objective indicators of the Tribunal's influence on expropriation in international investment law are the references to the Tribunal's awards as authority in (1) recognized commentaries on investment law, and (2) investment arbitration awards or decisions. References to the Tribunal jurisprudence on indirect expropriation by prominent investment law scholars as well as a diverse range of investment arbitration awards are discussed below.

6.1 INVESTMENT LAW COMMENTARIES

August Reinisch's chapter on "Expropriation" in the *Oxford Handbook of International Investment Law* expressly refers to the "Iran–US Claims Tribunal" no fewer than nineteen times.[70] This figure does not include his numerous references to the Tribunal simply as "the tribunal." Reinisch cites *Starrett*, *Amoco*, and *Phillips Petroleum* to support the proposition that intangible rights, such as those belonging to shareholders, or contractual rights could be the subject of an expropriation.[71] In connection with indirect expropriation, Reinisch asserts that "[i]n the rich jurisprudence of the Iran–US Claims Tribunal, the concept of an indirect expropriation has been repeatedly addressed."[72] He then proceeds to quote portions of the *Tippetts* and *Starrett* findings.[73] The *Phillips Petroleum* case is cited as authority for the proposition that a series of actions by the government, when viewed cumulatively, may give rise to a creeping expropriation.[74] *Tippetts* is also cited as authority for the absence of a need for "wealth increase" on the part of the expropriating government for an expropriation claim to be successful.[75] Factual circumstances in the *Tippetts*, *Starrett*, and *Phillips Petroleum* cases, in which the government appointed "temporary" managers for companies, are referenced by Reinisch to illustrate the type of interference that can amount to indirect expropriation.[76]

---

70 Reinisch, *supra* note 2.

71 *Id.* at 144. The same point is made in CAMPBELL MCLACHLAN, LAURENCE SHORE & MATTHEW WEINIGER, INTERNATIONAL INVESTMENT ARBITRATION: SUBSTANTIVE PRINCIPLES 308 (2007).

72 Reinisch, *supra* note 2, at 424.

73 *Id.* at 439.

74 *Id.* at 428.

75 *Id.* at 442, 444–45. Other cases referred to as supporting this proposition are Phelps Dodge Corp. et al v Iran, Award No. 217-99-2 (Mar. 19, 1986), 10 Iran–U.S. Cl. Trib. Rep. 121, at 130 (1986-I); Sedco, Inc, et al v National Iranian Oil Co, et al., Award No. ITL 55-129-3 (Oct. 28, 1985), 9 Iran–U.S. Cl. Trib. Rep. 248, at 276–9; Tehran, Inc, et al v Iran, Award No. 220-37/231-1 (Apr. 11, 1986), 10 Iran–U.S. Cl. Trib. Rep. 228, at 249–52; Thomas Earl Payne v Iran, Award No. 245-335-2 (Aug. 8, 1986), 12 Iran–U.S. Cl. Trib. Rep. 3, at 11; Harold Birnbaum v Iran, Award No. 549-967-2 (July 6, 1993), 29 Iran–U.S. Cl. Trib. Rep. 260, at 267–68.

76 Reinisch, *supra* note 2, at 454.

Newcombe and Paradell in their work *Law and Practice of Investment Treaties*[77] observe that a determination of indirect expropriation needs to look at the effect of government measures on the investor's property and that the "effects-based approach is reflected in commonly cited definitions of expropriation, including the Iran–US Claims Tribunal in *Starrett Housing Corporation v. Iran* and *Tippetts, Abbett, McCarthy, Stratton and TAMS-AFFA Consulting Engineers of Iran v. Iran*."[78] Immediately thereafter, significant portions of the *Tippetts* and *Starrett* findings are quoted. Their conclusion is that the two awards highlight that "the focus of the expropriation analysis is on the extent of the deprivation that the investor suffers and, to a far lesser degree, on the form or content of the state measure or the intent of the state."[79]

Much like the approach of Newcombe and Paradell, the text of Dolzer and Schreuer, *Principles of International Investment Law*,[80] discusses the notion that only the effect of the governmental measure and not the intention of the government is relevant to determine an expropriation (also known as the "sole effect" doctrine). On this issue, that text makes the comment that "[a]uthority for the 'sole effect doctrine' also comes from the practice of the Iran–US Claims Tribunal."[81] In support of this proposition, the *Starrett* finding is quoted.[82] Dolzer and Schreuer also refer to *Tippetts* in a footnote to support the related proposition that "[o]ther decisions have in various wordings and degrees also emphasized the effect of the measure."[83] Similarly, Schreuer, in an individual work on expropriation under the Energy Charter Treaty, refers extensively to the *Tippetts* and *Starrett* findings.[84] And Dolzer, likewise, in his article on new developments in indirect expropriations, also makes several references to the findings in *Tippetts* and *Starrett*.[85] Further, Dolzer's seminal coauthored work, *Bilateral Investment Treaties*, uses *Starrett* as a supportive citation in its discussion as to what constitutes indirect expropriation.[86]

The work *International Investment, Political Risk and Dispute Resolution* by Rubins and Kinsella trace the source of the "effects" doctrine back to the Tribunal. Those authors observe that "[w]here State action does not result in the direct seizure of investments, most arbitral tribunals seeking to determine whether a compensable expropriation has occurred have followed the 'effects' doctrine, established in a line of cases leading back to the *Phillips* case."[87] The footnote that follows immediately

[77] ANDREW NEWCOMBE & LLUÍS PARADELL, LAW AND PRACTICE OF INVESTMENT TREATIES: STANDARDS OF TREATMENT (2009).

[78] NEWCOMBE & PARADELL, *supra* note 77, at 326.

[79] *Id.* at 327.

[80] DOLZER & SCHREUER, *supra* note 2.

[81] *Id.* at 103.

[82] *Id.* at 102–03.

[83] *Id.* at 102.

[84] *See* C.H. Schreuer, *The Concept of Expropriation under the ETC and Other Investment Protection Treaties*, 2(5) TRANSNAT'L DISP. MGMT. (Nov. 2005).

[85] *See* Rudolf Dolzer, *Indirect Expropriations: New Developments?*, 11 N.Y.U. ENVIR. L.J. 64 (2002–2003).

[86] R. DOLZER & M. STEVENS, BILATERAL INVESTMENT TREATIES 100, n.271 (1995).

[87] RUBINS & KINSELLA, *supra* note 60, at 206.

afterward cites the *Tippetts* case as additional authority for the proposition. The authors also indicate that this "effects" approach reflects the dominant view in the field of indirect expropriation. Interestingly, in their discussion of the minority view, reference is made to another Tribunal award, *Sea-Land Service, Inc. v. Iran*.[88] On this minority view they observe that "a subsidiary line of case law has drawn inspiration from the U.S.–Iran Claims Tribunal's decision in *Sea-Land* to look beyond the effects of State action to the legitimacy of its motivations."[89] In *Sea-Land*, Chamber One determined that "[a] finding of expropriation would require, at the very least, that the Tribunal be satisfied that there was deliberate governmental interference with the conduct of Sea-Land's operation."[90]

In McLachlan, Shore, and Weiniger's treatise on substantive principles of investment law, many references are made to the Tribunal's awards. As would be expected in a work of this nature, parts of the *Tippetts* and *Starrett* findings are quoted.[91] Reference is also made to the *Phillips Petroleum* award, with the accompanying comment that "[t]he methods by which the Iranian Government progressively assumed control over foreign enterprises after the 1979 Revolution often did not involve outright seizure. The Iran–US Claims Tribunal therefore had occasion to give elaborate consideration to situations involving creeping expropriation."[92]

References to Tribunal awards in compendiums of cases and materials in related subject areas are also plentiful. The coverage of expropriation in the investment law case book *Foreign Investment Disputes* by Bishop, Crawford, and Reisman contains numerous excerpts from Iran–United States Claims Tribunal awards, which include the *Tippetts*, *Starrett*, and *Phillips* awards.[93] In the well-known public international law casebook, Harris's *Cases and Materials on International Law*, the *Tippetts* and *Starrett* awards are also quoted at length.[94]

Citations to Tribunal jurisprudence as indicators of the law on expropriation are also made in reports of prominent organizations in the field of investment law. The OECD, for example, in its report analyzing indirect expropriation and the right of states to regulate refers to *Starrett* and *Tippetts* in its discussion of the requisite degree of interference with property rights.[95]

---

88 Award No. 135-33-1 (Nov. 1, 1984), *reprinted in* 6 Iran–U.S. Cl. Trib. Rep. 149.

89 RUBINS & KINSELLA, *supra* note 60, at 209–10.

90 6 Iran–U.S. Cl. Trib. Rep. 149, at 166. See the further discussion on the *Sea-Land* case in Section 6.2 of this chapter relating to the *CMS v. Argentina* case. Dolzer and Bloch have argued that the NAFTA tribunal in *S.D. Myers, Inc v Canada*, UNCITRAL (NAFTA), First Partial Award, November 13, 2000, followed a similar approach to *Sea-Land* by giving weight to the purpose behind the governmental action under question. Rudolf Dolzer & Felix Bloch, *Indirect Expropriation: Conceptual Realignments?*, 5 INTERNATIONAL LAW FORUM DU DROIT INTERNATIONAL 155, 161, 163 (2003).

91 *See* MCLACHLAN ET AL., *supra* note 71, at 297, 301.

92 *Id.* at 293, n.112.

93 R. DOAK BISHOP, JAMES CRAWFORD & W. MICHAEL REISMAN, FOREIGN INVESTMENT DISPUTES: CASES, MATERIALS AND COMMENTARY 837–946 (2005).

94 HARRIS, *supra* note 64, at 477–79.

95 OECD, *"Indirect Expropriation" and the "Right to Regulate" in International Investment Law*, Directorate for Financial and Enterprise Affairs, WORKING PAPERS ON INTERNATIONAL INVESTMENT, NO. 2004/4

The above section demonstrates that prominent works on investment law cite the Tribunal's case law as an important reference point when defining or examining principles of indirect expropriation that are applicable in international investment disputes. We will now turn our attention to investment arbitration awards in order to assess the degree to which those awards consider Tribunal awards on expropriation.

6.2 INVESTMENT ARBITRATION AWARDS

This section reviews a selection of investment arbitration awards that have directly or indirectly referred to Tribunal awards when determining expropriation claims. A common feature of these awards is that they are required to apply investment treaty provisions relating to expropriation. Various terms are deployed in these treaties to denote expropriation provisions. Giorgio Sacerdoti's survey of investment treaties summarizes them as follows:

> The terminology in BITs refers to "expropriation", "nationalization" and "measures having similar effects", or "any measure having effect equivalent to nationalization or expropriation", or "any other measure the effects of which would be tantamount to expropriation or nationalization", or other equivalent ones.[96]

However, no further definition or guidance as to the meaning of these terms is usually provided in the treaties that contain them.[97] Consequently, the task often falls on investment tribunals to interpret these terms. The *Lauder* tribunal observed that BITs:

> generally do not define the term of expropriation and nationalization, or any of the other terms denoting similar measures of forced dispossession ("dispossession", "taking", "deprivation", or "privation"). Furthermore, the practice shows that although the various terms may be used either alone or in combination, most often no distinctions have been attempted between the general concept of dispossession and the specific forms thereof.[98]

In particular, older-generation investment treaties often do not clarify expressly whether their protection against "expropriation" relates to direct or indirect expropriation. The frequent practice of tribunals is to interpret this unqualified term as meaning both direct as well as indirect expropriation. The latter has been identified through the use of many terms. As Reisman and Sloane have put it: "Jurists and

(Sept. 2004), at 11–12, 14–15, http://www.oecd.org/dataoecd/22/54/33776546.pdf.

96 Giorgio Sacerdoti, *Bilateral Treaties and Multilateral Instruments on Investment Protection*, 269 RECUEIL DES COURS 251, 380 (1997) (footnotes omitted).

97 *See, e.g.*, Lauder v Czech Republic, UNCITRAL, Award (Final), Sept. 3, 2001, at para. 200.

98 *Id.*

scholars refer to indirect expropriations variously, and often interchangeably, as regulatory, constructive, consequential, disguised, de facto or creeping."[99]

Applying the customary rules of treaty interpretation codified in Articles 31 and 32 of the Vienna Convention on the Law of Treaties to interpret a seemingly simple treaty term such as expropriation is not altogether helpful. It is a term of art. Its "ordinary meaning" or related preparatory work (interpretative criteria contained in the Vienna Convention) usually will not illuminate fully the application of the term in complex factual scenarios. An interpretation of that term must necessarily refer to a linage of relevant international legal jurisprudence. However, a way to deploy the Vienna Convention on the Law of Treaties effectively is to apply Article 31(3)(c), which prescribes that an interpretation shall take into account "any relevant rules of international law applicable in the relations between the parties [to the treaty subject to interpretation]."[100] A source that helps identify those rules may be arbitral awards, which would include Tribunal awards that discuss expropriation and identify associated rules of international law.

As mentioned above, the study by Drahozal and Gibson found that twenty six (or 32 percent) of the eighty-one ICSID cases they examined cited Tribunal precedent.[101] Although non-ICSID cases were not covered , it is assumed for the purposes of this chapter that this figure is roughly representative of investment arbitration in general. A mix of ICSID, NAFTA, and UNCITRAL Rules investment arbitrations are reviewed below with the aim of highlighting how they utilize Tribunal awards on expropriation.

Santa Elena v. Costa Rica

The tribunal in *Compañía de Desarrollo de Santa Elena S.A. v. Costa Rica*[102] stated that "[t]here is ample authority for the proposition that a property has been expropriated when the effect of the measures taken by the state has been to deprive the owner of title, possession or access to the benefit and economic use of his property."[103] Immediately after this statement, the tribunal quoted two paragraphs of the *Tippetts* case, highlighting the passage that speaks of expropriation involving the deprivation of fundamental rights of ownership.

The *Santa Elena* tribunal was required to determine the date on which the expropriated property should be valued. Using *Tippetts* as supporting precedent, the tribunal held that the expropriated property must be valued at the date "the governmental 'interference' has deprived the owner of his rights or made those rights practically useless."[104] It is to be noted, however, that the actual words employed in the *Tippetts*

99 Reisman & Sloane, *supra* note 59, at 119.

100 On this point, see WEERAMANTRY, *supra* note 58, at 55–56.

101 Drahozal & Gibson, *supra* note 20, at 22.

102 *Compañía de Desarrollo de Santa Elena S.A. v Costa Rica*, ICSID Case No. ARB/96/1, Award on the Merits (Feb. 17, 2000).

103 *Id.* ¶ 77.

104 *Id.* ¶ 78.

award require "deprivation or taking of property…through *interference* by a state *in the use of that property or with the enjoyment of its benefits*" (emphasis added). The Tribunal did not add a phrase to the effect that interference must make the property practically or totally useless. Moreover, the award goes on to speak of the deprivation of "fundamental rights," not the deprivation of all rights.

On whether uselessness must be present to find expropriatory conduct, the tribunal in *GAMI Investments Inc. v. United Mexican States* indicated that the *Starrett* award required rights to be rendered "useless" (i.e., a full deprivation was needed). However, the *GAMI* award in a later passage suggests that in contrast the *Tippetts* may stand for the proposition that a less-than-complete deprivation is sufficient to establish an expropriation.[105] Notwithstanding the distinction made in *GAMI* as to the *Tippetts* and *Starrett* awards, it may be open to debate whether they adopt such different standards, particularly given the similar precedents on which the two awards rely.

CME v. Czech Republic

In its initial discussion as to whether an expropriation was present in the case before it, the *CME Czech Republic B.V. v. Czech Republic* tribunal stated:

> The expropriation claim is sustained despite the fact that the Media Council did not expropriate CME by express measures of expropriation. De facto expropriations or indirect expropriations, i.e. measures that do not involve an overt taking but that effectively neutralize the benefit of the property of the foreign owner, are subject to expropriation claims. This is undisputed under international law…[106]

At this juncture of the award, international law citations are provided to support this position but no explicit reference is made to the Tribunal. The *CME* tribunal does, however, make express reference to Giorgio Sacerdoti's Hague Academy lectures entitled "Bilateral Treaties and Multilateral Instruments on Investment Protection," which stated that de facto expropriations or nationalizations are "measures that do not involve an overt taking but that effectively neutralize the benefit of the property for the foreign owner."[107] When referring to Sacerdoti's lectures, the *CME* tribunal indicates that he refers "to numerous precedents such as the German Interests In Polish Upper Silesia case."[108] The point to note here is that in addition to this case, Sacerdoti in the same footnote quotes from the Tribunal case of *Sedco, Inc. v. National*

---

105 GAMI Investments Inc. v. United Mexican States, UNCITRAL, Final Award (Nov. 15, 2004), at paras. 123, 131.

106 CME Czech Republic B.V. (The Netherlands) v. Czech Republic, UNCITRAL, Partial Award (Sept. 13, 2001), at para. 604.

107 Sacerdoti, *supra* note 96, at 382.

108 CME Czech Republic B.V. (The Netherlands) v. Czech Republic, UNCITRAL, Partial Award (Sept. 13, 2001), at para. 604.

Iranian Oil Co.[109] Significantly, this quoted *Sedco* passage cites both Professor Christie's article and *Starrett*.

The *CME* tribunal went on in the immediately following paragraph to express the view that when determining expropriation, "it makes no difference whether the deprivation was caused by actions or by inactions."[110] One of the cases cited to support this view was *International Technical Products Corporation v. Iran*.[111] The tribunal also referred to the oft-quoted passage from the *Tippetts* finding, which held, as indicated earlier, that a deprivation must affect the "fundamental rights of ownership" and that the deprivation must not be ephemeral.[112] This jurisprudence was used by the *CME* tribunal to support its finding that

> [e]xpropriation of CME's investment is found as a consequence of the Media Council's actions and inactions as there is no immediate prospect at hand that ÈNTS will be reinstated in a position to enjoy an exclusive use of the licence as had been granted under the 1993 split structure (even if the Czech Supreme Court would re-instate the Regional Commercial Court decision).[113]

Interestingly, the *CME* tribunal after having quoted from the *Tippetts* case immediately proceeded to quote from *Sea-Land*. The quoted passage of the latter Tribunal award stated that there must be deliberate governmental interference for an expropriation to exist.[114] In what appears to be an application of *Sea-Land*, the *CME* tribunal found that the requisite government intent had been met, which qualified Media Council's actions as an expropriation.[115] However, *Sea-Land* is not fully consistent with the immediately preceding quotation from the *Tippetts* case, where the Tribunal stated that "the intent of the government is less important than the effects of the measures on the owner."[116] The *CME* tribunal's reference to *Sea-Land* may be explained on the basis that the tribunal believed that the action of the government in *CME* was

109 *See* Sedco, Inc, et al v National Iranian Oil Co, et al., Award No. ITL 55-129-3 (Oct. 28, 1985), *reprinted in* 9 Iran–U.S. Cl. Trib. Rep. 248, cited in Sacerdoti, *supra* note 96, at 382. Also to be noted is the quotation of *Tippetts* later in Sacerdoti's article. *Id.* at 384.

110 CME Czech Republic B.V. (The Netherlands) v. Czech Republic, UNCITRAL, Partial Award (Sept. 13, 2001), at para. 605.

111 Award No. 196-302-2 (Oct. 28, 1985), *reprinted in* 9 Iran–U.S. CTR Rep. 206, at 239, cited in CME Czech Republic B.V. (The Netherlands) v Czech Republic, UNCITRAL, Partial Award (Sept. 13, 2001), at para. 605. Also to be noted is that the International Technical Products award refers to the *Tippetts* award. The other case cited by the CME tribunal was Biloune, et al. v Ghana Investment Centre, 95 I.L.R. 183, 207–10 (1993).

112 CME Czech Republic B.V. (The Netherlands) v Czech Republic, UNCITRAL, Partial Award (Sept. 13, 2001), at paras. 608, citing *Tippetts*, at 225.

113 Id. ¶ 607.

114 Id. ¶ 608, citing Sea-Land Service, Inc v Iran, Award No. 135-33-1 (Nov. 1, 1984), *reprinted in* 6 Iran–U.S. Cl. Trib. Rep. 149, at 166.

115 *Id.* ¶ 609.

116 *Id.* ¶ 608, citing Tippetts, Abbett, McCarthy, Stratton v. TAMS-AFFA Consulting Engineers of Iran, Award No. 141-7-2 (June 29, 1984), *reprinted in* 6 Iran–U.S. Cl. Trib. Rep. 219, at 225.

sufficiently clear to make a finding either under the *Tippetts* test or on the higher threshold required under *Sea-Land*.

CMS v. Argentina

In discussing whether governmental measures constituted indirect expropriation under the 1991 Argentina–United States BIT, the tribunal in *CMS Gas Transmission Company v. Argentine Republic*[117] first quoted with approval the following passage in *Lauder v. Czech Republic*:

> The concept of indirect (or "*de facto*", or "*creeping*") expropriation is not clearly defined. Indirect expropriation or nationalization is a measure that does not involve an overt taking, but that effectively neutralized the enjoyment of the property.[118]

The *CMS* tribunal subsequently stated in its own words that "[t]he essential question is therefore to establish whether the enjoyment of the property has been effectively neutralized. The standard that a number of tribunals have applied in recent cases where indirect expropriation has been contended is that of substantial deprivation."[119] The NAFTA case of *Metalclad Corporation v. United Mexican States*[120] is then cited to support this point, and the tribunal follows by adding "[s]imilarly, the Iran–United States Claims Tribunal has held that deprivation must affect 'fundamental rights of ownership,' a criteri[on] reaffirmed in the *CME v. Czech Republic* case."[121] The quote relating to the Tribunal is from the *Tippetts* finding.

The *CMS* tribunal eventually held against the investor, finding that the "investor is in control of the investment; the Government does not manage the day-to-day operations of the company; and the investor has full ownership and control of the investment."[122]

Lauder v. Czech Republic

Some investment arbitration awards dealing with expropriation fail to make express reference to the Iran–United States Claims Tribunal. However, this does not necessarily mean that the Tribunal is totally irrelevant in such cases. For example, the award in *Lauder v. Czech Republic*[123] does not refer to the Tribunal. Nonetheless, a deeper

---

[117] CMS Gas Transmission Co. v. Argentine Republic, ICSID Case No. ARB/01/8, Award (May 12, 2005).

[118] Ronald S. Lauder v. Czech Republic, UNCITRAL, Final Award (Sept. 3, 2001), at para. 200, cited in CMS Gas Transmission Company v. Argentine Republic, ICSID Case No. ARB/01/8, Award (May 12, 2005), at para. 261.

[119] CMS Gas Transmission Company v. Argentine Republic, ICSID Case No. ARB/01/8, Award (May 12, 2005), at para. 262.

[120] ICSID Case No. ARB (AF)/97/1, Award (Aug. 30, 2000).

[121] CMS Gas Transmission Company v. Argentine Republic, ICSID Case No. ARB/01/8, Award (May 12, 2005), at para 262.

[122] *Id.* ¶ 263. An annulment proceeding was instituted in this case, but the expropriation finding was not at issue in those proceedings.

[123] Ronald S. Lauder v. Czech Republic, UNCITRAL, Final Award (Sept. 3, 2001).

examination of the award reveals links to the Tribunal's jurisprudence. *Lauder* is also of interest in this section given its close connection to the *CME* case discussed above. Both cases concerned the same acts of the Czech Republic and were brought in relation to the same entity—*CME* was instituted by a company and *Lauder* by a shareholder of that company.

The tribunal in *Lauder* explored the principle of indirect expropriation, noting that it was not defined in the BIT at issue. It concluded that "[i]ndirect expropriation or nationalization is a measure that does not involve an overt taking, but that effectively neutralizes the enjoyment of the property."[124] Although the *Lauder* tribunal failed to refer to Tribunal jurisprudence, two supportive references followed the award's conclusion as to the meaning of indirect expropriation: Dolzer and Steven's book *Bilateral Investment Treaties*,[125] and the Hague Academy lectures delivered by Sacerdoti on "Bilateral Treaties and Multilateral Instruments on Investment Protection."[126]

As discussed earlier, Sacerdoti referred to the *Sedco* case as support for his proposition that expropriations or nationalizations are "measures that do not involve an overt taking but that effectively neutralize the benefit of the property for the foreign owner."[127] Moreover, later in Sacerdoti's analysis, he refers specifically to the Tribunal and quotes a passage from the *Tippetts* case.[128]

Despite the absence of a direct reference to the Tribunal in the text of the *Lauder* award, a side note should be made that the *Lauder* tribunal Chairman, Robert Briner, was a former president of the Iran–United States Claims Tribunal. He would have had intimate knowledge of the Tribunal's jurisprudence on expropriation. It would have been insightful to have heard from him why no Iran–United States jurisprudence was referred to in the *Lauder* award, but, sadly, he recently passed away.

Pope & Talbot v. Canada

Another case in which an investment arbitration tribunal did not make a reference to a specific award of the Iran–United States Claims Tribunal is the NAFTA arbitration proceedings in *Pope & Talbot*.[129] The claimant there asserted that the NAFTA phrase "measure tantamount to . . . expropriation" in Article 1110 referred to measures broader than those falling within the sphere of customary international law notions of expropriation. This argument was rejected by the tribunal in the following terms:

> "Tantamount" means nothing more than equivalent. Something that is equivalent to something else cannot logically encompass more. No authority cited by

[124] *Id.* ¶ 200.

[125] DOLZER & STEVENS, *supra* note 86.

[126] Sacerdoti, *supra* note 96.

[127] *Id.* at 382.

[128] *Id.* at 384. Also mentioned in the footnote to the quotation extracted from *Tippetts* is a reference to the *Starrett* case.

[129] Pope & Talbot, Inc. v. Canada, UNCITRAL (NAFTA), Interim Award on Merits (June 26, 2000).

> the Investor supports a contrary conclusion. References to the decisions of the Iran–U.S. Claims Tribunal ignore the fact that the tribunal's mandate expressly extends beyond expropriation to include "other measures affecting property rights."[130]

Maurizio Brunetti has correctly observed that this statement by the *Pope & Talbot* tribunal was not entirely clear:

> If it meant that, because the jurisdiction of the Iran–United States Claims Tribunal over "other measures affecting property rights" [as granted in the Claims Settlement Declaration] extends beyond customary international law of expropriation, its decisions concerning "other measures" represent *lex specialis*—that is, they have no relevance outside the context of that Tribunal—then the NAFTA tribunal might have been right. If, however, it was implying that *all* decisions of the Iran–United States Claims Tribunal represent *lex specialis*, then the NAFTA tribunal was wrong. As the following survey of the Iran–United States Claims Tribunal's expropriation jurisprudence demonstrates, the Tribunal nearly always relied on customary international law for its conclusions, and its awards have practical relevance to a wide variety of factual situations that will arise under NAFTA. Thus, the Iran–United States Claims Tribunal's jurisprudence with respect to expropriation may be a relevant body of knowledge from which arbitral tribunals established under Chapter 11 of the NAFTA may draw.[131]

Notwithstanding the *Pope & Talbot* tribunal's negative position in relation to Iran–United States Claims Tribunal awards, Andrea Menaker has observed that although the *Pope & Talbot* tribunal "did not cite to any Iran–U.S. Claims Tribunal cases, in denying the expropriation claim, it echoed the reasoning of *Starrett Housing* and *Tippetts*."[132] Echoes of the Tribunal's case law are also apparent in the *Pope & Talbot* tribunal finding that the investor still retained control over its investment and continued to direct the day-to-day operations of the investment, that no officers or employees of the investment were supervised by Canada, that Canada did not take any of the company's proceeds, and that Canada did not otherwise act in a way that ousted the investor from full ownership and control of the investment.[133] This reasoning is consistent especially with the *Tippetts* criterion of a deprivation of fundamental rights of ownership and the *Tippetts* finding that the claimant no longer possessed the ability to participate in the day-to-day operation and control of the investment.

---

130 *Id.* ¶ 104.

131 Maurizio Brunetti, *The Iran–United States Claims Tribunal, NAFTA Chapter 11, and the Doctrine of Indirect Expropriation*, 2 CHI. J. INT'L L. 203, 204–05 (2001) (footnotes omitted).

132 Andrea J. Menaker, *The Enduring Relevance of the Expropriation Jurisprudence of the Iran–U.S. Claims Tribunal for Investo–r-State Arbitrations*, *in* THE IRAN-U.S. CLAIMS TRIBUNAL AT 25, *supra* note 20, at 340.

133 Pope & Talbot, Inc. v Canada, UNCITRAL (NAFTA), Interim Award on Merits (June 26, 2000), at para. 100.

Generation Ukraine v. Ukraine

The *Generation Ukraine v. Ukraine* award noted that "although international precedents on indirect expropriation are plentiful, it is difficult to find many cases that fall squarely into the more specific paradigm of creeping expropriation."[134] Immediately thereafter, the tribunal referred to *Tippetts*, stating that case "might be said to demonstrate the possibility of a taking through the combined effect of several acts."[135] The award in *Generation Ukraine* then recited in some detail the factual situation in *Tippetts*, namely, Iran's appointment of a temporary manager in August 1979, who made decisions without consulting the claimant (which held a 50 percent stakehold). But then a working relationship was restored, only to start deteriorating again once the U.S. embassy hostage crisis began in December 1979, and further worsening until the tentative cooperation between the temporary manager and the claimant came to an end in March 1980. The *Generation Ukraine* award noted that the taking of the claimant's property was consummated not in August 1979 when the temporary manager was appointed, but in March 1980 when the cooperation ended. The award also quoted two frequently cited paragraphs in *Tippetts*.

In the context of the *Generation Ukraine* tribunal observation that few cases fall squarely into the category of creeping expropriations, it is noteworthy that a number of other Tribunal cases concerned events that were akin to creeping expropriation were decided by the Tribunal. For example in *International Technical Products Corporation v. Iran*, the tribunal held "[w]here the alleged expropriation is carried out by way of a series of interferences in the enjoyment of the property, the breach forming the cause of action is deemed to have taken place on the day the interference has ripened into more or less irreversible deprivation of the property rather than on the beginning date of the events. The point at which interference ripens into a taking depends on the circumstances of the case and does not require that legal title has been transferred."[136]

If the evaluation is accurate in the *Generation Ukraine* award that cases on creeping expropriation are rare, then these other cases of the Tribunal should also provide useful guidance in the development of investment law on creeping expropriation.

---

134 Generation Ukraine, Inc. v. Ukraine, ICSID Case No. ARB/00/9, Award (Sept. 16, 2003), at para. 20.22.

135 *Id.* ¶ 20.23.

136 International Technical Products Corporation v. Iran, Award No. 196-302-2 (Oct. 28, 1985), *reprinted in* 9 Iran–U.S. CTR Rep. 206, at 240–41. *See also* the following observation by Aldrich:

> [B]y the time the first claims for expropriation or other takings of property began to be decided by the Tribunal in late 1983, the interference with property rights had endured for at least three years or more, and the continuation of strained relations between Iran and the United States gave the Tribunal little reason to believe that such interference would soon end. Consequently, the often difficult question of when allegedly temporary interference with rights of property owners should be considered to have ripened into a compensable taking or deprivation of those rights rarely troubled the Iran–United States Claims Tribunal.

ALDRICH, *supra* note 4, at 172.

6.3 TRIBUNAL'S JURISDICTION OVER "OTHER MEASURES AFFECTING PROPERTY RIGHTS"

It may be argued (as indicated in the above quoted passage by Brunetti) that the Tribunal's jurisprudence that applies the proviso in paragraph 1 of Article II of the Claims Settlement Declaration concerning the Tribunal's jurisdiction over claims arising out of "expropriations" reflects customary international law, but that its application of that paragraph's "other measures affecting property rights" proviso is broader than the mandate granted to tribunals in most investment treaties. Consequently, it may be said to represent a *lex specialis*. On this issue, Menaker has submitted that

> Iran–United States Tribunal decisions that concern measures affecting property rights not amounting to expropriation may be of limited utility in the investor–State context, and parties to investor–State arbitrations at times have urged tribunals to disregard cases on such grounds. Thus, when relying on Iran–U.S. Claims Tribunal cases, one needs to exercise caution and confirm that the Tribunal is interpreting the international law of expropriation, and not *lex specialis*.[137]

Nonetheless, this section argues that the Tribunal's decisions on "other measures" may be useful for investment arbitration tribunals. First, it may well be that the Tribunal's findings on "other measures" may have been treated differently and considered as expropriations if the other measures remedy was not included in the Claims Settlement Declaration.[138] "Other measures" findings may play a role in interpreting broad investment treaty provisions that speak of impairment of management and control of economic value.[139] Dolzer and Stevens comment that these types of provisions represent

> possibly the broadest scope in investment treaties with respect to indirect expropriation insofar as the inclusion of measures that cause the "impairment...of [the] economic value" of an investment, equates expropriation with a host of

---

[137] Menaker, *supra* note 132, at 337–38 (footnotes omitted). These Tribunal cases may have been treated differently and considered as expropriations if the other measures remedy was not included in the Claims Settlement Declaration. *See also* ALDRICH, *supra* note 4, at 182–83, as to his views on the tendency of certain Tribunal arbitrators to avoid findings of expropriation and instead make a finding of "other measures affecting property rights."

[138] *See, e.g.*, ALDRICH, *supra* note 4, at 182–83.

[139] *See, e.g.*, Article III of the United States–Zaire BIT (1984), which provides protection against "any other measure or series of measures, direct or indirect, tantamount to expropriation (including the levying of taxation, the compulsory sale of all or part of an investment, or the impairment or deprivation of its management, control or economic value)..."

> measures which might not otherwise be considered as such under general international law, let alone under liberal systems of domestic law.[140]

The Tribunal's "other measures" decisions could also assist investment arbitration tribunals that adopt broad definitions of expropriation, such as the *Metalclad* test for expropriation, which is aimed to protect "covert or incidental interference with the use of property which has the effect of depriving the owner, in whole or in significant part, of the use or reasonably to-be-expected economic benefit of property even if not necessarily to the obvious benefit of the host State."[141] Further they may also provide guidance in the determination of fair and equitable treatment provisions.

In *Karubian v. Iran*,[142] the claimant contended, among other things, that his land was expropriated as a result of legislation that made title deeds to certain types of undeveloped land (such as the claimant's) vulnerable to a determination that would cancel those deeds. The Tribunal held that the existence of those laws were insufficient of themselves to constitute *expropriation* because no governmental determination was made to cancel those title deeds. Nonetheless, that Tribunal held that even in the absence of such a determination, the legislation made title to the claimant's land subject to the risk of immediate cancellation, and that the claimant would have had difficulties in finding a buyer for his property.[143] This represented damage to the claimant's ownership interests resulting from "other measures affecting property rights" for which Iran was responsible (but the case failed on other grounds). The same Iranian land legislation was at issue in *Mohtadi v. Iran*.[144] The tribunal there held that its effect "was to impair the right and real possibility of the Claimant to transfer his property" and accordingly was held to be a compensable "other measure."[145]

The findings in these two Tribunal cases and others may be helpful in assessing the degree of governmental interference that may impair the use or reasonably to-be-expected economic benefit of property as is required under a *Metalclad*-type approach. For example, if a government passes a law that decrees that the property of an investor

---

140 DOLZER & STEVENS, *supra* note 86, at 102. On this point, *see also* Brunetti, *supra* note 131, at 205, 211.

141 Metalclad Corporation v. United Mexican States, ICSID Case No. ARB (AF)/97/1, Award (Aug. 30, 2000), at para. 103. Although the Supreme Court of British Columbia set aside part of the *Metalclad* award, it left the above part of the award undisturbed. *See* 5 ICSID REPORTS 260. Consider, however, criticisms as to this finding, for example, Michael Ewing-Chow, *Thesis, Antithesis and Synthesis: Investor Protection in BITs, WTO and FTAs*, 30 U. NEW S. WALES L.J. 548 (2007), at 557 (the "orthodox approach requires a deprivation of the fundamental rights of ownership, all that the *Metalclad* approach apparently requires is that the government measure deprived the investor of their anticipated profits, or significantly affected their business plans").

142 Award No. 569-419-2 (Mar. 6, 1996), *reprinted in* 32 Iran–U.S. Cl. Trib. Rep. 3.

143 Id. ¶¶ 143–44.

144 Award No. 573-271-3 (Dec. 2, 1996), *reprinted in* 32 Iran–U.S. Cl. Trib. Rep. 124.

145 Mohtadi v Iran, Award No. 573-271-3 (Dec. 2, 1996), *reprinted in* 32 Iran–U.S. Cl. Trib. Rep. 124, at paras. 68–69.

can at any future date be subject to instant cancellation without due compensation, this could be so damaging to its value that it would constitute an expropriation. Moreover, these decisions may also be helpful where, as mentioned above, investment treaties define "measures tantamount to expropriation" as including "impairment . . . of economic value." Alternatively, they may assist in evaluating the rights and wrongs of fair and equitable claims, for example, in circumstances such as in *Karubian* where a law creates a risk of sudden cancellation of title to property, which may be seen as unfair treatment of the investor.[146]

6.4 CONCLUSION

We see from the foregoing paragraphs that the Iran–United States Claims Tribunal jurisprudence, particularly the *Tippetts* and *Starrett* cases, has had a normative influence in international investment law. For a start, the case law of the Tribunal has been referenced frequently in major texts on expropriation in investment law. Perhaps more importantly, they have often been cited in investment arbitration decisions to support their decisions, particularly as to finding that the actual taking of title to property is not essential for an expropriation to occur, and that it is the effect of the measures taken rather than the intention of the government that is relevant. Moreover, investment arbitration awards on expropriation that do not directly cite Tribunal awards may also be seen to be consistent with the Tribunal jurisprudence if one is to delve behind the text of the award. The use of *Tippetts* or *Starrett* cannot be said to have "developed" international investment law because, as has been shown earlier, those awards themselves were based on well-established international law. Nonetheless, the Tribunal without doubt has played a significant and valuable role in informing investment tribunals as to the application of the law on indirect expropriation.

The future, however, remains uncertain because as the number of investment arbitration awards exponentially grow, the probabilities increase that the jurisprudence that future tribunals refer to will be that contained in investment arbitration awards.[147] Based on the growth trends in investment arbitration, reference rates to Tribunal awards may diminish and investment arbitration awards may assume a more prominent place when authorities need to be cited.

The other factor at play is that investment arbitration awards are starting to develop their own jurisprudence, which makes them less reliant on Tribunal awards. A good example is provided in *Tecnicas Medioambientales Tecmed S.A. v. United Mexican States* in which the award took into account considerations of legitimate expectations

146 *See also* Dolzer & Bloch, *supra* note 90, at 155 (stating that treatment standards such as "fair and equitable treatment," "full protection and security," and "national treatment" are "highly relevant and possibly overlapping in the context of indirect expropriation").

147 In this regard, see also Menaker, *supra* note 132, at 346 ("As the area of investor–State arbitration continues to grow, however, it is possible that these decisions will be overshadowed by the burgeoning number of decisions rendered by investor–State tribunals.").

in holding Mexico responsible for the expropriation that caused damage to the claimant.[148] Expectations created by the government of Iran has not been a feature (at least explicitly) that has been emphasized in Tribunal jurisprudence. This type of development of investment law may be susceptible to criticism. For example, the *Metalclad* definition of expropriation that included considerations of investor expectation (i.e., deprivation in whole or in significant part of the use or reasonably to-be-expected economic benefit of property) has been questioned by Dolzer because the award "laid down its definition without reference to any previous decision or codificatory norm."[149] Dolzer further comments that the starting point to interpret the term is to ascertain the "ordinary meaning" of the treaty term "indirect expropriation" pursuant to Article 31 of the Vienna Convention on the Law of Treaties. This approach, says Dolzer, can best be established by reference to case law, which includes Tribunal awards. Bearing in mind that Dolzer's article was published in 2002, it merits note that he adds

> The tendency by recent tribunals to ignore these cases[150] does not contribute to an organic growth of foreign investment law or to legal security based on jurisprudential consistency. Disagreement with previous cases will, of course, always remain an option, but ignoring them raises questions regarding whether there was a proper effort on the part of the deciding tribunal to place a judgment into the appropriate context.[151]

This critique by Dolzer illustrates that investment law jurisprudence needs to be linked to prior authority. Given that Tribunal jurisprudence is well-founded and has provided one of the cornerstones of the modern law on expropriation, it is important that its relevance be maintained, despite the high volume of expropriation-related decisions made in investment arbitration.

Notwithstanding the current deluge of investment arbitration awards, the Tribunal still continues to be relevant. As an illustration, one need go no further than to cite one of the most recent requests for investment arbitration (at the time of writing). In *Adel A Hamadi Al Tamimi v. Oman*, the request states that "An expropriation occurs when the 'owner was deprived of fundamental rights of ownership and

[148] Tecnicas Medioambientales Tecmed S.A. v. United Mexican States, ICSID Case No. ARB (AF)/00/2, Final Award (May 29, 2003), at para. 149 ("upon making its investment, the Claimant had legitimate reasons to believe that the Landfill would extend over the long term"). *See also* DOLZER & SCHREUER, *supra* note 2, at 104–06.

[149] Dolzer, *supra* note 85, at 72. *See also* Ewing-Chow, *supra* note 141, at 557.

[150] The cases referred to by Dolzer are the *Norwegian Shipowners* case and cases decided by the Permanent Court of International Justice and the International Court of Justice, ICSID tribunals and the Iran–United States Claims Tribunal, courts applying the European and American Conventions on Human Rights, and a number of ad hoc tribunals. Dolzer, *supra* note 85, at 72–73.

[151] *Id.* at 73.

it appears that this deprivation is not merely ephemeral.'"[152] The internal quotation is from *Biwater Gauff (Tanzania) Ltd. v. United Republic of Tanzania*,[153] which in turn quotes *Tippetts*.

In 2007, Drahozal and Gibson concluded that "there is little evidence that the precedential value of Tribunal awards has depreciated over time, or that Tribunal awards are being wholly displaced by the increasing stock of ICSID awards."[154] The recent *Adel A Hamadi Al Tamimi* request for arbitration demonstrates Tribunal jurisprudence on expropriation still continues to maintain its relevance and importance.

[152] Adel A Hamadi Al Tamimi v. Oman, ICSID Case No. ARB/11/33, Request for Arbitration (Dec. 5, 2011), para. 88.

[153] ICSID Case No. ARB/05/22, Award (Jul. 24, 2008), para. 438.

[154] Drahozal & Gibson, *supra* note 20, at 27.

12

AUSTRALIA'S REJECTION OF INVESTOR–STATE ARBITRATION: A SIGN OF GLOBAL CHANGE

Leon E. Trakman[*]

I. INTRODUCTION

Many countries have lately sought to reassess the efficacy of international investment agreements, and investment arbitration in particular. Nicaragua and Venezuela have both signaled their intention to terminate existing Bilateral Investment Treaties (BITs) including provisions for investment arbitration.[1] Ecuador has denounced the International Centre for Settlement of Investment Disputes (ICSID), the primary source of investment arbitration. Romania attempted to withdraw from the Swedish–Romanian BIT, only to then be subject to an investment arbitration award that purported to bind it "irrevocably" to that agreement. China traditionally restricted investor–state provisions in BITs until its more recent emergence as a leading capital exporter,[2] whereas the

* For related studies, *see* Leon E. Trakman, *Investor State Arbitration or Local Courts: Will Australia Set a New Trend?* 46 J. WORLD TRADE 83 (2012); Leon E. Trakman, *Choosing Domestic Courts over Investor–State Arbitration: Australia's Repudiation of the Status Quo,* 35 UNSW L.J. (forthcoming 2012). The author thanks the editors of these journals for their work on these related studies; Susan Franck, Jurgen Kurtz, Luke Peterson, Colin Picker, and Lisa Toohey for their comments on this chapter, and Kunal Sharma for his research assistance.

1 For commentary on these events, as well as investment arbitration in Latin America generally, see Scott Appleton, *Latin American Arbitration: The Story behind the Headlines*, International Bar Association, *available at* http://www.ibanet.org/Article/Detail.aspx?ArticleUid=78296258-3B37-4608-A5EE-3C92D5D0B979.

2 On China's shifting position in regard to investment arbitration, see VIVIENNE BATH & LUKE NOTTAGE, (EDS) FOREIGN INVESTMENT AND DISPUTE RESOLUTION LAW AND PRACTICE IN ASIA (2011) chs 1, 4 and 5.

Philippines negotiated to exclude investment arbitration in its free trade treaty with Japan in 2007.[3] One result is that bilateral investment agreements themselves are under attack. Another result is that investment arbitration is not assured as the pervasive medium through which investor–state disputes will be resolved in the future.

Although the Australian government's position is more moderate than the stance taken by these South American states, Australia is the first developed state to openly indicate that it will no longer agree to the adoption of arbitration within its Bilateral and Regional Trade Agreements (BRTAs). The effect of this policy shift is that henceforth the Australian government may negotiate that investment disputes with foreign investors be heard by domestic courts of law, rather than be resolved by international investment arbitration.[4] In a trade policy statement released on April 12, 2011, the Australian government confirmed that it would no longer negotiate treaty protections "that would confer greater legal rights on foreign businesses than those available to domestic businesses" or that would "constrain the ability of Australian governments to make laws on social, environmental and economic matters in circumstances where those laws do not discriminate between domestic and foreign businesses."[5]

This approach adopted by Australia reflects the view that domestic courts, not investment tribunals, are more appropriate bodies to resolve investment disputes between domestic states and foreign investors, in the same manner as domestic courts decide "other" domestic disputes.[6] The inference is that a domestic court can protect the rights of foreign investors while preventing them from receiving investment benefits beyond those provided to domestic investors. It is also presumed that, if investment arbitration privileges foreign investors, it undermines the national interest, and if it detracts from the national interest, local courts ought to replace it.[7] A third option is conceivable: that investors who feel that their rights have been violated can seek diplomatic intervention by their home states. However, that is not a practical mechanism

[3] *See* Shotaro Hamamoto & Luke Nottage, *Foreign Investment in and out of Japan: Economic Backdrop, Domestic Law, and International Treaty-Based Investor–State Dispute Resolution* (Sydney Law School Research Paper No 10/145); TRANSNAT'L DISPUTE MGMT. (2010), *available at* http://ssrn.com/abstract=1724999.

[4] *Trading Our Way to More Jobs and Prosperity* (Gillard Government Trade Policy Statement, released by Australia's Trade Minister, Craig Emerson, Apr. 2011), http://www.dfat.gov.au/publications/trade/trading-our-way-to-more-jobs-and-prosperity.html#investor-state [hereinafter Policy]. For a comment on the Australian government's Policy announced on Apr. 12, 2011, see Luke Peterson, *Australia Rejects ISA Provision in Trade Agreements: Don't Trade Our Lives Away* (Apr. 19, 2011), http://donttradeourlives-away.wordpress.com/2011/04/19/australia-rejects-investor-state-arbitration-provision-in-trade-agreements/. *See generally* Leon E. Trakman, *Foreign Direct Investment: Hazard or Opportunity?* 41 GEO. WASH. INT'L L. REV. 1 (2010).

[5] *See* Policy, *supra* note 4, at 1–2.

[6] *See* Leon E. Trakman, *Foreign Direct Investment: An Australian Perspective*, 13 INT'L TRADE & BUS. L. REV. 31, 48–53 (2010); Thomas Westcott, *Foreign Investment Issues in the Australia–United States Free Trade Agreement*, Australian Government: The Treasury, *available at* http://www.treasury.gov.au/documents/958/pdf/06_foreign_investment_policy_ausfta.pdf.

[7] On this view, see DAVID SCHNEIDERMAN, CONSTITUTIONALIZING ECONOMIC GLOBALIZATION: INVESTMENT RULES AND DEMOCRACY'S PROMISE chs. 2, 6 (2008).

for resolving all disputes, and governments are generally loath to intervene on behalf of private investors who are resource-intensive, as this may undermine state-to-state relations. A further option is for foreign investors to enter into contracts directly with states, including negotiating terms governing the settlement of investment disputes. However, that option is inaccessible to the vast majority of investors who lack the economic resources and political influence to negotiate such contracts with host countries. The further proposal by the Australian government is that "Australian business will need to make their own assessments about whether they to want to commit to investing in those countries [with greater risk]." This, too, is problematic because it leaves Australian investors to resolve investor–state disputes in the domestic courts of a myriad of host countries. A further risk, to Australia itself, is that Australian businesses will restructure their foreign investments through offshore entities that have more favorable BIT dispute resolution provisions, removing themselves from the regulatory and taxation regimes of Australia.

However, it is arguable that outbound Australian investors who bring ISA claims against recalcitrant states under BITs to which Australia is not a state party benefit both Australia and its outbound Australian investors. In particular, outbound investors can bring ISA, claims against states that have limited "rule of law" traditions, by relying on BITs between those states and intermediary states. This enables Australian investors to lodge claims against states whose courts those investors do not trust. An incidental benefit is that, given the resort by Australian outbound investors to intermediary states, the Australian government need not conclude BITs with ISA provisions with states that lack established rule-of-law traditions.

One can debate whether the Australian government is unqualifiedly committed to this policy. There has been no indication that it will seek to withdraw from existing BITs and FTAs that provide for investor–state arbitration (ISA). However, in the interests of uniformity, it may conceivably insist on renegotiating some or even all existing BITs that provide for ISA. It may also insist on negotiating more protective dispute resolution provisions with countries whose domestic standards of legal protection are lower than Australia's, in effect capping protection for foreign investors at Australia's domestic standard of protection. These interventions by the Australian government seem unlikely to eventuate given its comments that Australian businesses need to make their own assessment of the risks of investing in host countries abroad. It may also be that the Australian government has yet to arrive at firm responses to these issues. A successor Liberal government, in turn, may retreat from this policy, reverting to a widely accepted reliance on ISA, particularly with respect to developed countries. A particular difficulty for the Australian government is that it is currently negotiating a Trans–Pacific Strategic Partnership Agreement in which the United States is a dominant party. An issue will be whether Australia can negotiate to be included in this multilateral partnership that is likely to endorse ISA, while still being able to opt out of investor–state arbitration.

What is now known is that the Australian government's Policy Statement is based less on unremitting faith in domestic courts to resolve investor–state disputes than in disdain for ISA in particular. That disdain stems from the draft research and final Reports of the Australian Productivity Commission (APC), a public commission in Australia charged by the federal treasurer with the specific task of making recommendations on future trade and trade policy statements.[8] However, the APC's Report did more than challenge investor–state arbitration. It proposed more pervasively that Australia negotiate bilateral and regional trade and investment treaties in stages, that it first reach agreement on non-contentious issues, that it conclude treaties in order of their net benefit to Australia, that it cease to adopt ISA to resolve disputes in such treaties, and that it increase consultation with industry stakeholders and consumer representative groups.[9]

This chapter has several key objectives in relation to these matters. The first is to challenge the APC's contention that ISA should be rejected on grounds that it is objectively inferior to other mechanisms of dispute resolution. Although other methods, such as diplomatic intervention, political risk insurance, investor–state contracts, and so forth remain open, the most practical alternative to ISA is domestic litigation. However, domestic litigation is as open to criticism as is ISA. The second key objective of the chapter is to evaluate the consequences of resorting to domestic courts, as distinct from ISA to resolve investment disputes. The conclusion is that poking metaphorical holes in ISA is offset by the debilitating holes in domestic courts attempting to resolve investor–state disputes transparently, evenhandedly, and in particular, consistently and fairly. Indeed, ISA provisions in BITs provide a greater level of uniformity, predictability, and security than does resort to domestic courts. The chapter makes recommendations for changes to ISA that may reasonably accommodate some perceived deficiencies in it, that redress some of Australia's concerns, and that enable Australia to participate in investment treaties in which ISA is most likely to prevail. The chapter concludes by arguing against the Australian government's summary rejection of ISA because that rejection lacks an entirely justifiable basis. The government has also failed to provide a sustainable alternative, beyond open-ended reliance on domestic courts, once ISA is abandoned. The risk to Australia is in facing treaty isolation as a result of domesticating investment disputes before domestic courts in a manner that Australia's key partners in the region and elsewhere reject.

This chapter does not examine the economic costs of subjecting investment disputes to domestic litigation, given that insufficient time has elapsed since Australia's

---

[8] PRODUCTIVITY COMMISSION (AUSTRALIA), BILATERAL AND REGIONAL TRADE AGREEMENTS (Final Report, Nov. 2010, released Dec. 13, 2010), *available at* http://www.pc.gov.au/projects/study/trade-agreements [hereinafter PC FR]. For the Draft Research Report, *see* PRODUCTIVITY COMMISSION (AUSTRALIA), BILATERAL AND REGIONAL TRADE AGREEMENTS (Draft Research Report, July 16, 2010), *available at* http://www.apo.org.au/research/bilateral-and-regional-trade-agreements; Draft Research Report also on file with author [hereinafter PC RR]. On submissions invited by the Commission, see, for example, Patricia Ranald & Harvey Purse, *Supplementary Submission on behalf of the Australian Fair Trade and Investment Network (AFTINET) to the Productivity Commission Review into Bilateral and Regional Trade Agreements*, *available at* http://www.pc.gov.au/__data/assets/pdf_file/0015/102525/subdr068.pdf. *See also* Trakman, *supra* note 6.

[9] PC FR, *supra* note 8, Part D.

new policy statements to allow for such an analysis. However, it does maintain that the alleged economic costs that the Productivity Commission imputes to ISA are insufficiently established to justify rejecting ISA out of hand. Even if there are susceptible economic grounds to hold that the costs of ISA undermine its viability, and its fairness, these arguments need to be assessed on principled grounds. Doubts about ISA also need to take into account principled objections to its alternatives, notably to domestic courts, to resolve investor–state disputes.

II. BACKGROUND: THE APC REPORT

A primary consideration impelling the Australian government's policy stance is domestic public policy. The government's central concern is that foreign investors, notably foreign drug companies, will invoke investment arbitration to challenge Australia's sovereignty, and public interest in regulating industrial relations, public health, safety, and the environment. These concerns are understandable. Foreign drug companies are increasingly likely to challenge the Australian government's restrictions on access to and the price of foreign-manufactured drugs, such as under the Pharmaceutical Benefit Scheme (PBS). A related concern is a potential challenge to prospective Australian law requiring the plain packaging of tobacco products. Philip Morris has already initiated investment arbitration against the Republic of Uruguay under the Switzerland–Uruguay BIT, and has since launched a formidable challenge against Australia.[10]

Despite rhetoric about the national interest, the political and economic subtext behind Australia's new policy may be more complex in nature. There are growing doubts about the perceived economic merits of trade and investment arbitration. Reflecting these doubts are comments of the APC specifically making recommendations on

---

[10] On Australia's tobacco legislation, See *Tobacco Plain Packaging Act 2011* (Cth). See series of steps leading up to the passage of the Act, see <http://parlinfo.aph.gov.au/parlInfo/search/display/display.w3p;query=Id%3A%22legislation%2Fbillhome% *See generally* Matthew C. Porterfield & Christopher R. Byrnes, *Philip Morris v Uruguay: Will Investor–State Arbitration Send Restrictions on Tobacco Marketing up in Smoke?*, INV. TREATY NEWS, July 12, 2011, http://www.iisd.org/itn/2011/07/12/philip-morris-v-uruguay-will-investor-state-arbitration-send-restrictions-on-tobacco-marketing-up-in-smoke/ (last visited July 31, 2011); Andrew D. Mitchell & Sebastian M. Wurzberger, *Boxed In? Australia's Plain Tobacco Packaging Initiative and International Investment Law*, 27 ARB. INT'L 623 (2011), *available at* http://ssrn.com/abstract=1896125; Simon Chapman & Becky Freeman, *The Cancer Emperor's New Clothes: Australia's Historic Legislation for Plain Tobacco Packaging*, 340 BRIT. MED. J. 2436 (May 5, 2010); Tania Voon & Andrew Mitchell, *Implications of WTO Law for Plain Packaging of Tobacco Products*, PUBLIC HEALTH AND PLAIN PACKAGING OF CIGARETTES: LEGAL ISSUES (2011), http://ssrn.com/abstract=1874593. Philip Morris International, *Submission to the Office of the US Trade Representative*, Jan. 25, 2010, *available at* http://www.regulations.gov/search/Regs/home.html#documentDetail?R=0900006480a81289. On Philip Morris' initiation of an action against Australia in terms of the Australia–Hong Kong Free Trade Agreement, see http://www.pmi.com/eng/media_center/press_releases/pages/PM_Asia_plain_packaging.aspx. On Philip Morris' unsuccessful litigation against the prime minister of Australia, see Philip Morris Limited v Prime Minister [2011] AATA 556 (Aug. 2011). *See further Case S389/2411*, High Court of Australia <http://www.hcourt.gov.au/cases/case-s389/2011>; *JT International SA v Commonwealth of Australia* [2012] HCA 43 (5 October 2012).

future trade and investment policy. In essence, the Commission's report found no overwhelming economic rationale in support of ISA mechanisms in trade and investment agreements. Indeed, at its core the Commission found limited economic value in the BRTAs concluded to date. Craftily stated, the Commission noted that "current processes for assessing and prioritising BRTAs lack transparency and tend to oversell the likely benefits."[11] The APC's Report continued: "At a minimum, the economic value of Australia's preferential BRTAs has been oversold."[12] A recent analysis of the APC's report emphatically asserts that the APC's approach was based on a set of problematic assumptions and omissions, including a failure to fully understand the international legal and political implications of rejecting ISA, as well as a failure to take into account the effect of this rejection on outbound investment.[13]

At issue is whether the APC's assumptions are valid that the costs of ISA outweigh any ancillary benefits, whether declining to incorporate ISA into investment treaties will cause a "regulatory chill" on public authorities, whether reliance on domestic courts to resolve investment disputes will undermine the democratic process of law making, and whether ISA will distort the efficient flow of investments.[14] Further at issue are institutional impediments associated with ISA raised by the APC, as identified in Section VI below.

The reality is that it is speculative at best whether ISA does more to chill than encourage regulation of foreign direct investment (FDI). One can as readily hypothecate that governments may regulate foreign investment more efficiently and fairly by incorporating ISA into BITs than the contrary.

What, then, are the principled reasons in favor of domestic courts resolving investment disputes between host states and foreign investors? What are the principled arguments to the contrary? One answer is that the APC's concerns are defensible, at least in part.[15] Australia has a legitimate economic interest in reducing defensive costs that restrict its domestic policy space arising from entry into investment treaties. The problem is that the APC fails to balance these costs against the potential offensive gains to outbound Australian capital. For example, why would the Australian government avoid investment arbitration in its BITs with developed states that are net FDI importers from Australia, and that Australia perceives as having legal systems that are comparable to Australia's?

[11] PC RR, *supra* note 8, at xiv.

[12] *Id.* at xxii.

[13] Jurgen Kurtz, *Australia's Rejection of Investor–State Arbitration: Causation, Omission and Implication*, ICSID Rev. (forthcoming 2012).

[14] PC FR, *supra* note 8, 271–72.

[15] *See* Jurgen Kurtz, 'Australia's Rejection of Investor–State Arbitration: Causation, Omission and Implication' (2012) 27 *ICSID Review* 65. Aug. 2, 2011, *available at* http://www.asil.org/insights110802.cfm (noting that the Productivity Commission's Report, although offering a rigorous quantitative analysis of the net economic benefits of BITs, fails to take into account the dynamism of international law: "critical barriers to foreign investment do not usually take the form of simply border measures whose effects are easily quantifiable."); Hamamoto & Nottage, *supra* note 3.

The macroeconomic concern that dispute resolution mechanisms, especially investment arbitration, can be costly is a double-edged one. Investor–state arbitration does expose states to the risk of costly, fractious, and dysfunctional disputes with deep-pocket foreign investors of the likes of Philip Morris.[16] Weighed against this is the unfairness of denying foreign investors in general access to "neutral" arbitration, the cost to them of having to submit their investor–state disputes to domestic courts of host states in which proceedings are potentially more adversarial than arbitration, and the potential denial by domestic courts of natural justice on dubious national interest grounds. A further macro-political and economic cost to Australia is the prospect of being isolated from potentially lucrative investment treaties with leading trade partners that insist on the adoption of ISA. This concern is most likely to eventuate under the Trans-Pacific Partnership Agreement in which the vast majority of state parties are likely to prefer ISA over domestic litigation. Nor is Australia's rejoinder justified that at least Australian courts are preferable institutions to dispense natural justice than ad hoc investment tribunals in the absence of further legitimation.[17] These competing arguments are considered in greater detail below.

III. CHALLENGING ISA

An initial observation is that the Australian government and the Productivity Commission are not alone in their doubts about the value of ISA. Related concerns were expressed in a comparatively recent report by the UNCTAD:

> Moreover, the financial amounts at stake in investor–State disputes are often very high. Resulting from these unique attributes, the disadvantages of international trade and investment arbitration are found to be the large costs involved, the increase in the time frame for claims to be settled, the fact that ISDS cases are increasingly difficult to manage, the fears about frivolous and vexatious claims, the general concerns about the legitimacy of the system of investment arbitration as it affects measures of a sovereign State, and the fact that arbitration is focused entirely on the payment of compensation and not on maintaining a working relationship between the parties.[18]

---

[16] *See Philip Morris Asia Initiates Legal Action against the Australian Government over Plain Packaging, Phillip Morris International* (News Release, June 27, 2011), http://www.pmi.com/eng/media_center/press_releases/pages/PM_Asia_plain_packaging.aspx. On the prelude to this conflict, see Liv Casben, *Tobacco Companies Rally against Plain Packaging*, ABC NEWS (online), Apr. 29, 2011, http://www.abc.net.au/news/stories/2010/04/29/2885343.htm. *See also Tobacco Company Files Claim against Uruguay over Labeling Laws*, INTERNATIONAL CENTRE FOR TRADE AND SUSTAINABLE DEVELOPMENT, Mar. 10, 2010, http://ictsd.org/i/news/bridgesweekly/71988/.

[17] *See* Policy, *supra* note 4, at 1–2.

[18] *Investor–State Disputes: Prevention and Alternatives to Arbitration*, UNCTAD Series on International Investment Policies for Development (May 2010), at xxiii, *available at* http://www.unctad.org/en/docs/diaeia200911_en.pdf. *See also Investor–State Disputes: Prevention and Alternatives to Arbitration II*

The Australian government has asserted that it supports the principle of national treatment: that domestic and foreign businesses are to be treated equally under the law. An inference is that foreign investors ought not to benefit from investor–state arbitration as a dispute resolution process that is not ordinarily available to domestic investors and that would place local investors at a comparative disadvantage. Thus, APC's research report noted: "Dispute settlement processes should not afford foreign investors in Australia with access to litigation options not normally afforded to local investors."[19] These localized considerations notwithstanding, reliance on domestic courts to decide investment disputes carries its own risks. Can the Australian government be reasonably assured that foreign trade and investment partner states will respect the rule of law in deciding foreign investor–state disputes abroad? At a functional level, what framework would domestic courts apply in resolving investment disputes? Would they apply local laws? How would any claim for breach of BIT protections be presented to a domestic court? When would a foreign investor be entitled to bring a claim again a host state for breach of the fair and equitable treatment standard? When, if ever, would a domestic court directly apply international investment law to an investor–state dispute? To what extent could national courts be relied upon to demonstrate their willingness and ability to exercise discretion in displaying fairness toward foreign investors, conceivably at the expense of the host state?

The APC presents an ambitious answer to the rule of law question in particular. Its answer is for Australia to provide developing country partners with infrastructure and related financial support to reform their economies, including presumably by redressing Australian concerns about access to justice in investor–state disputes before the courts of "host" states.[20]

A further self-help remedy proposed is for Australian investors abroad to develop their own mechanisms to assess the risks of relying on foreign domestic courts to resolve investment disputes with foreign host states.[21] In this regard, political risk insurance is one conceivable, albeit underdeveloped, avenue of risk avoidance that is available to Australian investors abroad.[22]

Interestingly, the APC noted that it "received no feedback from Australian businesses or industry associations indicating that ISDS provisions were of much value or importance to them."[23] Nevertheless, the absence of feedback from the private sector does not necessarily imply acquiescence in the APC's inference that businesses do not value investor–state arbitration. The more likely inference is that businesses were not

(Proceedings of the Washington and Lee University and UNCTAD Joint Symposium on International Investment and Alternative Dispute Resolution, Lexington, VA, Susan D. Franck & Anna Joubin-Bret eds., Mar. 29, 2010), http://www.unctad.org/en/docs/webdiaeia20108_en.pdf.

19 PC RR, *supra* note 8, section [13.20].

20 PC RR, *supra* note 8, sections [13.19]–[13.20].

21 *See* PC FR, *supra* note 8, at 270–71.

22 Jurgen Kurtz, 'Australia's Rejection of Investor–State Arbitration: Causation, Omission and Implication' (2012) 27 *ICSID Review* 65.

23 *See* PC FR, *supra* note 8, at 270–71.

attuned to the Commission's project, did not appreciate its influence on government policy, or doubted their capacity to change the Commission's view.[24]

It is possible that Australia's rejection of ISA, along with that by other countries noted in the Introduction, will undermine the work of recognized investment arbitration institutions such as the ICSID. A related hazard is that the Australian government's rejection of ISA will encourage other states to adopt more nuanced dispute resolution mechanisms, not limited to domestic courts. These concerns are reflected in part in problematic dispute resolution clauses that are incorporated into the China–New Zealand Free Trade Agreement and the possibility that New Zealand will also opt for domestic courts over investor–state arbitration.[25] Linked to these concerns is the apprehension that other developed states will follow Australia's lead, not least of all as a result of entering into BITs with Australia in which domestic courts are chosen over ISA, as is already the case in the Australia–U.S. Free Trade Agreement. At its most basic, this risk is about international investment arbitration centers losing their business to domestic courts, not just about investor–state disputes being rendered parochial.

IV. FURTHER ALTERNATIVES

The Rejection of ISA does not mean that domestic courts are the only available avenue in resolving investor–state disputes. Investors may enter into investment partnerships with organizations such as the World Bank, regional banks, and international corporations with headquarters in Europe or the United States. They may purchase private investor insurance schemes. They may conclude ad hoc arrangements with home states, including access to government funded or private investor insurance schemes. Failing that, they may request their home states to intervene to resolve their investment disputes with host states.

The APC acknowledged these alternatives, but then discounted them in part. Although it recognized that investors may negotiate investment contracts with host countries that include dispute resolution clauses, the APC appropriately conceded that such a negotiated strategy "is more feasible for large businesses."[26] It identified

---

[24] Leon E. Trakman, *Investor State Arbitration or Local Courts: Will Australia Set a New Trend?*, 46 J. World Trade 83, 93 (2012). For the APC to infer that because no Australian business commented on ISDS, business interests did not value ISDS, constitutes a questionable leap of faith by the APC.

[25] Free Trade Agreement, New Zealand–China, signed Apr. 7, 2008 (entered into force Oct. 1. 2008), NZTS 19, *available at* http://chinafta.govt.nz/1-The-agreement/2-Text-of-the-agreement/index.php. On resistance to ISA in the Trans-Pacific Partnership Agreement, particularly in Australia and New Zealand, see, for example, Kyla Tienhaara, *Investor–State Dispute Settlement in the Trans-Pacific Partnership Agreement*, Submission to the Department of Foreign Affairs and Trade, May 19, 2010, *available at* www.pc.gov.au/__data/assets/pdf_file/.../subdr067-attachment1.pdf. *See also* Meredith Kolsky Lewis, *The Trans-Pacific Partnership: New Paradigm or Wolf in Sheep's Clothing?*, 34 B.C. Int'l & Comp. L. Rev. 27 (2011).

[26] PC FR, *supra* note 8, at 270.

the availability of political risks insurance against expropriation; however, it did not highlight the current short time frame, complexity, and limited coverage of such insurance.[27] By a process of elimination, the APC conceived that the most practical option was resort to domestic courts.

V. IN PURSUIT OF EQUALITY

In its research report, the APC criticizes international investment arbitration:

> Cases are generally not appealable and arbitration frequently operates without the benefit of precedents (an important component of legal certainty). Additionally, particular government actions that would otherwise be non-reviewable to domestic investors may be subject to ISDS actions by foreign investors.[28]

The APC's research report goes on to note that arbitration clauses in BRTAs often accord greater rights to foreign than domestic investors,[29] BRTAs diverge over the nature of arbitration mechanisms in agreements between developed and developing countries,[30] and they do not address potential conflicts arising from mixed regional agreements such as under the proposed Trans-Pacific Partnership Agreement.[31]

The APC's research report also challenges ISA clauses for restricting future governments from regulating foreign investment in the public interest.[32] It stresses, too, that the benefits arising from the econometric measurement of bilateral investment arbitration are likely to be scant.[33]

A large issue therefore is the appearance of ISA providing foreign investors with unmerited advantages while also unduly restricting the ability of the Australian government to pursue its policy—including equalitarian—goals.

This viewpoint may not be unique as countries sometimes diverge in their treatment of international trade and investment law, including in dispute resolution. Bilateral trade agreements occasionally refer investment disputes between foreign investors and host states to the domestic courts of host states, most notably in the Free Trade Agreement between Australia and the United States. There are proclivities, too, for the United States to opt for domestic courts in future bilateral and regional investment agreements, albeit less profoundly articulated than those of the

---

27 *Id.* at 320.

28 PC RR, *supra* note 8, section [13.20].

29 *Id.*

30 *Id.* at section [19].

31 *Id.* at section [13.20].

32 *Id.* at section [9.11], [13.20].

33 *Id.* at section [14.5].

Australian government.[34] In addition, legislatures sometimes prefer domestic courts to arbitration in resolving trade and investment disputes, notably under the U.S. Trade Act 2002.[35] The Australian government is also not alone in seeking to protect domestic investors from foreign investors. The Bipartisan Trade Promotion Authority Act of 2002 in the United States and the consequent 2004 U.S. Model BIT challenged trade-distorting barriers by which foreign investors acquired "greater substantive rights with respect to investment protections" than domestic investors.[36] However, although the legislative intent in the United States was to amend ISA in the interests of local investors, it fell markedly short of rejecting ISA out of hand.[37]

The Australian government's position is nevertheless distinctive in insistence on national treatment to investors in every investment treaty it concludes in order to ensure "that foreign and domestic businesses are treated equally under the law."[38] Whether domestic courts will accord equal treatment to domestic and foreign investors remains to be seen. Some scholars espouse the view that all countries engage in a measure of discrimination against foreign investors, however much the Australian Policy is based on equal treatment of foreign and domestic investors.[39]

The across-the-board submission of trade and investment disputes to domestic courts, enunciated by the Australian government, is unusual in two respects. First, countries historically resolved investment disputes diplomatically through negotiations between host and home states on behalf of their investors abroad. Though it remains a theoretical option, this diplomatic process is no longer prevalent, given the development of regional and bilateral treaties enabling foreign investors to proceed directly against host states. Second, countries with comparable cultural histories and legal systems have greater reason to conclude bilateral treaties in which they place mutual trust in each other's legal and judicial systems. The assumption is that such treaty partners are most likely to agree to each other's courts resolving investor–state

---

34 *See generally* Mark Kantor, *The New Draft Model U.S. BIT: Noteworthy Developments*, 21 J. INT'L ARB. 383 (2004); Trakman, *supra* note 6, at 79–81; Westcott, *supra* note 6; Peter Drahos & David Henry, *The Free Trade Agreement between Australia and the United States*, BRIT. MED. J. 1271 (May 29, 2004); Philippa Dee, The Australia–US Free Trade Agreement: An Assessment (Paper prepared for the Senate Select Committee on the Free Trade Agreement between Australia and the United States of America, June 2004), *Pacific Economic Papers* (No 345, 2005), http://crawford.anu.edu.au/pdf/pep/pep-345.pdf; Drusilla K. Brown, Kozo Kiyota & Robert M. Stern, *Computational Analysis of the US FTAs with Central America, Australia and Morocco*, 28 WORLD ECON. 1441 (2005). *See also Free Trade Agreements with Australia*, OFFICE OF THE UNITED STATES TRADE REPRESENTATIVE, http://www.ustr.gov/trade-agreements/free-trade-agreements/australian-fta.

35 The Trade Act was passed on Aug. 6, 2002. *See* Trade Act 2002, Pub. L. No. 107-210, 116 Stat. 933, 994 (2002) [hereinafter *Trade Act*].

36 *See* Trade Act div B (Bipartisan Trade Promotion Authority) § 2102(b)(3).

37 *See* Kantor, *supra* note 34, at 383.

38 Policy, *supra* note 4, at 14.

39 Jurgen Kurtz, 'Australia's Rejection of Investor–State Arbitration: Causation, Omission and Implication' (2012) 27 *ICSID Review* 65." Kurtz relies on the commentary of Joseph Stiglitz to assert that "'all countries engage in some discrimination' against foreign investors," and concedes that "protectionism is a political temptation that is not confined to any political or legal tradition."

disputes due to long-standing, and deeply engrained, trade and investment relationships, similarities in legal traditions, and "trust" that the others' courts will apply mutually affirmed rules of law and principles of natural justice. Despite the rhetoric, BITs that refer investment disputes to domestic courts, notably under the Australia–United States Free Trade Agreement are the exception, not the norm.[40] As such, the Australian government's stance that it will discontinue the practice of pursuing "investor–state dispute resolution procedures in trade agreements with *developing countries*" is surprising.[41]

One of the Australian government's key assumptions in specifying that domestic courts will resolve investment disputes in all future BITs is its insistence that Australian investors who invest abroad ought to take account of economic, political, and legal risks associated with such investments. Its advice to such Australians is to assess the likelihood of receiving less favorable treatment before foreign courts than they would before domestic Australian courts. If Australian investors abroad fail to do their homework in making investment choices, they ought to bear the consequences of their own actions. Defensively phrased, the Australian government ought not to be responsible for protecting Australian investors who assume foreign investment risks they ought to have avoided or mitigated.[42]

The Australian government's approach is nevertheless problematic. The expectation of Australian investors about the hazard of being subject to foreign courts abroad is likely to be informed, to varying degrees, by the conditions in BITs that are negotiated between the Australian government and its treaty partners. That conduct is likely to affirm the perception among Australian investors abroad that, if the Australian government is willing to conclude BITs with foreign governments, it is likely also to "trust" the courts of those partner countries to resolve investor–state disputes. If the Australian government has doubts, Australian investors could reasonably assume that it would not have concluded those treaties, or it would have provided economic infrastructure or other financial support to help investment partners deliver legal services judiciously to foreign investors from Australia. Alternatively, Australian investors could presuppose that the Australian government would have included appropriate conditions within its treaties to ensure that "national treatment" for Australian investors is both clearly articulated and implemented.[43] It is probable, too, that Australian investors might be more likely to submit an investor–state dispute to a court in a host state with whom Australia has a BIT relationship when compared to submitting such a dispute involving a host state that has no such BIT relationship.

---

40 *See* Trakman, *supra* note 6, at 39, 41–50, 79–81.

41 Policy, *supra* note 4 (emphasis added).

42 The government states in its Policy, *supra* note 4, at 16: "If Australian businesses are concerned about sovereign risk in Australian trading partner countries, they will need to make their own assessments about whether they want to commit to investing in those countries."

43 *See, e.g.*, Westcott, *supra* note 6; Trakman, *supra* note 6, at 39, 41–50, 79–81.

VI. THE CASE FOR NOT RELYING ON ISA

Any alleged flaws in the APC's analysis notwithstanding, it can be readily accepted that ISA institutions are far from perfect. There are numerous principled objections to reliance on ISA.[44] In fairness, the APC identifies some of its reasons for such objections: the large size of investor claims, the latitude of investment tribunals in determining the amount of compensation, the lack of rigorous rules governing the conduct of ISA, the absence of an appeals process, and the threat of "institutional biases and conflicts of interest, inconsistency and matters of jurisdiction, a lack of transparency and the costs incurred by participants."[45] The Commission concludes that "experience in other countries demonstrates that there are considerable policy and financial risks arising from ISDS provisions."[46]

I. THE CASE FOR RELYING ON DOMESTIC COURTS

There are numerous reasons also for preferring resort to domestic courts over ISA.

First, on principled grounds, domestic investors ought to be subject to the territorial sovereignty of the state in which they invest.[47] National law ought to govern the rights of foreign investors, and the jurisdiction of domestic courts ought to exclude other options such as diplomatic channels that bypass the judicial system of the host state.[48]

Second, a domestic court of the state that is party to an investment treaty is the appropriate forum to resolve an investment dispute, in the same manner as it resolves other disputes between that state and other private or corporate claimants.[49]

Third, foreign investors should not receive investment benefits beyond those provided to domestic investors. Such treatment is conceivably unfair, as is evidenced

---

44 Trakman, *supra* note 24, at 100 (for commentary on the principled objections to ISA).

45 PC FR, *supra* note 8, at 272.

46 *Id.* at 274.

47 On the complexity of sovereignty in international investment law, see, for example, WENHUA SHAN, PENELOPE SIMONS & DALVINDER SINGH, REDEFINING SOVEREIGNTY IN INTERNATIONAL ECONOMIC LAW (2008) (see especially pt. 4 for commentary on the complexity of sovereignty in international investment law); Robert Stumberg, *Sovereignty by Subtraction: The Multilateral Agreement on Investment*, 31 CORNELL INT'L L. J. 491 (1998), 503–04, 523–25. *See also* ROBERT H. JACKSON, QUASI-STATES: SOVEREIGNTY, INTERNATIONAL RELATIONS AND THE THIRD WORLD (1990); JOHN H. JACKSON, THE JURISPRUDENCE OF GATT AND THE WTO: INSIGHTS ON TREATY LAW AND ECONOMIC RELATIONS (2000); Michael Reisman, *International Arbitration and Sovereignty*, 18 ARB. INT'L (LCIA) 231 (2002); OPPENHEIM'S INTERNATIONAL LAW 927 (Robert Jennins & Arthur Watts eds., 1992).

48 On the history and resurgence of the Calvo Doctrine, *see infra* note 76.

49 On these arguments in relation to the Australia–United States Free Trade Agreement, see Trakman, *supra* note 6, at 48–53; Westcott, *supra* note 6.

historically by the privileges accorded by less-developed countries to multinational corporations at the expense of local subjects who were competitively disadvantaged.[50]

Fourth, domestic courts ought to decide cases involving foreign investors according to domestic law, including by incorporating international investment laws into that domestic law.[51]

Fifth, domestic courts are bound by established forum procedures and rules of evidence to protect the rights of foreign investor in accordance with domestic public policy that usually includes a right of appeal to a higher court.[52]

These arguments, for national courts to decide investor–state disputes, are buttressed by doubts about the legitimacy and sufficiency of ISA. In particular, ISA is not subject to comparable procedural and substantive constraints as are domestic courts. Investment arbitrators may decide in favor of foreign investors on grounds that undermine the public interest of home states. There are no appeals from ISA awards, except for an arbitrator's failure to exercise, or abuse of, jurisdiction, leading to a review by the ICSID Annulment Committee. Annulment proceedings are an extraordinary process and more limited in scope than an appeal to a domestic court.[53] In contrast,

---

[50] On these arguments buttressing the dispute resolution mechanisms adopted under the Australia–United States Free Trade Agreements, see Trakman, *supra* note 6, at 48–49; Westcott, *supra* note 6.

[51] On the contentious constraints on the jurisdiction of state courts in the *Mondev* and *Loewen* Chapter 11 cases, see *infra* note 106.

[52] On this contest between individual rights and public policy in the development of the "margin of appreciation" doctrine in European Union law, see Onder Bakircioglu, *The Application of the Margin of Appreciation Doctrine in Freedom of Expression and Public Morality Cases*, 8 GERMAN L.J. 711 (2007); Yuval Shany, *Toward a General Margin of Appreciation Doctrine in International Law?*, 16 EUR. J. INT'L L. 907 (2005); Eyal Benvenisti, *Margin of Appreciation, Consensus, and Universal Standards*, 31 N.Y.U. J. INT'L L. & POL'Y 843 (1999); R. St. J. Macdonald, *The Margin of Appreciation*, *in* THE EUROPEAN SYSTEM FOR THE PROTECTION OF HUMAN RIGHTS 125 (R. St. J. Macdonald, F. Matscher & H. Petzold eds., 1993).

[53] On the absence of an appeal from ICSID arbitration, see Convention on the Settlement of Investment Disputes between States and Nationals of Other States art. 53(1), http://icsid.worldbank.org/ICSID/StaticFiles/basicdoc/CRR_English-final.pdf [hereinafter ICSID Convention]. Article 53 provides:

> The award . . . shall not be subject to any appeal or to any other remedy except those provided for in this Convention. The most significant remedy under the ICSID is the annulment of an award under Article 53. The ICSID provides instead for a review of an investment award by an Annulment Committee which is set up specifically for that purpose, with the power to modify or nullify an ICSID award on limited procedural grounds under Art 75 of the ICSID Convention. Either party can request that the award be annulled. However, the grounds for such a challenge are restricted and fall short of an appeal. They include that:
>
> 1) the ICSID tribunal was not properly constituted;
> 2) the tribunal manifestly exceeded its powers;
> 3) there was corruption on the part of a tribunal member;
> 4) there was a serious departure from a fundamental rule of procedure; or
> 5) the award failed to state the reasons on which it was based.

ICSID Annulment Committees traditionally have interpreted these grounds for a challenge liberally, permitting a series of challenges, although such challenges have dissipated in recent years. Resort to domestic courts is not an option under the ICSID. *See* ICSID Convention, art 75. For ICSID documents generally, see http://icsid.worldbank.org/ICSID/Index.jsp. *See also* JAMES CRAWFORD & KAREN LEE, ICSID REPORTS VOL. 6 (2004). On the ICSID Additional Facility, see http://icsid.worldbank.org/

awards rendered by a tribunal established under the United Nations Commission on International Trade Law (UNCITRAL) Rules are subject to review by the national courts of the legal place of the arbitration.[54]

II. THE LEGITIMACY CRISIS OF PUBLIC/PRIVATE INVESTMENT ARBITRATION

Investor–state arbitration also faces a legitimacy crisis arising out of its public and private attributes.[55] It is the product of a public process insofar as it stems from investment treaties between countries and engages public interests that transcend the commercial interests of private parties. As a result, public considerations, not least of all public reactions, influence how readily states endorse, participate in, and comply with ISA determinations.[56] The other side of the legitimacy crisis is that ISA is "private." In the tradition of "private" commercial arbitration, ISA ordinarily is conducted with the consent of both parties to an ISA.[57] Third parties such as public interest groups are not permitted to participate in ISA proceedings without the consent of the investor–state parties.[58] Nor can ISA awards be published without the support of the investor and

---

ICSID/ICSID/AdditionalFacilityRules.jsp. *See generally Analysis of Key Obligations and Emerging Issues in International Investment Treaties, Foreign Investment Review Board*, http://www.firb.gov.au/content/international_investment/current_issues.asp?NavID=60>.

54 The UNCITRAL Rules are a general set of rules that can be applied flexibly to resolve any type of international dispute. Some of the 2010 amendments to the UNCITRAL rules were inspired by the rising use of the Rules in investor–state arbitrations. *See, e.g.*, United Nations Commission on International Trade Law, *2010 - UNCITRAL Arbitration Rules (as revised in 2010)*, http://www.uncitral.org/uncitral/en/uncitral_texts/arbitration/2010Arbitration_rules.html.

55 On this legitimacy crisis, see Susan D. Franck, *The Legitimacy Crisis in Investment Treaty Arbitration: Privatizing Public International Law through Inconsistent Decisions*, 73 FORDHAM L. REV. 1521, 1543–44 (2005).

56 For a description of this tension between the law governing treaties and their impact on state–investor disputes, see CHRISTOPH SCHREUER & RUDOLF DOLZER, PRINCIPLES OF INTERNATIONAL INVESTMENT LAW CH. 1 (2008); CHRISTOPH SCHREUER, THE ICSID CONVENTION: A COMMENTARY chs. 1– 2 (2001); STEPHAN W. SCHILL, THE MULTILATERALIZATION OF INTERNATIONAL INVESTMENT LAW, chs. 1–2 (2009).

57 On similarities and differences between international commercial arbitration and investment arbitration, see Luke Nottage & Kate Miles, "Back to the Future" for Investor–State Arbitrations: Revising Rules in Australia and Japan to Meet Public Interests (University of Sydney Legal Research Paper No 08/62, 25 June 2008), *available at* http://papers.ssrn.com/sol3/papers.cfm?abstract_id=1151167.

58 *Suez Sociedad General de Aguas de Barcelona S.A. and Vivendi Universal S.A. v. the Republic of Argentina* (Order in Response to a Petition by Five Non-Governmental Organizations for Permission to Make an Amicus Curiae Submission) (ICSID Arbitral Tribunal, Case No ARB/03/19, 12 February 2007); (Order in Response to a Petition for Transparency and Participation as Amicus Curiae) (ICSID Arbitral Tribunal, Case No ARB/03/19, May 19, 2005). The petition challenged the decision by the government of Argentina to accede to the ICSID treaty, on grounds that it violates the constitutional guarantees of citizens of Argentina to participate in proceedings. Although the government of Argentina was willing to hear the petition, the complainant company was not. However, the attorney general of Argentina published on the Internet the information in his possession on the related cases. *See also* Carlos E. Alfaro & Pedro M. Lorenti, *The Growing Opposition of Argentina to ICSID Arbitral Tribunals: A Conflict between International and Domestic Law?*, 6 J. WORLD INV. & TRADE 417 (2005).

state parties.[59] Typically, the Secretary General of the ICSID can publish reports of conciliation commissions or awards rendered by arbitral tribunals in ICSID proceedings, but only "with the consent of both disputing parties."[60] A related consequence is that investor and state parties to ISA proceedings can deny a public interest petition, amicus briefs, or other forms of participation by third parties in ISA proceedings. For example, in *Suez Sociedad General de Aguas de Barcelona S.A. and Vivendi Universal S.A. v. Republic of Argentina*, the arbitration tribunal acknowledged that the case "potentially involved matters of public interest and human rights" and that the public access "would have the additional desirable consequence of increasing the transparency of ISA."[61] It nevertheless declined to permit public participation under the petition. The perceived result of such private proceedings was the loss of public attributes for an ISA process that derives from treaties between states.

The problem is not only that one or both parties may choose to exclude third parties from ISA proceedings. A further difficulty arises from a perceived lack of transparency in ISA proceedings in the absence of comprehensive public information about the nature, content, and results of the full range of ISA disputes.[62] It is also difficult to draw inferences about the public benefits attributes to ISA in the absence of comprehensive access to investment proceedings and awards.

VII. THE CASE AGAINST RELIANCE ON DOMESTIC COURTS

That a case can be made against relying on ISA does not in itself imply that domestic courts ought to be preferred. What is required is a balancing exercise, including the ramifications of resorting to domestic courts. The intention in this section is to show

[59] *See, e.g., GEA Group Aktiengesellschaft v Ukraine (Award)* (ICSID Arbitral Tribunal, Case No ARB/08/16, Mar. 31, 2011); *Talsud, S.A. v. United Mexican States (Award)* (ICSID Arbitral Tribunal, Case No. ARB(AF)/04/4, June 16, 2010); *Gemplus, S.A., SLP, S.A. and Gemplus Industrial, S.A. de C.V. v United Mexican States (Award)* (ICSID Arbitral Tribunal, Case No. ARB(AF)/04/3, June 16, 2010).

[60] *See, e.g., GEA Group Aktiengesellschaft v. Ukraine* (Award) (ICSID Arbitral Tribunal, Case No. ARB(AF)/04/4, June 16, 2010); *Gemplus, S.A., SLP, S.A. and Gemplus Industrial, S.A. de C.V. v. United Mexican States* (Award) (ICSID Arbitral Tribunal, Case No. ARB(AF)/04/3, June 16, 2010); *Aguas del Tunari, S.A. v. Republic of Bolivia* (Order Taking Note of Discontinuance) (ICSID Case No ARB/02/3, March 28, 2006), *available at* http://ita.law.uvic.ca/documents/AguasdelTunari-jurisdiction-eng_000.pdf. These requirements, replicated on the ICSID Web site, are available at http://icsid.worldbank.org/ICSID/FrontServlet?requestType=CasesRH&actionVal=ShowHome&pageName=Cases_Home. *See also* ICSID Procedural Order of February 2, 2011 inviting third parties to apply to submit *amici curiae* briefs under ICSID Arbitration Rule 37(2). *See further* Kenneth J. Vandevelde, Aguas del Tunari, S.A. v. Republic of Bolivia, 101 AM. J. INT'L L. 179 (2007) (providing an overview and analysis of the case); A. de Gramont, *After the Water War: The Battle for Jurisdiction in* Aguas Del Tunari, S.A. v. Republic of Bolivia, TRANSNAT'L DISPUTE MGMT. (Dec. 2006), http://www.crowell.com/documents/After-the-Water-War_The-Battle-for-Jurisdiction-in-Aguas-del-Tunari_v_Bolivia.pdf.

[61] (Order in Response to a Petition for Transparency and Participation as Amicus Curiae) (ICSID Case No ARB/03/19, May 19, 2005) [19], [22].

[62] On criticism of the existence and sufficiency of international investment law, see M. Sornarajah, Chapter 16 in this book.

that the case for domestic courts, presented in Part VI, is based more on perception, preference, and semantic manipulation than objectively verified criteria. The author has noted elsewhere that, in the debate between ISA and domestic litigation, beauty lies in the eyes of the beholder.[63]

First, Australia's new investment policy raises a noteworthy complication. By insisting that Australian courts apply domestic law to foreign investors in Australia, the Australian government presumably accepts that foreign courts will apply their laws to Australian investors in those foreign countries, whatever those laws may be. In declining to agree to arbitration in investment treaties with both developed and developing countries, the Australian government also draws no distinction between countries that apply a "rule of law" jurisprudence that is comparable to the rules of law applied by Australian courts and those countries that do not subscribe to such a "rule."[64]

Attacking a plethora of domestic legal systems and courts is more doubtful than challenging a few ISA institutions such as the ICSID and UNCITRAL, especially where foreign investors may be subject to a multitude of domestic legal systems with divergent procedures and substantive investment jurisprudence. However, this multiplicity of domestic legal options is itself problematic, in forsaking uniformity among inevitably divergent legal systems. These deficiencies of domestic legal systems stand starkly in contrast to ISA institutions that seek to limit the proliferation of international investment law. As such, ISA serves as a unifying framework within which multiple bilateral investment treaties are subject to largely uniform ISA provisions that derive significantly from the global experience of foreign investors, host, and home states. Acting as a leveling force, ISA is founded on principles, standards, and rules of investment jurisprudence that are not ordinarily sublimated by domestic legal systems and rules of procedure. Investor–state arbitration is also conceived as more certain and stable than a myriad of different domestic laws and rules that might otherwise govern FDI.[65]

Whether ISA jurisprudence exists in a truly transcendental form is the subject of ongoing doubt.[66] Arguably, the failure of the community of states to reach a multilateral investment accord in the past demonstrates the difficulty of states finding common ground on the treatment of foreign investment, including on processes for

---

63 Trakman, *supra* note 24, at 114.

64 Trakman, *supra* note 6, at 39–43; *see also* Westcott, *supra* note 6.

65 Vandevelde writes that in 1969 there were only seventy-five BITs. During the 1970s, nine BITs were negotiated each year; that rate doubled in the 1980s and has been increasing geometrically until five years ago. *see* Kenneth Vandevelde, *A Brief History of International Investment Agreements*, 12 U.C. DAVIS J. INT'L L. & POL'Y 157, 172 (2005). *See also* World Investment Report 2010, *United Nations Conference on Trade and Development*, UNCTAD/WIR/2010 (July 22, 2010), at xxv, www.unctad.org/en/docs/wir2010_en.pdf.

66 *See generally* SCHILL, *supra* note 56, chs. 1–2; Sharun W. Mukand, *Globalization and the "Confidence Game"*, 70 J. INT'L ECON. 406 (2006); Steffen Hindelang, *Bilateral Investment Treaties, Custom and a Healthy Investment Climate—The Question of Whether BITs Influence Customary International Law Revisited*, 5 J. WORLD INV. & TRADE 789 (2004); Jeswald W. Salacuse, *The Treatification of International Investment Law*, 8 STUDIES INT'L FIN. ECON. & TECH. L. 241 (2007).

dispute resolution.[67] The counterargument is that ISA does respond to these concerns through standards of treatment that apply generally to foreign investors, even though ISA provisions vary among BITs and are sometimes construed differently by investment arbitrators.[68]

Notwithstanding the absence of a formalized system of judicial precedent in ISA as common lawyers conceive of it, ISA is still likely to be more coherent than a multiplicity of different state laws applied by local courts to foreign investment.[69] However difficult it is to identify cohesive ISA principles out of ad hoc and sometimes unpublished arbitration awards, and however arbitrators may fragment standards of treatment under different BITs, ICSID and UNCITRAL arbitrations have been used over a considerable period of time to resolve investment disputes in often complex cases.[70] That task of investment arbitration is accomplished notwithstanding the plethora of BITs in existence and their susceptibility to different kinds of interpretation.[71] Nor should institutions such as the ICSID be blamed for inconsistent reasoning that is sometimes adopted by ISA tribunals that, although guided by ICSID and UNCITRAL rules, exercise independent discretion in deciding investment disputes.[72]

The principled argument that the domestic courts of sovereign states ought to decide investment disputes based on domestic laws and judicial procedures is offset by the observation that international arbitrators are also subject to domestic laws that are encompassed within a BIT or investor–state agreement. Far from being insulated from domestic laws and procedures, ISA principles and standards of treatment accorded to foreign investors inhere not only in international jurisprudence, but both evolve from and are incorporated into domestic law as well. As a result, ISA arbitrators cannot summarily disregard domestic laws that are expressly or impliedly integrated into applicable BITs or investor–state agreements.[73]

---

67 *See MAI Negotiating Text*, ORGANISATION FOR ECONOMIC CO-OPERATION AND DEVELOPMENT (Apr. 24, 1998), http://italaw.com/documents/MAIDraftText.pdf; Katia Tieleman, *The Failure of the Multilateral Agreement on Investment (MAI) and the Absence of a Global Public Policy Network*, GLOBAL PUBLIC POLICY INSTITUTE (2000), http://www.gppi.net/fileadmin/gppi/Tieleman_MAI_GPP_Network.pdf.

68 On such issues, *see generally OECD Investment Committee*, FOREIGN INVESTMENT REVIEW BOARD, http://www.firb.gov.au/content/international_investment/current_issues.asp?NavID=60.

69 On the development of international investment norms, see *OECD Investment Committee*, INTERNATIONAL CENTRE FOR SETTLEMENT OF INVESTMENT DISPUTES, http://www.firb.gov.au/content/international_investment/current_issues.asp?NavID=60.

70 This capacity of international investment law to withstand its own fragmentation is a central attribute of this book. But see contra Sornarajah, Chapter 16 of this book; SCHREUER & DOLZER, *supra* note 56; SCHILL, *supra* note 56.

71 *See, e.g.*, Aurélia Antonietti, *The 2006 Amendments of the ICSID Rules and Regulations and the Additional Facility Rules*, 21 ICSID REV.—FOR. INV. L.J. 427 (2006); Edward Baldwin, Mark Kantor & Michael Nolan, *Limits to Enforcement of ICSID Awards*, 23 J. INT'L ARB. 1 (2006) (discussing "tactics" that may be employed in attempts to "delay" or "avoid" compliance with ICSID Awards).

72 On the development of international investment norms, see *OECD Investment Committee*, INTERNATIONAL CENTRE FOR SETTLEMENT OF INVESTMENT DISPUTES, http://www.firb.gov.au/content/international_investment/current_issues.asp?NavID=60.

73 *See, e.g.*, SCHREUER, *supra note* 56, at 357.

The rationale that domestic courts are expert in law including investment law is counterbalanced by the contention that investment arbitrators are expert in international investment law in a manner that domestic judges, even courts of commercial jurisdiction, are not.[74] Even the rationale that domestic courts are subject to tried and tested rules of evidence and procedure is offset by the observation that investment arbitration is guided by ICSID or UNCITRAL rules that focus specifically on the complexities of investment law. Insofar as the decisions of domestic courts are subject to appeal, the awards of investment arbitrators are subject to extraordinary challenge or annulment proceedings for noncompliance.[75]

VIII. THE ASSAULT ON ISA BY DEVELOPING COUNTRIES

As highlighted in the Introduction, the Australian government is not the only country to reject ISA. The Calvo Doctrine enunciated in Latin America was also intended to domesticate the resolution of investor–state disputes.[76] Some developing countries have also long resented ISA. This resentment is most vividly expressed by President Raphael Correa of Ecuador in his verbal onslaught in 2009 on the ICSID, the World Bank, and the American government.[77] Correa contended that investment arbitration under the ICSID is designed to protect capital exporter states and their investors at the expense of developing Latin American states. His subtext was that investment institutions such as the ICSID have disregarded the interests of capital importer states such as Ecuador that traditionally are economically and politically exploited by colonial powers and their investors.[78]

---

74 On the case for investor–state arbitration, see generally CHRISTOPHER DUGAN, DON WALLACE, JR. & NOAH RUBINS, INVESTOR-STATE ARBITRATION (2008); OXFORD HANDBOOK OF INTERNATIONAL INVESTMENT LAW (Peter Muchlinski, Federico Ortino & Christoph Schreuer eds., 2008) [hereinafter OXFORD HANDBOOK]; CAMPBELL MCLACHLAN, LAWRENCE SHORE & MATTHEW WEINIGER, INTERNATIONAL INVESTMENT ARBITRATION: SUBSTANTIVE PRINCIPLES (2008); NEW ASPECTS OF INTERNATIONAL INVESTMENT LAW (Philippe Kahn & Thomas W. Walde eds., 2007); GUS VAN HARTEN, INVESTMENT TREATY ARBITRATION AND PUBLIC LAW (2007); R. DOAK BISHOP, JAMES CRAWFORD & W. MICHAEL REISMAN, FOREIGN INVESTMENT DISPUTES: CASES, MATERIALS AND COMMENTARY (2005); INTERNATIONAL INVESTMENT LAW AND ARBITRATION: LEADING CASES FROM THE ICSID, NAFTA, BILATERAL TREATIES AND CUSTOMARY INTERNATIONAL LAW (Todd Weiler ed., 2005); ARBITRATING FOREIGN INVESTMENT DISPUTES (Norbert Horn ed., 2004).

75 On the ICSID, see *supra* note 54.

76 On the history and resurgence of the Calvo Doctrine, see, for example, Wenhua Shan, *From "North-South Divide" to "Private-Public Debate": Revival of the Calvo Doctrine and the Changing Landscape in International Investment Law*, 27 NW. J. INT'L L. & BUS. 631 (2007); Bernardo Cremades, *Resurgence of the Calvo Doctrine in Latin America*, 7 BUS. L. INT'L 53 (2006).

77 On these statements, see *ICSID in Crisis: Straight-Jacket or Investment Protection?*, BRETTON WOODS PROJECT (July 10, 2009), http://www.brettonwoodsproject.org/art-564878. *See also* Leon E. Trakman, "The ICSID and Investor–State Arbitration," Chapter 10 in this book.

78 On the history of this division between capital exporter and importer states, see generally M. SORNARAJAH, THE INTERNATIONAL LAW ON FOREIGN INVESTMENT 142, 177 (3rd ed. 2010).

A noteworthy difference is that Australia's new foreign investment policy represents a shift by a *developed* country against a political and economic tide when the opposite might have been expected, namely, for Australia to de-localize investment disputes. In prescribing that domestic courts decide investor–state disputes, Australia presumably was not motivated by the exploitative biases that some Latin American countries have ascribed to ISA. Australia is also unlikely to espouse these concerns of developing countries in making trade policy decisions that impact on its relations with both developing and developed BIT partners. Nevertheless, it is necessary to explore briefly the attack on ISA made by developing countries to detect the possibility of a more fundamental institutional objection to the ISA process.

A key cultural objection to ISA is that it is institutionally—and legally—biased against developing countries.[79] The concern is that "international" investment law, derived primarily from European civil law and Anglo-American common law traditions, favors parties and institutions from predominantly high and upper-middle income states.[80] The worry, too, is that ISA rules of evidence and procedure derive from the actions of developed countries and their multinational and international corporations, with significant European and American antecedents.[81]

These worries are accentuated by the virtually unlimited territorial reach exercised by courts in some developed countries. For example, American courts can invoke the U.S. Alien Tort Claims legislation to hold non-U.S. citizens abroad liable for harm to American interests there, so long as the non-U.S. citizen is in the United States to be served a subpoena (though admittedly cases suggest that there must be an international wrong amounting to a serious violation of international law).[82]

A related concern is that the beneficiaries of ISA are investors from developed countries who can afford to mount piecemeal claims against developing countries and

[79] On the U.S.' alleged double standard in favoring resort to arbitration to restrain interference by foreign governments with private investment while disfavoring arbitration filed against the U.S. government, see Guillermo Alvarez & William Park, *The New Face of Investment Arbitration: NAFTA Chapter 11*, 28 YALE J. INT'L L. 365, 368–69 (2003). *See also* Susan D. Franck, *The ICSID Effect? Considering Potential Variations in Arbitration Awards*, 51 VA. J. INT'L L. 825, 826, 909–14 (2011), http://papers.ssrn.com/sol3/papers.cfm?abstract_id=1842164.

[80] On the dominance by developed states over trade and investment and challenges by developing states, see, for example, James O. Gump, *The West and the Third World: Trade, Colonialism, Dependence, and Development* (Review), 11 J. WORLD HIST. 396 (2000); *The Theory of Capitalist Imperialism* (D.K. Fieldhouse ed., 1967); FREE TRADE AND OTHER FUNDAMENTAL DOCTRINES OF THE MANCHESTER SCHOOL (Francis Wrigley Hirst ed., [1902], 2009) (for a collection of speeches from the nineteenth century advocating the development of free trade); P.J. Cain, *J A Hobson, Cobdenism, and the Radical Theory of Economic Imperialism, 1898–1914*, 31 ECON. HIST. REV. 565, 576–80 (1978); Michael Freeden, *J. A. Hobson as a New Liberal Theorist: Some Aspects of His Social Thought until 1914*, 34 J. HIST. IDEAS 421 (1973).

[81] On limitations associated with traditional "international" principles of compensation for expropriation particularly in relation to developing countries, see M. Sornarajah, *The Clash of Globalizations and the International Law on Foreign Investment* (Norman Paterson School of International Affairs Simon Reisman Lecture in International Trade Policy, Ottawa, Sept. 12, 2002), *reprinted in* 10 CANADIAN FOREIGN POL'Y 1 (2003).

[82] 28 USC § 1350 (2010).

developed countries that can afford to defend ISA proceedings brought by investors from developing states. This concern is accentuated by the perceived cost and length of ISA proceedings, [83]

Reinforcing these concerns is the contention that investment arbitrators, often trained as commercial not public international lawyers, are less likely to pay regard to the broader public policy consequences of arbitration awards than to the literal texts of treaties that favor developed countries. ISA tribunals are also likely to marginalize broader state and multistate policies directed at remediating systemic and historical disadvantages among developing states and their investors. Added to this is concern about arbitration tribunals determining their own competence, and by the right of the chair of a tribunal to exercise a casting vote in awards on the merits.[84]

A perceived risk of ISA decision-making is that investment arbitrators, drawn primarily from developed states, will enshrine investment treaties that promote the national security, health, labor, environment, and market interests of developed countries. They will imbed the defense of necessity under customary international law that allegedly systemically disadvantages developing countries and their investors.[85] They will apply ISA rules that enable developed countries and their investors to immunize ISA from public scrutiny, for example by insisting on the confidentiality of both ISA proceedings and the ensuing awards.[86] Even if these attacks on ISA are overstated,[87]

---

83 On the absence of binding precedents, at least in principle, in international investment law, see Christoph Schreuer & Matthew Weiniger, *A Doctrine of Precedent? in* OXFORD HANDBOOK, *supra* note 74, at 1188. *See generally* OECD Investment Committee, Foreign Investment Review Board, http://www.firb.gov.au/content/international_investment/current_issues.asp?NavID=60.

84 On the influence of commercial law, as distinct from public international law, on the development of investment law, see VAN HARTEN, *supra* note 74, ch. 6. On procedural challenges to ISA proceedings, see, for example, Luke R. Nottage, *The Rise and Possible Fall of Investor–State Arbitration in Asia: A Skeptic's View of Australia's "Gillard Government Trade Policy Statement* 5, TRANSNAT'L DISPUTE MGMT. (2011), *available at* SSRN: http://ssrn.com/abstract=1860505.

85 On the defense of necessity in investment arbitration including under customary investment law, see Alberto Alvarez-Jiménez, *Foreign Investment Protection and Regulatory Failures as States' Contribution to the State of Necessity under Customary International Law*, 27 J. INT'L ARB. 141 (2010); Andrea K. Bjorklund, *Emergency Exceptions: State of Necessity and Force Majeure*, in OXFORD HANDBOOK, *supra* note 74, at 459; Nicholas Song, *Between Scylla and Charydbis: Can a Plea of Necessity Offer Safe Passage to States in responding to an Economic Crisis without Incurring Liability to Foreign Investors?*, 19 AM. REV. INT'L ARB. 235 (2008); *Panel Discussion: Is There a Need for the Necessity Defense for Investment Law?*, in *Investment Treaty Arbitration and International Law* 189 (T.J. Grierson Weiler ed., 2008).

86 *See further* Howard Mann et al., "Comments on ICSID Discussion Paper, "Possible Improvements of the Framework for ICSID Arbitration" (International Institute for Sustainable Development, Dec. 2004), http://www.iisd.org/publications/publication.asp?pno=667.

87 It is noteworthy that the ICSID amended its rules in 2006 to provide for greater transparency, including greater access of third parties to ICSID proceedings and the publication of arbitration awards. The UNCITRAL Rules did so as well through various articles. *See, e.g., UNCITRAL Arbitration Rules*, GA Res 65/22 (2010) arts 28(3), 34(5); *UNCITRAL Arbitration Rules*, GA Res 31/98 (1976) arts 25(4) and 32(5). In addition, UNCITRAL Working Group II is currently engaged in the "[p]reparation of a legal standard on transparency in treaty-based investor-State arbitration." See United Nations Commission on International Trade Law, *Working Group II* (2012), http://www.uncitral.org/uncitral/en/commission/working_groups/2Arbitration.html; *Settlement of Commercial Disputes: Preparation of a Legal Standard*

a residuary concern is that, in the absence of a uniform international investment convention or code, deciding international investment disputes will be fraught with conceptual and interpretative challenges for developing countries and their investors. In subscribing to textual methods of interpreting investment treaties, investment arbitrators will construe investment laws literally more than contextually. They will struggle to interpret complex property concepts,[88] and they will studiously avoid having their awards annulled for misconstruing such concepts.[89] Investment arbitrators will rely on their comprehension of the laws of developed countries in determining the "reasonable" or "legitimate" expectations of foreign investors,[90] in delineating the reach of the "margin of appreciation" doctrine,[91] and in providing investor and state parties with "fair and equitable" treatment.[92]

These concerns have some foundation. ISA tribunals that apply different methods of interpretation to investment treaties can lead to divergences in the treatment of foreign investors in comparable cases. The worry is that "plain word" methods of interpretation are likely to challenge even the most skilled, sophisticated, and erudite

---

on Transparency in Treaty-Based Investor–State Arbitration, 46th sess., A/CN.9/WG.II/WP.169 (Feb. 6–10, 2012).

88 On such differences, see, for example, *Salini Costruttori SpA and Italstrade SpA v. Kingdom of Morocco* (Decision on Jurisdiction) (ICSID Arbitral Tribunal, Case No ARB/00/4, July 23, 2001); 42 ILM 609 (2003). *See also* MONIQUE SASSON, SUBSTANTIVE LAW IN INVESTMENT TREATY ARBITRATION: THE UNSETTLED RELATIONSHIP BETWEEN INTERNATIONAL AND MUNICIPAL LAW (2010) (see especially chapter 4 for a discussion of property in investment treaty context); Omar E. Garcia-Bolivar, *Protected Investments and Protected Investors: The Outer Limits of ICSID's Reach*, 2 TRADE L. & DEV. 145 (2010) (discussing the requirements that must be met in order to invoke the ICSID's jurisdiction); SCHREUER, supra note 56, 90–91 (discussing jurisdictional requirements under Article 25 of the ICSID Convention).

89 For an articulation of this interpretative confusion in the trilogy of investment claims against the government of Argentina, see *infra* note 105 and associated discourse in text.

90 On such "legitimate expectations," see *Saluka Investments BV (The Netherlands) v. The Czech Republic* (Partial Award) (Arbitration under the UNCITRAL Rules, Mar. 17, 2006) [304], http://italaw.com/documents/Saluka-PartialawardFinal.pdf; *Waste Management, Inc. v The United Mexican States* (Final Award) (ICSID Arbitral Tribunal, Case No ARB(AF)/00/3 (NAFTA), Apr. 30, 2004) [98], http://italaw.com/documents/laudo_ingles.pdf; *International Thunderbird Gaming Corporation v. The United Mexican States* (arbitration under the UNCITRAL Rules (NAFTA), Jan. 26, 2006) [147] ("*Thunderbird*"), http://italaw.com/documents/ThunderbirdAward.pdf; *GAMI Investments Inc v The Government of the United Mexican States* (Final Award) (Arbitration under the UNCITRAL Rules, Nov. 15, 2004) [100], http://www.state.gov/documents/organization/38789.pdf. *See also* Stephan W. Schill, *Fair and Equitable Treatment under Investment Treaties as an Embodiment of the Rule of Law*, TRANSNAT'L DISPUTE MGMT. 16 (Dec. 2006).

91 On the "margin of appreciation" doctrine, see, for example, Bakircioglu, *supra* note 52; Shany, *supra* note 52; Benvenisti, *supra* note 52; R. St. J. Macdonald, *Margin of Appreciation*, *supra* note 52, at 125.

92 Illustrating these variable conceptions of "fair and equitable" treatment is a series of cases commencing with the ICSID award in *Maffezini v Kingdom of Spain* (Award on the merits) (ICSID Arbitral Tribunal, Case No ARB/97/7, Nov. 13, 2000) [64], http://icsid.worldbank.org/ICSID/FrontServlet?requestType=CasesRH&actionVal=showDoc&docId=DC566_En&caseId=C163; *MTD Equity Sdn Bhd and MTD Chile S.A. v Republic of Chile* (ICSID Arbitral Tribunal, Case No ARB/01/7, May 25, 2004) [178]. *See too* Ian A. Laird, *MTD Equity Sdn Bhd and MTD Chile S.A. v Republic of Chile—Recent Developments in the Fair and Equitable Treatment Standard*, TRANSNAT'L DISPUTE MGMT. (Oct. 2004).

investment arbitrators in attempting to construe marginally different clauses in BITs.[93] Their efforts to distinguish the interpretation of one BIT from another will impede the evolution of uniform principles of customary and treaty investment law;[94] ISA will also fail to resolve disputes between states and foreign investors in a transparent and evenhanded manner.[95]

A final objection to ISA is that it will produce a fragmented body of international investment law that favors states and investors that are sufficiently resourced to take advantage of that fragmentation against states and investors that lack such advantages. Nor, ironically, would the growth of an ISA *ius cogens* assuage these concerns. Given the institutional roots of ISA in the Western legal tradition, the worry is that a uniform system of ISA justice would deny corrective justice to developing countries and their investors. The perceived harm, arguably, exceeds the denial of justice to developing countries under a fragmented system of ISA justice.

These objections to ISA do add to the flaws already identified with it. However, enumerating ISA's failings does not in itself provide support for the contemplated alternative, namely, for resort to domestic courts. The Australian government's rejection of ISA may encourage the reform of ISA to address these flaws, as is discussed in the penultimate section of this chapter.

However, the Australian government's preference for domestic litigation to resolve ISA disputes protracts more than it remedies deficiencies in the resolution of investor–state disputes. The perception among some developing states is that the courts of wealthy developed states will rely on common or civil law traditions that, historically, were insulated from the plight of developing countries, and remain so insulated today. The likely harm is that such courts will be perceived as applying "their" laws in a discriminatory manner, to the disadvantage of investors from developing countries. The problem of perceived discrimination is therefore unlikely to dissipate by adopting this new route.

---

[93] *See, e.g.*, Luzius Wildhaber & Isabelle Wildhaber, *Recent Case Law on the Protection of Property in the European Convention on Human Rights*, *in* INTERNATIONAL INVESTMENT LAW FOR THE 21ST CENTURY: ESSAYS IN HONOUR OF CHRISTOPH SCHREUER 657 (Christina Binder et al. eds. 2009).

[94] *See* Franck, *supra* note 55. On the customary nature of international investment law and its contest with treaty-made law, see, for example, Campbell McLachlan, *Investment Treaties and General International Law*, 57 INT'L & COMP. L.Q. 361 (2008); Stephen Schwebel, *The Influence of Bilateral Investment Treaties on Customary International Law*, TRANSNAT'L DISPUTE MGMT. 1 (Nov. 2005); Patrick Dumberry, *Are BITs Representing the "New" Customary International Law in International Investment Law?*, 28 PENN. ST. INT'L L. REV. 675, 701 (2010) (for a rejection of the proposition that BITs represent customary law).

[95] On the varied and inconsistent interpretations of investment treaties, see Jurgen Kurtz, *Adjudging the Exceptional at International Investment Law: Security, Public Order and Financial Crisis*, 59 INT'L & COMP. L.Q. 325 (2010) (Kurtz identifies three different methodologies of interpretation). *But see* William W Burke-White & Andreas von Staden, *Investment Protection in Extraordinary Times: The Interpretation and Application of Non-Precluded Measures Provisions in Bilateral Investment Treaties*, 48 VA. J. INT'L L. 307 (2008) (considering the interpretive challenges posed by provisions for non-precluded measures, such as for maintenance of security and public order).

IX. THE BALANCING EXERCISE

It is difficult convincingly to resolve the perceived contest between investment arbitration and domestic courts of law. There are only a limited number of past investment arbitration cases to review. There is also scant experience of domestic courts displacing arbitration in deciding investment disputes.[96] Preferring ISA over domestic litigation is suspect in the absence of material information about the investment treaty parties, the investors, and the dispute in issue. Emphatic support for either ISA or domestic litigation will often be rooted in policy preferences more than in principles grounded in state sovereignty and its surrender by treaty.

Nor is the choice solely between ISA and litigation to resolve investment disputes. Conflict-preventive and avoidance measures sometimes are preferable to both.[97] "Multitiered" dispute resolution agreements can allow parties to agree upon a tiered process, varying from negotiating in good faith to mediation, and failing both, to arbitration or litigation, or conceivably, to both.[98] Neither the Productivity Commission nor the Australian government paid much heed to conflict-preventive alternatives, perhaps because such measures usually operate informally and often "under the radar" of investment dispute resolution. However, the UNCTAD considered conflict prevention and avoidance sufficiently important to devote a detailed study to it.[99]

Even ignoring these conflict prevention and avoidance options, ISA and litigation each have their beauty spots and warts. Insisting that domestic litigation preserves the sovereignty of countries is hardly credible when those same countries repeatedly surrender their sovereignty to one another under customary international and treaty law. Overstated, too, is the assertion that multilateral, regional, or bilateral investment negotiations signify a sharing of sovereignty by signatory states. An investment "agreement" in which one state dominates may well lead to "sovereignty by subtraction," including the loss of sovereignty by the subservient state. The threat of "sovereignty by subtraction" is one key reason the community of nation states failed to reach multilateral investment accord historically.[100]

---

96 On international investment claims and decisions generally, see *Investment Claims* (run by Oxford University Press), http://www.investmentclaims.com.

97 *Investor–State Disputes: Prevention and Alternatives to Arbitration*, UNCTAD Series on International Investment Policies for Development (May 2010), http://www.unctad.org/en/docs/diaeia200911_en.pdf. International investment claims and decisions are available at http://www.investmentclaims.com.

98 *See* Klaus Peter Berger, Private Dispute Resolution in International Business: Negotiation, Mediation, Arbitration 74–78 [Vol. II: Handbook] (2006).

99 *See* William S. Dodge, *Investor–State Dispute Settlement between Developed Countries: Reflections on the Australia-United States Free Trade Agreement*, 39 Vanderbilt J. Transnat'l L. 1 (2006) (commenting on the exhaustion of local remedies).

100 *See, e.g.*, Robert Stumberg, *Sovereignty by Subtraction: The Multilateral Agreement on Investment*, 31 Cornell Int'l L.J. 491, 503–04, 523–25 (1998). *See further* Kevin Kennedy, *A WTO Agreement on Investment: A Solution in Search of a Problem?* 24 U. Penn. J. Int'l Econ. L. 77 (2003). On the

Nor is it persuasive to insist that ISA is inherently superior to litigation because arbitrators are investment specialists, whereas domestic judges operate as courts of general jurisdiction. Neither resort to ISA nor to litigation ensures equitable and transparent procedures or sound substantive determinations. Evidence of an unjust state expropriation is factually informed: it calls for good judgment, not only investment expertise. Full-time national court judges arguably often have as much claim to good judgment as do part-time and often academically focused arbitrators.

What can be said in defense of ISA is that, although it does not lead to judicial precedent as common lawyers conceive of it, ISA is likely to be more stable in nature than a plethora of different local laws and procedures that domestic courts apply to foreign investment.[101] However fragmentary may be the application of different standards of treatment to foreign investors, and however difficult it may be to identify cohesive principles out of ad hoc and sometimes unpublished arbitration awards, an international investment jurisprudence has evolved, inconsistencies notwithstanding.[102] Given the multitude of BITs currently in existence and their disparate clauses, ICSID and UNCITRAL arbitrations have promoted the successful resolution of investment disputes in a series of complex cases.[103] As such, ISA has helped to develop a more cohesive construction of BITs internationally than has the jurisprudence of divergent domestic legal systems and their courts.

Nor should investment arbitrators or institutions such as the ICSID Secretariat be blamed if ISA proceedings sometimes are not transparent and investment awards are not published. The rules governing investment arbitration derive, not from the action of arbitration institutions such as the ICSID, but from the collective action of member countries that are signatories to the ICSID Convention and state signatories to BITs. It remains within the power of the multilateral community of states to pursue institutional change in international investment jurisprudence. Likewise, institutions such as the ICSID should not be blamed for inconsistent reasoning and determinations reached by investment arbitrators who, although guided by the ICSID, exercise discretion in making awards. Not unlike the authority of judges on the International Court of Justice, the coherence of ISA reasoning and awards depends on the persuasive authority of the awards rendered by ISA arbitrators. The cogency of those awards, in turn,

---

prospective impact of the Doha round of multilateral negotiations on Chapter 11 of the NAFTA, see Bryan Schwartz, *The Doha Round and Investment: Lessons from Chapter 11 of NAFTA* (2003) 3 ASPER REV. INT'L BUS. & TRADE LAW 1 (2003).

[101] On the development of international investment norms, see *OECD Investment Committee*, FOREIGN INVESTMENT REVIEW BOARD, http://www.firb.gov.au/content/international_investment/current_issues.asp?NavID=60.

[102] For the argument that. whatever are the limitations of domestic investment decision-making, international investment law is inherently biased in favor of developed countries, see Sornarajah, Chapter 16 of this book; SCHREUER & DOLZER *supra* note 56; SCHILL, *supra* note 56.

[103] *See, e.g.*, Aurélia Antonietti, *The 2006 Amendments of the ICSID Rules and Regulations and the Additional Facility Rules*, 21 ICSID REV.—FOR. INV. L.J. 427 (2006); Edward Baldwin, Mark Kantor & Michael Nolan, *Limits to Enforcement of ICSID Awards*, 23 J. INT'L ARB. 1 (2006) (discussing "tactics" that may be employed in attempts to "delay" or "avoid" compliance with ICSID Awards).

transcends the consent of the investor–state parties to disputes; it extends beyond the literal construction of conventions such as the ICSID; it surpasses the guidance of administrators of such conventions charged with overseeing ISA proceedings under disparate BITs.[104] It is also artificial to ground the authority of ISA tribunals solely in the mutual consent of state parties to BITs, given the discretion that is accorded to ISA arbitrators in both law and fact.[105]

Nor, too, is Australia's unwillingness to submit to investor–state arbitration necessarily a death knell for Australian outbound investors. Australian outbound investors have several choices. They can engage in foreign direct investment in states that have BITs with Australia, such as the United States, and in whose courts Australian investors are reasonably comfortable. They can invest in countries in whose courts they do not trust, relying instead on BITs between those and intermediary countries to bring ISA claims against countries with limited rule-of-law traditions. An incidental beneficiary of such investor resort to intermediary states is the Australian government itself, in not having to conclude BITs with ISA provisions with states that do not subscribe to the rule of law. The Australian government can also decline to intervene diplomatically on behalf of outbound Australian investors, on grounds that those investors have lodged their claims through intermediary states, not Australia. There is also no shortage of potential intermediary states to which outbound investors may resort. Notable among these states are the Netherlands Antilles or Mauritius that have stable financial systems and transparent and investor-friendly tax regimes.[106]

---

104 *See* Vandevelde, *supra* note 65 (discussing the exponential growth in BITs from 1969 to 2005). *See also Research Note: Recent Developments in International Investment Agreements*, UNITED NATIONS CONFERENCE ON TRADE AND DEVELOPMENT (Aug. 30, 2005), http://www.unctad.org/sections/dite_dir/docs/webiteiit20051_en.pdf. Although the ICSID administers ISA, the UNCITRAL is *not* an administering authority. The UNCITRAL Web site states: "UNCITRAL does not administer arbitration or conciliation proceedings, nor does it provide services ... in connection with dispute settlement proceedings." See United Nations Commission on International Trade Law, *FAQ - UNCITRAL and Private Disputes/Litigation* (2012), http://www.uncitral.org/uncitral/en/uncitral_texts/arbitration_faq.html#dispute. Other institutions, most notably the Permanent Court of Arbitration (PCA), administer investor–state disputes under the UNCITRAL Rules. A recent UNCTAD report states that "[b]y the end of 2011, the total number of ISDS cases administered by the PCA was 65, of which 32 are pending." *See* United Nations Conference on Trade and Development, *Latest Developments in Investor–State Dispute Settlement* (IIA Issues Note No 1, Apr. 2012), http://unctad.org/en/PublicationsLibrary/webdiaeia2012d10_en.pdf.

105 On allegedly inconsistent ICSID decisions in a series of investment claims against Argentina, commencing with the *CMS*, *Enron*, and *Sempra* cases, see *CMS Gas Transmission Co. v. The Argentine Republic* (Award) (ICSID Arbitral Tribunal, Case No ARB/01/8, May 12, 2005); *Enron Creditors Recovery Corporation and Ponderosa Assets, L.P. v. Argentine Republic* (Award) (ICSID Arbitral Tribunal, Case No ARB/01/3, May 22, 2007); *Sempra Energy International v. The Argentine Republic* (Award) (ICSID Arbitral Tribunal, Case No ARB/02/16, Sept. 28, 2007). *See further* August Reinisch, *Necessity in International Investment Arbitration—An Unnecessary Split of Opinions in Recent ICSID Cases? Comments on* CMS v. Argentina *and* LG&E v. Argentina, 8 *J. World Inv. & Trade* 191 (2007); Stephan W. Schill, *International Investment Law and the Host State's Power to Handle Economic Crises: Comment on the ICSID Decision in* LG&E v. Argentina, 24 J. INT'L ARB. 265 (2007); Michael Waibel, *Two Worlds of Necessity in ICSID Arbitration: CMS and LG&E*, 20 LEIDEN J. INT'L L. 637 (2007).

106 On the tax and related protection accorded foreign investors in the Netherlands Antilles, see, for example, http://www.ibcformations.com/index.php?menu=jurisdiction_17&trusts_foundations=1.

Nor is the practice of foreign investors bringing ISA or other claims through intermediary states unprecedented. Brazil has effectively insulated itself from investor–state arbitration by declining to ratify any of its investor–state treaties; its investors abroad have transacted through "good governance" intermediary states. As a result, Brazilian companies have gained access to resource wealthy countries such as Venezuela through intermediary states without exposing Brazil to investor–state claims in respect of which Brazil has assumed no treaty obligations in fact.[107]

However, treaty shopping by investors, not limited to outbound Australian investors, for intermediary states from which to launch an ISA claim is not risk free. In particular, treaty-shopping investors risk losing ISA claims on jurisdictional grounds, that their business connection to the intermediary state is insufficiently substantial to justify their ISA claim. That risk is conceivably accentuated as more states strive for intermediary status, seeking to resource investors with ever-ready means of establishing business connections domestically. Coupled with these risks is the prospect of regulators, including ISA tribunals, establishing rules to regulate such treaty shopping.

The final observation is not that investor-treaty arbitration is capable of resolving these various problems in a manner that domestic courts cannot accomplish: ISA is not a panacea. Dominant states and their investors may well perpetuate their economic and political influence by using ICSID and UNCITRAL proceedings to their advantage, including by protracting ISA proceedings and adding to their costs. Yet even if ISA is not beyond reproach, it is capable of transformation and improvement.

X. PROPOSALS FOR REGULATING ISA BY TREATY

The following are proposals to regulate the adoption of ISA by treaty. The purpose is to accommodate concerns about the unfairness and inefficiency of ISA. It is also to ensure that Australia is not excluded from participating in important multilateral treaties such as the strategic Trans-Pacific Partnership Agreement.

First, it is recommended that treaties expressly protect fundamental public interests such as those in natural resources, agriculture, and financial markets. This is consistent with the Australian government's legitimate interest in protecting the national identity, public health, and environment from erosion by foreign investors.

Second, investment chapters in treaties should stipulate for negotiation and conciliation between disputing parties prior to initiating investor–state arbitration. This is consistent with the recommendations of the UNCTAD.[108] It also reaffirms the importance in principle of encouraging cooperation between investor–state parties,

---

107 *See, e.g.*, Ricardo Ortíz, *The Bilateral Investment Treaties and the Cases at ICSID* (FOCO 2006), *available at* http://fdcl-berlin.de/fileadmin/fdcl/Publikationen/FOCO-ICSID-engl-2006.pdf. Table 2 notes that Brazil had entered into fourteen BITs by 2006, but had not ratified any of them.

108 See UNCTAD, *supra*, note 29.

especially because investor–state arbitration is potentially costly and time-consuming, and disputes can have devastating economic consequences for investors and a drastic social and economic impact on host states and their subjects.

Third, investment treaties should require that investor–state parties resort to alternative methods of dispute avoidance in good faith before embarking on ISA, such as by using mediation or conciliation. This is consistent with the recommendations of the UNCTAD.

Fourth, treaties should govern the standing of investors to bring claims against host states, in order to discourage premature, opportunistic, and pernicious claims by adventitious investors against vulnerable host states.

Fifth, investors should be required to initiate mediation or conciliation proceedings within specified time limits prior to initiating ISA and without which ISA should not be available, unless state parties decline to submit to mediation or conciliation, or mediation fails. Mediation or conciliation proceedings should be circumscribed by time lines and good faith requirements so as to avoid protracting and raising the costs of disputes. Although such requirements are ideally embodied in bilateral and regional investment agreements, insofar as they are not so embodied, it may be necessary to rely on the ICSID/ICSID Additional Facility or UNCITRAL to do so instead.

Sixth, and as a qualification to the first recommendation above, rules of procedure are needed to inhibit host states from expropriating foreign investment on overbroad grounds such as in relation to the protection of natural resources, agriculture, and financial markets. States should also be discouraged from discriminating against foreign investors on grounds of protection that extend beyond essential security, national identity, public health, and environmental safety.

Seventh, consistent with ICSID Rule 37 adopted in 2006, which provides for submissions by non-disputing parties,[109] further provision is needed to ensure that arbitration proceedings are transparent, while preserving confidential information of one or both direct parties to an ISA dispute. In particular, provision is needed for the publication of investor claims, for public access to ISA proceedings in the ordinary course, and for the publication of ISA proceedings and awards, including reasons for granting or denying third party intervener status in whole or in part. Provision should be made for the submission of *amici curiae* briefs and the participation of third-party interveners in proceedings. Social, economic, and environmental impact reports adduced into evidence should also be publicly available. These publications should be subject to requirements of confidentiality, as identified above.

Eighth, interim measures are needed to inhibit host states from imposing regulations that unreasonably interfere with investor claims. Such measures are appropriate, for example, to inhibit Australia from implementing fast track tobacco legislation to circumvent arbitration initiated against it by Philip Morris. Conversely, interim measures are appropriate to discourage Philip Morris from protracting investor–state

[109] On Rule 37 of the ICSID Regulations and Rules, see *supra*, note 76. *See further* Leon E Trakman, *The ICSID under Siege*, CORNELL INT'L L.J., Part V (forthcoming 2012).

arbitration in order to delay the implementation of public health regulations by Australia.

Ninth, rules are needed to streamline the mechanics of investor–state arbitration. In particular, challenges to an arbitrator should be decided by a challenge committee, not by arbitrators sitting on the same panel as the challenged arbitrator.

Tenth, rules are needed to monitor legal costs, including but not limited to: the use of contingency fees, capping the fees of arbitrators, and allocating costs between investor–state parties and conceivably, third parties. Related concerns about monitoring costs are expressed in the 2010 UNCITRAL Rules.

Eleventh, guidelines are needed for the stay of arbitration proceedings to allow investor–state parties to settle their disputes during the course of such proceedings.

Finally, standing panels are needed to interpret the ICSID Rules in order to redress the inconsistent construction and application of those Rules in tribunal decisions.

These recommendations, among others, are sustainable only if they are subject to ongoing scrutiny and refinement. In particular, signatories to investment treaties that adopt them need to monitor their interpretation and application to ensure that they are properly implemented.

XI. CONCLUSION

What can be said about a state-orchestrated movement away from ISA toward domestic courts in resolving investment disputes is that the choice is not entirely about the quality of decision making, or even about the operational virtues of judicial decisions over arbitral awards or vice versa. The choice of domestic courts over ISA is also about states exercising normative preferences based on macroeconomic and political assumptions. It is about states calculating that their foreign investors are more likely to succeed before a foreign court than an investment tribunal. Such a "win" is not grounded in objective economic rationality or dispassionate altruism, but in perceptible attempts by states to secure a strategic advantage for their subjects who invest abroad.[110] Nor should one expect countries to disregard their self-interest in electing among dispute resolution options. Indeed, countries are likely to adopt double standards in exercising those elections. A government that favors ISA to restrain "interference" by foreign

[110] These observations are exemplified in Chapter 11 jurisprudence under the NAFTA, notably under the *Mondev* and *Loewen* cases. *See Mondev International Ltd v United States of America* (Award) (ICSID Arbitral Tribunal, Case No. ARB (AF)/99/2, Oct. 11, 2002) ("*Mondev*"). *See also* Dana Krueger, *The Combat Zone:* Mondev International, Ltd v. United States *and the Backlash against NAFTA Chapter 11*, 21 B.U. INT'L L.J. 399 (2003) (arguing that, but for a technical time bar, two tribunal decisions—*Mondev* and *Loewen*—might have prevailed over U.S. judicial decisions). On the Loewen arbitration, see *Loewen Group, Inc v United States of America* (Award) (ICSID Arbitral Tribunal, Case No. ARB(AF)/98/3, June 26, 2003) ("*Loewen*"); William Dodge, Loewen v. United States: *Trials and Errors under NAFTA Chapter 11*, 52 DEPAUL L. REV. 563 (2002). On the judicial review of the *Loewen* Chapter 11 decision, see Bradford K. Gathright, *A Step in the Wrong Direction: The* Loewen *Finality Requirement and the Local Remedies Rule in NAFTA Chapter Eleven*, 54 EMORY L.J. 1093 (2005); Trakman, *supra* note 6, at 52.

governments with private investment may well disfavor ISA proceedings that are filed against it.[111]

However, it is precisely the risk to Australia's self-interest that throws doubt on the persuasiveness of the APC's blanket assertion that there are no truly cogent economic reasons for countries such as Australia to agree to ISA. More often than not states favor institutions for dispute resolution based on their capacity to deliver results that treat their subjects abroad "fairly," and according to "home" rather than "host" state standards.[112]

Australia's policy shift toward domestic courts resolving investor–state disputes is significantly driven by the APC's recommendations that espouse particular policy preferences without paying adequate regard to their practical ramifications. This chapter recommends that the government further examine the economic, political, and practical implications of rejecting ISA and look at the viability of alternative methods of resolving international investment disputes. A failure to do so could jeopardize Australia's participation in multilateral investment treaties such as the Trans-Pacific Partnership Agreement in which it has a strong economic incentive to be a party.

---

111 On the U.S. alleged double standard in favoring resort to arbitration to restrain interference by foreign governments with private investment while disfavoring arbitration filed against the U.S. governments, see Alvarez & Park, *supra* note 79, at 368–69. *See also* Franck, *supra* note 55.

112 *See, e.g.*, Charles Brower & Lee Steven, *NAFTA Chapter 11: Who Then Should Judge? Developing the International Rule of Law under NAFTA Chapter 11*, 2 CHI. J. INT'L L. 193, 193–95 (2001); Jack J. Coe, Jr., *Domestic Court Control of Investment Awards: Necessary Evil or Achilles Heel within NAFTA and the Proposed FTAA*, 19 J. INT'L ARB. 185 (2002); David A. Gantz, *An Appellate Mechanism for Review of Arbitral Decisions in Investor–State Disputes: Prospects and Challenges*, 39 VANDERBILT J. TRANSNAT'L L. 39 (2006). *But see* William S. Dodge, *Case Report:* Waste Management, Inc v Mexico, 95 AM. J. INT'L L. 186 (2001) (presenting the case for modeling Chapter 11 on the WTO appellate process). See also Gary R. Saxonhouse, *Dispute Settlement at the WTO and the Dole Commission: USTR Resources and Success, in* ISSUES AND OPTIONS FOR U.S.–JAPAN TRADE POLICIES 363 (Robert M. Stern ed., 2002).

13

THE RELATION OF THE EUROPEAN UNION AND ITS MEMBER STATES IN INVESTOR–STATE ARBITRATION

*Stephan W. Schill**

I. Introduction

The European Union (EU) has entered the stage as a full-fledged actor in international investment law and policy with the entry into force of the Lisbon Treaty on December 1, 2009. In Article 207(1), the Treaty on the Functioning of the European Union (TFEU)[1] now grants the Union, as part of the common commercial policy, a new exclusive competence in the field of "foreign direct investment."[2] The grant of this new competence has started a political process in which the EU is currently trying to define the scope and direction of its future international investment law policy. This process started with the Commission presenting a Communication entitled "Towards a Comprehensive European International Investment Policy,"[3] in which it outlined its

* Senior Research Fellow, Max Planck Institute for Comparative Public Law and International Law, Heidelberg; Rechtsanwalt; Attorney-at-Law (New York); LL.M. in European and International Economic Law (Universität Augsburg, 2002); LL.M. International Legal Studies (New York University, 2006); Dr. iur. (Johann Wolfgang Goethe-Universität Frankfurt am Main, 2008). This chapter partly draws on and further develops considerations first expressed in Stephan Schill, Arbitration Procedure: The Role of the European Union and the Member States in Investor-State Arbitration, in Le droit européen et l'arbitrage d'investissement/European Law and Investment Arbitration (Catherine Kessedjian ed., 2011) 129-147.

[1] *See* Consolidated Version of the Treaty on the Functioning of the European Union, May 9, 2008, O.J. (C 115) 47.

[2] For the exclusiveness of the competence, *see* Article 3(1)(e) TFEU.

[3] *Communication from the Commission to the Council, the European Parliament, the European Economic and Social Committee and the Committee of the Regions, Towards a Comprehensive European International*

own views on investment as the "new frontier for the common commercial policy,"[4] followed by generally positive conclusions by the Council in October 2010[5] and a somewhat more critical reception by the European Parliament.[6]

This process poses a great challenge as Commission, Parliament, and Member States struggle to balance the manifold and partly competing interests that are at stake.[7] Not only is the scope of the competence contested, and thus the relative power relations between the Union and the Member States,[8] but also the form, content, and direction of the future investment policy, including questions of dispute settlement, regulatory space, transparency, coherence, the relation of investment protection to social and environmental standard, and the relation between investment law and EU law. Given how important the EU is both as a capital-exporter but also as a capital-importer, it is likely that the outcome of this process will have a considerable impact on international investment law- and policy-making worldwide. In fact, the EU already is aiming to include provisions on investment protection in ongoing free trade agreement negotiations, inter alia with Canada, Singapore, and India.[9]

Furthermore, the grant of the new competence has raised the question as to the continued application of investment treaties already concluded by Member States. Although there is an argument to be made that Member States are entitled to keep investment treaties in place that they had concluded prior to the entry into force of the Lisbon Treaty with third states,[10] they are required to bring investment treaty obligations in line with their obligations under EU law, for example by renegotiating or even

---

Investment Policy, COM (2010) 343 final (July 7, 2010).

4 *Id.* at 2.

5 Council, *Conclusions on a Comprehensive European International Investment Policy*, 3041st Foreign Affairs Council Meeting, October 25, 2010, *available at* http://www.consilium.europa.eu/uedocs/cms_data/docs/pressdata/EN/foraff/117328.pdf.

6 European Parliament, *Resolution on the Future European International Investment Policy*, April 6, 2011, 32 (2010/2203(INI)).

7 For a discussion of the various issues involved, both from a legal and policy-making perspective, *see* Angelos Dimopoulos, EU Foreign Investment Law (2011); *see also* the contributions in International Investment Law and EU law, European Y.B. Int'l Econ. L. Special Issue (Marc Bungenberg, Joern Griebel & Steffen Hindelang eds., 2011); and Internationaler Investitionsschutz und Europarecht (Marc Bungenberg, Joern Griebel & Steffen Hindelang eds., 2010).

8 *See* Wenhua Shan & Sheng Zhang, *The Treaty of Lisbon: Half Way toward a Common Investment Policy*, 21 Eur. J. Int'l L. 1049, 1057–65 (2010).

9 The texts of the negotiating mandates are confidential. Yet, the Seattle to Brussels Network has released what is said to be the authentic text of the mandates on their website; *see* http://www.s2bnetwork.org/themes/eu-investment-policy/eu-documents/text-of-the-mandates.html.

10 This argument can be based on an analogous application of Article 351(1) TFEU. Although this provision applies only to "rights and obligations arising from agreements concluded before January 1, 1958 or, for acceding States, before the date of their accession, between one or more Member States on the one hand, and one or more third countries on the other," it can be understood as an expression of the more general principle that agreements concluded by Member States under their exclusive competence may stay in force even if that competence is later transferred to the EU. In this sense Thomas Eilmansberger, *Bilateral Investment Treaties and EU Law*, 46 CML Rev. 398 (2009), and the Bundesverfassungsgericht (BVerfG) (German Constitutional Court), 123 Entscheidungen des Bundesverfassungsgerichts (BVerfGE) 267 (421–22) (citing Christian Tietje, *Die Außenwirtschaftsverfassung der EU nach dem Vertrag*

terminating incompatible agreements, if possible.[11] In order to clarify the situation of extra-EU investment treaties and to ensure legal certainty for Member States and investors, the Commission has proposed a regulation, under which Member States can notify the Commission of those investment treaties they wish to keep in place despite the EU's new competence.[12] Furthermore, under the proposal, Member States would be able to continue concluding investment treaties with non-EU Member States under close supervision by the Commission for a transitory period. The draft regulation, however, has not yet been passed, and continues to be under consideration in the legislative process of the EU; this process has given rise to different views among Commission, Parliament, and Member States.[13] Even more complex is the question of whether intra-EU investment treaties are still applicable.[14]

A comprehensive analysis of the current political process within in the EU as well as of the EU-related questions relating to international investment law is beyond the scope of the present chapter. It focuses instead on one particularly important aspect of the new external competence of the EU for foreign direct investment, namely its impact on the settlement of international investment disputes, in particular

von Lissabon, 83 BEITRÄGE ZUM TRANSNATIONALEN WIRTSCHAFTSRECHT 17 (2009), *available at* http://www.wirtschaftsrecht.uni-halle.de/Heft83.pdf.).

[11] *Cf.* CJEU, Case C-205/06, Comm'n v. Austria, 2009 ECR I-1301, 24–46; Case C-249/06, Comm'n v. Sweden, 2009 ECR I-1335, 25–46; Case C-118/07, Comm'n v. Finland, 2009 ECR I-10889, 18–52. For a closer discussion of the cases in which the CJEU found incompatibilities between investment treaties and EU law, *see* Nikos Lavranos, *Protecting European Law from International Law*, 15 EUR. FOR. AFF. REV. 265 (2010); Nikos Lavranos, *New Developments in the Interaction between International Investment Law and EU Law*, 9 L. & PRAC. INT'L CTS. & TRIBUNALS 409, 416–24 (2010). *See also* CJEU, September 15, 2011, C-264/09, Comm'n v. Slovak Republic, 2011 ECR I-0000, 29–53 (where the Court accepted that the obligation of a Member State to protect investments under an investment treaty concluded prior to accession to the EU was an obligation that remained unaffected by EU law); *cf. also* CJEU, Mar. 15, 2011, Case C-264/09, AG Jääskinen, Comm'n v. Slovak Republic, 2011 ECR I-0000, 72–107.

[12] *See Proposal for a Regulation of the European Parliament and of the Council Establishing Transitional Arrangements for Bilateral Investment Agreements between Member States and Third Countries*, COM (2010) 344 final (July 7, 2010).

[13] *See* European Parliament, Legislative resolution of May 10, 2011 on the proposal for a regulation of the European Parliament and of the Council establishing transitional arrangements for bilateral investment agreements between Member States and third countries (COM (2010) 0344–C7-0172/2010–2010/0197(COD)).

[14] Although the Commission and some Member States are of the opinion that such treaties cannot be applied anymore, other Member States and investment treaty tribunals continue to apply them. For a comprehensive analysis of the legal questions involving investment treaties among Member States, *see* Christer Söderlund, *Intra-EU BIT Investment Protection and the EC Treaty*, 24 J. INT'L ARB. 455 (2007); Eilmansberger, *supra* note 9, at 383; Hanno Wehland, *Intra-EU Investment Agreements and Arbitration: Is European Community Law an Obstacle?*, 58 INT'L & COMP. L. Q. 297 (2009); Markus Burgstaller, *European Law and Investment Treaties*, 26 J. INT. ARB. 181 (2009); Nikos Lavranos, *New Developments in the Interaction between International Investment Law and EU Law*, 9 L. & PRACT. INT'L COURTS & TRIBS 409, 431–36 (2010); Christian Tietje, *Bilaterale Investitionsschutzverträge zwischen EU-Mitgliedstaaten (Intra-EU-BITs) als Herausforderung im Mehrebenensystem des Rechts*, 104 BEITRÄGE ZUM TRANSNATIONALEN WIRTSCHAFTSRECHT (2011), *available at* http://www.wirtschaftsrecht.uni-halle.de/Heft_104.pdf; Angelos Dimopoulos, *The Validity and Applicability of International Investment Agreements between EU Member States under EU and International Law*, 48 CML REV. 63 (2011).

investor–state arbitrations.[15] This issue is of particular importance in light of the significant backlash against investment arbitration that one can observe over the last few years,[16] most recently when Australia's government announced in April 2011 that it would discontinue including investor–state dispute settlement provisions in future investment treaties.[17]

In contrast to this position, the Commission,[18] the Council,[19] and also the European Parliament,[20] take a much more positive stance vis-à-vis investor–state arbitration and support that this well-established feature of Member State investment treaties should be maintained under future EU investment treaties. In fact, the Council's negotiating mandates for investment agreements with Canada, Singapore, and India state that the respective "agreement shall aim to provide for an effective investor-to-state dispute settement mechanism [that] should provide for investors a wide range of arbitration fora as currently available under the Member States' bilateral investment agreements."[21] Similarly, in a joint EU–U.S. Statement on Shared Principles for International Investment, the EU has affirmed its position that "[g]overnments should provide access to effective dispute settlement procedures, including investor-to-State

---

[15] To the extent the EU will become party to an investment treaty arbitration initiated by a foreign investor, the term investor–state arbitration, of course, is not entirely fitting, as the EU is not a state. Yet, the term is so well established that I will continue to use it in this chapter to include future arbitrations between foreign investors and the EU.

[16] *See* The Backlash against Investment Arbitration (Michael Waibel, Asha Kaushal, Kyo-Hwa Liz Chung & Claire Balchin eds., 2010). *See further* Peter Muchlinski, *Trends in International Investment Agreements, 2008/2009: Review of the Model Bilateral Investment Treaties of Norway, South Africa and the United States*, 2 Y.B. Int'l Inv. L. & Pol'y 35 (2009/2010).

[17] *See* Gillard Government Trade Policy Statement: Trading Our Way to More Jobs and Prosperity, at 14, *available at* http://www.dfat.gov.au/publications/trade/trading-our-way-to-more-jobs-and-prosperity.pdf. *See further* Luke R. Nottage, *The Rise and Possible Fall of Investor–State Arbitration in Asia: A Skeptic's View of Australia's "Gillard Government Trade Policy Statement,"* 8(5) Transnat'l Disp. Settlement (2011); Leon E. Trakman, *Investor State Arbitration or Local Courts: Will Australia Set a New Trend?*, 46 J. World Trade 83 (2012); Jürgen Kurtz, *Australia's Rejection of Investor–State Arbitration: Causation, Omission and Implication*, 27 ICSID Rev.—For. Inv. L.J. 65 (2012).

[18] Commission Communication of July 7, 2010, *supra* note 3, at 9–10 ("Investor–state dispute settlement, which forms a key part of the inheritance that the Union receives from Member State BITs, is important as an investment involves the establishment of a long-term relationship with the host state which cannot be easily diverted to another market in the event of a problem with the investment. Investor-state [sic] is such an established feature of investment agreements that its absence would in fact discourage investors and make a host economy less attractive than others. For these reasons, future EU agreements including investment protection should include investor–state dispute settlement.").

[19] Council, Conclusions, *supra* note 5, 18 ("stress[ing], in particular, the need for an effective investor-to-state dispute settlement mechanism in the EU investment agreements").

[20] *See* European Parliament, Resolution, *supra* note 6, 32 (stating that "in addition to state-to-state dispute settlement procedures, investor–state procedures must also be applicable in order to secure comprehensive investment protection"). The same resolution, however, also voices criticism of the current international investment protection regime and calls for adopting changes in the EU's future investment policy, such as the inclusion of social and environmental standards.

[21] *See supra* note 9.

arbitration, and ensure that such procedures are open and transparent, with opportunities for public participation."[22]

Notwithstanding, the grant of the new competence to the EU is not without problems in respect of investor–state dispute settlement. Beyond the fundamental question of whether investor–state arbitration is a desirable instrument, the new competence raises several questions in relation to the procedural status of the Union and of the Member States and as regards the legal framework EU law sets up for investor–state arbitration. Procedural status is distinct from responsibility[23] and concerns three separate issues: first, whether the Union or the Member States are the proper party to an investor–state arbitration; second, which entity will act for the respondent, and most importantly, appoint arbitrators and make written and oral submissions to the arbitral tribunal; and, third, how the cooperation between Member States and the Union, if any, will look like in relation to such arbitrations. In addition, it is important to consider the interaction between EU law and international investment law as a limit on procedural status and as a framework for investor–state arbitration of Member States and the EU.

When addressing the question of procedural status of the Union and the Member States, two perspectives need to be distinguished: a perspective *de lege ferenda* and a perspective *de lege lata*. The perspective *de lege ferenda* concerns the question of procedural status under future investment treaties, which are concluded based on the new competence in Article 207 TFEU. Some of the issues arising in this context under future investment treaties concluded by the EU are going to be addressed in an EU regulation for which the Commission presented a proposal in June 2012.[24] A *de lege*

---

22 *See* Statement of the European Union and the United States on Shared Principles for International Investment (April 10, 2012), Point 4, *available at* http://www.ustr.gov/webfm_send/3337.

23 Responsibility concerns the merits of a claim; it goes to the question of which public entity is the *right* party in an investor–state arbitration, the Union or its Member States. Procedural status, by contrast, concerns issues of jurisdiction, admissibility, and procedure, and goes to the question of which public entity is a *potential* party to an investor–state arbitration. The difference between responsibility and procedural status shows in respect of the consequences of a lack of procedural status respectively responsibility. The former will prompt a case to be dismissed on jurisdictional grounds (without prejudice to the merits of the case), whereas the latter results in dismissing the case on the merits with res judicata effect, thus precluding the dispute from being raised again against the same party. On the distinction between procedural status and substantive responsibility, *see also* JONI HELISKOSKI, MIXED AGREEMENTS AS A TECHNIQUE FOR ORGANIZING THE INTERNATIONAL RELATIONS OF THE EUROPEAN COMMUNITY AND ITS MEMBER STATES 194–97 (2001).

Determining responsibility is first and foremost a question of interpreting the substantive obligations and determining who owes what. Currently, for example, the EU does not owe any obligations under investment treaties to third countries because it is not bound by investment treaties of Member States. Instead, at present, the only question in an investor–state arbitration under existing investment treaties could be whether Member States are responsible vis-à-vis foreign investors for conduct by the EU, in case such conduct does not conform to the standards of treatment laid down in the applicable investment treaty.

24 *See*, most recently, the *Proposal for a Regulation of the European Parliament and of the Council Establishing a Framework for Managing Financial Responsibility Linked to Investor–State Dispute Settlement Tribunals Established by International Agreements to which the European Union is Party*, COM(2012) 335 final (June 21, 2012), which will address financial responsibility, procedural status, and cooperation between EU and Member States in investment arbitrations under future EU investment agreements. *See* on these

lata–perspective, by contrast, asks for the impact the new EU competence has on investor–state arbitrations under existing investment treaties concluded by Member States with third countries.[25] Both perspectives have to be distinguished, as the procedural status in future investment treaties will likely differ from that under present investment treaties. Accordingly, in respect of future investment treaties, it will be important to determine which questions regarding procedural status should be addressed in such treaties.

As regards existing investment treaties of Member States, the issue instead is whether Article 207 TFEU has an impact on the procedural status of Member States in investor–state arbitrations. The questions this chapter will address in this context thus are the following: Does the new competence affect or change the party status of Member States, now that the Union has exclusive competence in matters of foreign direct investment? If not, who will represent the Member State in an investment arbitration, the Member State itself or the Commission acting for the EU? And what else are, if any, the duties of cooperation between Member States and the Commission in conducting investment treaty arbitrations?

Against this background, the present chapter will proceed as follows: In a first step, it will sum up the reasons why the issue of procedural status is of considerable importance for the different actors involved (Section II). Second, this chapter will take a perspective on future EU investment treaties and highlight which issues concerning procedural status need to be considered and addressed in such treaties, including the limits on investor–state arbitration stemming from the interaction between EU law and international investment law, and the relations between investment arbitration and dispute settlement in the EU legal order (Section III). Finally, the impact of the new competence in Article 207 TFEU on investor-state arbitrations under existing investment treaties of Member States will be addressed (Section IV).

II. The Different Interests Regarding Procedural Status

The question of procedural status is important for a number of reasons. First, it is important from the investor's perspective, as he or she needs to know against whom to initiate arbitration. In this respect, there may be some uncertainty as to whether the new competence affects the party status of Member States—that is, whether Member

issues also the contributions in LE DROIT EUROPÉEN ET L'ARBITRAGE D'INVESTISSEMENT/EUROPEAN LAW AND INVESTMENT ARBITRATION (Catherine Kessedjian ed., 2011).

[25] The present chapter will not deal with how EU law affects intra-EU investment treaties. These treaties raise a number of specific questions and concerns that are different from those raised by investment treaties between Member States and third countries. The main difference lies in the fact that intra-EU investment treaties are not matters falling under the Common Commercial Policy; they are not matters of external competence. Yet, as regards the questions of procedural status of the Union and Member States in investor–state arbitration several findings of this chapter will apply mutatis mutandis also to arbitrations under intra-EU investment treaties. *See also supra* note 14.

States are still the named respondents in an investor–state arbitration, or whether such arbitrations now have to be directed against the Union.[26]

Second, for Member States the topic is important, because they will have an interest in defending a claim by a foreign investor themselves, or at least be in a position to influence the defense strategy, if they are ultimately liable for damages resulting from a breach of such a treaty. Member States, in other words, may be opposed to having the Commission defend claims, in case they will ultimately have to pay, as risk of liability and interest in an effective defense often correspond. At the very least, Member States will be interested in having sufficient opportunities to influence the defense strategy, including the appointment of arbitrators and the content of written and oral submissions to an arbitral tribunal, should the Union handle the defense of claims for which a Member State is liable.

Finally, questions of party status in investor–state arbitration are also important for the EU, above all for the Commission, for two reasons: one related to EU law and one related to international investment law. First, as regards the interrelation between EU law and international investment law, being able to appoint arbitrators and to participate in investor–state arbitration can be a way to persuade arbitral tribunals to adopt a harmonious interpretation of international investment law and EU law, which ensures that values of EU law, most importantly the uniform application of EU law, its primacy in relation to the law of Member States, and its autonomy are not compromised by the decision making of arbitral tribunals.[27] Party status, or at least procedural rights vested in the Union, could thus alleviate concerns about the threat of investor–state arbitration to the primacy and autonomy of EU law and the task of the Court of Justice of the European Union (CJEU) under Article 19(1)(2) TEU to ensure the correct interpretation and application of EU law.[28]

Second, from the broader perspective of international investment law- and policy-making the Union has an interest in being able to participate in investor–state arbitrations because these arbitrations do not only concern the settlement of an individual dispute, but also function as a mechanism of global governance.[29] Investment treaty tribunals, in other words, are not only dispute resolvers, but through the extensive

---

[26] Again, to clarify, the question in the present context is not who is ultimately responsible vis-à-vis a private investor for breaches of an investment treaty, but who to direct an arbitration against and who to name as respondent.

[27] For a detailed discussion of potential incompatibilities of international investment treaties with EU law, *see* Anca Radu, *Foreign Investors in the EU—Which "Best Treatment"? Interactions between Bilateral Investment Treaties and EU Law*, 14 Eur. L.J. 237 (2008).

[28] Comprehensively on the impact of the autonomy of the EU legal order on the design of investor–state arbitrations under EU investment treaties, *see* Steffen Hindelang, *Der primärrechtliche Rahmen einer EU Investitionsschutzpolitik: Zulässigkeit und Grenzen von Investor-Staat-Schiedsverfahren aufgrund künftiger EU Abkommen*, WHI-Paper 01/11, *available at* http://www.whi-berlin.de/documents/whi-paper0111.pdf.

[29] Benedict Kingsbury & Stephan Schill, *Investor–State Arbitration as Governance: Fair and Equitable Treatment, Proportionality, and the Emerging Global Administrative Law*, IILJ Working Paper 2009/6 (Global Administrative Law Series), *available at* http://www.iilj.org/publications/documents/2009-6.KingsburySchill.pdf.

use of precedent craft and concretize the content of international investment law and thereby function as significant lawmakers in international investment law. Investment treaty arbitration therefore has a significant influence on how the future body of international investment law is developing. Because of this wide-ranging effect of investment treaty arbitration on the whole of international investment law, and thus also on future EU investment policy-making, being able to influence investor–state arbitrations, including through the appointment of arbitrators and through written and oral submissions to arbitral tribunals—as party, as party representative, or because of an internal mechanism of coordination with the Member State involved—becomes crucial because of the spillover effects of investment treaty arbitration on investment treaty making.

It is against this background that the Commission in its Communication *Towards a Comprehensive European International Investment Policy* of July 7, 2010 has signaled its ambition, as regards future investment treaties, to be the sole entity appearing in investment treaty arbitrations:

> The European Union, represented by the Commission, will defend all actions of EU institutions. Given the exclusive external competence, the Commission takes the view that the European Union will also be the sole defendant regarding any measure taken by a Member State which affects investments by third country nationals or companies falling within the scope of the agreement concerned.[30]

Subsequently, the Commission has modified this seemingly categorical position and suggested in its *Proposal for a Regulation of the European Parliament and of the Council Establishing a Framework for Managing Financial Responsibility Linked to Investor-State Dispute Settlement Tribunals Established by International Agreements to which the European Union is Party* a more nuanced position on procedural status that would also allow Member States to defend claims under future EU investment treaties depending on the circumstances.[31] In any event, this proposal is based on the principle that Commission and Member States will closely cooperate in responding to investment treaty arbitrations.[32]

Similarly, the Commission's *Proposal for a Regulation of the European Parliament and of the Council Establishing Transitional Arrangements for Bilateral Investment Agreements between Member States and Third Countries* of July 7, 2010, envisages an active role of the Commission in investor–state arbitrations under investment treaties of Member States. It provides not only that Member States shall inform the Commission about prospective investor–state arbitrations and cooperate with the Commission in conducting such arbitrations, but also that the Commission may participate in the procedure.[33]

---

[30] Commission Communication of July 7, 2010, *supra* note 3, at 10.

[31] *See* Commission, Proposal on Financial Responsibility, *supra* note 24, ch. III.

[32] *Id.*, Articles 6, 7, 9, and 10. For cooperation in the context of settlements, *see id.*, ch. IV.

[33] *See* Commission, Proposal on Transitional Arrangements, *supra* note 12, Article 13(2) and (3).

The different perspectives and interests of the EU, the Member States, and foreign investors illustrate that finding a solution for questions relating to procedural status will not always be easy. Although foreign investors are above all concerned about legal certainty and will be rather agnostic as to whom to address in an investor–state arbitration, reconciling the at-times adverse interests of the EU and its Member States could be more difficult. It will be one of the objectives of future EU investment treaties and accompanying internal legislation to furnish a solution that meets the needs of both the EU and its Member States. Independent of the precise solution adopted regarding party status, the key will be, as envisaged by the Commission's proposed regulation on transitional arrangements and its proposed regulation on financial responsibility, the close cooperation between the EU and its Member States in conducting investor–state arbitrations.

III. Party Status under Future Investment Treaties

Regarding party status, *de lege ferenda* much will depend on the content and structure of future EU investment treaties and EU internal implementing legislation. As regards procedural status, the most crucial question is whether future investment treaties will be concluded as agreements only between the Union and third countries (in which case the Member States will likely not have any externally visible and legally relevant procedural role), whether individual Member States will continue to be allowed to conclude investment treaties with third countries in their own name (in which case the procedural role of the Union will likely not be different from the current status), or whether future investment treaties will be concluded as mixed agreements (in which case both the Member States and the EU might have procedural status, and thus their external coordination also in relation to third countries and their investors will become relevant).[34]

First, one needs to emphasize that there is an undeniable interest of foreign investors, both EU investors abroad and foreign investors in the EU, to be able to have recourse to investment treaty arbitration. Because of the complications recourse to domestic courts may entail, above all their real or perceived lack of independence, impartiality, and neutrality, or their real or perceived inability to settle investor–state

34 For discussion on the form of future EU investment treaties, *see* Jan A. Bischoff, *Just a Little Bit of "Mixity"? The EU's Role in the Field of International Investment Protection Law*, 48 CML REV. 1527 (2011); Christoph Herrmann, *Die Zukunft der mitgliedstaatlichen Investitionspolitik nach dem Vertrag von Lissabon*, 21 EUROPÄISCHE ZEITSCHRIFT FÜR WIRTSCHAFTSRECHT (EuZW) 207 (2010); Tietje, *supra* note 10, at 17; Joern Griebel, *Überlegungen zur Wahrnehmung der neuen EU-Kompetenz für ausländische Direktinvestitionen nach Inkrafttreten des Vertrags von Lissabon*, 55 RECHT DER INTERNATIONALEN WIRTSCHAFT (RIW) 469 (2009); Marc Bungenberg, *Going Global? The EU Common Commercial Policy after Lisbon*, 1 EUR. Y.B. INT'L ECON. LAW 123 (2010); Jan Ceyssens, *Towards a Common Foreign Investment Policy?—Foreign Investment in the European Constitution*, 32 LEGAL ISSUES OF EUR. INTEGRATION 259 (2005).

disputes efficiently and expediently, access to investor–state arbitration is one of the hallmarks effective investor–state cooperation and investment protection depends on.[35] Accordingly, the Commission,[36] the Council,[37] and even the European Parliament, which has taken a much more critical view of the current international investment protection regime than the Commission and the Member States,[38] have recognized that an investor's direct access to investor–state arbitration should be safeguarded also under future EU investment treaties. Which forum to entrust such disputes to, however, is a different, and as of now unresolved question.[39]

Second, party status under future investment treaties depends on who will consent to investor–state arbitration under those treaties. Consent, in other words, as a condition for jurisdiction of an international dispute settlement body under international law, determines party status.[40] If, for example, only the Union has consented to arbitration under such treaties, only the Union can be a party. Conversely, if only Member States have given consent to arbitration, only they can have party status. Yet, what is more likely is that future investment treaties will be concluded as mixed agreements that permit foreign investors to initiate arbitrations against both Union and Member States because both have consented to arbitration. In such a case, there are concerns

---

[35] On the importance of an investor's direct right of recourse against a state or public entity outside domestic courts, *see* Stephan Schill, *Private Enforcement of International Investment Law: Why We Need Investor Standing in BIT Dispute Settlement, in* The Backlash against Investment Arbitration, *supra* note 15, at 29.

[36] Commission, Communication of July 7, 2010, *supra* note 3, at 9–10 ("Investor–state dispute settlement, which forms a key part of the inheritance that the Union receives from Member State BITs, is important as an investment involves the establishment of a long-term relationship with the host state which cannot be easily diverted to another market in the event of a problem with the investment. Investor–state [sic] is such an established feature of investment agreements that its absence would in fact discourage investors and make a host economy less attractive than others. For these reasons, future EU agreements including investment protection should include investor–state dispute settlement.").

[37] Council, Conclusions, *supra* note 5, 18 ("stress[ing], in particular, the need for an effective investor-to-state dispute settlement mechanism in the EU investment agreements").

[38] *See* European Parliament, Resolution, *supra* note 6, 32 (stating that "in addition to state-to-state dispute settlement procedures, investor–state procedures must also be applicable in order to secure comprehensive investment protection"). The same resolution, however, also voices criticism of the current international investment protection regime and calls for adopting changes in the EU's future investment policy, such as the inclusion of social and environmental standards.

[39] *See* Commission, Communication of July 7, 2010, *supra* note 3, at 10 (pointing out that "[c]urrent structures are to some extent ill-adapted to the advent of the Union"). Most important, the Convention on the Settlement of Investment Disputes between States and Nationals of Other States, *opened for signature* Mar. 18, 1965, 17 U.S.T. 1270, 575 U.N.T.S. 159 [hereinafter ICSID Convention] is currently only open to states that are members of the World Bank or to states that are party to the Statute of the International Court of Justice; *see* Article 67 ICSID Convention. The EU does not fall under either category. Arbitration under the UN Commission on International Trade Law (UNCITRAL) Arbitration Rules or ad hoc arbitration, by contrast, would be possible.

[40] On the principle of consensuality as a basis for international dispute settlement, *see*, for example, *Armed Activities on the Territory of the Congo (New Application: 2002) (Democratic Republic of the Congo v. Rwanda), Jurisdiction and Admissibility*, Judgment, 2006 I.C.J. 6, 64, and 127. *See also* Bin Cheng, General Principles of Law as Applied by International Courts and Tribunals 259 *et seq.* (1953).

for legal certainty for foreign investors as to whom to sue, the Union or the Member States, and as to the criteria that are relevant to make that choice.

These issues must be addressed in future EU investment treaties and, as may be the case, in EU implementing legislation. In fact, the Commission's proposal for a regulation regarding financial responsibility provides that the respondent status under future EU investment treaties will depend on whether the act allegedly in breach of such a treaty emanates from the Union or from a Member State. In the former case, the Union shall act as respondent.[41] Where Member State conduct is at issue, the Member State may act as respondent, provided it so agrees, but the Commission may decide to assume party status within thirty days after receiving notice of an arbitration, if it is likely that the Union would bear some financial responsibility, if the dispute also concerns treatment afforded to the foreign investor by the Union, if similar claims are likely to be brought against other Member States and the Commission is in a better position to ensure an effective and consistent defense, or if the dispute raises issues that may also occur in other disputes under the same or other EU investment treaties.[42] This would provide an appropriate solution to managing the determination of party status at an EU internal level.

Furthermore, independently of who can serve as respondent under future EU investment treaties, the relationship between the Commission and the Member States in defending claims under such treaties requires regulation. Again, as an EU internal matter this is appropriately done through EU internal legislation, as now suggested in the Commission's proposal on financial responsibility. It provides that in defending claims, the Commission and the Member States are under a duty of cooperation. Thus, both the Commission and Member States have to inform each other of the initiation of arbitral proceedings by foreign investors.[43] Furthermore, both sides are required to provide each other with information about ongoing arbitrations, to consult on the defense in arbitral proceedings, to provide necessary assistance and documentation, and to permit each other to send members as part of the delegation to the proceedings; in addition, the Commission can require a Member State to take a specific position on a question of law and make use of remedies against an arbitral award, such as annulment or review.[44] Similarly, in the context of settlements of arbitral proceedings, Commission and Member State have to cooperate.[45]

Yet, at a more fundamental level, the inclusion of investor–state arbitration in future EU investment treaties also raises questions as to the permissibility of such a dispute settlement mechanism as a matter of EU constitutional law.[46] In fact, EU

---

41 *See* Commission, Proposal on Financial Responsibility, *supra* note 24, Article 4.

42 *Id.*, Article 8.

43 *Id.*, Article 7.

44 *Id.*, Articles 9 & 10.

45 *See id.*, ch. IV.

46 *See* more in-depth on this question Stephan Schill, *Luxembourg Limits: Conditions for Investor–State Dispute Settlement under Future EU Investment Agreements*, *in* EU AND INVESTMENTS AGREEMENTS—OPEN QUESTIONS AND REMAINING CHALLENGES (Marc Bungenberg, August Reinisch & Christian

law sets up certain criteria that may limit the participation of both the Union and the Member States in investor–state arbitrations. Although the CJEU has accepted the possibility for the EU and its Member States to subject themselves to international dispute settlement mechanisms in an international agreement,[47] it has also clarified that such dispute settlement mechanisms must be structured in a way so as not to affect the autonomy of the EU legal order and the CJEU's monopoly for the authoritative interpretation of EU law.[48]

The autonomy of the EU legal order and the CJEU's monopoly for the interpretation of EU law could be threatened if an international agreement permits an international dispute settlement mechanism to rule on questions that, from the perspective of EU law, fall into the exclusive competence of the CJEU. In the context of a mixed agreement, this would prevent, for example, the international dispute settlement mechanism from deciding questions relating to the distribution of competences between the EU and its Member States.[49] In addition, it would be contrary to the CJEU's monopoly

---

Tietje eds., forthcoming). *See further also* Jacqueline Dutheil de la Rochère, *Quel rôle pour la Cour de Justice?*, *in* LE DROIT EUROPÉEN ET L'ARBITRAGE D'INVESTISSEMENT, *supra* note 24, at 37; Hindelang, *supra* note 28; Markus Burgstaller, *Investor–State Arbitration in EU International Investment Agreements with Third States*, 39 LEGAL ISSUES ECON. INTEGRATION 207 (2012); Matthew Parish, *International Courts and the European Legal Order*, 23 EUR. J. INT'L L. 141 (2012); Nikos Lavranos, *Is an International Investor-to-State System under the Auspices of the ECJ Possible?*, *available at* http://ssrn.com/abstract=1973491 (Dec. 16, 2011); Angelos Dimopoulos, *The Compatibility of Future EU Investment Agreements with EU Law*, 39 LEGAL ISSUES ECON. INTEGRATION 447 (2012); Steffen Hindelang, *The Autonomy of the European Legal Order: EU Constitutional Limits to Investor-State Arbitration on the Basis of Future Investment-Related Agreements*, *in* COMMON COMMERCIAL POLICY OF THE EU "AFTER LISBON" (Marc Bungenberg & Christoph Herrmann eds., forthcoming).

47 CJEU, Opinion 1/91, Economic Area Agreement I, 1991 ECR I-6079, 39–40:

> Where . . . an international agreement provides for its own system of courts, including a court with jurisdiction to settle disputes between the Contracting Parties to the agreement, and, as a result, to interpret its provisions, the decisions of that court will be binding on the Community institutions, including the Court of Justice . . .
>
> An international agreement providing for such a system of courts is in principle compatible with Community law. The Community's competence in the field of international relations and its capacity to conclude international agreements necessarily entails the power to submit to the decisions of a court which is created or designated by such an agreement as regards the interpretation and application of its provisions.

48 *Id.* at 32–36; similarly, CJEU, Opinion 1/00, European Common Aviation Area, 2002 ECR I-3498, 11–13. *See now also* CJEU, March 8, 2011, Opinion 1/09, European and Community Patent Court, 2011 ECR I-0000, 64 *et seq.* Comprehensively on the restrictions the concept of the autonomy of the EU legal order imposes on dispute settlement under international law involving the EU and its Member States, *see* Hindelang, *supra* note 28, at 12–17.

49 CJEU, Opinion 1/91, Economic Area Agreement I, 1991 ECR I-6079, 34–36:

> . . . when a dispute relating to the interpretation or application of one or more provisions of the agreement is brought before it, the EEA Court may be called upon to interpret the expression "Contracting Party", within the meaning of Article 2(c) of the agreement, in order to determine whether, for the purposes of the provision at issue, the expression "Contracting Party" means the Community, the Community and the Member States, or simply the Member States. Consequently, the EEA Court will have to rule on the respective competences of the Community and the Member States as regards the matters governed by the provisions of the agreement.

if arbitral tribunals could bind the CJEU to a specific interpretation of EU law[50] or rule on the legality of conduct of EU institutions under EU law.[51] Equally, the CJEU considered that the autonomy of the EU legal order could be threatened if interpretations of non-EU law by an international dispute settlement mechanism had spillover effects on the interpretation of EU law; this is particularly the case when international agreements seek to extend the *acquis communautaire* to third countries by including provisions that are essentially identical to EU law.[52]

Furthermore, in a recent opinion on the compatibility with EU law of an envisaged European and Community Patents Court, the CJEU emphasized the importance of

---

> It follows that the jurisdiction conferred on the EEA Court under... the agreement is likely adversely to affect the allocation of responsibilities defined in the Treaties and, hence, the autonomy of the Community legal order, respect for which must be assured by the Court of Justice pursuant to Article 164 of the EEC Treaty. This exclusive jurisdiction of the Court of Justice is confirmed by Article 219 of the EEC Treaty, under which Member States undertake not to submit a dispute concerning the interpretation or application of that treaty to any method of settlement other than those provided for in the Treaty.... Consequently, to confer that jurisdiction on the EEA Court is incompatible with Community law.

Similarly, CJEU, Opinion 1/00, European Common Aviation Area, 2002 ECR I-3498, 12.

50 CJEU, Opinion 1/00, European Common Aviation Area, 2002 ECR I-3498, 12–13 ("... the autonomy of the Community legal order requires therefore... the procedures for ensuring uniform interpretation of the rules of the [international agreement] and for resolving disputes will not have the effect of binding the Community and its institutions, in the exercise of their internal powers, to a particular interpretation of the rules of Community law referred to in that agreement.").

51 CJEU, Opinion 1/00, European Common Aviation Area, 2002 ECR I-3498, 24 (stressing that conferring jurisdiction on an international dispute settlement body requires that "... the Court's exclusive task of reviewing the legality of acts of the Community institutions, whether the latter are acting under the Treaty or under another international instrument, conferred on it by *inter alia* Articles 230 EC and 234 EC, is not called into question.").

52 CJEU, Opinion 1/91, Economic Area Agreement I, 1991 ECR I-6079, 41–46:

> ... the agreement at issue takes over an essential part of the rules—including the rules of secondary legislation—which govern economic and trading relations within the Community and which constitute, for the most part, fundamental provisions of the Community legal order. Consequently, the agreement has the effect of introducing into the Community legal order a large body of legal rules which is juxtaposed to a corpus of identically-worded Community rules. Furthermore... the objective of uniform application and equality of conditions of competition... necessarily covers the interpretation both of the provisions of the agreement and of the corresponding provisions of the Community legal order.
>
> Although, under... the agreement, the EEA Court is under a duty to interpret the provisions of the agreement in the light of the relevant rulings of the Court of Justice given prior to the date of signature of the agreement, the EEA Court will no longer be subject to any such obligation in the case of decisions given by the Court of Justice after that date. Consequently, the agreement's objective of ensuring homogeneity of the law throughout the EEA will determine not only the interpretation of the rules of the agreement itself but also the interpretation of the corresponding rules of Community law.
>
> It follows that in so far as it conditions the future interpretation of the Community rules on free movement and competition the machinery of courts provided for in the agreement conflicts with Article 164 of the EEC Treaty and, more generally, with the very foundations of the Community.

Similarly, CJEU, Opinion 1/00, European Common Aviation Area, 2002 ECR I-3498, 13.

safeguarding the opportunity for courts and tribunals of the Member States to refer questions to the Court by means of the preliminary rulings procedure in Article 267 TFEU in order to ensure the correct and uniform application of EU law and to afford the protection granted to individuals under the EU legal order.[53] This aim would be vitiated if a dispute settlement mechanism with exclusive jurisdiction was established outside of the ordinary court system of Member States that was to interpret and apply EU law.[54]

In light of this jurisprudence, EU law sets up limits on how investor–state arbitration can be structured under future EU investment treaties. In case such treaties are concluded as mixed agreements, and both the EU and its Member States have consented to arbitrations under such agreements, the dispute settlement mechanism needs to be structured in a way that arbitral tribunals will not decide on who the proper respondent is in an investment arbitration, as this decision might touch upon the distribution of competences between the EU and its Member States, and thus falls into the exclusive competence of the CJEU.

Spillover effects of the jurisprudence of investment treaty tribunals on the interpretation of EU law, by contrast, will be less of a problem because international investment treaties do not intend to extend the *acquis communautaire* to third countries and do not intend to create a harmonized legal regime between EU law and international investment law. Instead, EU law and international investment treaties are sufficiently different in scope, object and purpose, and content of the rights and obligations concerned.[55] This would particularly be the case if arbitral tribunals established under future EU investment were limited to granting damages, not specific performance, as this would ensure that the CJEU remains competent to determine—de jure and de facto—the legality under EU law of acts of EU institutions and Member States.[56]

Furthermore, to the extent the interpretation of EU law becomes relevant in an investment treaty arbitration as a preliminary question, mechanisms are necessary to ensure that the resolution of that preliminary question is not only compatible with the interpretation of EU law by the CJEU, but also subject to the CJEU's jurisdiction.[57]

---

53 CJEU, March 8, 2011, Opinion 1/09, European and Community Patent Court, 2011 ECR I-0000, 80–84.

54 *Id.* at 80 (stating that "the Member States cannot confer the jurisdiction to resolve such disputes on a court created by an international agreement which would deprive those courts of their task, as 'ordinary' courts within the European Union legal order, to implement European Union law and, thereby, of the power provided for in Article 267 TFEU, or, as the case may be, the obligation, to refer questions for a preliminary ruling in the field concerned.").

55 *See* Tietje, *supra* note 14, at 12–15; Eureko B.V. v. The Slovak Republic, PCA Case No. 2008-13, UNCITRAL, Award on Jurisdiction, Arbitrability and Suspension, October 26, 2010, 239–67.

56 For a discussion of the situation that a measure allegedly in breach of an EU investment treaty is required by EU law and consists in the payment of money, *see* Schill, *supra* note 46.

57 *Cf.* CJEU, Case C-459/03, Commission/Ireland (MOX Plant), 2006 ECR I-4635, 177 ("The act of submitting a dispute of this nature to a judicial forum such as the Arbitral Tribunal involves the risk that a judicial forum other than the Court will rule on the scope of obligations imposed on the Member States pursuant to Community law."); CJEU, Opinion 1/00, European Common Aviation Area, 2002 ECR I-3498, 11 ("It is particularly important that the mechanisms in the agreement should prevent the Community, in the event of a dispute with a State Party, from being bound by a particular interpretation

For this purpose, access to the CJEU needs to be ensured whenever questions of EU law are affected, most importantly through the preliminary rulings proceeding under Article 267 TFEU, as the Court has stressed in Opinion 1/09.[58] Although the Court in that decision emphasizes the importance of the "ordinary" courts within the EU legal order to request such rulings,[59] and therefore suggests that dispute settlement systems that entirely exclude the jurisdiction of Member State courts, such as investor–state arbitration under the ICSID Convention, may be contrary to EU law, it is important to note that the envisaged European and Community Patents Court would have had to apply and interpret EU law routinely, above all as regards the Community Patent, and review the legality of acts of the EU under EU law.[60]

Investment treaty tribunals, by contrast, would determine international responsibility of the EU and of Member States under the applicable international investment treaty. Questions of EU law, by contrast, would regularly only constitute preliminary questions. This could be clarified through provisions in future EU investment treaties that clarify the applicable law in investor–state arbitrations to be the respective international treaty, not EU law. This would be another significant distinction with the envisaged European and Community Patents Court. In order to safeguard the correct and uniform interpretation of such preliminary questions, it may still be a viable option to introduce a preliminary reference procedure that would allow an investment treaty tribunal to submit requests to the CJEU concerning the interpretation of EU law.[61] In light of the CJEU's Opinion 1/91, the decision by the Court on such a request would need to be binding on the tribunal.[62]

In any event, potentially concurring party status and safeguarding the autonomy of the EU legal order are not issues that are specific to future investment treaties. Instead, the problem already exists at present in the context of international treaties to which both the Union and the Member States are parties, and which provide for international dispute settlement mechanisms. Thus, some environmental agreements as well as the Energy Charter Treaty provide examples for how questions of concurring party status can be resolved through an EU-internal procedure. This allows the Union and its Member States to submit to the jurisdiction of an international dispute settlement mechanism in relation to third countries, while at the same time upholding

of the rules of Community law referred to in the agreement. Thus, the agreement must make it possible to anticipate and prevent any such undermining of the objective enshrined in Article 220 EC [now Article 19(1)(2) TEU] that Community law should be interpreted uniformly and of the Court's function of reviewing the legality of the acts of the Community institutions.").

58 *See* CJEU, March 8, 2011, Opinion 1/09, European and Community Patent Court, 2011 ECR I-0000, 80–84.

59 *Id.* at 80.

60 *See id.* at 9 and 78.

61 On the question whether an investment treaty tribunal can be considered as "a court or tribunal of a Member State" in the sense of Article 267 TFEU, see *infra* Section IV.4.

62 CJEU, Opinion 1/91, Economic Area Agreement I, 1991 ECR I-6079, 61–65; similarly, CJEU, Opinion 1/00, European Common Aviation Area, 2002 ECR I-3498, 33.

the requirement under EU law to leave the unity of the EU legal order and the CJEU's jurisdiction to interpret EU law authoritatively untouched.

Thus, the Convention concerning the International Commission for the Rhine (Berne Convention) provides for the following EU-internal procedure to determine party status:

> In the case of a dispute between two Contracting Parties, only one of which is a Member State of the European Economic Community, which is itself a Contracting Party, the other party shall simultaneously transmit its request to that Member State and the Community, which shall jointly notify the party within two months following receipt of the request whether the Member State, the Community or the Member State and the Community together are parties to the dispute. If such notification is not given within the appointed time, both the Member State and the Community shall be regarded as constituting one and the same party to the dispute.[63]

A similar EU-internal procedure exists in the context of the Energy Charter Treaty, to which both the EU (as successor to the European Communities (EC)) and the Member States are parties. In a statement submitted by the EC to the Energy Charter Secretariat, the EC at the time of ratification invited investors seeking to initiate investor–state arbitration under the treaty to seek clarification as to whom to initiate arbitrations against. The statement provides:

> [T]he European Communities and their Member States have both concluded the Energy Charter Treaty and are thus internationally responsible for the fulfilment of the obligations contained therein, in accordance with their respective competences. The Communities and the Member States will, if necessary, determine among them who is the respondent party to arbitration proceedings initiated by an Investor of another Contracting Party. In such case, upon the request of the Investor, the Communities and the Member States concerned will make such determination within a period of 30 days.[64]

Through such a mechanism, the risk for investor-claimants arising out of the difficult legal relationship between the EU and its Member States under mixed agreements is shifted to those responsible for generating the underlying uncertainty, namely Member States and the EU. Such a distribution of risk is also in line with the rationale of Article 27 of the Vienna Convention on the Law of Treaties, which provides that a State cannot use its domestic law and its internal structure of organization to justify

[63] Convention concerning the International Commission for the Rhine (Berne Convention), adopted on December 3, 1976, 1977 O.J. (L 240) 50, Annex B, 8.

[64] Statement submitted by the European Communities to the Secretariat of the Energy Charter pursuant to Article 26(3)(b)(ii) of the Energy Charter Treaty, 1998 O.J. (L 69) 115.

noncompliance with international obligations. A procedure such as the one under the Berne Convention or the Energy Charter Treaty would also protect the autonomy of the EU legal order as the international dispute settlement mechanism in question would not need to decide on issues within the exclusive competence of the CJEU, in particular as regards the distribution of competences between the EU and its Member States. Problems relating to the lack of access to the CJEU via domestic courts through requests for preliminary rulings, finally, could be resolved if investment treaty tribunals were granted the right to make such requests in future EU investment treaties.[65]

IV. The Impact of Article 207 TFEU on Existing Investor–State Arbitration

The new competence in Article 207 TFEU does not only raise questions with respect to how investor–state arbitration will need to be structured under future EU investment treaties; it also raises questions as to existing investment treaties concluded by Member States. Although the treaties themselves, for the time being, will continue to stay in force,[66] the question is whether the new competence in Article 207 TFEU affects the procedural role of the Member States in investor–state arbitrations initiated under these treaties.[67] In this context, one will thus need to consider who is the proper party to an arbitration under existing investment treaties (the Member States or the EU), who will represent the party to the arbitration, and how the potentially conflicting interests of the EU and the Member States will be coordinated.[68]

1. ARTICLE 207 TFEU AND PARTY STATUS

The question of which entity, Member States or EU, will serve as the named party to an investor–state arbitration under existing Member State investment treaties is solely

65 This could be done by providing in a future EU investment agreement that investor–state tribunals established under that agreement can request preliminary rulings from the Court on questions relating to the interpretation of EU law. In fact, similar mechanisms have been considered in other international agreements and were considered as permissible by the Court. *See* CJEU, Opinion 1/91, Economic Area Agreement I, 1991 ECR I-6079, 59–65; Opinion 1/00, European Common Aviation Area, 2002 ECR I-3493, 19 and 32–33; *cf. also* CJEU, March 8, 2011, Opinion 1/09, European and Community Patents Courts, 2011 ECR I-0000, 77. The decision by the Court on such a request would need to be binding on the tribunal; *see* CJEU, Opinion 1/91, Economic Area Agreement I, 1991 ECR I-6079, 61–65; similarly, CJEU, Opinion 1/00, European Common Aviation Area, 2002 ECR I-3498, 33.

66 *See supra* note 10.

67 Note that the proposed regulation regarding financial responsibility would not cover arbitrations under existing Member States BITs. *See* Commission, Proposal on Financial Responsibility, *supra* note 24, Article 1(1). As a consequence, the questions dealt with in this section of this chapter are governed by primary EU law.

68 The relationship between Member States and the EU concerning investor–state arbitrations under investment treaties of Member States is also addressed in Article 13(2) and (3) of the Commission's proposed draft regulation; *see supra* note 12. Until such a regulation enters into force, questions concerning the relationship between Member States and the EU will remain questions of primary Union law.

one of consent under such agreements; it is therefore a question that is independent of any provisions of EU law. Existing investment treaties only contain the consent of Member States. Hence, only they can serve as named parties in investor–state arbitrations. Article 207 TFEU itself does not contain any consent by the EU and therefore has no impact on party status in investor–state arbitrations under existing investment treaties. Article 207 TFEU also does not have the effect of turning the Member States' consent in their investment treaties into consent of the EU. The transfer of external competences from the Member States to the Union as such therefore does not affect party status.

The situation in this context is not different from cases where party status of Member States in a dispute settlement proceeding under an international regime to which the EU is not a party has been upheld, even though the challenged act fell into the competence of the EU.[69] Similarly, the CJEU recently held, in a case involving conduct by Greece as a member of an international organization to which the EU was not a party, but whose activity fell into the exclusive competence of the EU, that Greece had breached its duty of cooperation (now enshrined in Article 4(3) TEU) by exercising its membership rights without prior coordination with the Commission; the CJEU did not consider, by contrast, that by virtue of the Union's exclusive competence in the field in question, the Union had either become a party to the international agreement in question, or was able to exercise the right of membership of the Member State.[70]

Thus, Member States may be under additional obligations under EU law in view of the Union's competence in a certain field, in particular obligations arising from the principle of sincere cooperation contained in Article 4(3) TEU. Yet, a transfer of competences from Member States to the EU as such does not have direct effect in relation to third states under international law. Anything else would contravene the principle of international law, enshrined in Article 34 of the Vienna Convention on the Law of Treaties, that "[a] treaty does not create either obligations or rights for a third State without its consent." The same rationale also applies to investor–state arbitration under existing investment treaties between Member States and third countries. Article 207 TFEU therefore does not affect party status under existing investment treaties of Member States.

---

[69] *See* ECHR, Senator Lines v. Austria, Belgium, Denmark, Finland, France, Germany, Greece, Ireland, Italy, Luxembourg, the Netherlands, Portugal, Spain, Sweden, and the United Kingdom, App. No. 56672/00, Decision, March 10, 2004; ECHR, Emesa Sugar v. The Netherlands, App. No. 62023/00, Decision, January 15, 2005. Similarly, the party status of Member States remains unaffected when they merely implement EU law. *See* ECHR, Melchior, App. No. 13258/87, Decision, February 9, 1990; ECHR, Matthews v. United Kingdom, App. No. 24833/94, Judgment, February 18, 1999; ECHR, Bosphorus v. Ireland, App. No. 43036/98, Judgment, June 30, 2005, 153. For an overview of different international dispute settlement systems and the way they deal with the EU and its Member States as respondents, *see* Frank Hoffmeister, *Litigating against the European Union and Its Member States—Who Responds under the ILC's Draft Articles on International Responsibility of International Organizations?*, 21 EUR. J. INT'L L. 723 (2010).

[70] *See* CJEU, Case C-45/07, Commission v. Greece, 2009 ECR I-701, 14 *et seq.*, in particular 28–31.

2. ACTING FOR THE NAMED PARTY

Although leaving party status unaffected, the question arises whether Article 207 TFEU nevertheless confers competence on the Union to act on behalf of the Member States in investor–state arbitrations, including the appointment of arbitrators and the right to make written and oral submissions to the arbitral tribunal. As a rule, party status encompasses the right to represent oneself in an international proceeding. Yet, one could consider whether Article 207 TFEU understands the competence in matters of foreign direct investment to encompass the competence to act for Member States in investor–state arbitrations.[71] This could be based on the argument that defending a claim under an international investment treaty is a matter relating to "foreign direct investment" in the sense of Article 207 TFEU, in particular as investment treaty arbitration involves more than just dispute settlement and contributes to the making of international investment law.[72]

Such a proposition, however, is not convincing for a number of reasons. First, if international agreements concluded by the Member States prior to a transfer of competence to the EU stay in place,[73] these agreements arguably stay in place *tel quel*, including the functioning of the dispute settlement mechanism under such treaties. If Member States were allowed to act for themselves in investor–state arbitrations prior to the entry into force of the Lisbon Treaty, they continue to do so also after December 1, 2009, because they are entitled to keep the treaties in question in place.

Second, Article 207 TFEU views foreign direct investment as part of the common commercial policy. This competence encompasses entering into international agreements as well as implementing autonomous measures under EU law. Article 207 TFEU, however, is primarily a policy-making competence, not a competence relating to dispute settlement. Although Article 207 TFEU allows the EU to conclude investment treaties that include dispute settlement provisions, it is not a competence to act on behalf of a Member State under existing international dispute settlement mechanisms.

Third, one has to consider that the substantive rights granted under investment treaties are essentially functional substitutes for the substantive and procedural protection of investors under domestic law against the misuse of public authority by host states; investment treaty arbitration, in turn, functionally replaces dispute settlement in domestic courts.[74] In respect of dispute settlement in the domestic courts of the Member States, it is, however, unheard of that an external competence of the EU

[71] In this sense Christian Tietje, *EU-Investitionsschutz und -förderung zwischen Übergangsregelungen und umfassender europäischer Auslandsinvestitionspolitik*, 21 EuZW 647, 652 (2010) (stating that the "participation in arbitral proceedings in the area of investment protection is no longer within the competence of Member States since December 1, 2009").

[72] *See supra* note 29 and accompanying text.

[73] *See supra* note 10.

[74] *See* STEPHAN SCHILL, *International Investment Law and Comparative Public Law: An Introduction in* INTERNATIONAL INVESTMENT LAW AND COMPARATIVE PUBLIC LAW 3, 10–17 (Stephan Schill ed., 2010).

should affect the right of a Member State, who is a party to a proceeding, to act on its own behalf.

Finally, although the CJEU has held conduct by Member States in the context of their membership in international organizations to violate EU law, for example because it contravenes the distribution of competences between the EU and its Member States, neither the Court, nor the Commission, have ever argued that the EU's competence would have direct effect vis-à-vis third states and override the right of the Member State to exercise rights under international law in its own name.[75] Article 207 TFEU, therefore, has to be understood as not affecting the right of a Member State to defend itself in an investor–state arbitration under existing investment treaties.

3. COORDINATING INTERESTS: THE DUTY TO COOPERATE UNDER ARTICLE 4(3) TEU

Although Member States continue to have party status in investor–state arbitrations, and continue to be able to act for themselves in such proceedings, the question arises as to how the EU is able to participate in investor–state arbitrations under existing investment treaties in order to safeguard its interests that could be affected by such proceedings. Of course, the Commission could intervene as a non-disputing party, as it already has in at least one investor–state arbitration under the ICSID Convention.[76] Likewise, an arbitral tribunal could take the initiative and request views of the Commission on certain issues relating to the operation of EU law, as happened in *Eureko v. Slovak Republic*.[77]

Although these arbitrations shed light on the practice regarding the relationship between the EU and investment treaty tribunals, they do not elucidate the relations between the Member States and the EU, in particular the Commission, in relation to such proceedings. Above all, this practice leaves unanswered important questions such as whether a Member State can prevent an arbitral tribunal from requesting the views of the Commission, or whether the Commission is at all allowed, without the consent of the Member State, to make submissions as a non-disputing third party. It also does not answer the question of whether the Commission has a right vis-à-vis the Member

---

[75] *See supra* note 69.

[76] *See* AES Summit Generation Limited and AES-Tisza Erömü Kft v. The Republic of Hungary, ICSID Case No. ARB/07/22, Award, September 23, 2010, 3.25. Such interventions are permissible under Rule 37(2) of the ICSID Arbitration Rules, but are also increasingly recognized in investor–state arbitrations outside the ICSID context. That the mere impact of decisions of investment treaty tribunals on the future direction of international investment jurisprudence (and the Union's abstract interest in having influence in shaping that direction through the appointment of arbitrators and submissions to arbitral tribunals) is sufficient to constitute "a significant interest in the proceeding" (Rule 37(2)(c) ICSID Arbitration Rules), however, is questionable as the impact of a single decision by an arbitral tribunal is probably comparatively small, and the interest of the EU accordingly rather remote. *Cf.* in the context of Article 62 of the ICJ Statute, Sovereignty over Pulau Ligitan and Pulau Sipadan (Indonesia/Malaysia), Application for Permission to Intervene, Judgment, 2001 I.C.J. 575 (October 23), 83. The issue is different, however, as regards legal issues concerning the relationship between EU law and international investment law, as the primacy and autonomy of EU law are at stake in this context.

[77] *See* Eureko v. Slovak Republic, *supra* note 55, 31.

States under primary EU law to be informed about the existence of investor–state arbitration and whether it can participate in the defense of a claim.

These questions are issues of EU law and are governed by the principle of sincere cooperation (or principle of loyalty) enshrined in Article 4(3) TEU, which provides:

> Pursuant to the principle of sincere cooperation, the Union and the Member States shall, in full mutual respect, assist each other in carrying out tasks which flow from the Treaties.
>
> The Member States shall take any appropriate measure, general or particular, to ensure fulfilment of the obligations arising out of the Treaties or resulting from the acts of the institutions of the Union.
>
> The Member States shall facilitate the achievement of the Union's tasks and refrain from any measure which could jeopardise the attainment of the Union's objectives.

The meaning of the principle of sincere cooperation in the context of external relations of the EU has been concretized further by the jurisprudence of the CJEU in numerous cases, above all in the context of mixed agreements.[78] As the Court recently held in *Commission v. Sweden*, under the principle of loyalty

> it is essential to ensure close cooperation between the Member States and the Community institutions, both in the process of negotiation and conclusion and in the fulfilment of the commitments entered into. That obligation to cooperate flows from the requirement of unity in the international representation of the Community.[79]

In this context, the CJEU has recognized that Member States and the Commission are subject to a duty of coordination, information, and consultation. This duty, in principle,

---

[78] The CJEU, in fact, has circumscribed the content of this duty in numerous cases mainly under mixed agreements. Although, of course, the situation in the foreign investment context at present is not identical to that under a mixed agreement, the present situation in the investment context, namely where treaties concluded by Member States continue to stay in force at times when an exclusive EU competence came into being, is structurally comparable to that of a mixed agreement because in both cases the power of Member States to act under international law needs to be coordinated with the EU's competence. Generally on the content of the principle of sincere cooperation in the context of the EU's external relations, *see* Eleftheria Neframi, *The Duty of Loyality: Rethinking Its Scope through Its Application in the Field of EU External Relations*, 47 CML REV. 323 (2010); Marise Cremona, *Defending the Community Interest: The Duties of Cooperation and Compliance, in* EU FOREIGN RELATIONS LAW—CONSTITUTIONAL FUNDAMENTALS 125, 157 *et seq.* (Marise Cremona & Bruno de Witte eds., 2008); Astrid Epiney, *Zur Tragweite des Art. 10 EGV im Bereich der Außenbeziehungen, in* INTERNATIONALE GEMEINSCHAFT UND MENSCHENRECHTE—FESTSCHRIFT FÜR GEORG RESS 441 (Jürgen Bröhmer, Roland Bieber, Christian Calliess, Christine Langenfeld, Stefan Weber & Joachim Wolf eds., 2005).

[79] CJEU, Case C-246/07, Comm'n v. Sweden, 2010 ECR I-0000, 73.

also applies in the context of dispute settlement under an international agreement.[80] In consequence, it can equally bear on the relationship between the Commission and Member States in investor–state arbitrations under existing investment treaties. It prohibits Member States to act, including in investment treaty arbitrations, in a way that affects the primacy and uniform application of EU law or that has negative impact on the future exercise of the EU's competence under Article 207 TFEU.

The relationship of the Union and the Member States as regards investor–state arbitration thus needs to be characterized by mutual information, coordination, and cooperation. The application of these principles can ensure that the Commission participates internally in investor–state arbitrations in order to monitor that Member States did abide by EU law in regard of the subject matter of an arbitration; to ensure that Member States abide by EU law in conducting the proceedings (e.g., by monitoring that a settlement in an investor–state arbitration does not constitute a prohibited state aid); to ensure that the activity of Member States and arbitral tribunals does not negatively affect the Union's future exercise of its competence in the field; and to observe whether investment treaty tribunals deal with EU law in ways that are incompatible with the CJEU's interpretative monopoly under Article 19(1)(2) TEU.

In practical terms, the duty of loyalty thus requires Member States to inform the Commission of the existence or initiation of investment treaty arbitrations, to inform it about the development of the proceedings, to provide to the Commission the written material submitted in the proceedings, to consult with the Commission regarding the defense of the claim, and, in case the Commission wishes to do so, to cooperate with it in the defense of the claim itself, for example by considering the integration of submissions the Commission would like to make to an arbitral tribunal into the written and oral submissions of the Member State. Likewise, a Member State could give representatives of the Commission the opportunity to make oral submissions to an arbitral tribunal as part of the Member State's team. In fact, these different aspects of the principle of sincere cooperation relating to investor–state arbitration are reflected in the Commission's proposal for a regulation establishing a transitional regime for the continued operation of investment treaties of Member States.[81]

4. RELATIONSHIP BETWEEN INVESTMENT TREATY TRIBUNALS AND THE CJEU

The coordination of investment treaty arbitration under existing investment treaties of Member States and the EU also needs to take into account the relations between the CJEU and investor–state arbitral tribunals. So far, these relations have been characterized by the lack of any institutional linkages. Although the CJEU has not yet had to pronounce itself on rulings of an investment treaty tribunal, but may soon have to do

[80] CJEU, Case C-459/03, Comm'n v. Ireland (MOX Plant), 2006 ECR I-4635, 176 *et seq.* (concerning, however, the case that a Member State is in a position to initiate, not, as is usually the case in investor–state arbitration, to defend a claim).

[81] *See* Commission, Proposal on Transitional Arrangements, *supra* note 12, Article 13(2) and (3).

so,[82] the arbitral tribunal in *Eastern Sugar B.V. v. Czech Republic* decided that it could not request a preliminary ruling from the CJEU under Article 267 TFEU, arguing that the Court would reject such a request as inadmissible.[83] In fact, the CJEU has rejected at several occasions requests by commercial arbitration tribunals for a preliminary ruling, arguing that such tribunals were not a "court or tribunal of a Member State" as required by Article 267(2) TFEU.[84] Moreover, it has not been necessary for the Court to accept requests for preliminary rulings by commercial arbitration tribunals to ensure the uniform and effective application of EU law because a domestic court of a Member State called to set aside an arbitral award or was involved in the enforcement of an award which could initiate such a request under Article 267 TFEU in case questions of EU law were involved.

Yet, the CJEU should consider classifying investment treaty tribunals as "courts or tribunals of a Member State" in the sense of Article 267(2) TFEU and not analogize them with commercial arbitration tribunals, as there are significant differences between investment treaty tribunals and commercial arbitration tribunals.[85] This is all the more the case if one considers investment treaties and investment treaty arbitration to pose a greater challenge to the autonomy and unity of EU law, and the EU's ordre public, than commercial arbitration awards. Moreover, the rationale for not allowing requests for preliminary rulings by commercial arbitration tribunals does not hold for investment treaty tribunals. First, unlike commercial arbitration, which constitutes a dispute settlement mechanism involving contractual disputes,[86] investment treaty arbitration is based on the participation of a public authority and involves, to a large extent, disputes under public law, that is, disputes involving review of the legality of the exercise of public power.[87] Functionally, investment treaty tribunals are equivalent to dispute settlement in domestic administrative or constitutional courts, and

---

82 A challenge to the jurisdictional award in Eureko v. Slovak Republic, *supra* note 55, was pending in the Court of Appeals in Frankfurt, Germany, which is the court exercising jurisdiction at the seat of arbitration. The Frankfurt court did not set aside the award, but a preliminary ruling remains possible if the Slovak Republic requests a revision of the judgment before the German Supreme Court (Bundesgerichtshof). *See* Luke E. Peterson, 5(9) INV. ARB. R., May 22, 2012, *available at* http://www.iareporter.com.

83 Eastern Sugar B.V. v. Czech Republic, SCC Case No. 088/2004, Partial Award, March 27. 2007, 130–39.

84 *See* CJEU, Case 102/81, Nordsee Deutsche Hochseefischerei, 1982 ECR 1095, 10–13; Case C-126/97, Eco Swiss, 1999 ECR I-3055, 34; Case C-125/04, Denuit v. Transorient, 2005 ECR I-923, 13.

85 For a similar argument, *see* Miloš Olík & David Fyrbach, *The Competence of Investment Arbitration Tribunals to Seek Preliminary Rulings from European Courts*, 2 CZECH Y.B. INT'L L. 191, 196–202 (2011).

86 This fact constituted one of the arguments for the CJEU to reject requests for preliminary rulings by commercial tribunals. *See, e.g.*, CJEU, Case C-126/97, Eco Swiss, 1999 ECR I-3055, 34 (observing "that an arbitration tribunal constituted pursuant to an agreement between the parties is not a 'court or tribunal of a Member State' within the meaning of Article 177 of the Treaty since the parties are under no obligation, in law or in fact, to refer their disputes to arbitration and the public authorities of the Member State concerned are not involved in the decision to opt for arbitration nor required to intervene of their own accord in the proceedings before the arbitrator").

87 On the public law nature of investment treaty arbitration, *see* Schill, *supra* note 74, at 14–17. On the nature of the state's consent to investment treaty arbitration as a sovereign act, *see* Gus Van Harten, *The Public–Private Distinction in the International Arbitration of Individual Claims against the State*, 56 ICLQ 371, 378–80 (2007).

therefore deal, unlike commercial arbitration, with matters pertaining to the limits to the exercise of public authority.

Second, the CJEU's rationale for rejecting requests for preliminary rulings by a commercial arbitration tribunal is that domestic courts that are competent for reviewing and enforcing arbitration awards can, or are even obliged to, request a preliminary ruling by the CJEU.[88] In investment treaty arbitrations, however, domestic courts are much less involved than in the context of commercial arbitration. Thus, the avenue for questions regarding the interpretation of EU law to come before the CJEU via domestic courts is much narrower than in the commercial arbitration context. In particular in arbitrations against Member States under the ICSID Convention, the domestic courts of that state, or the domestic courts of any other Member State, have no jurisdiction to review whether the investment treaty tribunal observed EU law,[89] and hence cannot request a preliminary ruling from the CJEU. Similarly, in non-ICSID arbitrations the seat of arbitration of an investment treaty tribunal may be outside the territory of the Member States, and enforcement of such an award could equally take place exclusively outside the EU.

Investment treaty tribunals, above all those established under the ICSID Convention, therefore replace domestic courts to a large extent. This does not, however, need to be seen negatively as depriving domestic courts of their jurisdiction, but rather as transferring their function to investment treaty tribunals. Investment treaty arbitration could thus be viewed as simply another form of granting access to justice. It is in this sense, for example, that the European Court of Human Rights has decided that Member States of the European Convention on Human Rights (ECHR) can satisfy the implied guarantee in Article 6(1) ECHR to grant individuals access to courts[90] by providing for recourse to arbitration. From the perspective of Article 6(1) ECHR, in other words, arbitration is equivalent to dispute settlement in a domestic court.[91] In this perspective, consenting to arbitration is a form of affording affected individuals the

---

[88] *See, e.g.*, Case C-126/97, Eco Swiss, 1999 ECR I-3055, 32 (observing that "where questions of Community law are raised in an arbitration resorted to by agreement, the ordinary courts may have to examine those questions, in particular during review of the arbitration award, which may be more or less extensive depending on the circumstances and which they are obliged to carry out in the event of an appeal, for setting aside, for leave to enforce an award or upon any other form of action or review available under the relevant national legislation").

[89] Under the ICSID Convention, the exclusive remedy against an ICSID award is a request for annulment under Article 52 ICSID Convention based on strictly limited, primarily procedural grounds; it is decided by an ad hoc Annulment Committee with members appointed by the Chairman of the ICSID Administrative Council. Domestic courts at the seat of arbitration, therefore, are not entitled to set aside the arbitral award or supervise the arbitral tribunal. Domestic courts in third countries, in turn, are obliged to recognize an ICSID award as binding. *See* Article 54(1) ICSID Convention.

[90] Golder v. United Kingdom, Judgment, February 21, 1975, ECHR Series A No. 18, at 28–36; recently confirmed in Cudak v. Lithuania, Judgment, March 23, 2010, at 54.

[91] Lithgow and Others v. United Kingdom, Judgment, July 8, 1986, ECHR Series A No. 102, 201 (observing that "the word 'tribunal' in Article 6 para. 1 (art. 6-1) is not necessarily to be understood as signifying a court of law of the classic kind, integrated within the standard judicial machinery of the country . . . ; thus, it may comprise a body set up to determine a limited number of specific issues, provided always that it offers the appropriate guarantees."); this argumentation recently has been confirmed in Regent Company v. Ukraine, Judgment, April 3, 2008, 54.

treatment they are entitled to receive under the Convention's substantive obligation, namely to have access to justice.

As a consequence, as the opportunity for courts of a Member State to submit a request for a preliminary ruling to the CJEU is significantly reduced in the investment treaty context, that right should be transferred to investment treaty tribunals together with the function to exercise judicial review and to provide access to justice.[92] This is another reason why the CJEU should not treat investment treaty arbitrations as commercial arbitrations, and accordingly view investment treaty tribunals as a "court or tribunal of a Member State" in the sense of Article 267 TFEU. In addition, the CJEU should not treat investment treaty tribunals differently from other international dispute settlement mechanisms set up by Member States, such as the Benelux Court,[93] or other courts established by other international treaties, to which Member States and third states are parties, and that the Court has found to be empowered to request preliminary rulings.[94]

V. Conclusion

The present chapter has examined the impact of the EU's new competence in matters of foreign direct investment in Article 207 TFEU on arbitrations under international investment treaties, both in regard of future EU treaties as well as existing treaties of the Member States. It addressed the questions of party status, representation of the state party, and the basis of cooperation between Member States and the EU.

In respect of future EU treaties, this chapter has highlighted that investor–state arbitration remains a desirable mode of dispute settlement, but that it needs to be set up in a way so that the autonomy of EU law, both as regards substantive law and dispute settlement procedure, is not affected. This requires that investment treaty tribunals remain sufficiently separate from the EU legal order and respect the CJEU's interpretative monopoly for questions of EU law. The CJEU, in turn, should limit its own role to deciding on EU-law-related questions and should exercise restraint in interfering with the dispute settlement activity of investment treaty tribunals. In any event, the CJEU's existing case law on the limits that EU law sets on international dispute settlement appears sufficiently flexible in permitting investor–state arbitration under future EU investment treaties provided applicable law, available remedies, and mechanisms of cooperation between investor–state dispute settlement bodies and the CJEU are structured in a way to ensure that the CJEU's exclusive jurisdiction in dealing with matters of EU law remains untouched.

Remaining conflicts between the CJEU and investment treaty tribunals should be resolved based on the principle of cooperation. As a practical matter, the institutional setup of investor–state arbitration under future EU investment treaties should draw

92 See above text accompanying notes 88–89.

93 CJEU, Case C-337/95, Dior v. Evora, 1997 ECR I-6013, 21.

94 CJEU, Opinion 1/91, Economic Area Agreement I, 1991 ECR I-6079, 59.

on how existing models in other international treaty regimes structure the relationship between Member States and the EU as well as the relations between the CJEU and other international dispute settlement bodies. In addition, the Commission's proposal on a regulation dealing with financial responsibility and procedural status of the Union and the Member States constitutes a further step toward stressing the importance of cooperation between Union and Member States in resolving investor–state disputes.

Furthermore, both in respect of future and existing investment treaties, it is necessary to distinguish between the internal relationship between the EU and its Member States and the external dimension, that is the relations vis-à-vis third states and their investors. While the former is the genuine domain of EU law, the latter is the domain of international law and international dispute resolution. Thus, according to the principles governing international dispute resolution, party status depends on consent. Issues concerning the distribution of competences between Member States and the EU, by contrast, should have no bearing on the rights and obligations and the procedural options of third states and their investors. As regards existing investment treaties, this means that Member States will continue to be party to investor–state arbitrations under their investment treaties and accordingly have to respond to claims by foreign investors. Likewise, this chapter has argued that the new competence of the EU does not affect the right of Member States to represent themselves in arbitration proceedings brought against them.

As a matter of EU law, however, Member States are under an obligation under Article 4(3) TEU to cooperate with the Union, in particular the Commission, in the defense of claims brought by foreign investors under an investment treaty, because such claims can affect the EU's new competence and the uniform application of EU law. Under the principle of sincere cooperation in Article 4(3) TEU, a Member State is therefore required to inform, to coordinate, and to cooperate with the Commission regarding investor–state arbitrations. Conversely, in case the Union will in the future participate as a party in investor–state arbitrations, it is under a duty to cooperate with Member States, in case their interests are affected by the proceedings. As a constitutional principle of the Union, the principle of sincere cooperation provides a fertile basis for the effective cooperation between the Union and its Member States in participating in investor–state arbitrations under present and future investment treaties and rightly features prominently in the Commission's proposal for a regulation dealing with financial responsibility and procedural status in investor–state arbitrations under future EU investment treaties.

14

INVESTORS' RIGHTS, LEGAL CONCEPTS, AND PUBLIC POLICY IN THE NAFTA CONTEXT

*Nicola W. Ranieri**

Introduction

With only a few hiccups, globalization is compelling the world toward a more interconnected existence.[1] In this context, countries have become more amenable to abandoning traditional notions of sovereignty to participate in bigger and more intricate international economic agreements.[2] This paradigm shift has propelled the debate over the benefits of trade agreements beyond the rudimentary arguments of jobs and living standards, reaching into fundamental issues of democratic principles, public regulation,

* The author is indebted to James Holbein and Dara Denson for their comments and insights.

1 There has been a proliferation of interconnected international economic agreements. However, this process is occasionally and temporarily halted by "sovereignty backlash" concerns as was evidenced by earlier European refusals to endorse the European Union Constitution.

2 There are presently several hundred free trade agreements (FTAs). *See* the WTO Regional Trade information at www.wto.org. The NAFTA partners are working on deeper integration within North America through the Security and Prosperity Partnership Initiative, which covers agreements on continental-wide standards dealing with consumer products, management of industries, law enforcement, and security agencies. Also, Mexico went from a model of import substitution and self-sufficiency to signing more than fourteen FTAs, involving over thirty countries, since 1994. These FTAs include NAFTA (1994), Colombia and Venezuela (1995), Costa Rica (1995), Bolivia (1995), Nicaragua (1998), Chile (1999), EU (2000), Israel (2000), El Salvador, Guatemala and Honduras (2001), EFTA (2001), Uruguay (2004), Japan (2005). Mexico is also in negotiations with Trinidad and Tobago, Mercosur, and Singapore. The Mexican FTAs are accessible at the Web site of the NAFTA Secretariat-Mexican Section, www.nafta-sec-alena.org.

and sovereignty. At the heart of the debate, strongly felt notions about the expansion of international commerce contend with an array of noneconomic concerns.[3]

A direct consequence of concluding more expansive trade agreements has been the obfuscation of foreign and domestic policy. The international commitments taken on by governments inevitably affect the relationship between the state and the citizen.[4] It has been noted that "as issues affecting the lives of citizens increasingly evolve outside the domestic sphere, non-state actors' control over their lives diminishes proportionally."[5] The divide between what is ruled by sovereign dominion and that which is subject to international agreement is increasingly at the center of debate.

Frustration with sovereign control, or the lack thereof, of the processes that affect the everyday lives of civil society has led many to question the legitimacy of the infrastructure on which global governance is based. That is, although civil society, in general, remains reluctant to concede the legality of the framework for global governance through the global institutions, certain groups within the movement have turned to question the legitimacy of that legal framework. As global institutions evolve, they have come to recognize the importance of citizen participation and have incorporated some forms of citizen participation in their processes. However, the reaction to this attempted democratization of global institutions has been disappointing. On the one side, citizen groups have argued that the measures undertaken to date do not go far enough. On the other side, many sovereign entities have begun questioning the legitimacy of these institutions to embrace such fundamental change without the consensus of their constituent members. The cultures and legal traditions of many countries may not value, and in fact have come to resent, the participation of citizens in what they deem to be exclusively a sovereign function.

Civil society has responded to this modern challenge by demanding a more vocal participation in global governance. Civil society activism is not by any means a recent phenomenon.[6] From the beginning of the twentieth century, individuals have been entitled to bring direct claims for the infringements of their rights, especially as they relate to property ownership, before international tribunals.[7] As international law evolved after World War II, the traditional approach, in limiting access to international

---

[3] *See* M. Sornarajah, The Clash of Globalizations and the International Law of Foreign Investment (Lecture at the Norman Paterson School of International Affairs) (Sept. 12, 2002) (on file at the Centre for Trade Law and Policy, Carleton University, Ottawa).

[4] Criticisms have arisen from opponents to recent trade agreements, that governments, at times, conclude such trade agreements as justification not to respond to their citizens' concerns.

[5] *See* Noemi Gal-Or, *Private Party Access: A Comparison of the NAFTA and the EU Disciplines*, 21 B.C. INT'L & COMP. L. REV. 1, 2 (1998), arguing that the resulting scenario from this democratic deficit is that economics might trump the functioning of representative democratic institutions, and that access to justice is varied among the citizenry of different countries even though they are all bound by the same treaty.

[6] The GATT negotiations saw the International Chamber of Commerce voice its displeasure of the lack of consultations with nongovernmental organizations, and the World Federation of Trade objected to the prevalence of neoliberalism in the draft texts.

[7] Gal-Or, *supra* note 5.

legal remedies to state actors, began to be replaced by the recognition that individuals had a necessary role to play. Particularly important in this process was the growth of the international human rights movement (e.g., the Nuremberg trials and recent war crimes tribunals). Over time, commentators came to see the separation between human rights and the rights of private parties in other contexts, such as trade, as artificial.[8]

More recently, the 1990s saw the galvanization of these forces at United Nations World Conferences. Today, the issue is no longer whether, but how, civil society will participate in global governance.[9] In this context, the right of citizens to bring an action and have standing (*locus standi*) to assert interests has become increasingly significant. The right of private parties to assert their rights and interests is relevant in two related, but different contexts: state-to-state adjudication and private party versus state adjudication.

The 1990s also bore witness to a newer phenomenon, the race to attract foreign direct investment (FDI). Developing countries came to rely on FDI as a means to develop while developed countries saw FDI as another lucrative export. Proponents of free trade agreements argue that given the interdependence of trade and investment flows, the development of investment safeguards is essential to providing a stable and predictable investment environment. They believe in a system that values private property and that fosters investment, free from political discrimination and judicial complacency. Investment provisions are contained in comprehensive trade agreements or in more limited stand-alone Bilateral Investment Treaties (BITs) containing provisions aimed at facilitating the flow of investments between countries and creating standard investor protection provisions.

An emboldened civil society collided with the world's insatiable need for FDI in the latter part of the 1990s. The proponents of globalization saw the need for a multilateral investment agreement, which would provide predictable and transparent investment rules in a world increasingly competing for FDI. The energized civil society groups actively sought to restrain the development of a multilateral investment regime that they saw as being corporate-driven and repugnant to the notions of sovereignty. This battle came to a head in 1998 when the Multilateral Agreement on Investment failed to materialize at the Organization for Economic Cooperation and Development (OECD).[10] Although this debate is continuing under the auspices of the World Trade Organization (WTO), recent rounds of multilateral negotiations have provided faint hope for progress.[11]

---

[8] *Id.* at 2.

[9] *See* The Future of the WTO: Addressing Institutional Challenges in the New Millennium, Report by the Consultative Board to the Director—General Supachai Panitchpakdi, 2004, at 41.

[10] *See* Katie Tieleman, *The Failure of the Multilateral Agreement on Investment and the Absence of a Global Public Policy Network* (2000), *available at* http://www.gppi.net.

[11] Doha Ministerial declaration, Fourth Ministerial Conference in Doha, Qatar, ¶¶ 20–22 (Nov. 2001), *available at* http://www.wto.org.

NAFTA and Chapter 11 on Investment

The result of this failed attempt to establish a multilateral agreement on investment has been a patchwork of bilateral investment agreements and regional agreements. In this light, the investment protection provisions found in Chapter 11 of the North American Free Trade Agreement (NAFTA)[12] came to be looked upon as a model or prototype for evolving investment protocols. However, although earlier agreements tracked NAFTA investment provisions, more recent agreements appear to be trying to cut back on many of the investor safeguards contained in NAFTA.[13]

The recently ratified U.S. FTAs with Panama, Peru, and Korea all contain a Chapter 11–type mechanism, but each has specific annexes to deal with special issues presented by each agreement. In addition, the Parties have included interpretative annexes that purport to address the problematic interpretative issues that have arisen in this chapter.[14]

The challenges faced by global institutions have affected NAFTA rules and their interpretation. Reduced to its most basic of terms, the NAFTA is an attempt to create more benefits for its constituent members by more efficiently allocating resources. It may be likened to the process of creating a larger pie from which its members may draw larger pieces. The NAFTA was negotiated in the context of the WTO and other global negotiations. Thus although progress in one arena necessarily encouraged progress in the other, problems that evolved in one arena necessarily percolated into the other.

NAFTA's Chapter 11 permits investors to sue host governments for property expropriated without fair compensation. Chapter 11 has become the focal point for the free trade debate in general and the evolution of investor protection protocols. Chapter 11 has become both the lightning rod for antiglobalization critics as well as the beacon of light for internationalists. Initially, Chapter 11 remained a relatively unknown NAFTA add-on. The Canada–U.S. Free Trade Agreement (CUSFTA) already had an investment chapter, and BITs contained investment protection clauses. For years, while Chapter 11 operated under the radar screen, internationalists hailed it as the future investment prototype or model and called for its insertion in the Free Trade Agreement of the Americas (FTAA). They see Chapter 11 as the logical extension of BITs and as a model to be developed and projected into other multilateral agreements, such as the

---

[12] Ca.-Mex.-U.S., 32 I.L.M. 289 (NAFTA). Available online at the NAFTA Secretariat Web site, www.nafta-sec-alena.org.

[13] Earlier agreements that appeared to track the NAFTA include: the Canada–Chile FTA, concluded Dec. 5, 1996, *reprinted in* 36 I.L.M. 1067, 1114 (1997) and the Mexico–Northern Triangle FTA. *See* Guillermo Pereira, *Mexico–Northern Triangle Free Trade Agreement*, 7 L. & BUS. REV. AM. 383 (2001). However, more recent agreements, based on the 2002 Trade Promotions Act, such as the U.S.–Central American Free Trade Agreement (CAFTA), appear to cut back on some of the NAFTA safeguards.

[14] Annex 11-B Expropriation, U.S.–Korea Free Trade Agreement, approved by Congress Oct. 12, 2011, available online at www.ustr.gov/trade-agreements/free-trade-agreements/korus-fta. Similar definitional annexes are found in the U.S.–Panama FTA and U.S.–Peru FTA.

Trans-Pacific Partnership (TPP).[15] Internationalists point to the TPP[16] as the next logical repository for these safeguards.

According to the outline provided by USTR on its public Web site, the TPP will include a Chapter 11–type mechanism:

> Investment. The investment text will provide substantive legal protections for investors and investments of each TPP country in the other TPP countries, including ongoing negotiations on provisions to ensure non-discrimination, a minimum standard of treatment, rules on expropriation, and prohibitions on specified performance requirements that distort trade and investment. **The investment text will include provisions for expeditious, fair, and transparent investor–State dispute settlement subject to appropriate safeguards, with discussions continuing on scope and coverage. The investment text will protect the rights of the TPP countries to regulate in the public interest.** (emphasis added)[17]

Proponents of Chapter 11 argue that it establishes a valid mechanism for balancing the rights of investors with those of the state, representing, at least nominally, the public interest. They stress that NAFTA does not call for the repeal of regulation.[18] They maintain that NAFTA distinguishes between legitimate and illegitimate regulations and sets out a time-tested arbitral mechanism to determine compensation for expropriation where governmental regulation is unjustified.

It was not until Chapter 11 questioned regulatory measures in the United States and Canada that commentators began to question its scope. Contrary to the intent of the U.S. and Canadian NAFTA negotiators, their respective governments appear to be bearing the brunt of the claims from dissatisfied nationals of each other's countries complaining about regulation that has the effect of expropriation. Chapter 11 evolved beyond a shield for U.S. and Canadian interests against Mexico's history of

---

15 Negotiations on the Multilateral Agreement on Investment (MAI), under the auspices of the Organization for Economic Cooperation and Development, failed in 1998, in large part due to effective public criticism. For an overview of the MAI and its implications on sovereignty and the federal–state balance of powers, See Robert Stumberg, *Sovereignty by Subtraction: The Multilateral Agreement on Investment*, 31 CORNELL INT'L L.J. 491 (1998). *See generally* MAI Negotiating Text (Apr. 24, 1998) *available at* http://www.oecd.org/daf/cmis/mai/maitext.pdf.

16 The FTAA contemplated a hemispheric wide trade agreement among thirty-four countries in the Americas. The draft FTAA text may be consulted at http: //www.ftaa.alca.org. The negotiations have been stalled while the governments in the region negotiate the Doha round multilateral agenda, which is also deadlocked on several issues, including agriculture and the appropriate role and obligations for developing countries.

17 http://www.ustr.gov/about-us/press-office/fact-sheets/2011/november/outlines-trans-pacific-partnership-agreement.

18 NAFTA Chapter 9, concerning technical barriers to trade or standards, confirms the rights of government to set a level of protection based on assessment of risk.

confiscation.[19] Chapter 11 could now be used as a sword to cut against governmental regulation in developed countries.

NAFTA was the first international agreement that led to expropriation claims being filed by foreigners directly against the United States. The Methanex case represents the first time that a U.S. regulatory measure was challenged by a foreigner investor for resulting in an expropriation.[20] This should not come as a surprise because NAFTA also represents the first time in recent history that the United States signed an investor-protection protocol with a developed country.

Prior to NAFTA, BITs were generally concluded between developed and developing countries. The United States and Canada, capital-exporting countries, always sought expansive investor protection to protect their nationals from the confiscatory practices of foreign governments. However, as NAFTA included Canada and the United States, both highly developed countries, these countries were put in the novel situation of being simultaneously both the capital-exporting and the capital-importing ones. As such, NAFTA was the first time that an agreement protected the investors of these countries while simultaneously circumscribing their government's behavior as it impacted on investors of the other country. In this light, it is perhaps not so surprising that these developed countries have borne the brunt of litigation from their respective nationals. For example, the United States is presently involved in litigation brought by foreign investors, all Canadian, complaining about environmental regulation.[21]

The price of the benefit of investor protection abroad is the cost inherent in ensuring that foreign investors receive the same treatment at home. Perhaps, not so unexpectedly, Canadian and U.S. investors continue to demand the investor protections afforded them under the agreement while their governments express outrage at having these safeguards used as the basis for a claim over regulatory measures. Clearly, this controversy emanates from a double standard[22] as well as familiarity of Canadian and U.S. investors benefiting from investment safeguards accruing to capital-exporting countries and their unfamiliarity with fulfilling the obligations of capital-importing nations.[23]

---

[19] The nationalization of the Mexican oil industry is perhaps the most notorious Mexican expropriation. However, there have also been other more subtle expropriations related to bouts of peso devaluations. *See* Callejo v. Bancomer, 764 F.2d 1101 (5th Cir.) (1985) (Mexican banks imposing foreign exchange controls amounting to partial loss of investment for U.S. nationals pursuant to law, and the hurdles posed by the Act of State Doctrine and the Foreign Sovereigns Immunities Act for American investors seeking recovery in U.S. courts for acts committed abroad by foreign sovereigns).

[20] Methanex Corporation and the United States of America, Statement of Claim, dated Dec. 3, 1999, *available at* http://www.naftalaw.org.

[21] Given the confidentiality of the arbitral proceedings to date, it is possible that there may be other cases pending that are not yet public. For a comprehensive compilation of the materials that are currently available, see http://www.naftalaw.org, edited by Todd Weiler.

[22] *See* Guillermo Alvarez & William Park, *The New Face of Investment Arbitration: NAFTA Chapter 11*, 28 Yale J. Int'l L. 365, 368–69 (2003) (noting the evolving U.S. double standard toward arbitration whereby arbitration is good when it corrects the misbehavior of foreign governments but bad when claims are filed for the alleged wrongdoing of the United States.)

[23] *See* Charles Brower, *NAFTA Chapter 11: Who Then Should Judge? Developing the International Rule of Law under NAFTA Chapter 11*, 2 Chi. J. Int'l L. 193, 194–95 (noting that some of the distress felt by U.S. and

Chapter 11 critics, while still hesitant to acknowledge its legality, have found fertile ground in questioning its legitimacy. To these detractors, Chapter 11 is symbolic of an illegitimate multinational conspiracy that attempts to elevate corporate interests over those of the general public. They argue that it goes far beyond its original mandate of protecting investors from arbitrary governmental expropriation. Critics fear that Chapter 11 will be used to promote a corporate agenda at the expense of democratic and constitutional principles. In allowing investors to sidestep local courts, constitutional guarantees and legitimate public regulation will be avoided by international panels established to protect the rights of investors.

Detractors argue that Chapter 11 will put a "chill" on public regulation in the areas of health and safety. They contend that Chapter 11's focus on protecting the rights of investors will provide compensation for regulatory takings that would not be compensable under local law or even international law. Critics reason that by broadly circumscribing expropriation, in terms of otherwise valid governmental regulation, Chapter 11 effectively permits multinational corporations to manipulate their corporate personalities to evade the legitimate regulation that binds their domestic counterparts. With the aid of Chapter 11, a NAFTA investor can either evade the regulation that controls a domestic company or force the government to underwrite its business interest in a fashion that is not available to local business. Critics fear that as a result of this perceived handicap, local corporate entities will join in the race to the bottom by seeking modification to local law so as not to be disadvantaged vis-à-vis their foreign competitors.

Chapter 11 has raised issues concerning the rights and obligations of the different levels of government to regulate in the public interest. Chapter 11 may violate fundamental principles of state sovereignty, federalism, core governmental functions, and constitutional safeguards by compensating investors when governments exercise their regulatory powers. These concerns are premised on the potentially broad investment protections found in the NAFTA as well as the private nature of investor dispute mechanisms.

Resolution of disputes that may affect public health and safety in the confines of traditional commercial arbitration, free from the pressures of public scrutiny, has sharpened tensions. Moreover, concern has been heightened by the fact that these private arbitral panels will adjudicate the potentially competing interests of investors and the public by reference to developing environmental law, which continues to struggle with the level of scientific proof necessary to justify governmental regulation in the public interest.

Canadian governments over Chapter 11 was caused by the novel and disconcerting fact of having to live up to the same substantive and procedural guarantees required from the BITs partners). *See also* Dana Krueger, *The Combat Zone:* Mondev International, LTD. v. United States *and the Backlash against Chapter 11*, 21 B.U. INT'L L.J. 399 (suggesting that the Chapter 11 controversy is arguably attributable to U.S. unfamiliarity with fulfilling the obligations of a capital-importing nation).

Chapter 11 has an incendiary history. It has spawned sensational lawsuits, claiming billions of dollars in damages, against NAFTA governments for failure to respect the investment rights of foreign nationals in sensitive regulatory areas, traditionally thought to be beyond the purview of litigation. The sensationalism has been heightened by the fact that many of these suits resulted from environmental regulation and were threatened to be litigated without public input. The flames were further fanned by the initial actions of some governments to conceal the existence of these suits, allegedly for reasons relating to political expediency and litigation tactics.

The resulting public pressure quickly attracted political concern.[24] Congress was particularly troubled by the way this litigation came to the forefront. Sensitive environmental litigation, replete with public policy concerns holding potentially hundreds of millions of tax revenue dollars in the balance, was revealed only indirectly through Securities and Exchange Commission disclosure filings. They expressed reservations about expanding this type of investor protection to other fora until more is known about its potential impact. Congress concluded that the USTR should enter into negotiations with its NAFTA partners to clarify definitions of expropriation, fair and equitable treatment, and national treatment, as well as to ensure greater disclosure and consultation for pending NAFTA cases.

These concerns continue to be timely, given ongoing American bilateral, regional, and multilateral negotiations. Moreover, the failed multilateral investment agreement, initially negotiated under the auspices of the OECD, continues to languish at the WTO.[25] The conclusion of these agreements could increase exponentially the pool of private investors willing and able to sue governments over otherwise legitimate regulation.

Much has passed in the years since the members of Congress raised their concerns.[26] However, notwithstanding these concerns and the scholarly treatment that they have received throughout the NAFTA region, Chapter 11 continues to provide both its proponents and detractors with sufficient grist to solidify their positions.[27] Chapter 11

---

[24] On August 6, 1996, five members of Congress wrote to Ambassador Charlene Barshefsky, then–U.S. Trade Representative (USTR), expressing concern about the manner in which Chapter 11 was being used by Methanex to challenge environmental regulations. These congressional members echoed public sentiments raising the following concern:

> ... [we didn't] think anyone believed that the expropriation protections in the NAFTA would be used to challenge environmental regulations in the way Methanex has ... (Letter of members of Congress Miller, Waxman, Pelosi, Starck and Dixon to USTR, dated August 6,1999).

[25] *See* Tieleman, *supra* note 10.

[26] In particular, negotiators will seek to ensure that standards for expropriation and compensation will be consistent with U.S. legal principles and practice. In the recently negotiated FTAs between Chile and Singapore, indirect expropriation provisions are included that reflect U.S. Supreme Court Decisions (*see* Celine Levesque, *Distinguishing Expropriation and Regulation under NAFTA Chapter 11: Making Explicit the Link to Property*, THE FIRST DECADE OF NAFTA: THE FUTURE OF FREE TRADE IN NORTH AMERICA 323 n.173, 174 (Kevin Kennedy ed., 2004).

[27] Canadian contributions include articles from WHOSE RIGHTS?: THE NAFTA CHAPTER 11 DEBATE (Laura Ritchie Dawson ed., 2002): Christopher Wilkie, *The Origins of the NAFTA Investment Provisions: Economic Policy and Considerations*; J. Anthony Van Duzer, *NAFTA Chapter 11 to Date: The Progress of a Work in*

tribunals have had the opportunity to adjudicate claims made against the three NAFTA governments.[28] As a result, decisions have been judicially reviewed,[29] an interpretive note has been delivered by the Free Trade Commission,[30] U.S. and Canadian BITs have been amended,[31] FTAs have been negotiated,[32] international agreements have been negotiated,[33] and Congress has passed reactive legislation.[34]

Interestingly, recent developments have all but the staunchest internationalists questioning the legitimacy of Chapter 11. Many Chapter 11 parties decried the illegitimacy of the process when NAFTA parties appeared to direct the result of the

---

Progress; Michael M. Hart & William A. Dymond, *NAFTA Chapter 11: Precedents, Principles and Prospects;* Maureen Appel Molot, *NAFTA Chapter 11: An Evolving Regime*. U.S. contributions include David Gantz, *Potential Conflicts between Investor Rights and Environmental Regulation under NAFTA Chapter 11*, 33 GEO. WASH. INT'L L. REV. 651 (2001); Frederick Abbott, *The Political Economy of NAFTA Chapter Eleven: Equality before the Law and the Boundaries of North American Integration*, 23 HASTINGS INT'L & COMPAR. REV. 303 (2000). Mexican contributions include Maximo Romero Jimenez, *Considerations of NAFTA Chapter 11*, 2 CHI. J. INT'L L. 243 (2001).

28 *See* Metalclad Corp. v. United Mexican States, Final Award, NAFTA/ICSID(AF) Tribunal, Case No. Arb(AF)/97/1, Aug.30, 2000, 40 I.L.M. 36 (2001) [hereinafter *Metalclad*]; Marvin Feldman v. Mexico, ICSID Case No. ARB(AF)/99/1, at 70 (Dec. 16, 2002), at ICSID, http://www.worldbank.org/icsid/cases/feldman_mexico-award-en.PDF [hereinafter *Feldman*]; Pope & Talbot, Inc. v Canada, NAFTA/UNCITRAL Tribunal, Final Merits Awards, Apr. 10, 2001, *available at* http://www.naftalaw.org [hereinafter *Pope*]; S.D. Myers Inc. v. Canada, NAFTA/UNCITRAL Tribunal, Oct. 21, 2002, *available at* http://www.naftalaw.org [hereinafter *S.D. Myers*].

29 *See Metalclad, Feldman, supra* note 28.

30 Free Trade Commission Interpretive Note, July 31, 2001, *available at* http:www.dfait-maeci.gc.ca/tna-nac/nafta_commission-en.asp.

31 2004 U.S. Model of Bilateral Investment Treat, *available at* http://www.state.gov/documents/organizations/29030.doc; http:www.state.gov/e/eb/rls//prsrl/2004/28923.htm. Updated Canada's model Foreign Investment Promotion and Protection Agreement (FIPA), *available at* http://dfait-maeci.gc.ca/tna-nac/what_fipa-en.asp.

32 More recent American FTAs include: U.S.–Australia FTA signed Mar. 1, 2004 [Annex11-B]; U.S.–Chile FTA signed June 6, 2003 (Annex 10-D); U.S.–Central American Free Trade Agreement (CAFTA) signed Jan. 28, 2004 (Annex 10 C) (the countries are Costa Rica, El Salvador, Guatemala, Honduras, Nicaragua, and Dominican Republic; U.S.–Morocco FTA signed June 15, 2004 (Annex 10-B); Korea–U.S. (KORUS) FTA (2011); U.S.–Peru FTA (2011); and U.S.–Panama FTA (2011).

33 For example, multilateral investment negotiations have been carried out under the auspices of the WTO Doha round. However, little progress has been realized. *See* Doha Ministerial Declaration, Fourth Ministerial Conference in Doha, Qatar, ¶¶ 20–22.(Nov. 2001), *available at* http: //www.wto.org.

34 19 U.S.C. § 3802(b)(3) (West 2003). Trade Act of 2002-Bipartisan Trade Promotion Authority (requires that U.S. trade agreements ensure that foreign investors do not get greater protection than U.S. property owners, and also requires the application of U.S. principles and practices concerning regulatory takings.)

> Recognizing that US law on the whole provides a high level of protection for investment, consistent with or greater than the level required by international law, the principle negotiating objective of the US regarding foreign investment are to reduce or eliminate artificial trade distorting barriers to foreign investment, while ensuring that foreign investors in the US are not accorded greater substantive rights with respect to investment protections than US investors in the US, and to secure for investors rights comparable to those that would be available under US legal principles and practice, by ... (D) seeking to establish standards for expropriation and compensation for expropriation, consistent with US legal principles and practice (Baucas-Grassely amendment—see Been and Beauvais).

Metalcald, *Methenex*, and *Feldman* cases through the interpretive notes of the Free Trade Commission. Some of the NAFTA parties have openly questioned the legitimacy of the Chapter 11 process in judicial proceedings at the municipal level, opening the door to conflict-of-interest allegations. Even Chapter 11 tribunals themselves have come to question the legitimacy of the process in the face of interpretive notes that have the effect of circumscribing their powers. The confluence of this criticism does not bode well for Chapter 11 at this critical juncture when it will either develop so as to adapt to new and larger agreements or atrophy from nonuse into a tried, but failed relic of the twentieth century.

Regulation is increasingly pervasive in modern society. The clash inherent in the interaction between traditional expropriation notions and the issues arising under Chapter 11 concepts of indirect expropriation, or actions tantamount to expropriation, has exposed an antiquated vocabulary. Scientific uncertainty, evaluation of risks, and the precautionary principle are concepts that do not easily fit in the classic expropriation analysis. Commentators have come to question which international law principles should guide the evaluation of the sovereign's conduct.[35]

This chapter will focus on NAFTA Chapter 11, arguing that its continued evolution as a cutting-edge dispute resolution mechanism to deal with private rights and public issues requires attention. Rather than discarding the mechanism entirely, the NAFTA Parties should focus on ameliorating its more controversial aspects. In this light, it is proposed that the Parties permit Chapter 11 jurisprudence to evolve and consider fine-tuning some of its procedural aspects, especially as they relate to permitting greater public access to its processes.

Section I of this chapter will explore the legitimacy crisis that now threatens the evolution of Chapter 11. Section II will propose a three-step test aimed at enabling tribunals to more accurately distinguish regulation from expropriation by identifying and balancing all the relevant interests. This test focuses on the relationship among expropriation, the police powers principle, and evolving property concepts.

This chapter will argue that although the NAFTA should be applauded for breaking new ground in promoting private party participation in proceedings involving public issues, it needs to evolve if it is to provide the framework for future more intricate trade agreements presently contemplated by the NAFTA Parties. This evolution will require both substantive and procedural changes. Chapter 11 jurisprudence must develop in a fashion to facilitate the perceived substantive conflicts between regulation and expropriation. Party intervention will also be required to bring about the procedural modifications necessary to ensure more effective public participation.

[35] Levesque, *supra* note 26, at 309, citing G.C. Christie, *What Constitutes a Taking of Property in International Law?* 38 BRIT. Y.B. INT'L L. 307, 338 (1962).

Section I: Legitimacy Crisis

Legitimacy, an open-ended concept in legal discourse, is highly dependent on subjective expectations and specific legal traditions.[36] Although usually defined in terms of a counter distinction to legality, it is often aimed more at undermining political will than at undermining the legality of the institution at issue. That is, although ideally legitimacy and legality coincide, neither is necessarily a precondition for the other. Legal commentators have noted that legitimacy is a form of legal discourse, often arising after legality is conceded.[37] In this sense, Chapter 11 critics seek to destabilize the political foundation upon which Chapter 11 is built.

It is trite to say that international legal regimes depend on perceptions of legitimacy. Perceptions of legitimacy are the glue that binds the political resolve of states and others into voluntary compliance with rules and decisions of institutions. Conversely, the failure of institutions to be perceived as legitimate can be the lightning rod that congeals criticism into contempt for institutions. Perceptions of legitimacy are founded on predictability, conformity with historical practice, and shared fundamental values within the community.[38]

Predictability of operation is the cornerstone underpinning the legitimate operation of legal institutions. The lack of predictable operation engenders claims of arbitrariness and unfairness that undermine the legitimacy of the institution. Predictability is, to a great extent, dependent on textual clarity and coherence of rules. However, the complexities of international relations and the dynamics of negotiations often lead to drafting a text that is less-than-clear in all essential facets. To this extent, Chapter 11's use of language that some have argued is textually indeterminate was bound to raise concerns.[39]

Legitimacy concerns brought on by a lack of textual clarity might be overcome by historical practice and shared values. These elements may serve to enhance the legitimacy of institutions by reinforcing predictability and by incorporating them into the temporal and ideological structure of the regulated community.[40] Historical practice provides a sense of continuity that enhances legitimacy through the use of name recognition and compliance with predictable patterns. The incorporation of shared values enhances legitimacy by increasing the likelihood that institutions will operate

---

[36] *See* Thomas M. Frank, *Legitimacy in the International System*, 82 AM. J. INT'L L. 705 (1988) (analyzing the concept of legitimacy in international law). Charles H. Brower, II, *Structure, Legitimacy and NAFTA's Investment Chapter*, 36 VAND. J. TRANSNAT'L L. 37 (2003) (applying Frank's legitimacy analysis to Chapter 11); Jeffery Atik, *Legitimacy, Transparency and NGO Participation in the NAFTAS Chapter 11 Process, in* NAFTA INVESTMENT LAW AND ARBITRATION: PAST ISSUES, CURRENT PRACTICE, FUTURE PROSPECTS (Todd Weiler ed., 2004) (exploring questions of legitimacy from the perspective of the legal traditions of the NAFTA Parties).

[37] Atik, *supra* note 36, at 137.

[38] *See* Brower, *supra* note 36, at 51–58.

[39] *Id.* at 59–63 (discussing Chapter 11's lack of textual clarity).

[40] *Id.* at 53–55.

predictably, and harmonizes the ideologies of the community and the institution. The use of accountable and transparent institutions that benefit from democratic participation is likely to be seen as more legitimate and as more likely to increase voluntary compliance.[41]

Claims of illegitimacy regarding Chapter 11, no longer exclusively the anarchist's battle cry, presently resound from all corners. In fact, antiglobalists, the NAFTA Parties, Chapter 11 participants, and Chapter 11 tribunals have all questioned the legitimacy of Chapter 11.

A. CRITICS: ANTIGLOBALISTS

Antiglobalists criticize Chapter 11 for being part of a corporate agenda aimed at elevating profits over the public interest through the creation of institutions that operate beyond domestic regulation. In this sense, Chapter 11 is seen as a business-friendly tool that stifles government regulation. This view holds that the NAFTA governments have knowingly ceded sovereignty to unaccountable secret panels because this then excuses the government from making politically unpopular decisions consistent with their international obligations.

Opponents allege that it transforms domestic issues into international agendas. Chapter 11 permits private individuals to bring actions against governments who regulate in the public interest. That is, Chapter 11 permits private individuals to sue governments on their international commitments, even if the regulation in question is one traditionally thought to be in the domestic domain, such as health and safety regulations. Exacerbating concerns is the fact that these public issues are then litigated through a private commercial arbitration process.

These critics argue that governments have lost control of the process. Governments do not appoint all the arbitrators and lack the mechanism by which to hold them accountable. Governments do not have a vetted list of arbitrators, as is the case in NAFTA Chapters 19 and 20. Moreover, although judges may have a broader public orientation, arbitrators chosen by the parties may not labor under such an orientation, and their mandate extends no further than the specific arbitration at hand.

Although these critics may acknowledge that Chapter 11 cannot force the repeal of regulations, they contend that it nonetheless results in a process that hinders the development of public regulation. They contend that, as a practical matter, forcing governments to pay for such regulation impedes the development and maintenance of such regulation.[42] Detractors allege that this has a "chilling effect" on public regulation as legislators, weary of litigation, hesitate to enact regulation that they might otherwise support.

These critics also decry uncertain judicial review. They contend that the commercial arbitration orientation of Chapter 11 narrows the judicial review available. As

---

41 *Id.*

42 *See S.D. Myers, supra* note 28.

Chapter 11 does not contain an appeal process, national courts have only limited ability to correct tribunal error. This shortcoming is compounded by lack of clarity relating to the relationship between courts and tribunals and their respective powers and jurisdiction.

Problems persist in the perception that foreign investors may receive compensation where locals are left without remedy. This perception creates issues of unjust enrichment and a belief that it creates a "race to the bottom" as locals seek legislative modification to level the playing field.[43] Chapter 11 awards are limited to the particular parties and facts before the tribunal. As such, local investors who lack recourse before the national courts and do not have standing before Chapter 11 tribunals would not benefit from a Chapter 11 finding that the regulations are compensable. Local investors are therefore limited to seeking legislative redress. Moreover, given that Chapter 11 tribunals are limited to looking at the interests of the parties before them, they may not seek to balance the offending regulation with the societal benefit.

Chapter 11 further exacerbates complicated questions of federalism. Given that the NAFTA regime holds the federal government responsible for the wrongs of other levels of government, the awkward situation arises where the federal government is the payer in areas where it might not have jurisdiction. This situation further exacerbates the NIMBY-type problems. For example, a municipal regulation prohibiting MTBE in a locality in California eventually led to the *Methanex* case. Another example is the municipal and state actions in Mexico that resulted in the *Metalclad* arbitration.

Critics of Chapter 11 also argue that the process labors under a democratic deficit. NAFTA was negotiated by the executive branch of each country with limited input by the public. In the United States, it was negotiated under fast-track authority where the executive presented the package for Congressional approval on a yes-or-no basis, with no congressional opportunity for input.

Critics also bemoan the asymmetry of obligations. While Chapter 11 gives private companies the right to question governmental regulation, there is no countervailing governmental right to question corporate activity. There is also some regret that Chapter 11, intended to hold the Mexican government's history of confiscation in check, has become a powerful tool capable of thwarting necessary government regulation. The intent of Chapter 11 was not to allow "entrepreneurial" lawyers to turn this shield against uncompensated expropriation into a sword against legitimate public regulation.

---

[43] Aside from the obvious problems entailed by a "race to the bottom," constitutional concerns have also been raised with respect to equality rights in Mexico and the United States. *See* Cesar De La Garza, *Constitutional Inconsistencies of NAFTA Chapter 19: A Mexican Perspective*, *in* DOING BUSINESS IN MEXICO (Leon Trakman, Nick Ranieri, & Marion O. Lopez, eds., 2006) (arguing that NAFTA violates equality provisions in the Mexican Constitution); Atik, *supra* note 36 (describing equality concerns in the United States)

Critics have also complained that Chapter 11 favors a privileged class of investors over the general public. The perception persists that choosing traditional commercial arbitration to resolve disputes of public regulation may underwrite bad deals or at least shield investors from the normal judicial and public scrutiny attendant with litigation. Critics have also argued that Chapter 11 benefits capital-exporting countries to the detriment of capital-importing ones. A variant to this argument also holds that it favored U.S. and Canadian investors more than their Mexican counterparts because it was the former (investors from capital- exporting countries) who were more likely to bring such claims.[44]

Additionally, critics decry the transparency deficit. They allege that Chapter 11 has been entrusted to secretive tribunals. Commercial arbitration has been selected as the repository for the settlement of disputes that concern the public interest. There is no real appeal process, and the supervisory function has been limited to the political will of the Free Trade Commission. Excessive secrecy has served to aggravate legitimacy concerns.

B. CRITICS: GOVERNMENT

Surprisingly, some of the harshest criticisms that have been leveled at Chapter 11 have come not from the traditional critics of globalization, but from the entities that created it and that otherwise espouse the benefits of free trade—the NAFTA Parties. Several provisions of Chapter 11 have generated great controversy. In attempting to delimit various provisions, the drafters inserted clarifying language that ironically appears to have invited expansionary interpretation.[45] Interpretation of investment, minimum standard of treatment consistent with international law, and "measure tantamount to nationalization or expropriation" have the potential to reach beyond the Parties' expectations of Chapter 11. This undermines the underlying consent of the Parties to the Agreement.[46]

Taken aback by the expansive interpretations that tribunals have given to the Chapter 11 provisions, the Parties have sought to rein in tribunals both at the court level and through the binding interpretations of the FTC. In so doing, the Parties have criticized Chapter 11 to its core and raised complicated issues of conflict of interest.

In the two annulment proceedings that occurred, the government of Canada appeared as an interested party to question the legitimacy of Chapter 11 and to request

---

[44] Critics have gone one step further in asserting that Chapter 11 perpetually impoverishes targeted races. *See* Jose E. Alvarez, *Critical Theory and the North American Free Trade Agreement's Chapter Eleven*, 28 U. MIAMI INTER-AM. L. REV. 303 (1997).

[45] *See* Atik, *supra* note 36, at 147. *See also* Brower, *supra* note 36, at 59–61 (describing Chapter 11's textual indeterminacy).

[46] Atik, *supra* note 36; Brower, *supra* note 36.

an exceedingly strict level of judicial review.[47] In one case, the government of Canada argued that:

> ...the awards of Chapter 11 tribunals about public measures are not supposed to be worthy of judicial deference and not supposed to be protected by a high standard of review. Chapter 11 tribunals do not exhibit the features of a specialized or expert tribunal. Chapter 11 tribunals are currently appointed ad hoc and for single cases. There is no Chapter 11 secretariat or in-house specialists or other institutional hallmark of expertise or special authority.[48]

These actions by the government of Canada in a judicial forum are certain to raise conflict-of-interest concerns. While attorneys for the interested Parties must have all the means available at their disposal to avoid liability, Parties to a treaty must perform treaty obligations in good faith and encourage their courts to do the same.[49] A forceful argument is made that this inevitable conflict of interest must be resolved in favor of the integrity of the international legal system.[50] However, the NAFTA Parties appear to have preferred a more cavalier approach, treating their lawyers as "hired guns."[51]

Arguably, when the Parties urge their own courts to second-guess the merits of a Chapter 11 award, they violate their treaty obligations, impair the effectiveness of arbitral proceedings by pushing them into the court system's endless maze of appeals, and undermine Chapter 11 by calling into question its legitimacy.[52] Indeed, one of the benefits of arbitration generally and Chapter 11 specifically is the avoidance of local courts and the attendant legal complications.

This situation is exacerbated by the uncertainty inherent in the court process itself. Although courts in the NAFTA countries have varying degrees of traditions of independence, they lack experience in international affairs and may adhere to a constitutional doctrine that permits greater judicial deference to their own government's handling of international matters. Although this proclivity may have worked well in the past, its application to this modern mechanism, which permits private citizens to sue national governments before tribunals, does not bode well

---

47 *See* Brower, *supra* note 36, at 75 (chiding the Canadian government for its criticisms of Chapter 11 tribunals and requesting "a level of judicial scrutiny which is not compatible with the letter or the spirit of NAFTA's investment chapter.")

48 Canada's Outline of Argument in *Metalclad available at* http://www.naftaclaims.com.

49 Brower, *supra* note 36, at 76.

50 *Id.* at 76, n.213, n.216 (citing *Pope & Talbot* and *Metalclad* Tribunal concerns over the positions taken by the governments at annulment proceedings, as well as citing to the LeGrande Case (Gr. v. US 2001, ICJ, ¶¶ 112, 115 (June 27), *available at* http://www.icj-cij.org/icjwww/idocket/igusframe.htm. [hereinafter *LeGrande Case*] (ruling that the United States breached its obligations by arguing against the ICJ order at the Supreme Court; Iran Claims Tribunal Rep., ¶¶ 67–71 (1998), *available at* 1998 WL 1157733 (holding that second-guessing a tribunal award violated the submission to arbitration), and n.217 (noting that extensive judicial review undermines the legitimacy of the process and impairs the tribunal's effectiveness, citing to Gantz and Collier and Lowe).

51 Brower, *supra* note 36, at 76 and n.214 and n. 215.

52 *Id.* at 76 and n.216, citing *LaGrande Case*, *supra* note 50.

for international litigants or enforcement of otherwise valid awards. Permitting national courts to review the tribunal awards in circumstances where the impugned government is permitted to appear as an interested party is bound to raise questions of conflict.

Inequality in the treatment of the participants calls into question the most fundamental tenet of procedural justice and rules of arbitration. Notwithstanding the Parties' best intentions at an annulment proceeding, their appearance as both a litigant and Party creates great potential not just with respect to the appearance of conflict of interest, but actual conflict.

C. CRITICS: PARTICIPANTS

On July 31, 2001, the FTC adopted interpretations of Chapter 11 to clarify and reaffirm the meaning of certain of its provisions.[53] The interpretations focused on access to documents and the minimum standard of treatment in accordance with international

---

[53] Free Trade Commission Clarifications Related to NAFTA Chapter 11 July 31, 2001:

> Having reviewed the operation of proceedings conducted under Chapter Eleven of the North American Free Trade Agreement, the Free Trade Commission hereby adopts the following interpretations of Chapter Eleven in order to clarify and reaffirm the meaning of certain of its provisions:
>
> **A. Access to documents**
>
> 1. Nothing in the NAFTA imposes a general duty of confidentiality on the disputing parties to a Chapter Eleven arbitration, and, subject to the application of Article 1137(4), nothing in the NAFTA precludes the Parties from providing public access to documents submitted to, or issued by, a Chapter Eleven tribunal.
>
> 2. In the application of the foregoing:
>
> (a) In accordance with Article 1120(2), the NAFTA Parties agree that nothing in the relevant arbitral rules imposes a general duty of confidentiality or precludes the Parties from providing public access to documents submitted to, or issued by, Chapter Eleven tribunals, apart from the limited specific exceptions set forth expressly in those rules.
>
> (b) Each Party agrees to make available to the public in a timely manner all documents submitted to, or issued by, a Chapter Eleven tribunal, subject to redaction of:
>
> (i) confidential business information;
>
> (ii) information which is privileged or otherwise protected from disclosure under the Party's domestic law; and
>
> (iii) information which the Party must withhold pursuant to the relevant arbitral rules, as applied.
>
> (c) The Parties reaffirm that disputing parties may disclose to other persons in connection with the arbitral proceedings such unredacted documents as they consider necessary for the preparation of their cases, but they shall ensure that those persons protect the confidential information in such documents.
>
> (d) The Parties further reaffirm that the Governments of Canada, the United Mexican States and the United States of America may share with officials of their respective federal, state or provincial governments all relevant documents in the course of dispute settlement under Chapter Eleven of NAFTA, including confidential information.3. The Parties confirm

law. Although the interpretation mechanism holds great theoretical potential for alleviating the problems of Chapter 11, it appears to be evolving as a quick-fix mechanism to rewrite the Parties' obligations without the necessary formalities. In so doing, it calls into question not merely the legitimacy of the Parties' intentions, but the whole Chapter 11 process.

Although the FTC suffers many problems of legitimacy,[54] its most obvious weakness appears to be the promulgation of interpretations that blatantly appear to favor the Parties. Interpretations have become the most recent and perhaps most serious development in the legitimacy crisis facing Chapter 11. Participants in the process have accused the Parties of using these processes in an illegitimate attempt to amend Chapter 11 in order to decrease their obligations. Commentators have noted that this mechanism has not been used to enhance Chapter 11, but have been subverted by the Parties to exploit short-term self-interest.[55]

Even more troubling than the fact that these interpretations may exacerbate textual indeterminacy,[56] and appear to be masked amendments,[57] is the fact that the Parties have argued that these interpretations should be given retroactive effect that impacts ongoing arbitrations.[58] Commentators have accused the Parties of intentionally blurring the amendment–interpretation line in a flagrant attempt to change the rules of the game in their favor.[59]

---

that nothing in this interpretation shall be construed to require any Party to furnish or allow access to information that it may withhold in accordance with Articles 2102 or 2105.

B. Minimum Standard of Treatment in Accordance with International Law

1. Article 1105(1) prescribes the customary international law minimum standard of treatment of aliens as the minimum standard of treatment to be afforded to investments of investors of another Party.

2. The concepts of "fair and equitable treatment" and "full protection and security" do not require treatment in addition to or beyond that which is required by the customary international law minimum standard of treatment of aliens.

3. A determination that there has been a breach of another provision of the NAFTA, or of a separate international agreement, does not establish that there has been a breach of Article 1105(1).

Closing Provision

The adoption by the Free Trade Commission of this or any future interpretation shall not be construed as indicating an absence of agreement among the NAFTA Parties about other matters of interpretation of the Agreement.

54 *See* Brower *supra* note 36, at 78 (describing the FTC's want of pedigree).

55 *Id.* at 78–82 (outlining the Interpretive Notes shortcomings with respect to want of pedigree, textual indeterminacy, violations of international law, and gratification of narrow self-interests).

56 *Id.* (describing ambiguities in the Notes).

57 Ian Laird, *Betrayal, Shock and Outrage—Recent Developments in NAFTA Article 1105*, *in* NAFTA Investment Law and Arbitration: Past Issues, Current Practice, Future Prospects 49 (Todd Weiler ed., 2004) (arguing that the Parties attempted to rewrite 1105 through the interpretation mechanism).

58 *See* Methanex Corporation v. United States of America, Fourth Opinion of Sir Robert Jennings, *The Meaning of Article 1105(1) of the NAFTA*, Sept. 6, 2001, at 4–5.

59 Brower, *supra* note 36; Laird, *supra* note 57.

Perhaps the problems associated with the FTC's 2001 Interpretive Notes stem from the fact that the FTC is itself saddled with limitations. Although it may adopt binding interpretations, it cannot amend the NAFTA. Article 1131(2) authorizes the FTC to make binding interpretations while Article 2202 permits the Parties to make modifications or amendments in accordance with the Party's applicable legal procedures. NAFTA amendment requires formal procedures and a higher degree of political scrutiny, particularly, congressional approval in the United States.

NAFTA does not address vital questions pertaining to interpretations. Chief among them is whether the interpretations are to be prospective or retrospective. Some argue that the FTC should be a legislative body with the power to formulate general rules of application, rather than directing specific outcomes in ongoing disputes.[60] Another view is that the FTC is an adjudicative body with the power to preclude a tribunal's interpretation in a particular dispute even if its governments are parties to the same disputes.[61]

The FTC's role is further complicated by its power to resolve questions pertaining to reservations and exceptions. NAFTA Article 1132 requires that the tribunal address all questions (pertaining to reservations and exceptions established by Annexes I–IV) to the FTC. An earlier Chapter 11 draft would have given the FTC an overall interpretive power in Chapter 11 cases, whereas the final version speaks of the FTC's power to issue interpretive statements of general application. A reasonable view is that the FTC is not empowered to resolve particular disputes.[62] This view is supported by the evolution of Chapter 11 into the newer FTAs. In addition, the Parties to the U.S.–Korea, U.S.–Peru, and U.S.– Panama FTAs have all included an annex permitting the negotiation of an appellate body within three years of the entry into force of the agreements.[63] So the tribunals are clearly empowered to resolve particular disputes in those agreements with the possibility of a new review body to discipline errant tribunals, if the need arises.

The difficulties in separating distinction from amendment, in general, further complicate the situation.[64] Such ambiguity facilitates allegations that the FTC impermis-

---

[60] Stephan Clarkson, *Systemic or Surgical?: Possible Cures for NAFTA's Investor–State Dispute Process*, 36 CAN. BUS. L.J. 368, 385 (2002); Brower, *supra* note 36, at 85.

[61] *See* Brower, *supra* note 36, at 85, citing U.S. Post-Hearing Submission in ADF at 8–9 (arguing that the FTC has the plenary power to overrule the tribunal, and that the tribunal plays a subsidiary role to the FTC). *See also* Charles Brower & Lee Steven, *Who Then Should Judge?: Developing the International Rule of Law under NAFTA Chapter 11*, 2 CHI. J. INT'L L. 193, 193–94 (2001) (describing Canada's support for interpretive statements as an attempt by the NAFTA Parties to take power from the tribunals).

[62] Brower, *supra* note 36, at 85, n.259. *See also* Gary Horlick & Alicia Marti, *NAFTA Chapter 11 B—A Private Right of Action to Enforce Market Access through Investments*, 14 J. INT'L ARB. 43,49, n.47 (1997) (comparing the FTC's adjudicative roles under the draft and final texts of Chapter 11).

[63] Annex 11-D, U.S.–Korea FTA, and identical provisions in the other FTAs, www.ustr.gov/trade-agreements/free-trade-agreements.

[64] *See* Brower, *supra* note 36, at 85, citing ANTHONY MUST, MODERN TREATY LAW AND PRACTICE 193 (2000) and RESTATEMENT (THIRD) OF THE FOREIGN RELATIONS OF THE UNITED STATES § 325 (1987)

sibly engaged in amendment under the guise of interpretation.[65] Commentators have noted that the procedures for determining where the line lies are as indeterminate as the standard itself.[66] Although tribunals might assert the right to determine whether the text is an interpretation or amendment, the Parties contend that the tribunals lack this power and must accept the FTC's interpretation as conclusive. Absent rules demarking respective authority, or a mechanism for establishing same, problems will continue and legitimacy concerns will increase.[67]

The jurisdictional fog between the tribunals and the FTC will likely exacerbate the problems between the courts and the tribunals. Professor Brower posits the circumstance where a tribunal rules that an interpretive note is a de facto amendment and therefore void. Such an award would certainly be challenged by the Parties through an annulment proceeding, where the court, at the behest of the government, might likely find that the tribunal acted beyond its jurisdiction, and annul the award. If the claimant were to resubmit the claim, the new tribunal might find that the annulment was an unwarranted intrusion into the arbitral process. The result would be a never-ending cascade of allegations of ultra vires conduct. Such an eventuality is sure to weaken the legitimacy of the Chapter 11 process.[68]

Ironically, these interpretations, like the original text, appear to worsen the textual ambiguity rather than alleviate it. Critics of the original text have argued that the Parties' attempts to clarify the text through extra language actually made it more open to debate Similarly, these interpretations, which attempt to clarify the terms of the agreement, may contain significant ambiguities that could actually invite more debate. As discussed, commentators have argued that the FTC has not proven adept at formulating legitimate interpretations.[69] There remains ample room for tribunals to interpret these interpretations differently.[70]

(explaining that the distinction between interpretation and amendment may be imperceptible is some cases).

65 Brower, *supra* note 36, at 85, n.261, citing participants' briefs. Todd Weiler, *NAFTA Investment Arbitration and the Growth of International Economic Law*, 36 CAN. BUS. L.J. 405, 429 (2002).

66 Brower, *supra* note 36, at 85.

67 *Id.*

68 *Id.* at 86.

69 *Id.* (arguing that The FTC's interpretations create more ambiguity. He argues that tribunals can take various approaches to the suggestion that: (1) international law means customary law; (2) fair and equitable treatment is restricted to dated customary rules prohibiting only the most egregious and shocking government conduct and that external treaty provisions have no relevance to the application of Article 1105(1)).

70 Tribunals could interpret these Notes to confirm the view that Article 1105(1) represents a statement of *opinio-juris* to the effect that, through widespread incorporation into BITs, the conventional standard of fair and equitable treatment has become a rule of customary international law. Similarly, even if tribunals are precluded from seeing breaches of other treaty obligations as not per se establishing a breach of Article 1105(1), tribunals might still view it as relevant if not a strong indication of unfair and inequitable treatment. *Id.*; *see* Charles Brower, *Fair and Equitable Treatment under NAFTA's Investment Chapter*, 96 AM. SOC'Y INT'L L. PROC. 9, 11 (2002).

It has also been argued that the Parties have violated their obligation to interpret the NAFTA "in accordance with the applicable rules of international law" (Article 102(2)). The argument has been made that the prescribed rules of construction cannot uphold an interpretation that circumscribes "fair and equitable treatment" to the most egregious forms of governmental conduct.[71] The argument holds that the applicable rules of international law must necessarily include reference to the Vienna Convention on the Law of Treaties, which calls for the customary rules of treaty interpretation. The Vienna Convention therefore compels the FTC to interpret the NAFTA language according to its ordinary meaning within the context of NAFTA's objectives and purposes and with reference to the relevant international obligations of the NAFTA Parties.[72]

The FTC's Interpretative Notes, as qualified by the NAFTA Parties in their submissions to tribunals, appear to be more consistent with routine claims made by the Parties that tribunals strictly construe Chapter 11 to work the least intrusion on sovereignty as possible.[73] The argument is made that although strict construction prevailed in an earlier era, it is no longer sustainable in modern treaty interpretation. Commentators have argued that if the Notes rest on the principle of strict interpretation, then the FTC has deviated from ritual in a way that undermines the legitimacy of its work and the Chapter 11 process.[74]

Even if the NAFTA Parties followed the rituals of interpretation, the Notes, delivered at pivotal junctures in ongoing arbitrations, would still fall short of the values of accountability, transparency, and democratic participation.[75] These Notes did not have the benefit of public consultation and were delivered without any notice to the Chapter 11 stakeholders. Given that the Notes were delivered at critical junctures in ongoing arbitrations and that the Parties have insisted on retroactive effect in the pending arbitrations, commentators have referred to the work of the FTC as more of a clever fait accompli to avoid liability than a principled exercise in international governance. It has been argued that the Parties are using the FTC in a secretive, nonparticipatory fashion to advance short-term narrow self-interest. The FTC has been called a "mere hunting license" for the NAFTA Parties to do whatever they wish.[76]

---

[71] *See* Brower, *supra* note 36.

[72] Vienna Convention Article 31.

[73] *See* Brower, *supra* note 36, at 80 and n.235, citing the *Loewen* and *Ethyl* cases. *See also* Andrea Bjorklund, *Contract without Privity: Sovereign Offer and Investor Acceptance*, 2 CHI. J. INT'L L. 183 191 (2001) (arguing that the Parties are justified in urging a narrow construction of Chapter 11).

[74] *See supra* note 70; *see also* Brower, *supra* note 36, at 80–1, n.236 (citing to *Loewen* and *Ethyl* filings).

[75] *See* Brower, *supra* note 36; Laird, *supra* note 57.

[76] *See* Brower, *supra* note 36, at 82; *see also* David A. Gantz, *Government-to-Government Dispute Resolution under NAFTA's Chapter 20: A Commentary on the Process,* 11 AM. REV. INT'L. ARB. 481 (2000) indicating that the FTC lacks the capacity to act independently of the Parties; Robert Paterson, *A New Pandora's Box? Private Remedies for Foreign Investors under the North American Free Trade Agreement*, 8 WILLAMETTE J. INT'L. L. & DISP. RESOL. 77 (2000).

Section II: A Three-Part Test

The eye of the storm brewing between the proponents and detractors of expanded investment protection is centered squarely in NAFTA's expropriation provisions. Both in the international context and the NAFTA context, the debate over the appropriateness of and amount of compensation for direct expropriation has been displaced by a growing debate over the requirement to pay for governmental regulation. This evolving debate is now centered on determining the point where otherwise legitimate governmental regulation in furtherance of the state's police powers becomes compensable expropriation because it diminishes the value of foreign investments.[77]

NAFTA does not define expropriation, police powers, or property. Although expropriation implies a societal balance and burden sharing, NAFTA does not specifically address these issues, choosing instead to fall back on an amorphous international standard. The application of this international standard, in the NAFTA context, has entangled the debate in an expropriation and regulation conundrum.

The key to unraveling this conundrum contains three discreet, but related steps that must be addressed. First, a test for expropriation needs to be established. Second, the police powers exception must be analyzed. Third, an analysis must be undertaken in relation to property rights in the context of the need to regulate, without engaging compensation liability.

The first step is to establish a test for expropriation. However, defining such a test does not by itself establish what types of regulation escape compensation. Therefore, the test needs to be refined to exclude from the compensation requirement bona fide regulatory measures pursuant to the state's police powers. Finally, this test needs to be further refined so that its applicability precisely targets legitimate property expectations by balancing competing interests consistent with the societal burden sharing that expropriation entails. The test needs to go beyond an effects analysis and address the purpose, if not the intent, behind the regulation.[78]

Although an FTC interpretation could theoretically assist in this endeavor, practice has shown that the Parties' use of this mechanism in the past has been arguably shortsighted and self-serving. As such, the tribunals will need to develop a jurisprudence that remains sensitive to the needs of all stakeholders. As tribunal jurisprudence is not binding, it must remain logically compelling and persuasive if it is to evolve.

---

[77] The debate is equally strong in the United States. The doctrine of regulatory takings might be traced back to 1922 when Justice Holmes first announced that compensation must be paid when governmental regulation "goes too far" in diminishing the value of private property. Pennsylvania Coal v. Mahon, 260 U.S. 393, 415 (1922). Since then U.S. courts have strived to define what goes too far. More recent Supreme Court rulings in Lucas v. South Carolina, 112 S. Ct. 2286 (1992) and Dolan v. City of Tigard, 114 S. Ct. 2309 (1994) have created a body of case law that has been referred to as a "mess." *See* William Michael Treanor, *The Original Understanding of the Takings Clause and the Political Process*, 95 COLUM. L. REV. 782 (1995); J. Peter Byrne, *Ten Arguments for the Abolition of the Regulatory Takings Doctrine*, 22 ECOLOGY L.Q. 89 (1995).

[78] *See* J. Soloway, *NAFTA's Chapter 11: Issues and Perspectives, in* CANADIAN YEARBOOK OF INTERNATIONAL LAW (2000). *See also* H. MANN & K. VON MOLTE, NAFTA'S CHAPTER 11AND THE ENVIRONMENT (1999).

Step I: Test for Expropriation

The expropriation debate is now shaped by those advocating a bright-line test for distinguishing regulation from expropriation[79] and those who argue that it must be left to a case-by-case contextualized analysis of the facts.[80] In both the domestic and international context, a usual point of departure in trying to draw the line between regulation and expropriation may be to examine the property component.[81] Regulation will often have property-deprivation effects, at times amounting to expropriation.

In the international context, not unlike the domestic arena, the key to understanding when regulation becomes expropriation may lie in better understanding how property rights have been affected. Property law has traditionally been the domain of domestic law, and rarely the subject of international consensus. However, given that investors now are encouraged to deal with property interests around the globe, in the context of expanding governmental regulation and increased civil society activism, it may be time to revisit the development of property rights in the international expropriation context.[82] Arguably, this is already occurring in some areas, such as in the development of modern international economic and human rights law.[83]

The nature and degree of the property deprivation is a useful analysis to employ in determining whether compensable expropriation has occurred. A deprivation of rights can be something less than complete. In such circumstances, an analysis focusing on degrees continues to be relevant.[84] One difficulty with this approach is the "denominator" problem that tries to define the different strands or bundles of property. Property can be refined, subdivided, or broken up in such a way as to ensure that a taking is always found and compensation payable.[85] In other words, if the degree of deprivation is evaluated against a sufficiently narrow component of property, there will always be a sufficient finding of deprivation.[86]

---

79 Levesque, *supra* note 26.

80 Marc C. Poirier, *The NAFTA Chapter 11 Expropriation Debate through the Eyes of a Property Theorist*, 33 ENVTL. L. 851 (2003).

81 Levesque, *supra* note 26.

82 *Id.* (arguing that an exploration of expropriation without a consideration of property is necessarily incomplete).

83 Todd Weiler, *The Potential for Overlap in NAFTA Chapter 11 Obligations*, *in* THE FIRST DECADE OF NAFTA: THE FUTURE OF FREE TRADE IN NORTH AMERICA (Kevin Kennedy ed., 2004).

84 *See* Levesque, *supra* note 26; John Herz, *Expropriation of Foreign Property*, 35 AM. J. INT'L L. 243, 251 (1941); Francisco Orrego Vicuna, *Regulatory Expropriations in International Law: Carlos Calvo, Honorary NAFTA Citizen*, 11 N.Y.U. ENVT'L L.J. 19, 23–25 (2002).

85 Kevin Banks, *NAFTA's Article 1110: Can Regulation be Expropriation?*, 5 NAFTA L. & BUS. REV. AM. 499, 508–09 (1999).

86 *See* Weiler, *supra* note 83, suggesting that businesses split up subsidiaries, and *NAFTA Investment and Arbitration and the Growth of Economic International Law*, 36 CAN. BUS. L.J. 405 (2000) advocating that the test of substantial interference not be applied to the entire business of an investor.

A case-by-case approach can be relevant[87]within basic parameters. The analysis should begin by taking down the straw men. The extreme cases should be quickly discarded from the analysis. On the one extreme—the state's unjustified and total deprivation of property rights—compensation is clear. On the other extreme, a minor and temporary deprivation of property rights with potential justification is clearly a case that does not warrant compensation.

The wide gray area between these two extremes provides the circumstances that challenge arbitrators. In these cases, arbitrators grapple with the question of whether the governmental measure presents a sufficiently serious interference with property rights to justify compensation. Different international tribunals have used different parameters to decide this issue, including Chapter 11 tribunals.[88] The United States has attempted to clarify the parameters by the inclusion of explicit provisions in the annexes to its newer FTAs.[89]

Understanding what types of expropriations fall into the purview of Chapter 11 requires a close reading of the relevant NAFTA provisions and an understanding of international legal standards as they relate to expropriations. As a practical matter, understanding expropriation law in the NAFTA countries might also shed light on what the NAFTA negotiators intended, as well as assisting in clarifying the analyses of Chapter 11 arbitrators. [90]

Chapter 11 does not apply to all expropriations. The language of Article 1110 makes it clear that only certain expropriations are actionable. It notes that the Parties cannot expropriate except: (1) for a public purpose; (2) on a nondiscriminatory basis; (3) in accordance with due process of law and pursuant to Article 1105(1) (minimum standard of treatment); and (4) on payment of compensation.[91] Therefore, an expropriation is beyond the purview of Chapter 11 if it is for a public purpose, on a nondiscriminatory basis, in accordance with due process of law, compliant with minimal standards of treatment, and compensation is paid.

The language of Article 1110 also refers to different types of expropriations that are actionable. It speaks to "directly or indirectly nationalize or expropriate" or "take a measure tantamount to nationalization or expropriation."[92] Understanding the relationship between these types of expropriations and how they have evolved under traditional BITs is crucial to comprehending the scope of Chapter 11.

---

[87] *See* Christie, *supra* note 35, at 338 (1962); Rudolf Dolzer, *Indirect Expropriation of Alien Property*, 1(1) ICSID Rev.–For. Inv. L.J. 41, 42 (1986).

[88] *See* Levesque, *supra* note 26, at 301; CHARLES BROWER & JASON BRUEKSCHKE, THE IRAN–US CLAIMS TRIBUNAL 378–79 (1998).

[89] Annex 11-B in the Korea–U.S. FTA, http://www.ustr.gov/trade-agreements/free-trade-agreements/korus-fta/final-text, and related annexes in the Peru and Panama agreements.

[90] For a review of expropriation law in NAFTA countries, *see* Poirier, *supra* note 80, at 65 n.105.

[91] NAFTA Chapter 11, Article 1110.

[92] NAFTA, Chapter 11.

Direct expropriation, indirect expropriation, as well as measures tantamount to expropriation, are terms that are found in many BITs. All of these investment accords were negotiated in the absence of a global framework for investment. They were generally negotiated between developed countries and developing countries where the former were able to wield their economic clout to ensure the most comprehensive protection for their investors by limiting the latter's ability to frustrate the investments in the course of fulfilling their governmental functions. That is, given the inequality of bargaining powers, developed countries were able to extract expansive definitions of takings and make them compensable. Given that investors of developing countries were less likely to invest in developed countries, developed countries had little fear that these definitions would be used against them.[93]

Direct expropriation is a relatively settled concept in international law. Although direct expropriation is often not defined in traditional BITs, the interpretation relies on customary international law. Expropriation is often given its ordinary meaning as the act of stripping property from the owner's hands by the public authority. Although the act of direct expropriation is relatively settled in terms of it constituting an actionable taking by the government, the issue of what is the appropriate level of compensation appears to be evolving in the direction of full compensation, measured where possible by reference to market value.[94]

Indirect expropriation continues to develop in the absence of a doctrinal basis.[95] Indeed, despite numerous decisions of international tribunals, there appears to be no universally recognized definition. It appears to be generally accepted that a wide variety of measures may lead to a finding of indirect expropriation and that this is usually determined on a case-by-case basis. Particularly important to the analysis appears to be the effect that the measure had on the investor's rights. As a measure draws closer to having more of the effect of depriving the owner of the benefits or the value of his or her property, it also draws closer to being a compensable taking. Arguably, the recent tendency among international arbitral tribunals has been to shift the focus of the analysis away from the context and purpose of the governmental regulation toward the effect on the owner.[96]

The OECD Draft Convention on the Protection of Foreign Property and the Resolution of the Council of the OECD on the draft Convention provide some insight

---

[93] *See* Kenneth J. Vandevelde, *The Bilateral Investment Treaty of the United States*, 21 CORNELL INT'L L.J. 201 (1988), and Andrew T. Guzman, *Why LDCs Sign Treaties That Hurt Them: Explaining the Popularity of Bilateral Investment Treaties*, 38 VA. J. INT'L L. 639 (1998).

[94] It has been argued that with few exceptions more recent international arbitral awards have affirmed that customary international law requires that a state expropriating the property of a foreign national pay the full value of the property with an intention to make the foreign national "whole." *See* Patrick M. Norton, *A Law of the Future or a Law of the Past? Modern Tribunals and the International Law of Expropriation*, 85 AM. L. INT'L L.474 (1991).

[95] *See* Soloway, *supra* note 78; *see also* Dolzer, *supra* note 87.

[96] Rudolf Dolzer, *Indirect Expropriations: New Developments*, 11 N.Y.U. ENVT'L L.J. 64 (2002).

into the expansive nature of expropriation. Examples of indirect expropriation include excessive or arbitrary taxation, prohibition of dividend distribution, compulsory loans, use of required administrators, prohibitions on staff dismissals, refusal of access to raw materials, or denial of required export or import licenses.[97]

Measures "tantamount to expropriation," the more recent addition to the family of expropriation terms, is the least universally understood. This term may, on its face, be redundant with "indirect expropriation," or it may mean something even more encompassing. Assuming that the drafters of the NAFTA did not mean it to be redundant, then measures tantamount to expropriation have the potential to apply to an even greater number of government measures than measures that have the effect of indirectly expropriating an investment. Although this term is explicitly qualified with respect to intellectual property matters[98] and to debt securities, the presence of these restrictions in these fields may suggest an otherwise ample and unfettered interpretation in other fields, based on customary international law concepts.

The potentially wide definitions of direct or indirect expropriation, coupled with the potentially even wider definition of measures tantamount to expropriation, suggest that there is ample scope for the application of the compensable-takings concept. This imprecise definition of expropriation has created doubts as to when government regulation becomes compensable expropriation.[99] This uncertainty has led to the suggestion that the NAFTA governments, in the course of undertaking environmental regulation in the face of the threat of massive lawsuits, may be inhibited from legislating in the public interest.[100]

Whether this fear is justified requires an examination of the potential interpretations applicable to Chapter 11.

INTERPRETATION

The interpretation of Chapter 11's substantive provisions begins with an analysis of the governing law provided by the NAFTA drafters. Article 1131(1) is, essentially, a choice-of-law clause that states the tribunals "shall decide the issues in dispute in accordance

---

97 The OECD Draft Convention on the Protection of Foreign Property and the Resolution of the Council of the OECD. *See also* OECD Working Papers on International Investment, *Indirect Expropriations* and the *Right to Regulate* in INT'L INV. L. (Sept. 2004).

98 NAFTA, Chapter 17.

99 Some commentators have suggested that the imprecise NAFTA investor protection language obscures the point at which regulatory actions that adversely affect NAFTA foreign investment are to be deemed violations of the NAFTA requiring compensation. *See, e.g.*, David A. Gantz, *Reconciling Environmental Protection and Investor Rights under Chapter 11 of the NAFTA*, 31 ENVTL. L. REP. 10646 (2001).

100 *See* J. Martin Wagner, *International Investment, Expropriation and Environmental Protection*, 29 GOLDEN GATE U.L. REV. 465 (1999) (suggesting that giving companies the right to base compensation claims on the economic impact of environmental regulations has a chilling effect on the willingness of governments to implement such regulation of governments).

with this Agreement and applicable rules of international law." Additionally, NAFTA Article 102 provides:

1. The objectives of this Agreement, as elaborated more specifically through its principles and rules, including national treatment, most favored nation treatment and transparency, are to:

   a. eliminate barriers to trade in, and facilitate the cross-border movement of goods and services between the territories of the Parties;
   b. promote conditions of fair competition in the free trade area;
   c. increase substantially investment opportunities in the territories of the Parties;
   d. provide adequate and effective protection and enforcement of intellectual property rights in each Party's territory;
   e. create effective procedures for the implementation and application of this Agreement, for its joint administration and for the resolution of disputes; and
   f. establish a framework for further trilateral, regional and multilateral cooperation to expand and enhance the benefits of this Agreement.

2. The Parties shall interpret and apply the provision of this Agreement in light of its objectives set out in paragraph 1 and in accordance with the applicable rules of international law.[101]

This interpretive guidance has led NAFTA Chapter 11 tribunals to adopt similar interpretive approaches to those of the WTO Appellate Body.[102] The WTO Appellate Body has stated that Articles 31 and 32 of the Vienna Convention on the Laws of Treaties (Vienna Convention) are a codification of the applicable rules of customary international law for treaty interpretation.[103]

Article 31 of the Vienna Convention provides:

1. A treaty shall be interpreted in good faith in accordance with the ordinary meaning to be given to the terms of the treaty in their context and in light of its object and purpose.
2. The context, for the purpose of the interpretation of a treaty shall comprise, in addition to the text, including its preamble and annexes:

   a. any agreement relating to the treaty which was made between all the parties in connection with the conclusion of the treaty;

[101] NAFTA, Article 102.

[102] *See* Ethyl Corp v. Canada, Award on Jurisdiction, NAFTA /UNCITRAL Tribunal, June 24, 1998; Mondev International LTD. v. USA, ICSID No. ARB(AF)/99/2, Final Award, Oct. 11, 2002.

[103] United States—Standards for Reformulated and Conventional Gasoline, WT/DS2/AB/9 (May 20, 1996) at 17.

b. any instrument which was made in by one or more parties in connection with the conclusion of the treaty and accepted by the other parties as an instrument related to the treaty.

3. There shall be taken into account together with the context:

a. Any subsequent agreement between the parties regarding the interpretation of the Treaty or the application of its provisions;
b. Any subsequent practice in the application of the Treaty which establishes the agreement of the parties regarding its interpretation;
c. Any relevant rules of international law applicable in the relations between the parties.

4. A special meaning shall be given to a term if it is established that the parties so intended.

Vienna Convention Article 31(1) provides what some have called the golden rule of treaty interpretation—focus on the plain meaning of the text while being mindful of its placement in the context of the treaty as well as the objectives and purposes of the treaty.[104] NAFTA Article 102(1) makes the objectives and goals of the NAFTA clear. An early Chapter 11 tribunal noted the importance of transparency and the objective of increasing investment opportunities in the NAFTA region.[105]

The Preamble of the NAFTA may be used to establish the context for interpretation.[106] NAFTA has objectives that go beyond trade and investment liberalization. The Preamble of NAFTA states:

The Government of Canada, the Government of the United Mexican States and the Government of the United States of America, resolved to:

STRENGTHEN the special bonds of friendship and cooperation among their nations;
CONTRIBUTE to the harmonious development and expansion of world trade and provide a catalyst to broader international cooperation;
CREATE an expanded and secure market for the goods and services produced in their territories;
REDUCE distortions to trade;
ESTABLISH clear and mutually advantageous rules governing their trade;
ENSURE a predictable commercial framework for business planning and investment;

104 *See* Weiler, *supra* note 83.
105 *Metalclad, supra* note 28, ¶¶ 70–71.
106 *See S.D. Myers, supra* note 28.

BUILD on their respective rights and obligations under the General Agreement on Tariffs and Trade and other multilateral and bilateral instruments of cooperation;
ENHANCE the competitiveness of their firms in global markets;
FOSTER creativity and innovation, and promote trade in goods and services that are the subject of intellectual property rights;
CREATE new employment opportunities and improve working conditions and living standards in their respective territories;
UNDERTAKE each of the preceding in a manner consistent with environmental protection and conservation;
PRESERVE their flexibility to safeguard the public welfare;
PROMOTE sustainable development;
STRENGTHEN the development and enforcement of environmental laws and regulations; and
PROTECT, enhance and enforce basic workers' rights;

NAFTA Article 102 is specific in the manner in which it lays out the appropriate context for the interpretation of the NAFTA text. It states that the objectives are "elaborated more specifically through its principles and rules," which include national treatment, most-favored-nation treatment, and transparency. These three principles and rules represent the foundations of international economic law that are found in many treaty provisions and the growing jurisprudence of international economic law, which includes WTO Panel and Appellate Body Reports. Commentators have argued that it is therefore appropriate for NAFTA tribunals to have recourse to other trade and investment treaties, as well as the wider jurisprudence of economic law, in interpreting the NAFTA consistently with its broadly liberalizing objectives.[107]

The NAFTA adopts a model of multiple liabilities in terms of state responsibility. The NAFTA is noticeably silent in many cases of internal overlap (i.e., between the chapters) permitting state responsibility to theoretically emanate from several sources.[108]

However, NAFTA addresses potential conflicts with the provisions of other treaties, as well as other NAFTA provisions.[109] NAFTA Article 103(2) provides that NAFTA provisions will trump other treaties, unless provided otherwise in the NAFTA. NAFTA Article 104(1) provides that various environmental treaties will trump NAFTA provisions to the extent that the least-NAFTA-inconsistent approach is adopted. NAFTA Article 1103(1) provides that Chapter 11 is inapplicable to measures covered by Chapter 14 (financial services), and Article 1112 states that in the event of inconsistency between

107 Weiler, *supra* note 83.

108 *Id.* at 330 (suggesting that "this silence bespeaks an obvious preference for overlapping obligations to cover the conduct of state—as they do in the WTO context").

109 *Id.* (arguing that Chapter 11 is poorly tuned to deal with the scope and import of the NAFTA, but that none of its substantive provisions are internally inconsistent whereas overlap is minor and complimentary).

this Chapter and another Chapter, the other Chapter shall prevail to the extent of the inconsistency.

Chapter 11 Jurisprudence

Chapter 11 tribunals have given its provisions a wide application. Chapter 11 tribunal jurisprudence has made it clear that Chapter 11 is applicable even where the measures are not specifically aimed at investors or their investments, but also to goods (Chapter 3)[110] and services (Chapter 12),[111] which are arguably covered by other treaties or other NAFTA provisions. Commentators have noted that the key to identifying the scope and application of an individual Chapter 11 obligation, in relation to others, is to ascribe a meaning to the provision that does not result in redundancy or inutility.[112] This is consistent with the Vienna Convention, which requires that the interpreter adopt a reading that would not result in reducing whole clauses or paragraphs of a treaty to redundancy or inutility.[113]

As Chapter 11 was modeled on BITs, which are themselves based on language that was developed during the middle of the twentieth century, some of the wording has undergone a long process of evolution that may at times appear dated. However, commentators have argued that although the substantive provisions of Chapter 11 are not precise, they are not open-ended and reflect an evolving jurisprudence on expropriations and regulatory takings, both internationally and in the United States.

The commentators argue that Chapter 11 provisions are sufficiently grounded in international jurisprudence and will not prevent NAFTA Parties from implementing necessary environmental and social regulation.[114] That is, although the substantive provisions of Chapter 11 might be capable of being applied in a manner that might impose significant constraints on sovereignty, by enlarging the scope of governmental activity that could be labeled as expropriation, they have not been so applied. Rather, these provisions have been used judicially to sanction only the more egregious state

110 *See* Pope & Talbot, *supra* note 28, (Tribunal rejecting Canadian government argument that the measure at question was an export quota aimed at trade in goods and therefore beyond the purview of Chapter 11).

111 *See S.D. Myers*, *supra* note 28, at ¶¶ 123–38, where the tribunal concluded that an investor could use Chapter 11 to seek compensation for business activity harmed in breach of Articles 1102 and 1105 even though the activity might also be characterized as a cross-border service within the auspices of NAFTA Chapter 12. *See also* ADF v. United States, Final Award, NAFTA/ICSID (AF) Tribunal, Case No. ARB(AF)/00/1, Jan. 9, 2003, at ¶ 155.

112 *See* Weiler, *supra* note 83, at 332.

113 *See* United States—Standards for Reformulated and Conventional Gasoline, WT/DS2/9, adopted May 20, 1996, at 23.

114 *See* Jason Gudofsky, *Shedding Light on Article 1110 of the North American Free Trade Agreement (NAFTA) Concerning Expropriations: an Environmental Case Study*, 21 NW. J. INT'L L. & B. 243 (2000) and Wagner, *supra* note 100.

actions that were unfair, arbitrary, overly protectionist, or unjustifiable under the circumstances.[115]

It has also been argued that Chapter 11 goes beyond the regulatory takings principles established by U.S. law.[116] Others have suggested that U.S. regulatory takings law and international expropriations jurisprudence might draw on each other as sources for guidance for future development.[117] However, drawing parallels between Chapter 11 expropriations and regulatory takings law in the United States must be approached with caution, paying heed to the inherent differences between a domestic regulatory takings regime designed to protect the property rights of citizens from their own government and the international expropriations jurisprudence based on protecting the rights of foreign investors against host governments.[118]

Such caution is further justified by the structural differences between arbitrating international expropriations claims and litigating takings claims in the United States. These differences include the use of ad hoc arbitration versus judicial litigation, differences in intergovernmental liability, and differences in appeal mechanisms, as well as the lack of stare decisis in the context of international arbitration.[119] Moreover, trying to import the jurisprudence of one country into Chapter 11 might be inappropriate given that the negotiators chose not to do so and that the three NAFTA countries do not share common jurisprudence on regulatory takings.[120]

---

[115] Anthony Van Duzer, *NAFTA Chapter 11 to Date: The Progress of a Work in Progress*, *in* WHOSE RIGHTS? THE NAFTA CHAPTER 11 DEBATE (Laura Ritchie Dawson ed., 2002).

[116] *See* William T. Warren, *Paying to Regulate: Guide to* Methanex v. United States *and the NAFTA Investor Rights*, 31 ENVT'L. R. 10986 (2001). *See generally* William Michael Treanor, *The Original Understanding of the Takings Clause and the Political Process*, 95 COLUM. L. REV. 782 (1995); J. Peter Byrne, *Ten Arguments for the Abolition of the Regulatory Takings Doctrine*, 22 ECOLOGY L. Q. 89 (1995); Matthew P. Harrington, *"Public Use" and the Original Understanding of the So-Called "Takings" Clause*, 53 HASTINGS L.J. 1245 (2002); and Gavin M. Erasmus, *Eminent Domain Jurisprudence*, C791 ALI-ABA 1 (1993).

[117] *See* Paul B. Stephan, *Redistributive Litigation—Judicial Innovation, Private Expectations, and the Shadow of International Law*, 88 VA. L. REV. 789 (2002). *See also* Joseph Strazzeri, *A Lucas Analysis of Regulatory Expropriations under NAFTA Chapter Eleven*, 14 GEO. WASH. INT'L L. REV. 837 (2002), suggesting that Chapter 11 might benefit from the application of the "Lucas Principle," which holds that some rights that are never acquired along with the investment do not require compensation when the government later regulates to restrict them).

[118] *See* Vicki Been & Joel C. Beauvais, *The Global Fifth Amendment? NAFTA's Investment Protections and the Misguided Quest for an International "Regulatory Takings" Doctrine*, 78 N.Y.U. L. REV. 30 (2003) (arguing that a global regulatory takings doctrine is neither beneficial nor necessary, and expropriation provisions should be limited to the traditional investor concerns. *See also,* Joel C. Beauvais, *Regulatory Expropriations under NAFTA: Emerging Principles & Lingering Doubts*, 10 N.Y.U. ENVTL. L. J. 245 (arguing that the investor–state dispute resolution mechanism needs to be replaced or redesigned to provide greater accountability in balancing investor protection with environmental and social regulation).

[119] Although both the takings doctrine and expropriation law deal with government encroachments on private property, the takings doctrine rests on the U.S. Constitution, both expressly through the Fifth Amendment and implicitly through incorporation into the Fourteenth. Expropriations law rests on a developing international customary law and on a variety of international instruments. *See* Ethan Shenkman, *Could Principles of Fifth Amendment Takings Jurisprudence Be Helpful in Analyzing Regulatory Expropriation Claims under International Law?*, 11 N.Y.U. ENVT'L L.J. 174 (2002).

[120] For example, the constitutional property protections found in the United States have no counterpart in Canada. *See* Kevin Banks, *NAFTA's Article 1110—Can Regulation Be Expropriation?*, 5 NAFTA: L. &

Of the three notable cases that were decided on the merits, the tribunal in *Metalclad*[121] gave expropriation its broadest interpretation, but this decision was subsequently overturned, in part, upon judicial review.[122] The tribunals in *S.D. Myers*[123] and *Pope*[124] narrowly interpreted the expropriation provisions, finding for the investors on other grounds.

The *Metalclad* tribunal found a breach of Article 1110 and ordered compensation.[125] The Tribunal cited Article 1110 and stated:

> Thus, expropriation under NAFTA includes not only open, deliberate and acknowledged takings of property, such as outright seizure or formal or obligatory transfer of title in favor of the host State, but also covert or incidental interference with the use of property which has the effect of depriving the owner, in whole or in significant part, of the use or reasonably-to-be-expected economic benefit of property even if not necessarily to the obvious benefit of the host state.[126]

On two sets of facts, the *Metalclad* tribunal ruled that an expropriation. The tribunal ruled that the Mexican government had expropriated the foreign investment by refusing to grant a building permit and by adopting an ecological decree that effectively prevented the investor from operating his business.[127]Although the award was eventually narrowed on appeal, the finding of expropriation resulting from the ecological decree was upheld.[128]

This remains the only Chapter 11 case to find an expropriation. Although the facts of the *Metalclad* case tilted strongly in favor of this finding, a dearth of citation by the tribunal to sources for the propositions it appeared to hold as true remains troubling.[129] This lack of citation strongly suggests that the tribunal justified its perceptions with expropriation language.

BUS. REV. AM. 499 (1999). The Bush administration was looking at ways to incorporate into NAFTA principles mandated by the Trade Act of 2002. For a comparison of the expropriations law in the NAFTA countries, see Poirier, *supra* note 80 at fn 104 and 105.

121 *Metalclad, supra* note 28.

122 *Id.*

123. *S. D. Myers, supra* note 28.

124 *Pope &Talbot, supra* note 28.

125 *Metalclad, supra* note 28.

126 *Id.* ¶ 103.

127 *Id.* ¶ ¶ 109–12.

128 Mexico v. Metalclad, British Columbia Supreme Court, Reasons for Judgment, Justice Tysoe, May 2, 2001, *available at* http://www.dfait-maeci.gc.ca/tna-nac/documents/trans-2may.pdf.

129 *See* Levesque, *supra* note 26 (even though the tribunal referred to the *Biloune* case, it was distinct on the facts and not used as a source for the definition of expropriation. *See also* J.C. Thomas, *Reflections on Article 1105 of NAFTA: History, State Practice and the Influence of Commentators*, 17 ICSID Rev.—FOR. INV. L.J. 21–101 (2002).

Based on the perceived success of the expropriation claims in *Metalclad*, expropriation claims appear to have become the weapon of choice in many claims.[130] In response to an onslaught of cases filed after the *Metalclad* ruling, many tribunals quickly dismissed expropriation claims when the issue was no more than a breach of contract with local authorities[131] or when the issue was more properly founded on another Chapter 11 provision, such as 1105.[132] Other tribunals, having accepted the applicability of Article 1110 to the claim, have gone on to limit the potential scope of its application.[133] The tribunals in *Pope* and *Feldman*[134] also held that "tantamount" meant equivalent, an interpretation consistent with the French and Spanish versions of Article 1110.[135]

The *Pope* tribunal noted that regulation could be disguised expropriation. It stated:

> Regulations can indeed be characterized in a way that would constitute creeping expropriation... Indeed, much creeping expropriation could be conducted by regulation, and a blanket exception for regulatory measures would create a gaping loophole in international protection against expropriation.[136]

However, the *Pope* tribunal narrowed the definition of expropriation in finding that the regulatory measure in question did not constitute an expropriation under international law.[137] The *Pope* tribunal referenced the Harvard Draft and the U.S. *Restatement of Law* as sources of guidance. The analysis used by this tribunal revolved around the degree of interference caused by the measure to the investor's property. The tribunal confirmed that under international law, the interference had to be substantial.[138]

This tribunal looked for "an interference with the investment's business activities substantial enough to be characterized as an expropriation".[139] This Tribunal elaborated:

> The test is whether that interference is sufficiently restrictive to support a conclusion that the property has been "taken" from the owner... Action that is confiscatory, or that prevents, unreasonably interferes with or unduly delays, effective enjoyment of an alien's property.[140]

---

[130] *See* Weiler, *supra* note 83, at 325 (arguing that the time has come to avoid the kitchen sink approach to Chapter 11 claims).

[131] *See* Robert Azinian et al. v. the United Mexican States, Final Award, Nov. 1, 1999, *available at* www.naftalaw.org. (tribunal refusing to elevate contract breach with municipal authority to expropriation claim).

[132] *See* R. Loewen and Loewen Corp. v. USA, Final Award, June 23, 2003 (tribunal dismissing expropriation claim as Article 1105 adds nothing to the Article 1105 claim).

[133] *Pope* and *Feldman*, *supra* note 28.

[134] *Feldman*, *supra* note 28.

[135] Levesque, *supra* note 26, at 300.

[136] *Pope*, *supra* note 28.

[137] *Id.* at 96.

[138] *Id.* at 102.

[139] *Id.* ¶ 96.

[140] *Id.* ¶ 102.

The factors used by the tribunal further support this test. In finding that an expropriation had not occurred, the tribunal considered the fact that there was no nationalization or loss of control, and exports and profits by Pope and Talbot continued under the scheme. The tribunal focused on the fact that the investor was capable of maintaining part of its business in a profitable state of affairs.[141]

These extracts suggest that the principle test rests on the degree or significance of the interference with the use of the property. The tribunal concluded that because there was no substantial interference, no expropriation had occurred.

The *Myers* tribunal followed the reasoning of the *Pope* tribunal in its analysis of the necessary degree of deprivation to property rights to invoke a finding of expropriation. It stated:

> Expropriations tend to involve the deprivation of ownership rights; regulations a lesser interference. The distinction between expropriation and regulation screens out most potential cases of complaints concerning economic intervention by a state and reduces the risk that governments will be subject to claims as they go about their business of managing public affairs.[142]

Myers went further to impose a temporal qualification on the measure in question. It stated:

> An expropriation usually amounts to a lasting removal of the ability of an owner to make use of its economic rights although it may be that, in some contexts and circumstances, it would be appropriate to view a deprivation as amounting to an expropriation, even if it were partial or temporary.[143]

Myers found that temporary restrictions will usually not amount to an expropriation. On the facts of this case, the tribunal found that a temporary border closing does not constitute an expropriation. Although the outcome of this case on the facts is not assailable, the reasoning of the tribunal has not advanced the thinking on the subject.[144] The minority opinion, which follows the majority, but deletes the qualifiers, is arguably more helpful. It states:

> Expropriations tend to be severe deprivations of ownership rights; Regulations tend to amount to much less interference.[145]

---

141 *Pope, supra* note 28, at 101.

142 *Myers, supra* note 28, ¶ 282.

143 *Id.* ¶ 283.

144 Levesque, *supra* note 26, at 303 (Noting that the degree-based distinction offered by the tribunal is fairly meaningless, as both expropriation and regulation can result in a deprivation of rights. The fact that the regulation "interferes less" is not helpful.)

145 *Myers, supra* note 28, ¶ 211.

The *Feldman* tribunal charted its own course by undertaking an analysis that did not focus on the degree or threshold of deprivation, but looked at factors that tend to distinguish expropriation from regulation. In so doing, this tribunal appears to reject the possibility of a bright-line test that distinguishes regulation from expropriation. Instead, this tribunal held that expropriation is a finding that is fact-specific.

The *Feldman* tribunal stated:

> With regard to this case, Article 1110 deals not only with direct takings, but indirect expropriations and measures "tantamount to expropriation," which potentially encompass a variety of government regulatory activity that may significantly interfere with an investors property rights.... However, it is much less clear when governmental action that interferes with broadly-defined property rights—an "investment" under NAFTA, Article 1139—crosses the line from valid regulation to a compensable taking, and it is fair to say that no one has come up with a full satisfactory means of drawing this line.[146]

The *Feldman* tribunal held that expropriation was fact-specific and declined to find an expropriation on the facts of this case.[147]

> In some circumstances government regulatory activity can be a violation of Article 1110. [148]... [N]ot all government regulatory activity that makes it difficult or impossible for an investor to carry out a particular business, change in the law or change in the application of existing laws that makes it uneconomical to continue a particular business, is an expropriation under Article 1110. Governments, in their exercise of regulatory power, frequently change their laws and regulations in response to changing economic circumstances or changing political, economic or social considerations. Those changes may well make certain activities less profitable or even uneconomic to continue.[149]

The *Feldman* tribunal then proceeded to undertake a contextual analysis of the regulatory scheme and the rights and entitlements of the investor. The tribunal analyzed whether an expropriation under Article 1110(1) had taken place, and noted that subparagraphs (a) through (e) did not add much to the analysis.[150] Most of the measures can be reviewed under the nondiscrimination and fair and equitable treatment provisions that are covered in two of those subparagraphs.[151]

The *Feldman* tribunal appears to have given short shrift to the subparagraphs, perhaps violating the principle of effectiveness. This might have been inevitable

146 *Feldman, supra* note 28, ¶ 100.

147 *Id.* ¶ 102; *see* Poirier, *supra* note 80.

148 *Id.*

149 *Id.* ¶ 112.

150 *Id.* ¶ 135.

151 *Pope, supra* note 28, Damages Award, ¶ 111.

given that the tribunal was trying to apply archaic language to a modern regulatory taking. However, the tribunal's approach might be beyond criticism given that the subparagraphs do not constitute an exception to Article 1110 because the language of "and" at the end of subparagraph (c) suggests compensation is payable notwithstanding a measure that might otherwise be balanced, fair, and nondiscriminatory. Discriminatory measures that violate fundamental norms of due process may be pursued via Article 1102 or 1105 without requiring proof of a total deprivation of the value of an investment.[152]

The *Pope* and *Feldman* tribunals looked for a substantial degree of government interference and its effective confiscation of the investment. Any interference caused by a measure that affects merely a portion of an investor's business will normally not be considered "sufficient" if the investment continues to operate.[153] Commentators have suggested that large corporate investors might circumvent this limitation by structuring their investments so that different corporate entities are responsible for different lines of the business. This may rebut the successful arguments of governments that because the investment continues to operate, the taking of part of the business does not constitute expropriation under 1139 and 1110.[154]

Tribunals are helping to shape the takings jurisprudence developing both on the international plane and in the United States. Although the development of this jurisprudence cannot be isolated, troubling questions arise when international concepts, NAFTA concepts, and U.S. concepts are either blended without due consideration, or are artificially separated to make findings that may be valid under one set of norms and questionable under another. This discussion will be limited to the problems arising when U.S. takings concepts are imposed on Chapter 11 cases.

To a certain extent the Americanization of Chapter 11 is inevitable. To the extent that Chapter 11 cases involve the United States as a host state or U.S. investors, there will be U.S. jurists appointed to serve as Chapter 11 arbitrators. This will inevitably bring a U.S. focus to the analysis. However, the process may be better served if these tribunals focus more on generic property principles than specific takings principles developed in the context of the distinct constitutional traditions of the NAFTA Parties.

Both the *Pope* and *Feldman* tribunals narrowly focused their analysis on the American legal tradition. The Feldman tribunal relied on the U.S. Restatement of Law. The *Pope* tribunal relied on both the Restatement and the Harvard Draft. Both might be legitimately referred to as a subsidiary source of law under the Statute of the International Court of Justice.[155]

---

152 *See* Weiler, *supra* note 83, at 350.

153 *Feldman, supra* note 28, ¶ 152.

154 *See* Weiler, *supra* note 83, at 349.

155 ICJ Statute, Article 38(d) refers to "the teachings of the most highly qualified publicists of various nations" to help determine the rules of law. *See* http://www.icj-cij.org/cijwww/cdocumentbase/cba-sictext/cbasicstatute.html.

These sources should be recognized as being an American perspective of international law. Therefore, although these may accurately reflect certain aspects of international law, they will offer a distinctly American perspective on others.[156] The Comments in the Restatement state that the "line to be drawn in international law is similar to that drawn in US jurisprudence for the purposes of the Fifth and Fourteenth amendments."[157] This line is by no means clear, and the values underpinning those amendments of the U.S. Constitution are not given the same weight in international law as they are given under U.S. law.[158]

In sum, these cases suggest that the question of expropriation rests on a reference to an interference scale, where substantial interference is required to ground a finding of expropriation. Regrettably, the question of how much interference is substantial is influenced by the context and is not susceptible to a bright-line test. These cases further suggest that the expropriation test is merely the first step in the analysis. If the analysis ends with the question of expropriation, all measures that substantially interfered with investor property rights (however defined) would attract compensatory liability. As such, legitimate government regulation would not be exempt.

Step II: The Police Powers Exception

It might fairly be said that although one might expect recourse for expropriation, one should not expect compensation for legitimate regulation. This raises an interesting question as to who should bear the burden of regulation: society as a whole or affected individuals? The limits set on property, by other public interests, are determined by what has been labeled as the police power of the state.[159]

Customary international law recognizes the exercise of police power by the state and specifically exempts it from the compensation liability that attaches to expropriation. Its scope is understood to include all aspects of governing, such as measures affecting taxation, monetary policy, fiscal policy, penal codes and enforcement, public health and safety, and so forth. This police powers principle has evolved as an exception in international trade law. Bona fide measures adopted pursuant to the police

[156] *See* Levesque, *supra* note 26, at 303–04.

[157] *Id.* at 304, and David Gantz, *Potential Conflicts between Investor Rights and Environmental Regulation under NAFTA Chapter 11*, 33 GEO. WASH. INT'L L. REV. 651 (2001).

[158] Levesque, *supra* note 26, at 304.

[159] Courts have long grappled with the question of where property rights end and regulation begins. Hudson Water Co. v. McCarter, 209 U.S. 349, 355 (1908) (Holmes, J), "The boundary at which the conflicting interests balance cannot be determined by any general formula in advance, but points in the line, or helping to establish it, are fixed by decisions that this or that concrete case falls on the nearer or farther side."

powers principles should not attract compensatory liability.[160] The principle has been described as follows:

> The conclusion that a particular interference is an expropriation might also be avoided if the State whose actions are the subject of complaint had a purpose in mind which is recognized in international law as justifying even severe, although by no means complete, restrictions on the use of property. Thus . . . actions in the interest of the public health and morality, will all serve to justify actions which because of their severity would not otherwise be justifiable; subject to . . . the action in question not be . . . discriminatory.[161]

The internal law of all countries recognizes the right of the sovereign to regulate in the public interest. Similarly, the NAFTA countries each recognize the right of expropriation and the police power of the state. However, the NAFTA countries have different legal and constitutional traditions that preclude a harmonized vision of expropriation, the police power of the state, and property rights.[162] Thus, the use of one country's law is inappropriate in the Chapter 11 context.

The need to exempt certain governmental regulations from compensation liability is necessary if a sovereign is to govern. However, defining the parameters of such measures is a much more involved exercise. Measures regarding public health are as necessary to governing as are measures relating to fiscal, monetary, and penal provisions. Although taxation, monetary, and fiscal issues might ground an expropriation, penal measures are generally excluded from compensation liability because the punitive nature of such a measure is antithetical to the concept of compensation.[163]

Other less well studied, but equally important areas might reside in developing sovereign activity in areas of trade law, consumer protection, and so forth. Although the scope of government regulation is expanding, one thing is certain—not all government regulation should be exempt from compensation liability. That is, the police power exemption to compensation should not attach to every governmental measure. Although sovereigns are granted much discretion in regulating for the public good, this discretion is not unfettered. To find otherwise would be exclude compensation for expropriation in all cases, irrespective of purpose or motivation.

Public interest and police power are not synonymous under international law. Although "public interest" is a useful criterion to establish exemptions to expropriation compensation liability, it cannot operate to the exclusion of other factors.[164]

Governmental measures have the potential of being disguised expropriation. Both customary international law and general principles of law may give guidance as to

160 George Aldrich, *What Constitutes a Compensable Taking of Property: The Decisions of the Iran–US Claims Tribunal*, 88 AJIL 585–610, 609 (1994).

161 Christie, *supra* note 35, at 338 (1962).

162 Poirier, *supra* note 80, n.104 and n. 105.

163 Levesque, *supra* note 26, at 305.

164 *Id.* at 306, quoting Higgins and Schwarzenberger.

drawing the appropriate distinction. The discriminatory character of a measure is perhaps the most obvious example of a taint that would convert an otherwise exempt measure into one attracting compensation liability. Other red flags include excessive and arbitrary measures, as well as the abuse of individually guaranteed rights by a state.[165]

Chapter 11 jurisprudence will benefit from the guidance found in international law on this issue and will also shape its evolution. Chapter 11 tribunals have, implicitly and explicitly, recognized that the police power of the state may shield certain ostensible expropriation measures from attracting compensatory liability. These tribunals have used international law to interpret Article 1110. Chapter 11 jurisprudence does not create stare decisis under international law or even under the Chapter 11 regime. However, decisions of other tribunals can be reviewed during subsequent analyses of Chapter 11 matters, and their reasoning may prove persuasive to subsequent tribunals.[166]

In finding an expropriation, *Metalclad* appears to have set the watershed mark of expropriation claims. Although this decision did not specifically reject the police powers exemption, its analysis focused on the effects, rather than the purpose of the measures. In so doing, it tended to elevate the concerns of impacted investors and downplay the need of governments to regulate.

The *Metalclad* tribunal focused on the potential expropriatory qualities of regulation. It noted that regulation may amount to expropriation. It stated that an expropriation might arise when:

> . . . any covert or incidental interference with the use of property which has the effect of depriving the owner, in whole or in significant part, of the use or reasonably to be expected economic benefit of property even if not necessarily to the obvious benefit of the host state.[167]

One reading of this award is that the tribunal, in focusing on the interference of the regulation on the property, totally vitiated the applicability of the purpose-and-effect analysis. It has been argued that in so doing, for all practical purposes, this had the effect of precluding the police power principle, which is a purpose-based analysis.[168]

Another view is that although not specifically rejecting the police power principle, the *Metalclad* tribunal noted the importance of the effect of the regulation and diminished the importance of motivation or intent behind the regulation. The tribunal stated:

> The Tribunal need not decide or consider the motivation or intent of the Ecological Decree. Indeed, a finding of expropriation on the basis of the Ecological Decree is

165 *Id.*
166 *See* MANN, *supra* note 78; Soloway, *supra* note 78.
167 *Metalclad*, *supra* note 28, ¶ 102.
168 *See* MANN, *supra* note 78; Soloway, *supra* note 78.

> not essential to the Tribunal's finding of a violation under Article 1110. However, the Tribunal considers that the implementation of the Ecological Decree would, in and of itself, constitute an act tantamount to expropriation. [169]

A cursory analysis may suggest that the *Metalclad* tribunal rejected the police power principle. However, a closer examination may offer an alternate explanation. This view holds that the tribunal recognized that an indirect expropriation may have the equivalent effect as an expropriation, regardless of the intent or motivation of the regulation in question.[170] However, although the intent of the sovereign was discounted, the purpose of the measure is not irrelevant. The tribunal's limited analysis renders it difficult to determine whether the tribunal rejected the purpose of the statute or merely confirmed that the effect trumped intent in this case because, by the tribunal's own characterization, the expropriation resulting from the measure was direct, and therefore the police power principle was inapplicable as it relates only to indirect expropriations.[171]

The *Metalclad* decision remains controversial. There is widespread disagreement among commentators on the finding of facts and the impact that those findings might have had on different parts of the arbitral decision. One thing is certain: this award missed the opportunity to examine the ecological decree in light of the police powers principle. Such an analysis could have assisted in distinguishing measures whereby governments regulate to create a state asset—here an ecological reserve—from measures that prevent the use of property in an environmentally injurious manner.

It has been suggested that in cases where the government sets land aside for public use, it might well fall into the expropriation category outside the scope of the police powers principle. Such an analysis could reach the same result while expressly recognizing the role of the police powers principle. The tribunal's decision to, deliberately or not, end the analysis at the first step remains troubling.[172]

A closer look at the facts of the case may well explain the tribunal's focus. *Metalclad* was one of the first cases to get to the adjudication of the expropriation claim. Therefore it might have been looked upon as a test of the expropriation protection mechanism. This might explain the focus on the effect of the measure. Additionally, the case rang with allegations of old-fashioned corruption politics. The responsible level of government had given the environmental permit, the local authority requested a building permit for the first time in history, and there were allegations that politically influential family members had a direct interest in a competing investment.[173] Given the tenor of these allegations, it is not difficult to understand the tribunal's focus.

---

169 *Metalclad*, *supra* note 28, ¶ 111.

170 Levesque, *supra* note 26, citing Herz, Christie, and Higgins.

171 *See Feldman* Award, *supra* note 28, at n.29 and ¶ 148.

172 Solway, *supra* note 78; MANN, *supra* note 78.

173 *Metalclad*, *supra* note 28.

The *Pope* tribunal recognized the delicate nature of regulations. In describing the police powers principle, it stated:

> Canada appears to claim that, because the measures under consideration are cast in the form of regulations, they constitute an exercise of police powers, which if nondiscriminatory, are supposedly beyond the reach of the NAFTA rules regarding expropriations. While the exercise of police powers must be analyzed with special care, the Tribunal believes that Canada's formulation goes too far. Regulations can indeed be exercised in a way that would constitute creeping expropriation.... Indeed, much creeping expropriation could be conducted by regulation, and a blanket exception for regulatory measures would create a gaping loophole in international protections against expropriation.[174]

The tribunal properly rejected the Canadian argument. The claim that simply because it was regulation, it was automatically protected under the police power principle is too narrow a reading of international law on this issue. As well, nondiscriminatory regulation could nonetheless constitute expropriation if arbitrary or excessive, or if it substantially deprives the owner of property rights. Moreover, an able argument might be made that the export management scheme does not fall within the traditional police powers rubric.[175]

The *Pope* award states that nondiscriminatory measures, within the scope of police powers, are covered by Article 1110. It reasoned that a blanket exemption would permit creeping expropriation or indirect expropriation to go unchallenged due to its form. Unfortunately its reasoning as to the distinction between bona fide regulation under the police powers principle and confiscatory protectionist regulation is not sufficiently developed as this tribunal did not find the substantial interference to go beyond the first part of the expropriation test.

The *Feldman* tribunal also appeared to recognize the applicability of the police powers principle. It stated:

> The Tribunal notes that the ways in which governmental authorities may force a company out of business, or significantly reduce the economic benefits of its business, are many...At the same time governments must be free to act in the broader public interest through protection of the environment, new or modified tax regimes, the granting or withholding of government subsidies, reduction or increases in tariff levels, imposition of zoning restrictions and the like. Reasonable governmental regulation of this type cannot be achieved if any business that is adversely affected may seek compensation, and it is safe to say that customary international law recognizes this.[176]

---

[174] *Pope, supra* note 28, ¶ 99.

[175] Levesque, *supra* note 26 at 307.

[176] *Feldman* award, *supra* note 28, ¶ 103.

Although the tribunal noted that not all business problems amount to expropriation, there are some circumstances under which regulation could amount to expropriation.[177] Citing *Azinian*,[178] the tribunal noted that not all regulatory activity that makes it difficult or impossible to carry on business, or changes in law that make it economically unfeasible to carry on business, constitute expropriation under Article 1110. Governments, pursuant to their regulatory power, need to adjust their regulations to changing circumstances. These changes, in turn, may affect the economic well-being of an investor.[179] The tribunal concluded that although no one factor was conclusive, taken together the factors tipped the balance toward a finding of no expropriation.[180]

The *Myers* tribunal remains the only tribunal to have gone beyond the expropriation question and analyzed the potential applicability of the police power principle. This tribunal went beyond the significant impact analysis. The Myers decision recognizes that some cases of regulation may well amount to expropriation, with the caveat however that most cases of regulation will not amount to expropriation.[181]

This tribunal formally noted the importance of looking at the purpose and effect of a measure when analyzing whether an expropriation has occurred.[182] This analysis confirms both the role of the police powers principle, which might be gleaned through a purposive analysis, and at the same time a substance-over-form analysis looking at the effect rather than the intent of the measure. The tribunal stated:

> The Tribunal accepts that...international law makes it appropriate for tribunals to examine the purpose and effect of governmental measures. The Interim Order and the Final Order were regulatory acts that imposed restrictions on SDMI. The general body of precedent usually does not treat regulatory action as amounting to expropriation. Regulatory conduct by public authorities is unlikely to be the subject of legitimate complaint under Article 1110 of the NAFTA, although the Tribunal does not rule out that possibility.[183]

Having noted the importance of a purpose analysis as well as an effects test, the *Myers* tribunal then turned to an examination of the factors and tests that follow. The tribunal noted that the following factors deserved consideration:

- whether a deprivation of ownership rights or a lesser interference were at issue;
- whether the interference was lasting or temporary(noting that expropriation might at times be temporary); and
- whether the state received some benefit from the measure.[184]

---

177 *Id.* ¶ 110.
178 *Supra* note 131.
179 *Id.* ¶ 112.
180 *Feldman, supra* note 28, ¶ 111.
181 *Myers, supra* note 28, ¶ 280–81.
182 *Id.* ¶¶ 281, 285.
183 *Id.* ¶ 281.
184 *Id.*

The tribunal found that the measure was temporary, did not involve a deprivation of ownership rights, and did not confer any benefit to the state. The tribunal therefore concluded that the measure did not constitute an expropriation.[185] This analysis was similar to the analysis used by the other tribunals in that the focus appeared to be based on effects—namely the degree of impact. The tribunal's interpretation of the facts, finding that the measure was a disguised protectionist measure, limited its development of the analysis on the question of the police powers principle in terms of the bona fides of the measure. However, although the tribunal made mention of a purpose component to the analysis, its actual analysis fell short in this regard. Its analysis focused on criteria that, in the end, focused on effect and not purpose. Therefore, the promised effect-and-purpose distinction did not materialize in the analysis. Unfortunately, from an analytical perspective, having not found an expropriation the tribunal did not have to explore whether this regulation was pursuant to the state's police powers and as such could shield the state from a liability to pay compensation. Also, there was no guidance as to whether the facts of this case could support an exception to the police power principle if the measure was discriminatory or arbitrary (i.e., there was no legitimate environmental reason for the regulation).[186]

The dissenter in *Myers* came closer to addressing the critical distinction between effect and purpose. He noted that regulation is something that owners ought to expect.[187] He argued that Article 110 must be read in light of NAFTA's overall environmental construction, including the preamble, Article 1114, and the NAAEC. He argued that the government has a right to protect the environment, and noted that Article 1110 "does not constitute a generous invitation to impose liability for regulatory activity in the ordinary course of government business."[188]

The dissenter stated that regulatory conduct is remotely the subject of legitimate complaint, but undermined the strength of this finding with the qualification that this is the case most of the time.[189] He noted the need for a purposive analytical approach to complement the focus on effects. He also noted criteria that might be useful in distinguishing regulatory measures from nonregulatory confiscatory measures. Specifically, he mentioned:

- severe versus lesser forms of deprivation;[190]
- whether the state or third party is enriched by the measure[191]

[185] *Id.* ¶¶ 287–88.

[186] *See* Levesque, *supra* note 26, at 309.

[187] *Myers*, Schwartz Dissent, *supra* note 28, ¶ 213.

[188] *Id.* ¶ 214.

[189] *Id.* ¶ 207.

[190] *Id.* ¶ 211.

[191] *Id.* ¶ 212.

- unjust deprivation upon one party with a corresponding unjust enrichment on the other party.[192]
- regulation that tends to prevent the use of property in a way that that unjustly enriches the owner.[193]

The dissenter concluded his analysis by finding that there had not been a transfer of wealth and that the measure was temporary. He concluded by stating that he "would refrain from characterizing the export ban as an expropriation" due to political concerns that expropriations issues were inflammatory, and thus rulings on expropriations should not be made unless necessary.[194] Regrettably, because this decision did not rule on the expropriation versus regulation issue, it will probably undermine the relevance and weight that subsequent tribunals accord to the criteria used to distinguish between expropriation and regulation. Perhaps even more regrettable is the fact that by not ruling on the expropriation, after extensive reasoning and analysis, a chance was lost to clarify the criteria or tests applicable to his introductory caveat of "in most cases."[195]

These cases confirm that the expropriation test is merely the first step in the analysis. If the analysis stopped with the question of expropriation, all measures that substantially interfered with investor property rights would attract compensatory liability and read the police powers principle out of existence. The cases further suggest that international law recognizes the police power principle under which various forms of government regulation, which would otherwise be indirect expropriation, are exempted from compensation liability. However, this principle is not unfettered where a regulation, pursuant to the state's police power, can be shown to be discriminatory, arbitrary, excessive, or abusive.

However, these cases also confirm that there is no simple definition of the police power principle. Once again, the analysis fails to develop a bright-line test and remains fact-sensitive, turning on evidentiary standards and on "degree." Commentators have noted that the absence of a test to distinguish the bona fides of regulation does not imply a trumping of the police powers principle. They note the difficulty in reducing a "smell test" into a series of discreet legal questions. Commentators argue that arbitrators are imbued with discretion to provide flexibility in making this determination.[196]

Whether existing tests implicitly recognize the police powers principle is yet to be explicitly developed in the cases. While Chapter 11 jurisprudence develops in this regard, a focus on the investor's "reasonable to be expected benefit" from the property may inform the debate. Such an analysis would evaluate whether certain regulations,

---

192 *Id.*

193 *Id.*

194 *Id.* ¶ 222–23.

195 *See* Solway, *supra* note 78, and MANN, *supra* note 78.

196 *Id.*

designed to protect the public interest, may be "reasonably expected" and therefore not compensable. The classic example is the toxic polluter who is eventually stopped; he could not reasonably expect to be permitted to pollute perpetually.[197] Such a scenario would also provide a second line of defense to regulation, after passing the substantial interference hurdle. Although not yet addressed in the case, this analysis can be derived through a property rights analysis.

Step III: The Property Link

Traditionally, a foreign investor's protected property rights have included the rights to: remain in possession and operate and manage, and not to be stripped of indirect beneficial interests such as profits. Commentators have begun to debate whether Chapter 11 has expanded the pool of protected property rights.[198] As the array of property rights broadens, the scope for Chapter 11's application grows proportionately. Whether the expansion of property rights narrows the ability of governments to regulate, without engaging compensation liability, is an exercise that requires analysis of evolving property principles.[199]

International tribunals have looked at many attributes in determining whether an expropriation has resulted. These attributes have included the right to use and dispose of property,[200] as well as the direction and management of property.[201] Although lawyers may use different terminology to describe property's attributes, the common law rights to use, exploit, and dispose of property are consonant with the civil law's focus on *usus*, *fructus*, and *abusus*.[202] Most arbitrators, international or NAFTA, generally refer to these elements, but rarely state their origin or sources.

Commentators have questioned whether these property elements are general principles of law or a selective transposition in international law of domestic law concepts.[203] Although property is central to expropriation law, it is a concept whose definition has eluded an international elaboration. As a consequence, investment disputes that turn on the definition of property might be resolved on the basis of an arbitrator's implicit values, which are susceptible to wide variations.[204] Such an approach is unsustainable

---

197 The *Feldman* tribunal, *supra* note 28, essentially ruled that Feldman had not complained when the government closed a questionably legitimate tax loophole.

198 *Id.*

199 Levesque, *supra* note 26, at 309.

200 *Id.* at 313, citing Carreau and Juillard.

201 *Id.* citing Laviec, Herz, Christie, and Solway.

202 *See* the application of this at Libyan Oil v. Government of Libya, 20 I.L.M. 1 (1981), §§ 89–92.

203 Levesque, *supra* note 26, at 314, citing PAUL E. COMEAUX & N. STEPHAN KINSELLA, PROTECTING FOREIGN INVESTMENT UNDER INTERNATIONAL LAW 1–2 (1996) (succinct description of civil and common law terminology on property).

204 Levesque, *supra* note 26, at 310–11.

in that it fosters a perception of arbitrariness and inhibits the evolution of analytical rigor.

Chapter 11 tribunals have begun to evaluate investor rights within a framework that goes beyond traditional analysis. The *Pope* tribunal found that access to market share was a protected right, noting the key export component of its business.[205] Similarly, the dissent in *Myers* explored the protected rights in market share.[206] If market share is a protected right, then any measures that shifts, directly or indirectly, market share could arguably be confiscatory.

International law has developed a definition of expropriation to provide a minimal standard of treatment across borders. However, a complementary elaboration of the definition of property has not been developed on the international plane. Notwithstanding the concerns raised by commentators, international legal analysis has failed to adequately analyze the conceptual aspects of property in the context of expropriation.[207] This remains perplexing because a narrow definition of property could have the same effect on investors as a narrow definition of expropriation.[208]

There are many reasons explaining why the concept of property has not been developed on the international plane. At the root of this phenomenon is the traditional notion that property is a matter that is limited to national laws. This is consistent with the conflict-of-laws rules, which designated the law of property to the jurisdiction in which the land was situated.[209] However, the expansion of property rights to objects beyond land, and the increasingly transnational nature of investment, requires that the thinking on this issue be revisited.

The relatively modern notion of indirect expropriation is another reason international law failed to develop a more comprehensive definition of property. Indirect expropriation was not recognized until well into the nineteenth century when traditional property notions had already taken root.[210] However, given sovereign recognition of property rights and the growing claims of indirect expropriation, traditional notions of property may need to be reconsidered.

Yet another reason that tends to explain the lack of development of the property notion in international law is that the BITs were negotiated among sovereigns that were more concerned with the notion of "investment." NAFTA Chapter 11 is such an example, where the Parties defined investment, but not property. However, given that investments are objects of property, any analysis of expropriation without reference to property rights remains incomplete.

It is simply not feasible to determine whether an investor has been substantially deprived of property rights without defining what constitutes property. In defining

---

205 *Pope*, *supra* note 28, ¶¶ 96–98.

206 *Myers*, *supra* note 28 (Schwartz dissent at 45–46).

207 Levesque, *supra* note 26, at 310, citing Herz and Higgins.

208 *Id.*, citing Bindschedler and Brownlie.

209 *Id.*

210 *Id.*

property, its objects and essential attributes need to be identified. The object of property relates to the kind of things that can be expropriated. Understanding the attributes of the property in question enables discussion of whether the measures substantially deprive owners of rights.[211]

International law respecting compensation and restitution has given a broad definition to the objects of property and the interests therein that are protected.[212] Chapter 11 follows this tradition by giving "investment" an expansive definition.[213] Notwithstanding this broad definition of the objects of property, tribunals will benefit from further guidance, relating to the norms regarding the actual character of property rights.[214]

The *Pope* tribunal grappled with this inherent difficulty in defining property rights. Despite the Canadian government's opposition, the tribunal held that the investment's access to the U.S. market was a protected property right. It held:

> While Canada suggests that the ability to sell softwood lumber from British Columbia to the US is an abstraction, it is in fact, a very important part of the business of the investment. Interference with that business would necessarily have an adverse effect on the property... which... constitutes the investment... the true interests that are at stake are the investors asset base, the value of which is largely dependent on it export business.[215]

The *Pope* tribunal also referred to the Harvard Draft citing the right to "use, enjoy and dispose of the property."[216] In its analysis, it considered the attributes of property, including the control of the investment, direction of day-to-day operations, and lack of interference with management.[217]

The *Feldman* tribunal similarly dealt with troubling questions relating to property rights. In evaluating the right to export, the tribunal noted that neither the NAFTA nor the principles of customary international law permit gray-market exports. In so doing, it referred to the *Pope* and *Myers* tribunals in analyzing the objects of property, as well as the essential attributes of property and related denominator problem. It held:

> It may be questioned as to whether the claimant ever possessed a right to export that has been taken... the regulatory action... has not deprived the claimant of control of its investment.... The claimant is free to pursue other continuing lines of export....[218]

---

211 *Id.*, at 311, citing Higgins, Michelman, and Munzer.
212 *See, e.g.*, Harvard Draft, *infra*.
213 *See* Chapter 11, Article 1139.
214 Levesque, *supra* note 26, at 312 (as opposed to potential, and its durability as opposed to revocability).
215 *Pope, supra* note 28, ¶ 98.
216 *Id.* ¶ 102.
217 *Pope, supra* note 28, ¶ 100.
218 *Feldman, supra* note 28, ¶ 152.

The *Feldman* tribunal, in its discussion of direct expropriation, noted the necessity of finding a deprivation of all meaningful benefits of control and ownership.[219] It also considered whether there had been a deprivation of control, an interference with management, and so forth.[220] It held that although Mexico may have violated Article 1102 in administering its tax regime by treating the foreign investor to audits that locals did not need to endure, it did not commit a compensable taking because it closed a loophole through which the investor had been profiting.

Feldman appears to stand for the proposition that the question of whether an expropriation has taken place is tied to whether the investor had a legitimate expectation of deriving an economic benefit from the allegedly expropriated right (the polluter example). This approach is in keeping with the reasoning in *Metalclad*. The *Metalclad* test included an interference with the use of the property that had the effect of depriving the owner of the reasonably to be expected economic benefit of the property.[221] Similarly, the *Myers* tribunal referenced reasonable expectations when it noted that an expropriation usually amounted to a lasting removal of the ability of the owner to make economic use of its rights.[222] Implicit in this reasoning is that although an investor, doing business in a regulated society, might reasonably expect a temporary curtailment of economic rights, it might well expect compensation for measures that go further.

The evolution of a modern international property standard could provide Chapter 11 tribunals with an additional tool to draw the distinction between expropriation and regulation. This would be particularly helpful in cases where the value of an investment is diminished as a result of a measure, or where profits have diminished. It may also help in understanding what use of the property is protected—optimal or reasonable? Is it the existing or planned use? Similar questions arise with respect to the management of a company—is it exclusive or relative? Such a standard is dynamic and requires a contextual analysis in terms of the changing social norms that shape its evolution.

Property: The Social Context

The notion of property is best understood in the context of the society in which it evolves. A thorough discussion of the evolution of property is clearly beyond the parameters of this chapter.[223] For our limited purposes, a discussion of the role property plays in our social order may help provide context for the analysis of who should bear the

[219] *Id.* ¶ 100.

[220] *Id.* ¶¶ 142, 152.

[221] *Metalclad*, *supra* note 28, ¶ 103.

[222] *Myers*, *supra* note 28, ¶ 283.

[223] For a discussion of the role of property in society, see Eric A. Kaes, *Foreword: Property Rights and Economic Development*, 45 WM. & MARY L. REV. 815 (2004).

burden of regulation and how it should be apportioned. These questions cannot be answered without consideration of the social function of property.[224]

The general principles of law and customary international law recognize that a foreign investor submits itself to the laws of the jurisdiction, with its concomitant risks, of the home state.[225] However, this submission is not unfettered because international law recognizes the applicability of certain minimum standards, which includes the rules on expropriation. The difficulty in applying this standard is that the foreign investor often complains about the amendments made to regulations subsequent to its investment.

Similarly, another legal standard, risk allocation, is of limited utility in this exercise. Risk allocation burdens the party best able to deal with the risk. However, transposing this contract analysis to property principles, in the context of expropriation, is insufficient. The party best able to diversify the risk, the investor, is not the party best able to control it, the government. [226]

Investors must act on the basis of risk evaluation. This evaluation in turn depends on a number of factors that influence the investor's expectations. An investor will analyze the risk of regulation based on the level of development of a country, the relevant industry, and the type of regulation. That is, investors might expect more regulation from an advanced country than a developing one. An investor might expect more regulation in the chemical industry than in the textile industry. An investor might expect more regulation as the measure nears the sphere of national security or health and safety. An investor might expect more scrutiny from governmental measures as the activity moves away from the common or legal and enters the risky and loophole-driven.[227]

Such an analysis focuses on the reasonable expectations of an investor. As Bentham noted, "Property is nothing but a basis of expectations."[228] Property is not absolute, and is subject to limitations. It is better to have reasonable or limited expectations.[229] The expectations of the investor, which are tied to the social function of property, act as a fulcrum for the expropriation–regulation debate. It is difficult to evaluate the quality and degree of a deprivation of property rights resulting from the measure until the property is identified. Even when the object and attributes of the property are identified, this might not suffice.

The laws of many Western developed countries do not generally guarantee the optimal use of property, but recognize that a prohibition of an existing use of property

[224] Levesque, *supra* note 26, at 315.

[225] *Id.* at 316, citing Higgins and Cheng.

[226] *Id.*

[227] *See* Thomas Walde, *Investment Arbitration as a Discipline for Good-Governance, in* NAFTA INVESTMENT LAW AND ARBITRATION: PAST ISSUES, CURRENT PRACTICE, FUTURE PROSPECTS (Todd Weiler ed., 2004) (providing an overview of the emerging jurisprudence and analytical approaches).

[228] JEREMY BENTHAM, THE THEORY OF LEGISLATION 111–12 (C.K. Ogden ed., 1931).

[229] Frank Michelman, *Property, Utility, and Fairness: Comments on the Ethical Foundations of "Just Compensation" Law*, 80(6) Harv. L. Rev. 1165, 1213 (1967).

can give rise to compensation.[230] Although property rights are not limitless, reasonable expectations of the owners can help distinguish between the situations where the owner of the property should bear the burden and where society should share in the burden of regulation and use. Gauging the degree of arbitrariness or excessiveness in the context of scientific uncertainty has compromised the analytical development of the modern police power.

This expectations analysis remains relevant even in the context of the state's exercise of its police power. Reasonable expectations analysis suggests that in certain situations, an investor who invests in a highly regulated or potentially dangerous sector might expect high profits in return for the assumption of certain regulatory risks. The reasonable expectations analysis suggests that, in some cases, the cost of the regulation should be borne by the investor and not apportioned to society.[231]

An expectations-type analysis was present in the *Feldman* award. In *Feldman*, the tribunal focused on Feldman's expectations and implied that he should have been aware and accepting of the law of the jurisdiction where the investment was made. In denying Feldman compensation, the tribunal recognized that the measure was part of a rational tax policy, was not an unreasonable measure, and was in place at all relevant times. The tribunal reasoned that Feldman could have sought professional tax guidance, which should have confirmed an objective reasonable expectation that tax loopholes could be closed. Such a conclusion did not warrant compensation, even though it might appear that foreigners were selected for its application.[232]

Perhaps, most telling on the issue of reasonable expectations is the contrast between the *Feldman* award and the *Metalclad* award. The *Feldman* tribunal implied that it was unreasonable to expect that tax loopholes enjoyed perpetual existence. The *Metalclad* tribunal implied that the investor had a reasonable expectation of noninterference with its investment after the appropriate level of government (federal) sanctioned its activity (hazardous waste landfill).[233] The difficulty generally, and in the NAFTA context specifically, is whether the different legal traditions recognize common elements in the definition of property and the role of regulation that can be reliably applied by multinational tribunals.

The NAFTA definition of investment refers to expectations.[234] Some commentators argue that this reference is insufficient to form the basis of a broad analysis.[235] Further support might be found in U.S. court decisions that have applied the concept

---

230 Dolzer, *supra* note 87.

231 *See* Walde, *supra* note 227.

232 *Feldman*, *supra* note 28.

233 Contrast *Metalclad*, *supra* note 28, at 103 with *Feldman*, *supra* note 28, at 114–34.

234 NAFTA Article 1139(g).

235 Levesque, *supra* note 26.

of "investment-backed expectations."[236] International tribunals have also started looking at expectations.[237]

Detailed international property law is both unfeasible and unwelcome. It is unfeasible because of the different variations in legal traditions. It is unwelcome in that the purpose is not to trump domestic property regimes, but rather to explore the viability of minimum standards in property matters from general principles of law applied to the international expropriations context. Such an approach permits the reconciliation of the international definition of property (general principles of law) with the domestic definition, in the context of differentiating expropriation from regulation.[238] Focusing on the reasonable expectations of the investor, in the context of the host country and minimal broad standards of property, would give real protection to the foreign investor while respecting the host country's regulation.

Conclusions

Chapter 11 awards have, for the most part, been in accordance with international law. The analysis, of the nature and degree of deprivation necessary to ground expropriation, has been consistent with international law. However, the present analysis could be greatly enhanced through further exploration, in the awards, of the principles relating to the police powers and property. Such expanded analysis would serve to strengthen the intellectual rigor of the award and ameliorate the legitimacy concerns.

The dearth in analysis of the principles relating to police powers and property can be attributed to many factors. Perhaps, the proper case to explore the police powers principle has not presented itself. That is, a case where a general measure is adopted that is of general application, bona fide, and nondiscriminatory. However, this is certainly not the case with property principles where tribunals have declined to seize the opportunity to exploit the property analysis in differentiating between regulation and expropriation. Rather, tribunals have been prone to offer subjective property notions, which are lacking in citation. Although identifying international property law concepts is difficult given the different legal traditions, ignoring international cases, which might assist in the analysis, is a missed opportunity.[239]

Chapter 11 awards appear to have relied, directly and indirectly, on property notions when distinguishing between expropriation and regulation. However, the tribunals have done so with insufficient reference to their legal sources, giving the

---

236 *Id.* at 321.

237 *Id.* at 321, citing Dolzer.

238 *See* Todd Weiler, *Prohibitions against Discrimination in NAFTA Chapter 11*, *in* NAFTA INVESTMENT LAW AND ARBITRATION, *supra* note 227.

239 Dolzer, *supra* note 96, at 72–73.

appearance that they drew on their own subjective values as to the nature of property and the role it plays in society. From a legal and systemic point of view, this is unacceptable. From a legitimacy point of view, this further undermines confidence in the system.

Some have suggested that an interpretation from the FTC would assist in demarcating regulation from expropriation.[240] Although Canada suggested this approach, it acknowledged that there is no simple formula for drawing distinctions between expropriation and regulation, and that any attempt to draw a hard-and-fast clarification could be arbitrary and at odds with existing instruments and practice.[241] Other ideas include reversing the burden of proof and listing governmental activities that are illustrative of non-compensable government regulation.

Any notion of having the Parties "fix" the situation should be avoided because it would be potentially more harmful to the process than beneficial. As noted, past FTC interpretations have only furthered the legitimacy crisis. Moreover, the mandatory application of hard-and-fast rules to an evolving and contextually sensitive area of law is sure to work more injustice than it alleviates. The cure, if one is to be found, may rest in addressing the procedural shortcomings of Chapter 11 and developing an analysis that balances all the interests involved.

Although commentators may debate the legal effects of the imprecision in the wording of the substantive provisions of Chapter 11, the legitimacy concerns are certainly exacerbated. Fears remain over the definitional uncertainty of what constitutes a compensable expropriation. These fears, in the context of investment claims, which have overarching public regulation concerns, are magnified by the lack of public participation and transparency contemplated under the presently applicable arbitral regimes.[242] Until such time as a bright-line test evolves, capable of distinguishing between compensable taking and non-compensable regulation, any attempt to create an arbitrary rule in this regard could have the damaging effect of stripping investors from the appropriate protection in some instances, while precluding legitimate government regulation in others.

In summary, the substantive provisions in Chapter 11, as they relate to indirect expropriation, have attracted much attention for their potential to disrupt or chill bona fide regulation. In practice, however, these potentially expansive theoretical musings have been contained by reasoned analysis in the tribunal proceedings. The need to contain this potentially expansive definition of expropriation is best handled through the development of an expropriations jurisprudence that remains fact-

---

240 Mann and Von Molke, *NAFTA Chapter 11 and the Environment: Addressing the Impacts of the Investor–State Process on the Environment* (1999), *available at* IISDnet http://iisd.ca/trade/chapter 11.htm at 48–49; *see also* Wagner, *supra* note 100, at 537–38.

241 17(6) Inside US Trade, summary and 18–23 (Feb. 12, 1999).

242 *See* Abbott, *supra* note 27, at 308; Henri Alvarez, *Arbitration under the North American Free Trade Agreement*, 16 ARB. INT'L 393 (2000).

sensitive. In this regard, the development of Chapter 11 jurisprudence would be aided through the use of a three-step analysis focused on the relationship amongst expropriation, police powers, and evolving property principles. As these panels are not, in theory, tied to any political or judicial structure, substantive issues might enjoy the same level of development as have questions of procedure.[243]

---

[243] Seigfried H. Elsing & John M. Townsend, *Bridging the Common Law–Civil Law Divide in Arbitration*, 18(1) ARB. INT'L, (LCIA 2002) (arguing that international arbitration is bridging common law–civil law difference with respect to commencing, developing, and presenting disputes. Converging practices embracing elements from both systems are quickly becoming an acceptable middle ground).

15

CONSUMER PRODUCT SAFETY REGULATION AND INVESTOR–STATE ARBITRATION POLICY AND PRACTICE AFTER *PHILIP MORRIS ASIA v. AUSTRALIA**

*Luke Nottage**

Justice Oliver Wendell Holmes famously remarked in *Northern Securities Co. v. United States*, 193 U.S. 197, 400 (1904) that:

> Great cases like hard cases make bad law. For great cases are called great, not by reason of their importance... but because of some accident of immediate overwhelming interest which appeals to the feelings and distorts the judgment.

We might take this reasoning a step further: big cases make or entrench bad policy. A contemporary example is the first-ever arbitration claim brought by a foreign investor against Australia pursuant to an investment treaty.

* This is an extensively updated and expanded version of an article that appeared in 22(1 & 2) Australian Prod. Liab. R. 154 (2011). I thank Eriko Kadota for research and editorial assistance, and, for helpful discussion, participants at the seminar on "Australia's New Policy on Investor–State Dispute Settlement," hosted on August 3, 2011 at Sydney Law School (supported by the Australian Centre for International Commercial Arbitration and the Chartered Institute of Arbitrators—Australian Branch) and the International Trade Law workshop hosted by the Attorney General's Department and Law Council of Australia on September 21 in Canberra. This work draws on research for the project, "Fostering a Common Culture in Cross-Border Dispute Resolution: Australia, Japan and the Asia-Pacific," supported by the Commonwealth through the Australia–Japan Foundation, which is part of the Department of Foreign Affairs and Trade. All views presented are my own. Also, for the record, I am a non-smoker with little sympathy in general for the tobacco industry; and I have been heavily involved in pressing for consumer law reforms in Australia since 2005—particularly to improve product safety regulation and product liability regimes.

On June 27, 2011, Philip Morris Asia Limited (PMA) delivered to the Commonwealth government a notice of intent to commence arbitration (proposing Singapore as the seat for the arbitral proceedings), if its dispute could not be resolved.[1] This Notice of Claim invoked the "Agreement between the Government of Australia and the Government of Hong Kong for the Promotion and Protection of Investments" (signed in 1993). PMA is the Hong Kong subsidiary of the tobacco giant, and holds all shares in Philip Morris (Australia) Limited (PM Australia), which in turn owns all shares of Philip Morris Limited (PML). Through PML, PMA and PM Australia supply cigarettes and other tobacco products in Australia and elsewhere, and PML holds various intellectual property rights and goodwill in Australia related to those tobacco products. PMA alleged primarily that enactment of the Tobacco Plain Packaging Bill 2011, foreshadowed by an Exposure Draft released by the Australian government on April 7, 2011, would amount to "expropriation" of these investments (Art. 6) and a violation of the government's "fair and equitable treatment" (FET) obligations (Art. 2(2)).[2] The dispute has escalated to full-scale arbitration proceedings, after the Bill passed both Houses of Parliament on November 21, 2011.[3]

I. Treaty-Based Investor–State Arbitration

Australia has concluded twenty-one Bilateral Investment Treaties (BITs) since 1988, and four out of six Free Trade Agreements (FTAs) with Investment Chapters since 2003, which include investor–state arbitration (ISA) provisions.[4] ISA protections allow a home state's investor to bring claims directly against the host state for illegally interfering with its investment, rather than imploring its home state to bring a "diplomatic protection" inter-state claim on its behalf. The home state's other interests may make it reluctant to espouse its investors' claims, when the investment dispute happens to

---

[1] Chris Kenney, *Big Tobacco Ignites Legal War*, AUSTRALIAN, June 27, 2011, http://www.theaustralian.com.au/national-affairs/big-tobacco-ignites-legal-war/story-fn59niix-1226082403380 (accessed July 31, 2011).

[2] Notice of Claim, ¶ 10, *available at* http://www.ag.gov.au/www/agd/agd.nsf/page/8F5B65DEBCAED226CA25796D006B4857 (last visited Jan. 27, 2012). The Agreement is also available via that website, as is other information related to this claim; and the Agreement is also available directly via http://www.austlii.edu.au/au/other/dfat/treaties/1993/30.html. *See also* Tania Voon & Andrew Mitchell, *Time to Quit? Assessing International Investment Claims against Plain Tobacco Packaging in Australia*, 14 J. INT'L ECON. L. 515 (2011). They remark that PMA also rely on provisions (in Art. 2(2)) dealing with "full protection and security" and "unreasonable impairment," which are unlikely to prove decisive.

[3] See the Bill's progress via http://parlinfo.aph.gov.au/parlInfo/search/display/display.w3p;query=Id%3A%22legislation%2Fbillhome%2Fr4613%22. *See generally also* PUBLIC HEALTH AND PLAIN PACKAGING OF CIGARETTES (Tania Voon, Andrew D. Mitchell, Jonathan Liberman & Glen Ayres eds., 2012).

[4] Mark Mangan, *Australia's Investment Treaty Program and Investor–State Arbitration*, *in* INTERNATIONAL ARBITRATION IN AUSTRALIA 191 (Luke Nottage & Richard Garnett eds., 2010). The FTA with the United States (signed in 2004) omits ISA provisions. So does the Investment Protocol (signed Feb. 16, 2011) for the ("Closer Economic Relations") FTA with New Zealand. There was also an Exchange of Letters between Australia and New Zealand to exclude bilaterally the operation of the entire Investment Chapter contained in the ASEAN Australia New Zealand FTA (signed in 2009): *see* http://www.dfat.gov.au/fta/aanzfta/index.html.

arise, so foreign investors have increasingly pressed for direct ISA protections to be added to treaties that host states conclude with home states. This phenomenon, combined with the proliferation of investment treaties and the explosion of cross-border foreign investment world-wide especially since the early 1990s, has resulted in hundreds of disputes being submitted to formal arbitration proceedings. The Asian region is no longer an exception, although so far relatively few arbitrations have involved Asian investors or host states.[5]

Overall, foreign investors have had considerable success in claiming compensation, especially under earlier treaties that have broadly worded definitions of expropriation or "fair and equitable treatment" (FET), such as the Australia–Hong Kong BIT. By contrast, for example, Australia's FTA with Chile (signed fifteen years later, in 2008) follows recent U.S. treaty practice in adding an Annex (10-B) on Expropriation that states:

> Except in rare circumstances, non-discriminatory regulatory actions by a Party that are designed and applied to protect legitimate public welfare objectives, such as public health, safety and the environment, do not constitute indirect expropriations.[6]

The arbitrators in the PMA case may be influenced, at least subconsciously, by the omission of such declared intentions in the Hong Kong BIT—although, from a legal point of view, this should not really be relevant. Even under earlier treaties with unqualified provisions similar to those found in the Hong Kong BIT, most decided cases do not find an indirect "regulatory expropriation,"[7] but the reasoning adopted has varied and analysis is necessarily very fact-specific.[8] One line of (mostly earlier) awards tends to view regulatory measures, even for bona fide protection of the environment or public

---

5 Vivienne Bath & Luke Nottage, *Foreign Investment and Dispute Resolution Law and Practice in Asia: An Overview*, SYDNEY LAW SCHOOL RESEARCH PAPER 11/20 (2011), http://papers.ssrn.com/sol3/papers.cfm?abstract_id=1789306; Luke Nottage & J. Romesh Weeramantry, *Investment Arbitration in Asia: Five Perspectives on Law and Practice*, *in* FOREIGN INVESTMENT LAW AND DISPUTE RESOLUTION LAW AND PRACTICE IN ASIA 25 (Vivienne Bath & Luke Nottage eds., 2011) (with a longer version also in 28(1) ARB. INT'L 19 (2012)); Vivienne Bath & Luke Nottage, The ASEAN Comprehensive Investment Agreement and "ASEAN Plus"—The Australia–New Zealand Free Trade Area (AANZFTA) and the PRC–ASEAN Investment Agreement, in INTERNATIONAL INVESTMENT LAW (Marc Bundenberg, Jörn Griebel, Stephen Hobe & August Reinish eds., 2013).

6 Australia–Chile FTA (signed July 30, 2008), Art 3(b).

7 August Reinisch, *Expropriation*, *in* THE OXFORD HANDBOOK OF INTERNATIONAL INVESTMENT LAW 407, 456 (Peter Muchlinski, Federico Ortino & August Reinisch eds., 2008); Katia Yannaca-Small, *Indirect Expropriation and the Right to Regulate: How to Draw the Line?*, *in* ARBITRATION UNDER INTERNATIONAL INVESTMENT AGREEMENTS: A GUIDE TO THE KEY ISSUES 445, 460–76 (Katia Yannaca-Small ed., 2009).

8 CAMPBELL MCLACHLAN, LAURENCE SHORE & MATTHEW WEINIGER, INTERNATIONAL INVESTMENT ARBITRATION: SUBSTANTIVE PRINCIPLES 311 (2008); ANDREW NEWCOMBE & LLUIS PARADELL, LAW AND PRACTICE OF INVESTMENT TREATIES: STANDARDS OF TREATMENT 366–68 (2009); Anne Hoffmann, *Indirect Expropriation*, *in* STANDARDS OF INVESTMENT PROTECTION 151, 169 (August Reinisch ed., 2008).

health, as similar to other potentially expropriatory measures.[9] Other awards tend to exclude such measures, unless for example the host state has committed not to introduce them.[10] The former also generally emphasize the effect of the regulation on the investor (a factor still acknowledged as one of the most important in deciding where to draw the line[11]), whereas the latter cases highlight the purpose or intent behind the host state's measure. A third set of cases tries to steer a middle course, invoking factors such as the proportionality of the measure relative to its objective as well as the legitimate investment-based expectations of the investor.[12] Difficult issues remain concerning which party bears what burden of proof.[13] PMA therefore does seem to have a viable claim against Australia for regulatory expropriation, under the "plain vanilla" Hong Kong BIT, but Australia also certainly has a viable defense.[14]

In addition, the Hong Kong BIT lacks a provision expressly limiting FET obligations to the standards set by customary international law. PMA may argue under this rubric, for example, that its "legitimate expectations" about the regulatory framework (when making its investment) have been frustrated. However, this usually requires showing that specific assurances induced the investment.[15] Australia's defense relating to FET is probably stronger, but the scope of this obligation is also quite fluid.

It should also be noted that even Australia's earlier treaties (such as the Hong Kong BIT in Art. 1(e)(iv)) tend to define "investment" liberally, typically encompassing intellectual property rights as well. The Hong Kong BIT further defines "investor" broadly (Art. 1(b)). This helps explain why the Philip Morris group has been able to initiate this treaty claim, while its Swiss-based company has initiated parallel arbitration proceedings challenging different tobacco control measures undertaken by Uruguay pursuant

---

[9] *E.g.*, Compania del Desarollo de Santa Elena, SA v. Republic of Costa Rica, Final Award, Feb. 17, 2000, ¶ 171. *See also* Metalclad Corporation v. Mexico, Award, Aug. 30, 2000.

[10] Most prominently in Methanex v. USA, Award, Aug. 2, 2005, 44 ILM (2005).

[11] Reinisch, *supra* note 7, at 444.

[12] *See, e.g.*, Azurix Corp v. Argentine Republic, ICSID ARB/01/12, Award, July 14, 2006; Hoffmann, *supra* note 8, at 163–68; Newcombe & Paradell, *supra* note 8, at 364.

[13] It remains unclear what level of scientific evidence is appropriate for the host state to be able to invoke its "police powers" related to environmental or other protective measures. In addition, tribunals have generally required the state to prove justification for invoking powers, although it can be argued that this should only be a prima facie burden: Newcombe & Paradell, *supra* note 8, at 365–66. Some similar issues arise even under the more specific provisions found in WTO agreements: *see, e.g.*, Michael Ming Du, *Autonomy in Setting Appropriate Level of Protection under the WTO Law: Rhetoric or Reality?*, 13 J. Int'l Econ. L. 1077 (2010) and Meredith Kolsky Lewis, *Australians Get Their First Taste of New Zealand Apples in Ninety Years*, 15 ASIL Insights (2011), http.//www.asil.org/insights110912.cfm.

[14] A "strong" defense may be putting it too highly. *Cf.* Voon and Mitchell, *supra* note 2, and generally Andrew Mitchell & Sebastian Wurzberger, *Boxed in? Australia's Plain Tobacco Packaging Initiative and International Investment Law*, 27 Arb. Int'l 623 (2011).

[15] *Id.* at 16–22.

to that bilateral FTA.[16] However, after PMA filed a "Notice of Arbitration" on November 21, 2011, Australia's "Response" dated December 21, argues that:[17]

> 6. [...PMA] acquired its shares in PM Australia on 23 February 2011, both in full knowledge that the decision had been announced [on 29 April 2011] by the Australian Government to introduce plain packaging, and also in circumstances where various other members of the Philip Morris group had repeatedly made clear their objections to the plain packaging legislation, whereas such objections had not been accepted by the Australian Government.
>
> 7. Against this backdrop, [PMA's] claims under the BIT inevitably fail, both as to jurisdiction and the merits:
>
> a) Article 10 of the BIT does not confer jurisdiction on an arbitral tribunal to determine pre-existing disputes that have been re-packaged as BIT claims many months after the relevant governmental measure has been announced.
> b) The plain packaging legislation cannot be regarded as a breach of any of the substantive protections under the BIT. [PMA] made a decision to acquire shares in PM Australia in full knowledge that the decision had been announced by the Australian Government to introduce plain packaging. An investor cannot make out a claim for breach of (say) the fair and equitable treatment standard or of expropriation in circumstances where (i) a host State has announced that it is going to take certain regulatory measures in protection of public health, (ii) the prospective investor—fully advised of the relevant facts—then acquires some form of an interest in the object of the regulatory measures, and (iii) the host State then acts in the way it has said it is going to act.

Accordingly, Australia's Response contends:[18]

> [T]there could be no "investment" for the purposes of Article 10 of the BIT and any reliance on Article 10 of the BIT would constitute an abuse of right. It follows

---

16 ICSID Case No. ARB/10/17 (filed Feb. 19, 2010). *See generally also* Matthew C. Porterfield & Christopher R Byrnes, *Philip Morris v. Uruguay: Will Investor–State Arbitration Send Restrictions on Tobacco Marketing up in Smoke?*, INV. TREATY NEWS, July 12, 2011, http://www.iisd.org/itn/2011/07/12/philip-morris-v-uruguay-will-investor-state-arbitration-send-restrictions-on-tobacco-marketing-up-in-smoke/ (last visited July 31, 2011).

17 Response, ¶¶ 6–7, *available* (with the Notice of Arbitration) *at* http://www.ag.gov.au/Internationallaw/Pages/Investor-State-Arbitration—Tobacco-Plain-Packaging.aspx (last visited Nov. 18, 2013).

18 Australia also objects to jurisdiction (*id.*, ¶ 32) by noting that under Art. 1(e) investments are protected only to the extent "admitted" by the host state "subject to its law and investment policies applicable from time to time." Requirements that investments be "approved" arguably created a stumbling block to investors considering claims under earlier treaties concluded by ASEAN member states: *see* M. Sornarajah, *Review of Asian Views on Foreign Investment Law*, *in* FOREIGN INVESTMENT LAW AND DISPUTE RESOLUTION LAW AND PRACTICE IN ASIA 242, 246–47 (Vivienne Bath & Luke Nottage eds., 2011).

that the arbitral tribunal lacks jurisdiction or that the claims that [PMA] now seeks to bring under the BIT are inadmissible.

As one commentator points out, this interesting threshold objection is similar to a defense in another recent investment arbitration, where the host state objected (unsuccessfully on this point) to the investor seeking treaty protections via corporate restructuring that occurred allegedly after the dispute arose.[19] In a Decision on Jurisdiction rendered on June 1, 2012, in that case, the arbitrators suggested that there would only be an abuse of process, at least where the host state introduces a measure constituting a continuing act (such as an omission to act on mining permit requests), if the investor "can see an actual dispute or can foresee a specific future dispute as a very high probability and not merely as a possible controversy."[20] It remains to be seen where this sort of approach can and will be extended, and applied on the proven facts, in the PMA–Australia case.

II. Impact of the PMA Claim on Australia's Policy Debate

For many, therefore, PMA's treaty-based ISA claim will seem like a "big bad company" cleverly manipulating procedures to claim against a government trying to pass a "good law"—aimed at addressing the serious public health problems and expenses still associated with cigarette sales. These issues persist despite the Australian government already having tried many other measures to curb consumption: graphic warnings on cigarette packaging and in television or print advertisements, restrictions on displays and promotion, and increasingly high consumption taxes.[21]

PMA's claim will also lead some to acclaim the April 2011 "Gillard Government Trade Policy Statement,"[22] which blew cold on ISA provisions in future treaties. On

[19] Pac Rim Cayman LLC v. Republic of El Salvador, ICSID Case No ARB/09/12; *see* Luke Peterson, *Australian Defense Strategy Puts Spotlight on Timing of Philip Morris's Corporate Restructuring Moves, Claims "Abuse" of Investment Treaty*, 4(9) INV. ARB. R. (Dec. 31, 2011), *available at* http://www.iareporter.com. On that case, see further, for example, Robert Cavooris, *National Sovereignty of Tiny El Salvador at Stake as it Considers El Dorado Mining Project*, THE CUTTING EDGE (Mar. 28, 2011), *available at* http://www.thecuttingedgenews.com/index.php?article=51659&pageid=&pagename= (both last visited Jan. 27, 2012). On forum shopping generally, see (by lawyers from the law firm now representing PMA in the claim against Australia) Matthew Skinner, Cameron Miles & Sam Luttrell, *Access and Advantage in Investor–State Arbitration: The Law and Practice of Treaty Shopping*, 3(3) J. WORLD ENERGY L. & BUS. 260–85 (2010).

[20] Luke Eric Peterson, *Arbitrators Reject El Salvador's Contention That Pac Rim's 2007 Change of Nationality Was an "Abuse of Process,"* INV. ARB. R. (June 4, 2012).

[21] *See generally* Simon Chapman & Becky Freeman, *The Cancer Emperor's New Clothes: Australia's Historic Legislation for Plain Tobacco Packaging*, 340 BRIT. MED. J. (2010); and Tania Voon & Andrew Mitchell, *Implications of WTO Law for Plain Packaging of Tobacco Products*, PUBLIC HEALTH & PLAIN PACKAGING OF CIGARETTES: LEGAL ISSUES (2011), http://ssrn.com/abstract=1874593.

[22] *Available at* http://www.dfat.gov.au/publications/trade/trading our way-to-more-jobs-and-prosperity.html. *See also* Jürgen Kurtz, *The Australian Trade Policy Statement on Investor–State Dispute Settlement*, 15 ASIL INSIGHTS (2011), http://www.asil.org/insights110802.cfm (both last visited Jan. 27, 2012); and Leon Trakman, *Investor State Arbitration or Local Courts: Will Australia Set a New Trend?*, 46(1) J. WORLD TRADE (2012) 83.

one interpretation it means simply that Australia will no longer agree to ISA in any future treaty—even with developing countries. That effectively means no more ISA in treaties with anyone. This follows because Australian investors anyway are less concerned about ISA protections where the host state has a more developed legal system—offering a reliable court system applying domestic substantive law supportive of the rights of all investors.

However, read in the context of Productivity Commission (PC) recommendations from its Inquiry into FTA policy for Australia, finalized in December 2010,[23] an alternative interpretation is that the Statement still allows scope for the Gillard government to include ISA in future treaties on certain conditions. In particular, this can happen provided foreign investors are not accorded better rights than local investors. Thus, if the partner country's domestic law protections are lower than Australia's, then future treaties can therefore at least include substantive protections (aimed at Australian investors abroad) capped at the Australian domestic standard of protection. Yet even this policy stance generates complex implications, and the theory and evidence contained in the PC's analysis have significant weaknesses, as I outline elsewhere.[24]

There has been ongoing confusion about what precisely the Gillard government intended by its Statement. On the one hand, at a public seminar organized by the International Chamber of Commerce, hosted on August 15, 2011, by the Canberra office of Norton Rose, an official from the Department of Foreign Affairs (DFAT) explained that the Statement drafted by the Trade Minister and approved by the Cabinet indicated the government's intention to eschew ISA in future treaties, in light of evidence set out in the PC's Report.[25] Asked by the current author why the government had decided to go beyond the PC's specific recommendation, which could allow scope for ISA on certain conditions at least with countries with less-developed legal systems, the official responded that the govern-

[23] *Available at* http://www.pc.gov.au/projects/study/trade-agreements.

[24] Luke Nottage, *The Rise and Possible Fall of Investor–State Arbitration in Asia: A Skeptic's View of Australia's "Gillard Government Trade Policy Statement"*, 5 (2011) TRANSNATIONAL DISPUTE MANAGEMENT / SYDNEY LAW SCHOOL RESEARCH PAPER 11/32, http://papers.ssrn.com/sol3/papers.cfm?abstract_id=1860505. The Commission arguably understates problems encountered by outbound (Australian) investors, while overstating evidence suggesting that offering ISA does not significantly increase inbound FDI, and overstating risks of "regulatory chill." *See also* Trakman, *supra* note 22; and more generally Jürgen Kurtz, *Australia's Rejection of Investor–State Arbitration: Causation, Omission and Implication*, 27(1) ICSID REV. 65 (2012). The PC's recommendation echoes aspects of s2102(b)(3) of the Bipartisan Trade Promotion Authority Act 2002, enacted by the U.S. Congress and influencing the 2004 U.S. Model BIT. However, the Act balanced various interests in a more nuanced way. It stated that the principal negotiating objectives were to reduce artificial or trade-distorting barriers to foreign investment while ensuring that foreign investors in the United States are "not accorded greater *substantive* rights with respect to investment protections" than U.S. investors in the United States, and to secure for investors important rights comparable to those available under U.S. law. It then urged various improvements for ISA provisions. *See generally* Mark Kantor, *The New Draft Model U.S. BIT: Noteworthy Developments*, 21 J. INT'L ARB. 383 (2004).

[25] The Seminar was entitled "Facing the Present and Predicting the Future—Issues in International Arbitration": *see* http://www.iccaustralia.com.au/events.html.

ment believes strongly in nondiscrimination in its treaty relations.[26] However, asked then whether this stance implies that the government would terminate existing investment treaties containing ISA provisions, the official stated that this was not envisaged because it might adversely affect investments already made (by Australians abroad or by foreigners into Australia), which would otherwise be covered by relevant treaties.[27]

On the other hand, on September 6, 2011, the media reported that Australia and the European Union were intending to commence negotiations to elevate a nonbinding framework agreement on economic cooperation into a binding treaty, although apparently leaving to WTO multilateral negotiations the vexed issue of trade in goods (especially market access for agricultural products). DFAT was reported to be expecting the treaties to "be fairly general [...but...] likely to commit both sides to arbitration of disputes and facilitating investments."[28] On one view, this suggests some scope to include ISA relating to any liberalization provisions or protections in a future Australia–EU treaty. However, a more probable interpretation is that DFAT was referring instead to inter-state arbitration procedures.[29] Indeed, at a session on Australia's

---

26 This response is hard to follow. The reason the government favors nondiscrimination in international trade derives from a particular economic theory set out in the Statement, namely mutual gains from free trade derived from comparative (not absolute) advantage. Tariffs or other measures discriminating against imports, for example, can reduce economic welfare for both the home country as well as the exporting country. By contrast, the Statement does not put forth any economic theory as to why discrimination in the form of tailored ISA protections in treaties with developing countries could not increase net welfare for Australia. On the contrary, following the approach of the PC, Australian investors abroad (and indirectly, for example, through higher tax revenues, their home state) would be likely to benefit from such protections, even if this meant no additional inbound FDI from the partner state, with Australia not giving away greater rights to foreign investors, and thereby incurring direct costs or indirect ("regulatory chill") disadvantages from agreeing to ISA provisions. Thus, the Gillard government's criticism of "discrimination" extended to ISA in investment treaties must be based on a non-economic rationale, such as the perceived illegitimacy of having effectively "one-sided" provisions in treaties that only or overwhelmingly benefit Australian interests. Such a stance would be understandable, and indeed I have expressed sympathy with it (in my Submission relating to the PC's draft Report, *available at* http://www.pc.gov.au/projects/study/trade-agreements/submissions). But this legitimacy-based rationale jars with the rest of the Trade Policy Statement—setting out *economic* reasons for nondiscrimination and free trade with a renewed focus on multilateral and even unilateral liberalization—let alone the PC's Report, which the Statement essentially purports to adopt.

27 Again, this response is far from convincing. Australia's investment treaties typically contain a "sunset clause," such as Art. 14(4) of the Hong Kong BIT, which extends protections to preexisting investments for fifteen years following unilateral termination. Indeed, this term could be extended by mutual agreement between Australia and a partner country, while eschewing ISA for subsequent investments.

28 David Uren, *Australia, European Union Plan Investment Treaty*, AUSTRALIAN, Sept. 6, 2011, http://www.theaustralian.com.au/business/markets/australia-european-union-plan-investment-treaty/story-e6frg916-1226130055831.

29 After all, even if the Gillard government were to apply the PC recommendation in treaty negotiations, it would only really press for ISA in countries with less-developed legal systems—not those of EU Member States (even after the EU's recent expansion into Eastern Europe). As noted *supra* note 4, even under existing treaty practice, Australia has not included ISA in treaties with states with developed legal systems such as the United States and New Zealand—although Singapore and Chile do of course have sophisticated legal systems as well. Anyway, the existing arrangement between Australia and the EU largely contains only exhortatory provisions, encouraging efforts to promote cooperation in various fields; turning such broad provisions into binding treaty obligations will not significantly expand the obligations assumed by both sides.

ISA policy at the annual "International Trade Law Conference" co-hosted in Canberra on September 23, 2011, by the Attorney-General's Department and Law Council of Australia, the same DFAT official reiterated the Trade Policy Statement could be read as signaling that the Gillard government would press for the omission of ISA in all future treaties. The official also indicated that government negotiators had already advanced that position in subsequent treaty negotiations. Consistently with this approach, all forms of investor–state dispute settlement were omitted in the Australia–Malaysia FTA signed on May 22, 2012[30] (although such protections remain available anyway under the ASEAN-Australia-New Zealand FTA signed in 2009).

Unfortunately, the recent PMA claim against Australia makes it more difficult for casual observers to realize that ISA proceedings may also quite often be initiated by smaller and/or "good" investors complaining about "bad laws" enacted by the host state.[31] After all, larger investors typically have political clout even in the host state, and/or within their home state, to facilitate a negotiated settlement (including via an inter-state process typically also offered by treaties) without filing formal arbitration claims.[32] Indeed, PMA perhaps approached its home state to encourage it to launch a World Trade Organization (WTO) claim alleging breaches of the TRIPS (Trade-Related Aspects of Intellectual Property Rights) Agreement or other WTO Agreements, and tobacco companies are allegedly supporting the Dominican Republic, Honduras, and the Ukraine in their WTO claims now lodged against Australia.[33] But at the level of substantive law, that legal avenue anyway seems weaker than their BIT claim,[34] thus providing a further reason for a direct ISA claim brought by PMA against Australia.[35]

---

30 *See* http://www.dfat.gov.au/fta/mafta/.

31 *See, e.g.*, the cases listed on the ICSID Web site at http://icsid.worldbank.org/ICSID/FrontServlet?requestType=CasesRH&actionVal=ShowHome&pageName=Cases_Home, and casenotes available at http://www.investmentclaims.com/, although it would be difficult to prove this point through quantitative analysis. Nonetheless, a recent study by the Organization for Economic Cooperation and Development notes that a significant proportion of both ICSID and non-ICSID ISA claims appear to be initiated by small and medium-sized investors; see its Scoping Paper (2012), at 15–16, *available at* http://www.oecd.org/investment/internationalinvestmentagreements/publicconsultationoninvestor-statedisputesettlement.htm (all last visited Aug. 13, 2012).

32 *See, e.g.*, some significant associations between Woodside and DFAT that became apparent when the investment by this large Australian oil and gas company into Mauritania encountered difficulties: Richard Baker & Julia May, *Woodside Drill Deep into an African Money Pit*, AGE, July 5, 2008, http://www.theage.com.au/national/woodside-drill-deep-into-an-african-money-pit-20080704-31x9.htm.

33 Stephanie Nebehay, *Australia Says Big Tobacco Aiding WTO Challengers*, REUTERS, May 22, 2012, http://www.reuters.com/article/2012/05/22/trade-tobacco-idUSL5E8GMHBW20120522; Simon Chapman, *Big Tobacco Crashes at First Legal Hurdle on Plain Packaging*, CONVERSATION, Aug. 15, 2012, http://theconversation.edu.au/big-tobacco-crashes-at-first-legal-hurdle-on-plain-packaging-8807 (also criticizing Philip Morris for "forum shopping" in their pending ISA claim against Australia). *See also* Chris Zappone, *Tobacco Fight Not Over, Philip Morris Says*, SYDNEY MORNING HERALD, Aug. 15, 2012, http://www.smh.com.au/business/tobacco-fight-not-over-phillip-morris-says-20120815-2488s.html (all last visited Aug. 13, 2012).

34 Voon & Mitchell, *supra* note 2.

35 Interestingly, however, PMA's Notice of Claim (¶ 10(b)) and seemingly the Notice of Arbitration (¶ 7.7, referring to "breaches of international law") alleges that the plain packaging legislation is contrary to Australia's WTO treaty obligations and thereby violates the FET obligation under the Hong Kong BIT.

PMA may also have considered that the substantive rights under the treaty with Hong Kong provided greater protection than public law rights offered by Australian courts, including the constitutional prohibition on the government acquiring property without paying compensation. British American Tobacco (BAT), Japan Tobacco International, and Imperial Tobacco had pursued that option,[36] perhaps instead because they did not have holding companies in jurisdictions such as Hong Kong with ISA-equipped investment treaties with Australia. However, in December 2011 PMA also filed a constitutional claim in the High Court of Australia.[37] On August 15, 2012, the Court rejected the tobacco companies' challenge, ruling that the legislation did not constitute a compensable "acquisition" of the tobacco companies' rights.[38]

Various problems with the Gillard government's recently announced policy stance on ISA would have received a fairer hearing if the first arbitration claim against the Australian government had been brought not by a tobacco company for this sort of legislation. Imagine instead, for example, if a Malaysian solar power panel manufacturer had claimed violation of the FET obligation, due to New South Wales legislation retrospectively changing feed-in tariffs that the state government had promised to retain for at least five years, based on ISA protections contained in the 2009 ASEAN–Australia–NZ FTA. As I explain in another paper, the NSW government did back down

---

The Notice of Arbitration (¶¶ 7.15–7.17) seeks to bring in such alleged violations of other international treaties by invoking the "umbrella clause" set out in the BIT (Art 2(2)). Australia's Response to the Notice of Arbitration rejects both claims as "plainly outside the scope of protection of the BIT" (¶ 34), and anyway argues (¶ 35):

> It is not the function of a dispute settlement provision such as that contained at Article 10 of the BIT to establish a roving jurisdiction that would enable a BIT tribunal to make a broad series of determinations that would potentially conflict with the determinations of the agreed dispute settlement bodies under the nominated multilateral treaties. This is all the more so in circumstances where such bodies enjoy exclusive jurisdiction.

36 Nicola Berkovic, *Big Tobacco's Pre-Emptive Strike Raises Stakes*, AUSTRALIAN, July 2, 2011, http://www.theaustralian.com.au/national-affairs/big-tobaccos-pre-emptive-strike-raises-stakes/story-fn59niix-1226085121167 (last visited July 31, 2011). On July 6, 2012, JTI also initiated a public campaign against the UK Department of Health's consultation on standardized packaging of tobacco products: *see* http://www.jti.com/7-0-stories/challenge-uk-plain-cigarette-packs/ (last visited Aug. 13, 2012). JTI is headquartered in Switzerland and was formed in 1999 when its parent, Japan Tobacco Inc. (still government-linked), purchased the non-U.S. operations of R.J. Reynolds. That was then the largest-ever overseas acquisition by a Japanese company, as was JTI's purchase in 2007 of Gallaher in the UK (http://www.jti.com/our-company/history/our-company/). Despite Japan's (growing) interest in the tobacco industry, however, it has not joined consultations or initiated its own WTO claim against Australia regarding plain packaging—perhaps because of pending bilateral FTA negotiations.

37 Lenore Taylor, *Roxon Accuses Tobacco Giant of Trick in Packaging Fight*, SYDNEY MORNING HERALD, Dec. 22, 2011, http://www.smh.com.au/national/health/roxon-accuses-tobacco-giant-of-trick-in-packaging-fight-20111221-1p5p9.html (last visited Jan. 27, 2012). Note that the Hong Kong BIT, unlike Australia's more recent investment treaties (Mangan, *supra* note 4, at 205), does not contain a "fork in the road" provision requiring an investor to elect international arbitration or litigation before host state courts.

38 Reasons were reserved, and eventually delivered on October 5, 2013. *See* http://www.hcourt.gov.au/assets/publications/judgment-summaries/2012/hca30-2012-08-15.pdf. *See also* Mark Metherell, *Big Tobacco Loses High Court Battle over Plain Packaging*, BRISBANE TIMES, Aug. 15, 2012, http://www.brisbanetimes.com.au/opinion/political-news/big-tobacco-loses-high-court-battle-over-plain-packaging-20120815-247kz.html (last visited Aug. 15, 2012).

on such proposed legislation, and anyway the chances of success would not necessarily have been high.[39] But if such a claim had been made, then we arguably would have had a more high-profile example of a smaller "good" company complaining about a "bad law."

Instead, Australians (and others) will now tend to remember the PMA claim whenever ISA is mentioned. That will entrench the Gillard government's policy stance rather than creating opportunities to properly reconsider more targeted ISA reform options, such as those I have outlined in Appendix A of that paper—with some options elaborated further below (especially in Section IV). After all, social psychologists and now behavioral economists have long warned about "availability bias": we usually give too much weight to high-profile or memorable events. They also point to "confirmation bias": we discount counterexamples and instead are disproportionately influenced by evidence that seems to support our existing preferred theories.[40]

Other psychological factors may be involved too. The Trade Policy Statement (and even aspects of the PC's Report) could reflect the powerful "Not-Invented Here" bias in decision making: "if I (or we) didn't invent it, then it's not worth much."[41] That is, Australia has been a relative latecomer in incorporating ISA protections into treaties (since 1988) and not heavily involved in developing the ICSID system (except for a few high-profile arbitrators particularly in recent years), so its policy makers may feel less "ownership" in the ISA regime. Also at play in Australia may be an "emotional cascade." More emotional responses (such as policy-makers' reactions to the PMA claim or early threats thereof) can interrupt the usual decision-making process (the government developing and responding to a PC recommendation), triggering a short-term decision (adopting a highly negative view of ISA provisions), which then gets entrenched over the long term (eschewing such provisions in future treaties).[42]

III. Further Practical Implications and Lessons from the PMA Claim

Unfortunately, the PMA claim also highlights risks of disputes rapidly escalating in ISA, compared to disputes in international commercial arbitration (ICA). In a typical ICA dispute (say, for anticipated breach of an underlying sales contract), the parties might quietly agree to defer the original timetable (putting back a delivery date, for example)

---

39 Nottage, *supra* note 24. Treaty protections are never intended to provide insurance against all investment risks, as many tribunals and commentators have pointed out. *See, e.g.*, NEWCOMBE & PARADELL (*supra* note 8, at 347, quoting Generation Ukraine Inc. v. Ukraine, Award of September 16, 2003, at ¶ 20.30) and Reinisch, *supra* note 7, at 434.

40 *Cf.* generally Luke Nottage & Souichirou Kozuka, *Lessons from Product Safety Regulation for Reforming Consumer Credit Markets in Japan and Beyond*, 34 SYDNEY L. REV. 129 (2012).

41 DAN ARIELY, THE UPSIDE OF IRRATIONALITY 109 (2011).

42 *Id.* at 265. More generally, experiments conducted by Professor Ariely and other behavioral economists show how such "predictably irrational" responses frequently afflict not just random individuals in everyday situations, but also professionals faced with specific decision-making tasks.

to resolve or minimize the problem, or at least make the consequences reversible or less severe (adjusting contracts with other parties, for example). Equivalent "dispute avoidance" measures are often more difficult when state action is involved. This is particularly true when such action is premised on a formal legislative process (such as enacting a bill through Parliament), but the problem also arises when the government publically announces what it intends to do (for example, when a minister wishes to exercise discretion or other delegated authority). Backing down from publicly declared policy positions will often appear weak or inconsistent to voters.

This factor helps explain why the Gillard government pressed forward with the Tobacco Plain Packaging Bill. Shortly after PMA's Notice of Claim, on July 6, 2011, the government introduced the Bill to Parliament. It passed the House of Representatives on August 24, 2011, and was introduced to the Senate the next day.[43] On September 12, 2011, almost three months after the Notice of Claim, representatives of PMA and the Australian government met in Canberra to discuss amicable settlement or procedures for resolving the dispute, but no settlement could be reached.[44] On November 21, 2011, the Senate and House of Representatives reached agreement on a somewhat amended Bill, and PMA filed its Notice of Arbitration on the same day. The Bill received Royal Assent and became final on December 1, 2011. The requirement that retailers sell only plain-packaged tobacco products comes into effect from December 1, 2012 (six months later than originally envisaged by the government).[45] Any major compromise, such as enacting the law but deferring implementation for several years, would probably have been widely viewed as an instance of dithering or caving in to powerful business interests.[46] Once the Bill passed the Senate, it would have become even harder for the government to defer implementation or compromise in other ways, virtually ensuring that PMA will commence formal arbitration proceedings.

This highlights another difference between ISA and ICA practice. In commercial cross-border practice between firms, it has become increasingly common to include "multitiered" dispute resolution agreements, whereby the parties agree first to

---

43 Max Blenkin & Katina Curtis, *Aussies Lead World with Plain Cig Packages*, SYDNEY MORNING HERALD, Aug. 24, 2011, http://news.smh.com.au/breaking-news-national/aussies-lead-world-with-plain-cig-packages-20110824-1ja9s.html. Concerns had been expressed about the Bill only a week before it passed the House of Representatives: *Plain Packaging Laws for Tobacco in Doubt*, SYDNEY MORNING HERALD, Aug. 17, 2011, http://news.smh.com.au/breaking-news-national/plain-packaging-laws-for-tobacco-in-doubt-20110817-1iww4.html?skin=text-only.

44 Notice of Arbitration, ¶ 3.5.

45 In relation to the original implementation date of July 1, 2012, at least one company (BAT) had asserted in an earlier parliamentary inquiry that this time frame would lead to a tobacco shortage. Tim Lester, *Tobacco Shortage Fear*, SYDNEY MORNING HERALD, Aug. 5, 2011, http://www.smh.com.au/national/tobacco-shortage-fear-20110804-1idh4.html (last visited Aug. 9, 2011). To be sure, such predictions may well be self-serving.

46 The Gillard government had already been criticized for backtracking on the "mining super profits tax" soon after it took over in 2010 from the Rudd government. The latter was itself undermined when former prime minister Kevin Rudd agreed to defer implementation of a proposed carbon emissions trading scheme. *See generally, e.g.*, NICHOLAS STUART, RUDD'S WAY: NOVEMBER 2007—JUNE 2010 (2010). But other governments face similar risks of voter discontent when the governments backtrack from major publicly announced policy positions.

negotiate in good faith, then perhaps to attempt mediation through the offices of a third party neutral, and only then to proceed to arbitration for a binding decision. This typically works well, if each of the stages or processes before arbitration involves a reasonable time limit, as parties have little to lose by exploring settlement options among themselves. Indeed, often the trick to effective settlement is for parties to expand the avenues for innovative "win-win" outcomes.[47]

In ISA practice, by contrast, scrutiny by third parties (such as voters) and other considerations (such as institutional procedures or practices constraining government entities) may well reduce the scope for innovative solutions. Decisions taken, such as enactment of legislation in dispute, therefore may be—or seem—more irreversible. Compared to multitiered dispute resolution clauses in commercial contracts, this undermines the efficacy of provisions commonly found in investment treaties that provide for investor–state negotiations prior to arbitration. For example, Art. 10 of the Australia–Hong Kong BIT essentially envisages a "cooling off" period of up to three months of negotiations to seek amicable settlement (or agreement on other dispute resolution procedures), before committing the host state to any arbitration claim filed by the investor, and PMA precipitated this initial stage through its Notice of Claim dated June 27, 2011. Enactment of the Tobacco Plain Packaging Bill made it highly likely that PMA would proceed with arbitration, as an opportunity for creative settlement of the dispute had passed by. Indeed, PMA might well have been able to initiate the arbitration even within the three-month period, as arbitral tribunals interpreting similar provisions in other treaties have sometimes held that expiry of the specified period for negotiations is not necessarily intended to be "jurisdictional"—that is, a condition precedent to commencement of the arbitration.[48]

Similar differences from ICA practices hamper the potential for the arbitral tribunal, in an ISA case such as the PMA claim, to actively facilitate settlement between the parties during the arbitral proceedings. Such "Arb-Med" has become more popular in ICA circles, even among practitioners from common law jurisdictions, where the traditional conceptions of both arbitrators and judges has been viewed as fundamentally different from those of a mediator facilitating settlement among the parties.[49] Combining the two roles—subject to appropriate safeguards, especially by prohibiting ex parte "caucusing"—is

[47] The classic work remains ROGER FISHER & WILLIAM URY, GETTING TO YES (1982). *See also generally* KLAUS PETER BERGER, PRIVATE DISPUTE RESOLUTION IN INTERNATIONAL BUSINESS: NEGOTIATION, MEDIATION, ARBITRATION (VOLUME II: HANDBOOK) (2006), especially at 74–84.

[48] *See, e.g.*, CHRISTOPHER DRAHOZAL & RICHARD NAIMARK, TOWARDS A SCIENCE OF INTERNATIONAL ARBITRATION: COLLECTED EMPIRICAL RESEARCH 248 (2005). Again, this represents a distinction from ICA law and practice. Most courts require completion of the other agreed dispute process(es) before allowing the arbitral process to be initiated; *see generally* Simon Chapman, *Multi-Tiered Dispute Resolution Clauses: Enforcing Obligations to Negotiate in Good Faith*, 27 J. INT'L ARB. 90 (2010).

[49] *See* Luke Nottage & Richard Garnett, *The Top 20 Things to Change In or Around Australia's International Arbitration Act*, in INTERNATIONAL ARBITRATION IN AUSTRALIA 149, 179–84 (Luke Nottage & Richard Garnett eds., 2010); Micah Burch, Luke Nottage & Brett Williams, Appropriate Treaty-Based Dispute Resolution for Asia-Pacific Commerce in the 21st Century, SYDNEY LAW SCHOOL RESEARCH PAPER 12/37 (2012), *available at* http://ssrn.com/abstract=2065636 (also in 35(3) U. NEW SOUTH WALES L.J. 1013 (2012)).

increasingly viewed as one appropriate way to help address burgeoning costs and delays in conventional ICA proceedings. Admittedly, there are also growing concerns about costs and delays in ISA, creating more incentive to settle cases.[50] Yet cases such as Philip Morris show that the dynamics in this field generally tend to make settlements more difficult than in ICA, where confidentiality of proceedings and outcomes is still perceived as a significant advantage.[51] A further complication in this particular case is that Nicola Roxon, the Health Minister who strongly pressed for the Tobacco Plain Packaging legislation over 2010–2011, was moved to the position of Attorney-General (responsible for representing the Australian government in claims such as these) in a subsequent Cabinet reshuffle.[52]

Greater public scrutiny involved in many contemporary ISA proceedings, and the various public statements made by the Australian government regarding the strength of its defense against the PMA claim, will also make it more difficult to achieve settlement based on an agreed quantum of damages. The Gillard government may consider that even multibillion compensation payouts to PMA, and even other tobacco companies such as BAT that have also reportedly considered filing legal action against the legislation, are economically justified in the long term anyway. After all, Australia's entire tobacco market was worth A$10.4 billion in 2009, while the health costs from smoking are thought to amount to A$30 billion.[53]

---

[50] Such perceptions remain and are important. An earlier study based on (limited) empirical data had suggested that these problems in ISA may not be as large as commonly believed: Susan Franck, *Empirically Evaluating Claims about Investment Treaty Arbitration*, 86 N.C. L. REV. 1 (2007). But in a more recent detailed analysis, albeit still of publicly available awards through to mid-2006, the same commentator accepts that the problems remain significant: Susan Franck, *Rationalizing Costs in Investment Treaty Arbitration*, 88 WASH. U. L. REV. (2011), *available at* http://ssrn.com/abstract=1781844. *See also* Otylia Babiak, *Rationalizing Costs in Investment Treaty Arbitration (S. D. Franck)—Article Review*, June TRANSNAT'L DISP. MGMT. (June 2011), *available at* http://www.transnational-dispute-management.com/journal-advance-publication-article.asp?key=405.

[51] Proportions of settlements or withdrawals in ICSID claims, for example, appear lower than in ICA claims. *Cf.* Nottage & Weeramantry, *supra* note 5, at 33 (rates ranging typically between one-quarter to one-third, for ICSID arbitration filings) with Drahozal & Naimark, *supra* note 48, at 258 (rates over one-half, in cases resolved through ICC arbitrations between 1998 and 2003). For empirical research noting the persistent significance of confidentiality in ICA, especially in Asia, see Shahla Ali, *Approaching the Global Arbitration Table: Comparing the Advantages of Arbitration as Seen by Practitioners in East Asia and the West*, 28 REV. LIT. 799, 833 (2009).

[52] *Gillard Reshuffes Cabinet*, SYDNEY MORNING HERALD, Dec. 12, 2011, http://www.smh.com.au/national/gillard-reshuffles-cabinet-20111212-1oqov.html (last visited Jan. 27, 2012).

[53] Nick Bryant, *Big Tobacco Takes on Australia over Bland Branding*, BBC NEWS, July 3, 2011, http://www.bbc.co.uk/news/business-13986740; and Christian Kerr, *Trade Minister Blasts Tobacco Companies over Claims Government Plan in Breach*, AUSTRALIAN, May 19, 2011, http://www.theaustralian.com.au/national-affairs/trade-minister-blasts-tobacco-companies-over-claims-government-plan-in-breach/story-fn59niix-1226058538247 (both last visited July 31, 2011). Yet Philip Morris gained notoriety for its cost–benefit analysis in 2000 that argued that the Czech government (which had been considering an increase in cigarette taxes) made *net gains* from cigarette smoking—because smokers died earlier, thereafter reducing the burden on the state despite higher health care costs caused by illness. *See* MICHAEL SANDEL, JUSTICE: WHAT'S THE RIGHT THING TO DO? 42 (2009) (with further references and a critique of such utilitarianism). Furthermore, in the case of Australia recently, it is unclear whether claims by other companies could be initiated under other investment treaties. It is also unclear whether PMA will seek only compensation, or instead a "suspension" of the legislation in its case—a possibility

More cynically, the Gillard government may be calculating that it will get votes in the short term by coming down hard on tobacco companies with this legislation, without having to take much responsibility for a compensation payment if and when the tribunal reaches a final decision—which may take several years. A similar phenomenon arguably can be observed in inter-state WTO disputes, such as the one Australia recently lost against New Zealand over apple imports.[54] A state can persist with a dispute that it is unlikely to win in order to maximize votes in the short term, and later blame the tribunal for an adverse ruling—by which time, anyway, a different government may have taken power. For its part, PMA may wish to pursue a final award to serve as a warning (from itself or the tobacco industry as a whole) to other states considering similar legislation, such as New Zealand, if they are party to similar investment treaties.[55]

Of course, similar considerations may also come into play in ICA proceedings. A claim may be initiated by a CEO of a company who does not expect to be around in a few years, or where even a loss in the proceedings will bring offsetting greater benefits,[56] or where a party wants to "send a message" to others—despite greater confidentiality in ICA. Yet this does not prevent skilled negotiators, mediators, or even arbitrators prepared to attempt Arb-Med from finding innovative ways to prompt settlement. Interest is belatedly emerging also regarding dispute avoidance and management in the context of international investment treaties.[57] Even if particularly difficult to introduce into a scenario such as that raised by the PMA claim, and for ISA generally compared to ICA, for future disputes—and therefore revisions of conventional treaty provisions or Arbitration Rules—more attention should be paid to such considerations.[58]

---

not expressly excluded by the Hong Kong BIT: *see* Jürgen Kurtz, *Big Tobacco v. Australia: Taking the Battle to the Global Stage*, The CONVERSATION, June 27, 2011, http://theconversation.edu.au/big-tobacco-v-australia-taking-the-battle-to-the-global-stage-2027 (last visited July 31, 2011).

54 *See generally* Kolsky Lewis, *supra* note 13.

55 *See generally* Professor Mike Daube, quoted (with others including the current author) in *World First Plain Packaging for Tobacco Products a Step Closer to Becoming Law*, The CONVERSATION, Aug. 25, 2011, http://theconversation.edu.au/world-first-plain-packaging-for-tobacco-products-a-step-closer-to-becoming-law-3053 (last visited Jan. 27, 2011). On interest in similar legislation expressed in countries such as New Zealand, see *Australia Inches Closer to Plain Cigarette Packaging Law*, INT'L BUS. TIMES, Aug. 25, 2011, http://au.ibtimes.com/articles/203675/20110825/cigarette-plain-packaging-bill-health-minister-nicolo-roxon.htm.

56 In the common law of contract, for example, damages are typically assessed by reference to what the innocent party would have enjoyed except for the breach (its "expectation interest"), not by reference to the amount that the breaching party may gain ("restitutionary damages"). *See generally* Sam Doyle & David Wright, *Restitutionary Damages—The Unnecessary Remedy?*, 25 MELBOURNE U. L. REV. 1 (2001).

57 In the context of the Asia Pacific Economic Cooperation (APEC) forum, see for example the materials for APEC's "Workshop on Dispute Prevention and Preparedness," Washington D.C., July 26–30, 2010, 2010/IEG/WKSP1/, http://aimp.apec.org/MDDB/default.aspx.

58 For some innovative proposals for reducing costs and delays in ICA, and thereby perhaps encouraging settlement, see, for example, Luke Nottage, *Drafting Arbitration Clauses to Minimise Costs and Delays in International Commercial Arbitration: An Asia-Pacific Perspective*, SCIL WORKING PAPER NO. 28 (2011), http://sydney.edu.au/law/scil/publications/working_papers.shtml.

If arbitration does proceed, and PMA and Australia cannot agree otherwise, the procedure shall follow UNCITRAL Arbitration Rules "as then in force." This means the 2010 version of those Rules (as provided in Art. 1 thereof), recently agreed to by the United Nations Commission on International Trade Law. This version has been praised for many significant improvements compared to the original 1976 Rules.[59] However, because Hong Kong is still not a member of the World Bank/ICSID family, treaties such as this one with Australia do not provide for ICSID Arbitration Rules. The 2006 revisions of the ICSID Rules, in particular, offer greater transparency compared to the UNCITRAL Arbitration Rules. ICSID Rules arbitrations involve public notifications about important steps in the proceedings through the ICSID Web site and a requirement for ICSID promptly to publish "excerpts of legal reasoning" from awards.[60]

Nonetheless, the Hong Kong BIT (Art. 10) allows for PMA and Australia to agree in writing to modify the UNCITRAL Rules. It may be in PMA's short-term interest to agree to greater transparency in the arbitral proceedings, if an aim is to "warn off" other states contemplating legislation similar to Australia's plain-packaging legislation. Agreeing to greater transparency may also be in PMA long-term interest, namely avoiding problems when seeking to enforce and execute any favorable arbitral award against the Australian government. This possibility arises because, for instance, social psychologists have also shown that a process perceived as fairer is more likely to generate one side's compliance with an outcome, even if substantively adverse to that party.[61] Meanwhile, the UNCITRAL Rules only impose confidentiality obligations relating to arbitration awards (Art. 35(5)) and the duty to hold hearings in private (Art. 28(3)), except in certain circumstances (such as party consent). This is presumably why the Australian government has been able to make the pleadings and other information relating to the PMA claim freely available online.[62]

If the parties can agree on changes to UNCITRAL Rules allowing for even greater transparency, and perhaps others such as requiring arbitrators actively to facilitate

---

[59] *E.g.* Clyde Croft & Christopher Kee, *The UNCITRAL Arbitration Rules Revision: Implications for Australia*, *in* INTERNATIONAL ARBITRATION IN AUSTRALIA 137 (Luke Nottage & Richard Garnett eds., 2010).

[60] *Supra* note 31. Issues of confidentiality and transparency proved too controversial to be resolved for the 2010 revisions of the UNCITRAL Rules, which are aimed at ICA proceedings as well as ISA ones. Possibilities for new norms, especially for ISA, are still being explored by UNCITRAL Working Group II; *see* http://www.uncitral.org/uncitral/commission/working_groups/2Arbitration.html.

[61] TOM R. TYLER, WHY PEOPLE OBEY THE LAW (2006).

[62] *See supra*, note 2. The Web site notes:

> As the proceedings brought by Phillip Morris Asia concern the Government's right to take regulatory measures to protect public health, it is important that the public have access to information relating to the proceedings. The Government is committed to achieving transparency in these proceedings. This website will be used to provide relevant information and available documents.

> The government reportedly uploaded on this new website certain documents that it had released to a Canberra-based academic (Dr. Kyla Tienhaara) on 15 November 2011 pursuant to her Freedom of Information Act request: see Luke Peterson, *Australia Opts for Transparency in Philip Morris Arbitration; Uruguay Faces Similar Claim, But Has Yet to Follow Suit*, 4(9) INVESTMENT ARBITRATION REPORTER (31 December 2011) via http://www.iareporter.com.

settlement throughout proceedings ("Arb-Med"), this may point the way more generally toward alternative policy initiatives by Australia (and indeed other countries) regarding ISA. For example, rather than throwing the baby out with the bathwater and omitting ISA provisions completely in future treaties, states could encourage arbitral institutions and others to develop more tailored sets of Arbitration Rules for ISA, and include them in future treaties. States could then require or encourage their investors to invoke those Rules in any future disputes—appealing to those firms' short- and long-term interests, including commitments to broader Corporate Social Responsibility. In fact, Dr. Kate Miles and I proposed such reforms in detail in 2009.[63]

IV. Where to Now?

In our earlier study, Dr. Miles and I also suggested that reforms to Arbitration Rules available for ISA proceedings would not preclude other substantive law improvements to the ISA system. The latter could include adding to investment treaties broader express exceptions for nondiscriminatory regulation bona fide in the public interest, such as for public health purposes. These are already found in WTO Agreements, and indeed in some of Australia's more recent FTAs and investment treaties.[64] Elsewhere, I have suggested that treaties could also simply exclude certain matters from the scope of ISA provisions, as with investments in natural resources pursuant to the ICSID Convention regime.[65] Another example is certain prudential measures relating to financial services under Art. 7(7) of the Japan–Korea BIT signed in 2002, apparently influenced by experiences during the Asian Financial Crisis of 1997.[66] A more subtle approach is Art. 13(5) of the Canadian Model BIT of 2003: expropriation of intellectual property rights held by investors can be enforced via ISA, but such a claim is expressly limited to the standard of protection provided under WTO law.[67]

It could be argued that treaties should simply include an exception for investments involving "dangerous goods."[68] But a difficulty arises if states try to be too specific, by listing certain types of goods as outside the scope of ISA provisions, because treaties last often for decades, yet they are infrequently renegotiated. At first blush, in light of now-evident health risks, it may seem obvious that tobacco products could and should be listed as "dangerous," and thus be excluded from ISA protections. But the

63 Luke Nottage & Kate Miles, *"Back to the Future" for Investor–State Arbitrations: Revising Rules in Australia and Japan for Public Interests*, 26 J. INT'L ARB. 25 (2009), summarized at 56–58.

64 As with Chile, *supra* note 6.

65 *Supra* note 24, Appendix A.

66 Luke Nottage & Shotaro Hamamoto, *Foreign Investment in and out of Japan: Economic Backdrop, Domestic Law, and International Treaty-Based Investor–State Dispute Resolution*, SYDNEY LAW SCHOOL RESEARCH PAPER 10/145 (2010), at 32.

67 NEWCOMBE & PARADELL, *supra* note 8, at 336.

68 In a quite similar vein, for example, Mitchell and Wurzberger (*supra* note 14, at 21) suggest that "Investors dealing with dangerous products must, in our view, meet a higher threshold than investors in other areas to prove that they had 'legitimate' expectations concerning future regulation by the host state."

fact remains that even Australia does not ban their sale outright—unlike, for example, asbestos products.[69] It is not simply the inherent features of tobacco products, such as addictiveness to significant proportions of the population and links to lung disease, which are of concern. Health regulators in Australia and elsewhere are mainly worried about the ways in which tobacco products are marketed, appealing particularly to certain vulnerable groups such as young people, without warnings sufficient to assure consumers' informed consent to assuming health risks.

In terms of product liability law, therefore, the problem with tobacco products is primarily one of a "warning defect," and in some limited respects a "design defect." Such situations are much more difficult for a legal system to address than a case of a one-off "manufacturing defect," where a particular product deviates from the supplier's own prescribed safety standards. This is why in the United States the 1998 *Restatement (Third) of Torts—Products Liability* essentially retains a strict liability regime for manufacturing defects, but reinstates aspects of a risk-benefit–based negligence test for design or warning defects.[70]

Authorities developing product safety regulations, not just courts adjudicating civil claims for product liability, also find it harder to deal with products potentially involving the latter types of defects. The usual pattern is for regulators gradually to become aware of harms arising from certain products, thanks to product liability litigation, accident reports from the media, or (recently) mandatory disclosure duties placed on suppliers. From this information, regulators may decide to introduce outright bans (for inherently or clearly dangerous goods), mandatory product safety standards (for goods that can be redesigned to avoid or minimize harm), or information standards (for goods that essentially cannot be redesigned, but involve "warning defects").[71] Occasionally, as further information becomes available, goods that have been banned or subjected to mandatory safety standards are made subject to less-onerous safety regulations.

Thus, listing specific types of products in long-term investment treaties as too dangerous to enjoy ISA protections is an approach that is often too blunt. An alternative is to have a general exception for genuine and nondiscriminatory public health measures.[72]

---

[69] In its media campaign against the Tobacco Plain Packaging Bill, the industry pressed this point strongly. *See e.g.*, Rob Moodie, *Nanny Knows Best: Why Big Tobacco's Attack on Mary Poppins Ought to Backfire*, CONVERSATION, June 21, 2011, http://theconversation.edu.au/nanny-knows-best-why-big-tobaccos-attack-on-mary-poppins-ought-to-backfire-185. However, although cigarettes are not currently banned, Nicola Roxon (when still Australia's Health Minister) stated that "There isn't any safe amount of tobacco that you can smoke [; it] will kill you eventually"; *supra* note 55.

[70] LUKE NOTTAGE, PRODUCT SAFETY AND LIABILITY LAW IN JAPAN: FROM MINAMATA TO MAD COWS ch. 3 (2004); Geraint Howells & David Owen, *Products Liability Law in America and Europe*, *in* HANDBOOK OF RESEARCH ON INTERNATIONAL CONSUMER LAW 224, 233–37 (Iain Ramsay & Thomas Wilhelmsson eds., 2010).

[71] *See generally* Luke Nottage, *Product Safety Regulation*, *in* HANDBOOK OF INTERNATIONAL CONSUMER LAW AND POLICY 256 (Geraint Howells, Iain Ramsay & Thomas Wilhelmsson eds., 2010).

[72] Indeed, Art 8(3) of the Hong Kong–New Zealand BIT (*available at* http://www.unctadxi.org/templates/DocSearch.aspx?id=779), signed on July 6, 1995, not long after the Australia–Hong Kong BIT now subject to the PMA claim, already included an express and quite broadly worded exemption for "measures directed to the protection of public health."

The main problem here is that this provision can lead to complicated claims, decided by ad hoc arbitral tribunals, with no appellate review mechanism for substantive error of law, such as the permanent Appellate Body available for WTO disputes. Along with several other commentators, Dr. Miles and I have suggested developing various forms of appellate review to incorporate into treaties directly or via amendments to the Arbitration Rules.[73] This innovation could be particularly well-suited for the complex legal and factual inquiries needed to determine whether a good is or has become "dangerous" enough to justify a host state's regulatory response.

Instead or in addition, however, some other innovations seem worthwhile exploring in this field. One inspiration comes from the way many countries now deal with frequently sensitive and complex issues arising from international taxation disputes. For example, U.S. and Canadian BITs commonly exclude from coverage taxation measures adopted by the host state, unless they are arguably "expropriatory." The U.S. Model BIT 2004 went on to exclude ISA unless the investor has asked the tax authorities of both states to determine whether the measure constitutes an expropriation, and the authorities fail to agree within 180 days that it does not.[74] In other words, the states perform a screening function by deciding whether the host state's taxation measure constitutes expropriation.

Rather similarly, future investment treaties could allow ISA claims by investors against a host state introducing measures aimed at promoting public health based on its assessment that the investors' goods are "dangerous," but the treaties could add that ISA protections become unavailable if both states party to the treaty agree that the host state's measure did genuinely promote nondiscriminatory public health objectives by regulating dangerous products. (Of course, such agreement would also preclude an inter-state claim.) This approach has the advantage of encouraging states to work together to try to reach consensus on emerging consumer product safety issues, thus promoting deeper cross-border economic integration.[75] One could well imagine that if there had been such a provision in the Australia–Hong Kong BIT, the respective governments would have worked very hard to try to reach agreement on whether the Australian Bill was justified.[76] A possible further consequence would be that Hong Kong might also then introduce similar legislation there.

---

73 *Supra* note 63, at 43–44.

74 Newcombe & Paradell, *supra* note 8, at 336. A precursor can be found in Art. 2103(6) of NAFTA, signed in 1993. *See also generally* Abba Kolo & Thomas Wälde, *Investor–State Disputes: The Interface between Treaty-Based International Investment Protection and Fiscal Sovereignty*, 35 Intertax 424 (2007). A similar provision is also found in Art. 21(2) of the U.S. Model BIT of 2012, *available at* http://www.state.gov/e/eb/ifd/bit/index.htm.

75 *See generally* Luke Nottage, *Asia-Pacific Regional Architecture and Consumer Product Safety Regulation for a Post-FTA Era*, Sydney Law School Research Paper 09/125 (2009), *available at* http://ssrn.com/abstract=1509810 (updated and forthcoming in Trade Agreements at the Crossroads, Meredith Kolsky Lewis and Susy Frankel, eds., 2013); and Philomena Murray, *Regionalism and Community: Australia's Options in the Asia-Pacific*, Australian Strategic Policy Institute (Nov. 23, 2010), *available at* http://www.aspi.org.au/publications/publication_details.aspx?ContentID=273&pubtype=.

76 In the PMA case, Australia and Hong Kong could also agree to amend their treaty to prevent the claim proceeding. *See* Voon & Mitchell, *supra* note 2. However, absent provisions set out in advance such as those suggested here, this is difficult from both international law and practical perspectives. *See further* Burch et al., *supra* note 49.

Another approach is also worthy of consideration. It derives also from recent developments in resolving cross-border tax disputes, but is inspired by Double Tax Treaty practice.[77] The Model Treaty promoted by the Organization for Economic Cooperation and Development (OECD), to provide a template for thousands of bilateral tax treaties, had provided only for a "Mutual Agreement Procedure" (MAP). This allowed a taxpayer finding itself subject to tax both in its home state and the other state, contrary to the intention of the treaty aimed at *avoiding* such double taxation, to initiate a process of mutual negotiations between the states party to the treaty in the hope that they would reach agreement on who had the sole right to impose tax. However, taxpayers and their peak associations became increasingly concerned about delays involved in the MAP procedure. In 2007, drawing also on developments within the EU, the OECD Model Treaty was amended to provide that if the MAP did not lead to a negotiated settlement between the respective tax authorities within two years, the taxpayer could force them to commence arbitration generating a decision binding on the states—thus resolving the taxpayer's double tax problem. Australia and New Zealand introduced such "Nego-Arb" provisions in their revised tax treaty of 2008; Japan first did so with Hong Kong in 2009.[78]

Similarly, the Australia–Hong Kong BIT could have provided that any claim by an investor that a host state's measure was not a justified public health measure, regulating a dangerous product, could not be pursued through ISA. Instead, (1) the investor could trigger inter-state negotiations to see if they could agree on whether the host state's measure was justified, and (2) if no agreement was reached within a set period (say, six or twelve months), the investor could trigger inter-state arbitration to resolve the issue. Various further permutations are possible on this model. For example, consideration would need to be given to whether and how the investor could be involved—although not as a party per se—in the negotiation phase, and especially any consequent inter-state arbitration phase.[79]

Adding exceptions or exclusions to ISA coverage, as well as more carefully drafted definitions for "investment" or "investor," were options generally acknowledged in the PC's final report in December 2010 as possible ways forward in minimizing excessive "regulatory chill" on government policy making.[80] But the PC did not fully appreciate the various options available to rebalance private and public interests in the investment treaty regime, such as those sketched above drawing inspiration from cross-

---

[77] Micah Burch & Luke Nottage, *Novel Treaty-Based Approaches to Resolving International Tax and Investment Disputes*, 18 AUSTRL. INT'L L.J. 127 (2011), *available at* http://ssrn.com/abstract=1938758.

[78] *Available at*, respectively, http://www.ato.gov.au/businesses/content.aspx?doc=/content/61011.htm and http://www.ird.gov.hk/eng/tax/dta_inc.htm.

[79] A particular issue could arise regarding inter-state settlement, which the investor may feel is disadvantageous. Similar concerns arise in the tax treaty arbitration arena: *see* Marcus Desax & Mark Veit, *Arbitration of Tax Treaty Disputes: The OECD Proposal*, 23 ARB. INT'L 405 (2007). In the context of investment treaty dispute resolution, we might also want to include a clear discretion for the state's party or the arbitrators to receive evidence or submissions from NGOs. *See generally* Nottage & Miles, *supra* note 63, at 41–42.

[80] PC draft Report, *supra* note 26, at 276–77.

border tax treaty dispute resolution. In addition, when blowing even colder on ISA provisions in future treaties, the Gillard government Trade Policy Statement in April 2011 seemed particularly concerned about the chill factor. It reiterated concerns raised by the Commission about possible claims not just on the part of tobacco companies, but also by foreign pharmaceutical companies related to Australia's Pharmaceutical Benefits Scheme (PBS) regime.

Both industries certainly had been lobbying the U.S. government and others to press for significant protections in the Trans-Pacific Partnership Agreement (TPPA).[81] Initially agreed in 2005 among New Zealand, Singapore, Brunei, and Chile, negotiations are now underway to add an Investment Chapter and bring in Australia, the United States, Malaysia, Vietnam, Peru, Canada, Mexico, and possibly Japan—creating the first Asia–Pacific regional FTA.[82] Both the United States and Singapore have been particularly strong proponents of ISA in their other respective investment treaties, although the United States did agree to omit ISA in its FTA with Australia signed in 2004.[83] It therefore remains to be seen whether Australia's new policy stance will prevail in the ongoing TPPA negotiations.[84]

On the one hand, we now have an "Open Letter from Lawyers to the Negotiators of the Trans-Pacific Partnership Urging the Rejection of Investor–State Dispute Settlement" released on May 8, 2012, by a group comprised mostly of Australia and New Zealand law professors. However, as one (non-signatory) New Zealand lawyer expert in international law promptly responded:[85]

> The letter is backed by well-meaning, and several well-known, signatories; most of whom are not especially well-informed about investor–state arbitration. The fact of the letter is welcome, as the issues are important. But the letter itself contains several overstatements and does not make a balanced contribution to the debate.

---

81 Thomas Faunce & Ruth Townsend, *Public Health and Medicine Policies*, NO ORDINARY DEAL: UNMASKING THE TRANS-PACIFIC PARTNERSHIP 149, 157–61 (Jane Kelsey ed., 2010).

82 *See also generally* Nottage, *supra* note 75.

83 *Supra* note 4. *See also* William S. Dodge, *Investor–State Dispute Settlement between Developed Countries: Reflections on the Australia–United States Free Trade Agreement*, 39 VAND. J. TRANSNAT'L L. 1 (2006); *and generally* Kantor, *supra* note 24. Japan has also almost always included ISA provisions in its investment treaties; *see* Hamamoto & Nottage, *supra* note 66.

84 Deborah Gleeson, for example, hopes for that outcome; *see* http://theconversation.edu.au/world-first-plain-packaging-for-tobacco-products-a-step-closer-to-becoming-law-3053 (*supra* note 55). The DFAT official who had spoken at the ICC seminar in Canberra on Aug. 15, 2011 (*supra* note 22) stated publicly, at the annual International Trade Law Conference in Canberra on Sept. 23, 2011, that in recent TPPA negotiations the Australian government had "politely declined" a proposal to add ISA provisions in the new Investment Chapter. *See also generally* Leon Trakman, Resolving Investor-State Disputes under a Transpacific Partnership Agreement (September 2012) University of New South Wales Faculty of Law Research Series, Working Paper 46, available at http://law.bepress.com/unswwps-flrps12/46.

85 Daniel Kalderimis, *Investor–State Arbitration Not Deal Breaker for TPP Negotiations*, BRIEF COUNSEL (May 11, 2012), http://www.chapmantripp.com/publications/Pages/Investor-state-arbitration-not-deal-breaker-for-TPP-negotiations.aspx.

On July 28, 2012, moreover, I co-organized the release of an Open Letter that instead mainly urged various improvements to aspects of the Investor–State Dispute Settlement system,[86] responding partly also to a detailed scoping paper and a Public Consultation process provided by the Organization for Economic Cooperation and Development over May–July 2012.[87] In early August 2012 the Australian Chamber of Commerce and Industry made public a July 13 letter to Prime Minister Julia Gillard,[88] urging a return to Australia's past treaty practice allowing for some investor–state dispute settlement provisions in treaties, depending on a case-by-case assessment.

Nonetheless, this industry-led public response in Australia has been slower and less visible than the efforts of NGOs and other local groups that object strongly to any forms of ISA. It has also prompted a spirited reaction by an Australia-based academic.[89] Australia's policy shift away from ISA, reinforced by the ongoing tobacco company claims, therefore could still precipitate the unraveling of a growing acceptance of the ISA system throughout the Asia–Pacific region.[90] The Gillard government Trade Policy Statement may also now rub up again an emerging tendency on the part of the EU, like the United States, to view investment chapters or treaties as stepping-stones toward comprehensive arrangements.[91] At least at this stage, however, it seems unlikely that the Australian government will heed calls—prompted partly by the PMA claim—to terminate some of its existing treaties that have gone past their initial term.[92]

---

86 *Available at* http://blogs.usyd.edu.au/japaneselaw/2012/07/assessing_treatybased_investor.html.

87 *See* http://www.oecd.org/investment/internationalinvestmentagreements/publicconsultationoninvestor-statedisputesettlement.htm (last visited Aug. 13, 2012). This webpage also discloses other Public Comments provided to the OECD, including an endorsement of ISDS by a peak business body in New Zealand.

88 ACCI, *Australian Foreign Investment Requires Right to Sue Foreign Governments* (Aug. 9, 2012), http://acci.asn.au/Research-and-Publications/Media-Centre/Media-Releases-and-Transcripts/Global-Engagement/Australian-Foreign-Investment-Requires-Right-to-Su (last visited Aug. 13, 2012). *See also* Chris Merritt, *Labor Facing Business Revolt on Trade Pacts*, AUSTRALIAN, Aug. 6, 2012; Geoff Kitney, *Business Push for Sovereign Risk Protection*, AUSTRL. FIN. REV., Aug. 9, 2012.

89 Kyla Tienhaara, *ACCI's Right to Sue Campaign Not Supported by the Facts*, CONVERSATION, Aug. 13, 2012, http://theconversation.edu.au/accis-right-to-sue-campaign-not-supported-by-the-facts-8800. For a preliminary reaction, see Luke Nottage, *Abandoning All Investor–State Dispute Settlement Mechanisms Also Not Supported by the Facts*, Aug. 15, 2012, blogs.usyd.edu.au/japaneselaw/2012/08/abandoning_all_investor-state.html (with a version also at www.eastasiaforum.org, all last visited Sept. 27, 2012).

90 *See generally* FOREIGN INVESTMENT, See Chapter by Bath *supra* note 5; Nottage & Weeramantry, *supra* note 5.

91 *See* KENNETH HEYDON & STEPHEN WOOLCOCK, THE RISE OF BILATERALISM 120 (2009); and compare the media report discussed *supra* note 28. The EU is playing a more active role partly due to its expanded competence over foreign investment pursuant to the Lisbon Treaty. *See generally* Thomas Eilmansberger, *Bilateral Investment Treaties and EU Law*, 46 COMMON MKT. L. REV. 383 (2009); and especially now its Mandate on investment treaty issues (dated Sept. 12, 2011, unofficially *available at* http://www.bilaterals.org/spip.php?article20272), intended to cover negotiations ongoing for example with Singapore, India, and Canada.

92 *Cf.* Kyla Tienhaara & Thomas Faunce, *Gillard Must Repel Big Tobacco's Latest Attack*, CANBERRA TIMES, June 28, 2011, http://www.canberratimes.com.au/news/opinion/editorial/general/gillard-must-repel-big-tobaccos-latest-attack/2209168.aspx (last visited July 31, 2011), and Tienhaara, *supra* note 89, with the discussion *supra* note 27.

Unfortunately, PMA filed its claim against Australia at a bad time for this broader policy debate. This has made it even harder for the Gillard government to heed calls to reinterpret or restate its Trade Policy Statement (at least in light of one possible interpretation of the PC's recommendation)—let alone to revisit the PC's underlying theories and evidence—to determine whether there may be an even stronger case for ISA protections incorporating a variety of innovative aspects. Instead, the PMA claim in June 2011 seems to have spurred the government to forge ahead to introduce the Tobacco Plain Packaging legislation into Parliament. This meant forgoing one opportunity for compromise, and that legislation's enactment without major amendments now makes it more difficult for settlement to occur during arbitral proceedings. Regarding the substantive law, moreover, the PMA case raises some very difficult questions—similar to those that bedeviled the WTO dispute resolution system, especially in its earlier years. The claim has also raised the procedural issue of the circumstances in which cross-border corporate restructuring is permissible to claim the benefit of treaty-based ISA protections.

All these aspects will probably entrench a view in Australia that the ISA system itself is fatally flawed and therefore should simply be abandoned. A tentative interest group analysis suggests that there may be fewer-than-expected constituencies that are prepared instead to seek more tailored reforms to the system.[93] Yet abandoning it altogether risks throwing the baby out with the bathwater.[94]

93 Nottage, *supra* note 24, Part IV.

94 *See further* Luke Nottage, *Throwing the Baby with the Bathwater: Australia's New Policy on Treaty-Based Investor–State Arbitration and Effects on Cross-Border Investment in Asia*, 37 ASIAN STUDIES REV. (forthcoming 2013), updating Nottage, *supra* note 24, in a special issue on "International Politics of Resources: China, Japan and Korea's Demand for Energy, Minerals and Food."

16

THE CASE AGAINST A REGIME ON INTERNATIONAL INVESTMENT LAW

Muthucumaraswamy Sornarajah[*]

Yet another state, and that too a developed one, has withdrawn from the practice common in investment treaties of providing for investor–state dispute settlement. The Gillard government announced such a policy in a policy report on international trade in April 2011. Unlike the Latin American states, which had withdrawn earlier from submitting investment disputes to arbitration under treaties, Australia has not had any adverse arbitral awards made against it.[1] However, given the climate that prevailed in the area of investment arbitration, Australia thought it prudent to make this withdrawal. One of the reasons given in the report was to ensure that foreign investors in Australia did not have greater access to dispute settlement than local businesses. Many commentators in other developed states have noted the anomaly that results from the existence of this device in investment treaties.[2] Yet the fact is that these devices have existed in treaties for a considerable period of time—it is only now that developed states are reacting to the existence of these mechanisms. The explanation for the lateness of the reaction of developed states lies in the fact that they are now becoming targets of mechanisms that were devised against developing states in a past era of foreign

* CJ Koh Professor of Law, National University of Singapore. The Tunku Abdul Rahman Professor of Public International Law, University of Malaya, Kuala Lumpur

[1] One possible episode concerned the cancellation of the license of Dillingham Moore to mine for sand on Fraser Island. The contract had been made with the state government of Queensland but cancelled by the federal government due to effects of the sand mining on the Great Barrier Reef. It was an early case of a clash between environmental interests and investment interests. The Australian government stood firm, and the matter was settled. For litigation involving the incident, see *Murphyores Ltd v. Commonwealth of Australia* (1976) 136 CLR 1.

[2] David Schneiderman, *Constitutionalizing Economic Globalization: Investment Rules and Democracy's Promise* (2008).

investment relations. As flows of investment from the BRIC states (Brazil, Russia, India, and China) into the developed states set in, there will be more anxious rethinking of the bases of investment treaties by the developed countries. An instrument that was designed against developing states now targets the interests of developed states. The boot is on the other foot, and it is beginning to pinch quite a bit. Developed states may evince a keenness to dismantle the system of investment protection they had laboriously created over the years. The process will be accelerated as the neoliberal basis on which the law was created itself goes into reverse.[3]

These withdrawals and retreats of developed states make the case for the creation of a regime of international law grow weaker. By retreat is meant the fact that the developed country treaties are becoming less focused on investment protection. They contain many preclusionary provisions enabling avoidance of responsibility.[4] The argument for a regime in international investment law is couched in the language of the regime theories, which postulate the existence of institutional arrangements for compliance with definite rules backed by a hegemonic state.[5] Regimes succeed when there is a commitment by a hegemonic leader to maintain the regime of rules. The idea of a regime for the international law on foreign investment in this sense becomes weak as the hegemonic state, the United States, which was foremost in shaping the law from its inception, itself is now in retreat from these principles, its treaties becoming weaker and its position as a recipient rather than as an exporter of capital increasing. Its hegemonic status is in decline. Its European allies are in no better position. With their economies in recession, the aim of fostering regimes with absolute investment protection will hinder the regulatory measures that may have to be taken to lead these states out of their economic crises. The European Union is currently considering a European investment treaty that will be common to all Member States. It is likely that the treaty will be a balanced one, for the Union will be bound by the investment treaty to capture its comprehensive jurisprudence on human rights and the environment. It will also have to provide for the fact that the region is a recipient of capital from newly industrializing states such as China and India. There are obvious tensions afoot that make the evolution of a regime in the area of foreign investment unlikely. There is an insufficient communality of interests to support the evolution of such a regime.[6]

---

3 M. Sornarajah, *The Ravage and Retreat of Neo-Liberalism in International Investment Law*, *in* 2 YEARBOOK OF INTERNATIONAL INVESTMENT LAW 60 (2010).

4 The classic instance would be the Canadian and U.S. Model Treaties (2004), which apart from subjective national security preclusions, contain statements regarding regulatory expropriation being non-compensable and create defenses for measures taken to promote the health and welfare of citizens.

5 For a statement of the regime theory, see VOLKER RITTBURGER, REGIME THEORY AND INTERNATIONAL RELATIONS (1993). For its use in explaining international investment law, see JESWALD SALACUSE, THE LAW OF INVESTMENT TREATIES 1–16 (2010). The work does not contain an adequate statement of the regime theories or explain why a regime on foreign investment would succeed.

6 Classic regimes, such as those in the areas of civil aviation, international health, meteorology, or the postal services, develop when there are sufficient shared interests to make them successful. A characteristic is that there is a constitutional document with an international organization in such regimes. Exclusion from membership works as a deterrent as the excluded state becomes unable to share in the mutual benefits that membership in the regime brings.

A regime must also be driven by a definite political aim or philosophy. A philosophy driving the law toward the goal of establishing a regime with common aims of investment protection through firm standards of investment protection enforced by a system of arbitration could have been constructed during the period when the market-oriented neoliberalist ideas were ascendant.[7] A regime would require the total acceptance by all of its participants of a common philosophy. For a few fleeting years, such acceptance of a common philosophy did exist.[8] The so-called "Washington Consensus" ensured that neoliberalism was driven by the single hegemonic state and the international financial institutions it controlled. But, soon, with a succession of economic crises and the realization that there was no single prescription to solve them, neoliberalism became hugely dented and abandoned even in the states that had adhered to it. Nationalization of foreign banks became the norm in developed countries, which witnessed bank failures.[9] Increasing state regulation was seen as necessary for dealing with the economic chaos. Neoliberalism was abandoned in the very states in which it had ascendancy.

Compulsory arbitration at the unilateral insistence of the foreign investor may be a powerful compliance mechanism under treaties but increasing challenges to jurisdiction of arbitral tribunals on a variety of grounds has rendered this mechanism of less significance.[10] Though announced as significant in that an investor, an entity lacking personality could take a state to an international tribunal, the system generated many systemic imperfections, such as inconsistent awards, allegations of arbitral bias,

---

7 Neoliberalism was ascendant after the fall of the Soviet Union in 1990. As the sole hegemonist committed to this philosophy under President Reagan, the United States was able to drive it into the global order it led. Though initially successful, such efforts failed as the power of the United States began to wane and a global economic crisis set in. JOSEPH STIGLITZ, FREE FALL: AMERICA, FREE MARKETS AND THE SINKING OF THE GLOBAL ECONOMY (2010).

8 See the euphoric proclamations of the triumph of the market philosophy in MICHAEL MANDELBAUM, THE IDEAS THAT CONQUERED THE WORLD: PEACE, DEMOCRACY AND FREE MARKETS IN THE TWENTY-FIRST CENTURY (2002). The title of the book itself was misplaced. Market fundamentalism was seen as the cause of the succession of economic crises that has characterized the first decade of the twenty-first century. The only relevance of the book is the euphoria that characterizes the thinking of a group that led neoliberalism. It is such euphoria for a nonexistent consensus behind market fundamentalism that characterizes efforts at multilateralization of international investment norms.

9 For the nationalization of foreign banks in the United Kingdom, see Jason Calamita, *British Bank Nationalizations: An International Law Perspective*, 58 ICLQ 119 (2009). The argument in this article that compensation was due for the nationalization of the foreign banks is untenable. None was sought, and none was given. It was understood that the taking was regulatory, particularly because of the mismanagement of the foreign banks in their lending practices. It is necessary to compare this taking with the Malaysian restrictions following the Asian economic crisis and the Argentinian restrictions following the crisis there. The legal outcomes were markedly different.

10 States have successfully explored various grounds on which the jurisdiction of the arbitral tribunal can be challenged. These include claims that the investment did not fall within the category of protected investments (Grueslin v. Malaysia (2000) 5 ICSID Rpts 483) that it did not conform to the laws of the host state and hence moved out of treaty protection (Fraport v. Philippines ICSID Case No ARB 03/25, Aug. 16, 2007) and that the investment did not promote economic development (Malaysian Salvors v. Malaysia ICSID Case ARB/05/10, May 17, 2007).

and charges of expansionary interpretations of treaties that resulted in its legitimacy being queried.

A successful regime for international trade was created when the World Trade Organization came into existence with its effective dispute settlement mechanism and secure treaty rules. The dispute settlement mechanism is regarded as the most efficient so far devised in international law. There is no such regime on foreign investment protection. The opportunity that may have existed at the highpoint of the acceptance of neoliberalism did not result in an investment regime, though the proposed Multilateral Agreement on Investment sought to create one. The fact that such a regime could not be set up within an organization that consisted only of developed states, and that too when circumstances were most propitious, indicates the difficulties that attend the formation of a regime for foreign investment. With successive economic crises culminating in the global economic crises in 2008,[11] the driving philosophy for the emergence of a regime has been significantly dented. It is unlikely that a similar situation that is suitable for the construction of a regime for investment law will emerge in the immediate future. When states have failed to create a regime, it is not appropriate that such a regime should be conjured up through magical processes of reasoning such as those based on customary international law or through reliance on interpretations of investment treaty activity. The several attempts that are currently being made to revive the moribund effort at multilateralization of foreign investment law through the creation of theoretical constructs on the basis of selective facts is an indication of the last gasps of neoliberalism. The modern phase is characterized by the new mutations that have begun to appear, just as the main system that existed during the heyday of neoliberalism begins to disintegrate. The efforts to shore up the system have thrown up novel arguments that seek to justify the continuation of the system. These efforts are discussed below.

With these comments in mind, it would be appropriate to begin considering the case for a regime by starting with a short statement of the history of the international law on foreign investment. The history will illustrate that the law, even at the zenith of the neoliberal phase, was not characterized by any uniform set of norms that would have promoted the formation of a regime. The consideration of the matter will also involve analysis of the current literature, which seeks to conserve methods of creating a global regime on investment law. It concludes that the techniques that have been resorted to are weak. It ends with the argument that, since the global economic crises, the developed states have reined in the offensive nature of investment treaties so as to make the possibility of a regime such a mirage. As a result, none of the mutations to conserve the construction of norms based on neoliberalism could survive without resistance from interests that are opposed to the imposition of a regime through indirect means.

---

[11] The global economic crisis is attributed to the failures of neoliberalism. STIGLITZ, *supra* note 7.

1. The Four Phases of the International Law on Foreign Investment.

The present represents a stage in the post-colonial phase of international investment law. As far as norm conflict is concerned, it is akin to the very first phase of international law relating to foreign investment, which involved a conflict between two normative prescriptions.[12]

I. THE FIRST PHASE

In this early period, the contest was between the United States and Latin America, as investments in the rest of the world largely took place within the colonial context. The U.S. view was that there was an international minimum standard that applied to foreign investment, and that this standard mandated that disputes between foreign investors and host states in Latin America should be settled in accordance with an external standard by neutral tribunals sitting overseas. The central concept through which this prescription was advanced was the international minimum standard, which had to be maintained by international law. This view was rejected by Latin American states, the recipients of U.S. investments. They argued that a national treatment standard applied, and that this standard of treatment permitted national courts to dispose of disputes between foreign investors and their host states according to national law. International law had no role to play, or if it did, it merely referred the disputes to national law to be settled by national courts as the final arbiters. The standard was no different from that applied to local investors. The Latin American view was stated in the form of the Calvo Doctrine.[13] This conflict in the first phase of international investment law became internationalized with the decolonization of African and Asian states. The latter states espoused the Latin American view, whereas the former colonial powers of Europe adopted the U.S. position. The cleavage of views existed between the capital-exporting states of America and Europe and the capital-importing states of Asia and Africa.[14]

---

[12] Trade and investment were the foundations of international law from early times. The Spanish conquest of Latin America and the British conquests in Asia had much to do with trade and investments. The use of force was intertwined with trade and investment. This period is excluded. The modern period begins with the developments in the Americas that did not operate under a colonial system. It was in the context of an absence of a colonial relationship that international law on the protection of investments became relevant. The rest of the world was still under colonialism when this first phase of the international law on foreign investment developed. This phase is described well in CHARLES LIPSON, STANDING GUARD: PROTECTING CAPITAL IN THE NINETEENTH AND TWENTIETH CENTURIES (1985).

[13] Wenhua Shan, *Is Calvo Dead?*, 55 AM. J. COMP. L. 123 (2007) (a tempting conclusion that Calvo has been revived by no less than the United States). It could be argued that the 2004 Model Treaty is the best representation of what the developing states argued for through the New International Economic Order.

[14] The first two phases of the international law on foreign investment are described in M. SORNARAJAH, THE INTERNATIONAL LAW ON FOREIGN INVESTMENT (3rd ed. 2010).

II. THE SECOND PHASE

It is during the second phase that the newly independent states of Asia and Africa joined with the Latin American states to espouse the New International Economic Order (NIEO), which, among other things, sought to universalize the Calvo doctrine. The affirmation of the Calvo doctrine was even stronger in the associated resolution containing the Charter of Economic Rights and Duties of States. The developing states also had over the years passed resolutions asserting the doctrine of permanent sovereignty over natural resources. These developments were hotly resisted by the developed states. Thus, the compromise resolution accepting the permanent sovereignty over natural resources contained the promise that contracts should be honored and that disputes arising from the violation of contracts should be settled in accordance with international law. But, this compromise did not last long. The developing countries returned to assert the doctrine of permanent sovereignty over natural resources without any qualifications. They adopted the principle in their national constitutions and in their domestic legislation such as their foreign investment codes and mining acts.

The developed states sought to blunt these changes. There were discussions as to whether international norms could be created by resolutions of the General Assembly.[15] During this second phase, the law was kept in a fine balance, for much of the law that had been built up by the developed states also relied on weak sources of international law. They were contained in arbitral awards and in the writings of publicists, which in terms of opposability would be weaker law-creating sources than solemn resolutions of states made at their general assembly indicating their preferred norms of law. States alone can create practice, and such practice can become law. Opinions of individual arbitrators and publicists, however highly qualified, cannot claim such status in the law. The U.S. assertion of norms had been resisted by Latin American practice, but these norms were later adopted by the newly independent states of Africa and Asia. The decisions of arbitrators and writings of publicists are only subsidiary sources of international law, at best. They can hardly stand against frequently approved resolutions of states and the conversion of these principles into their constitutions and investment codes.

[15] These norms were advanced through General Assembly resolutions. The reaction was to treat these resolutions as not norm-creating despite the fact that they were supported by a large majority of countries. The principal resolutions are the Charter of economic rights and duties of states, United Nations General Assembly Resolution 3281(xxix) of Dec. 12, 1974, UN GAOR, 29th Sess., Supp. No. 31 (1974) 50, UN Doc. A/9631, reproduced in 14 I.L.M.251 (1975) (120 votes in favor; 6 against; 10 abstentions); United Nations General Assembly Resolution 3201 (S-VI) of May 1, 1974 on the New International Economic Order, UN doc. A/res/S-6/3201, text at (1974) 13 ILM 715. The major countries that did not subscribe must be regarded as persistent objectors subscribing to the alternate system of investment protection. This supports the view regarding normlessness. In *Texaco Overseas Petroleum Co./California Asiatic Oil Co. v. the Government of the Libyan Arab Republic* (1978) ILM 1, at 88, the resolutions were regarded as *lex ferenda*. NICO SCHRIJVER, SOVEREIGNTY OVER NATURAL RESOURCES: BALANCING RIGHTS AND DUTIES (1997).

III. THE THIRD PHASE

The law is presently in the third phase but is emerging into a fourth phase. So, it is very much a period of transition. That transition and the course the fourth phase will take will be important in considering the future course of the law. But, the failures of the law in its third phase make a multilateral regime unlikely until a cyclical change takes place. The third phase is therefore important and deserves closer attention.

The third phase related to the changes that the preference toward market-based solutions brought about. The ascendancy of neoliberalism ensured that a halt be put on the movement of the developing world to sovereign control over foreign investment and the development of secure norms of investment protection through international law on the ground that investment flows would be promoted through the existence of such norms. The triumph of neoliberalism could be dated from the dissolution of the Soviet Union as this signaled the end of communism and left democracy and its economic concomitant, the free market theory, as the prevailing philosophies that were left standing with the end of the Cold War. It also found the developing world without other sources of external capital. The sovereign debt crisis of the preceding years resulting from the recycling of petrodollars had eliminated banks as the source of capital. Reaganism and Thatcherism cut down aid not only to their own poor but to the developing world. The only source of funds was from the multinational corporations that were willing to invest. Developing countries began competing for the funds. With the advent of new states of the dissolved Soviet Union also joining in, the competition soon undid the Third World cohesion supporting projects such as the New International Economic Order. The scramble for investment capital set off the third phase, which was guided largely by the objective of stabilizing neoliberal norms relating to property and contract protection.

International law became an instrument through which the dominant philosophies could be expressed. In the political sphere, moves were made to ensure the triumph of democracy, such as the articulation of doctrines that permitted forcible intervention to promote it.[16] The dominance of the United States as the single hegemonic power in a rapidly globalizing world ensured that it was able to push through norms based on its own political and economic system.[17] The role that a hegemonic power has in shaping international law through infusion of its preferred norms is evident in the international law on foreign investment as well as in other areas of international law.[18]

---

[16] DEMOCRATIC GOVERNANCE AND INTERNATIONAL LAW (Gregory Fox & Brad Roth eds., 2000).

[17] There are many examples, particularly in international trade where the instruments on intellectual property and services are widely regarded as serving U.S. interests and being based on U.S. law. SUSAN SELL, PRIVATE POWER, PUBLIC LAW: THE GLOBALIZATION OF INTELLECTUAL PROPERTY LAW (2008); for trade, see DONATELLA ALESSANDRINI, DEVELOPING COUNTRIES AND THE MULTILATERAL TRADE REGIME (2010).

[18] Jose Alvarez, *Hegemonic International Law Revisited*, 97 AJIL 873 (2003); MICHAEL BYERS, UNITED STATES HEGEMONY AND THE FOUNDATIONS OF INTERNATIONAL LAW (2005).

Trends within international law also favored the change that was taking place. The overmuch fragmentation that has taken place later in the field has resulted in a plethora of works that have looked at the subject in isolation from the general principles of international law and without regard to the changes that were taking place in the climate in which international law had to operate.[19] As a result of this fragmentation, the law came to be dominated by arbitrators and commentators who did not have much of a grounding in public international law but were more inclined to see it as an extension of international commercial law.

Consequently, contract-based solutions dominated over concerns with the public interest of states.[20] It has also resulted in the emphasis on the analytical exposition of the awards and the texts of treaties on which they are based. Again, technically competent arbitrators are more prone to interpret the words of contracts and treaties that are relevant without regard to the desirable outcomes in the law. Alternatively, the only preferable outcome they would have in mind is to ensure that the contract is given effect on the ground that international commerce cannot function unless parties respect the obligations they assumed. They may also believe in the single model of development that neoliberalism prescribes and see the treaty as seeking to establish that model of economic development. In the latter case, it would be prudent to indicate that they have a religious zeal for the course as it will ensure reappointments. In a profession that depended on influence and patronage, arbitrators accepted the prevailing political tendencies geared to the views favorable to international business and ignored the higher values such as neutrality and fidelity to the trust placed in them by the parties.

In a climate that saw greed as a good thing,[21] it was human to err. The schisms that have arisen in the field of investment arbitration are best explained in the context of the attitudinal differences that have characterized developments in this area of the law.[22] There was a struggle between two camps. There were those committed to neoliberal views that required expansion of a system of foreign investment protection based on the values of promoting the free market ideals of sanctity of property, the importance of preserving commercial obligations and free flows of investment. These were promoted to the detriment of other values such as neutrality in arbitration, confining

---

19 Moshe Hirsch, *The Interaction between International Investment Law and Human Rights Treaties: A Sociological Perspective*, *in Multi-Sourced Equivalent Norms in International Law* 211 (Tomer Broude & Yuval Shany eds., 2011). Hirsch argues that arbitrators and human rights lawyers belong to different systemic communities, applying different norms. The first group believes in capital flow, legal predictability, and market economy ideology whereas the second has universal values based on the primacy of human rights.

20 The point is strongly made in GUS VAN HARTEN, INVESTMENT TREATY ARBITRATION AND PUBLIC LAW (2007).

21 Muthucumaraswamy Sornarajah, *A Law for Need or a Law for Greed: Restoring the Lost Law in the International Law of Foreign Investment*, 6 INT'L ENV'T AGREEMENTS 329 (2006).

22 It is acknowledged that there is a problem but most of the works that acknowledge it quickly set out to be apologetic. Some even justify the schism on the basis of the vigor of the system, arguing that only a vigorous system can survive such schisms. BACKLASH AGAINST INVESTMENT ARBITRATION: PERCEPTIONS AND REALITY (Mark Waibel et al. eds., 2010).

decisions to the consent of the parties, and being aware of other values such as the protection of the environment and human rights and the primacy that must be attached to *ius cogens* principles of international law.

The idea that investment protection had to operate within a system of law, which had hierarchies of interests and conflicting obligations, did not come easily to arbitrators coming from a background in commercial arbitration where contractual sanctity was the sole determinant. It was natural that another camp should emerge that gave priority to these values over the values of neoliberalism. The fact that arbitrators brought different visions to their tasks resulted in wide divergences in the law stated in their awards. Important also was the need for self-promotion by the arbitrator because repeated appointments as an arbitrator become possible only if the arbitrator toes the lines drawn by the appointing authorities of arbitral institutions or ties in with the goals of multinational corporations and their counsel. Big law firms with specialized departments on investment arbitration had a say in the developments. The schisms that have occurred within the international law on foreign investment generally, and foreign investment arbitration in particular, are the result of ideological clashes that took place during years of the dominance of neoliberalism. These clashes have ravaged the law to such an extent that a regime for the area can scarcely be contemplated. They also took the law into a fourth phase. Though its exact contours are unclear, some trends in this phase can be identified.

IV. THE FOURTH PHASE

As neoliberalism retreated, with increasing evidence of failure manifested finally in the global economic crisis in 2008, the schism became more pronounced, with many arbitrators showing a willingness to beat back the gains that neoliberalism had made within the field.[23] States were beginning to assert themselves by pursuing vigorous defenses to liability, as a result of which arbitrators had to decide issues in a context outside the ambit of an inflexible and absolute law on investment protection.[24] Instead

---

23 The manner in which the defense of necessity was treated in the various Argentine arbitrations is illustrative of this. There was a gradual movement away from exclusion of the defense of necessity to qualified and then total acceptance of it. *CMS v. Argentina* adopted an exclusionary view, but *LGE v Argentina* and *Continental v Argentina* were tolerant of this argument based on necessity.

24 Thus, the fair and equitable standard was restricted to the meaning ascribed to the international minimum standard in customary law during the *Pope & Talbot v. Canada* arbitration by an interpretive note issued by the NAFTA Commission. Later, the U.S. and Canadian Model Investment Treaties adopted the restriction. After *Methanex v. United States*, the exception regarding regulatory expropriation also came to be stated in U.S. and Canadian investment treaties. In addition, the list of preclusionary factors in investment treaties is increasing. There are subjective statements of national security in the U.S. and Canadian Models as in other model treaties. Security issues are nonjusticiable under the India–Singapore CECA. There is a GATT-style exception on health, morals, and welfare, imported into investment treaties from international trade instruments in the U.S. Model. Exceptions also relate to sustainable development. These preclusions knock down the force of protection of foreign investment. Further, see ANDREW NEWCOMBE, GENERAL EXCEPTIONS IN INTERNATIONAL INVESTMENT AGREEMENTS, IN SUSTAINABLE DEVELOPMENT IN WORLD INVESTMENT LAW 355 (Marie-Claire Cordonier Segger et al. eds., 2011).

of rejecting them offhand as in the past,[25] some tribunals gave sympathetic considerations to the reasons given for the measure of the state in the context of the circumstances. Around the same time, there was increasing questioning of the benefits of entering into investment treaties. Some states withdrew from the system of treaty arbitration. Others made treaties, which whittled the scope for investment protection by curtailing the interpretative extensions that neoliberal arbitrators had made on the text of investment treaties and by providing for increasingly broad defenses that justified state interference with foreign investment. The vestiges of the law created through neoliberal thinking will remain until dismantled, and the conflict will continue to affect the law for a longer period. But, the advances that were made during the ascendancy of the period of neoliberal thinking will be subjected to greater scrutiny. Though the principles may not disappear altogether, their force will come to be dented considerably. One may even argue that it would be so dented that foreign investors may not have the same confidence in treaty-based arbitration that they initially had and they may look to contractual and other means of protecting their investments.

What will accelerate the change into a fourth state of norm clashes similar to the first phase is the attitude of states and the changes in the picture relating to the flows of foreign investment. The need for investment treaties is increasingly challenged. The economic literature is not conclusive on this point, but it casts considerable doubt on the rationale that foreign investment flows into developing countries are promoted by the existence of such treaties. If so, the need for a multilateral treaty creating a uniform regime must also be doubted. As indicated, some states have pulled out of the investment treaty system.

Other states are beginning to doubt the need for investor–state arbitration in the treaties. The case law so far does not inspire confidence in the system. Through expansive interpretations of treaty provisions it has derogated from the rights of states in a manner that states could never have intended. The costs to states involved in contesting even the jurisdictional phases of these arbitrations and the possible annulment phases challenging the jurisdictional award are considerable.[26] States, like Australia, have indicated that they will not sign treaties with investor–state dispute settlement clauses any longer.[27]

V. CONCLUSIONS FROM THE FOUR PHASES

It is obvious from the statement of these four phases of the international law on foreign investment that the most opportune time for devising a regime on foreign investment was the third phase when the neoliberal ideology supported by a single

---

25 *See, e.g.*, the blanket statement in *Santa Helena v Costa Rica* (2002) 5 ICSID Rpts 153 that competing environmental considerations cannot sway the object of investment protection.

26 The Philippines press reported that the costs involved for the state in the different phases of *Frapport v. Philippines* exceeded 53 million dollars.

27 The Japan–Philippines treaty also does not contain an investor–state dispute settlement provision. This may reflect the negative experience of the Philippines with investment arbitration.

hegemonic power was at the zenith of its influence. The regime did not come to pass, as the two efforts at creating one through multilateral instruments—the MAI and the draft instrument of the WTO—resulted in failure.

Despite the fact that neoliberalism suffered a decline with the global economic crisis, the rules it established during its period of dominance will retain their vitality for a considerable period of time. Indeed, efforts will be made to ensure that they are retained through the formulation of new theoretical and other constructs for considerable interests had profited by the system that was devised and maintain an interest in conserving the uncreated regime. As a result of the system, a closed circle of arbitrators have had a great run. Systemic communities were created during the third phase that profited from the rules that were devised and in turn, contributed greatly to building up the rules. Large global law firms witnessed great economic development though the developing countries did not. Arbitral institutions such as ICSID, the ICC, and other arbitral centers, which suddenly saw a spurt in arbitrations, will not want to see a decline. A coterie of academics who interacted with the arbitration community in the hope of securing work, and young scholars who see a path in the field with a pot of gold at the end, all have an interest in resuscitating a system that promised so much. Practitioners became professors at leading universities without the usual requirement of publications. If the system declines, some have much to lose.

One must remember that in other fields too it is not the powerful who pay for their follies. It is the public that pays to erase the economic ills that neoliberalism created while the elite classes still continue to profit. The law of greed that was devised had to be preserved. Hence, despite the reversal, like the hydra-headed monster, neoliberalism will find new ways of being kept afloat. There have been many efforts made to do this in the literature, with the methods having much to do with the argument relating to the creation of a global regime on investment protection. It is necessary to look at these arguments to see whether the project at the creation of a global regime for investment continues to remain viable. It is through various arguments as to the creation of a global regime through the developments that had taken place during the third phase that the prescriptions of neoliberalism are given a new lease of life.

II. Struggling for Regime Creation

The tenacity as to the struggle to maintain the vigor for the creation of a global regime for investment protection is evident in the generation of profuse literature offering various techniques for the preservation of the system that was attempted during the period of dominance of neoliberalism. These efforts muddy the emergence of a fourth phase. As the states recede from the treaty system, there is still an enterprise that seeks to keep alive what it considers are the gains made during the third, neoliberal phase through advocating various theories that do not reflect the reality that the state practice emerging in the fourth phase seeks either a withdrawal or a change in the older treaty practices by creating as much regulatory space as possible. As indicated, there are powerful interest groups that stand to lose much if the system that had been created is dismantled. These interest groups will mount powerful campaigns and advance new theories in the face of competing groups, which have become ascendant as a result of the decline of neoliberalism. These competing groups consist of nongovernmental organizations, particularly in the areas of the environment and human rights. There is also a vigorous group of academic opinion that has come out against the norms created in the third phase.[28] In addition, as indicated, states themselves are withdrawing from the system with which they were enamored during the period of neoliberalism. The task of conserving the package of rules generated during the third phase of law is undertaken vigorously. It is only a holding exercise that cannot stem the tide of opposition to the system that was built during the third phase. It assumes certain forms, which may be examined critically.

I. THE TREATY RULES AND THEIR INTERPRETATIONS HAVE BECOME CUSTOMARY INTERNATIONAL LAW AND HENCE CONSTITUTE PART OF A GLOBAL REGIME

This is an obvious nonstarter, but yet it is pressed with vigor.[29] The view proceeds largely on two grounds. The first is that there are some 2700 bilateral investment treaties and that they contain common principles. The second is that the various arbitrations interpreting them have produced a "jurisprudence constante" supporting the treaties' role as congealing a law that is universal. Both are false premises. The form of the treaties is not the same for them to give rise to customary law principles. Though the outward shell of the treaties seems similar and tracks similar areas, their content is not the same.

To take but one example, one would expect that the treaties uniformly protect all foreign investments. If they do not, a case for a customary law in the area cannot be made out. It is easy to demonstrate that the types of investments that are protected vary in the different treaties. The South-East Asian treaties confine protection to investments that are "approved in writing."[30] This means that the treaties do not protect non-approved investments. It would appear that no investments have been approved for protection of investment treaties in these Asian states so that the category of unprotected

[28] An indication of this academic opposition is seen in the Osgoode Hall *Statement on the International Investment Regime*" (Aug. 31, 2010, *available at* http://www.osgoode.yorku.ca/public_statement.) The statement begins with the following paragraph: "We have a shared concern for the harm done to the public welfare by the international investment regime, as currently structured, especially its hampering of the ability of governments to act for their people in response to the concerns of human development and environmental sustainability."

[29] Its most vigorous supporter is the former president of the International Court, Judge Stephen Schwebel. Stephen Schwebel, *The Influence of Bilateral Investment Treaties on Customary International Law*, 98 ASIL PROCEEDINGS 27 (2004).

[30] For the interpretation of the provision, see *Grueslin v. Malaysia* (2000) 5 ICSID Rpts 483 and *Yaung Chi Oo Ltd v. Myanmar* (2003) 8 ICSID Rpts 463.

foreign investments in these states is high.[31] Some treaties confine protection only to investments made in "accordance with the laws and regulations from time to time in being."[32] The extent of the uncertainty as to the types of investments protected under these treaties is huge. There is also the view stated in some arbitral awards that even in the absence of such an express qualification of the type of protected investment, it must be inferred that the treaty can only protect investments that conformed to the law at the time of entry.[33] Now, it would be obvious that there can be no agreement even as to the type of investments these treaties protect—hardly the basis on which it can be claimed that they can be the foundations for the creation of customary international law.

Arbitral awards have shown that there is an absence of uniformity as to the interpretation of a whole array of provisions of treaties, and these divergences in interpretations between awards are often explained by those who seek to conserve legitimacy in the system as being due to the difference in the terminology used in the treaties. If, indeed, the differences in formulations provide the explanation for the divergence in interpretations, it cannot also be that these different formulations giving rise to different interpretations and results can give rise to customary international law. Despite this, the vigorous assertion that the treaties form a source of customary law displays the paucity of evidence in support of the creation of uniform global norms in investment law.

There has been a lack of uniformity as to basic issues of interpretation of the provisions of the treaties. The differences relating to the application of the necessity defense have arisen in the different Argentinian awards.[34] There is disagreement on the scope of the umbrella clause. The interpretation of the most favored nation clause has also resulted in confusion. It would be foolhardy to say in the context of all these schisms that a customary international law has resulted from investment treaties or that a constant jurisprudence has emerged from the interpretation placed on these treaties.

The primary difficulty as to why custom cannot come about is because investment protection is about the protection of property. A diversity of ideological and cultural stances exists in the world relating to property. The notion that these could be made

---

31 In fact, as lead counsel in *Yaung Chi Oo Ltd v. Myanmar*, the present author inquired from all ASEAN states as to whether they had procedures for giving approval for foreign investments. Except for one state, none of the others had such procedures. The inevitable conclusion is that despite the existence of the treaties, there was no foreign investment that was approved for protection.

32 Such formulations appear in Asian treaties. Its interpretation was considered in *Fraport v. Philippines* ICSID Case ARB/ 03/25 (Aug. 16, 2007).

33 *Inceysa Vallisoletana v El Salvador* (ICSID Case ARB/03/26 (Aug. 2, 2006).

34 The five Argentinian cases (three of them, CMS, Enron, and Sempra, decided by tribunals having the same president) have three different interpretations of the necessity provision. Jurgen Kurtz, *Adjudging the Exceptional at International Investment Law: Security, Public Order and Financial Crisis*, 59 ICLQ 353 (2010). The annulment tribunal had a strongly worded statement that CMS interpreted the provision wrongly by equating the treaty statement of necessity with customary law as stated in the ILC Code on State Responsibility. Enron and Sempra were annulled. Andreas von Staden, *Towards Greater Doctrinal Clarity in Investor–State Arbitration: The CMS, Enron and Sempra Annulment Decisions*, 2 CZECH Y.B. INT'L LAW 207 (2011).

into a homogenous concept is one that is theoretically possible, for any matter that is domestic could be converted into the international sphere through a treaty. But, whether such a feat could be performed by an accumulation of bilateral treaties, which do not contain the exact words or concepts, is conjectural. Besides, none of the treaties exclude the application of domestic law altogether.[35] The exact relationship of domestic law and the treaty principles differ from treaty to treaty, making the extraction of common principles extremely difficult. Property is a concept that is rooted in domestic law. Title to property can only be created in terms of domestic law, international law having no procedures for the creation of such title. It is therefore difficult to think in terms of customary rules that could be created in respect of recognition of the rights to property and their termination. What the treaties seek to achieve is to specify standards and procedures for the treatment of property but in these standards too there are so many variations that it would be difficult to contemplate the growth of customary rules on the basis of their statements in the various treaties.

II. THE NEED FOR GOOD-GOVERNANCE STANDARDS OF TREATMENT OF FOREIGN INVESTMENT REQUIRES GLOBALLY UNIFORM RULES ON FOREIGN INVESTMENT

This is an argument that very much resembles the old standard of civilization argument of colonial times. The assumption is that a favor is being done to developing countries by ensuring that proper standards of investment protection are maintained at the global level so that there can be greater flows of foreign investment, which enhances the economic development of the poorer states. The poorer countries lack such standards and the altruistic object of the arbitrators interpreting the investment treaties is to further the objectives of these treaties in such a manner as to build a structure of rules that ensure good governance rules are followed by developing countries that would ensure greater flows of foreign investment into such countries. This is an assumption that lacks proof as the ability of investment treaties to ensure foreign investment flows is seriously doubted in the literature. Besides, it promotes the idea of wisdom in matters of economic development as the preserve of certain groups of persons who subscribe to the neoliberal theories relating to internationalization of capital flows. There are other economic views on development. Whereas neoliberalism mandates a single path to economic development for all states, many economists believe that each state should fashion its own plans to achieve its goals of development.[36] The neoliberal standards of governance deny such choice to states. These largely enhance the objectives of multinational corporations, often to the detriment of developing countries.

The developing countries do not subscribe to the standards of governance that have been articulated by the neoliberal lobbies. Though evidence for this neoliberal view is

[35] MONIQUE SASSON, SUBSTANTIVE LAW IN INVESTMENT TREATY ARBITRATION: THE UNSETTLED RELATIONSHIP BETWEEN INTERNATIONAL LAW AND MUNICIPAL LAW (2010).

[36] Dani Rodrik, *Growth Strategies*, *in* HANDBOOK OF ECONOMIC GROWTH (Aghion & Durlauf eds., 2005).

to be found in the dissenting award in *International Thunderbird*,[37] there is little overt support for the idea in arbitral awards. Much support for the notion of the imposition of the standards of governance comes from official reports of the World Bank and is reflected in writings. The failure of neoliberal models indicates that there are other ways in which development could be enhanced. The so-called, "Beijing Consensus" may indicate that the restrictions controlling investments and strict direction and control over foreign investment into appropriate projects may have more salutary effects than the standards of governance models advanced by neoliberal institutions. The case advanced for the building of a regime on the basis of a neoliberal model and the altruistic justification advanced for the model would hardly be accepted at a time when the developed states themselves are embarking on regulation and control over business in order to overcome the global economic crisis. Economists have stated other models of development that may prove to be as effective.[38] It is no longer possible to return to the days when one section of the world could impose its preferred standards under the cloak of altruistic objectives while in reality achieving its own objectives of securing the investments of multinational corporations. Though it could well be that the project could come to be repeated in the future, the structure of power within the world, which is becoming multipolar, may not permit such a return.

III. THE RULE OF LAW REQUIRES STABILITY OF NORMS OF INVESTMENT PROTECTION JUSTIFYING THE EVOLUTION OF A REGIME OF FOREIGN INVESTMENT PROTECTION

The use of the doctrine of the rule of law is the most creative and perhaps the oldest of the justifications advanced for the absolute protection of foreign investment.[39] As no one can quarrel with the rule of law, the disguising of the rules of investment protection in the garb of the rule of law is seen as giving it legitimacy. It is a strategy that has been pursued at various stages of the history of the subject. The attempt has made a fresh appearance in recent times, demonstrating that whenever the system that promotes private power is under attack, a defense comes to be made through the use of lofty ideals relating to the rule of law, which is seen as guaranteeing property rights.

The rule-of law justification is an old one. The "rustics" in the developing world were treated to this charade from old times when the Europeans, themselves relatively new to the idea of civilization, sought to impose the "standard of civilization" on the rest of the world.[40] The introduction of the idea of the rule of law into investment law was

---

37 The dissenting arbitrator was the late Thomas Wälde. *See* International Thunderbird Gaming Corp. v. the United Mexican States (Jan. 26, 2006), *available at* http://www.naftaclaims.com/Disputes/Mexico/Thunderbird/Thunderbird_Award.pdf

38 HA-JOON CHANG, KICKING AWAY THE LADDER: DEVELOPMENT STRATEGY IN HISTORICAL PERSPECTIVE (2005).

39 For such justifications, see generally, INTERNATIONAL INVESTMENT LAW AND COMPARATIVE PUBLIC LAW (Stephan Schill ed., 2010).

40 GERRITT GONG, THE STANDARD OF CIVILIZATION IN INTERNATIONAL SOCIETY (1984).

identified, in the initial phase, with the World Bank. It was reflected in the writings of the first two Secretaries-General of the International Centre for the Settlement of Investment Disputes.[41]

The notion of the rule of law has a special status, initially for the common lawyer, and later for the rest of the world due to the work of the International Commission of Jurists. Dicey, the foremost constitutional lawyer of his time, had popularized the phrase "the rule of law" as a bulwark of liberty against the power of the state, and prescribed it a meaning that had been generally accepted within the common law world. The Diceyan concept of the rule of law meant the equality of all before the law and the subjection of state to the courts so that exercise of power could be reviewed. The Diceyan concept has animated the work of the International Commission of Jurists, which, in struggling to establish the rights of people against dictatorships around the world, has used an elaborate notion of the Diceyan rule of law.

It is this principle of the rule of law as a bulwark against state power and its abuse against citizens that is subverted to serve the interests of the multinational corporations, themselves wielders and abusers of power both within their home and host communities. Such abuse of power takes place within developed states, which do have democratic institutions and mechanisms capable of correcting such abuse. But, such abuse, within developing countries, cannot easily be rectified as it takes place either with the collaboration of local elites or in states, which fear that they may drive away desirable foreign investment by taking action against deleterious foreign investors.[42] Besides, it may well be the case that adequate institutional machinery does not exist to deal with abuses of multinational corporations even in the more sophisticated developing countries.[43] The extent of human rights violations, pillage, and murder for which multinational corporations are responsible is made evident by a long list of cases that have been brought in the United States under the Alien Torts Act.[44] The discussion of the foreign investment arbitration awards and the concentration on this lucrative area of the law seeking to protect the assets of multinational corporations fails to mention the extent of abuse that is revealed by the expanding list of cases under the Alien Torts Act. Textbooks devote attention to foreign investment arbitration and the law under the subject without considering the impact of the case law involving the commission of international wrongs under laws such as the Alien Torts Act[45] or the work of the

---

41 IBRAHIM SHIHATA, TOWARDS A GREATER DEPOLITICIZATION OF INVESTMENT DISPUTES: THE ROLES OF ICSID AND MIGA (1993).

42 The spate of cases under the Alien Torts Act demonstrates the extent of this malaise.

43 The sad incident of the escape of gas at the Union Carbide factory at Bhopal remains the classic example. The thousands of people affected by it remain largely uncompensated either through Indian or U.S. law.

44 Alien Tort Claims Act (ATCA), 28 U.S.C. § 1350 (2006).

45 A string of books has appeared on international investment law and arbitration. None of them consider in any detail the human rights abuses of multinational corporations or their relevance to such arbitration. They are intent on considering the construction of rules on investment protection by treaties or by arbitration awards, giving the impression that the role of international law is devoted entirely

United Nations in considering the making of law to control human rights abuses by multinational corporations.[46]

The rule-of-law argument in the context of the international law on investment does not even recognize the principle of equality, one of the basic tenets of the rule of law in that it privileges the foreign investor over local entrepreneurs and the interests of the local citizenry. It does not permit the same access to foreign arbitration that the foreign investor has so that the home state could institute arbitrations against abusive conduct of multinational corporations. The Diceyan concept of the rule of law as requiring equality before the law is violated by the investment treaty system because it clearly privileges the foreign investor over domestic entrepreneurs and hinders the regulatory powers of the state to protect its citizens in times of crisis.

The system does not recognize equality between local entrepreneurs and foreign investors.[47] The protection of the foreign investor is at the higher standard he would be entitled to regarding treatment standards in a treaty and compensation according to the treaty formula. Quite apart from this, international investment law, which is designed to protect investment stability, may work against the interests of the public of the state when it comes to taking measures relating to the protection of the environment or human rights. International investment law may prevent regulatory measures being taken by the state as treaty provisions may prohibit such measures without full compensation. In any event, the ability to so intervene may have to be tested before a foreign arbitral tribunal. To the extent that it privileges the foreign investors, norms of international investment law, as presently developed, violate the rule of law, as traditionally understood to include equality before the law, by privileging the interests of the foreign investor. They may also violate democratic norms such as those relating to freedom of expression[48] or the right to health care.[49]

There is a newer version of the rule of law that is formulated with developing countries in mind. This version prescribes stability of rules in business, which would be enforced by neutral arbitration. This version is particularly tailor-made for investment in that its prescriptions precisely fit the mechanisms that have been developed in the third phase of the law identified above. It was formulated at the time of the ascen-

---

to this end. *See, e.g.*, CHRISTOPH SCHREUER & RUDOLPH DOLZER, INTERNATIONAL INVESTMENT LAW (2008).

[46] A United Nations Rapporteur has been in existence to study the human rights violations of multinational corporations and devise methods of dealing with them. The present Rapporteur, Professor John Ruggie, had issued several reports.

[47] The point is more fully developed in David Schneiderman, *Promoting Equality: Black Empowerment and the Future of Investment Rules*, 25 S. AFRICAN J. HUMAN RIGHTS 246 (2009).

[48] In *Ethyl Corporation v. Canada*, the argument was that a statement announcing the suspicion that ethyl was carcinogenic and was to be banned was held to be expropriatory. In Biwater Gauff v Tanzania (2008) ICSID Case ARB/05/22 at ¶ 696, adverse comments were made by the tribunal against negative ministerial statements, which were considered as expropriatory. Arbitrations on the basis of treaties have been threatened against Australia, Canada, and Thailand by cigarette manufacturers on the ground that labeling requirements indicating the hazards of smoking violate treaty standards.

[49] Legislation requiring mandatory labeling of cigarette cartons warning of health hazards was discontinued in Canada partly due to the view that such labeling may violate investment treaties.

dancy of neoliberalism and concentrated on stability of the regulatory framework so that contract and property relationships could be kept stable. The thinking was that such stability was essential for meaningful business relationships, and that the function of the rule of law was to promote such stability.

The property and the other assets of the foreign investor become sacrosanct under this revised concept of the rule of law. However, such a view is a deception. Not only is it a perversion of the original concept of the rule of law, but it subverts an idea that the rule of law was intended to protect the powerless mass of humanity against tyrants and dictators by channeling it to aid entities that keep alive such tyrants and dictators in many ways in their own search for profits at the cost of human suffering.

It is interesting to trace the manner of this development and its present mutation. An early statement of the rule-of-law argument appears in the writings of Aaron Broches, the first Secretary-General of ICSID, credited with the origins of the ICSID Convention.[50] It was continued in the writings of Ibrahim Shihata, the second Secretary-General, showing the commitment of the World Bank to make the linkage between the rule of law and foreign investment protection.[51] The World Bank has consistently acted on the basis of the classical belief that sound institutional protection of property and contract are the fundamentals on which economic development could be built. It has promoted a regime of rules that would ensure this. ICSID was seen as the central cog in the regime. But, realizing that it was pitching it too high to link the rule of law with foreign investment protection, it soon changed in tone and spoke in terms of the role of law in foreign investment in presenting its program of law reform, particularly in commercial law, as the basis for economic development. This modesty was not to be retained in the age when neoliberalism saw its absolute triumph. The early formulations merely made the link by indicating that the state, which maintained the rule of law, would attract more foreign investment because of the stability which that rule provided.

This was a truism. But, of course, with the spectacular success of China, a country which could hardly be associated with the rule of law in any traditional sense, the myth that a state needed a strong rule of law for economic progress has become dented. A distinction began to be drawn between rule-of-law light and rule-of-law strong.[52]

The rule of law took a new turn when it became directly incorporated into the agenda of foreign investment with the statement of the view that the idea of the rule of law itself contained the protection of foreign investment as one of its aims.[53] This notion came in different guises. One was that the rule of law required the protection of the right to property. It took the Lockean thesis that the protection of the right to property was the most important function of organized society, and supported

50 As cited in Margrete Stevens, *The ICSID Convention and the Origins of Investment Treaty Arbitration, in* 50 YEARS OF THE NEW YORK CONVENTION (Albert van den Berg ed. 2008).

51 SHIHATA, *supra* note 41.

52 RANDAL PEERENBOHM, CHINA'S LONG MARCH TOWARDS THE RULE OF LAW (2007).

53 Susan Franck, *Foreign Direct Investment, Investment Treaty Arbitration, and the Rule of Law*, 19 PAC. MCGEORGE GLOBAL BUS. & DEV. L.J. 337 (2007).

the protection of the assets of the foreign investor as an important function of both domestic and international law. Put in this way, it was easy to incorporate the right to property within the rule of law. Another method was to argue that the rule of law contained basic standards of governance and that because it was important for them to be recognized globally, the function of international law was to ensure that these standards, which importantly contained rules as to the treatment of the foreign investor, should be maintained. These arguments are also reminiscent of the standard of civilization that existed during colonial times. The argument then was that the burden rested on the "civilized" states of Europe to ensure that those in other parts of the world, particularly Asia and Africa, should be led to the same standard of civilization that the Europeans enjoyed. As is well-known, this seemingly altruistic justification cloaked centuries of plunder of the peoples of Africa and Asia.[54]

A third strategy has been to show that the constitutional systems of the Western world recognize property protection as a central feature of the rule of law, through a selective reading of the constitutional developments. It ignores constitutional developments in other parts of the world such as Africa or Asia that treat property as being subject to public interests, or even the democratic view of property in the Western tradition that is inclined to view property as being subject to prior social interests. As in older times, it is as if these systems do not exist or do not matter, and the world must subscribe entirely to Western standards.

The question that must now be asked is whether the new altruism purveyed through the rule of law and standards of governance seeks to cloak another bout of multinational plunder of the less-powerful parts of the world. In the context of a changing world, this is unlikely to eventuate. The arguments that are made for the evolution of a multilateral system will be seen to be surreptitious methods of introducing a regime of law that would have adverse consequences for the large majority of the people of the world and would be resisted. They are the last-gasp arguments in favor of neoliberal models of foreign investment protection.

IV. INTERNATIONAL INVESTMENT LAW IS A PART OF GLOBAL ADMINISTRATIVE LAW

All the new arguments coalesce in the attempt to argue that foreign investment arbitration is a facet of global administrative law and that foreign investment arbitration seeks to be a part of global governance. It is a sophisticated argument that sees in the explosion of investment treaties as well as the in the number of arbitral awards interpreting their provisions a genesis of a global multilateral system of foreign investment protection.

The argument is that the regime institutes what is in effect the review of the measures taken by a state against the foreign investor much in the mold of an administrative tribunal in domestic law. The difference is that the venue is shifted to an external

[54] For the view that new laws continue to justify plunder, see UGO MATTEI & LAURA NADER, PLUNDER: WHEN THE RULE OF LAW IS ILLEGAL (2008).

location in order to facilitate neutrality. Rules that have been developed for such review are similar to domestic administrative law. Heavy reliance is placed on the existence of the fair and equitable standard into which arbitrators have read the rule that where legitimate expectations of the foreign investor are violated by the state, liability for such violations should arise. The linkage between domestic administrative law and the development of the fair and equitable standard to include the protection of legitimate expectations enables the conclusion to be drawn that investment arbitration is a species of global administrative law.

The development of the link between the fair and equitable standard and legitimate expectations in itself is interesting. The genesis of the idea may be found in a talk that Professor Orego-Vicuna gave at the annual meeting of the American Society of International Law in 2004.[55] In it, he drew the connection between some English cases in which the courts had used the concept of legitimate expectations and provided relief on the basis of the violation of these expectations. But, English courts have seldom held that there is a substantive principle of administrative law that damages must result when a state or an administrative agency goes back on a commitment made to the citizen. Instead, the remedy provided is only that there must be due process remedies available to a citizen whose expectations are interfered with.[56] The case in English law where legitimate expectations were held to create a substantive principle has since been distinguished by subsequent cases. In *R v. North and East Devon Health Authority, ex parte Coughlan*,[57] it was held that a health authority must honor a commitment given by the health authority to a paraplegic who was promised that she would not be shifted from a care home close to her parent's home. Later cases have regarded *Coughlan* to be a singular instance and have not followed the decision.

The courts have explained the refusal to follow *Coughlan* in the following terms: "Here lies the importance of that fact that in the *Coughlan* case that few individuals were affected by the promise in question. The case's facts may be discrete and limited having no implications for an innominate class of persons. There may be no wide-ranging issues of general policy or none with multi-layered effects, upon whose merits the court is asked to embark."[58] Investment cases are also quite different from the *Coughlan*-type situation. Because of the public interest implications of the decisions the state has to make in these situations, the tribunals that decide such cases will have to make decisions that implicate concerns that transcend the immediate interests of the foreign investor and his or her operations within the state. The investment arbitrations that have used the notion of legitimate expectations have made decisions

---

55 Francisco Orrego-Vicuna, *Foreign Investment Law: How Customary Is Custom?*, ASIL Proceedings 98 (2005) ("Fair and equitable treatment is not really different from the legitimate expectations doctrine as developed, for example by the English court and also recently by the World Bank Administrative Tribunal").

56 *See further* PAUL CRAIG, *Administrative Law* 639–56 (5th ed. 2005). Professor Craig's writings pressed the idea of substantive relief.

57 [2001] QB 213.

58 *Begum v. The Returning Officer of the London Borough of Tower Hamlets* [2006] EWCA civ 733 (para. 68, citing with approval earlier cases, distinguishing *Coughlan*).

that implicate public interests. They have applied a notion purportedly derived from national legal systems, but providing remedies that are based on the violation of substantive standards. National systems simply do not go that far simply because of the fact that administration will become impossible if administrative policies relating to taxation, environmental regulation, labor issues, and a host of other matters have to be changed in order to meet new and unanticipated circumstances. It cannot be expected that a state should be constrained by solicitude to prior commitments to the foreign investor when such circumstances arise.

The formulations in investment awards of legitimate expectations are so broad that a writer described the rule that is formulated in the awards can only apply in "perfect public regulation in a perfect world to which all states should aspire but very few (if any) would attain."[59] Clearly, the law is made simply with the intention of ensuring investment protection, discarding all other considerations.

The European Court of Justice also generally avoids imposing substantive obligations on the basis of legitimate expectations. They would seek to balance overriding public interests with the expectations of individuals.[60] In contrast, the breadth of the rule that has been stated by investment arbitral tribunals is so staggering that states could not have expected that the provision on the fair and equitable standard could be used in this expansive manner. They could also not have expected an interpretation linking this standard with the notion of legitimate expectations. The suspicion also arises that investment tribunals have been loaded with arbitrators inclined to entrench the notion of legitimate expectations in international investment law. The repeat appointments of such persons to investment tribunals causes concerns, and leads to the inference that arbitrators partial to the acceptance of neoliberal tenets find appointments so that new, emergent mutations can be confirmed and the hydra-headed monster continues to live.

Other problems arise when principles that apply in domestic law are elevated to the global level where the exact parallels do not exist. It is evident that global administrative law seeks to achieve something more than domestic administrative law as known to common lawyers. Common lawyers view domestic administrative law as involving the protection of the rights of the common man against the awesome might of the state so that a part of the common law is devoted to ensuring that interferences with the facilities that the state provides are not withdrawn from any particular individual without observing the principles of natural justice; another part requires that there should be reasonableness in the exercise of delegated discretionary powers by administrative officials. In the case of foreign investment protection, if administrative law principles can in fact be employed, the results envisaged are the protection of large multinational corporations, significant bases of economic power, from a developing state that is seeking to regulate its economy for the benefit of its people as a result of changes necessitating regulatory

---

[59] Campbell McLachlan, *Investment Treaties and General International Law*, 57 ICLQ 361 (2008).

[60] *See generally* SOREN SCHONBERG, LEGITIMATE EXPECTATIONS IN ADMINISTRATIVE LAW (2000).

intervention. The interests that stand in opposition are those of the multinational corporations and the interests of the people of the state for whose benefit the state seeks to act. It is not the issue that domestic administrative law is devised to decide. It is difficult to justify the basis on which such a conflict of interests can be decided by an arbitral tribunal that cannot take into consideration the local issues that are relevant. It is obvious that local courts are more competent to deal with such issues.

It is interesting that the developed states, Canada and the United States, put an end to the possibility of the fair and equitable standard being developed through the notion of legitimate expectations as a basis for review of their administrative measures. This was done when the three NAFTA partners, the United States, Canada, and Mexico, sought an interpretive statement from the NAFTA Commission confirming the belief of these states that the fair and equitable statement meant no more than what the international minimum standard in customary international law meant. In their model treaties, these states describe the fair and equitable standard as indistinct from the international minimum standard of customary international law. That practice has been followed by other states as well. Some states leave out the fair and equitable standard from their newer treaties. Thus, states have evinced a desire to put an end to the arbitral adventurism that has led to the possibility of arguments relating to global administrative law. In this field, ideas of global administrative law devised to keep neoliberalism alive will fade away with time, when support from states for such ideas disappear. Already one can see that the standard of fair and equitable treatment is left out of the newer treaties or appears with qualifications limiting its use.

Conclusions

The lessons of the episode relating to the construction of regimes in international investment law are clear. International law in this area, as in many areas, undergoes a cyclical change. In the first period of the formation of international investment law, the contest between the international minimum standard formulated by the United States and the Calvo doctrine resulted in a stalemate and a balance as neither set of norms was able to dominate. The balance was somewhat tilted during the period after decolonization and the numerical strength of the Third World to push through normative packages containing the New International Economic Order. During this phase too, the balance was retained though the norms of the developing states did gather considerable support. In the third phase of neoliberalism, there was a movement away from the norms that were articulated previously by the developing states. Though not complete, the period saw an ascendancy of the norms of neoliberalism through a proliferation of investment treaties. Arbitral tribunals took the neoliberal tenets in the treaties further than was intended by the states. Schisms resulted within the arbitral community as a result. States also reacted by introducing defenses into investment treaties. With a succession of economic crises, neoliberalism, which accelerated the trend toward absolute investment protection, was dented. The global economic crisis in 2008 considerably eroded the reliance states placed on neoliberal theories. States assumed a greater regulatory role, which meant that they could not adhere to standards of protection of foreign investment as in the past. The developed countries were in the forefront of leading the changes. The nongovernmental organizations clamored for the restriction of a system that ignored environmental and human rights issues. The locus of power in matters relating to foreign investment was shifting to newly industrializing countries such as China and India.

In the context of these changes, it was necessary for the developed states to change their stances on investment protection. They began moving toward a position that gave rise to the view that what was desired was a balance between protection of foreign investment and the regulatory concerns of states. The pursuit of such a balance would prove to be a chimera. It will not satisfy foreign investors, and states will want to decide for themselves the regulatory concerns that justify their action. The treaty system will fade away. Those who argue for multilateralization of treaty principles should also consider whether the preclusionary factors and exceptions also get multilateralized on the basis of the most-favored-nation clauses or on the basis that they constitute custom. It is more likely that because these exceptions are linked to territorial control as well as newly evolving principles of international law such as those on the environment and human rights, they will be more readily accepted as being based on universally accepted principles of international law.

It is in this period of change that developing country international lawyers should assess their own future roles in this area. It is clear that China and India will have a greater role to play, but equally, it may well be that in their rush to prosperity and great power status, they may act as all-powerful states have done in the past. China's newer treaties indicate its desire to protect its outgoing investments through newer types of treaties that enlarge the scope of dispute resolution well beyond what the older treaties permitted. Although the older treaties confined arbitration by foreign tribunals to disputes involving compensation for expropriation, the newer treaties do not contain such a restriction. This announces China's interest is joining the capitalist states that rely on investment foreign arbitration. India's practice is more recent. But, it will also make more treaties. The indications are that China and India will join the developed states and participate in their model of investment protection. If this pattern develops, China and India would effectively abandon their earlier positions as champions of developing countries and follow the pattern set by developed states. The search for energy in these countries may make them do exactly what the European powers did in the extraction sectors: they may seek absolute protection for their investments. One hopes that such a scenario does not eventuate and that the two states remain steadfast to their earlier policies relating to the Third World interest in development.

The developing countries left behind must take firm stands in opposition to the systems of absolute protection that have been built up. They must ensure that their ability to control their natural resources is not surrendered through the making of inflexible treaties that confer absolute protection upon foreign investment. The problem may lie not in the treaties, which are transparent interests and are subject to the scrutiny of many interested parties, local interests as well as foreign, such as nongovernmental organizations. Developing countries should not get picked off individually but must remain united in presenting desirable norms such as the permanent sovereignty over natural resources, the ability to change arrangements when fluctuations in surrounding circumstances of a foreign investment occur, or the ability to change taxation regimes so that the full benefits of the foreign investment as it unfolds can be captured for the benefit of its people.

APPENDIX

A Polemic: The Cases For and Against Investment Liberalization

Leon E. Trakman: The Case for Investment Liberalization

Muthucumaraswamy Sornarajah: The Case against Investment Liberalization

TRAKMAN

The case for a transnational—or international—investment regime is political and economic as much as it is legal. It is political and economic in the assertion that foreign investment ought to be subject to protection not only by, but also from, nation-states. The rationale is that nation-states, acting in economic self-interest, ought not to be unduly constrained by a system of laws or rules that transcend and supersede the authority of those states to act in the public interest. The converse rationale is that foreign investors ought to be subject to treatment by host states that is transparent in nature and evenhanded in application, and that is not arbitrarily imposed on public interest grounds. Foreign investors ought to have the reasonable expectation that rights granted them to invest in a host state are not arbitrarily denied. Host states should have the power to curtail those rights on principled grounds not inconsistent with obligations assumed by treaty or investor–state agreement.

The case for protecting foreign investors from state incursion is sometimes identified with economic rationalism that is embodied in liberal discourse. Encouraging the free flow of foreign investment with minimal governmental interference is more likely to profit not only foreign investors, but also the domestic states in which they invest. This result is not assured, as when a foreign investor takes advantage of the host state and its subjects through the unreasonable exploitation of natural resources, or if a host state fails to pass on to domestic consumers the economic benefits derived from foreign investment. However, subject to these qualifications, it is assumed that investment treaties that grant transactional rights to foreign investors will advantage both host states and those investors. Constraints imposed on foreign investors, such as those grounded in national health and public policy, are ways in which states protect their national interests from investor incursions that are deemed to undermine the national good.

SORNARAJAH

It is important to take historical factors into account. The law cannot be viewed in the present context alone. Its rules were fashioned at a time when investments were exploitative and were designed in the context of Africa and Asia existing as providers of raw materials and markets for products. In that sense, the states that emerged from colonialism have had little opportunity to reframe the laws that had been devised in colonial times. If these rules continue to frame the regulatory structure that transcends sovereign authority of the developing states, they would have to be in continuing subservience to the interests of the developed states.

Nation-states do not have economic motives alone. They need to conserve their natural resources and utilize them in the interests of their own posterity as well as have international community interests in environmental protection in mind. The nation-state must ensure its economic development, but the paths to development are not uniform, and are not the ones prescribed by the international financial institutions alone. Some developing countries have successfully adopted their own models regarding development, which are based on alternative economic models—China being the obvious example.

TRAKMAN

The extent to which foreign investors reasonably enjoy rights and host states owe them duties depends significantly but not exclusively on the treaties governing foreign investment and any contractual relationship between foreign investors and host states. In issue is not only whether host states act in a formally legal manner, but also whether their actions are substantively fair. However, fairness should be grounded in a context that is informed, not only by macro-historical facts, but also by immediate treaty and contractual undertakings.

None of this denies the need for states to act in the national interest, including by preserving the cultural heritage of local communities. States need to regulate markets that are vulnerable to foreign competition. They need also to maintain public health programs and environmental protection schemes. The purpose is rather to ensure that states do not use national interest arguments arbitrarily to attract and then renege on undertakings made to foreign investors, such as through an expropriation or other government taking that is substantively inconsistent with the duties they have assumed by international convention, treaty, or investor–state agreement. The greater good does not exclude the good of individual states, but the good of the whole is ultimately more than the sum of its parts.

SORNARAJAH

Altruistic ideas as to global progress through liberalization may be a subterfuge for advancing the interests of multinational corporations. Such sentiments were expressed in order to justify free trade and investment from colonial times. Grotius justified free trade on the ground of the brotherhood of man. He advanced the doctrine of the freedom of the high seas so that the Dutch could enter the Malacca Straits and then exercise maritime power in the Asian oceans. In modern times, the magic mantra of neoliberalism is that free flow of investment through protection will bring economic development. It has not been shown to happen. Instead, there continues to be exploitation of the poorer areas of the world in collusion with elite groups. The law becomes a pliant instrument that would facilitate and justify the continuing advantages that are bestowed on multinational corporations, and a network of protection of foreign investment is created that limits the regulatory power of the state to act in the interests of its people. The global economic crisis has resulted in skepticism of the neoliberal view.

TRAKMAN

The risk of wealthy investors from developed home states using their economic and political power to dictate foreign investment is real. Nevertheless, account must also be taken of the converse risk of nation-states, not limited to developed states, invoking arguments based on sovereignty and the national "good" ex post facto, namely after having opened their doors to foreign investors. It is true that historical and ongoing economic disadvantage should be a factor in considering whether a host state has acted unreasonably in its treatment of foreign investors. However, that argument should not serve as a mantra to justify states using arguments grounded in the national self-interest to transform arbitrary takings into doubtful means of legitimating the regulation of foreign investment.

Nor it is appropriate to treat multinational corporations as representing all foreign investors in poor countries. There is a history of multinationals taking economic advantage of poor states and their subjects. Small and medium sized foreign investors often lack the political, economic and legal capabilities to effectively complain about receiving unfair treatment from host states, including by developing states. In addition, states also sometimes rely on the incapacity of foreign investors to mount investor–arbitration claims. States can also feign the grounds on which those states avoid duties on which foreign investors reasonably rely in investing in a host state. It is true that poor states often conclude treaties and agreements because of economic and social need. However, this should not lead to an open door to disregarding treaty or contractual obligations insofar as states ought reasonably to have foreseen and redressed those issues *before* assuming obligations by treaty or agreement. What is sauce for the goose is also sauce for the gander. In principle at least, states—rich and poor—cannot have it both ways. They cannot conclude treaties and contracts that invite foreign investment into host states, and then deny their voluntary action in making those invitations.

SORNARAJAH

Noninterventionism in foreign investment will not be a desired goal of states after the global economic crisis. In Asia, noninterventionism is passé because measures taken to deal with the earlier Asian economic crisis involved direct interventions by the state. Foreign investment was affected by expropriatory measures in both Europe and the United States. The argument that government interference is not advisable no longer holds as a result of the demonstration effect of the measures that were taken to confront the various economic crises. In the area of foreign investment, though success models such as China and India are dressed up often as triumphs of the neoliberal model, the fact is that in both countries there is heavy control of sectors of the investments that are thought vital to the economy. In Asia, though "open door" policies were announced by the various states of the region, restrictive laws controlling entry of investment remained. They were liberalized to the extent, for example, that higher percentages of shares in joint ventures could be held by the foreign investor but controls still were maintained. The few cases from Asia, such as *Frapport v Philippines,* demonstrate the extent of regulatory control. Some sectors such as oil have a heavy presence of the state oil company, and it is unlikely that such dominance will be dismantled in the near future.

TRAKMAN

It is true that neoliberal conceptions of international investment perpetuated by developed states for several centuries diverge from the so-called liberalization of investment in developing countries, such as in Asia. However, neoliberalism does not deny the virtue of regulation. Nor does it insist that regulation of investment should always prevail, any more than it pretends that markets are always "free." What is challenged is the argument that neoliberal models of international investment law are passé because they deny the capacity of states to regulate investment. It is true that state regulation of international investment expanded globally after the 2008 recession. It is also true that some Asian countries, not limited to China, for ideological and functional reasons insist on a closer regulation of foreign investment than most Western states. However, neither postulation denies the common view that foreign investors should enjoy a semblance of freedom in order to facilitate an investment. It requires that foreign investors enjoy a level of freedom accorded to them by customary or investment treaty law, constrained by the economic and social disadvantages of poor states in relation to wealthy investors.

The fact that this level of enjoyment is contentious is entirely explicable in fact. No standard of treatment accorded to foreign investors is absolute. Minimal standards of treatment, most-favored-nation, and national treatment, along with the right of investors to receive fair and equitable treatment, are all contextually determined. A foreign investor does not enjoy unqualified privileges that, once granted, states cannot limit thereafter. Developing states in particular often have reasonable grounds for regulating foreign investors in response to comparatively unforeseen circumstances giving rise to material disadvantage, including but not limited to economic recessions and civil insurrection. However, these grounds for states to regulate investment, including through expropriation, do not mean that foreign investors who are granted the right to invest in host states should have their rights summarily disregarded without compensation.

Determining when nation-states have unfairly exercised their regulatory powers is inevitably contestable. Under a socialized twenty-first–century human rights discourse, nation-states that enjoy unequal power over foreign investors should be accountable for exploiting that power, just as dominant investors should be accountable for exploiting the economic and social vulnerability of less-developed states. This does not imply that less-developed states that conclude investment treaties or investor–state agreements should be wholly unaccountable for expropriating foreign investments. It does mean that, in interpreting investment treaties and agreements, account should be given to their discrete circumstances.

SORNARAJAH

The human rights argument is not appropriate. The object of human rights law is to protect the weakest individuals of society against the powerful state or other agglomerations of political and economic power within society. A law that is designed to promote the interests of the flotsam of humanity against power should not be used to privilege multinational corporations, which have colossal economic power and are able to buy elites in both their home and host states. The human rights argument is strong with neoliberals as the Lockean notion that the right to property is the most central of rights and forms the basis of political organization lies at the foundation of the neoliberal creed. But, this argument is not accepted even in the best texts of human rights generated in the developed world, where the right to property is always made subject to the social interest in property.

TRAKMAN

Human rights protection against exploitation of property "rights," including but not limited to the rights asserted by foreign investors, is also about the social, economic, and political rights that provide the context in which "human rights" are exercised. Viewed in relation to international investment, the context in which "human rights" are exercised includes the object or purpose of the states in regulating those "rights" and the impact of that regulation upon the enjoyment of those rights.

SORNARAJAH

The case for an international body of investment law can be made only on the basis that there is but one way toward economic development that serves all of mankind. Unfortunately, neither in practice nor in economic theory can such a case be made. A uniform body of global investment law existed when hegemonic leaders desired that this be so. But, in the modern multipolar structure of global politics, it is unlikely that a global investment law can be built up as there is no single hegemon that could drive such a law on the basis of its own desired theory. The movement from a unipolar world to a multipolar world itself demonstrates that declining powers are backtracking on their construct of a universal system. Institutions are driven by the dictates of hegemonic powers, which control them and are inclined to instrumental solutions favored by these powers.

National biases are present at both ends. The dominant system is based on the hegemonic model that privileges protection of property of multinational corporations to the same or even higher extent than found in the national systems of developed states. Developing states would prefer to emphasize the social function of property, as developed states in fact did during the earlier stages of their development.

The argument about the denial of natural justice again presupposes the existence of a uniform idea of natural justice. The concept has no fixed meaning apart from principles of procedural law, and has a changing quality depending on a variety of factors even within the common law. As such, it would be difficult to construct a body of rules that has global significance based on natural justice.

TRAKMAN

The conception of a uniform, coherent, and fixed body of international investment law is idealistic at best. However, greater uniformity in international investment law can help to level the playing field among developed and developing states, as much as it serves hegemonic forces that seek uniformity in their own image. Ensuring that foreign investors are treated fairly according to norms that are identified with and endorsed by a coherent international community, including a community of disadvantaged states, can assist in redressing such hegemony. Greater uniformity can also promote investment laws that are not only more transparent in nature, but that also help to avoid the impact of dislocated—and dislocating—national laws devised by rich and poor states alike. However, such an eventuality is only truly tenable when the investment laws that result are built on a consensus among states that reflects, rather than discounts, their economic and social differences. It may be that taking account of such differences, particularly in want and need, may lead to disparate constructions of concepts such as expropriation, just and equitable treatment, and local requirements. However, far from diminishing the value of international investment law, these differences ought to inhere in the contextual interpretation of investment treaties and investor–state agreements. They ought also to take into account economic and social disadvantage rather than exclude them a priori as incidental or immaterial to the "plain words" of a treaty or agreement.

Ultimately, perfect symmetry in international investment law is an aspiration only. It is not realistic to expect states with diffuse political and socioeconomic traditions to agree upon narrowly defined principles of investment law. Nor are efforts to universalize investment law an abiding virtue. The disparate regulation of foreign investors may well be justified both on grounds of ideological and functional differences and in response to disparate expectations of foreign investors and states alike.

It is also doubtful that a single body of international investment law that includes protections for investors resembling human rights is capable of transcending the discrete—and sometimes unduly domestically fixated—national laws and regulations. Nor do commonly accepted conceptions of investment law, such as relate to "national treatment" of investors, mandate treating formally like cases alike in accordance with some transcendental principle of international investment law. This is not to deny that investment tribunals should apply commonly accepted conceptions of expropriation, insofar as they exist, in a manner that is fair to both states and investors. A state's fear of being denuded of its natural resources by acquisitive and destructive foreign investors is entirely defensible. A foreign investor's fear of being subject to national law biases, caprice, or the summary confiscation of investment property is equally defensible.

The fact that states diverge over the nature and significance of conceptions such as "natural justice" are also not reasons to deny the significance of treating states and investors justly. What is necessary is recognition that even though conceptions of justice are subject to different constructions in light of divergent legal cultures and traditions, concepts such as "natural justice" should not be discounted so long as they are subject to interpretations that take account of those differences. Nor are such conceptions inherently doubtful because they happen to have originated in the Western or any other legal system. The test is whether they are intractably contingent upon their origins and incapable of being adapted to other contexts, legal cultures, and states.

SORNARAJAH

Value-neutral principles are difficult to find in this area of the law. Given the division in political ideologies, a value-neutral system did not emerge during the Cold War. The developing states had a third vision, which was articulated in the form of the New International Economic Order. It generally denied the existence of an international minimum standard of treatment through which the United States sought to establish its preferred model. The NIEO universalized the Calvo doctrine, a earlier prescription developed by Latin American lawyers in opposition to the U.S. model that sought to create an international law that applied to foreign investment disputes. Despite the interlude that marked the triumph of neoliberalism in the "roaring nineties," this ideological schism has remained to thwart the possibility of value-neutral norms. The positivist tendency has been to utilize the argument that all law is value neutral so that the absence of neutrality could be effectively hidden behind a curtain. Law, especially the international law on foreign investment, given its history of conflict, cannot be value neutral. The continuing schisms within the law is evident even among arbitrators who would normally be expected to subscribe to the same code of values that are conducive to property protection. That being so, it is too great an expectation that value-neutral norms can be constructed in the field.

It should also be noticed that the aim is the protection of the investment from the power of the host state. The protection of the host state interests from the predation of the foreign investor is hardly mentioned in the efforts at creating a value-free law. This, in itself, indicates a value preference for property protection at the cost of social interests in property.

TRAKMAN

Liberalism is an outgrowth of the sixteenth-century liberal state based on the emancipation of the individual from the absolute rule of monarchs. An unfortunate result was the invocation of this same liberty by subjects of liberated states to exploit the subjects of other states who were not so emancipated. It is also true that this status of colonial domination has not entirely passed. More than vestiges of it remain in trade and investment law and practice. However, there are signals of a changing world order led by influential developing states, not limited to China, that have sought to reconstitute liberalism more than disavow it. Their assault is less on the foundations of liberalization of investment than on balancing "free" against "regulated" trade so that neither excludes the other. Nor is the conception of regulated trade and investment entirely novel. The liberalization of investment never was absolute in nature or application, even in the heyday of liberalism. What is different today is that the blend between free and regulated trade is subject to changing ideological and functional influences. These changes reflect, among others, the ideological influence of planned economies balanced against the functional need to facilitate foreign investment. Such a regime change, so called, is often more incremental than pervasive, and more diffuse than uniform in operation. However, this change is part of a new order in which the meaning and significance of liberalized investment has changed and will continue to change in treaty law as in investment practice.

SORNARAJAH

The notion of regime creation itself connotes a hegemonic leader. Effective regimes, according to regime theories, can only be created in circumstances where national interests coincide, and there is also an hegemonic leader who will ensure either through persuasion or through direct and indirect sanctions that others do not break ranks. Increasingly, the possibility of such a regime, though commented on by writers, is a mirage because the hegemonic leaders themselves are deviating from the model they once espoused. The seeming regime that was created during the highpoint of neoliberalism did not last longer than the three years of euphoria for the Multilateral Agreement on Investment proposed in 1995 and given up by 1998. Since then, there have been further futile attempts. It is unlikely that official efforts would be made until the next bout of neoliberalism comes about in the cycle. In the meantime, commentators inclined toward neoliberalism will seek to keep the tenets alive through other means, such as the creation of a global administrative law, the multilateralization of norms on investment protection as a result of treaty practice, and investment arbitration precedents based on treaties and the argument that recent trends create customary international law. These arguments are not supportable for a variety of reasons. They will continue to be made because there is a powerful lobby consisting initially of multinational corporations, arbitrators who depend on the existence of a regime for their business, law firms who also need the business in the area, academics who expect to join the bandwagon to supplement their relatively meager incomes, and an army of neophytes who see lucrative careers in the field. But, this group is met by an equally committed group that pursues the interests of the environment and human rights and sees foreign investors as the major spoilers of both interests.

In this conflict, the state is a participant both because of international pressures exerted by the two camps of actors as well as by domestic pressures. No longer are developed countries exporters of capital. They are among the largest importers of capital from the BRIC countries, and are conscious of sovereignty-based legal rights that vest control over entry and subsequent conduct of multinational investment. The old cry that sovereignty has diminished can no longer be heard in loud terms because the developed countries are more intent on sovereignty-based rights to control the influx of investments into their states and the impact they have on labor, security concerns, and the environment. As the boot gets increasingly to be on the other foot, the invasive hand of the hegemonic states will be more visible and the demand for an international regime will subside as there will be no exemplars practicing restraint who could demand such a regime.

TRAKMAN

We may agree more than we disagree on this issue. However, I do not believe that there is, or ever was, a single conception of the liberalized state, or the liberalization of investment. Historically, as today, so-called liberals have articulated and re-articulated the option malleable core values of liberalism. Even in the so-called highpoint of the Western liberal tradition until the early twentieth century, liberalism underwent a transformation including in the very meaning ascribed to liberalism.

Certainly, libertarians continue to insist that free, as distinct from freer, investment is not only efficient but is a "good" in itself. They argue, too, that any infraction by regulators on a free market threatens the foundations of a self-regulating investment order. This view of liberalized investment markets is not only overstated: it also exaggerates the extent to which liberal "realists" subject the exercise of liberty to qualifying conditions. Socially conscious liberals, too, have long insisted that market "choice" is not "free" in the absence of substantive voluntariness. That same viewpoint persists today. If one party—an investor or state—is subject to economic or political duress, that party's "consent" is conceivably absent. The conception of consent, so central to investment liberalization, is thereby suspect if it is coerced by a dominant state, or unconscionably extracted by a dominant investor in an investor–state by agreement.

These refinements of liberalism as applied to foreign investment are more than a by-product of the so-called "neoliberal welfare state" following World War II. They are formally manifest, however imperfectly, in declarations of human rights, as well as in multilateral, regional, and bilateral treaties, not limited to conceptions ascribed to the fair and equitable treatment of investors.

It is true that conceptions such as just and equitable treatment in international investment law often favor wealthy investors in disputes with poor states. However, the application of these principles is not cast in stone. Investment treaties and investor–state agreements are subject to variable interpretation. ICSID tribunals frequently dismiss the claims of foreign investors, not only on jurisdictional grounds, but because foreign investors have failed to establish that they were unjustly or unfairly treated. Indeed, almost half of ICSID awards reject the claims of a foreign investor, and more uphold their claims in part only. Given that many respondents in ICSID proceedings are developing states, the notion that ICSID investor–state agreements inevitably benefit wealthy claimants from developed states is simply wrong.

Added to this is the observation that ICSID respondents are themselves signatory states to the ICSID. It may be that some respondent states concluded investment treaties and investor–state agreements to attract foreign investment so as to redress their dire economic disadvantages. It may also be that expecting them to be "compliant" with a transcendental body of international investment law, such as by adopting expensive environmental programs and social reforms, is unreasonable in their circumstances. It may also be that, by signing multilateral investment protocols and investment treaties, developing countries were able to gain status and avoid being labeled "rogue" states. However, choices that states make, sometimes regrettably, lead to countervailing risks and liabilities.

It is also difficult to plead, after the fact, that a state was totally unaware of the economic, social, and legal implications of an investment treaty that it signed. However, it is plausible to take into account a state's disadvantaged capacity in interpreting such a treaty or agreement.

SORNARAJAH

There is an absence of perfect equality in knowledge, negotiating power, and lack of coercion to support the view that there is a voluntary surrender of sovereignty. The experience of the developed states themselves indicate that they had no understanding of the manner in which the treaties they were making would be used. Illustrations are the manner in which the fair-and-equitable standard was used in NAFTA and the subsequent interpretive statement. In the case of developing countries, there is little understanding of the effects of treaties that are entered into at the instigation of international organizations that may make such treaties a condition for assistance. In a perfect world, the argument relating to voluntary surrender of sovereignty may work, but not in a world full of asymmetries as to power and knowledge.

Supranational institutions themselves may be proxies for the power of hegemonic states. The widespread allegation against the World Bank is well-known. The ICSID Convention must also be viewed in this light. The manner in which this dormant institution became the focus of formulating neoliberal viewpoints into propositions of law provides interesting examples of law creation in directions favored by developed states.

TRAKMAN

This proposition about the unequal bargaining power of states that negotiated investment treaties is well-taken. However, taken to extremes it gives rise to an untenable consequence. The assumption behind a wholly "unbargained" treaty is that a developing state did not appreciate its terms and conditions and is therefore justified in disregarding it ex post facto.

Reinforcing this problematic approach is the assertion that sovereign states are immune from liability to foreign investor claims. The pitfall is the appearance of lawlessness in the hands of sovereign states on the one hand and the loss of an opportunity to remediate deficiencies—and undoubtedly there are many—in the development of international investment law on the other. The result is that respondent states could summarily disregard foreign investor claims for compensation arising out of the expropriation of property; they could also deny investor claims such as the right to be heard.

SORNARAJAH

The human rights argument is the weakest in the construction of support for a global system of property protection. A law designed to protect the weakest in the society against the power of governments is traduced to secure the protection of multinational corporations. International law had no law on property, which is always subject to domestic law, but with the emergence of human rights law, there came about rules on the protection of a right to property in qualified terms. The strength of the qualification varies in the different documents on human rights. It depends much on the purpose of the protection. The rules on the protection of the property of refugees are strong as the meager property that the flotsam of humanity holds must be given secure protection. One cannot extrapolate from such documents to the protection of the assets of multinational corporations.

Domestic parallels of property protection vary from the Canadian Bill of Rights, which does not mention the right to property, to its neigbor, the United States, which requires just compensation. Regional treaties also vary. The practice of the European Court indicates that social concerns must be taken into account and a balanced view taken as to the relevant compensation. There is no strong commitment to market value as compensation.

The revival of the notion of non-compensable regulatory taking in *Methanex v. United States* is an interesting erosion of the notion of an absolute right to property. The impact of this award and the subsequent inclusion of the exception as to regulatory takings in the U.S. Model Treaty (2004) is yet to be assessed. But, the fact is that there is a retreat into sovereignty-based arguments by developed states, which makes the possibility of binding regulatory regimes extremely remote, even if considered desirable. The experience of the MAI shows that it will not be considered desirable by many within the developed world.

TRAKMAN

I do not suggest that multinational corporations should receive the same rights or entitlements as poverty-stricken human subjects. Nor do I suggest that international standards of treatment devised by wealthy states should prevail over domestic standards, including the rights of states to self-determination and economic development. Indeed, even if nation-states owe responsibilities to foreign investors, this does not necessarily entail subjecting them to international laws that sublimate domestic requirements in order to act responsibly. No one would expect a nation-state to forsake its national legal requirements in trying a foreign national for murder or fraud. Why, then, should nation-states be subject prima facie to international laws that wholly forsake national requirements in their treatment of foreign investors?

SORNARAJAH

Murder and fraud are obvious instances of national concern. But, the list is broader, and even the U.S. Restatement accepts a longer list, including taxation, customs duties, antitrust, and similar regulation. The list is obviously longer as a result of *Methanex* and later developments, which would include measures taken to protect health, welfare, and morals, which is a short form for indicating a range of regulatory laws. The law is open now, and the impact of the so-called balance that has to be effected is uncertain. No foreign investor is going to be comfortable with the uncertainty with which this "balanced approach" begins.

TRAKMAN

This argument cuts both ways. The proposition that developed states ought not to over-regulate foreign investment on grounds of public health and environmental safety is balanced against the right of developing and less-developed states to raise comparable objections more forcefully. The limitation in a state's infrastructure relating to its financial, health, and environmental safety is material in determining whether its actions are legitimate. A less-developed state that lacks the financial resources to redress the negative impact of foreign investor mining companies upon public health or environmental safety may itself well be a material factor in denying a mining license.

The residual question, albeit difficult to answer in the abstract, is in the manner in and extent to which less-developed countries should be bound by duties arising from investment treaties or investor–state agreements. The answer, arguably, lies somewhat in the method of interpretation that is applied to such treaties or agreements. If such treaties or agreements are construed restrictively so that their "plain words" meaning prevails over a wider social context that includes social disadvantage, the result may be unduly harsh for developing and particularly less-developed states. If duties imposed upon states by treaty or agreement are construed expansively, taking into account the relative capabilities of the parties, the case for applying international investment jurisprudence remains tenable.

If the duties assumed by states by treaty or agreement are interpreted in light of their domestic constitutions or laws, and those constitutions or laws include the right to expropriate property in the national interest, these domestic laws, again, are part of the context in which investment treaties and agreements ought to be construed. If developing states are required to apply international standards of treatment to foreign investors in disregard of such domestic constitutions or laws, incongruous results may eventuate. One such eventuality is that foreign investors would receive treatment that is consistently more favorable than the treatment accorded to nationals of that state under domestic law.

SORNARAJAH

This is an issue that has been raised largely in the rich countries (such as Canada or the United States) where the populace is mature enough to understand the implications of investment rules. Constitutionality of investment treaties has been the focus of attention of scholars in Canada and the United States. People within the developing states are seldom concerned with low visibility instruments such as investment treaties. It does not affect their daily existence of drudgery. It is unlikely that the man in the street knows the extent to which his home state has tied up its sovereignty in order to protect the rights of foreign investors. These issues concern only the elite in the developing states who also stand to profit from the flows of foreign investment. But, in Colombia, the Supreme Court has ruled on the issue of whether investment treaties that were made are constitutional.

TRAKMAN

Homelessness, destitution, and drudgery are tragic global phenomenon. However, if these tragedies mean eradicating international investment law on grounds that it protects only the elite, it also means eradicating the certainty and stability upon which global investment depends. If global investment is relegated to the junk heap, an unfortunate result may be that those who are poor will become poorer. None of this denies that the benefits of global investment do not necessarily "trickle down" to the destitute and downtrodden. Nor does it assert that international investment law is directly concerned with the distribution and redistribution of investment wealth. What it does assert is that eliminating international investment law is unlikely to redress global problems of hunger and poverty. Indeed, its elimination may well make a bad situation worse.

Nor is it self-evident that developing states should have the right to disregard duties assumed by investment treaty or investor–state agreement as of right. Domestic constitutional law notwithstanding, developed and developing states alike repeatedly agree to devolve their sovereignty to international institutions, whether through the World Trade Organization or specific bilateral agreements. Just as states agree to accord international standards of treatment to discrete, insular, and vulnerable minorities, they also agree to accord international standards of treatment to foreign investors. This is not to contend that such duties are intractable. What is contended is that duties assumed by treaty or agreement cannot be dismissed out of hand if international investment is to be, or is perceived to be, an integral part of a "global good."

SORNARAJAH

It is not proper to draw parallels between the distinct types of treaty activity. In the area of minority protection, ethical pressures motivate states to enter into such treaties. In the area of trade and investment, there are other considerations associated sometimes with duress, and at other times with a belief that a course of activity will lead to economic prosperity. Competition for investment may also be a factor. Duress is exerted. TRIPS was an example of such duress. Developing countries had to reverse the effects of TRIPS on generic drugs for certain diseases such as AIDS. In the investment sphere, there was an unspoken assumption that aid will not be provided if investment treaties would not be signed or that outgoing investment would not be insured. Financial institutions also exerted pressure. Institutions such as UNCTAD promoted investment treaties in indirect ways while the mission of this body was to assist developing countries.

TRAKMAN

Treaty making unavoidably involves "have" states negotiating with "have not" states. The needier the state, the more likely it is to accept terms of agreement it might otherwise have avoided. However, this also oversimplifies global investment politics and economics. Both Mexico and Canada, a developing and a developed state respectively, wanted to join the Trans-Pacific Partnership Agreement. Both had to make concessions in order to gain admission. The rationale is not that developed, developing, and less-developed states should all be treated alike. The argument is that any appeal to a unifying "international" standard is also an appeal to the domestication of those standards in different settings, including in light of different levels of development.

If nation-states incorporate international standards into their national legal systems, through legislative, administrative, or judicial action, they affirm those standards without rendering them any less international. Certainly, international standards can serve as swords that challenge states that fail to incorporate those standards into national law, or do so selectively, as when national legislatures restrict their application in domestic law. If domestic laws serve as shields, they can protect states from international investment laws that become transcendental only because domestic laws are not part of the interpretative context.

SORNARAJAH

This cannot be borne out in evidence. There is no reception of international investment law principles in domestic law. Rather, the domestic systems, particularly of resource-rich countries, have received the contrarian norms such as permanent sovereignty over natural resources. There has been no effort made to dismantle these constitutional norms.

TRAKMAN

The future of international investment law is surely to acquire legitimacy and efficiency in the laws of the states that are a part of it. If it exists only as a supranational body of precepts that have no meaning in domestic law, it is doomed from inception. The "nationalization" of international investment law not only legitimizes international investment requirements, it also provides an efficacious basis upon which to assess the responses of states accused of violating those standards to the claims of foreign investors. The underlying goal is to establish a balance in investment law between international requirements and national law challenges to those requirements. That challenge inheres in determining whether a stabilization clause in a foreign investment agreement is subject to a constitutional challenge before a national court. However, that challenge to international investment law goes beyond stabilization clauses.

SORNARAJAH

There must be a precedential agreement as to what are the rules of the international order. Absent such agreement, it would be difficult to expect the national order to be proactive. The stabilization clause does not constitute a good example of the problem. There must be an international law on contracts between foreign investors and states to support such clauses. There is an absence of such law. A foreign investment contract and the rights created by it exist in domestic law alone. The internationalization of the contract is a myth for which there is little support outside the limited number of awards. Its protection under treaties also remains contentious.

Index

Printed in the USA/Agawam, MA
February 12, 2016
630625.004